Table of Contents

Chapter 4: Dressing and Dips Recipes

Chapter 7: Lunch Recipes

Join The Plant-Based Health, Fitness, And Nutrition Facebook Group

Looking for a community of like minded individuals who love all things plant base, working out, fitness, nutrition and health? If so, then check out my Facebook community: The Plant-Based, Health, Fitness and Nutrition Community.

This is an amazing group of plant-based health enthusiast who focus on getting results with their lives. Here you can discover simple strategies along your health journey, build powerful habits and relationships, find accountability partners, and ask questions about your struggles. I also host free book giveaways and share other helpful free resources that will be the key to reaching your health and fitness goals as fast as possible. If you want to "level up" in your health and fitness journey then this is the place to be.

Just scan the QR code below
to join The Plant-Based, Health, Fitness and Nutrition Community

Attention

Do Not Turn The Page Until You Have Read Everything Below

Scan the QR code below to receive the ebook version of this cookbook that includes all the pictures of each receipe!

Scan W/ Camera Now!

Due to printing costs, we are not able to provide you with a print book with colors and pictures. Instead, I have provided you the ebook version for you to download completely for free with the full cookbook for your ultimate plant-based experience. I want my book to be easily accessible for everyone in the world and since we are a small publishing company, this is the best we can offer to still keep the price for you as low as possible. Hopefully, in the near future, we would like to change this by offering the best quality of books in the world for the lowest prices. Thank you for your understanding and we greatly appreciate your support.

Introduction

Worldwide, millions of people lose their lives because of the lethal combination of unhealthy dietary practices, and sedentary lifestyles. This is happening despite the continuous advancements in medical care, medicine, and technology. Why is this occurring? Why does it only seem to be getting worse?

The foremost contributor to chronic life-threatening diseases can be traced back to the lack of nutritious, and balanced diets. Increased consumption of refined carbohydrates, processed meats, sugars, and a multitude of preservatives has unnaturally affected our biologies. The situation is alarming, dire, and seemingly without a solution.

The good news is that these negative trends can be reversed. We can all do something to prevent their re-emergence in the future. All we need to do is choose a healthier diet and lifestyle. By eating nutrient-dense food with a proper mix of macro, micro, and phytonutrients we can start our journey out of this ongoing health crisis.

A plant-based lifestyle has emerged as one of the best options in dealing with this health crisis. It recommends the necessary dietary changes. The nutritional sciences have agreed that plant-based food has a myriad of health benefits that can delay or even prevent these negative effects on our health. If you are interested in being a healthier, better-functioning human being, then the diet plan outlined in this book is the perfect fit for you!

When I started my plant-based diet journey, there were lots of challenges that came along the way- the first being ignorance and lack of awareness. During my 20s, I was never really a health enthusiast; eating healthy was never my priority. Weight gain came next. As soon as I crossed 30, I experienced the effects of my unhealthy food choices on my physical health. Obesity, high blood pressure, and high cholesterol became my reality. The medication worked, but that was not a permanent fix. These health conditions would have only gotten worse if my doctor had not suggested me a plant-based diet.

I tried this diet and soon lost 30 pounds in a couple of months, and I never looked back. After two years, my blood cholesterol dropped to normal levels, and I finally got rid of medications, and my insulin sensitivity improved! It has been six years since, and I am still sticking to this dietary regime. I never felt this healthy and active ever in my life.

Anyone who tells you that following a health-oriented diet plan is easy is lying to you. It's a difficult path, rewarding, but difficult. This is only made harder by all those delicious (but not nutritious) temptations everywhere we look. To make matters worse, truly healthy choices are hard to find and limited. Unless you live in a big city, restaurants

The Plant Based Cookbook For Beginners
650 Easy, Quick, & Simple Plant Based Vegan Diet Recipes With A 31 Day Meal Plan To Lose Weight & Live A Long Healthy Life

25

with vegetarian/vegan options can be rare leaving only salad and pasta as viable options. And when you go to a friends' house to eat, the struggle gets real. You have to bring your own homemade plant-based food. The good news is that this cookbook will offer you all your favorite delights, and more, in one place.

Open up most plant-based cookbooks and you're likely to feel overwhelmed. The complexity and involvement of each recipe are too much work for daily use. We all live busy lives. So, I compiled a collection of beginner-friendly recipes that are delicious and incorporate plant-based ingredients necessary for the new lifestyle we're embarking on together.

This whole food plant-based cookbook is written for all my fellow health enthusiasts! Over 600 recipes in this comprehensive book provides you with a world full of options to make your plant-based menu more diverse and flavorsome. The ingredients for all of the recipes can be easily found in grocery stores and I provide pictures for each recipe to aid beginner cooks. Eating healthy and delicious food is now possible for anyone with this plant-based recipe collection.

It's important that a beginner on this path to a healthier plant-based diet, not only has the required recipes, but also has a well-written meal plan and the information to back it all up. Having a meal plan is the easiest way to keep on the right track and introduce a variety of foods to your regular menu. The thirty-one-day meal plan included in this cookbook is simple to follow, healthy, and absolutely delicious. These plans are divided into weeks making meal-prep and grocery shopping simple and easy. Along with those plans are more details on the different food groups and the benefits of this new, healthier lifestyle.

All the recipes in this book are provided with a complete nutritional profile, making it easier for you to keep track of your daily caloric intake. Lastly, all the ingredients from this recipe collection are listed in an organized index, given at the end of the book, to help you find a recipe with a particular ingredient.

So, what are you waiting for? If you value your health or are currently suffering from chronic disease, you have nothing to lose. You have nothing to lose but weight and unhealthy habits. This cookbook is your key, your passport to a better, healthier lifestyle. Give it a read. Pick your favorite plant-based meals. See and more importantly, feel the results!

26

The Plant Based Cookbook For Beginners
650 Easy, Quick, & Simple Plant Based Vegan Diet Recipes With A 31 Day Meal Plan To Lose Weight & Live A Long Healthy Life

CHAPTER 01

WHAT IS A PLANT-BASED LIFESTYLE?

Most human civilizations started their journey on this planet with a diet primarily consisting of plant-based foods. Found in the Great Plains of the Central United States, the jungles of Brazil, mountainous Alps, and even the deserts of North Africa, the Earth provided all the nutrition we as a species needed. Our bodies functioned properly, limiting animal-based consumption and maximizing a more natural, healthy, and harmonious lifestyle.

With human progress came the degradation of our diets. Instead of hunting and earning each bite of meat, we buy it wrapped in cellophane and styrofoam off a refrigerated grocery store shelf. Pumped full of hormones and preservatives, it doesn't even carry the same nutrients the wild game we used to consume provided us.

Human ingenuity sparked an industrial revolution that spread to what we eat. Mass production and mass consumption led to the exploding prevalence of

processed foods. All it takes is a glance at the back label of almost anything you buy from the store, and you're guaranteed to see a long list of words that are hard to even read, let alone understand what they are. Why put something you can't pronounce into your body? And that doesn't even take the added sugar, sodium, and fats into account.

Luckily there is an alternative to this harmful modern Western diet. That is a plant-based lifestyle, a return to our roots as a species. Proponents argue that the rise and prevalence of chronic disease that plagues humanity today is at least partially due to the high consumption of meat, animal-based foods and processed meals. Scientists and doctors believe that minimizing the intake of these unhealthy foods and increasing the intake of plant-based items rich with antioxidants, phytonutrients, micro and macronutrients lowers the risks of cancer development, prevents diabetes and heart strokes while keeping a well-maintained body weight.

28

The Plant Based Cookbook For Beginners
650 Easy, Quick, & Simple Plant Based Vegan Diet Recipes With A 31 Day Meal Plan To Lose Weight & Live A Long Healthy Life

For me, the plant-based lifestyle worked like a miracle. No other diet I tried was as effective in losing weight and optimizing my health. It's more than just a restrictive regime designed to cut down my daily caloric intake. Instead, it takes the human body's needs into consideration and offers solutions through progressive and all-natural dietary changes. Working in conjunction with an active lifestyle, the results have been excellent. I want to share this revelation with you!

This is coming from someone who has read and learned extensively about plant-based food and tried and tested it to fight my obesity and high blood sugar levels. The most satisfying thing about this diet is that it does not offer a fixed formula to stick to; in this diet, the only condition is to eat healthy plant-based foods, which allows the dieter to work gradually on his dietary habits and create a lifestyle based on those principles. The results of this dietary plan will take time to show up, but they tend to last for a long time.

The Plant Based Cookbook For Beginners
650 Easy, Quick, & Simple Plant Based Vegan Diet Recipes With A 31 Day Meal Plan To Lose Weight & Live A Long Healthy Life

29

Five Plant-Based Food Groups

Every health-oriented dietary approach promotes the use of certain food items deemed healthy. On a plant-based diet, there are five main food groups that support this approach. These essential ingredients are utilized to prepare complete and nutritious plant-based meals packed with a balanced mix of ingredients. The recipes shared in this cookbook will further suggest different ways to incorporate various items from these food groups.

 **Fruits**

"An apple a day keeps the doctor away" this adage proves to be true when you study the health impact of a plant-based diet. Fruits have an important place in this diet plan, as they offer lots of nutrients that no other group in this list provides. Fruits are loaded with fibers, healthy carbs, vitamins, and minerals. Their natural sweetness can make various desserts and smoothies without using artificial flavors and sweeteners. Fresh fruit juices and flesh can be served between meals to keep your energy levels elevated. Some of the most commonly used fruits on this diet include:

- Banana
- Mango
- Berries
- Peaches
- Nectarines
- Passion fruit
- Persimmons
- Melons
- Kiwi fruit
- Apples
- Oranges
- Lime
- Papaya
- Lemons

30

The Plant Based Cookbook For Beginners
650 Easy, Quick, & Simple Plant Based Vegan Diet Recipes With A 31 Day Meal Plan To Lose Weight & Live A Long Healthy Life

 Vegetables

Vegetables add a diversity of flavors and nutrients to your food. Some veggies are packed with carbs, others with minerals like potassium, phosphorous, or magnesium, and some are a rich source of vitamins and antioxidants. The mix of all vegetables makes a plant-based diet healthy and nutritious. Here is a list of some vegetables you can add to your soups, stews, and stir-fry to make them taste even more delicious and nutritious.

- Carrots
- Broccoli
- Cauliflower
- Capsicum
- Cucumber
- Purple Cabbage
- Kale

- Bok Choy
- Spinach
- Tomato
- Eggplant
- Sweet Potato
- Pumpkin
- Corn

Tubers

Tubers are an instant source of energy, and they are added to increase the average caloric intake. They are also a great source of healthy carbohydrates.

- Potatoes
- Yam or Sweet Potatoes
- Parsnips
- Beets
- Squashes

The Plant Based Cookbook For Beginners
650 Easy, Quick, & Simple Plant Based Vegan Diet Recipes With A 31 Day Meal Plan To Lose Weight & Live A Long Healthy Life

31

 Whole Grains

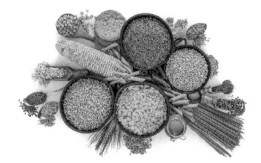

Whole grains offer you complex carbohydrates, which are slow-digesting and help control blood sugar levels. This group forms an integral part of this diet as all whole grains offer much-needed proteins, vitamins, minerals, fibers, and some essential fatty acids. There are endless ways to put these grains to use and can be made into various recipes to diversify your plant-based menu. Whole grain flour is used in making several breads and baking items. Other grains like buckwheat, millet, and quinoa are known as Pseudo Grains as they are actually 'seeds' but considered as grains due to their uses in meals. These pseudo-grains are low in carbohydrates and rich in fibers. They are great to use in salads and other vegetable mixes. These are a list of some common whole grains.

- Oats
- Wheat
- Spelt
- Barley
- Rice
- Rye
- Millet
- Buckwheat
- Quinoa

 Legumes

Legumes form a fundamental and vital part of the plant-based diet. They greatly compliment the other plant-based ingredients as they are rich in both carbs, proteins, and vitamins. Legumes are the underground part of a plant used to store most of its nutrients and are rich in vitamins. The following are the major legumes mostly consumed on the plant-based diet.

- Chickpeas
- Black Beans
- Lentils
- Split Peas
- Green Peas
- Kidney Beans
- Butter Beans
- Tempeh
- Mung Beans

32

The Plant Based Cookbook For Beginners
650 Easy, Quick, & Simple Plant Based Vegan Diet Recipes With A 31 Day Meal Plan To Lose Weight & Live A Long Healthy Life

Other Plant-Based Ingredients

Seeds, even when consumed in a small amount, are rich in a lot of vitamins and minerals. For instance, sesame seeds contain significant vitamin E content. Other edible seed varieties include:

- Pumpkin seeds
- Chia seeds
- Hemp seeds
- Flax seeds etc.

Like seeds, nuts are another plant-based ingredient rich in vitamins, special oils, and antioxidants. Here is the list of the nuts usually consumed on the plant-based diet.

- Almonds
- Pecans
- Brazil
- Cashews
- Macadamia
- Pistachios

The Plant Based Cookbook For Beginners
650 Easy, Quick, & Simple Plant Based Vegan Diet Recipes With A 31 Day Meal Plan To Lose Weight & Live A Long Healthy Life

33

Foods Not to Have on A Plant-Based Diet

There are several diet plans often associated with a plant-based dietary approach, and has fueled some misconceptions about this diet. Since we have discussed the food groups recommended on this dietary plan, here, for clarity, we shall see that besides meat and dairy, what other food items are not suitable to have on a whole food plant-based diet. Eggs, and caviar or roe, are animal-based food products that must be avoided on this diet since they are not plant-based. Similarly, honey is produced by bees, so it can not be consumed on this diet. Gelatin, meat or bone broths, animal-based preservatives, animal-based protein powders, and any other animal market-bought item is not suitable for this plant-based whole food diet.

Plant-Based Substitutes

Reduced protein intake is a major reason that keeps people fearful when switching to a plant-based diet. On a plant-based diet, you will be having considerably limited choices, especially with protein intake. Although, adding suitable substitutes to the diet will keep your body healthy and balanced, just as you want to be. Here are some common vegan substitutes to add to your plant-based diet grocery list:

 **Meat And Fish**

Meat and fish are rich sources of proteins, and their possible plant-based substitutes include some soy-sourced products such as:

— Tofu

— Tempeh

— Seitan

34

The Plant Based Cookbook For Beginners
650 Easy, Quick, & Simple Plant Based Vegan Diet Recipes With A 31 Day Meal Plan To Lose Weight & Live A Long Healthy Life

Dairy Free Milk

Since milk is an essential ingredient, it must be replaced with a suitable alternative to have a similar taste and consistency. Here are some plant-based milk options you can incorporate into your dietary regime. Use sugar and preservative-free variety of these nuts and seeds milk to keep your meals and drinks healthy.

- Almond Milk
- Coconut Milk
- Cashew Milk
- Soy Milk
- Hemp Milk
- Rice Milk
- Pea Protein Milk
- Flax Milk

Eggs And Cheeses

You can not find an absolute substitute for eggs, but to have a similar consistency in different recipes, it can be replaced with a mixture of flaxseed and water. Equal parts of flaxseeds and water are mixed together and left for 5-10 minutes until they make a thick mixture. This plant-based egg substitute can be used in a variety of dishes!

A variety of vegan cheeses are now available in the market. For instance, vegan cheddar cheese! It is dairy free and made out of tofu. There is vegan parmesan that can also be added to your plant-based menu. Such cheeses are non-diary and yet give a good taste and texture to food

The Plant Based Cookbook For Beginners
650 Easy, Quick, & Simple Plant Based Vegan Diet Recipes With A 31 Day Meal Plan To Lose Weight & Live A Long Healthy Life

35

 Gelatin

Gelatin is an animal-sourced product used in various desserts and can be replaced with a plant-based substitute called agar powder. This powder gives a gelatin-like consistency, has no taste, and can be substituted in a 1 to 1 proportion.

Using these substitutes is optional. They are just another way to balance out your daily nutritional intake and keep you from depriving yourself of essential proteins and some flavors you miss on a strictly plant-based diet. Every dieter can add the above-mentioned alternatives to this diet as per his/her needs.

36

The Plant Based Cookbook For Beginners
650 Easy, Quick, & Simple Plant Based Vegan Diet Recipes With A 31 Day Meal Plan To Lose Weight & Live A Long Healthy Life

The Benefits of A Plant-Based Diet

Have you ever heard about the concept of 'reversing disease'? In this age of chronic diseases where every fifth person is suffering from some health disorder, it's important to learn all the non-medicinal ways to prevent and effectively reverse disease to counter its harmful effects. With a diet as healthy as the plant-based approach, several of these health problems can be treated and prevented.

After having to try a plant-based diet for years and studying the concept in-depth, I only recommend this diet to all for its following proven benefits:

The Plant Based Cookbook For Beginners
650 Easy, Quick, & Simple Plant Based Vegan Diet Recipes With A 31 Day Meal Plan To Lose Weight & Live A Long Healthy Life

37

01.
Lowers High Blood Pressure

Over 80 million individuals over the age of twenty are suffering from hypertension or high blood pressure in the United States alone (2021). Insidious and deadly, this health problem is closely linked to our dietary habits and an inactive lifestyle. Using a whole-food plant-based diet is an effective prevention technique to control or reduce blood pressure, especially among those suffering from hypertension. A study published in 2017 has clearly stated the effects of a plant-based diet on blood pressure. It concluded that people living on plant-based foods are 34 percent less likely to have high blood pressure or to develop hypertension than those not living on this diet. (Joshi et al., 2019)

02.
Lowers Blood Cholesterol Levels

All plant-sourced food contains unsaturated fats, unsaturated oils, and a good source of high-density lipoproteins (HDL or good cholesterol). Unlike and animal-based diet, the plant-based diet is free from bad cholesterol (the low-density lipoproteins). Bad cholesterol is mainly responsible for elevating the blood cholesterol levels due to its accumulation in the vessels, which leads to several cardiac diseases and strokes. Since the plant-based diet is free from LDL and rich in HDL, its long-term use can aid in reducing or controlling blood cholesterol levels.

03.
Controls Blood Sugar Levels

The plant-based diet can also keep diabetes at bay as it can maintain blood sugar levels. Researches have shown that a plant-based diet can reduce the risks of developing diabetes by 23 percent. On a plant-based diet, a person receives a greater portion of fibers, minerals, phytonutrients, and vitamins, effectively reducing type 2 diabetes by 30 percent. (Upham et al.) The diet promotes the use of healthy whole food and restricts the intake of added and

38

The Plant Based Cookbook For Beginners
650 Easy, Quick, & Simple Plant Based Vegan Diet Recipes With A 31 Day Meal Plan To Lose Weight & Live A Long Healthy Life

processed or refined sugars and carbs, which are mainly responsible for increasing blood glucose levels. Diabetic patients can therefore rely on this diet to control their sugar levels as a non-medicinal treatment. In a study published in 2008, the risk of diabetes among 8,401 research participants was studied. The results showed that people living on the plant-based diet for over seventeen years were 70 percent less likely to develop diabetes than people not living on it. (McMacken & Shah, 2017)

04.
Aids Weight Loss

What causes weight gain? Poor lifestyle choices and a diet loaded with refined carbs, sugar and calories contribute to excessive weight gain and obesity. The rate of obesity has sky-rocketed to a level beyond any point in human history. A plant-based diet with its balanced mix of nutrients, a greater proportion of whole food, and a lack of processed meat and saturated animal fats make this approach effective for weight maintenance and weight loss. A plant based diet is also very low in calories.

In a study published in 2018, 75 obese individuals having a high body mass index were given a plant-based diet on a regular basis. Their results were compared with those consuming an animal-based diet. After four months of this experiment, the group consuming the plant-based diet showed a marked decrease in body weight. They all effectively lost their fat mass and experienced an increase in insulin sensitivity. (Tuso et al., 2013)

The Plant Based Cookbook For Beginners
650 Easy, Quick, & Simple Plant Based Vegan Diet Recipes With A 31 Day Meal Plan To Lose Weight & Live A Long Healthy Life

39

05.
Makes You More Active and Energetic

The plant-based diet sure makes you active! The main reason is the lack of processed carbs and saturated fats in the diet. The absence of these elements and the presence of antioxidants, minerals, and vitamins together in the diet helps keeps a person active and energetic all the time.

06.
Lighter Environmental Footprint

Another good reason to switch to a plant-based diet is that it has a lighter environmental footprint. According to a study published in 2018, increased consumption of a Western diet, including red meats and processed food, has dramatically strained the world's food system, and has disrupted the entire ecosystem. This contributes to global climate change. But, a plant-based diet can lead to a sustainable future while conserving the ecosystem. (Clark et al., 2019)

How to Transition to A Plant-Based Diet?

Managing expectations is important when switching or starting a new diet. You can't expect results overnight. That just isn't the way it works.

Everyone has different body mass indexes, lifestyles, and dietary routines. That means that everyone is in different physical shape and has varying existing health conditions. These all need to be considered before changing your dietary approach and mentally forecasting your results.

The best approach is to start implementing your lifestyle changes gradually. Start by cutting off basic animal-based food items from your menu and replace them with equally delicious vegan alternatives. For instance, replace meat with vegan meat-like tofu, and tempeh, etc. Focus on one group of food at a time and then work on it for a few days. It will take 2-3 weeks for you to adapt to this new diet and once you get a hold of it, work on its management to achieve lasting healthy results. Also, consult your doctor beforehand to make sure if these diet changes is safe for you.

The Plant Based Cookbook For Beginners
650 Easy, Quick, & Simple Plant Based Vegan Diet Recipes With A 31 Day Meal Plan To Lose Weight & Live A Long Healthy Life

41

My Plant-Based Recipe Collection

As someone following a plant-based diet, I recommended sticking to a well-planned diet plan and keep your kitchen ready for it. Stock up the pantry with required items and keep them organized as per your meal plan. Introduce balance into your diet, and don't let your weight loss goals deprive you of the essential nutrients, especially proteins. It is advised to keep your caloric intake and the nutritional content of your meals in check.

The entire collection of plant-based recipes shared in this cookbook gives balanced and nutritionally proportionate meals for various serving sizes. It covers all the essential daily meals along with some special entrees. Some recipes will provide you with ways to prepare plant-based substitutes for eggs, yogurt, cheese, and meat. From something as basic as salad dressings to various condiments, spread, burgers, snacks, dinner, lunch, and breakfast meals, you can find them all in different chapters of this book. Your plant-based dietary lifestyle is about to get a little more exciting and full of flavors. So, let's get started!

42

The Plant Based Cookbook For Beginners
650 Easy, Quick, & Simple Plant Based Vegan Diet Recipes With A 31 Day Meal Plan To Lose Weight & Live A Long Healthy Life

CHAPTER 02

31 DAY PLANT BASED DIET

Meal Plan (2000 Calories/Day)

Week 1

DAY 01

Meal	Food	Calories	Proteins (g)	Carbs (g)	Fats (g)
Breakfast	Chocolate Chia Pudding	212	4.5	37	7
	Turmeric Eggnog	145	1.1	21.8	7.1
Lunch	Avocado Bean Salad Wraps	105	4.7	13.5	5.5
	Chickpea Salad	240	5.3	28	6.4
Snack	Chickpea Salad	240	5.3	28.9	6.4
	Pina Colada	279	2.2	42.2	10.8
Dinner	Sweet Potato Penne Pasta	356	7	37.6	14
	Cabbage Mango Slaw	288	3.2	13	12.1
Dessert	Vanilla-Maple Ice Cream	182	12.3	7.2	5
TOTAL		**2047**	**45.6**	**229.2**	**67.9**

44

The Plant Based Cookbook For Beginners
650 Easy, Quick, & Simple Plant Based Vegan Diet Recipes With A 31 Day Meal Plan To Lose Weight & Live A Long Healthy Life

DAY 02

Meal	Food	Calories	Proteins (g)	Carbs (g)	Fats (g)
Breakfast	Chickpea Omelet with Mushrooms	249	17.5	40.3	3.9
	Cashew Creamer	100	1.3	16.2	3.1
Lunch	Spinach-Potato Tacos	243	4.6	20.8	5.8
	Cabbage Mango Slaw	288	3.2	12.1	13
Snack	Quinoa Crunch Salad	172	0.8	28	0.3
	Cherry Moon Milk	211	4.5	27.2	10.2
Dinner	Butternut Squash Lasagna	378	5.6	24.4	2.7
	Fennel Salad with Cucumber	161	4.8	10.3	14.7
Dessert	Banana Cream Pie	234	7	17	21.2
TOTAL		2036	49.3	196.1	74.9

The Plant Based Cookbook For Beginners
650 Easy, Quick, & Simple Plant Based Vegan Diet Recipes With A 31 Day Meal Plan To Lose Weight & Live A Long Healthy Life

45

DAY 03

Meal	Food	Calories	Proteins (g)	Carbs (g)	Fats (g)
Breakfast	Almond Granola	355	9.8	65.4	7.7
	Mango Lassi	181	6.9	32	3.9
Lunch	Slow-Cooker Chili	268	15.5	49.7	1.2
	Fennel Salad with Cucumber	161	4.8	10.3	14.7
Snack	Curry Tofu Salad	255	3.7	19.7	2.5
	Spiced Chai	135	4.1	25.5	2.2
Dinner	Taco Pasta with Sweet Corn	393	8.6	31	4.5
	Farro Tabbouleh Salad	238	4	25	3.7
Dessert	Chocolate Hazelnut Energy Bites	144	4.5	23	13.2
	TOTAL	**2130**	**61.9**	**281.6**	**53.6**

46

The Plant Based Cookbook For Beginners
650 Easy, Quick, & Simple Plant Based Vegan Diet Recipes With A 31 Day Meal Plan To Lose Weight & Live A Long Healthy Life

DAY 04

Meal	Food	Calories	Proteins (g)	Carbs (g)	Fats (g)
Breakfast	Chocolate Chip Pancakes	348	8.6	56.2	12.5
	Spiced Almond Milk	344	4.5	13	33.2
Lunch	Black Bean Burgers	389	18.6	75.2	2.2
	Kohlrabi Slaw with Cilantro	182	4.5	14.4	4.2
Snack	Cabbage Mango Slaw	288	3.2	12.1	13
	Coconut Orange Chai	158	2.8	23.9	6.3
Dinner	Roasted Butternut Squash Pasta	346	7.2	22.9	13
Dessert	Watermelon Coconut Sorbet	142	1	11	1
TOTAL		2197	50.4	205.8	85.4

The Plant Based Cookbook For Beginners
650 Easy, Quick, & Simple Plant Based Vegan Diet Recipes With A 31 Day Meal Plan To Lose Weight & Live A Long Healthy Life

47

DAY 05

Meal	Food	Calories	Proteins (g)	Carbs (g)	Fats (g)
Breakfast	Polenta with Saucy Pears	470	7.1	110.4	1.2
	Tahini Hot Chocolate	260	5.8	29.2	15.4
Lunch	Sweet Potato Quesadillas	324	13.6	59.3	4.4
	Winter Kale Salad	285	4.9	32.9	4.8
Snack	Coconut Milk Hot Chocolate	244	4.2	18.5	20.7
Dinner	Cashew Mac and Cheese	326	11.3	29	20.4
Dessert	Gingerbread Freezer Fudge	244	4.2	28.5	20.7
TOTAL		**2153**	**51.1**	**307.8**	**87.6**

48

The Plant Based Cookbook For Beginners
650 Easy, Quick, & Simple Plant Based Vegan Diet Recipes With A 31 Day Meal Plan To Lose Weight & Live A Long Healthy Life

DAY 06

Meal	Food	Calories	Proteins (g)	Carbs (g)	Fats (g)
Breakfast	Oatmeal with Mixed Fruit	274	7.2	50.5	6.6
	Pumpkin Spice Drink	161	3.1	32.6	3.2
Lunch	Sweet Potato Chili with Kale	391	16.2	83.4	1.9
	Beet Salad	206	1.1	22.3	1,9
Snack	Farro Tabbouleh Salad	238	4	25	3.7
Dinner	Vegetarian Lentil Loaf	367	3.3	22.8	27.4
	Chickpea Salad	240	5.3	28	6.4
Dessert	Strawberry Cheesecake Parfaits	160	1	29.2	1.4
	TOTAL	2037	41.2	292.8	50.6

The Plant Based Cookbook For Beginners
650 Easy, Quick, & Simple Plant Based Vegan Diet Recipes With A 31 Day Meal Plan To Lose Weight & Live A Long Healthy Life

49

DAY 07

Meal	Food	Calories	Proteins (g)	Carbs (g)	Fats (g)
Breakfast	French Toast with Berry Compote	215	5.1	30.6	8.4
	Turmeric Latte	142	1.9	13	4.4
Lunch	Potato-Cauliflower Curry	505	20.7	94.9	6.6
	Fennel Asparagus Salad	160	11.7	12.1	2.9
Snack	Kohlrabi Slaw with Cilantro	182	4.5	14.4	4.2
	Choco Banana Chai Latte	269	3.2	65.2	2.8
Dinner	Black Bean Loaf with Avocado Sauce	338	18	30.2	5.8
	Poke Beets Salad	178	2.1	23.8	0.9
Dessert	Pumpkin Cheesecake	159	4.1	25.5	2.2
TOTAL		**2148**	**71.3**	**309.7**	**38.2**

50

The Plant Based Cookbook For Beginners
650 Easy, Quick, & Simple Plant Based Vegan Diet Recipes With A 31 Day Meal Plan To Lose Weight & Live A Long Healthy Life

WEEK 1
GROCERY LIST

 **Grains**

- Oats
- Rice
- Quinoa
- Barley
- Whole wheat pasta
- Quinoa
- Farro
- Corn tortillas

 Flours

- Whole wheat flour
- Almond flour
- Corn flour
- Almond meal
- Flaxseed flour

 **Legumes**

- Kidney beans
- Pinto beans
- Garbanzo
- White beans
- Black beans
- Black-eyed peas
- Split peas
- Lentils

 **Nuts and Seeds**

- Almonds
- Cashews
- Brazil nuts
- Raw macadamia nuts
- Walnuts
- Pinenuts
- Hazelnuts
- Pecans
- Flaxseeds
- Pumpkin seeds

The Plant Based Cookbook For Beginners
650 Easy, Quick, & Simple Plant Based Vegan Diet Recipes With A 31 Day Meal Plan To Lose Weight & Live A Long Healthy Life

51

 **Vegetables**

- Potatoes
- Broccoli
- Butternut squash
- Beets
- Eggplants
- Sweet potatoes
- Tomatoes
- Carrots
- Radishes
- Artichokes
- Asparagus
- Lettuces
- Spinach
- Kale
- Cabbages
- Cauliflower

- Zucchini
- Brussels sprouts
- Bean sprouts
- Leeks
- Garlic
- Fennel
- Ginger
- Beets
- Bell peppers
- Pepper
- Onions
- Corn
- Cilantro
- Parsley
- Mint leaves

 Fruits

- Cherry
- Apples
- Pears
- Peaches
- Oranges
- Grapes
- Pineapple
- Peach

- Bananas
- Strawberries
- Mangoes
- Blueberries
- Raspberries
- Avocado
- Watermelon

 Condiments

- Blackstrap molasses
- Balsamic vinegar
- Apple cider vinegar
- Red wine vinegar
- Tahini
- Dijon mustard
- Yellow mustard
- Ketchup
- Soy sauce or tamari

- Worcester sauce
- Nutritional yeast
- Baking powder
- Cocoa powder
- Baking soda
- Corn starch or arrowroot powder
- Vanilla extract

Dried fruits

- Cranberries
- Raisins

Sweeteners

- Agave nectar
- Brown sugar
- Coconut sugar
- Dates

- Date syrup
- Maple syrup
- Palm sugar

 Vegan Dairy

- Almond milk
- Cashew milk
- Coconut milk
- Vegan cream cheese
- Oat milk
- Soy milk

- Vegan Feta
- Vegan Cheddar
- Vegan Parmesan
- Coconut yogurt
- Coconut cream

The Plant Based Cookbook For Beginners
650 Easy, Quick, & Simple Plant Based Vegan Diet Recipes With A 31 Day Meal Plan To Lose Weight & Live A Long Healthy Life

53

 Spices

- Sea salt
- Kosher salt
- Italian seasoning
- Garlic powder
- Onion powder
- Paprika
- Turmeric
- Cayenne

- Chili powder
- Cumin
- Bay leaf
- Parsley
- Basil
- Oregano
- Red pepper flakes

 Canned Products

- Beans
- Tomato paste
- Tomato sauce
- Artichoke hearts
- Water chestnuts
- Chipotles

- Cream corn
- Pimentos
- Baby corn
- Veggie broth
- Fire-roasted tomatoes
- Apple sauce

 Refrigerator foods

- Hummus
- Firm tofu
- Tempeh
- Lemon juice
- Lime Juice
- Flax meal

- Salsa
- Whole Grain Bread
- Dark chocolate chips
- Peanut Butter
- Vegan Margarine

54

The Plant Based Cookbook For Beginners
650 Easy, Quick, & Simple Plant Based Vegan Diet Recipes With A 31 Day Meal Plan To Lose Weight & Live A Long Healthy Life

 **Frozen foods**

- Chopped spinach
- Green peas
- Mixed veggies
- Stir fry veggies
- Whole-grain bagels
- Whole-grain buns

 **Plant-based oils and fats**

- Almond oil
- Avocado oil
- Canola oil
- Coconut oil
- Olive oil
- Sesame oil

The Plant Based Cookbook For Beginners
650 Easy, Quick, & Simple Plant Based Vegan Diet Recipes With A 31 Day Meal Plan To Lose Weight & Live A Long Healthy Life

55

Week 2

DAY 08

Meal	Food	Calories	Proteins (g)	Carbs (g)	Fats (g)
Breakfast	Mushroom Cauliflower Breakfast	123	10.2	22.8	1.3
	White Hot Chocolate	249	3	20.1	30.2
Lunch	Mushroom Asada Tacos	220	13.1	25.2	29.3
	Citrus Salad with Dates	185	5.9	23.6	8.2
Snack	Winter Kale Salad	285	4.9	32.9	4.8
	Peppermint Hot Chocolate	285	4.2	33	15
Dinner	Lentil Sloppy Joes with Spaghetti Squash	321	2.3	22	10
	Creamy Broccoli Salad	190	9.1	10.9	5.4
Dessert	Choc-Mint Cups	142	4.5	7.2	10.2
TOTAL		**2000**	**59.9**	**190.5**	**114.2**

56

The Plant Based Cookbook For Beginners
650 Easy, Quick, & Simple Plant Based Vegan Diet Recipes With A 31 Day Meal Plan To Lose Weight & Live A Long Healthy Life

DAY 09

Meal	Food	Calories	Proteins (g)	Carbs (g)	Fats (g)
Breakfast	Sweet Potato Hash with Black Beans	277	12.7	55.6	1.2
	Matcha Latte	157	1.4	8.1	14.3
Lunch	Raw Collard Wraps	293	6	13.2	5.2
Snack	Curry Chickpea Salad	219	7.2	21.9	5.1
	Boba Tea	260	1.1	58.5	2.5
Dinner	Sweet Potato Zoodles	310	5.6	23	5.1
	Chickpea Salad	240	5.3	28	6.4
Dessert	Tart Cherry Mint Sorbet	247	6	27	4.9
	TOTAL	2003	45.3	235.3	44.7

The Plant Based Cookbook For Beginners
650 Easy, Quick, & Simple Plant Based Vegan Diet Recipes With A 31 Day Meal Plan To Lose Weight & Live A Long Healthy Life

57

DAY 10

Meal	Food	Calories	Proteins (g)	Carbs (g)	Fats (g)
Breakfast	Apple-Walnut Bread	314	5.8	58.1	7.7
	Beetroot Latte	144	1	28.4	2.6
Lunch	Pita Pockets with Roasted Veggies	210	4.9	22.9	2.8
	Cabbage Mango Slaw	288	3.2	13	12.1
Snack	Thai Noodle Salad	240	10.9	19.2	4
	Ginger Pineapple Smoothie	303	3.9	25.1	23
Dinner	Broccoli and Potato Curry	238	4	25	3.7
	Quinoa Crunch Salad	172	0.8	28	0.3
Dessert	Banana Cream Pie	234	7	17	21.2
TOTAL		2143	41.5	236.7	77.3

58

The Plant Based Cookbook For Beginners
650 Easy, Quick, & Simple Plant Based Vegan Diet Recipes With A 31 Day Meal Plan To Lose Weight & Live A Long Healthy Life

DAY 11

Meal	Food	Calories	Proteins (g)	Carbs (g)	Fats (g)
Breakfast	Breakfast Beans	222	14.1	41	1
	Cranberry Smoothie	168	2.5	30.8	3.1
Lunch	Gazpacho Soup	215	6.8	20.9	3.2
	Fennel Salad with Cucumber	161	4.8	10.3	14.7
Snack	Pasta Salad with Asparagus	242	5.3	27	1.3
	Raspberry Apple Smoothie	221	3.1	44.8	4.6
Dinner	Butternut Squash Enchiladas	241	3	22.6	4.8
	Curry Tofu Salad	255	3.7	19.7	2.5
Dessert	Apple Crumble	281	6.9	9	19
TOTAL		2006	50.2	226.1	54.2

The Plant Based Cookbook For Beginners
650 Easy, Quick, & Simple Plant Based Vegan Diet Recipes With A 31 Day Meal Plan To Lose Weight & Live A Long Healthy Life

59

DAY 12

Meal	Food	Calories	Proteins (g)	Carbs (g)	Fats (g)
Breakfast	Brown Rice Pudding	509	9.4	108.4	5.6
Lunch	Mediterranean Pinwheels	233	14.4	21.6	7.6
	Farro Tabbouleh Salad	238	4	25	3.7
Snack	Beet Salad	206	1.1	22.3	1.9
	Pina Colada	279	2.2	42.2	10.8
Dinner	Sesame-Orange Chickpea Stir-Fry	366	13	34	3.4
Dessert	Coconut Lime Cheesecakes	201	13	16.2	3.1
	TOTAL	2032	57.1	269.7	39.1

60

The Plant Based Cookbook For Beginners
650 Easy, Quick, & Simple Plant Based Vegan Diet Recipes With A 31 Day Meal Plan To Lose Weight & Live A Long Healthy Life

DAY 13

Meal	Food	Calories	Proteins (g)	Carbs (g)	Fats (g)
Breakfast	Overnight Chia Oats	281	7.1	35.3	13.5
Lunch	Avocado Chickpea Lettuce Cups	257	9.4	20	9.5
	Thai Noodle Salad	240	10.9	19.2	4
Snack	Fennel Asparagus Salad	160	11.7	12.1	2.9
	Cherry Moon Milk	211	4.5	27.2	10.2
Dinner	Tofu Tikka Masala	331	18	29	17
	Winter Kale Salad	285	4.9	32.9	4.8
Dessert	Raspberry Cheesecake	280	9	19	24
TOTAL		**2145**	**75.5**	**194.7**	**85.9**

The Plant Based Cookbook For Beginners
650 Easy, Quick, & Simple Plant Based Vegan Diet Recipes With A 31 Day Meal Plan To Lose Weight & Live A Long Healthy Life

61

DAY 14

Meal	Food	Calories	Proteins (g)	Carbs (g)	Fats (g)
Breakfast	Potato Broccoli Frittatas	282	14.2	47.2	5.5
	Mango Lassi	181	6.9	32	3.9
Lunch	Lime Bean Artichoke Wraps	288	7	28	8
	Pasta Salad with Asparagus	242	5.3	27	1.3
Snack	Citrus Salad with Dates	185	5.9	23.5	8.2
	Spiced Chai	135	4.1	25.5	2.2
Dinner	Puerto Rican Rice and Beans	248	13	26	5.6
	Beet Salad	206	1.1	22.3	1,9
Dessert	Chocolate Pudding Pops	278	12	23	9
TOTAL		**2045**	**69.5**	**229**	**45.6**

62

The Plant Based Cookbook For Beginners
650 Easy, Quick, & Simple Plant Based Vegan Diet Recipes With A 31 Day Meal Plan To Lose Weight & Live A Long Healthy Life

WEEK 2 GROCERY LIST

 **Grains**

- Tapioca pearls
- Oats
- Rice
- Bulgur
- Quinoa
- Barley
- Whole wheat pasta
- Quinoa
- Farro

 **Flours**

- Whole wheat flour
- Almond flour
- Corn flour
- Almond meal
- Flaxseed flour

 **Legumes**

- Kidney beans
- Pinto beans
- Garbanzo
- White beans
- Black beans
- Black-eyed peas
- Split peas

 **Nuts and Seeds**

- Almonds
- Cashews
- Brazil nuts
- Raw macadamia nuts
- Walnuts
- Pinenuts
- Hazelnuts
- Pecans
- Flaxseeds
- Pumpkin seeds

The Plant Based Cookbook For Beginners
650 Easy, Quick, & Simple Plant Based Vegan Diet Recipes With A 31 Day Meal Plan To Lose Weight & Live A Long Healthy Life

63

 **Vegetables**

- Broccoli
- Spaghetti Squash
- Potatoes
- Sweet potatoes
- Tomatoes
- Carrots
- Radishes
- Artichokes
- Lettuces
- Beets
- Spinach
- Eggplants
- Kale
- Asparagus
- Cabbages
- Cauliflower
- Brussels sprouts
- Bean sprouts
- Leeks
- Garlic
- Butternut squash
- Ginger
- Bell peppers
- Pepper
- Onions
- Zucchini
- Cilantro
- Parsley
- Mint leaves

 Fruits

- Cherry
- Apples
- Pears
- Peaches
- Oranges
- Grapes
- Pineapple
- Peach
- Bananas
- Strawberries
- Mangoes
- Blueberries
- Raspberries
- Avocado

64

The Plant Based Cookbook For Beginners
650 Easy, Quick, & Simple Plant Based Vegan Diet Recipes With A 31 Day Meal Plan To Lose Weight & Live A Long Healthy Life

 Condiments

- Vinegar
- Peppermint extract
- Tahini
- Maple syrup
- Blackstrap molasses
- Dijon mustard
- Yellow mustard
- Ketchup
- Vanilla extracts
- Soy sauce
- Worcester sauce
- Nutritional yeast
- Baking powder
- Baking soda
- Cocoa powder
- Corn starch

Dried fruits

- Currants
- Cranberries
- Raisins

Sweeteners

- Agave nectar
- Brown sugar
- Coconut sugar
- Dates
- Date syrup
- Maple syrup
- Palm sugar

Vegan Dairy

- Almond milk
- Cashew milk
- Coconut milk
- Vegan cream cheese
- Oat milk
- Soy milk
- Vegan Feta
- Vegan Cheddar
- Vegan Parmesan
- Coconut yogurt
- Coconut cream

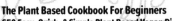
The Plant Based Cookbook For Beginners
650 Easy, Quick, & Simple Plant Based Vegan Diet Recipes With A 31 Day Meal Plan To Lose Weight & Live A Long Healthy Life

65

 Spices

- Sea salt
- Kosher salt
- Italian seasoning
- Garlic powder
- Onion powder
- Paprika
- Smoked paprika
- Turmeric
- Tarragon

- Cayenne
- Chili powder
- Cumin
- Fennel seeds
- Bay leaf
- Parsley
- Basil
- Oregano
- Red pepper flakes

 Canned Products

- Beans
- Tomato paste
- Tomato sauce
- Artichoke hearts
- Chipotles
- Cream corn

- Pimentos
- Baby corn
- Veggie broth
- Fire-roasted tomatoes
- Apple sauce

 Refrigerator foods

- Hummus
- Firm tofu
- Tempeh
- Lemon juice
- Lime Juice
- Flax meal

- Salsa
- Whole Grain Bread
- Dark chocolate chips
- Peanut Butter
- Vegan Margarine

66

The Plant Based Cookbook For Beginners
650 Easy, Quick, & Simple Plant Based Vegan Diet Recipes With A 31 Day Meal Plan To Lose Weight & Live A Long Healthy Life

 **Frozen foods**

- Green peas
- Mixed veggies
- Stir fry veggies
- Whole-grain bagels
- Whole-grain buns

Plant-based oils and fats

- Almond oil
- Avocado oil
- Canola oil
- Coconut oil
- Olive oil
- Sesame oil

The Plant Based Cookbook For Beginners
650 Easy, Quick, & Simple Plant Based Vegan Diet Recipes With A 31 Day Meal Plan To Lose Weight & Live A Long Healthy Life

67

Week 3

DAY 15

Meal	Food	Calories	Proteins (g)	Carbs (g)	Fats (g)
Breakfast	Sweet Potato and Blueberry Flatbreads	242	6.9	48.3	4.4
	Spiced Almond Milk	344	4.5	13	33.2
Lunch	Veggie Sushi Rolls	221	4.6	21.7	4.7
	Curry Chickpea Salad	219	7.2	21.9	5.1
Snack	Creamy Broccoli Salad	180	9.1	10.9	5.4
	Coconut Orange Chai	158	2.8	23.9	6.3
Dinner	Chickpeas in Sofrito	324	34	4.4	20
	Fennel Asparagus Salad	160	11.7	12.1	2.9
Dessert	Tahini Pomegranate Cookies	242	13	21	3
TOTAL		**2090**	**93.8**	**177.2**	**85**

68

The Plant Based Cookbook For Beginners
650 Easy, Quick, & Simple Plant Based Vegan Diet Recipes With A 31 Day Meal Plan To Lose Weight & Live A Long Healthy Life

DAY 16

Meal	Food	Calories	Proteins (g)	Carbs (g)	Fats (g)
Breakfast	Chocolate Pancakes	307	9.1	48.1	11.2
	Tahini Hot Chocolate	260	5.8	29.2	15.4
Lunch	Vegetarian Pancit Bihon	314	10.1	23.1	4.9
	Poke Beets Salad	178	2.1	23.8	0.9
Snack	Kale Chips	201	13	16.2	3.1
	Coconut Milk Hot Chocolate	244	4.2	18.5	20.7
Dinner	Potato Stuffed Peppers	338	14.2	18	15
Dessert	Summer Strawberry Crumble	238	4	25	3.7
	TOTAL	**2080**	**62.5**	**201.9**	**74.9**

The Plant Based Cookbook For Beginners
650 Easy, Quick, & Simple Plant Based Vegan Diet Recipes With A 31 Day Meal Plan To Lose Weight & Live A Long Healthy Life

69

DAY 17

Meal	Food	Calories	Proteins (g)	Carbs (g)	Fats (g)
Breakfast	Tofu Tortilla	196	12.6	28.8	4.9
	Pumpkin Spice Drink	161	3.1	32.6	3.2
Lunch	Chickpeas in Sofrito	324	34	4.4	20
	Creamy Broccoli Salad	180	9.1	10.9	5.4
Snack	Zucchini Chips	181	6.9	9	19
	Lavender London Fog	182	4.2	17.2	5
Dinner	Herb Pasta Salad	348	9	35.1	6.6
	Kale Farro Salad	177	6.4	20.7	14.9
Dessert	Vegan Lemon Muffins	261	8	23	14.7
TOTAL		2010	93.3	181.7	93.7

70

The Plant Based Cookbook For Beginners
650 Easy, Quick, & Simple Plant Based Vegan Diet Recipes With A 31 Day Meal Plan To Lose Weight & Live A Long Healthy Life

DAY 18

Meal	Food	Calories	Proteins (g)	Carbs (g)	Fats (g)
Breakfast	Millet and Squash Parfaits	474	9.7	79.7	13.4
	White Hot Chocolate	249	3	20.1	30.2
Lunch	Butternut Squash Lasagna	278	5.6	24.4	2.7
Snack	Kale Farro Salad	137	6.4	20.7	14.9
	Peppermint Hot Chocolate	285	4.2	33	15
Dinner	Sweet Potato Buddha Bowl	362	13	21	11
Dessert	Pistachio Oat Squares	246	8	32	9
TOTAL		2031	49.9	232.9	96.2

The Plant Based Cookbook For Beginners
650 Easy, Quick, & Simple Plant Based Vegan Diet Recipes With A 31 Day Meal Plan To Lose Weight & Live A Long Healthy Life

71

DAY 19

Meal	Food	Calories	Proteins (g)	Carbs (g)	Fats (g)
Breakfast	Berry Muffins	323	5.3	57.6	7.3
	Turmeric Latte	142	1.9	13	4.4
Lunch	Thai Coconut Cauliflower	306	3.6	13.6	0.1
	Chickpea Salad	240	5.3	28	6.4
Snack	Poke Beets Salad	178	2.1	23.8	0.9
	Choco Banana Chai Latte	269	3.2	65.2	2.8
Dinner	Curried Brown Rice with Tofu	314	13	28	18
Dessert	Creamy Butternut Squash Pudding	285	11	16	8
TOTAL		**2057**	**45.4**	**245.2**	**47.9**

72

The Plant Based Cookbook For Beginners
650 Easy, Quick, & Simple Plant Based Vegan Diet Recipes With A 31 Day Meal Plan To Lose Weight & Live A Long Healthy Life

DAY 20

Meal	Food	Calories	Proteins (g)	Carbs (g)	Fats (g)
Breakfast	Banana-Fig Bread	382	7.4	71.5	8.7
	Matcha Latte	157	1.4	8.1	14.3
Lunch	Spiralized Vegetable Lo Mein	280	2.3	21.7	2.4
	Curry Tofu Salad	255	3.7	19.7	2.5
Snack	Carrot Chips	141	4.5	7.2	10.2
	Boba Tea	260	1.1	58.5	2.5
Dinner	Tofu Hummus Buddha	287	9	26	7
Dessert	Peach Cobbler	327	10	25	12
	TOTAL	**2089**	**39.4**	**237.7**	**59.6**

The Plant Based Cookbook For Beginners
650 Easy, Quick, & Simple Plant Based Vegan Diet Recipes With A 31 Day Meal Plan To Lose Weight & Live A Long Healthy Life

73

DAY 21

Meal	Food	Calories	Proteins (g)	Carbs (g)	Fats (g)
Breakfast	Quinoa Bowls with Pears	482	14.1	95	7.2
	Beetroot Latte	144	1	28.4	2.6
Lunch	Eggplant Parmesan	339	14	29.4	1.1
	Kohlrabi Slaw with Cilantro	182	4.5	14.4	4.2
Snack	Banana Chips	159	4.1	25.5	2.2
Dinner	Vegan Burrito	363	7	23	11.1
Dessert	Golden Milk Cheesecake	340	13	28.2	14
TOTAL		2009	53.2	243.9	42.4

74

The Plant Based Cookbook For Beginners
650 Easy, Quick, & Simple Plant Based Vegan Diet Recipes With A 31 Day Meal Plan To Lose Weight & Live A Long Healthy Life

WEEK 3
GROCERY LIST

 **Grains**

- Tapioca pearls
- Oats
- Farro
- Rice
- Barley
- Millet
- Cornmeal
- Whole wheat pasta

 Flours

- Whole wheat flour
- Almond flour
- Corn flour
- Almond meal
- Flaxseed flour

 **Legumes**

- Kidney beans
- Pinto beans
- Garbanzo
- White beans
- Black beans
- Black-eyed peas
- Split peas

 **Nuts and Seeds**

- Almonds
- Cashews
- Brazil nuts
- Raw macadamia nuts
- Walnuts
- Pinenuts
- Hazelnuts
- Pecans
- Flaxseeds
- Pumpkin seeds

The Plant Based Cookbook For Beginners
650 Easy, Quick, & Simple Plant Based Vegan Diet Recipes With A 31 Day Meal Plan To Lose Weight & Live A Long Healthy Life

75

 ## Vegetables

- Butternut squash
- Potatoes
- Broccoli
- Sweet potatoes
- Beets
- Tomatoes
- Carrots
- Radishes
- Artichokes
- Lettuces
- Spinach
- Kale
- Cabbages
- Cauliflower
- Brussels sprouts
- Bean sprouts
- Leeks
- Garlic
- Zucchini
- Ginger
- Eggplants
- Bell peppers
- Red Peppers
- Jalapenos
- Onions
- Corn
- Cilantro
- Parsley
- Mint leaves

Fruits

- Figs
- Apples
- Pears
- Peaches
- Oranges
- Pineapple
- Peach
- Bananas
- Strawberries
- Mangoes
- Blueberries
- Raspberries
- Kiwi
- Pomegranate seeds
- Avocado

76

The Plant Based Cookbook For Beginners
650 Easy, Quick, & Simple Plant Based Vegan Diet Recipes With A 31 Day Meal Plan To Lose Weight & Live A Long Healthy Life

 Condiments

- Peppermint extract
- Honey
- Tahini
- Vegan fish sauce
- Balsamic vinegar
- Apple cider vinegar
- Maple syrup
- Blackstrap molasses
- Dijon mustard
- Yellow mustard
- Ketchup
- Soy sauce
- Vanilla extracts
- Worcester sauce
- Nutritional yeast
- Baking powder
- Baking soda
- Corn starch
- Cocoa powder

Dried fruits

- Cranberries
- Raisins

Sweeteners

- Agave nectar
- Brown sugar
- Coconut sugar
- Dates
- Date syrup
- Maple syrup
- Palm sugar

 Vegan Dairy

- Almond milk
- Cashew milk
- Coconut milk
- Vegan cream cheese
- Oat milk
- Soy milk
- Vegan Feta
- Vegan Cheddar
- Vegan Parmesan
- Coconut yogurt
- Coconut cream

The Plant Based Cookbook For Beginners
650 Easy, Quick, & Simple Plant Based Vegan Diet Recipes With A 31 Day Meal Plan To Lose Weight & Live A Long Healthy Life

77

 **Spices**

- Sea salt
- Kosher salt
- Italian seasoning
- Garlic powder
- Onion powder
- Smoked paprika
- Paprika
- Turmeric
- Cayenne pepper
- Chili powder
- Cumin
- Bay leaf
- Parsley
- Basil
- Oregano
- Fennel seeds
- Red pepper flakes

 **Canned Products**

- Beans
- Tomato paste
- Tomato sauce
- Artichoke hearts
- Chipotles
- Pimentos
- Veggie broth
- Fire-roasted tomatoes
- Apple sauce

 **Refrigerator foods**

- Hummus
- Olives
- Firm tofu
- Tempeh
- Lemon juice
- Lime Juice
- Flax meal
- Salsa
- Whole Grain Bread
- Dark chocolate chips
- Peanut Butter
- Vegan Margarine

78

The Plant Based Cookbook For Beginners
650 Easy, Quick, & Simple Plant Based Vegan Diet Recipes With A 31 Day Meal Plan To Lose Weight & Live A Long Healthy Life

 **Frozen foods**

- Green peas
- Mixed veggies
- Stir fry veggies
- Whole-grain bagels
- Whole-grain buns

Plant-based oils and fats

- Almond oil
- Avocado oil
- Canola oil
- Coconut oil
- Olive oil
- Sesame oil

The Plant Based Cookbook For Beginners
650 Easy, Quick, & Simple Plant Based Vegan Diet Recipes With A 31 Day Meal Plan To Lose Weight & Live A Long Healthy Life

79

Week 4

DAY 22

Meal	Food	Calories	Proteins (g)	Carbs (g)	Fats (g)
Breakfast	Blueberry Freekeh Breakfast	368	11.9	72.4	7.6
	Cranberry Smoothie	168	2.5	30.8	3.1
Lunch	Grilled Zucchini with Pine Nuts	201	5	10.8	2.4
	Winter Kale Salad	285	4.9	32.9	4.8
Snack	Stir-Fried Asparagus	142	1	11	1
	Raspberry Apple Smoothie	221	3.1	44.8	4.6
Dinner	Buffalo Tofu Wrap	250	6	20	7.8
	Pasta Salad with Asparagus	242	5.3	27	1.3
Dessert	Raspberry Ice Cream	191	9	19	12
TOTAL		**2068**	**48.7**	**272.3**	**44.6**

80

The Plant Based Cookbook For Beginners
650 Easy, Quick, & Simple Plant Based Vegan Diet Recipes With A 31 Day Meal Plan To Lose Weight & Live A Long Healthy Life

DAY 23

Meal	Food	Calories	Proteins (g)	Carbs (g)	Fats (g)
Breakfast	Blueberry Freekeh Breakfast	368	11.9	72.4	7.6
	Cashew Creamer	100	1.3	16.2	3.1
Lunch	Szechuan Tofu and Veggies	226	11.3	19	20.4
	Fennel Asparagus Salad	160	11.7	12.1	2.9
Snack	Sweet and Sour Kale	157	1.4	21	14.3
	Cherry Moon Milk	211	4.5	27.2	10.2
Dinner	Red Pesto Pasta	394	6	31	9
	Poke Beets Salad	178	2.1	23.8	0.9
Dessert	Chocolate Peanut Fat Bombs	246	7.2	29.4	7.4
	TOTAL	2040	57.4	252.1	75.8

The Plant Based Cookbook For Beginners
650 Easy, Quick, & Simple Plant Based Vegan Diet Recipes With A 31 Day Meal Plan To Lose Weight & Live A Long Healthy Life

81

DAY 24

Meal	Food	Calories	Proteins (g)	Carbs (g)	Fats (g)
Breakfast	Peanut Butter Granola Bars	246	7.2	29.4	7.4
	Mango Lassi	181	6.9	32	3.9
Lunch	Spaghetti Squash with Eggplant Puttanesca	380	4.9	15.1	14.7
	Citrus Salad with Dates	185	5.9	23.6	8.2
Snack	Cauliflower Mash	121	3.1	4.8	4.6
	Spiced Chai	135	4.1	25.5	2.2
Dinner	Peanut Noodles with Tofu	384	14	29	19
	Creamy Broccoli Salad	180	9.1	10.9	5.4
Dessert	Banana Walnut Muffins	265	5	26	14
TOTAL		2077	60.2	196.3	79.4

82

The Plant Based Cookbook For Beginners
650 Easy, Quick, & Simple Plant Based Vegan Diet Recipes With A 31 Day Meal Plan To Lose Weight & Live A Long Healthy Life

DAY 25

Meal	Food	Calories	Proteins (g)	Carbs (g)	Fats (g)
Breakfast	Muesli with Roasted Peanuts	451	14.5	70.9	14.3
Lunch	Pita Pizzas	413	19.9	71.6	1.4
	Kale Farro Salad	137	6.4	20.7	14.9
Snack	Spiced Corn	249	3	20.1	10.2
	Coconut Orange Chai	158	2.8	23.9	6.3
Dinner	Wraps with Cauliflower Rice	361	8	23	14.7
Dessert	Blueberry Crisp	246	0.8	31.1	0.6
TOTAL		**2015**	**55.4**	**261.3**	**62.4**

The Plant Based Cookbook For Beginners
650 Easy, Quick, & Simple Plant Based Vegan Diet Recipes With A 31 Day Meal Plan To Lose Weight & Live A Long Healthy Life

83

DAY 26

Meal	Food	Calories	Proteins (g)	Carbs (g)	Fats (g)
Breakfast	Sweet Potato Corn Hash	265	6	21.6	8.3
	Tahini Hot Chocolate	260	5.8	29.2	15.4
Lunch	Rainbow Taco Boats	245	7.2	22.9	3.5
	Cabbage Mango Slaw	288	3.2	13	12.1
Snack	Sweet and Sour Kale	157	1.4	21	14.3
	Coconut Milk Hot Chocolate	244	4.2	18.5	20.7
Dinner	Peruvian Sandwich	315	8	28	17
Dessert	Avocado filling Cake	398	1.8	53.6	13.8
TOTAL		2015	40.4	215.3	105.1

84

The Plant Based Cookbook For Beginners
650 Easy, Quick, & Simple Plant Based Vegan Diet Recipes With A 31 Day Meal Plan To Lose Weight & Live A Long Healthy Life

DAY 27

Meal	Food	Calories	Proteins (g)	Carbs (g)	Fats (g)
Breakfast	Oatmeal Cups with Berries	230	6.6	43.1	4.3
	Pumpkin Spice Drin	161	3.1	32.6	3.2
Lunch	Instant Pot Mujadara	266	10.7	22	12
	Curry Tofu Salad	255	3.7	19.7	2.5
Snack	Steamed Green Beans	161	3.1	16	3.2
	Lavender London Fog	182	4.2	17.2	5
Dinner	Broccoli Pesto Pasta	330	6	18.3	4.9
	Farro Tabbouleh Salad	238	4	25	3.7
Dessert	Protein Fat Bombs	293	4.2	25.2	16
TOTAL		2116	45.6	209.1	54.8

The Plant Based Cookbook For Beginners
650 Easy, Quick, & Simple Plant Based Vegan Diet Recipes With A 31 Day Meal Plan To Lose Weight & Live A Long Healthy Life

85

DAY 28

Meal	Food	Calories	Proteins (g)	Carbs (g)	Fats (g)
Breakfast	Sweet Waffles	488	7.3	92.5	11.4
	Turmeric Latte	142	1.9	13	4.4
Lunch	Warm Lentils with Roasted Beets	393	8.6	31	4.5
	Kohlrabi Slaw with Cilantro	182	4.5	14.4	4.2
Snack	Choco Banana Chai Latte	269	3.2	65.2	2.8
Dinner	Chickpea Lavash Wrap	391	9	19	12
Dessert	Carrot Flaxseed Muffins	172	4	45.8	11.8
TOTAL		**2035**	**38.5**	**280.9**	**51.1**

86

The Plant Based Cookbook For Beginners
650 Easy, Quick, & Simple Plant Based Vegan Diet Recipes With A 31 Day Meal Plan To Lose Weight & Live A Long Healthy Life

DAY 29

Meal	Food	Calories	Proteins (g)	Carbs (g)	Fats (g)
Breakfast	Peanut Butter Granola Bars	303	9.3	42.1	12.6
	White Hot Chocolate	249	3	20.1	30.2
Lunch	No-Tuna Salad Sandwich	307	15	47.3	7.4
	Kohlrabi Slaw with Cilantro	182	4.5	14.4	4.2
Snack	Eggplant Chips	293	6	13.2	5.2
	Peppermint Hot Chocolate	285	4.2	33	15
Dinner	Sesame Broccoli	138	5.8	20.2	5.8
Dessert	Applesauce Muffins	298	2	31	6
	TOTAL	**2055**	**49.8**	**221.3**	**86.4**

The Plant Based Cookbook For Beginners
650 Easy, Quick, & Simple Plant Based Vegan Diet Recipes With A 31 Day Meal Plan To Lose Weight & Live A Long Healthy Life

87

DAY 30

Meal	Food	Calories	Proteins (g)	Carbs (g)	Fats (g)
Breakfast	Overnight Apple Oats	347	5.7	43.7	18.1
	Matcha Latte	157	1.4	8.1	14.3
Lunch	Angel Hair Pasta with Watercress	246	8	22	9
	Beet Salad	206	1.1	22.3	1,9
Snack	Tomato Kebabs	233	4.4	11.6	17.6
Dinner	Moroccan Lentils	350	7	20	11
	Curry Chickpea Salad	219	7.2	21.9	5.1
Dessert	Oatmeal Cranberry Muffin	280	2.3	21.7	2.4
TOTAL		2038	37.1	171.3	79.4

88

The Plant Based Cookbook For Beginners
650 Easy, Quick, & Simple Plant Based Vegan Diet Recipes With A 31 Day Meal Plan To Lose Weight & Live A Long Healthy Life

DAY 31

Meal	Food	Calories	Proteins (g)	Carbs (g)	Fats (g)
Breakfast	Zucchini Bread	402	13.7	65.7	12.2
	Turmeric Eggnog	145	1.1	21.8	7.1
Lunch	Chickpea Salad Bites	356	7	37.6	13.6
	Beet Salad	206	1.1	22.3	1,9
Snack	Roasted Brussels Sprout				
	Pina Colada	279	2.2	42.2	10.8
Dinner	Peanut Noodles with Tofu	384	14	29	19
Dessert	Green Popsicle	261	3.3	29.3	16.3
	TOTAL	2033	42.2	248.94	80.9

The Plant Based Cookbook For Beginners
650 Easy, Quick, & Simple Plant Based Vegan Diet Recipes With A 31 Day Meal Plan To Lose Weight & Live A Long Healthy Life

89

WEEK 4
GROCERY LIST

 **Grains**
- Steel cut oats
- Rice
- Farro
- Bulgur
- Quinoa
- Millet
- Whole wheat pasta
- Quinoa
- Angel hair pasta

 Flours
- Coconut flour
- Whole wheat flour
- Almond flour
- Corn flour
- Almond meal
- Flaxseed flour

 **Legumes**
- Kidney beans
- Pinto beans
- Garbanzo
- White beans
- Black beans
- Black-eyed peas
- Split peas
- Lentils

 **Nuts and Seeds**
- Almonds
- Cashews
- Brazil nuts
- Raw macadamia nuts
- Walnuts
- Pinenuts
- Hazelnuts
- Pecans
- Flaxseeds
- Pumpkin seeds

 **Vegetables**

- Butternut squash
- Cabbage
- Spaghetti Squash
- Potatoes
- Fennel
- Broccoli
- Sweet potatoes
- Beets
- Tomatoes
- Carrots
- Eggplants
- Radishes
- Artichokes
- Lettuces
- Fennel
- Spinach

- Zucchini
- Kale
- Cauliflower
- Brussels sprouts
- Bean sprouts
- Leeks
- Garlic
- Ginger
- Bell peppers
- Pepper
- Onions
- Eggplants
- Corn
- Cilantro
- Parsley
- Mint leaves

 Fruits

- Cherry
- Pears
- Peaches
- Oranges
- Apples
- Pineapple
- Peach

- Bananas
- Strawberries
- Mangoes
- Blueberries
- Raspberries
- Avocado

The Plant Based Cookbook For Beginners
650 Easy, Quick, & Simple Plant Based Vegan Diet Recipes With A 31 Day Meal Plan To Lose Weight & Live A Long Healthy Life

91

 Condiments

- Pesto
- Vegan Protein powder
- Matcha Powder
- Balsamic vinegar
- Apple cider vinegar
- Red wine vinegar
- Tahini
- Maple syrup
- Blackstrap molasses
- Dijon mustard
- Yellow mustard
- Ketchup
- Soy sauce
- Worcester sauce
- Nutritional yeast
- Baking powder
- Baking soda
- Cocoa powder
- Corn starch or arrowroot powder
- Vanilla extract

Dried fruits

- Raisins
- Cranberries
- Dates

 Sweeteners

- Brown sugar
- Coconut sugar
- Dates
- Date syrup
- Maple syrup
- Palm sugar

 Vegan Dairy

- Almond milk
- Cashew milk
- Coconut milk
- Vegan cream cheese
- Oat milk
- Soy milk
- Vegan Feta
- Vegan Cheddar
- Vegan Parmesan
- Coconut yogurt
- Coconut cream

92

The Plant Based Cookbook For Beginners
650 Easy, Quick, & Simple Plant Based Vegan Diet Recipes With A 31 Day Meal Plan To Lose Weight & Live A Long Healthy Life

 Spices

- Sea salt
- Kosher salt
- Italian seasoning
- Garlic powder
- Onion powder
- Paprika
- Turmeric
- Tarragon

- Cayenne
- Chili powder
- Cumin
- Bay leaf
- Parsley
- Basil
- Oregano
- Red pepper flakes

 Canned Products

- Sun-dried tomatoes
- Watercress
- Beans
- Tomato paste
- Tomato sauce
- Artichoke hearts

- Chipotles
- Cream corn
- Pimentos
- Veggie broth
- Fire-roasted tomatoes
- Apple sauce

 Refrigerator foods

- Hummus
- Firm tofu
- Tempeh
- Lemon juice
- Lime Juice

- Flax meal
- Whole Grain Bread
- Dark chocolate chips
- Peanut Butter
- Vegan Margarine

Frozen foods

- Hash browns
- Chopped spinach
- Corn nibbles
- Green peas

- Mixed veggies
- Stir fry veggies
- Whole-grain bagels
- Whole-grain buns

The Plant Based Cookbook For Beginners
650 Easy, Quick, & Simple Plant Based Vegan Diet Recipes With A 31 Day Meal Plan To Lose Weight & Live A Long Healthy Life

93

 **Plant-based oils and fats**

- Almond oil
- Avocado oil
- Canola oil
- Coconut oil
- Olive oil
- Sesame oil

94

The Plant Based Cookbook For Beginners
650 Easy, Quick, & Simple Plant Based Vegan Diet Recipes With A 31 Day Meal Plan To Lose Weight & Live A Long Healthy Life

CHAPTER 03

PLANT-BASED BREAKFAST RECIPES

Chocolate Chia Pudding

SERVINGS	PREPARATION TIME	FRIDGE TIME
2	15 minutes	3 hours

Nutritional Values Per Serving

Calories	212
Total Fat	7g
Saturated Fat	1.1g
Cholesterol	0mg
Sodium	96mg
Total Carbohydrate	37.1g
Dietary Fiber	8.5g
Total Sugars	19.5g
Protein	4.5g

Ingredients:

- 1 cup unsweetened almond milk
- 4 tablespoons chia seeds
- 2 tablespoons cocoa powder
- 1 teaspoon vanilla extract
- 1 banana
- 2 tablespoons maple syrup

Instructions:

1. Blend cocoa powder, vanilla extract, maple syrup, banana, chia seeds and almond milk in a blender.
2. Divide the mixture into two small jars, cover and refrigerate for 3 hours.
3. Garnish with desired nuts and coconut cream.
4. Serve.

96

The Plant Based Cookbook For Beginners
650 Easy, Quick, & Simple Plant Based Vegan Diet Recipes With A 31 Day Meal Plan To Lose Weight & Live A Long Healthy Life

Chocolate Chip Banana Muffins

SERVINGS	PREPARATION TIME	COOKING TIME
8	10 minutes	20 minutes

Nutritional Values Per Serving

Calories	272
Total Fat	0.3g
Saturated Fat	0g
Cholesterol	0mg
Sodium	2mg
Total Carbohydrate	46g
Dietary Fiber	2.3g
Total Sugars	6g
Protein	12.1g

Ingredients:

- 4 tablespoons ground flaxseed
- 4 tablespoons warm water
- 1 ¾ cups whole-wheat pastry flour
- 1 teaspoon cinnamon
- ¼ teaspoon nutmeg
- 1 teaspoon baking powder
- ½ teaspoon baking soda
- ½ teaspoon sea salt
- ⅔ cup almond milk
- 1 tablespoon apple cider vinegar
- ⅓ cup maple syrup
- ⅓ cup olive oil
- 1 teaspoon vanilla
- 1 cup ripe banana, mashed
- ½ cup dark chocolate chips

Instructions:

1. At 350 degrees F, preheat your oven.
2. Grease a suitable 12-cup muffin pan with cooking spray.
3. Mix flaxseed with warm water in a bowl and leave for 5 minutes.
4. Mix flour with cinnamon, almond milk, nutmeg, baking soda, salt, baking powder, maple syrup, oil, vanilla and apple cider vinegar in a bowl.
5. Stir in a flaxseed mixture and mix until smooth.
6. Fold in chocolate chips and bananas, then stir well.
7. Divide this batter into the prepared muffin tray.
8. Bake these muffins for 20 minutes in the oven.
9. Allow them to cool, then serve.

The Plant Based Cookbook For Beginners
650 Easy, Quick, & Simple Plant Based Vegan Diet Recipes With A 31 Day Meal Plan To Lose Weight & Live A Long Healthy Life

97

Chocolate Chip Pancakes

SERVINGS	PREPARATION TIME	COOKING TIME
6	15 minutes	20 minutes

Nutritional Values Per Serving

Calories	348
Total Fat	12.5g
Saturated Fat	9.4g
Cholesterol	0mg
Sodium	56mg
Total Carbohydrate	56.2g
Dietary Fiber	7.5g
Total Sugars	12.9g
Protein	8.6g

Serving Suggestion:

Enjoy these pancakes with coconut yogurt and maple syrup.

Ingredients:

- 1 tablespoon flaxseed meal
- 1¼ cups buckwheat flour
- ¼ cup old-fashioned rolled oats
- 2 tablespoons coconut flakes
- 1 tablespoon baking powder
- Pinch of sea salt
- 1 cup almond milk
- ½ cup unsweetened applesauce
- ¼ cup pure maple syrup
- 1 teaspoon pure vanilla extract
- ⅓ cup mini dark chocolate chips
- Sliced bananas, for serving

Instructions:

1. Mix flaxseed meal with ½ cup of water in a small saucepan and cook for 4 minutes on medium heat.

2. Strain the mixture and discard the seeds.

3. Mix buckwheat flour with salt, baking powder, coconut flakes and oats in a large bowl.

4. Beat milk with 2 tablespoons flaxseed liquid, vanilla, maple syrup and apple sauce in a suitable bowl.

5. Pour this milk-liquid mixture into the flour mixture and mix well until smooth.

6. Fold in chocolate chips and mix evenly.

7. Set a non-stick griddle over medium-low heat.

8. Pour ⅓ cup prepared batter into the griddle, spread it around and cook for 5 minutes per side.

9. Transfer this pancake to a plate and cook more pancakes with the remaining batter.

10. Serve with sliced bananas on top.

98

The Plant Based Cookbook For Beginners
650 Easy, Quick, & Simple Plant Based Vegan Diet Recipes With A 31 Day Meal Plan To Lose Weight & Live A Long Healthy Life

Oatmeal Cranberry Muffins

SERVINGS
4

PREPARATION TIME
10 minutes

COOKING TIME
35 minutes

Nutritional Values Per Serving

Calories	280
Total Fat	2.4g
Saturated Fat	0g
Cholesterol	0mg
Sodium	99mg
Total Carbohydrate	21.7g
Dietary Fiber	10.2g
Total Sugars	49.7g
Protein	2.3g

Ingredients:

- 2 ½ cups rolled oats
- ½ cup oat flour
- 1 teaspoon baking powder
- ½ teaspoon baking soda
- ½ teaspoon salt
- 1 tablespoon cinnamon
- ½ teaspoon ground nutmeg
- 4 ripe bananas, mashed
- 1 apple, grated
- ½ cup almond milk
- 2 teaspoons vanilla extract
- ½ cup cranberries
- ½ cup chopped walnuts

Instructions:

1. At 350 degrees F, preheat your oven.
2. Whisk the dry muffin ingredients in a mixing bowl.
3. And beat the wet ingredients in a separate bowl.
4. Combine and beat the two mixtures together until smooth.
5. Fold in apples, walnuts and cranberries then give it a gentle stir.
6. Line a suitable muffin tray with muffin cups and evenly divide the muffin batter among the cups.
7. Bake for nearly 35 minutes and serve.

The Plant Based Cookbook For Beginners
650 Easy, Quick, & Simple Plant Based Vegan Diet Recipes With A 31 Day Meal Plan To Lose Weight & Live A Long Healthy Life

99

Applesauce Muffins

SERVINGS	PREPARATION TIME	COOKING TIME
4	15 minutes	25 minutes

Nutritional Values Per Serving

Calories	298
Total Fat	6g
Saturated Fat	7g
Cholesterol	632mg
Sodium	497mg
Total Carbohydrate	31g
Dietary Fiber	3g
Total Sugars	83g
Protein	2g

Ingredients:

- 2 cups whole wheat flour
- 1 teaspoon baking powder
- 1 teaspoon baking soda
- ½ teaspoon salt
- 1 teaspoon cinnamon
- ½ teaspoon ground allspice
- ½ cup brown sugar
- 15 ounces apple sauce
- ½ cup almond milk
- 1 teaspoon vanilla
- 1 teaspoon apple cider vinegar
- ½ cup raisins
- ½ cup apple, diced

Instructions:

1. At 350 degrees F, preheat your oven.
2. Separately, whisk together the dry ingredients in one bowl and wet ingredients in another bowl.
3. Combine and beat the two mixture together until smooth.
4. Fold in apples and raisins then give it a gentle stir.
5. Line a muffin tray with muffin cups and evenly divide the muffin batter among the cups.
6. Bake for nearly 25 minutes and serve

100

The Plant Based Cookbook For Beginners
650 Easy, Quick, & Simple Plant Based Vegan Diet Recipes With A 31 Day Meal Plan To Lose Weight & Live A Long Healthy Life

Chickpea Omelet with Mushrooms

SERVINGS	PREPARATION TIME	COOKING TIME
4	15 minutes	20 minutes

Nutritional Values Per Serving

Calories	249
Total Fat	3.9g
Saturated Fat	0.4g
Cholesterol	0mg
Sodium	183mg
Total Carbohydrate	40.3g
Dietary Fiber	13.1g
Total Sugars	6.7g
Protein	17.5g

Serving Suggestion:

Try this omelet with toasted whole wheat bread slices.

Ingredients:

- 1 cup chickpea flour
- ½ teaspoon onion powder
- ½ teaspoon garlic powder
- ¼ teaspoon white pepper
- ¼ teaspoon black pepper
- ⅓ cup nutritional yeast
- ½ teaspoon baking soda
- 3 green onions, chopped
- 4 ounces sautéed mushrooms

Instructions:

1. Mix chickpea flour with baking soda, nutritional yeast, black pepper, white pepper, garlic powder, and onion powder in a small bowl.

2. Pour in 1 cup water, then mix well until smooth.

3. Set a suitable deep skillet over medium heat.

4. Add the chickpea batter to the skillet and top it with mushrooms and green onions.

5. Cook for 3-5 minutes, then fold it in half and cook for another 5 minutes.

6. Slice and serve warm.

The Plant Based Cookbook For Beginners
650 Easy, Quick, & Simple Plant Based Vegan Diet Recipes With A 31 Day Meal Plan To Lose Weight & Live A Long Healthy Life

101

Banana Walnut Muffins

SERVINGS	PREPARATION TIME	COOKING TIME
4	10 minutes	18 minutes

Nutritional Values Per Serving

Calories	265
Total Fat	14g
Saturated Fat	7g
Cholesterol	632mg
Sodium	497mg
Total Carbohydrate	26g
Dietary Fiber	3g
Total Sugars	10g
Protein	5g

Ingredients:

- 4 large pitted dates, blended
- 1 cup almond milk
- 2 tablespoons lemon juice
- 2 ½ cups rolled oats
- 1 teaspoon baking powder
- 1 teaspoon baking soda
- 1 teaspoon cinnamon
- ¼ teaspoon nutmeg
- ⅛ teaspoon salt
- 1 ½ cups mashed banana
- ¼ cup maple syrup
- 1 tablespoon vanilla extract
- 1 cup walnuts, chopped

Instructions:

1. At 350 degrees F, preheat your oven.

2. Separately, whisk together the dry ingredients in one bowl and the wet ingredients in another bowl.

3. Combine and beat the two mixtures together until smooth.

4. Fold in walnuts and give it a gentle stir.

5. Line a suitable muffin tray with muffin cups and evenly divide the muffin batter among the cups.

6. Bake for 18 minutes and serve.

102

The Plant Based Cookbook For Beginners
650 Easy, Quick, & Simple Plant Based Vegan Diet Recipes With A 31 Day Meal Plan To Lose Weight & Live A Long Healthy Life

Carrot Flaxseed Muffins

SERVINGS   **PREPARATION TIME**   **COOKING TIME**
4   **10 minutes**   **20 minutes**

Nutritional Values Per Serving

Calories	172
Total Fat	11.8g
Saturated Fat	4.4g
Cholesterol	62mg
Sodium	871mg
Total Carbohydrate	45.8g
Dietary Fiber	0.6g
Total Sugars	2.3g
Protein	4g

Ingredients:

- 2 tablespoons ground flax
- 5 tablespoons water
- ¾ cup almond milk
- ¾ cup applesauce
- ½ cup maple syrup
- 1 teaspoon vanilla extract
- 1 ½ cups whole wheat flour
- ½ cup rolled oats, crushed
- 1 teaspoon baking soda
- 1 ½ teaspoons baking powder
- ½ teaspoon salt
- 1 teaspoon ground cinnamon
- ¼ teaspoon ground ginger
- 1 cup grated carrot

Instructions:

1. Whisk flaxseed with water in a bowl and leave it for 10 minutes
2. At 350 degrees F, preheat your oven.
3. Separately, whisk together the dry ingredients in one bowl and the wet ingredients in another bowl.
4. Combine and beat the two mixtures together until smooth.
5. Fold in flaxseed and carrots then give it a gentle stir.
6. Line a suitable muffin tray with muffin cups and evenly divide the muffin batter among the cups.
7. Bake for 20 minutes and serve.

The Plant Based Cookbook For Beginners
650 Easy, Quick, & Simple Plant Based Vegan Diet Recipes With A 31 Day Meal Plan To Lose Weight & Live A Long Healthy Life

103

Polenta with Saucy Pears

SERVINGS	PREPARATION TIME	COOKING TIME
4	10 minutes	10 minutes

Nutritional Values Per Serving

Calories	470
Total Fat	1.2g
Saturated Fat	0g
Cholesterol	0mg
Sodium	16mg
Total Carbohydrate	110.4g
Dietary Fiber	5.1g
Total Sugars	23.7g
Protein	7.1g

Ingredients:

- ¼ cup brown rice syrup
- 2 pears, peeled, cored, and diced
- 1 cup dried cranberries
- 1 teaspoon ground cinnamon
- 4 cups polenta, cooked
- Shredded coconut, to garnish

Instructions:

1. Add brown rice syrup to a saucepan and heat it over medium heat.

2. Stir in pears, cinnamon and cranberries, then cook for 10 minutes with occasional stirring.

3. Divide the polenta into the four serving cups and top it with the pears.

4. Garnish with coconut shreds.

5. Serve.

104

The Plant Based Cookbook For Beginners
650 Easy, Quick, & Simple Plant Based Vegan Diet Recipes With A 31 Day Meal Plan To Lose Weight & Live A Long Healthy Life

Almond Granola

SERVINGS **PREPARATION TIME** **COOKING TIME**
12   10 minutes   50 minutes

Nutritional Values Per Serving	
Calories	355
Total Fat	7.7g
Saturated Fat	0.9g
Cholesterol	0mg
Sodium	198mg
Total Carbohydrate	65.4g
Dietary Fiber	9.4g
Total Sugars	22.1g
Protein	9.8g

Serving Suggestion:

Enjoy this granola with coconut yogurt and berries.

Ingredients:

- 8 cups rolled oats
- 2 cups dates, pitted and chopped
- 2 ripe bananas, peeled and chopped
- 1 teaspoon almond extract
- 1 teaspoon salt
- 1 cup almonds

Instructions:

1. At 275 degrees F, preheat your oven.
2. Layer 2 (13x18 inch) baking sheets with parchment paper.
3. Boil dates with 1 cup water in a saucepan, reduce the heat and cook for 10 minutes on medium heat.
4. Remove the hot pan from the heat and blend these dates with bananas, salt and almond extract in a blender until smooth.
5. Mix oats and dates mixture in a bowl and mix well.
6. Spread this oats granola mixture in the prepared baking sheets.
7. Bake the granola for 40-50 minutes in the preheated oven. Stir after every 10 minutes.
8. Add on top and serve.

The Plant Based Cookbook For Beginners
650 Easy, Quick, & Simple Plant Based Vegan Diet Recipes With A 31 Day Meal Plan To Lose Weight & Live A Long Healthy Life

105

Oatmeal Breakfast Cookies

SERVINGS	PREPARATION TIME	COOKING TIME
6	15 minutes	22 minutes

Nutritional Values Per Serving

Calories	219
Total Fat	5g
Saturated Fat	3.1g
Cholesterol	14mg
Sodium	354mg
Total Carbohydrate	29g
Dietary Fiber	7g
Total Sugars	5g
Protein	7g

Ingredients:

- 2 tablespoons ground flaxseed
- 5 tablespoons warm water
- 1 cup oat flour
- 1 cup whole rolled oats
- ½ cup almond flour
- zest of 1 lemon
- ½ teaspoon baking powder
- ½ teaspoon baking soda
- ½ teaspoon cinnamon
- ½ teaspoon sea salt
- ½ cup almond butter
- ¼ cup coconut oil, melted
- ½ cup maple syrup
- ⅓ cup walnuts
- ¾ cup fresh blueberries

Instructions:

1. At 350 degrees F, preheat your oven.
2. Layer a suitable baking sheet with wax paper.
3. Mix flaxseed with water in a bowl and leave for 5 minutes.
4. Mix almond salt, cinnamon, baking soda, baking powder, lemon zest, 1 cup rolled oats and oat flour in a bowl.
5. Stir in flaxseed mixture, maple syrup, coconut oil, and almond butter, then mix well.
6. Fold in blueberries and walnuts, then mix evenly.
7. Divide this cookie dough into ¼ cup balls on the baking sheet.
8. Flatten each cookie ball and bake for 22 minutes.
9. Serve.

106

The Plant Based Cookbook For Beginners
650 Easy, Quick, & Simple Plant Based Vegan Diet Recipes With A 31 Day Meal Plan To Lose Weight & Live A Long Healthy Life

Oatmeal with Mixed Fruit

SERVINGS	PREPARATION TIME	COOKING TIME
2	10 minutes	5 minutes

Nutritional Values Per Serving

Calories	274
Total Fat	6.6g
Saturated Fat	1g
Cholesterol	0mg
Sodium	182mg
Total Carbohydrate	50.5g
Dietary Fiber	7.2g
Total Sugars	14.1g
Protein	7g

Ingredients:

- ¾ cup rolled oats
- 1 ½ cup of oat milk
- ¼ teaspoon ground cinnamon
- Pinch of sea salt
- ¼ cup fresh blueberries
- ½ ripe banana, sliced
- 2 tablespoons chopped nuts
- Maple syrup
- Sliced strawberries

Instructions:

1. Mix 1 ½ cup water and oats in a small saucepan.
2. Boil the oats on high heat, then reduce the heat to medium-low and cook or 5 minutes.
3. Stir in salt, and cinnamon then mix well.
4. Garnish with apple, maple syrup, dried fruit, nuts, banana and berries.
5. Serve.

The Plant Based Cookbook For Beginners
650 Easy, Quick, & Simple Plant Based Vegan Diet Recipes With A 31 Day Meal Plan To Lose Weight & Live A Long Healthy Life

107

French Toast with Berry Compote

SERVINGS **PREPARATION TIME** **COOKING TIME**
8 20 minutes 16 minutes

Nutritional Values Per Serving

Calories	215
Total Fat	8.4g
Saturated Fat	0.6g
Cholesterol	0mg
Sodium	259mg
Total Carbohydrate	30.6g
Dietary Fiber	3.3g
Total Sugars	15.7g
Protein	5.1g

Ingredients:

French Toast

- 1 ½ cup almond milk
- ½ cup almond flour
- 1 cup aquafaba
- 2 tablespoons pure maple syrup
- ¼ teaspoon ground cinnamon
- 2 pinches of salt
- ½ tablespoon orange zest
- 8 whole-grain bread slices

Berry Compote

- 1 cup raspberries
- ½ cup applesauce
- 1 teaspoon pure maple syrup

Instructions:

1. At 400 degrees F, preheat your oven. Set a wire rack on a suitable baking sheet.

2. Mix milk with flour, salt, cinnamon, maple syrup and aquafaba in a bowl until smooth.

3. Stir in orange zest, mix and spread this mixture in a shallow pan.

4. Set a skillet over medium heat and grease it with cooking spray.

5. Dip each bread slice in the milk mixture and sear the slice for 2-3 minutes per side until golden brown.

6. Transfer the cooked bread slices to a wire rack and bake for 10 minutes in the oven.

7. Blend berries with maple syrup and applesauce in a blender until chunky.

8. Spread this compote on top of the bread slices.

108

The Plant Based Cookbook For Beginners
650 Easy, Quick, & Simple Plant Based Vegan Diet Recipes With A 31 Day Meal Plan To Lose Weight & Live A Long Healthy Life

Breakfast Beans

SERVINGS	PREPARATION TIME	COOKING TIME
4	10 minutes	2 hours 5 minutes

Nutritional Values Per Serving

Calories	222
Total Fat	1g
Saturated Fat	0.1g
Cholesterol	0mg
Sodium	532mg
Total Carbohydrate	41g
Dietary Fiber	10.6g
Total Sugars	5.5g
Protein	14.1g

Serving Suggestion:

Try these beans with toasted whole wheat bread slices.

Ingredients:

- 1 ½ pounds dried fava beans, soaked
- 1 tablespoon tomato paste
- 1 medium yellow onion, peeled and diced
- 4 garlic cloves, peeled and minced
- 1 teaspoon ground cumin
- Zest and juice of 1 lemon
- Sea salt, to taste
- 1 lemon, quartered

Instructions:

1. Rinse and drain the fava beans then transfer to a large pot.
2. Pour water to cover the beans, boil and reduce the heat to medium.
3. Cover these beans and cook for 2 hours until beans are soft.
4. Meanwhile, sauté onion in a medium skillet for 10 minutes until golden brown.
5. Stir in lemon juice and zest, cumin and garlic, then sauté for 5 minutes.
6. Drain the cooked beans and keep ½ cup cooking liquid.
7. Add beans, tomato paste and cooking liquid to the onion mixture, then mix well.
8. Cook for 5 minutes.
9. Garnish with lemon quarters.
10. Serve warm.

The Plant Based Cookbook For Beginners
650 Easy, Quick, & Simple Plant Based Vegan Diet Recipes With A 31 Day Meal Plan To Lose Weight & Live A Long Healthy Life

109

Mushroom Breakfast

SERVINGS	PREPARATION TIME	COOKING TIME
4	10 minutes	19 minutes

Nutritional Values Per Serving

Calories	123
Total Fat	1.3g
Saturated Fat	0.2g
Cholesterol	0mg
Sodium	588mg
Total Carbohydrate	22.8g
Dietary Fiber	8.5g
Total Sugars	7.8g
Protein	10.2g

Serving Suggestion:

Enjoy this breakfast meal with tortillas.

Ingredients:

- 1 red onion, peeled and cut into julienned
- 1 red bell pepper, seeded and julienned
- 1 yellow bell pepper, seeded and julienned
- 2 cups mushrooms, sliced
- Salt, to taste
- ½ teaspoon black pepper
- 1½ teaspoons turmeric
- ¼ teaspoon cayenne pepper
- 3 garlic cloves, peeled and minced
- 2 tablespoons soy sauce
- ¼ cup nutritional yeast

Instructions:

1. Sauté mushrooms, bell peppers and onion in a medium skillet for 8 minutes.
2. Add 2 tablespoons water into the peppers if needed then cook for 6 minutes.
3. Add nutritional yeast, soy sauce, garlic, cayenne, turmeric, black pepper, and salt.
4. Mix and cook for 5 minutes with occasional stirring.
5. Serve warm.

110

The Plant Based Cookbook For Beginners
650 Easy, Quick, & Simple Plant Based Vegan Diet Recipes With A 31 Day Meal Plan To Lose Weight & Live A Long Healthy Life

Rice Berry Pudding

SERVINGS	PREPARATION TIME	COOKING TIME
6	10 minutes	12 minutes

Nutritional Values Per Serving

Calories	498
Total Fat	5.6g
Saturated Fat	0.7g
Cholesterol	0mg
Sodium	79mg
Total Carbohydrate	89.4g
Dietary Fiber	7.5g
Total Sugars	26.4g
Protein	9.4g

Serving Suggestion:

Enjoy this pudding with raspberry syrup or jam on top.

Ingredients:

- 3 cups rice, cooked
- 2 cups almond milk
- 1 cinnamon stick
- ¼ teaspoon ground cloves, to taste
- 2 tablespoons maple syrup
- 1 tart apple, cored and chopped
- ¼ cup raisins
- Salt to taste
- ½ frozen mixed berries

Instructions:

1. Mix cloves, cinnamon stick, almond milk and rice to a medium saucepan.
2. Cook for 12 minutes on medium-low heat with occasional stirring until it thickens.
3. Remove and discard the cinnamon stick and cloves.
4. Add apple, salt and maple syrup then mix well.
5. Garnish with berries.
6. Serve.

The Plant Based Cookbook For Beginners
650 Easy, Quick, & Simple Plant Based Vegan Diet Recipes With A 31 Day Meal Plan To Lose Weight & Live A Long Healthy Life

111

Sweet Potato Hash with Black Beans

SERVINGS
4

PREPARATION TIME
15 minutes

COOKING TIME
18 minutes

Nutritional Values Per Serving

Calories	277
Total Fat	1.2g
Saturated Fat	0.3g
Cholesterol	0mg
Sodium	88mg
Total Carbohydrate	55.6g
Dietary Fiber	11.7g
Total Sugars	3g
Protein	12.7g

Serving Suggestion:

Enjoy this sweet potato hash with tortillas.

Ingredients:

- 1 cup onion, chopped
- 2 garlic cloves, minced
- 2 cups sweet potatoes, peeled and chopped
- 2 teaspoons mild chili powder
- ⅓ cup vegetable broth
- 1 cup black beans, cooked
- 1 teaspoon salt, or to taste
- ¼ cup green onions, chopped
- Splash of hot sauce
- Chopped cilantro, for garnish

Instructions:

1. Sauté onions in a non-stick skillet over medium heat for 3 minutes.
2. Stir in garlic, sweet potatoes and chili powder then sauté for 1 minute.
3. Add broth then cook for 12 minutes with occasional stirring.
4. Stir in salt, green onions, and black beans then cook for 2 minutes.
5. Stir in hot sauce and mix well.
6. Garnish with chopped cilantro.
7. Serve warm.

112

The Plant Based Cookbook For Beginners
650 Easy, Quick, & Simple Plant Based Vegan Diet Recipes With A 31 Day Meal Plan To Lose Weight & Live A Long Healthy Life

Overnight Chia Oats

SERVINGS
2

PREPARATION TIME
10 minutes

FRIDGE TIME
Overnight

Nutritional Values Per Serving	
Calories	281
Total Fat	13.5g
Saturated Fat	7.2g
Cholesterol	0mg
Sodium	11mg
Total Carbohydrate	35.3g
Dietary Fiber	8.8g
Total Sugars	7.3g
Protein	7.1g

Serving Suggestion:

Enjoy this oatmeal with fresh fruit compote on top.

Ingredients:

- ¾ cup rolled oats
- ¼ cup almond milk
- ½ cup of water
- 1 tablespoon chia seeds
- 1 tablespoon maple syrup
- ¼ teaspoon cinnamon
- Dash of vanilla bean powder
- Fruits, to serve

Instructions:

1. Add oats, vanilla, cinnamon, maple syrup, chia seeds, and liquid to a 16 oz. mason jar.
2. Cover the jar and refrigerate it overnight.
3. Garnish with your choice of fruits.
4. Serve.

The Plant Based Cookbook For Beginners
650 Easy, Quick, & Simple Plant Based Vegan Diet Recipes With A 31 Day Meal Plan To Lose Weight & Live A Long Healthy Life

113

Apple-Walnut Bread

SERVINGS	PREPARATION TIME	COOKING TIME
8	15 minutes	30 minutes

Nutritional Values Per Serving

Calories	314
Total Fat	7.7g
Saturated Fat	2.5g
Cholesterol	0mg
Sodium	460mg
Total Carbohydrate	58.1g
Dietary Fiber	4g
Total Sugars	30.6g
Protein	5.8g

Serving Suggestion:

Enjoy this bread with peanut butter spread or strawberry jam.

Ingredients:

- 1 ½ cups unsweetened applesauce
- ¾ cup brown sugar
- ⅓ cup almond milk
- 1 tablespoon ground flax seeds
- 2 tablespoons warm water
- 2 cups whole wheat flour
- 1 teaspoon baking soda
- ½ teaspoon baking powder
- 1 teaspoon salt
- 1 teaspoon ground cinnamon
- ½ cup walnuts, chopped

Instructions:

1. At 375 degrees F, preheat your oven.
2. Mix flax seeds with warm water in a large bowl and soak for 15 minutes.
3. Stir in almond milk, brown sugar and applesauce then mix well.
4. Add salt, cinnamon, baking powder, baking soda and flour then mix well until smooth.
5. Fold in walnuts then spread the batter evenly in a 9x5 inch loaf pan.
6. Bake the walnuts batter for 30 minutes in the oven.
7. Allow the bread to cool then slice.
8. Serve.

114

The Plant Based Cookbook For Beginners
650 Easy, Quick, & Simple Plant Based Vegan Diet Recipes With A 31 Day Meal Plan To Lose Weight & Live A Long Healthy Life

Potato Broccoli Frittatas

SERVINGS
6

PREPARATION TIME
10 minutes

COOKING TIME
35 minutes

Nutritional Values Per Serving

Calories	282
Total Fat	5.5g
Saturated Fat	0.4g
Cholesterol	0mg
Sodium	162mg
Total Carbohydrate	47.2g
Dietary Fiber	10.7g
Total Sugars	12.3g
Protein	14.2g

Serving Suggestion:

Enjoy this frittata with toasted whole wheat bread slices.

Ingredients:

- 1 ½ cups mushrooms, sliced
- 1 ¼ cups red potatoes, sliced
- ½ cup red bell pepper, chopped
- ¼ cup red onion, chopped
- 4 cups frozen broccoli florets, chopped
- 1 ½ cups almond milk
- 2 tablespoons flaxseed meal
- 1 cup chickpea flour
- 2 tablespoons nutritional yeast
- 1 teaspoon baking powder
- 1 teaspoon dried dill weed
- ¼ teaspoon ground turmeric
- Black pepper, to taste
- Chopped herbs like tarragon, chives, or parsley

Instructions:

1. At 350 degrees F, preheat your oven.
2. Grease 12 muffin cups with foil cups.
3. Sauté onion, bell pepper, potatoes and mushrooms then sauté for 10 minutes.
4. Add 2 tablespoons water if needed, then add broccoli.
5. Mix milk with flaxseed meal in a bowl and leave for 5 minutes.
6. Add sautéed vegetables, chickpea flour, yeast, baking powder, dill weed, turmeric and black pepper.
7. Mix well until the chickpea mixture is smooth and lump-free.
8. Divide the batter into the prepared muffin cups and bake for 25 minutes in the oven.
9. Garnish with herbs and black pepper.
10. Serve warm.

The Plant Based Cookbook For Beginners
650 Easy, Quick, & Simple Plant Based Vegan Diet Recipes With A 31 Day Meal Plan To Lose Weight & Live A Long Healthy Life

115

Sweet Potato and Blueberry Flatbreads

SERVINGS	PREPARATION TIME	COOKING TIME
6	15 minutes	19 minutes

Nutritional Values Per Serving	
Calories	242
Total Fat	4.4g
Saturated Fat	0.1g
Cholesterol	0mg
Sodium	333mg
Total Carbohydrate	48.3g
Dietary Fiber	5.1g
Total Sugars	8.9g
Protein	6.9g

Ingredients:

- Cornmeal, for dusting
- 1 premade vegan pizza dough
- 1 cup sweet potato, cubed and peeled
- Salt and black pepper, to taste
- ¾ cup fresh blueberries
- 4 teaspoons pure maple syrup
- Ground cinnamon

Instructions:

1. At 400 degrees F, preheat your oven. Dust a large baking sheet with cornmeal.
2. Divide the pre-made pizza dough into 4 equal portions.
3. Roll each portion into an 8-inch round on a floured surface.
4. Place the flatbreads on the prepared pan and bake for 13 minutes.
5. Boil sweet potato with water in a cooking pot, reduce its heat, cover and cook for 10 minutes.
6. Drain the sweet potatoes then transfer to a bowl.
7. Mash the sweet potatoes then add black pepper and salt then mix well.
8. Spread the sweet potato mash on top of the flatbreads.
9. Top them blueberries.
10. Garnish with cinnamon and maple syrup.
11. Serve.

116

The Plant Based Cookbook For Beginners
650 Easy, Quick, & Simple Plant Based Vegan Diet Recipes With A 31 Day Meal Plan To Lose Weight & Live A Long Healthy Life

Tapioca Pudding with Mango

SERVINGS	PREPARATION TIME	COOKING TIME
5	15 minutes	25 minutes

Nutritional Values Per Serving

Calories	333
Total Fat	24g
Saturated Fat	8.9g
Cholesterol	0mg
Sodium	11mg
Total Carbohydrate	32g
Dietary Fiber	2g
Total Sugars	17g
Protein	3.5g

Ingredients:

- 6 cups water
- ⅓ cup small pearl tapioca
- 13.5 ounces full-fat coconut milk
- 2 tablespoons maple syrup
- ½ teaspoon vanilla extract
- ⅛ teaspoon kosher salt
- 1 mango, peeled and diced
- ¼ cup unsweetened toasted coconut flakes
- Sliced almonds

Instructions:

1. Add 6 cups water to a large saucepan and cook to a boil.
2. Stir in tapioca and cook for 20 minutes on a simmer.
3. Drain and rinse this tapioca in a fine mesh sieve.
4. Heat coconut milk with maple syrup, salt and vanilla in a saucepan.
5. Stir in tapioca and mix evenly.
6. Allow this tapioca pudding to cool.
7. Divide this pudding in the serving cups and garnish with mango, coconut flakes, and sliced almonds.
8. Serve.

The Plant Based Cookbook For Beginners
650 Easy, Quick, & Simple Plant Based Vegan Diet Recipes With A 31 Day Meal Plan To Lose Weight & Live A Long Healthy Life

117

Chocolate Pancakes

SERVINGS	PREPARATION TIME	COOKING TIME
6	15 minutes	66 minutes

Nutritional Values Per Serving

Calories	307
Total Fat	11.2g
Saturated Fat	8.8g
Cholesterol	0mg
Sodium	109mg
Total Carbohydrate	48.1g
Dietary Fiber	8.7g
Total Sugars	4.7g
Protein	9.1g

Serving Suggestion:

Enjoy these pancakes with fresh fruits on top.

Ingredients:

- 1¼ cups whole-grain flour
- 2 tablespoons unsweetened cocoa powder
- 1 tablespoon baking powder
- 1 tablespoon ground flaxseed
- 1 tablespoon mini chocolate chips
- ¼ teaspoon salt
- 1 cup almond milk
- 1 tablespoon pure maple syrup
- 1 teaspoon vanilla extract
- 1 tablespoon apple cider vinegar
- ¼ cup applesauce

Instructions:

1. Mix flour, cocoa powder, ground flaxseed, salt, chocolate chips, and baking powder in a medium bowl.
2. Beat almond milk with vinegar, vanilla and maple syrup in a bowl.
3. Pour this liquid into the flour mixture, then mix well until smooth.
4. Stir in applesauce, then mix well.
5. Leave this batter for 10 minutes until it thickens.
6. Set a suitable griddle over medium heat and grease it with cooking spray.
7. Pour enough batter into the griddle to get a 3-inch round.
8. Cook for 3 minutes per side and cook 11 more pancakes in the same way.
9. Serve warm.

Banana-Fig Bread

SERVINGS
6

PREPARATION TIME
10 minutes

COOKING TIME
60 minutes

Nutritional Values Per Serving

Calories	382
Total Fat	8.7g
Saturated Fat	4.6g
Cholesterol	0mg
Sodium	9mg
Total Carbohydrate	71.5g
Dietary Fiber	5.7g
Total Sugars	26.8g
Protein	7.4g

Serving Suggestion:

Enjoy this bread with peanut butter spread and fresh berry jam.

Ingredients:

- 4 ripe bananas
- ½ cup almond milk
- 4 teaspoons apple cider vinegar
- 4 teaspoons pure vanilla extract
- 2 cups whole wheat flour
- ¼ cup coconut sugar
- 1 tablespoon baking powder
- ⅛ teaspoon salt
- ½ cup dried figs, chopped
- ¼ cup walnuts, chopped

Instructions:

1. At 350 degrees F, preheat your oven.
2. Layer a 9x5 inch loaf pan with parchment paper.
3. Mash 4 ripe bananas in a bowl with a fork.
4. Stir in vanilla, vinegar and milk then mix well.
5. Add salt, baking powder, sugar and flour then mix well until smooth.
6. Fold in walnuts and figs then mix evenly.
7. Spread this batter in the loaf pan and bake for 1 hour in the preheated oven.
8. Allow the bread to cool then slice.
9. Serve.

The Plant Based Cookbook For Beginners
650 Easy, Quick, & Simple Plant Based Vegan Diet Recipes With A 31 Day Meal Plan To Lose Weight & Live A Long Healthy Life

119

Tofu Potato Cubes

SERVINGS	PREPARATION TIME	COOKING TIME
2	15 minutes	57 minutes

Nutritional Values Per Serving

Calories	196
Total Fat	4.9g
Saturated Fat	1g
Cholesterol	0mg
Sodium	643mg
Total Carbohydrate	28.8g
Dietary Fiber	7g
Total Sugars	10g
Protein	12.6g

Serving Suggestion:

Try this tortilla with sautéed mushrooms

Ingredients:

- 1 ½ cup potatoes, sliced
- 7 oz. tofu, drained
- ¼ cup 2 tablespoons aquafaba
- 2 tablespoons all-purpose flour
- 1 tablespoon chickpea flour
- ⅛ teaspoon ground turmeric
- 2 onions, chopped
- 2 garlic cloves, minced
- 3 tablespoons fresh parsley, chopped
- ½ teaspoon black salt
- Black pepper, to taste

Instructions:

1. At 425 degrees F, preheat your oven.

2. Set a suitable saucepan filled with water over medium heat and set a steamer basket in it.

3. Add potato pieces to the basket, cover and cook for 15 minutes then transfer to a bowl.

4. Crumble the tofu in this bowl then add aquafaba, chickpea flour, and turmeric then mix well until smooth.

5. Sauté onions, ¼ cup water and garlic in a skillet for 10 minutes.

6. Add rest of the ingredients then sauté for 2 minutes.

7. Spread potatoes and tofu mixture on top and mix well.

8. Bake the batter for 30 minutes in the oven.

9. Allow the tortilla to cool and cut into cubes

10. Serve.

120

The Plant Based Cookbook For Beginners
650 Easy, Quick, & Simple Plant Based Vegan Diet Recipes With A 31 Day Meal Plan To Lose Weight & Live A Long Healthy Life

Quinoa Bowls with Pears

SERVINGS	PREPARATION TIME	COOKING TIME
2	10 minutes	10 minutes

Nutritional Values Per Serving

Calories	482
Total Fat	7.2g
Saturated Fat	1.2g
Cholesterol	0mg
Sodium	56mg
Total Carbohydrate	95.8g
Dietary Fiber	12.4g
Total Sugars	27.6g
Protein	14.1g

Serving Suggestion:

Enjoy this quinoa bowl with mixed nuts, coconut cream and berries on top.

Ingredients:

- 1 ½ cups quinoa, rinsed
- ¼ cup raisins
- 3 tablespoons pure maple syrup
- 2 cups almond milk
- 2 pears, peeled and sliced
- Sliced almonds

Instructions:

1. Warm almond milk in a cooking pot to a boil.
2. Stir in quinoa and cook until the liquid is absorbed.
3. Add maple syrup and raisins then mix well.
4. Divide the quinoa into the serving bowls.
5. Garnish with sliced pears and almonds.
6. Serve.

The Plant Based Cookbook For Beginners
650 Easy, Quick, & Simple Plant Based Vegan Diet Recipes With A 31 Day Meal Plan To Lose Weight & Live A Long Healthy Life

121

Berry Muffins

SERVINGS	PREPARATION TIME	COOKING TIME
6	10 minutes	26 minutes

Nutritional Values Per Serving

Calories	323
Total Fat	7.3g
Saturated Fat	5.8g
Cholesterol	0mg
Sodium	352mg
Total Carbohydrate	57.6g
Dietary Fiber	3.2g
Total Sugars	20.9g
Protein	5.3g

Ingredients:

- ⅔ cup almond milk
- 1 tablespoon ground flaxseeds
- 1 teaspoon apple cider vinegar
- 2 cups whole-wheat flour
- 2 teaspoons baking powder
- ¼ teaspoon baking soda
- ¾ teaspoon salt
- ½ cup unsweetened applesauce
- ½ cup pure maple syrup
- 1½ teaspoons pure vanilla extract
- 1 cup blueberries

Instructions:

1. At 350 degrees F, preheat your oven.
2. Layer a 12 cups muffin tray with silicone liners.
3. Mix vinegar, flaxseeds, and milk in a suitable bowl.
4. Mix flour with salt, baking soda, and baking powder in a bowl.
5. Stir in milk mixture, then mix well until smooth.
6. Add vanilla, maple syrup, and applesauce, then mix well.
7. Fold in berries, mix gently and divide the batter into the muffin tray.
8. Bake these berry muffins for 26 minutes in the oven.
9. Allow the muffins to cool and serve.

122

The Plant Based Cookbook For Beginners
650 Easy, Quick, & Simple Plant Based Vegan Diet Recipes With A 31 Day Meal Plan To Lose Weight & Live A Long Healthy Life

Blueberry Freekeh Breakfast

SERVINGS	**PREPARATION TIME**	**COOKING TIME**
2	10 minutes	10 minutes

Nutritional Values Per Serving

Calories	368
Total Fat	7.6g
Saturated Fat	0.5g
Cholesterol	0mg
Sodium	4mg
Total Carbohydrate	72.4g
Dietary Fiber	9.8g
Total Sugars	34.5g
Protein	11.9g

Serving Suggestion:

Enjoy this breakfast meal with fresh blueberry smoothie on the side.

Ingredients:

- 1 ¼ cups freekeh
- 1 lemon
- 3 tablespoons pure maple syrup
- 4 tablespoons almonds, toasted and chopped

Instructions:

1. Cook and boil freekeh as per the package's directions.
2. Add lemon juice and zest, and maple syrup, then cover and leave for 5 minutes.
3. Divide the freekeh in the serving bowls.
4. Top the freekeh with chopped almonds.
5. Serve.

The Plant Based Cookbook For Beginners
650 Easy, Quick, & Simple Plant Based Vegan Diet Recipes With A 31 Day Meal Plan To Lose Weight & Live A Long Healthy Life

123

Zucchini Bread

SERVINGS	PREPARATION TIME	COOKING TIME
8	15 minutes	70 minutes

Nutritional Values Per Serving	
Calories	402
Total Fat	12.2g
Saturated Fat	3.7g
Cholesterol	0mg
Sodium	206mg
Total Carbohydrate	65.7g
Dietary Fiber	13.6g
Total Sugars	1.6g
Protein	13.7g

Ingredients:

- ⅓ cup almond milk
- 1 avocado, pitted, peeled, and mashed
- 1 tablespoon ground flaxseeds
- ½ cup coconut sugar
- 2 teaspoons pure vanilla extract
- 1 teaspoon lemon zest
- 1 ½ cups whole wheat flour
- ½ teaspoon baking powder
- ½ teaspoon baking soda
- ½ teaspoon sea salt
- 1 ½ teaspoon ground cinnamon
- ¼ teaspoon ground allspice
- 1 small zucchini, shredded
- ⅓ cup walnuts, chopped

Instructions:

1. At 350 degrees F, preheat your oven.
2. Layer an 8x4 inch loaf pan with parchment paper.
3. Blend milk with avocado, flaxseeds and coconut sugar in a food processor.
4. Add lemon zest and vanilla and blend again.
5. Stir in whole wheat flour, baking powder, baking soda, sea salt, cinnamon and allspice.
6. Mix well until smooth, then fold in zucchini and walnuts.
7. Pour this batter into the reared loaf pan and bake for 70 minutes in the preheated oven.
8. Allow the baked zucchini bread to cool on a wire rack.
9. Serve.

124

The Plant Based Cookbook For Beginners
650 Easy, Quick, & Simple Plant Based Vegan Diet Recipes With A 31 Day Meal Plan To Lose Weight & Live A Long Healthy Life

Oatmeal Cups with Berries

SERVINGS	PREPARATION TIME	COOKING TIME	FREEZE TIME
4	15 minutes	58 minutes	6 hours

Nutritional Values Per Serving	
Calories	230
Total Fat	4.3g
Saturated Fat	0.6g
Cholesterol	0mg
Sodium	237mg
Total Carbohydrate	43.1g
Dietary Fiber	6.9g
Total Sugars	11.4g
Protein	6.6g

Ingredients:

- 2 cups rolled oats
- ¼ cup date paste
- ½ teaspoon of sea salt
- ½ teaspoon orange zest
- ¼ cup dried cranberries
- 1 teaspoon ground cinnamon
- 1 cup fresh blueberries
- 2 tablespoons almonds, toasted, sliced

Instructions:

1. Boil oats with 5 cups water, orange zest, sea salt, and date paste in a large saucepan.

2. Cook for 5 minutes with occasional stirring, then remove from the heat.

3. Stir in cinnamon and cranberries, then allow the mixture to cool for 45 minutes.

4. Layer 12 muffin cups with foil cups and divide the oats batter into the muffin cups.

5. Top the batter with almonds and blueberries, then press them gently.

6. Cover the batter and freeze for 6 hours.

7. Heat the frozen oatmeal cups for 3 minutes in the microwave.

8. Serve.

The Plant Based Cookbook For Beginners
650 Easy, Quick, & Simple Plant Based Vegan Diet Recipes With A 31 Day Meal Plan To Lose Weight & Live A Long Healthy Life

125

Banana Teff Bread

SERVINGS	PREPARATION TIME	COOKING TIME
6	15 minutes	45 minutes

Nutritional Values Per Serving

Calories	405
Total Fat	6.9g
Saturated Fat	2.4g
Cholesterol	0mg
Sodium	195mg
Total Carbohydrate	85.6g
Dietary Fiber	7.5g
Total Sugars	47.9g
Protein	7.3g

Serving Suggestion:

Enjoy this bread with a fresh berry compote or coconut cream spread.

Ingredients:

- 2 ripe bananas
- ¼ cup almond milk
- 2 teaspoons apple cider vinegar
- 2 teaspoons pure vanilla extract
- 1 cup teff flour
- 2 tablespoons coconut sugar
- ¼ cup walnuts, chopped
- 1 teaspoon baking powder
- ½ teaspoon baking soda
- ½ teaspoon ground cinnamon
- 2 pinches sea salt
- 15 raisins, soaked and drained

Instructions:

1. At 350 degrees F, preheat your oven.

2. Layer an 8x4 inch loaf pan with parchment paper.

3. Mash bananas in a bowl, then stir in vanilla, vinegar, and milk, then mix well.

4. Add rest of the ingredients then mix until smooth and lump-free.

5. Spread the batter in the loaf pan.

6. Bake the bread for 45 minutes in the oven.

7. Allow the bread to cool and slice.

8. Serve.

126

The Plant Based Cookbook For Beginners
650 Easy, Quick, & Simple Plant Based Vegan Diet Recipes With A 31 Day Meal Plan To Lose Weight & Live A Long Healthy Life

Strawberry Rhubarb Oatmeal

SERVINGS
4

PREPARATION TIME
10 minutes

COOKING TIME
7 minutes

Nutritional Values Per Serving	
Calories	465
Total Fat	30.7g
Saturated Fat	25.6g
Cholesterol	0mg
Sodium	61mg
Total Carbohydrate	48.2g
Dietary Fiber	10.4g
Total Sugars	23.6g
Protein	7.4g

Ingredients:

- 2 cups almond milk
- 1 cup rolled oats
- 1 cup fresh rhubarb, sliced
- ⅓ cup pitted dates, chopped
- Salt, to taste
- 1½ cups fresh strawberries, sliced

Instructions:

1. Boil milk with oats, dates and rhubarb in a saucepan, then reduce the heat.
2. Cook on a simmer for 5 minutes with occasional stirring.
3. Remove the oats from the heat, and cover for 2 minutes.
4. Add some salt, then mix well.
5. Garnish with strawberries and serve.

The Plant Based Cookbook For Beginners
650 Easy, Quick, & Simple Plant Based Vegan Diet Recipes With A 31 Day Meal Plan To Lose Weight & Live A Long Healthy Life

127

Spinach Blueberry Smoothie

SERVINGS	PREPARATION TIME	COOKING TIME
2	5 minutes	0 minutes

Nutritional Values Per Serving

Calories	176
Total Fat	6g
Saturated Fat	0.6g
Cholesterol	0mg
Sodium	85mg
Total Carbohydrate	29.2g
Dietary Fiber	7.6g
Total Sugars	13.9g
Protein	4.2g

Serving Suggestion:

Enjoy this smoothie with freshly baked blueberry muffins.

Ingredients:

- 1 cup almond milk
- 1 cup raw spinach
- 1 frozen banana, chopped
- ½ cup frozen blueberries
- 1 tablespoon chia seeds

Instructions:

1. Blend all the berries, spinach and rest of the ingredients in a blender until smooth.
2. Serve.

128

The Plant Based Cookbook For Beginners
650 Easy, Quick, & Simple Plant Based Vegan Diet Recipes With A 31 Day Meal Plan To Lose Weight & Live A Long Healthy Life

Sweet Potato Chocolate Waffles

SERVINGS	PREPARATION TIME	COOKING TIME
6	10 minutes	40 minutes

Nutritional Values Per Serving

Calories	488
Total Fat	11.4g
Saturated Fat	8.7g
Cholesterol	0mg
Sodium	115mg
Total Carbohydrate	92.5g
Dietary Fiber	10.7g
Total Sugars	47.8g
Protein	7.3g

Ingredients:

- 1 ½ cups rolled oats
- ⅔ cup all-purpose flour
- ¼ cup cocoa powder
- 2 tablespoons coconut sugar
- 1 ½ teaspoons baking powder
- ¼ teaspoon sea salt
- 1 cup almond milk
- ¾ cup mashed sweet potato
- ¼ cup aquafaba
- 1 tablespoon apple cider vinegar
- 1 ½ teaspoons ginger, grated

Instructions:

1. Blend salt, cocoa powder, baking powder, sugar, flour and oats in a food processor.
2. Add milk, sweet potato mash, aquafaba, apple cider vinegar and ginger.
3. Blend again and mix until smooth.
4. Add a dollop of this batter into a preheated waffle iron and cook for 10 minutes.
5. Cook more waffles the same way.
6. Serve.

The Plant Based Cookbook For Beginners
650 Easy, Quick, & Simple Plant Based Vegan Diet Recipes With A 31 Day Meal Plan To Lose Weight & Live A Long Healthy Life

129

Peanut Butter Granola Bars

SERVINGS	PREPARATION TIME	COOKING TIME
6	15 minutes	18 minutes

Nutritional Values Per Serving	
Calories	303
Total Fat	12.6g
Saturated Fat	2.5g
Cholesterol	0mg
Sodium	173mg
Total Carbohydrate	42.1g
Dietary Fiber	4.1g
Total Sugars	18.5g
Protein	9.3g

Ingredients:

- ½ cup smooth peanut butter
- ¼ cup pure maple syrup
- ¼ cup brown rice syrup
- 1 teaspoon vanilla
- 2 cups rolled oats
- ½ teaspoon sea salt
- ½ teaspoon ground cinnamon

Instructions:

1. At 350 degrees F, preheat your oven.
2. Layer an 8-inch baking pan with 10-inch square wax paper.
3. Mix rice syrup, maple syrup and peanut butter in a saucepan on medium heat for 3 minutes with occasional stirring.
4. Add vanilla, oats, salt and cinnamon then mix well.
5. Spread this oats mixture in the prepared pan and bake for 18 minutes in the oven.
6. Allow the granola to cool and cut into bars.
7. Serve.

130

The Plant Based Cookbook For Beginners
650 Easy, Quick, & Simple Plant Based Vegan Diet Recipes With A 31 Day Meal Plan To Lose Weight & Live A Long Healthy Life

Muesli with Roasted Peanuts

SERVINGS	PREPARATION TIME	FRIDGE TIME
2	10 minutes	Overnight

Nutritional Values Per Serving	
Calories	451
Total Fat	14.3g
Saturated Fat	2.1g
Cholesterol	0mg
Sodium	71mg
Total Carbohydrate	70.9g
Dietary Fiber	10.3g
Total Sugars	13.5g
Protein	14.5g

Serving Suggestion:

Try this muesli with bananas on top.

Ingredients:

- 1 ½ cups rolled oats
- ½ cup whole-grain puffed cereal
- ½ cup whole-grain cereal flakes
- ¼ cup roasted peanuts, chopped
- ½ cup almond milk
- 2 tablespoons maple syrup
- 1 cup dried fruit, cranberries, raisins, or cherries

Instructions:

1. Mix oats with all the ingredients in a mason jar, cover and refrigerate overnight.
2. Serve.

The Plant Based Cookbook For Beginners
650 Easy, Quick, & Simple Plant Based Vegan Diet Recipes With A 31 Day Meal Plan To Lose Weight & Live A Long Healthy Life

131

Overnight Apple Oats

SERVINGS	PREPARATION TIME	FRIDGE TIME
4	10 minutes	8 hours

Nutritional Values Per Serving

Calories	347
Total Fat	18.1g
Saturated Fat	13g
Cholesterol	0mg
Sodium	11mg
Total Carbohydrate	43.7g
Dietary Fiber	6.6g
Total Sugars	23.5g
Protein	5.7g

Serving Suggestion:

Try these oats with fresh berries on top.

Ingredients:

- 1 cup rolled oats
- 1 cup apple, chopped
- 1 cup almond milk
- 2 pitted whole dates, chopped
- 2 tablespoons walnuts, toasted, chopped
- 1 tablespoon pure maple syrup
- ½ teaspoon orange zest
- ¼ teaspoon ground ginger
- Dash sea salt

Instructions:

1. Mix all the ingredients including oats in a mason jar and cover.
2. Refrigerate the overnight for 8 hours.
3. Serve.

132

The Plant Based Cookbook For Beginners
650 Easy, Quick, & Simple Plant Based Vegan Diet Recipes With A 31 Day Meal Plan To Lose Weight & Live A Long Healthy Life

Banana Oat Waffles

SERVINGS	PREPARATION TIME	COOKING TIME
4	10 minutes	28 minutes

Nutritional Values Per Serving

Calories	266
Total Fat	6.5g
Saturated Fat	0.9g
Cholesterol	0mg
Sodium	58mg
Total Carbohydrate	42.9g
Dietary Fiber	7.6g
Total Sugars	4.5g
Protein	8.6g

Serving Suggestion:

Enjoy these waffles with soy yogurt on the side.

Ingredients:

- 2 ½ cups rolled oats
- ¼ cup ground flaxseeds
- 2 teaspoons lemon zest, grated
- ½ teaspoon ground cinnamon
- 1 ½ cups almond milk
- ⅓ cup banana, mashed
- Sliced bananas or fresh fruit

Instructions:

1. Blend oats with flaxseeds, lemon zest, cinnamon, almond milk, and banana in a blender until smooth.
2. Preheat the waffle iron and add a dollop of the batter into the iron.
3. Cook the waffle for 7 minutes then transfer to a plate.
4. Continue cooking more waffles in the same way.
5. Garnish with sliced bananas or fresh fruit.
6. Serve.

The Plant Based Cookbook For Beginners
650 Easy, Quick, & Simple Plant Based Vegan Diet Recipes With A 31 Day Meal Plan To Lose Weight & Live A Long Healthy Life

133

Carrot Cake Oatmeal

SERVINGS	PREPARATION TIME	FRIDGE TIME
4	10 minutes	2 hours

Nutritional Values Per Serving	
Calories	245
Total Fat	16.6g
Saturated Fat	13.1g
Cholesterol	0mg
Sodium	20mg
Total Carbohydrate	23.5g
Dietary Fiber	4.6g
Total Sugars	11.9g
Protein	4.2g

Ingredients:

- ½ cup rolled oats
- ½ cup carrot, shredded
- 2 Medjool dates, pitted and chopped
- 1 tablespoon ground flaxseeds
- 1 tablespoon pumpkin seeds
- 1 teaspoon ground cinnamon
- Pinch of ground nutmeg
- 1 cup almond milk

Toppings

- Hemp seeds
- Chopped pecans
- Almond butter
- Raisins

Instructions:

1. Add almond milk, nutmeg, cinnamon, pumpkin seeds, flaxseeds, dates, carrot and oats to a mason jar.
2. Cover the jar and refrigerate for 2 hours.
3. Garnish with suggested toppings and serve.

134

The Plant Based Cookbook For Beginners
650 Easy, Quick, & Simple Plant Based Vegan Diet Recipes With A 31 Day Meal Plan To Lose Weight & Live A Long Healthy Life

Blueberry Oat Muffins

SERVINGS
4

PREPARATION TIME
15 minutes

COOKING TIME
20 minutes

Nutritional Values Per Serving

Calories	364
Total Fat	3.7g
Saturated Fat	0.2g
Cholesterol	0mg
Sodium	534mg
Total Carbohydrate	75.2g
Dietary Fiber	8.4g
Total Sugars	24.9g
Protein	8.9g

Ingredients:

- 1 banana, mashed
- 1 (15-ounce) can sweet potato puree
- ¼ cup pure maple syrup
- 1 teaspoon vanilla extract
- 2 cups whole oat flour
- ½ teaspoon baking soda
- ½ teaspoon baking powder
- ½ teaspoon salt
- 1 teaspoon ground cinnamon
- ½ teaspoon ground nutmeg
- ¼ teaspoon ground ginger
- 1 cup fresh blueberries

Instructions:

1. At 375 degrees F, preheat your oven.
2. Mix mashed banana with vanilla, maple syrup, and sweet potato puree in a large bowl.
3. Mix ginger, nutmeg, cinnamon, salt, baking powder, baking soda and oat flour in a small bowl.
4. Stir in the banana mash then mix well until smooth and fold in blueberries.
5. Divide this batter into muffin cups and bake for 20 minutes in the oven.
6. Allow the muffins to cool and serve.

The Plant Based Cookbook For Beginners
650 Easy, Quick, & Simple Plant Based Vegan Diet Recipes With A 31 Day Meal Plan To Lose Weight & Live A Long Healthy Life

135

Avocado Sprout Toast

SERVINGS	PREPARATION TIME	COOKING TIME
6	10 minutes	0 minutes

Nutritional Values Per Serving

Calories	165
Total Fat	8.3g
Saturated Fat	1.5g
Cholesterol	0mg
Sodium	157mg
Total Carbohydrate	21.6g
Dietary Fiber	5.6g
Total Sugars	4.1g
Protein	6g

Ingredients:

- 6 whole wheat bread slices, toasted
- 1 avocado, pitted and sliced into 6 wedges
- 2 ripe tomatoes, sliced
- 1½ cups cucumber, sliced
- 2 cups baby romaine lettuce
- ⅔ cup fresh alfalfa sprouts
- Salt and black pepper, to taste
- 2 tablespoons lemon juice

Instructions:

1. Place avocado wedges on top of the toasted bread slice.
2. Add tomato, lettuce, cucumber and alfalfa sprouts on top.
3. Drizzle lemon juice, black pepper, and salt on top.
4. Serve.

136

The Plant Based Cookbook For Beginners
650 Easy, Quick, & Simple Plant Based Vegan Diet Recipes With A 31 Day Meal Plan To Lose Weight & Live A Long Healthy Life

Blue Corn Waffles

SERVINGS	PREPARATION TIME	COOKING TIME
4	15 minutes	28 minutes

Nutritional Values Per Serving

Calories	417
Total Fat	3.2g
Saturated Fat	0.1g
Cholesterol	0mg
Sodium	310mg
Total Carbohydrate	90.9g
Dietary Fiber	2.8g
Total Sugars	29g
Protein	6.8g

Ingredients:

- 2 cups almond milk
- ¼ cup applesauce
- ½ cup maple syrup
- 1 teaspoon apple cider vinegar
- 1½ cups blue cornmeal
- 1 cup whole wheat flour
- 1 teaspoon baking powder
- ½ teaspoon of sea salt
- ¼ cup frozen blueberries
- ¼ cup small walnut pieces

Instructions:

1. Preheat your waffle iron as per the package's instructions.
2. Mix apple cider vinegar, maple syrup, applesauce, and almond milk in a large bowl.
3. Stir in cornmeal, baking powder, salt and whole wheat flour then mix well until smooth.
4. Fold in walnut and blueberries then mix gently.
5. Add a dollop of this batter into the waffle iron.
6. Cook for 7 minutes then transfer the waffle to a plate.
7. Continue cooking more waffles with the remaining batter.
8. Serve.

The Plant Based Cookbook For Beginners
650 Easy, Quick, & Simple Plant Based Vegan Diet Recipes With A 31 Day Meal Plan To Lose Weight & Live A Long Healthy Life

137

Pumpkin Chia Pudding

SERVINGS	PREPARATION TIME	FRIDGE TIME
4	15 minutes	4 hours

Nutritional Values Per Serving	
Calories	320
Total Fat	29.3g
Saturated Fat	25.5g
Cholesterol	0mg
Sodium	21mg
Total Carbohydrate	15.2g
Dietary Fiber	3.7g
Total Sugars	10.3g
Protein	3.1g

Serving Suggestion:

Enjoy this pudding with freshly baked walnut bread slices.

Ingredients:

- ¼ cup chia seeds
- 2 cups almond milk
- 2 cups pumpkin purée
- 1 teaspoon ground cinnamon
- ½ teaspoon ground ginger
- ¼ teaspoon ground nutmeg
- ¼ teaspoon ground cloves
- 1 pinch chili powder
- Black pepper, to taste
- 2 teaspoons vanilla extract
- 2 tablespoons maple syrup
- Coconut flakes for garnish

Instructions:

1. Add almond milk and chia seeds to a jar, cover and leave for 5 minutes.
2. Stir again, cover and refrigerate for 4 hours.
3. Mix black pepper, chili powder, cloves, nutmeg, ginger, and cinnamon in a small bowl.
4. Add this mixture, maple syrup, vanilla extract and pumpkin puree to the chia seeds.
5. Mix gently and garnish with coconut flakes.
6. Serve.

138

The Plant Based Cookbook For Beginners
650 Easy, Quick, & Simple Plant Based Vegan Diet Recipes With A 31 Day Meal Plan To Lose Weight & Live A Long Healthy Life

Pancakes with Raspberry Syrup

SERVINGS	PREPARATION TIME	COOKING TIME
6	10 minutes	16 minutes

Nutritional Values Per Serving

Calories	603
Total Fat	27.6g
Saturated Fat	18g
Cholesterol	0mg
Sodium	130mg
Total Carbohydrate	81.6g
Dietary Fiber	12.9g
Total Sugars	16.2g
Protein	14.4g

Ingredients:

Pancakes

- 2 cups almond milk
- 2 oz. pitted dates, chopped
- 1½ cups rolled oats
- ½ cup cornmeal
- 1½ teaspoons baking powder
- ½ teaspoon baking soda
- ½ teaspoon ground cinnamon
- 1 tablespoon lemon zest
- 3 tablespoons lemon juice
- Fresh raspberries

Raspberry-Date Syrup

- 4 oz. pitted dates, chopped
- ½ cup fresh raspberries

Instructions:

1. For raspberry date syrup, mix all its ingredients with 1½ cups water in a blender.
2. Leave this mixture for 15 minutes then blend until smooth.
3. Mix milk with remaining dates in a small bowl and leave it for 15 minutes.
4. Grind oats in a food processor to get a flourlike powder.
5. Transfer to a bowl then add cinnamon, baking soda, baking powder and cornmeal.
6. Mix oats mixture with milk mixture in a blender until smooth.
7. Set a griddle over medium heat and grease it with cooking spray.
8. Pour ½ cup oats batter into the griddle, spread and cook for 2 minutes per side.
9. Transfer to a plate, and cook more pancakes in the same way.
10. Serve the pancakes with raspberry syrup on top and garnish with berries.
11. Enjoy.

The Plant Based Cookbook For Beginners
650 Easy, Quick, & Simple Plant Based Vegan Diet Recipes With A 31 Day Meal Plan To Lose Weight & Live A Long Healthy Life

139

Tofu Frittata

SERVINGS
6

PREPARATION TIME
15 minutes

COOKING TIME
1 hr. 15 minutes

Nutritional Values Per Serving

Calories	199
Total Fat	5.2g
Saturated Fat	1g
Cholesterol	0mg
Sodium	413mg
Total Carbohydrate	28.2g
Dietary Fiber	5.3g
Total Sugars	8.1g
Protein	13.5g

Ingredients:

- 1 (14-ounce) package firm tofu, crumbled
- ¾ cup aquafaba
- ¼ cup all-purpose flour
- 2 tablespoons chickpea flour
- 2 tablespoons nutritional yeast
- 1½ tablespoons mild miso
- 1 tablespoon garlic powder
- 1 tablespoon onion powder
- ¼ teaspoon turmeric
- ¼ teaspoon black salt
- ¼ teaspoon crushed red pepper flakes
- 1 Yukon potato, scrubbed and diced
- 1 medium red bell pepper, diced
- 2 zucchinis, diced
- 8 green onions, sliced
- ¼ cup cilantro, chopped

Instructions:

1. At 325 degrees F, preheat your oven.

2. Blend tofu, red pepper flakes, black salt, turmeric, onion powder, garlic powder, miso, yeast, flours and aquafaba in a food processor until smooth.

3. Sauté bell pepper and potatoes in a skillet or 10 minutes, add 2 tablespoons water if needed.

4. Stir in cilantro, green onions, and zucchini then sauté for 5 minutes.

5. Spread the veggies in an 8-inch pie pan.

6. Pour the prepared tofu batter on top and bake for 60 minutes in the oven.

7. Slice and serve.

Banana Blueberry Bake

SERVINGS	PREPARATION TIME	COOKING TIME
6	20 minutes	35 minutes

Nutritional Values Per Serving

Calories	457
Total Fat	9.5g
Saturated Fat	1g
Cholesterol	0mg
Sodium	16mg
Total Carbohydrate	90g
Dietary Fiber	9.4g
Total Sugars	48g
Protein	9.4g

Serving Suggestion:

Enjoy these berry bars with a berry smoothie on the side.

Ingredients:

- 1 cup dates, pitted and halved
- 1½ cups apple juice
- 3 cups rolled oats
- ¾ teaspoon ground cinnamon
- ¼ teaspoon ground nutmeg
- 1½ tablespoons baking powder
- 2 small bananas
- 1 teaspoon vanilla extract
- 1 cup fresh blueberries
- ½ cup walnuts

Instructions:

1. Mix dates with apple juice in a small bowl and leave for 15 minutes.
2. At 375 degrees F, preheat your oven.
3. Layer a 9x9 inch baking pan with wax paper.
4. Mix baking powder, nutmeg, cinnamon and 2 cups rolled oats in a medium bowl.
5. Puree the dates and apple juice in a blender until smooth.
6. Add remaining 1 cup oats, vanilla extract and bananas to the dates, then blend
7. Stir in both mixtures to the bowl then mix evenly.
8. Fold in walnuts and blueberries, then spread the batter in the prepared pan.
9. Bake for 35 minutes in the preheated oven.
10. Allow the baked berry cake to cool then cut into bars.
11. Serve.

The Plant Based Cookbook For Beginners
650 Easy, Quick, & Simple Plant Based Vegan Diet Recipes With A 31 Day Meal Plan To Lose Weight & Live A Long Healthy Life

141

Banana Muffins

SERVINGS	PREPARATION TIME	COOKING TIME
6	15 minutes	20 minutes

Nutritional Values Per Serving

Calories	210
Total Fat	2.8g
Saturated Fat	0.5g
Cholesterol	0mg
Sodium	109mg
Total Carbohydrate	42.9g
Dietary Fiber	5.9g
Total Sugars	14.4g
Protein	4.9g

Ingredients:

- 4 bananas
- 2 cups oats, ground
- ½ cup unsweetened apple juice
- ½ cup unsweetened applesauce
- 2 tablespoons ground flax seeds
- 1 teaspoon ground cinnamon
- ½ tablespoon vanilla extract
- ½ tablespoon apple cider vinegar
- ½ tablespoon baking powder
- ½ teaspoon baking soda

Instructions:

1. At 350 degrees F, preheat your oven.
2. Layer a muffin tray with muffin liners.
3. Grind oats with all the dry ingredients and bananas in a food processor until smooth.
4. Stir in apple cider vinegar, extract, apple sauce and apple juice then mix evenly.
5. Divide the prepared oats batter into the muffin cups and bake for 20 minutes in the oven.
6. Allow the muffins to cool.
7. Serve.

Cranberry Pumpkin Muffins

SERVINGS **PREPARATION TIME** **COOKING TIME**
6 15 minutes 35 minutes

Nutritional Values Per Serving

Calories	288
Total Fat	7g
Saturated Fat	0.9g
Cholesterol	0mg
Sodium	8mg
Total Carbohydrate	48.5g
Dietary Fiber	9.1g
Total Sugars	10.4g
Protein	8.5g

Ingredients:

- 2 bananas
- ½ cup of orange juice
- Zest of one orange
- 1 (15-ounce) can of pumpkin
- ½ cup date paste
- 2 tablespoons ground flax seeds
- 1 tablespoon pumpkin pie spice
- 1 tablespoon vanilla extract
- 1 cup dried cranberries
- 3 cups oats
- ¼ cup walnuts, chopped
- ½ teaspoon cinnamon

Instructions:

1. At 350 degrees F, preheat your oven.
2. Blend bananas, juices, pumpkin, pumpkin spices, flaxseeds, orange zest, extract and date paste in a food processor until smooth and creamy.
3. Pour this batter into a large bowl, then fold in dried cranberries and oats.
4. Divide the batter into a muffin tray lined with cupcake liners.
5. Sprinkle cinnamon and nuts on top of the muffin batter.
6. Bake these muffins for 35 minutes in the oven.
7. Serve once cooled.

The Plant Based Cookbook For Beginners
650 Easy, Quick, & Simple Plant Based Vegan Diet Recipes With A 31 Day Meal Plan To Lose Weight & Live A Long Healthy Life

143

Oat Raisins Snackles

SERVINGS	PREPARATION TIME	COOKING TIME
6	15 minutes	15 minutes

Nutritional Values Per Serving

Calories	221
Total Fat	4.7g
Saturated Fat	2.5g
Cholesterol	1mg
Sodium	87mg
Total Carbohydrate	41.7g
Dietary Fiber	4.2g
Total Sugars	17.7g
Protein	4.6g

Ingredients:

- 1 cup rolled oats
- ¾ cup oat flour
- ¼ cup hemp seeds
- ⅓ cup raisins
- ¼ cup coconut, shredded
- 1 teaspoon baking powder
- 1 teaspoon cinnamon
- 1 teaspoon lemon zest
- ¼ teaspoon sea salt
- 2 pinches grated nutmeg
- ½ cup unsweetened applesauce
- ¼ cup pure maple syrup
- 3 tablespoons dark chocolate chips

Instructions:

1. At 350 degrees F, preheat your oven.
2. Layer a baking sheet with wax paper.
3. Mix oats, nutmeg, salt, zest, cinnamon, baking powder, hemp seeds, raisins, and oat flour.
4. Stir in maple syrup and apple sauce then mix evenly.
5. Fold in chocolate chips and mix well.
6. Divide the cookie batter into cookie mounds into the baking sheet.
7. Bake these cookies for 15 minutes in the oven.
8. Allow the cookies to cool and serve.

Cinnamon Raisin Oatmeal

SERVINGS
4

PREPARATION TIME
10 minutes

COOKING TIME
10 minutes

Nutritional Values Per Serving	
Calories	178
Total Fat	2.7g
Saturated Fat	0.5g
Cholesterol	0mg
Sodium	157mg
Total Carbohydrate	34.4g
Dietary Fiber	4.5g
Total Sugars	5.8g
Protein	5.6g

Serving Suggestion:

Enjoy this oatmeal with a peanut butter smoothie on the side.

Ingredients:

- 4 cups of water
- ½ cup raisins
- 2 cups old-fashioned rolled oats
- ½ teaspoon cinnamon
- ¼ teaspoon salt
- Coconut shreds, to garnish

Instructions:

1. Mix water, oats, raisins, cinnamon, and salt in a saucepan.
2. Boil first, then reduce the heat and cook for 10 minutes with occasional stirring.
3. Garnish with coconut shreds.
4. Serve.

The Plant Based Cookbook For Beginners
650 Easy, Quick, & Simple Plant Based Vegan Diet Recipes With A 31 Day Meal Plan To Lose Weight & Live A Long Healthy Life

145

Corn Black Bean Cakes

SERVINGS	PREPARATION TIME	COOKING TIME
6	10 minutes	32 minutes

Nutritional Values Per Serving

Calories	514
Total Fat	4.9g
Saturated Fat	0.7g
Cholesterol	0mg
Sodium	240mg
Total Carbohydrate	107.1g
Dietary Fiber	14.3g
Total Sugars	13.1g
Protein	20.1g

Ingredients:

- 1 ½ cups whole wheat flour
- ½ cup cornmeal
- 1 tablespoon baking powder
- ½ teaspoon sea salt
- 1 ½ cups almond milk
- ¼ cup applesauce
- 1 red bell pepper, seeded and diced
- 1 (10-ounce) package corn kernels
- 1 cup canned black beans, drained
- 6 green onions, sliced
- Tomato salsa, for serving
- Sour cream for serving
- Chopped fresh cilantro for serving

Instructions:

1. At 200 degrees F, preheat your oven.

2. Mix baking powder, salt, cornmeal and flour in a bowl.

3. Stir in milk, bell pepper, apple sauce, black beans, green onions, and corn then mix well until lump-free.

4. Set a griddle over medium heat and grease it with cooking spray.

5. Pour ½ cup batter into the griddle and cook for 4 minutes per side.

6. Cook the remaining bean pancakes in the same way.

7. Garnish the cooked pancakes with salsa, cilantro and sour cream.

8. Serve warm.

146

The Plant Based Cookbook For Beginners
650 Easy, Quick, & Simple Plant Based Vegan Diet Recipes With A 31 Day Meal Plan To Lose Weight & Live A Long Healthy Life

Raspberry Blueberry Smoothie

SERVINGS	PREPARATION TIME	COOKING TIME
1	10 minutes	0 minutes

Nutritional Values Per Serving

Calories	280
Total Fat	2.4g
Saturated Fat	0g
Cholesterol	0mg
Sodium	99mg
Total Carbohydrate	67.7g
Dietary Fiber	10.2g
Total Sugars	49.7g
Protein	2.3g

Ingredients:

- 1 apple, peeled, cored and chopped
- 2 ½ oz. frozen raspberries
- 2 ½ oz. frozen blueberries
- ⅔ cup almond milk
- ½ teaspoon agave syrup

Instructions:

1. Add apple, raspberries, blueberries, almond milk and agave syrup in a blender until smooth.
2. Serve.

The Plant Based Cookbook For Beginners
650 Easy, Quick, & Simple Plant Based Vegan Diet Recipes With A 31 Day Meal Plan To Lose Weight & Live A Long Healthy Life

147

Banana Pancakes

SERVINGS	PREPARATION TIME	COOKING TIME
4	15 minutes	20 minutes

Nutritional Values Per Serving

Calories	278
Total Fat	2.4g
Saturated Fat	0.1g
Cholesterol	0mg
Sodium	291mg
Total Carbohydrate	59.4g
Dietary Fiber	3.7g
Total Sugars	13.2g
Protein	6.4g

Ingredients:

- 1 ½ cups whole wheat flour
- 2 teaspoons baking powder
- ½ teaspoon of sea salt
- ½ tablespoon flaxseed
- ½ tablespoon water
- 2 bananas, mashed
- 1 ½ cups almond milk
- 1 cup of sparkling water

Instructions:

1. Soak flaxseed in ½ tablespoon water in a bowl for 5 minutes.
2. Mix flour with salt, baking powder and flaxseed mixture in a bowl.
3. Stir in mashed bananas, milk and water then mix evenly.
4. Set a griddle over medium heat and grease it with cooking spray.
5. Pour ¼ cup prepared batter into the griddle and cook for 5 minutes per side.
6. Transfer to a plate and make more pancakes with remaining batter.
7. Serve.

148

The Plant Based Cookbook For Beginners
650 Easy, Quick, & Simple Plant Based Vegan Diet Recipes With A 31 Day Meal Plan To Lose Weight & Live A Long Healthy Life

Potato Zucchini Hash

SERVINGS	PREPARATION TIME	COOKING TIME
4	15 minutes	24 minutes

Nutritional Values Per Serving

Calories	139
Total Fat	1.1g
Saturated Fat	0.3g
Cholesterol	0mg
Sodium	16mg
Total Carbohydrate	29.4g
Dietary Fiber	5g
Total Sugars	3.2g
Protein	4.5g

Serving Suggestion:

Try these patties with some soy sauce.

Ingredients:

- 2 russet potatoes, grated
- 1 large zucchini, grated
- ½ yellow onion, grated
- ½ cup oat flour
- 1 teaspoon baking powder
- ½ teaspoon black pepper

Instructions:

1. At 425 degrees F, preheat your oven.
2. Layer 2 baking sheets with wax paper.
3. Mix oat flour, black pepper and baking powder in a bowl.
4. Toss in veggies and mix evenly.
5. Take ¼ cup of the potato mixture and shape it into a patty.
6. Repeat the same steps to make more patties.
7. Place the patties in the baking sheets and cook for 12 minutes.
8. Flip the patties and bake for another 12 minutes.
9. Serve warm.

The Plant Based Cookbook For Beginners
650 Easy, Quick, & Simple Plant Based Vegan Diet Recipes With A 31 Day Meal Plan To Lose Weight & Live A Long Healthy Life

149

Hash Browns

SERVINGS	PREPARATION TIME	COOKING TIME
4	10 minutes	15 minutes

Nutritional Values Per Serving	
Calories	106
Total Fat	0.1g
Saturated Fat	0g
Cholesterol	0mg
Sodium	176mg
Total Carbohydrate	23.6g
Dietary Fiber	3.5g
Total Sugars	1.3g
Protein	3.6g

Ingredients:

- 2 ½ potatoes, shredded
- ¼ teaspoon salt
- ½ teaspoon black pepper
- 6 garlic cloves, minced

Instructions:

1. At 375 degrees F, preheat your oven.

2. Mix shredded potatoes with black pepper, garlic, and salt in a bowl.

3. Spread the shredded potatoes in a baking sheet and bake for 10 minutes.

4. Enjoy.

150

The Plant Based Cookbook For Beginners
650 Easy, Quick, & Simple Plant Based Vegan Diet Recipes With A 31 Day Meal Plan To Lose Weight & Live A Long Healthy Life

Chocolate Chip Pumpkin Muffins

SERVINGS	PREPARATION TIME	COOKING TIME
6	10 minutes	20 minutes

Nutritional Values Per Serving

Calories	201
Total Fat	2.4g
Saturated Fat	0.7g
Cholesterol	0mg
Sodium	303mg
Total Carbohydrate	40.8g
Dietary Fiber	5.8g
Total Sugars	12.7g
Protein	5g

Ingredients:

- 1 banana, mashed
- 1 (15-ounce) can pumpkin puree
- ¼ cup pure maple syrup
- 1 teaspoon vanilla extract
- 2 cups oat flour
- ½ teaspoon baking soda
- ½ teaspoon baking powder
- ½ teaspoon salt
- 1 teaspoon ground cinnamon
- ½ teaspoon ground nutmeg
- ¼ teaspoon ground ginger
- 1 cup dark chocolate chips

Instructions:

1. At 375 degrees F, preheat your oven.
2. Mix pumpkin puree with vanilla, maple syrup and mashed banana in a bowl.
3. Stir in ginger, nutmeg, cinnamon, salt, baking powder, baking soda and oat flour.
4. Mix well until smooth and lump-free then fold in chocolate chips.
5. Divide this batter into muffin cups and bake for 20 minutes in the oven.
6. Serve.

The Plant Based Cookbook For Beginners
650 Easy, Quick, & Simple Plant Based Vegan Diet Recipes With A 31 Day Meal Plan To Lose Weight & Live A Long Healthy Life

151

Corn Muffins

SERVINGS	PREPARATION TIME	COOKING TIME
6	15 minutes	20 minutes

Nutritional Values Per Serving	
Calories	366
Total Fat	13.6g
Saturated Fat	9.1g
Cholesterol	0mg
Sodium	420mg
Total Carbohydrate	57.6g
Dietary Fiber	7.1g
Total Sugars	19.9g
Protein	7g

Ingredients:

- 1 ½ tablespoons ground flaxseed
- 1 cup almond milk
- ½ cup applesauce
- ½ cup pure maple syrup
- 1 cup corn meal
- 1 cup oat flour
- 1 teaspoon baking soda
- 1 teaspoon baking powder
- ½ teaspoon salt
- 1 cup corn kernels

Instructions:

1. At 375 degrees F, preheat your oven.
2. Mix almond milk with flaxseed in a large bowl then leave it for 5 minutes.
3. Stir in maple syrup and applesauce then mix well.
4. Add salt, baking powder, baking soda, oat flour and cornmeal then mix until smooth.
5. Add corn kernels and mix evenly.
6. Divide the corn batter into 12 muffin cups and bake for 20 minutes in the oven.
7. Allow the muffins to cool and serve.

Chickpea Flour Scramble

SERVINGS	PREPARATION TIME	COOKING TIME
4	10 minutes	13 minutes

Nutritional Values Per Serving

Calories	145
Total Fat	3.5g
Saturated Fat	0.4g
Cholesterol	0mg
Sodium	159mg
Total Carbohydrate	22.9g
Dietary Fiber	6.6g
Total Sugars	6.2g
Protein	7.2g

Serving Suggestion:

Enjoy this scramble with toasted whole wheat bread slices and hash browns.

Ingredients:

Veggies

- ½ teaspoon oil
- 1 clove of garlic
- ¼ cup onions, chopped
- 2 tablespoons asparagus, chopped
- 2 tablespoons yellow bell pepper, chopped
- 2 tablespoons zucchini, chopped
- ½ green chile, chopped
- 2 tablespoons red bell pepper, chopped
- Cilantro and black pepper for garnish

Chickpea Batter

- ½ cup chickpea flour
- ½ cup water
- 1 tablespoon nutritional yeast
- 1 tablespoon flaxseed meal
- ½ teaspoon baking powder
- ¼ teaspoon salt
- ¼ teaspoon turmeric
- ¼ teaspoon or less paprika
- ⅛ teaspoons black salt
- Dash of black pepper

Instructions:

1. Mix chickpea batter ingredients in a bowl until lump-free.
2. Set a skillet over medium heat and grease it with ½ teaspoons oil.
3. Sauté garlic and onion in the skillet for 3 minutes.
4. Stir in chile and veggies then sauté for 2 minutes.
5. Pour in chickpea batter then cook for 2 minutes and scramble it.
6. Cook for 5 minutes with stirring.
7. Serve and garnish with cilantro.

The Plant Based Cookbook For Beginners
650 Easy, Quick, & Simple Plant Based Vegan Diet Recipes With A 31 Day Meal Plan To Lose Weight & Live A Long Healthy Life

153

Morning Congee

SERVINGS	PREPARATION TIME	COOKING TIME
4	45 minutes	60 minutes

Nutritional Values Per Serving

Calories	266
Total Fat	2g
Saturated Fat	0.5g
Cholesterol	0mg
Sodium	1802mg
Total Carbohydrate	52g
Dietary Fiber	4.3g
Total Sugars	4.8g
Protein	10.7g

Ingredients:

Congee

- 1 cup jasmine rice
- 6 dried shiitake mushrooms
- 4 cups water
- 5 cups vegetable broth
- 3 stalks lemongrass, sliced
- 2-inch piece ginger, peeled and sliced
- 1 teaspoon salt

Toppings

- Soy sauce
- Chili oil
- Ground pepper
- Furikake
- Fried onions
- Green onions, sliced

Instructions:

1. Boil about 2 cups water in a suitable cooking pot and then remove it from the heat.
2. Soak mushrooms in the water for 45 minutes
3. Transfer mushrooms, rice and water to a cooking pot.
4. Add 2 cup water, broth, ginger slices, lemon grass and salt.
5. Cover and cook the rice for 1 hour on a simmer.
6. Garnish with desired toppings.
7. Serve.

154

The Plant Based Cookbook For Beginners
650 Easy, Quick, & Simple Plant Based Vegan Diet Recipes With A 31 Day Meal Plan To Lose Weight & Live A Long Healthy Life

Tofu Scramble Toast

SERVINGS **4**

PREPARATION TIME **15 minutes**

COOKING TIME **8 minutes**

Nutritional Values Per Serving

Calories	326
Total Fat	20.4g
Saturated Fat	3.7g
Cholesterol	0mg
Sodium	173mg
Total Carbohydrate	29g
Dietary Fiber	8g
Total Sugars	10.4g
Protein	11.3g

Serving Suggestion:

Enjoy this scramble with toasted whole wheat bread slices.

Ingredients:

- 12 oz. silken tofu
- 2 green onions, sliced
- 1 garlic clove, chopped
- 10 cherry tomatoes, halved
- ½ fresh red chili, sliced
- 1 avocado, sliced
- 1 teaspoon ground turmeric
- Salt and black pepper, to taste
- 2 tablespoons olive oil
- 8 bread slices, toasted

Instructions:

1. Sauté garlic with olive oil in a cooking pan over medium-low heat for 30 seconds.

2. Add tomatoes and sauté for 2 minutes.

3. Toast and grill the bread slices in a grill pan over medium heat or in a toaster oven.

4. Sauté green onions with chili slices in the same pan as the tomatoes over medium-low heat until soft.

5. Stir in tofu and crumble it with a fork.

6. Add black pepper, salt and turmeric then sauté for 2 minutes.

7. Divide the tofu scramble on top of the toast slices.

8. Serve.

The Plant Based Cookbook For Beginners
650 Easy, Quick, & Simple Plant Based Vegan Diet Recipes With A 31 Day Meal Plan To Lose Weight & Live A Long Healthy Life

155

Red Pesto and Kale Porridge

SERVINGS	PREPARATION TIME	COOKING TIME
4	10 minutes	6 minutes

Nutritional Values Per Serving	
Calories	193
Total Fat	4.5g
Saturated Fat	0.8g
Cholesterol	1mg
Sodium	42mg
Total Carbohydrate	31g
Dietary Fiber	4.8g
Total Sugars	1.7g
Protein	8.6g

Serving Suggestion:

Try this porridge with toasted whole wheat bread slices.

Ingredients:

- ½ cup of oats
- ½ cup of couscous
- 2 cups of veggie stock
- 1½ teaspoons dried oregano
- 1 teaspoon dried basil
- 1 cup of kale, chopped
- 1 cup of cherry tomatoes, sliced
- 1 green onion, sliced
- 1 teaspoon tahini
- 1 tablespoon pesto
- 2 tablespoons nutritional yeast
- 1 tablespoon pumpkin seeds
- 1 tablespoon hemp seeds
- Salt and black pepper, to taste

Instructions:

1. Add black pepper, salt, basil, oregano, vegetable stock, couscous and oats to a small pot.

2. Cook the couscous and oats for 5 minutes on medium heat.

3. Add chopped kale, tomatoes and green onions then cook for 1 minute.

4. Stir in yeast, pesto and tahini then mix well.

5. Garnish with seeds and serve.

156

The Plant Based Cookbook For Beginners
650 Easy, Quick, & Simple Plant Based Vegan Diet Recipes With A 31 Day Meal Plan To Lose Weight & Live A Long Healthy Life

Waffle Strawberry Pizza

SERVINGS	PREPARATION TIME	COOKING TIME
4	15 minutes	24 minutes

Nutritional Values Per Serving

Calories	274
Total Fat	13.6g
Saturated Fat	12.8g
Cholesterol	0mg
Sodium	12mg
Total Carbohydrate	29.9g
Dietary Fiber	3g
Total Sugars	5.7g
Protein	4.9g

Ingredients:

Waffle

- 1 ripe banana
- 1 cup flour
- 1 cup almond milk
- 2 teaspoons baking powder

Toppings

- 2 cup strawberries
- ½ cup maple syrup

Instructions:

1. Mix all the waffle ingredients in a bowl until smooth and thick.
2. Preheat your waffle iron and add a dollop of the batter into the iron.
3. Cook the waffle for 6 minutes then transfer to a plate.
4. Continue cooking more waffles with remaining batter.
5. Add strawberries and maple syrup on top of each waffle and serve.

The Plant Based Cookbook For Beginners
650 Easy, Quick, & Simple Plant Based Vegan Diet Recipes With A 31 Day Meal Plan To Lose Weight & Live A Long Healthy Life

157

Mango Chia Pudding

SERVINGS	PREPARATION TIME	FRIDGE TIME
2	15 minutes	4 hours

Nutritional Values Per Serving

Calories	367
Total Fat	27.4g
Saturated Fat	23.3g
Cholesterol	0mg
Sodium	19mg
Total Carbohydrate	32.8g
Dietary Fiber	4.9g
Total Sugars	26g
Protein	3.3g

Ingredients:

- 1 (15 ½ ounce) can coconut milk
- 10 ounces fresh mango chunks
- ¼ cup maple syrup
- 1 tablespoon lime zest, grated
- ¼ cup lime juice
- ⅓ cup chia seeds
- ¼ cup hemp seeds

Toppings

- Mango, chopped

Instructions:

1. Mix coconut milk, lime juice, lime zest, maple syrup, and mango chunks in a blender until smooth.

2. Stir in hemp seeds, and chia seeds then mix well.

3. Divide this mixture into mason jars and cover.

4. Refrigerate the pudding for 4 hours and garnish with mango.

5. Serve.

158

The Plant Based Cookbook For Beginners
650 Easy, Quick, & Simple Plant Based Vegan Diet Recipes With A 31 Day Meal Plan To Lose Weight & Live A Long Healthy Life

Cashew Chia Toast

SERVINGS	PREPARATION TIME	COOKING TIME
4	10 minutes	20 minutes

Nutritional Values Per Serving

Calories	138
Total Fat	5.8g
Saturated Fat	1.1g
Cholesterol	0mg
Sodium	270mg
Total Carbohydrate	20.2g
Dietary Fiber	4.6g
Total Sugars	2.7g
Protein	5.8g

Serving Suggestion:

Enjoy this chia toast with maple syrup and fruits on top.

Ingredients:

- 1 cup 2 tablespoons almond milk
- 1 tablespoon chia seeds
- ⅓ cup cashews, soaked and drained
- ¾ teaspoon cinnamon
- ½ teaspoon vanilla extract
- ⅛ teaspoon sea salt
- 1 medium bread loaf, sliced

Instructions:

1. Blend milk with salt, vanilla extract, cinnamon, cashews and chia in a blender until smooth.
2. Set a skillet with some oil over medium heat.
3. Dip the bread slices in the prepared batter and sear the slices for 3-5 minutes per side until golden brown.
4. Serve warm.

The Plant Based Cookbook For Beginners
650 Easy, Quick, & Simple Plant Based Vegan Diet Recipes With A 31 Day Meal Plan To Lose Weight & Live A Long Healthy Life

159

Chickpea Omelet

SERVINGS	PREPARATION TIME	COOKING TIME
2	15 minutes	11 minutes

Nutritional Values Per Serving

Calories	111
Total Fat	1.8g
Saturated Fat	0.2g
Cholesterol	0mg
Sodium	9mg
Total Carbohydrate	17.9g
Dietary Fiber	5.7g
Total Sugars	2.8g
Protein	7.2g

Ingredients:

- ¼ cup chickpea flour
- 1 tablespoon nutritional yeast
- ½ teaspoon baking power
- ¼ teaspoon turmeric
- ½ teaspoon chives, chopped
- ¼ teaspoons garlic powder
- ⅛ teaspoons black pepper
- ½ teaspoons flaxseed
- ¼ cup 1 tablespoon water
- Handful of leafy greens of your choice

Instructions:

1. Soak flaxseed in 1 tbsp water in a bowl for 5 minutes.
2. Mix chickpea flour with yeast, baking powder, turmeric, chives, garlic powder, black pepper, flaxseed mixture, and water in a bowl until smooth.
3. Stir in green and mix evenly then leave the batter for 5 minutes.
4. Set a skillet, greased with oil, over medium heat.
5. Pour the omelet batter into the skillet and cook for 3 minutes.
6. Flip the omelet and cook for 3 minutes.
7. Serve.

160

The Plant Based Cookbook For Beginners
650 Easy, Quick, & Simple Plant Based Vegan Diet Recipes With A 31 Day Meal Plan To Lose Weight & Live A Long Healthy Life

Green Chia Pudding

SERVINGS	PREPARATION TIME	COOKING TIME
1	5 minutes	0 minutes

Nutritional Values Per Serving	
Calories	141
Total Fat	4.8g
Saturated Fat	0.3g
Cholesterol	0mg
Sodium	165mg
Total Carbohydrate	22.6g
Dietary Fiber	4.1g
Total Sugars	15.1g
Protein	3.5g

Ingredients:

- 1 Medjool date, pitted
- 1 cup almond milk
- 1 handful fresh spinach
- 3 tablespoons chia seeds
- Fruit for topping, banana, kiwi, mango, berries

Instructions:

1. Blend milk with date and spinach in a blender until smooth.
2. Add chia seeds to the milk and leave for 15 minutes.
3. Serve.

The Plant Based Cookbook For Beginners
650 Easy, Quick, & Simple Plant Based Vegan Diet Recipes With A 31 Day Meal Plan To Lose Weight & Live A Long Healthy Life

161

Matcha Green Tea Smoothie

SERVINGS	PREPARATION TIME	COOKING TIME
2	5 minutes	0 minutes

Nutritional Values Per Serving

Calories	221
Total Fat	2.3g
Saturated Fat	0.4g
Cholesterol	20mg
Sodium	128mg
Total Carbohydrate	41.5g
Dietary Fiber	4.9g
Total Sugars	24.6g
Protein	10g

Ingredients:

- 2 bananas, frozen
- 1 cup almond milk
- 1 cup spinach, frozen
- ½ cup zucchini, chopped
- ½ cup coconut yogurt
- 1 scoop vanilla protein powder
- 1 tablespoon matcha green tea powder
- 2 pitted dates
- 2 teaspoons vanilla extract

Instructions:

1. Blend all the green tea smoothie in a blender until smooth.
2. Serve.

162

The Plant Based Cookbook For Beginners
650 Easy, Quick, & Simple Plant Based Vegan Diet Recipes With A 31 Day Meal Plan To Lose Weight & Live A Long Healthy Life

Turmeric Oats

SERVINGS
2

PREPARATION TIME
10 minutes

COOKING TIME
19 minutes

Nutritional Values Per Serving

Calories	166
Total Fat	3.4g
Saturated Fat	0.3g
Cholesterol	0mg
Sodium	224mg
Total Carbohydrate	61.4g
Dietary Fiber	2.5g
Total Sugars	3.2g
Protein	3.3g

Serving Suggestion:

Try this oatmeal with toasted whole wheat bread slices.

Ingredients:

- ¼ teaspoon olive oil
- ½ cup steel-cut oats
- 1 ½ cups water
- 1 cup almond milk
- ⅓ teaspoons turmeric
- ½ teaspoon cinnamon
- ¼ teaspoon cardamom
- ⅛ teaspoons salt
- 2 tablespoons maple syrup
- Goji berries, to garnish

Instructions:

1. Toast oats with oil in a saucepan for 2 minutes.
2. Boil water with milk in a saucepan, reduce the heat and cook for 10 minutes.
3. Stir in toasted oats, maple syrup, salt and spices then cook for 7 minutes.
4. Garnish with goji berries.
5. Serve warm.

The Plant Based Cookbook For Beginners
650 Easy, Quick, & Simple Plant Based Vegan Diet Recipes With A 31 Day Meal Plan To Lose Weight & Live A Long Healthy Life

163

Chocolate Chip Oatmeal Bars

SERVINGS
6

PREPARATION TIME
10 minutes

COOKING TIME
20 minutes

Nutritional Values Per Serving

Calories	210
Total Fat	5.1g
Saturated Fat	1.6g
Cholesterol	1mg
Sodium	89mg
Total Carbohydrate	37.3g
Dietary Fiber	3.4g
Total Sugars	13.6g
Protein	5.6g

Serving Suggestion:

Enjoy these oatmeal bars with a peanut butter smoothie on the side.

Ingredients:

- 1½ cups rolled oats
- 1¼ cups oat flour
- 4 tablespoons pumpkin seeds
- 3 tablespoons dark chocolate chips
- 1 teaspoon cinnamon
- ¼ teaspoon salt
- ¼ teaspoon grated nutmeg
- ¼ cup 2 tablespoons almond milk
- ⅓ cup brown rice syrup
- 2 tablespoons pure maple syrup

Instructions:

1. At 350 degrees F, preheat your oven.

2. Layer an 8x8 inch baking dish with parchment paper.

3. Mix oats with nutmeg, sea salt, cinnamon, chocolate chips, pumpkin seeds, and oat flour in a large bowl.

4. Stir in milk, maple syrup and brown rice syrup then mix well until smooth.

5. Pour this batter into the prepared pan and bake for 20 minutes in the preheated oven.

6. Slice into bars and serve.

164

The Plant Based Cookbook For Beginners
650 Easy, Quick, & Simple Plant Based Vegan Diet Recipes With A 31 Day Meal Plan To Lose Weight & Live A Long Healthy Life

Blueberry Buckwheat Porridge

SERVINGS	PREPARATION TIME	FRIDGE TIME
4	15 minutes	Overnight

Nutritional Values Per Serving

Calories	390
Total Fat	20.3g
Saturated Fat	1.4g
Cholesterol	0mg
Sodium	68mg
Total Carbohydrate	46.6g
Dietary Fiber	8.3g
Total Sugars	19.7g
Protein	12.3g

Ingredients:

- ⅓ cup buckwheat groats
- ⅓ cup amaranth
- 1 cup raw walnuts
- 1 tablespoon lemon juice
- 4 cups blueberries
- 1 tablespoon agave
- ½ teaspoon ground cardamom
- ¼ teaspoon cinnamon
- Dash of sea salt
- ½ teaspoon pure vanilla extract
- 1½ cups warm water

Instructions:

1. Mix buckwheat with warm water, amaranth, walnuts and lemon juice in a bowl.
2. Cover this mixture and soak it overnight.
3. Blend 3 cups of blueberries with agave in a blender until smooth and transfer half of the puree to a bowl.
4. Mix blueberry puree with buckwheat mixture, ½ cup water, spices and vanilla in the blender.
5. Divide the pureed porridge in the serving bowls and stir in rest of blueberries.
6. Serve.

The Plant Based Cookbook For Beginners
650 Easy, Quick, & Simple Plant Based Vegan Diet Recipes With A 31 Day Meal Plan To Lose Weight & Live A Long Healthy Life

165

Pumpkin Smoothie

SERVINGS	PREPARATION TIME	COOKING TIME
2	5 minutes	0 minutes

Nutritional Values Per Serving

Calories	131
Total Fat	1.7g
Saturated Fat	0.2g
Cholesterol	0mg
Sodium	75mg
Total Carbohydrate	29.5g
Dietary Fiber	3.4g
Total Sugars	18.2g
Protein	1.8g

Ingredients:

- 1 banana frozen
- ½ cup pumpkin puree
- 1 cup almond milk
- ½ teaspoon pumpkin pie spice
- 1 tablespoon maple syrup
- ½ cup ice cubes

Instructions:

1. Blend pumpkin puree and rest of the ingredients in a blender until smooth.
2. Serve.

166

The Plant Based Cookbook For Beginners
650 Easy, Quick, & Simple Plant Based Vegan Diet Recipes With A 31 Day Meal Plan To Lose Weight & Live A Long Healthy Life

Banana Cream Chia Pudding

SERVINGS
2

PREPARATION TIME
15 minutes

FRIDGE TIME
1 hour

Nutritional Values Per Serving

Calories	248
Total Fat	15.6g
Saturated Fat	12.9g
Cholesterol	0mg
Sodium	17mg
Total Carbohydrate	28.6g
Dietary Fiber	5.6g
Total Sugars	9.2g
Protein	3g

Ingredients:

- ¼ cup chia seeds
- ½ cup full-fat coconut milk
- ½ cup almond milk
- 1 tablespoon agave syrup
- 1 teaspoon cinnamon
- 1 banana, mashed
- 1 banana, chopped
- Coconut flakes, garnish

Instructions:

1. Mix mashed banana with cinnamon, agave, almond milk, coconut milk and chia seeds in a bowl.
2. Cover and refrigerate this pudding for 1 hour.
3. Divide the prepared pudding into the serving bowls.
4. Garnish with coconut flakes and chopped bananas.
5. Serve.

The Plant Based Cookbook For Beginners
650 Easy, Quick, & Simple Plant Based Vegan Diet Recipes With A 31 Day Meal Plan To Lose Weight & Live A Long Healthy Life

167

Mint Chocolate Smoothie

SERVINGS	PREPARATION TIME	COOKING TIME
2	5 minutes	0 minutes

Nutritional Values Per Serving

Calories	114
Total Fat	1.8g
Saturated Fat	0.5g
Cholesterol	10mg
Sodium	54mg
Total Carbohydrate	18g
Dietary Fiber	4.8g
Total Sugars	7.9g
Protein	7.3g

Ingredients:

- 1 scoop vegan protein powder
- 1 tablespoon ground flaxseed
- 1 medium banana
- 1 cup fresh spinach
- ¼ teaspoons peppermint extract
- 4 ice cubes
- ¾ cup almond milk
- 1 tablespoon coconut nectar

Instructions:

1. Blend all the green smoothie ingredients in a blender until smooth.
2. Serve.

168

The Plant Based Cookbook For Beginners
650 Easy, Quick, & Simple Plant Based Vegan Diet Recipes With A 31 Day Meal Plan To Lose Weight & Live A Long Healthy Life

Strawberry Cream Cheese Spread

SERVINGS	PREPARATION TIME	FRIDGE TIME
4	5 minutes	1 hour

Nutritional Values Per Serving

Calories	134
Total Fat	10g
Saturated Fat	1.7g
Cholesterol	0mg
Sodium	81mg
Total Carbohydrate	7.5g
Dietary Fiber	0.8g
Total Sugars	2.9g
Protein	4.4g

Serving Suggestion:

Try this strawberry spread on top of bread slices.

Ingredients:

- 1 oz. strawberries
- ⅓ cup raw cashew butter
- ⅓ cup 2 tablespoons coconut yogurt
- 1 teaspoon apple cider vinegar
- 2 teaspoons fresh lemon juice
- ⅛ teaspoon salt

Instructions:

1. Blend all the strawberry cream cheese ingredients in a bowl.
2. Cover and refrigerate for 1 hour to set.
3. Serve.

The Plant Based Cookbook For Beginners
650 Easy, Quick, & Simple Plant Based Vegan Diet Recipes With A 31 Day Meal Plan To Lose Weight & Live A Long Healthy Life

169

Green Avocado Smoothie

SERVINGS	PREPARATION TIME	COOKING TIME
2	15 minutes	0 minutes

Nutritional Values Per Serving	
Calories	162
Total Fat	10.1g
Saturated Fat	2.1g
Cholesterol	0mg
Sodium	23mg
Total Carbohydrate	18.9g
Dietary Fiber	5.2g
Total Sugars	7.9g
Protein	2.3g

Ingredients:

- 1 banana
- ½ avocado
- 1 cup baby spinach
- ½ cup coconut yogurt
- ½ lemon, juiced
- 1 cup water

Instructions:

1. Blend avocado with rest of the ingredients in a blender until smooth.
2. Serve.

170

The Plant Based Cookbook For Beginners
650 Easy, Quick, & Simple Plant Based Vegan Diet Recipes With A 31 Day Meal Plan To Lose Weight & Live A Long Healthy Life

Mushroom Avocado Toast

SERVINGS
4

PREPARATION TIME
10 minutes

COOKING TIME
5 minutes

Nutritional Values Per Serving

Calories	338
Total Fat	13.5g
Saturated Fat	2.8g
Cholesterol	0mg
Sodium	472mg
Total Carbohydrate	45.8g
Dietary Fiber	13.9g
Total Sugars	5.7g
Protein	14.2g

Ingredients:

- 1 medium avocado, mashed
- 1 tablespoon lemon juice
- 4 ounces mushrooms
- ¼ cup cooked cannellini beans
- 1-ounce microgreens
- 1 tablespoon miso paste
- 1 tablespoon balsamic vinegar
- 4 whole grain bread, slices, toasted
- 1 tablespoon sesame seeds

Instructions:

1. Mash peeled and pitted avocado with lemon juice in a bowl.
2. Sauté mushrooms with oil in a skillet for 5 minutes.
3. Stir in microgreens and beans then mix well.
4. Mix 1 tablespoon water with miso paste in a small bowl.
5. Pour this mixture over mushrooms along with balsamic vinegar.
6. Spread the prepared avocado mash on top of the toasted bread.
7. Add mushrooms mixture on top and garnish with sesame seeds.
8. Serve.

The Plant Based Cookbook For Beginners
650 Easy, Quick, & Simple Plant Based Vegan Diet Recipes With A 31 Day Meal Plan To Lose Weight & Live A Long Healthy Life

171

Green Apple Smoothie

SERVINGS	PREPARATION TIME	COOKING TIME
2	5 minutes	0 minutes

Nutritional Values Per Serving

Calories	116
Total Fat	0.5g
Saturated Fat	0.1g
Cholesterol	0mg
Sodium	37mg
Total Carbohydrate	29.5g
Dietary Fiber	5g
Total Sugars	22.4g
Protein	2g

Ingredients:

- 1 large green apple
- 4 Mejdool dates
- 3 cups spinach
- 8 ice cubes
- ½ cup water
- 1 teaspoon lemon juice

Instructions:

1. Blend all of the ingredients in a blender until smooth.
2. Serve.

172

The Plant Based Cookbook For Beginners
650 Easy, Quick, & Simple Plant Based Vegan Diet Recipes With A 31 Day Meal Plan To Lose Weight & Live A Long Healthy Life

French Toast with Caramelized Bananas

SERVINGS	PREPARATION TIME	COOKING TIME
4	10 minutes	26 minutes

Nutritional Values Per Serving

Calories	366
Total Fat	18.5g
Saturated Fat	13g
Cholesterol	0mg
Sodium	486mg
Total Carbohydrate	47g
Dietary Fiber	4.5g
Total Sugars	15.2g
Protein	5.8g

Ingredients:

- 1 cup almond milk
- 1 ripe banana
- 2 tablespoons pure maple syrup
- 1 teaspoon vanilla extract
- 1 tablespoon chia seeds
- 1 teaspoon ground cinnamon
- ¼ teaspoon kosher salt
- 8 sandwich bread slices
- 2 tablespoons coconut oil

Caramelized Bananas

- 2 bananas, sliced
- ¼ cup coconut sugar

To Serve

- 2 tablespoons crushed raw pecans
- Pure maple syrup
- Almond butter

Instructions:

1. Mix milk with salt, cinnamon, chia seeds, vanilla, maple syrup, and banana in a blender.

2. Pour this mixture into a shallow dish.

3. Place the bread slices in a baking dish and pour the milk mixture on top.

4. Set a medium sized skillet over medium heat and grease it with 2 tablespoons coconut oil.

5. Sear the bread slices for 3-5 minutes per side.

6. Mix banana slices with coconut Sugar in a bowl to coat evenly.

7. Spread the bananas in a large skillet and sear for 2-3 minutes per side until golden brown.

8. Serve the toasts with caramelized banana on top, pecans, maple syrup and almond butter.

The Plant Based Cookbook For Beginners
650 Easy, Quick, & Simple Plant Based Vegan Diet Recipes With A 31 Day Meal Plan To Lose Weight & Live A Long Healthy Life

173

Carrot Cake Cookies

SERVINGS	PREPARATION TIME	COOKING TIME
8	15 minutes	17 minutes

Nutritional Values Per Serving

Calories	263
Total Fat	11.1g
Saturated Fat	3.8g
Cholesterol	0mg
Sodium	250mg
Total Carbohydrate	38.5g
Dietary Fiber	2.5g
Total Sugars	15.6g
Protein	3.5g

Ingredients:

- 1 cup oats
- 1 cup whole wheat flour
- 1 teaspoon baking powder
- 1 teaspoon ground cinnamon
- ½ teaspoon salt
- ¼ teaspoon ground ginger
- 1 ½ cups grated carrots, peeled
- 1 cup roughly raw pecans, chopped
- ¼ cup golden raisins
- ½ cup maple syrup
- ½ cup melted coconut oil

Instructions:

1. At 375 degrees F, preheat your one.
2. Layer a suitable rimmed baking sheet with parchment paper.
3. Mix oats with ginger, salt, cinnamon, baking powder and flour in a bowl.
4. Add in maple syrup and coconut oil then mix until smooth.
5. Fold in raisins, pecans and carrots then mix evenly.
6. Divide dough on the baking sheet into ¼ cup cookie rounds.
7. Bake these cookies for 17 minutes in the oven then allow the cookies to cool.
8. Serve.

(174)

The Plant Based Cookbook For Beginners
650 Easy, Quick, & Simple Plant Based Vegan Diet Recipes With A 31 Day Meal Plan To Lose Weight & Live A Long Healthy Life

Strawberry Oatmeal Bites

SERVINGS
8

PREPARATION TIME
15 minutes

COOKING TIME
25 minutes

Nutritional Values Per Serving

Calories	318
Total Fat	6.6g
Saturated Fat	1.9g
Cholesterol	1mg
Sodium	97mg
Total Carbohydrate	55.1g
Dietary Fiber	8.2g
Total Sugars	10.5g
Protein	9g

Serving Suggestion:

Enjoy these oatmeal bites with a peanut butter smoothie on the side.

Ingredients:

- 2 bananas, mashed
- 1 cup almond milk
- 1 teaspoon vanilla extract
- 3 cups old fashioned oats
- 2 tablespoons flax meal
- 1½ teaspoons baking powder
- ¼ teaspoons salt
- 1 teaspoon cinnamon
- 2 cups fresh strawberries, chopped
- ¼ cup of dark chocolate chips

Instructions:

1. At 350 degrees F, preheat your oven.
2. Grease the muffin tray.
3. Mix mashed bananas with vanilla and milk in a medium bowl.
4. Stir in oats, cinnamon, salt, baking powder, and flax meal, then mix well until smooth.
5. Fold in chocolate chips and strawberries, then mix evenly.
6. Divide this oatmeal mixture into the muffin tray.
7. Bake the oat-muffins for 25 minutes in the oven.
8. Allow the muffins to cool and serve.

The Plant Based Cookbook For Beginners
650 Easy, Quick, & Simple Plant Based Vegan Diet Recipes With A 31 Day Meal Plan To Lose Weight & Live A Long Healthy Life

175

Snickerdoodle Bars

SERVINGS	PREPARATION TIME	COOKING TIME
6	10 minutes	0 minutes

Nutritional Values Per Serving

Calories	250
Total Fat	17.8g
Saturated Fat	4.1g
Cholesterol	0mg
Sodium	150mg
Total Carbohydrate	20g
Dietary Fiber	5.2g
Total Sugars	12.8g
Protein	6g

Ingredients:

- 1 cup unsweetened coconut
- 2 cup almonds
- 2 cups pecans
- 1 tablespoon cinnamon
- 12 Medjool dates, pitted and quartered
- 1 tablespoon vanilla extract
- ½ teaspoon salt
- 2 tablespoons maple syrup
- 2 tablespoons water

Instructions:

1. Blend dates, cinnamon, pecans, almonds and coconut in a food processor for 45 seconds.
2. Stir in maple syrup, water, salt and vanilla, then blend for 20 seconds.
3. Layer baking sheet with plastic wrap and spread the dough into ½ inch thick sheet.
4. Cut the set batter into 30 bars of equal size.
5. Cover the bars with a plastic sheet and refrigerate for 30 minutes.
6. Serve.

176

The Plant Based Cookbook For Beginners
650 Easy, Quick, & Simple Plant Based Vegan Diet Recipes With A 31 Day Meal Plan To Lose Weight & Live A Long Healthy Life

Coconut Pancakes with Banana

SERVINGS	PREPARATION TIME	COOKING TIME
4	15 minutes	20 minutes

Nutritional Values Per Serving	
Calories	215
Total Fat	0.7g
Saturated Fat	0.1g
Cholesterol	0mg
Sodium	6mg
Total Carbohydrate	48.7g
Dietary Fiber	5.2g
Total Sugars	11.3g
Protein	5.1g

Ingredients:

- 5 oz. flour
- 2 teaspoons baking powder
- Pinch of salt
- 3 tablespoons golden caster sugar
- 1 ½ cups can coconut milk
- Vegetable oil, for frying
- 2 bananas, sliced

Instructions:

1. Mix flour, a pinch of salt, baking powder, and sugar in a bowl
2. Stir in coconut milk then mix well until smooth.
3. Set a shallow frying pan, greased with oil, over medium heat.
4. Add 2 tablespoons of coconut batter to the pan and cook for 2-3 minutes per side.
5. Make more pancakes and transfer them to a plate.
6. Serve with sliced bananas on top.
7. Enjoy.

The Plant Based Cookbook For Beginners
650 Easy, Quick, & Simple Plant Based Vegan Diet Recipes With A 31 Day Meal Plan To Lose Weight & Live A Long Healthy Life

177

Jelly Chia Pudding

SERVINGS	PREPARATION TIME	COOKING TIME	FRIDGE TIME
3	15 minutes	10 minutes	1 hour

Nutritional Values Per Serving

Calories	284
Total Fat	11.9g
Saturated Fat	2g
Cholesterol	0mg
Sodium	456mg
Total Carbohydrate	39.4g
Dietary Fiber	6.1g
Total Sugars	30.7g
Protein	6.5g

Ingredients:

Chia Pudding

- 1 cup almond milk
- ½ cup coconut milk
- 1 teaspoon vanilla
- 2 tablespoons maple syrup
- 3 tablespoons peanut butter
- ⅓ cup chia seeds

Compote

- 1 cup wild blueberries
- 1 tablespoon orange juice
- 1 tablespoon chia seeds

Instructions:

1. Mix blueberries with orange juice in a small skillet and cook until bubbles.
2. Reduce the heat and cook for 2 minutes with occasional stirring.
3. Remove it from the heat and add chia seeds, then mix.
4. Now blend peanut butter, maple syrup, vanilla, and almond and coconut milk in a blender.
5. Add chia seeds to the milk mixture and leave for 10 minutes.
6. Divide the chia pudding into the serving bowls and add the compote on top.
7. Cover and refrigerate for 1 hour.
8. Serve.

Chocolate Peanut Butter Smoothie

SERVINGS
1

PREPARATION TIME
5 minutes

COOKING TIME
0 minutes

Nutritional Values Per Serving

Calories	315
Total Fat	7.1g
Saturated Fat	2.6g
Cholesterol	1mg
Sodium	97mg
Total Carbohydrate	70.3g
Dietary Fiber	10.9g
Total Sugars	34.3g
Protein	6.6g

Ingredients:

- 2 frozen bananas
- 3 tablespoons cacao powder
- 3 tablespoons peanut butter
- 1 cup almond milk

Instructions:

1. Blend bananas and rest of the ingredients in a blender until smooth.
2. Serve.

The Plant Based Cookbook For Beginners
650 Easy, Quick, & Simple Plant Based Vegan Diet Recipes With A 31 Day Meal Plan To Lose Weight & Live A Long Healthy Life

179

Tofu Banh Mi

SERVINGS	PREPARATION TIME	COOKING TIME
1	15 minutes	20 minutes

Nutritional Values Per Serving

Calories	194
Total Fat	9.3g
Saturated Fat	1.6g
Cholesterol	0mg
Sodium	255mg
Total Carbohydrate	19.8g
Dietary Fiber	1.7g
Total Sugars	2.1g
Protein	9.4g

Ingredients:

Tofu

- 1 tofu, sliced
- 1 teaspoon olive oil
- Turmeric, to taste
- Salt and black pepper, to taste

To Assemble

- Bread slice, toasted
- Carrots, julienned
- Veggies, shredded

Instructions:

1. Rub the tofu with black pepper, salt and turmeric.
2. Set a pan with olive oil over medium-high heat.
3. Sear the tofu slices for 3-5 minutes per side until golden brown.
4. Place the seared tofu slices on top of the toasted bread.
5. Serve with veggies.

180

The Plant Based Cookbook For Beginners
650 Easy, Quick, & Simple Plant Based Vegan Diet Recipes With A 31 Day Meal Plan To Lose Weight & Live A Long Healthy Life

Breakfast Fig Toast

SERVINGS
8

PREPARATION TIME
10 minutes

COOKING TIME
10 minutes

Nutritional Values Per Serving

Calories	213
Total Fat	4.9g
Saturated Fat	1.1g
Cholesterol	0mg
Sodium	248mg
Total Carbohydrate	38.3g
Dietary Fiber	3.7g
Total Sugars	16g
Protein	6.6g

Ingredients:

Cinnamon Butter

- ¼ cup peanut butter
- ¼ teaspoon vanilla extract
- ½ teaspoon cinnamon
- 2 tablespoons maple syrup
- ¹⁄₁₆ teaspoon cardamom

Fig Toast

- 8 sourdough bread slices
- 10 fresh figs, sliced
- Roasted pistachios, crushed
- Sea salt
- Fresh mint, chopped
- Coconut cream, to serve

Instructions:

1. Mix all the ingredients for cinnamon butter in a bowl, cover and refrigerate.
2. Toast the bread in a skillet or toaster until golden brown.
3. Spread cinnamon butter on top of the bread.
4. Add sliced figs, mint, pistachios, and salt on top of the bread.
5. Garnish with a dollop of coconut cream.
6. Enjoy.

The Plant Based Cookbook For Beginners
650 Easy, Quick, & Simple Plant Based Vegan Diet Recipes With A 31 Day Meal Plan To Lose Weight & Live A Long Healthy Life

181

Tangelo Marmalade

SERVINGS	PREPARATION TIME	COOKING TIME
16	10 minutes	1 hour

Nutritional Values Per Serving

Calories	246
Total Fat	0.8g
Saturated Fat	0g
Cholesterol	0mg
Sodium	1mg
Total Carbohydrate	61.1g
Dietary Fiber	1.7g
Total Sugars	59.3g
Protein	0.8g

Serving Suggestion:

Try this marmalade on top of whole wheat bread slices.

Ingredients:

- 3 lb. tangelos, quarter
- 1 vanilla bean
- 4 cups sugar
- 1 cup water
- ½ Granny Smith apple, chopped

Instructions:

1. Juice the tangelos over a medium bowl.
2. Peel the rinds from the leftover tangelos and cut the rinds into 14-inch-wide strips.
3. Mix tangelos juice, rinds, vanilla pods, sugar, vanilla seeds, apple and water in a saucepan.
4. Cook this tangelo mixture for 1 hour, then remove the heat.
5. Discard apple, vanilla pods from this mixture.
6. Allow the marmalade to cool and serve.

182

The Plant Based Cookbook For Beginners
650 Easy, Quick, & Simple Plant Based Vegan Diet Recipes With A 31 Day Meal Plan To Lose Weight & Live A Long Healthy Life

Sweet Potato Breakfast

SERVINGS	PREPARATION TIME	COOKING TIME
2	10 minutes	60 minutes

Nutritional Values Per Serving

Calories	191
Total Fat	6.9g
Saturated Fat	0.7g
Cholesterol	0mg
Sodium	70mg
Total Carbohydrate	29.9g
Dietary Fiber	5.2g
Total Sugars	10.8g
Protein	4.9g

Serving Suggestion:

Enjoy this breakfast meal with toasted whole wheat bread slices.

Ingredients:

- 16 oz. sweet potato
- Agave to taste
- Cinnamon, to taste
- 2 tablespoons almond butter

Instructions:

1. At 375 degrees F, preheat your oven.
2. Poke all the sweet potatoes with a fork and wrap them with an aluminum foil.
3. Place these sweet potatoes on a baking sheet and bake for 60 minutes.
4. Allow the baked potatoes to cool, then transfer to a bowl.
5. Mash the potatoes with a fork then add agave, cinnamon, and almond butter.
6. Stir and serve.

The Plant Based Cookbook For Beginners
650 Easy, Quick, & Simple Plant Based Vegan Diet Recipes With A 31 Day Meal Plan To Lose Weight & Live A Long Healthy Life

183

Avocado Toast

SERVINGS	PREPARATION TIME	COOKING TIME
4	15 minutes	0 minutes

Nutritional Values Per Serving

Calories	110
Total Fat	6.4g
Saturated Fat	1.2g
Cholesterol	0mg
Sodium	219mg
Total Carbohydrate	11.9g
Dietary Fiber	4.1g
Total Sugars	3g
Protein	5.3g

Ingredients:

- ½ teaspoon garlic powder
- 1 teaspoon coriander powder
- ½ teaspoon salt
- Cayenne or black pepper to taste
- 4 of Bread Slices
- 2 ripe avocados mashed
- 2 tablespoons olive oil

Instructions:

1. Mash avocados with cayenne, salt, coriander powder and garlic powder in a bowl.
2. Toast the bread in a skillet or toaster until golden brown.
3. Spread this avocado mash on the toast.
4. Drizzle with olive oil.
5. Enjoy.

Tater Tot Waffles

SERVINGS
6

PREPARATION TIME
10 minutes

COOKING TIME
24 minutes

Nutritional Values Per Serving

Calories	288
Total Fat	13g
Saturated Fat	2.8g
Cholesterol	0mg
Sodium	751mg
Total Carbohydrate	42.1g
Dietary Fiber	3.8g
Total Sugars	0.4g
Protein	3.2g

Ingredients:

- 1 (32-ounce) bag vegan tater tots
- 1 tablespoon Cajun seasoning
- Salt and black pepper, to taste
- 2 tablespoons parsley leaves, chopped

Instructions:

1. Blend tater tots with parsley, Cajun, black pepper and salt in a blender.
2. Spread a ladle of the tater tot batter into the waffle iron.
3. Close and cook for 6 minutes then transfer to a plate.
4. Cook more waffles in the iron.
5. Garnish with a pinch of parsley.
6. Serve.

The Plant Based Cookbook For Beginners
650 Easy, Quick, & Simple Plant Based Vegan Diet Recipes With A 31 Day Meal Plan To Lose Weight & Live A Long Healthy Life

185

Strawberry Balsamic Jam

SERVINGS	PREPARATION TIME	COOKING TIME
4	15 minutes	30 minutes

Nutritional Values Per Serving

Calories	72
Total Fat	0.3g
Saturated Fat	0g
Cholesterol	0mg
Sodium	2mg
Total Carbohydrate	17.8g
Dietary Fiber	2.3g
Total Sugars	14.6g
Protein	0.8g

Serving Suggestion:

Try this jam with freshly baked apple walnut bread slices.

Ingredients:

- 1-pound strawberries, hulled and diced
- 3 tablespoons sugar
- 2 tablespoons balsamic vinegar

Instructions:

1. Mix balsamic vinegar, sugar and strawberries in a saucepan.
2. Cook the mixture to a boil, reduce the heat and cook for 30 minutes on a simmer.
3. Allow jam to cool and serve.

186

The Plant Based Cookbook For Beginners
650 Easy, Quick, & Simple Plant Based Vegan Diet Recipes With A 31 Day Meal Plan To Lose Weight & Live A Long Healthy Life

Pumpkin Pancakes

SERVINGS	PREPARATION TIME	COOKING TIME
4	15 minutes	32 minutes

Nutritional Values Per Serving

Calories	261
Total Fat	14.7g
Saturated Fat	12.8g
Cholesterol	0mg
Sodium	161mg
Total Carbohydrate	30.3g
Dietary Fiber	2.7g
Total Sugars	2.6g
Protein	4.8g

Ingredients:

- 1 cup whole wheat flour
- 1 tablespoon baking powder
- ½ teaspoon pumpkin pie spice
- ¼ teaspoon salt
- 4 tablespoons pumpkin puree
- 1 cup almond milk

Instructions:

1. Mix whole wheat flour with salt, pumpkin pie spice, and baking powder in a bowl.
2. Stir in pumpkin puree, and almond milk, then mix well until smooth.
3. Leave the batter for 15 minutes.
4. Set a skillet, greased with cooking oil, over medium heat.
5. Add ¼ cup batter into the skillet and cook for 4 minutes per side.
6. Make more pancakes in the same way.
7. Serve.

The Plant Based Cookbook For Beginners
650 Easy, Quick, & Simple Plant Based Vegan Diet Recipes With A 31 Day Meal Plan To Lose Weight & Live A Long Healthy Life

187

Mango Pancakes

SERVINGS	PREPARATION TIME	COOKING TIME
4	15 minutes	32 minutes

Nutritional Values Per Serving

Calories	155
Total Fat	2.5g
Saturated Fat	1.2g
Cholesterol	0mg
Sodium	340mg
Total Carbohydrate	29.7g
Dietary Fiber	1.7g
Total Sugars	3.1g
Protein	3.7g

Serving Suggestion:

Try these pancakes with a glass of a mango smoothie.

Ingredients:

- 1 cup whole wheat flour
- 2 tablespoons coconut Sugar
- 1 tablespoon baking powder
- ½ teaspoon salt
- 1 cup unsweetened almond milk
- 1 tablespoon apple cider vinegar
- 1 teaspoon vanilla extract
- ¼ teaspoon nutmeg
- ¼ teaspoon ginger
- ½ teaspoon cinnamon
- ½ cup mango
- 1 teaspoon coconut oil

Toppings

- 2 tablespoons coconut flakes
- ¼ cup mango, diced
- Maple syrup

Instructions:

1. Puree the mango flesh in a blender until smooth.
2. Mix cinnamon, ginger, nutmeg, salt, baking powder, sugar and whole wheat flour in a large bowl.
3. Stir in vanilla, apple cider vinegar, and almond milk, then mix well until smooth.
4. Fold in mango puree and mix evenly.
5. Set a skillet, greased with 1 teaspoon coconut oil, over medium-high heat.
6. Add ⅓ cup mango batter into the skillet and cook for 4 minutes per side.
7. Transfer to a plate and cook for pancakes in the same way.
8. Serve with diced mangos, coconut flakes, and maple syrup.

Brownie Oatmeal

SERVINGS	PREPARATION TIME	COOKING TIME
2	15 minutes	8 minutes

Nutritional Values Per Serving

Calories	138
Total Fat	3.7g
Saturated Fat	1.2g
Cholesterol	0mg
Sodium	19mg
Total Carbohydrate	23.5g
Dietary Fiber	3g
Total Sugars	7.4g
Protein	4g

Serving Suggestion:

Enjoy this oatmeal with a peanut butter smoothie on the side.

Ingredients:

- 1 cup water
- ½ cup rolled oats
- ¼ teaspoon salt
- 1 tablespoon cacao powder
- 1 tablespoon maple syrup
- ½ teaspoon vanilla extract

Toppings

- Peanut butter
- Dark chocolate
- Fresh blueberries
- Shredded coconut

Instructions:

1. Boil 1 cup water in a saucepan and then add oats and ¼ teaspoons salt.
2. Reduce the heat, cook for 8 minutes until the mixture thickens.
3. Stir in vanilla extract, maple syrup and cacao powder.
4. Mix well then remove from the heat.
5. Garnish with peanut butter, dark chocolate, blueberries, and coconut.
6. Serve.

The Plant Based Cookbook For Beginners
650 Easy, Quick, & Simple Plant Based Vegan Diet Recipes With A 31 Day Meal Plan To Lose Weight & Live A Long Healthy Life

189

Mango Banana Smoothie

SERVINGS	PREPARATION TIME	COOKING TIME
2	5 minutes	0 minutes

Nutritional Values Per Serving

Calories	182
Total Fat	4.2g
Saturated Fat	1.9g
Cholesterol	0mg
Sodium	91mg
Total Carbohydrate	34.4g
Dietary Fiber	3.5g
Total Sugars	25.6g
Protein	4.5g

Ingredients:

- 1 cup frozen mango, cubed
- 1 frozen banana, chopped
- 1 cup unsweetened almond milk
- ¼ cup coconut yogurt
- 1 scoop pea protein powder

Instructions:

1. Blend mango and the rest of the ingredients in a blender until smooth.
2. Serve.

190

The Plant Based Cookbook For Beginners
650 Easy, Quick, & Simple Plant Based Vegan Diet Recipes With A 31 Day Meal Plan To Lose Weight & Live A Long Healthy Life

Tofu Scramble

SERVINGS	PREPARATION TIME	COOKING TIME
1	10 minutes	15 minutes

Nutritional Values Per Serving

Calories	140
Total Fat	4g
Saturated Fat	0.8g
Cholesterol	0mg
Sodium	650mg
Total Carbohydrate	19.2g
Dietary Fiber	6.5g
Total Sugars	7.7g
Protein	10.9g

Serving Suggestion:

Enjoy this scramble with toasted whole wheat bread slices and sliced vegetables on the side.

Ingredients:

- 2 blocks of silken tofu
- 1 small onion diced
- ¼ cup vegetable stock
- ½ teaspoon turmeric
- ¼ teaspoon salt
- ¼ teaspoon black pepper
- ¼ teaspoon dried herbs
- ¼ teaspoon garlic powder

Instructions:

1. Cook diced onions with vegetable stock in a cooking pan for 5 minutes.
2. Add tofu to the skillet, break into chunks and cook for 5 minutes.
3. Stir in black pepper, salt, herbs, garlic powder, and turmeric, then mix well.
4. Cover and cook for 5 minutes, then stir gently.
5. Serve warm.

The Plant Based Cookbook For Beginners
650 Easy, Quick, & Simple Plant Based Vegan Diet Recipes With A 31 Day Meal Plan To Lose Weight & Live A Long Healthy Life

191

Zucchini Muffins

SERVINGS	PREPARATION TIME	COOKING TIME
8	15 minutes	35 minutes

Nutritional Values Per Serving

Calories	185
Total Fat	4.8g
Saturated Fat	1.3g
Cholesterol	1mg
Sodium	168mg
Total Carbohydrate	32.9g
Dietary Fiber	3.7g
Total Sugars	13.4g
Protein	4.9g

Ingredients:

- 1 ½ cup white whole wheat flour
- 1 teaspoon baking powder
- ½ teaspoon baking soda
- 1 teaspoon cinnamon
- ½ teaspoon nutmeg
- ¼ teaspoon salt
- 1 ripe banana mashed
- ⅓ cup maple syrup
- ⅓ cup unsweetened almond milk
- 1 tablespoon apple cider vinegar
- 1 tablespoon ground flax
- 2 ½ tablespoon warm water
- 1 cup grated zucchini
- ¼ cup dark chocolate chips
- ¼ cup walnuts, chopped

Instructions:

1. At 350 degrees F, preheat your oven.
2. Mix the 2 ½ tablespoons water with 1 tablespoon ground flax in a small bowl and leave for 5 minutes.
3. Mix almond milk with apple cider vinegar in a bowl and leave for 5 minutes.
4. Stir in flaxseed mixture, then add grated zucchini, nutmeg, cinnamon, salt, baking soda, baking powder and flour, then mix until smooth.
5. Stir in mashed banana and maple syrup, then mix evenly.
6. Fold in chocolate chips or nuts, then mix well.
7. Divide the muffin batter into greased muffin cups.
8. Bake these muffins for 35 minutes in the oven.
9. Allow the muffins to cool and serve.

French Toast Casserole

SERVINGS	PREPARATION TIME	COOKING TIME
6	20 minutes	40 minutes

Nutritional Values Per Serving

Calories	242
Total Fat	1.3g
Saturated Fat	0.1g
Cholesterol	0mg
Sodium	281mg
Total Carbohydrate	53.7g
Dietary Fiber	6.7g
Total Sugars	30.6g
Protein	5.3g

Ingredients:

- 16 oz loaf whole-grain bread
- 15 oz can coconut milk
- ⅓ cup maple syrup
- 1 cup pumpkin puree
- 2 tablespoons corn starch
- 1 teaspoon pumpkin pie spice
- 1 teaspoon vanilla extract
- ¼ teaspoon salt

Pumpkin Glaze

- ½ cup organic sugar
- 1 tablespoon pumpkin puree
- ¼ cup pecans, chopped

Instructions:

1. Blend pumpkin puree, vanilla, salt, cornstarch, pumpkin pie spice, maple syrup and coconut milk in a blender.
2. Cut the bread loaf into 1-inch pieces.
3. Place these bread pieces in a 9x13 inch baking dish.
4. Pour the pumpkin mixture over the bread pieces, cover and refrigerate for 4 hours.
5. Bake the pumpkin pieces for 40 minutes at 350 degrees F in the oven.
6. For pumpkin glaze, mix all the ingredients in a bowl.
7. Pour this pumpkin glaze over the toasts.
8. Serve.

The Plant Based Cookbook For Beginners
650 Easy, Quick, & Simple Plant Based Vegan Diet Recipes With A 31 Day Meal Plan To Lose Weight & Live A Long Healthy Life

193

Turmeric Coffee Latte

SERVINGS	PREPARATION TIME	COOKING TIME
1	5 minutes	5 minutes

Nutritional Values Per Serving	
Calories	117
Total Fat	2.7g
Saturated Fat	0g
Cholesterol	0mg
Sodium	142mg
Total Carbohydrate	22.3g
Dietary Fiber	0.3g
Total Sugars	17.9g
Protein	1.1g

Ingredients:

- 1 cup almond milk
- ¼ teaspoon ground turmeric
- ⅛ teaspoon cardamom
- ¼ teaspoon coffee powder
- 1 tablespoon maple syrup

Instructions:

1. Boil 1 cup almond milk in a saucepan over medium heat.
2. Stir in maple syrup, coffee powder, cardamom and turmeric.
3. Blend the mixture until foamy and serve.

194

The Plant Based Cookbook For Beginners
650 Easy, Quick, & Simple Plant Based Vegan Diet Recipes With A 31 Day Meal Plan To Lose Weight & Live A Long Healthy Life

Breakfast Panini

SERVINGS
2

PREPARATION TIME
15 minutes

COOKING TIME
10 minutes

Nutritional Values Per Serving

Calories	279
Total Fat	5.1g
Saturated Fat	1.1g
Cholesterol	0mg
Sodium	244mg
Total Carbohydrate	57.9g
Dietary Fiber	7.5g
Total Sugars	25.5g
Protein	7.2g

Ingredients:

- ¼ cup of raisins
- ¼ cup of hot water
- 1 tablespoon cinnamon
- 2 teaspoons cacao powder
- ¼ cup of peanut butter
- 1 ripe banana, sliced
- 2 whole-grain bread slices

Instructions:

1. Mix cacao powder, cinnamon, hot water and raisins in a bowl.
2. Brush peanut butter over one whole grain bread slice.
3. Add banana slices and raisin mixture on top.
4. Place the other bread slice on top, then grill the panini sandwich for 3-5 minutes per side.
5. Serve.

The Plant Based Cookbook For Beginners
650 Easy, Quick, & Simple Plant Based Vegan Diet Recipes With A 31 Day Meal Plan To Lose Weight & Live A Long Healthy Life

195

Sweet Potato Waffles

SERVINGS	PREPARATION TIME	COOKING TIME
4	15 minutes	5 minutes

Nutritional Values Per Serving

Calories	360
Total Fat	2.9g
Saturated Fat	0.3g
Cholesterol	0mg
Sodium	229mg
Total Carbohydrate	72.1g
Dietary Fiber	3.8g
Total Sugars	10.6g
Protein	11.7g

Serving Suggestion:

Enjoy these waffles with coconut cream on top or with tobacco sauce.

Ingredients:

- 2 cups soy milk
- 1 teaspoon cider vinegar
- 2 tablespoons rapeseed oil
- 3 ½ oz. cooked sweet potato, mashed
- 5 oz. polenta
- Pinch of salt
- 4 ½ oz. plain flour
- 1 tablespoon baking powder
- Small bunch chives, snipped
- 1 tablespoon maple syrup
- 2 teaspoons soy sauce
- 6 large mushrooms, sliced
- Olive oil, for frying

Instructions:

1. Mix milk with rapeseed oil, vinegar and sweet potatoes mash in a bowl.
2. Stir in baking powder, flour, a pinch of salt, and polenta, then mix evenly.
3. Stir in chives and add a dollop of the batter into a preheated waffle iron.
4. Cook the waffle for 5 minutes and transfer it to a plate.
5. Continue cooking more waffles with the remaining batter.
6. Sauté mushrooms with soy sauce, maple syrup and black pepper in a pan with olive oil until brown.
7. Serve the waffles with mushrooms.
8. Enjoy.

(196)

The Plant Based Cookbook For Beginners
650 Easy, Quick, & Simple Plant Based Vegan Diet Recipes With A 31 Day Meal Plan To Lose Weight & Live A Long Healthy Life

Kiwi Smoothie

SERVINGS
4

PREPARATION TIME
5 minutes

COOKING TIME
0 minutes

Nutritional Values Per Serving

Calories	178
Total Fat	0.9g
Saturated Fat	0.1g
Cholesterol	0mg
Sodium	5mg
Total Carbohydrate	43.8g
Dietary Fiber	4.1g
Total Sugars	32.7g
Protein	2.1g

Ingredients:

- 3 peeled kiwi fruit
- 1 mango, peeled, pitted and chopped
- 2 cups pineapple juice
- 1 banana, sliced

Instructions:

1. Blend kiwi, mango and the rest of the ingredients in a blender until smooth.
2. Serve.

The Plant Based Cookbook For Beginners
650 Easy, Quick, & Simple Plant Based Vegan Diet Recipes With A 31 Day Meal Plan To Lose Weight & Live A Long Healthy Life

197

Tofu Pancakes

SERVINGS	PREPARATION TIME	COOKING TIME
6	15 minutes	10 minutes

Nutritional Values Per Serving

Calories	345
Total Fat	8.2g
Saturated Fat	1.5g
Cholesterol	0mg
Sodium	72mg
Total Carbohydrate	63.6g
Dietary Fiber	4.5g
Total Sugars	51.5g
Protein	5.9g

Ingredients:

- 12 oz. pack firm silken tofu
- 2 teaspoons vanilla extract
- 2 teaspoons lemon juice
- 1 ½ cups almond milk
- 1 tablespoon vegetable oil
- 9 oz. buckwheat flour
- 4 tablespoons muscovado sugar
- 1 ½ teaspoon ground mixed spice
- 1 tablespoon baking powder

Instructions:

1. Preheat a pan on stove top on medium heat.
2. Blend milk with lemon juice and tofu in a blender until smooth.
3. Stir in oil and remaining ingredients then mix well.
4. Set a pan with 1 teaspoon oil over medium heat.
5. Pour a ladle of the prepared batter into the pan, swirl and cook for 2 minutes per side.
6. Transfer the pancake to a plate and cook more pancakes with the remaining batter.
7. Serve.

 198

The Plant Based Cookbook For Beginners
650 Easy, Quick, & Simple Plant Based Vegan Diet Recipes With A 31 Day Meal Plan To Lose Weight & Live A Long Healthy Life

Peach Quinoa Porridge

SERVINGS	PREPARATION TIME	COOKING TIME
2	15 minutes	15 minutes

Nutritional Values Per Serving

Calories	280
Total Fat	5.4g
Saturated Fat	0.6g
Cholesterol	0mg
Sodium	93mg
Total Carbohydrate	50.9g
Dietary Fiber	6.7g
Total Sugars	16.1g
Protein	9.1g

Ingredients:

- 3 oz. quinoa
- ⅔ oz. porridge oats
- 4 cardamom pods
- 1 cup unsweetened almond milk
- 2 ripe peaches, cut into slices
- 1 teaspoon maple syrup

Instructions:

1. Mix almond milk, water, cardamom pods, oats and quinoa in a cooking pot.
2. Cook to a boil, reduce the heat and cook for 15 minutes on a simmer with occasional stirring.
3. Discard the cardamom pods and transfer the porridge to a serving bowl.
4. Garnish with maple syrup and peaches.
5. Serve.

The Plant Based Cookbook For Beginners
650 Easy, Quick, & Simple Plant Based Vegan Diet Recipes With A 31 Day Meal Plan To Lose Weight & Live A Long Healthy Life

199

Blueberry Apple Bircher

SERVINGS	PREPARATION TIME	FRIDGE TIME
4	5 minutes	Overnight

Nutritional Values Per Serving

Calories	377
Total Fat	14.9g
Saturated Fat	4.7g
Cholesterol	194mg
Sodium	607mg
Total Carbohydrate	60.7g
Dietary Fiber	1.4g
Total Sugars	3.3g
Protein	6.4g

Serving Suggestion:

Enjoy this Bircher with nuts and apple slices and fresh fruits on top.

Ingredients:

- 7 oz. quick cooking oats
- ½ teaspoons ground cinnamon
- 2 cups apple juice
- 4 apples, grated
- 7 oz. blueberries

Instructions:

1. Mix oats with cinnamon in a large bowl.
2. Add apples, apple juice and blueberries.
3. Mix well, cover and refrigerate overnight.
4. Serve.

200

The Plant Based Cookbook For Beginners
650 Easy, Quick, & Simple Plant Based Vegan Diet Recipes With A 31 Day Meal Plan To Lose Weight & Live A Long Healthy Life

Blackcurrant Compote

SERVINGS
8

PREPARATION TIME
10 minutes

COOKING TIME
10 minutes

Nutritional Values Per Serving	
Calories	139
Total Fat	0.2g
Saturated Fat	0.1g
Cholesterol	0mg
Sodium	568mg
Total Carbohydrate	33.6g
Dietary Fiber	2g
Total Sugars	33.6g
Protein	0.6g

Serving Suggestion:

Try this compote with freshly baked apple walnut bread slices.

Ingredients:

- 2 tablespoons water
- Juice from ½ lemon
- 1 lb. blackcurrants
- 3 ½ oz. golden caster sugar

Instructions:

1. Mix 2 tablespoons of water, lemon juice and blackcurrants in a large pan.
2. Cook this mixture on a simmer until soft and crushed.
3. Stir in golden caster sugar, insert a cooking thermometer and cook until compote's temperature reaches to 221 degrees F.
4. Pour this compote into a mason jar and allow it to cool.
5. Serve.

The Plant Based Cookbook For Beginners
650 Easy, Quick, & Simple Plant Based Vegan Diet Recipes With A 31 Day Meal Plan To Lose Weight & Live A Long Healthy Life

201

Sheet Pan Pancakes

SERVINGS	PREPARATION TIME	COOKING TIME
4	10 minutes	15 minutes

Nutritional Values Per Serving	
Calories	212
Total Fat	7g
Saturated Fat	1.1g
Cholesterol	0mg
Sodium	96mg
Total Carbohydrate	17.1g
Dietary Fiber	8.5g
Total Sugars	19.5g
Protein	4.5g

Ingredients:

- 2 cups old-fashioned oats
- 4 tablespoons chia seeds
- 1 teaspoon salt
- 1 tablespoon baking powder
- 2 tablespoons coconut sugar
- 2 cups soy milk
- 2 ripe bananas
- ¼ cup almonds, sliced
- ¼ cup sugar-free chocolate chip

Instructions:

1. At 425 degrees F, preheat your oven.

2. Blend oats with chia seeds in a blender for 1 minute.

3. Add baking powder, sugar, and salt to a small bowl then mix well.

4. Mix soy with bananas in a large bowl and stir in almonds, dry oats mixture, and baking powder mixture.

5. Whisk well until smooth.

6. Spread the batter in a 16x12 inch baking sheet evenly and sprinkle the sugar-free chocolate chips on top.

7. Bake this pancake for 15 minutes.

8. Slice and serve with maple syrup.

202

The Plant Based Cookbook For Beginners
650 Easy, Quick, & Simple Plant Based Vegan Diet Recipes With A 31 Day Meal Plan To Lose Weight & Live A Long Healthy Life

Date Applesauce

SERVINGS	PREPARATION TIME	COOKING TIME
12	15 minutes	22 minutes

Nutritional Values Per Serving	
Calories	148
Total Fat	12.5g
Saturated Fat	9.4g
Cholesterol	0mg
Sodium	56mg
Total Carbohydrate	6.2g
Dietary Fiber	7.5g
Total Sugars	12.9g
Protein	8.6g

Ingredients:

- 3 Fuji apples chopped
- ⅓ cup pitted Medjool dates, chopped
- ½ cup water
- ½ teaspoon cinnamon

Instructions:

1. Mix apples with the rest of the ingredients in a Dutch oven and cook to a boil.
2. Reduce its heat then cover and cook for 20 minutes on a simmer.
3. Blend and puree the apple mixture.
4. Serve.

The Plant Based Cookbook For Beginners
650 Easy, Quick, & Simple Plant Based Vegan Diet Recipes With A 31 Day Meal Plan To Lose Weight & Live A Long Healthy Life

203

Chia Seed Pumpkin Muffins

SERVINGS	PREPARATION TIME	COOKING TIME
6	15 minutes	25 minutes

Nutritional Values Per Serving

Calories	249
Total Fat	3.9g
Saturated Fat	0.4g
Cholesterol	0mg
Sodium	183mg
Total Carbohydrate	13g
Dietary Fiber	13.1g
Total Sugars	6.7g
Protein	17.5g

Ingredients:

- ¼ cup chia seeds
- ½ cup water
- 2 ½ oz. oat flour
- 3 oz. whole wheat flour
- 3 ½ oz. coconut sugar
- 1 teaspoon pumpkin pie spice
- 1 teaspoon cinnamon
- ½ teaspoon baking powder
- ½ teaspoon baking soda
- ½ teaspoon salt
- 3 oz. soften peanut butter
- 4 oz. canned pumpkin

Instructions:

1. At 325 degrees F, preheat your oven.
2. Layer a muffin tray with muffin tins.
3. Soak chia seeds in ½ cup water and leave for 10 minutes.
4. Mix oat flour with the rest of the ingredients in a large bowl.
5. Stir in chia seeds mixture and mix until smooth.
6. Divide the batter in the muffin tray, then bake for 25 minutes.
7. Allow the muffins to cool and serve.

204

The Plant Based Cookbook For Beginners
650 Easy, Quick, & Simple Plant Based Vegan Diet Recipes With A 31 Day Meal Plan To Lose Weight & Live A Long Healthy Life

Pumpkin Pie Spice Pancakes

SERVINGS	PREPARATION TIME	COOKING TIME
4	10 minutes	16 minutes

Nutritional Values Per Serving

Calories	270
Total Fat	1.2g
Saturated Fat	0g
Cholesterol	0mg
Sodium	16mg
Total Carbohydrate	20.4g
Dietary Fiber	5.1g
Total Sugars	23.7g
Protein	7.1g

Serving Suggestion:

Enjoy these pancakes with fresh fruits or a fruit compote on top on top.

Ingredients:

- 1 cup oat bran
- 2 tablespoon chia seeds
- ½ teaspoon salt
- 1 teaspoon baking powder
- 1 ½ cup water
- 2 teaspoon pumpkin pie spice
- 1 tablespoon olive oil

Toppings

- Pancake syrup
- Pumpkin butter

Instructions:

1. Blend chia seeds with oat bran in a blender for 1 minute.
2. Sift this mixture through a strainer into a mixing bowl.
3. Now stir in the rest of the pumpkin pancake ingredients and mix well.
4. Set a suitable skillet over medium heat and add a little oil to grease it.
5. Pour a dollop of the batter into the skillet and cook for 4 minutes per side.
6. Make more chia pancakes in the same way.
7. Serve.

The Plant Based Cookbook For Beginners
650 Easy, Quick, & Simple Plant Based Vegan Diet Recipes With A 31 Day Meal Plan To Lose Weight & Live A Long Healthy Life

205

Peanut Tofu Scramble

SERVINGS	PREPARATION TIME	COOKING TIME
2	10 minutes	11 minutes

Nutritional Values Per Serving

Calories	255
Total Fat	7.7g
Saturated Fat	0.9g
Cholesterol	0mg
Sodium	198mg
Total Carbohydrate	15.4g
Dietary Fiber	9.4g
Total Sugars	22.1g
Protein	9.8g

Serving Suggestion:

Enjoy this scramble with toasted bread slices.

Ingredients:

- 8 oz. firm tofu
- 1 teaspoon peanut butter
- 1 tablespoon nutritional yeast
- ¼ teaspoon turmeric powder
- ¼ teaspoon garlic powder
- Salt to taste

Instructions:

1. Crumble the tofu in a skillet and mix it with peanut butter.
2. Sauté this mixture for 3 minutes over medium heat.
3. Stir in the rest of the seasonings and ingredients.
4. Sauté for 8 minutes then serve warm.

206

The Plant Based Cookbook For Beginners
650 Easy, Quick, & Simple Plant Based Vegan Diet Recipes With A 31 Day Meal Plan To Lose Weight & Live A Long Healthy Life

Cranberry Oats Smoothie Bowl

SERVINGS	PREPARATION TIME	COOKING TIME
1	5 minutes	0 minutes

Nutritional Values Per Serving	
Calories	310
Total Fat	9.3g
Saturated Fat	3.7g
Cholesterol	20mg
Sodium	128mg
Total Carbohydrate	46g
Dietary Fiber	6.3g
Total Sugars	30.3g
Protein	9.3g

Ingredients:

- ½ cup instant oats
- 1 cup almond milk
- 1 cup fresh cranberries
- ⅛ teaspoon cinnamon
- ½ cup coconut yogurt
- 1 apple, peeled and diced

Instructions:

1. Blend ½ cup cranberries, almond milk, cinnamon, yogurt, and apple in a blender until smooth.
2. Pour into a bowl and garnish with oats and remaining cranberries.
3. Serve.

The Plant Based Cookbook For Beginners
650 Easy, Quick, & Simple Plant Based Vegan Diet Recipes With A 31 Day Meal Plan To Lose Weight & Live A Long Healthy Life

207

Chocolate Raspberry Smoothie

SERVINGS	PREPARATION TIME	COOKING TIME
2	5 minutes	0 minutes

Nutritional Values Per Serving

Calories	215
Total Fat	8.4g
Saturated Fat	0.6g
Cholesterol	0mg
Sodium	259mg
Total Carbohydrate	20.6g
Dietary Fiber	3.3g
Total Sugars	15.7g
Protein	5.1g

Serving Suggestion:

Enjoy this smoothie with fresh raspberries on top.

Ingredients:

- ½ cup frozen raspberries
- 1 frozen banana
- ¼ cup cocoa powder
- 1 ½ cup of soy milk
- 2 tablespoons agave

Instructions:

1. Blend raspberries and the rest of the ingredients in a blender until smooth.
2. Serve.

208

The Plant Based Cookbook For Beginners
650 Easy, Quick, & Simple Plant Based Vegan Diet Recipes With A 31 Day Meal Plan To Lose Weight & Live A Long Healthy Life

Grilled Raisin Sandwich

SERVINGS	PREPARATION TIME	COOKING TIME
1	10 minutes	10 minutes

Nutritional Values Per Serving	
Calories	222
Total Fat	1g
Saturated Fat	0.1g
Cholesterol	0mg
Sodium	532mg
Total Carbohydrate	21g
Dietary Fiber	10.6g
Total Sugars	5.5g
Protein	14.1g

Ingredients:

- 2 bread slices
- Peanut butter
- 1 teaspoon raspberry jam
- 1 pinch of cinnamon
- 2 teaspoons chia seeds
- 1 tablespoons raisin

Instructions:

1. Spread peanut butter on top of one bread slice.
2. Mix raisins with chia seeds, cinnamon and raspberry jam in a bowl.
3. Add this mixture on top of the peanut butter and place the other bread slice on top.
4. Cut into triangles and keep them aside.
5. Grease a grill pan with a little bit of coconut oil and grill the sandwich for 5 minutes per side.
6. Serve.

The Plant Based Cookbook For Beginners
650 Easy, Quick, & Simple Plant Based Vegan Diet Recipes With A 31 Day Meal Plan To Lose Weight & Live A Long Healthy Life

209

Chocolate Banana Bread

SERVINGS	PREPARATION TIME	COOKING TIME
6	10 minutes	1 hour 15 minutes

Nutritional Values Per Serving

Calories	233
Total Fat	1.3g
Saturated Fat	0.2g
Cholesterol	0mg
Sodium	588mg
Total Carbohydrate	22.8g
Dietary Fiber	8.5g
Total Sugars	7.8g
Protein	10.2g

Ingredients:

- 2 tablespoons chia seeds
- 6 tablespoons water
- 3 ripe bananas
- ½ cup almond milk
- 2 cups oat bran flour
- ½ cup brown sugar
- 4 tablespoons cocoa powder
- 2 teaspoons baking powder
- ¼ cup peanut butter, melted

Instructions:

1. Soak chia seeds in water, in a bowl and leave it for 15 minutes.
2. At 350 degrees F, preheat your oven.
3. Layer an 8-inch loaf pan with wax paper.
4. Blend banana with milk in a blender and pour into a bowl.
5. Stir in the rest of the ingredients, and mix well until smooth.
6. Spread the prepared batter in the loaf pan.
7. Bake the bread for 1 hour 15 minutes.
8. Allow the bread to cool, then slice.
9. Serve.

210

The Plant Based Cookbook For Beginners
650 Easy, Quick, & Simple Plant Based Vegan Diet Recipes With A 31 Day Meal Plan To Lose Weight & Live A Long Healthy Life

Cream of Rice with Cinnamon

SERVINGS	PREPARATION TIME	COOKING TIME
4	10 minutes	10 minutes

Nutritional Values Per Serving	
Calories	209
Total Fat	5.6g
Saturated Fat	0.7g
Cholesterol	0mg
Sodium	79mg
Total Carbohydrate	18.4g
Dietary Fiber	7.5g
Total Sugars	28.4g
Protein	9.4g

Ingredients:

- 1 cup white rice
- 1 cup of coconut milk
- 3 cups of water
- 1 teaspoon cinnamon
- 2 tablespoons brown sugar

Instructions:

1. Grind rice in a blender and keep them aside.
2. Boil coconut milk in a suitable saucepan, then reduce its heat.
3. Stir in rice, sugar, cinnamon, and water then cook the mixture for 10 minutes with occasional stirring.
4. Serve.

The Plant Based Cookbook For Beginners
650 Easy, Quick, & Simple Plant Based Vegan Diet Recipes With A 31 Day Meal Plan To Lose Weight & Live A Long Healthy Life

211

Banana Nut Bread

SERVINGS	PREPARATION TIME	COOKING TIME
6	15 minutes	60 minutes

Nutritional Values Per Serving

Calories	277
Total Fat	1.2g
Saturated Fat	0.3g
Cholesterol	0mg
Sodium	88mg
Total Carbohydrate	55.6g
Dietary Fiber	11.7g
Total Sugars	3g
Protein	12.7g

Ingredients:

- 2 cups whole wheat flour
- 1 ½ teaspoon baking powder
- ½ teaspoon baking soda
- ¼ teaspoon salt
- 1 teaspoon cinnamon
- 1 cup canned coconut milk
- 1 cup brown sugar
- ½ cup water
- 2 teaspoons flaxseed
- 1 cup mashed bananas
- 1 cup chopped walnuts

Instructions:

1. At 350 degrees F, preheat your oven.
2. Soak flaxseed in ½ cup water, in a bowl for 5 minutes.
3. Layer an 8-inch loaf pan with wax paper.
4. Mix cinnamon, flour, salt, baking soda and baking powder in a bowl.
5. Beat coconut milk with sugar, flaxseed mixture and mashed bananas in a large bowl.
6. Stir in flour mixture and mix well until smooth.
7. Fold in chopped walnuts and mix evenly.
8. Spread the prepared batter in the loaf pan and bake for 60 minutes.
9. Allow the bread to cool and slice.
10. Serve warm.

212

The Plant Based Cookbook For Beginners
650 Easy, Quick, & Simple Plant Based Vegan Diet Recipes With A 31 Day Meal Plan To Lose Weight & Live A Long Healthy Life

Cucumber Sandwich

SERVINGS	PREPARATION TIME	COOKING TIME
2	10 minutes	0 minutes

Nutritional Values Per Serving	
Calories	193
Total Fat	16g
Saturated Fat	9.1g
Cholesterol	0mg
Sodium	11mg
Total Carbohydrate	19.8g
Dietary Fiber	10g
Total Sugars	5.3g
Protein	9.8g

Ingredients:

- ¼ cucumber, thinly sliced
- 4 whole-wheat bread, slices
- 4 tablespoons alfalfa sprouts
- 2 tablespoons vegan cheese, shredded
- Salt and black pepper to taste

Instructions:

1. Pat dry the thin cucumber slices with a paper towel.
2. Divide alfalfa sprouts, and cheese over two bread slices and place the cucumber on top.
3. Sprinkle black pepper and salt on top.
4. Place the over two bread slices on top to make two sandwiches.
5. Slice and serve.

The Plant Based Cookbook For Beginners
650 Easy, Quick, & Simple Plant Based Vegan Diet Recipes With A 31 Day Meal Plan To Lose Weight & Live A Long Healthy Life

213

Cherry Smoothie Bowl

SERVINGS	PREPARATION TIME	COOKING TIME
2	5 minutes	0 minutes

Nutritional Values Per Serving	
Calories	214
Total Fat	7.7g
Saturated Fat	2.5g
Cholesterol	0mg
Sodium	460mg
Total Carbohydrate	21.1g
Dietary Fiber	4g
Total Sugars	30.6g
Protein	5.8g

Ingredients:

- 2 cups almond milk
- 2 cups frozen peaches
- 1 cup frozen cherries
- 3 pitted dates

Toppings

- Shredded coconut
- Sliced almonds
- 1 tablespoon chia seeds
- 3 fresh ripe cherries, pits removed

Instructions:

1. Blend milk with dates and fruits in a blender until smooth.
2. Pour this smoothie into serving bowls.
3. Garnish with coconut, almonds, chia seeds and cherries.
4. Serve.

Protein Tropical Smoothie

SERVINGS	PREPARATION TIME	COOKING TIME
1	5 minutes	0 minutes

Nutritional Values Per Serving	
Calories	282
Total Fat	5.5g
Saturated Fat	0.4g
Cholesterol	0mg
Sodium	162mg
Total Carbohydrate	17.2g
Dietary Fiber	10.7g
Total Sugars	12.3g
Protein	14.2g

Ingredients:

- 1 (11 ½ oz) package Silken Tofu
- ½ banana, sliced
- ½ cup frozen pineapple
- ½ cup frozen mango
- 1 teaspoon agave
- 1 cup of coconut milk

Instructions:

1. Blend all ingredients in a blender until smooth.
2. Serve.

The Plant Based Cookbook For Beginners
650 Easy, Quick, & Simple Plant Based Vegan Diet Recipes With A 31 Day Meal Plan To Lose Weight & Live A Long Healthy Life

215

Blueberry White Bean Smoothie

SERVINGS
6

PREPARATION TIME
5 minutes

COOKING TIME
0 minutes

Nutritional Values Per Serving

Calories	242
Total Fat	4.4g
Saturated Fat	0.1g
Cholesterol	0mg
Sodium	333mg
Total Carbohydrate	13g
Dietary Fiber	5.1g
Total Sugars	8.9g
Protein	6.9g

Ingredients:

- 1 cup strawberries
- 1 cup blueberries
- 1 banana, cut into slices
- ½ cup white beans, cooked
- ½ cup almond milk
- 1 teaspoon vanilla extract

Toppings

- Fresh blueberries

Instructions:

1. Blend wihite beans with the rest of the ingredients in a blender until smooth.
2. Garnish with blueberries.
3. Serve.

216

The Plant Based Cookbook For Beginners
650 Easy, Quick, & Simple Plant Based Vegan Diet Recipes With A 31 Day Meal Plan To Lose Weight & Live A Long Healthy Life

Chocolate Cherry Smoothie Bowl

SERVINGS	PREPARATION TIME	COOKING TIME
1	15 minutes	0 minutes

Nutritional Values Per Serving

Calories	474
Total Fat	14.4g
Saturated Fat	8.9g
Cholesterol	0mg
Sodium	11mg
Total Carbohydrate	21.7g
Dietary Fiber	8.4g
Total Sugars	37.6g
Protein	9.7g

Ingredients:

- 2 frozen bananas, sliced
- ¾ cup frozen cherries, pitted
- ¾ cup almond milk
- 3 Medjool dates, pitted
- 2 tablespoons cocoa powder
- 1 teaspoon chia seeds
- ½ tablespoon maple syrup
- 1 teaspoon vanilla extract
- 1 tablespoon vegan protein powder

Toppings

- Cherries
- Dark chocolate

Instructions:

1. Blend banana with the rest of the ingredients in a blender until smooth.
2. Serve this bowl with fresh cherries and dark chocolate on top.

The Plant Based Cookbook For Beginners
650 Easy, Quick, & Simple Plant Based Vegan Diet Recipes With A 31 Day Meal Plan To Lose Weight & Live A Long Healthy Life

217

Pumpkin Oatmeal

SERVINGS	PREPARATION TIME	COOKING TIME
2	15 minutes	45 minutes

Nutritional Values Per Serving

Calories	207
Total Fat	11.2g
Saturated Fat	8.8g
Cholesterol	0mg
Sodium	109mg
Total Carbohydrate	18.1g
Dietary Fiber	8.7g
Total Sugars	4.7g
Protein	9.1g

Ingredients:

- 2 ½ cups rolled oats
- 3 tablespoons chia seeds
- 1 teaspoon baking powder
- 1 teaspoon cinnamon
- ½ teaspoon cardamom
- ½ teaspoon salt
- 1 ¾ cups almond milk
- 1 (15 oz.) can pumpkin
- ⅓ cup maple syrup
- 1 tablespoon pure vanilla extract

Instructions:

1. At 350 degrees F, preheat your oven.
2. Layer an 8x8 inch baking dish with wax paper.
3. Mix oats with salt, cardamom, cinnamon, baking powder, and chia seeds in a bowl.
4. Now, stir in the rest of the ingredients and mix well until smooth.
5. Spread this batter in the baking dish and bake for 45 minutes.
6. Allow the oatmeal to cool and serve.

218

The Plant Based Cookbook For Beginners
650 Easy, Quick, & Simple Plant Based Vegan Diet Recipes With A 31 Day Meal Plan To Lose Weight & Live A Long Healthy Life

Cauliflower Oatmeal

SERVINGS	PREPARATION TIME	COOKING TIME
2	10 minutes	15 minutes

Nutritional Values Per Serving	
Calories	282
Total Fat	8.7g
Saturated Fat	4.6g
Cholesterol	0mg
Sodium	9mg
Total Carbohydrate	21.5g
Dietary Fiber	5.7g
Total Sugars	26.8g
Protein	7.4g

Ingredients:

- 1 cup cauliflower rice
- ½ cup unsweetened almond milk
- ½ teaspoon cinnamon
- 1 tablespoon agave
- ½ tablespoons peanut butter
- Strawberries, sliced

Instructions:

1. Mix milk with peanut butter, cauliflower rice, agave and cinnamon in a saucepan.
2. Cook this rice mixture to a boil then reduce the heat to low.
3. Now cook this mixture for 10 minutes on a simmer.
4. Allow the oatmeal to cool, then garnish with strawberries.
5. Serve.

The Plant Based Cookbook For Beginners
650 Easy, Quick, & Simple Plant Based Vegan Diet Recipes With A 31 Day Meal Plan To Lose Weight & Live A Long Healthy Life

219

Breakfast Berry Cobbler

SERVINGS	PREPARATION TIME	COOKING TIME
4	15 minutes	35 minutes

Nutritional Values Per Serving

Calories	196
Total Fat	4.9g
Saturated Fat	1g
Cholesterol	0mg
Sodium	643mg
Total Carbohydrate	18.8g
Dietary Fiber	7g
Total Sugars	10g
Protein	12.6g

Serving Suggestion:

Try this cobbler with a blueberry smoothie.

Ingredients:

- 1 cup fresh blueberries
- 1 cup fresh blackberries
- 1 cup fresh raspberries
- 1 cup of water
- 3 tablespoons tapioca starch
- ½ teaspoon cinnamon
- ¼ cup coconut sugar

Cobbler Topping

- 1 cup rolled oats
- ⅔ cup whole wheat flour
- ¼ cup coconut sugar
- 1 tablespoon flaxseed
- 1 tablespoon hemp seeds
- 1 tablespoon chia seeds
- 3 tablespoons coconut oil, melted
- ⅓ cup almond milk
- ¼ teaspoon pure vanilla extract
- ¼ teaspoon cinnamon
- ¾ teaspoons baking powder
- 1 pinch of pink salt

Instructions:

1. At 375 degrees F, preheat your oven.
2. Mix all the berry filling ingredients in a saucepan and cook on a simmer until it thickens.
3. Remove this filling from the heat and spread it in a baking dish.
4. Mix oats with coconut sugar with cinnamon, hemp shells, chia seeds, flour, flaxseeds, salt and baking powder in a large bowl.
5. Stir in vanilla, milk and coconut oil, then mix well.
6. Spread this batter on top of the filling.
7. Bake this cobbler for 30 minutes at 375 degrees F.
8. Allow it to cool and serve.

220

The Plant Based Cookbook For Beginners
650 Easy, Quick, & Simple Plant Based Vegan Diet Recipes With A 31 Day Meal Plan To Lose Weight & Live A Long Healthy Life

Protein Bars

SERVINGS
6

PREPARATION TIME
10 minutes

COOKING TIME
20 minutes

Nutritional Values Per Serving

Calories	182
Total Fat	7.2g
Saturated Fat	1.2g
Cholesterol	0mg
Sodium	56mg
Total Carbohydrate	18g
Dietary Fiber	12.4g
Total Sugars	27.6g
Protein	14.1g

Ingredients:

- 1 ½ cup quick-cooking oats
- ½ cup almond meal
- ½ cup flaxseed meal
- 2 teaspoons cinnamon
- ½ teaspoon salt
- 4 tablespoons vegan protein powder
- 1 teaspoon pure vanilla extract
- 2 bananas, ripe and mashed
- ½ cup applesauce
- ¼ cup creamy peanut butter
- 2 tablespoons maple syrup

Instructions:

1. At 350 degrees F, preheat your oven.
2. Layer an 8x8 inch square baking dish with parchment paper.
3. Mix all the ingredients in a large bowl.
4. Spread this mixture in the prepared baking dish.
5. Bake the batter for 20 minutes in the oven.
6. Allow the mixture to cool, then slice into bars.
7. Serve.

The Plant Based Cookbook For Beginners
650 Easy, Quick, & Simple Plant Based Vegan Diet Recipes With A 31 Day Meal Plan To Lose Weight & Live A Long Healthy Life

221

Hemp Breakfast Cookies

SERVINGS	PREPARATION TIME	COOKING TIME
6	1 hour 10 minutes	15 minutes

Nutritional Values Per Serving

Calories	223
Total Fat	7.3g
Saturated Fat	5.8g
Cholesterol	0mg
Sodium	352mg
Total Carbohydrate	17.6g
Dietary Fiber	3.2g
Total Sugars	20.9g
Protein	5.3g

Ingredients:

- 3 cups almond flour
- 1 cup dates, pitted
- ½ cup hemp seeds
- 1 cup almond milk

Instructions:

1. Mix almond milk with hemp seeds and dates in a bowl and let it sit for 1 hour.

2. Blend almond flour with the rest of the ingredients and milk mixture in a mixer until it makes a smooth dough.

3. At 350 degrees F, preheat your oven

4. Divide the dough into 9 portions and shape each into a cookie.

5. Place these cookies in a baking sheet, lined with wax paper.

6. Bake the cookies for 15 minutes in the oven and flip them once cooked halfway through.

7. Serve.

Strawberry Coconut Chia Pudding

SERVINGS	PREPARATION TIME	FRIDGE TIME
2	10 minutes	Overnight

Nutritional Values Per Serving

Calories	268
Total Fat	7.6g
Saturated Fat	0.5g
Cholesterol	0mg
Sodium	4mg
Total Carbohydrate	12.4g
Dietary Fiber	9.8g
Total Sugars	34.5g
Protein	11.9g

Serving Suggestion:

Enjoy this breakfast pudding with fresh strawberries on the top.

Ingredients:

- 2 tablespoons chia seeds
- 1 cup of canned coconut milk
- ¼ cup strawberries, chopped
- ½ teaspoon vanilla extract
- ½ teaspoon stevia

Instructions:

1. Add strawberries and all the ingredients to a mason jar.
2. Cover its lid and refrigerate overnight.
3. Serve.

The Plant Based Cookbook For Beginners
650 Easy, Quick, & Simple Plant Based Vegan Diet Recipes With A 31 Day Meal Plan To Lose Weight & Live A Long Healthy Life

223

Zucchini Instant Pot Oatmeal

SERVINGS	PREPARATION TIME	COOKING TIME
4	15 minutes	4 minutes

Nutritional Values Per Serving

Calories	302
Total Fat	12.2g
Saturated Fat	3.7g
Cholesterol	0mg
Sodium	206mg
Total Carbohydrate	20g
Dietary Fiber	13.6g
Total Sugars	1.6g
Protein	13.7g

Ingredients:

- 2 cups rolled oats
- 6 tablespoons pea protein
- 2 teaspoons coconut oil
- 2 teaspoons cinnamon
- 1 teaspoon nutmeg
- 2 ¼ cups almond milk
- 1 cup zucchini, grated
- ¼ cup maple syrup
- 1 teaspoon vanilla extract

Toppings

- Zucchini shreds

Instructions:

1. Sauté oats with coconut oil in an Instant Pot for 2 minutes on Sauté mode.
2. Stir in the rest of the ingredients, cover and seal its lid.
3. Cook for 2 minutes on High pressure.
4. When done, release all the pressure and remove the lid.
5. Allow the oatmeal to cool and garnish with desired toppings.
6. Garnish with zucchini shreds.
7. Serve.

224

The Plant Based Cookbook For Beginners
650 Easy, Quick, & Simple Plant Based Vegan Diet Recipes With A 31 Day Meal Plan To Lose Weight & Live A Long Healthy Life

Peanut Butter Muffins

SERVINGS	PREPARATION TIME	COOKING TIME
6	15 minutes	27 minutes

Nutritional Values Per Serving

Calories	230
Total Fat	4.3g
Saturated Fat	0.6g
Cholesterol	0mg
Sodium	237mg
Total Carbohydrate	23.1g
Dietary Fiber	6.9g
Total Sugars	11.4g
Protein	6.6g

Ingredients:

- ¾ cup oat flour
- ¼ cup coconut sugar
- 2 tablespoons pea protein powder
- 1 tablespoon baking powder
- 2 teaspoons baking soda
- 3 large bananas, mashed
- ½ cup peanut butter
- 2 tablespoons flaxseed
- ½ cup water
- ½ cup almond milk
- 1 teaspoon vanilla extract

Instructions:

1. Preheat the oven to 350F and layer two muffin trays with cupcake liners.
2. Soak flaxseed with ½ cup water in a bowl for 5 minutes.
3. Mix mashed banana with milk, peanut butter and flaxseed mixture in a large bowl.
4. Now, stir in the rest of the muffin ingredients and mix well evenly.
5. Divide the prepared batter into the muffin tray and bake for 27 minutes.
6. Allow the muffins to cool and serve.

The Plant Based Cookbook For Beginners
650 Easy, Quick, & Simple Plant Based Vegan Diet Recipes With A 31 Day Meal Plan To Lose Weight & Live A Long Healthy Life

225

Gingerbread Loaf

SERVINGS	PREPARATION TIME	COOKING TIME
6	15 minutes	50 minutes

Nutritional Values Per Serving

Calories	205
Total Fat	6.9g
Saturated Fat	2.4g
Cholesterol	0mg
Sodium	195mg
Total Carbohydrate	25.6g
Dietary Fiber	7.5g
Total Sugars	47.9g
Protein	7.3g

Ingredients:

- 2 cups whole wheat flour, sifted
- ⅓ cup coconut sugar
- 1 ½ teaspoon ginger
- 1 teaspoon cinnamon
- ½ teaspoon cardamom
- ¼ teaspoon allspice
- ¼ teaspoon nutmeg
- 2 teaspoons baking powder
- 1 teaspoon baking soda
- 1 cup almond milk
- ½ cup molasses
- ½ cup unsweetened applesauce

Instructions:

1. At 350 degrees F, preheat your oven and layer a 9-inch loaf pan with olive oil.
2. Mix molasses, applesauce, and milk in a bowl.
3. Stir in the rest of the dry ingredients and mix well until smooth.
4. Spread this batter into the prepared loaf pan.
5. Bake this batter for 50 minutes in the oven.
6. Allow the baked bread to cool on a wire rack.
7. Slice and serve.

226

The Plant Based Cookbook For Beginners
650 Easy, Quick, & Simple Plant Based Vegan Diet Recipes With A 31 Day Meal Plan To Lose Weight & Live A Long Healthy Life

Chocolate Zucchini Bread

SERVINGS
6

PREPARATION TIME
15 minutes

COOKING TIME
55 minutes

Nutritional Values Per Serving

Calories	265
Total Fat	30.7g
Saturated Fat	25.6g
Cholesterol	0mg
Sodium	61mg
Total Carbohydrate	48.2g
Dietary Fiber	10.4g
Total Sugars	23.6g
Protein	7.4g

Ingredients:

- 1 ¼ cup whole wheat flour
- ¾ cup coconut sugar
- ½ cup raw cacao powder
- 3 teaspoons baking powder
- 2 teaspoons baking soda
- 1 cup zucchini, shredded
- ½ cup almond milk
- ⅓ cup unsweetened applesauce
- 2 teaspoons vanilla extract
- ⅔ cup sugar-free chocolate chip

Instructions:

1. At 350 degrees F, preheat your oven and layer a 9-inch loaf pan with wax paper.
2. Pat dry the shredded zucchini and keep it aside.
3. Mix flour with baking soda, baking powder, cacao powder, coconut sugar and flour in a bowl.
4. Stir in vanilla, applesauce, and milk, then mix until smooth.
5. Fold in sugar-free chocolate chips and zucchini shreds.
6. Spread this batter in the prepared loaf pan.
7. Bake this bread for 55 minutes in the oven.
8. Allow the bread to cool, then slice.
9. Serve.

The Plant Based Cookbook For Beginners
650 Easy, Quick, & Simple Plant Based Vegan Diet Recipes With A 31 Day Meal Plan To Lose Weight & Live A Long Healthy Life

227

Breakfast Sweet Potatoes

SERVINGS	PREPARATION TIME	COOKING TIME
3	10 minutes	60 minutes

Nutritional Values Per Serving

Calories	276
Total Fat	6g
Saturated Fat	0.6g
Cholesterol	0mg
Sodium	85mg
Total Carbohydrate	29.2g
Dietary Fiber	7.6g
Total Sugars	13.9g
Protein	4.2g

Ingredients:

- 3 large sweet potatoes
- Black pepper, to taste
- ½ teaspoon salt

Instructions:

1. At 400 degrees F, preheat your oven and layer a baking sheet with tin foil.
2. Wash and pat dry the sweet potatoes.
3. Place these potatoes in the baking sheet and bake for 1 hour.
4. Cut the sweet potato from the top and make a slit.
5. Sprinkle black pepper and salt on top of the sweet potato.
6. Serve.

Pumpkin Pie Smoothie

SERVINGS	PREPARATION TIME	COOKING TIME
2	5 minutes	0 minutes

Nutritional Values Per Serving

Calories	188
Total Fat	11.4g
Saturated Fat	8.7g
Cholesterol	0mg
Sodium	115mg
Total Carbohydrate	15g
Dietary Fiber	10.7g
Total Sugars	47.8g
Protein	7.3g

Ingredients:

- 1 frozen ripe banana, mashed
- ½ cup pumpkin puree
- ¼ cup sprouted oats
- 2 tablespoons pea protein powder
- 1 tablespoon maple syrup
- 2 teaspoons pumpkin pie spice
- 1 teaspoon cinnamon
- 1 teaspoon vanilla extract
- 1 cup oat milk

Instructions:

1. Blend oats in a blender until powdered.
2. Add the rest of the ingredients and blend well.
3. Serve.

The Plant Based Cookbook For Beginners
650 Easy, Quick, & Simple Plant Based Vegan Diet Recipes With A 31 Day Meal Plan To Lose Weight & Live A Long Healthy Life

229

Hazelnut Chocolate Smoothie

SERVINGS	PREPARATION TIME	COOKING TIME
1	5 minutes	0 minutes

Nutritional Values Per Serving

Calories	203
Total Fat	12.6g
Saturated Fat	2.5g
Cholesterol	0mg
Sodium	173mg
Total Carbohydrate	32.1g
Dietary Fiber	4.1g
Total Sugars	18.5g
Protein	9.3g

Serving Suggestion:

Enjoy this smoothie bowl with granola bars on the side.

Ingredients:

Smoothie

- 1 frozen banana, mashed
- 1 tablespoon hazelnuts, soaked
- 1 scoop Detox Chocolate Superfoods
- 1 tablespoon hemp seeds
- ⅓ cup almond milk
- 2 Medjool dates, pitted

Toppings

- 2 teaspoons hazelnuts, chopped
- 1 teaspoon cacao nibs
- 1 teaspoon hemp seeds

Instructions:

1. Blend bananas with hazelnuts and milk, dates, chocolate and hemp seeds in a blender until smooth.

2. Pour this smoothie into the serving bowl.

3. Garnish with hazelnuts, hemp seeds and cacao nibs.

4. Enjoy.

230

The Plant Based Cookbook For Beginners
650 Easy, Quick, & Simple Plant Based Vegan Diet Recipes With A 31 Day Meal Plan To Lose Weight & Live A Long Healthy Life

Huevos Rancheros

SERVINGS	PREPARATION TIME	COOKING TIME
4	10 minutes	24 minutes

Nutritional Values Per Serving

Calories	351
Total Fat	14.3g
Saturated Fat	2.1g
Cholesterol	0mg
Sodium	71mg
Total Carbohydrate	19g
Dietary Fiber	10.3g
Total Sugars	13.5g
Protein	14.5g

Ingredients:

Rancheros

- 1 tablespoon olive oil
- 4 small corn tortillas
- 8 oz. fresh salsa
- ½ (15-oz.) can black beans

Toppings

- ½ small avocado, diced
- ½ fresh lime, juiced
- A few sprigs of cilantro
- Hot sauce

Instructions:

1. Cook salsa with olive oil in a saucepan for 15 minutes on a simmer then transfer to a bowl.

2. Add black beans to a pan and cook for 5 minutes.

3. Sear the tortillas in another pan for 2 minutes per side.

4. Spread the tortillas on the serving plate.

5. Top them with beans, lime juice, avocado, cilantro and hot sauce.

6. Serve.

The Plant Based Cookbook For Beginners
650 Easy, Quick, & Simple Plant Based Vegan Diet Recipes With A 31 Day Meal Plan To Lose Weight & Live A Long Healthy Life

231

Carrot Orange Smoothie

SERVINGS	PREPARATION TIME	COOKING TIME
2	5 minutes	15 minutes

Nutritional Values Per Serving

Calories	147
Total Fat	18.1g
Saturated Fat	13g
Cholesterol	0mg
Sodium	11mg
Total Carbohydrate	13.7g
Dietary Fiber	6.6g
Total Sugars	23.5g
Protein	5.7g

Ingredients:

- 1 cup carrots, sliced
- ½ teaspoon orange peel, shredded
- 1 cup orange juice
- 1½ cups ice cubes
- 3 (1 inch) pieces Orange peel curls

Instructions:

1. Boil carrots in a saucepan with water, for 15 minutes then drain.
2. Blend the boiled carrots with the rest of the ingredients in a blender.
3. Add ice cubes and serve.

232

The Plant Based Cookbook For Beginners
650 Easy, Quick, & Simple Plant Based Vegan Diet Recipes With A 31 Day Meal Plan To Lose Weight & Live A Long Healthy Life

Cinnamon Roll Oats

SERVINGS	PREPARATION TIME	FRIDGE TIME
4	10 minutes	Overnight

Nutritional Values Per Serving

Calories	226
Total Fat	6.5g
Saturated Fat	0.9g
Cholesterol	0mg
Sodium	58mg
Total Carbohydrate	12.9g
Dietary Fiber	7.6g
Total Sugars	4.5g
Protein	8.6g

Serving Suggestion:

Enjoy this oatmeal with soy yogurt or berries on top.

Ingredients:

- 2 ½ cups old-fashioned rolled oats
- 2 ½ cups almond milk
- 8 teaspoons light brown sugar
- 2 ½ teaspoon vanilla extract
- 1 ¼ teaspoons cinnamon
- ½ teaspoon salt

Instructions:

1. Add oats and all the ingredients to a large bowl.
2. Divide this mixture into 8 mini mason jars.
3. Cover their lids and refrigerate overnight.
4. Serve.

The Plant Based Cookbook For Beginners
650 Easy, Quick, & Simple Plant Based Vegan Diet Recipes With A 31 Day Meal Plan To Lose Weight & Live A Long Healthy Life

233

Blueberry Chia Pudding

SERVINGS	PREPARATION TIME	FRIDGE TIME
2	**10 minutes**	**Overnight**

Nutritional Values Per Serving

Calories	245
Total Fat	16.6g
Saturated Fat	13.1g
Cholesterol	0mg
Sodium	20mg
Total Carbohydrate	13.5g
Dietary Fiber	4.6g
Total Sugars	11.9g
Protein	4.2g

Ingredients:

- ½ cup unsweetened almond milk
- 2 tablespoons chia seeds
- 2 teaspoons pure maple syrup
- ⅛ teaspoon almond extract
- ½ cup fresh blueberries
- 1 tablespoon toasted almonds, sliced

Instructions:

1. Add almond milk, chia, almond extract and maple syrup to a mason jar.
2. Mix well, cover its lid and refrigerate overnight.
3. Garnish with almonds and blueberries.
4. Serve.

234

The Plant Based Cookbook For Beginners
650 Easy, Quick, & Simple Plant Based Vegan Diet Recipes With A 31 Day Meal Plan To Lose Weight & Live A Long Healthy Life

Apple Chia Pudding

SERVINGS	PREPARATION TIME	FRIDGE TIME
1	5 minutes	Overnight

Nutritional Values Per Serving

Calories	264
Total Fat	3.7g
Saturated Fat	0.2g
Cholesterol	0mg
Sodium	534mg
Total Carbohydrate	15.2g
Dietary Fiber	8.4g
Total Sugars	24.9g
Protein	8.9g

Ingredients:

- ½ cup unsweetened almond milk
- 2 tablespoons chia seeds
- 2 teaspoons pure maple syrup
- ¼ teaspoon vanilla extract
- ¼ teaspoon cinnamon
- ½ cup apple, diced
- 1 tablespoon granola

Instructions:

1. Add almond milk, chia, vanilla extract, cinnamon and maple syrup to a mason jar.
2. Mix well, cover its lid and refrigerate overnight.
3. Garnish with apples and granola.
4. Serve.

The Plant Based Cookbook For Beginners
650 Easy, Quick, & Simple Plant Based Vegan Diet Recipes With A 31 Day Meal Plan To Lose Weight & Live A Long Healthy Life

235

Sweet Potato Corn Hash

SERVINGS	PREPARATION TIME	COOKING TIME
2	10 minutes	23 minutes

Nutritional Values Per Serving

Calories	265
Total Fat	8.3g
Saturated Fat	1.5g
Cholesterol	0mg
Sodium	157mg
Total Carbohydrate	21.6g
Dietary Fiber	5.6g
Total Sugars	4.1g
Protein	6g

Ingredients:

- 2 teaspoons canola oil
- 2 medium onions, chopped
- 1 sweet potato, peeled and cubed
- 2 garlic cloves, minced
- 1 jalapeno pepper, seeded and minced
- 4 teaspoons cumin
- ½ teaspoon salt
- ¾ cup water
- ¾ cup frozen corn kernels
- 1 (15-oz.) can black beans, rinsed
- 2 tablespoons fresh cilantro, chopped
- Black pepper, to taste
- 1 lime, cut into wedges

Instructions:

1. Sauté onions with oil in a skillet over medium high heat for 5 minutes.
2. Stir in sweet potatoes and sauté for 7 minutes.
3. Add cumin, salt, jalapenos and garlic then sauté for 30 seconds.
4. Stir in water and cook for 5 minutes.
5. Add black beans, corn, cilantro, black pepper and salt then cook for 5 minutes.
6. Garnish with a little bit of lime juice from the lime wedges.
7. Serve warm.

236

The Plant Based Cookbook For Beginners
650 Easy, Quick, & Simple Plant Based Vegan Diet Recipes With A 31 Day Meal Plan To Lose Weight & Live A Long Healthy Life

Chickpea Avocado Toast

SERVINGS	PREPARATION TIME	COOKING TIME
1	5 minutes	0 minutes

Nutritional Values Per Serving

Calories	217
Total Fat	3.2g
Saturated Fat	0.1g
Cholesterol	0mg
Sodium	310mg
Total Carbohydrate	20.9g
Dietary Fiber	2.8g
Total Sugars	29g
Protein	6.8g

Ingredients:

- 1 whole-wheat bread slice, toasted
- ¼ avocado, mashed
- ½ cup chickpeas
- Salt to taste
- Black pepper to taste
- 1 pinch crushed red pepper

Instructions:

1. Spread mashed avocado on top of the toasted bread.
2. Add chickpeas, red pepper, black pepper and salt on top.
3. Serve.

The Plant Based Cookbook For Beginners
650 Easy, Quick, & Simple Plant Based Vegan Diet Recipes With A 31 Day Meal Plan To Lose Weight & Live A Long Healthy Life

237

Chia Berry Jam Muffin

SERVINGS	PREPARATION TIME	COOKING TIME
1	5 minutes	5 minutes

Nutritional Values Per Serving

Calories	220
Total Fat	29.3g
Saturated Fat	25.5g
Cholesterol	0mg
Sodium	21mg
Total Carbohydrate	15.2g
Dietary Fiber	3.7g
Total Sugars	10.3g
Protein	3.1g

Serving Suggestion:

Enjoy this muffin with strawberry smoothie.

Ingredients:

- ½ cup strawberries
- 2 teaspoons chia seeds
- 2 teaspoons natural peanut butter
- 1 whole-wheat English muffin, toasted

Instructions:

1. Mix strawberries with chia seeds in a saucepan, cover and cook for 5 minutes on low heat.
2. Stir well and mash the berries with a spoon.
3. Spread peanut butter over the English muffin.
4. Add chia berry mixture on top.
5. Serve.

Zucchini Bars

SERVINGS	PREPARATION TIME	COOKING TIME
6	10 minutes	30 minutes

Nutritional Values Per Serving

Calories	233
Total Fat	27.6g
Saturated Fat	18g
Cholesterol	0mg
Sodium	130mg
Total Carbohydrate	21.6g
Dietary Fiber	12.9g
Total Sugars	16.2g
Protein	14.4g

Ingredients:

- ¾ cup almond butter
- 1 cup zucchini, grated
- ¼ cup flax egg
- ¼ cup pure maple syrup
- 1 teaspoon vanilla extract
- ¾ teaspoons baking soda
- 2 teaspoons cinnamon
- ¼ teaspoons nutmeg
- ¼ teaspoons salt
- ⅓ cup sugar-free chocolate chips

Instructions:

1. At 350 degrees F, preheat your oven.
2. Mix zucchini with the rest of the ingredients in a bowl.
3. Spread this mixture in a 8x8 inches baking pan and bake for 30 minutes.
4. Allow the bars to cool and slice into bars.
5. Serve.

The Plant Based Cookbook For Beginners
650 Easy, Quick, & Simple Plant Based Vegan Diet Recipes With A 31 Day Meal Plan To Lose Weight & Live A Long Healthy Life

239

Matcha Smoothie with Pineapples

SERVINGS	PREPARATION TIME	COOKING TIME
2	5 minutes	0 minutes

Nutritional Values Per Serving

Calories	199
Total Fat	5.2g
Saturated Fat	1g
Cholesterol	0mg
Sodium	413mg
Total Carbohydrate	18.2g
Dietary Fiber	5.3g
Total Sugars	8.1g
Protein	13.5g

Ingredients:

- 1 cup almond milk
- 1 cup ice cubes
- ½ cup frozen pineapples
- 1 teaspoon matcha powder
- 1 frozen banana
- 1 scoop of soy yogurt
- 1 teaspoon agave

Instructions:

1. Blend pineapples with the rest of the ingredients in a blender until smooth.
2. Serve.

240

The Plant Based Cookbook For Beginners
650 Easy, Quick, & Simple Plant Based Vegan Diet Recipes With A 31 Day Meal Plan To Lose Weight & Live A Long Healthy Life

Tropical Salad

SERVINGS
2

PREPARATION TIME
10 minutes

COOKING TIME
0 minutes

Nutritional Values Per Serving	
Calories	257
Total Fat	9.5g
Saturated Fat	1g
Cholesterol	0mg
Sodium	16mg
Total Carbohydrate	20g
Dietary Fiber	9.4g
Total Sugars	48g
Protein	9.4g

Ingredients:

- 1 large mango, peeled and diced
- ½ cup kiwi sliced
- ½ strawberries, sliced
- 2 limes, juiced
- 2 teaspoons agave
- 1 tablespoon coconut oil, melted

Instructions:

1. Mix mango, kiwi with the rest of the ingredients in a salad bowl.
2. Serve.

The Plant Based Cookbook For Beginners
650 Easy, Quick, & Simple Plant Based Vegan Diet Recipes With A 31 Day Meal Plan To Lose Weight & Live A Long Healthy Life

241

Lemon Chia Muffins

SERVINGS	PREPARATION TIME	COOKING TIME
6	15 minutes	25 minutes

Nutritional Values Per Serving

Calories	210
Total Fat	2.8g
Saturated Fat	0.5g
Cholesterol	0mg
Sodium	109mg
Total Carbohydrate	22.9g
Dietary Fiber	5.9g
Total Sugars	14.4g
Protein	4.9g

Ingredients:

- 6 tablespoons warm water
- 2 tablespoons flaxseed
- ⅔ cup almond milk
- ½ cup maple syrup
- ¼ cup coconut oil
- 2 teaspoons lemon zest, grated
- 2 tablespoons lemon juice
- 1 teaspoon vanilla extract
- 2 cups whole wheat flour
- 1½ teaspoon baking soda
- ¼ teaspoon salt
- ¼ cup chia seeds

Instructions:

1. At 375 degrees F, preheat your oven.
2. Layer a muffin tray with muffin cups.
3. Soak flaxseeds in ½ water and leave for 5 minutes.
4. Mix water and the rest of the muffin ingredients in a large bowl until smooth.
5. Stir in flaxseed mixture and mix well.
6. Divide the batter in the prepared muffin tray and bake for 25 minutes.
7. Allow the muffins to cool.
8. Serve.

242

The Plant Based Cookbook For Beginners
650 Easy, Quick, & Simple Plant Based Vegan Diet Recipes With A 31 Day Meal Plan To Lose Weight & Live A Long Healthy Life

Tofu Egg Bites

SERVINGS	PREPARATION TIME	COOKING TIME
6	10 minutes	30 minutes

Nutritional Values Per Serving

Calories	288
Total Fat	7g
Saturated Fat	0.9g
Cholesterol	0mg
Sodium	8mg
Total Carbohydrate	28.5g
Dietary Fiber	9.1g
Total Sugars	10.4g
Protein	8.5g

Ingredients:

- 19 oz. firm tofu, drained
- ¼ cup nutritional yeast
- ½ teaspoon turmeric
- 4 green onions, chopped
- 3 mushrooms, chopped
- ½ large tomato, chopped
- ½ bell pepper, chopped
- ¾ cup broccoli, chopped
- 1 pinch of black salt
- Black pepper, to taste
- Olive oil spray

Instructions:

1. At 375 degrees F, preheat your oven.
2. Layer a muffin tray with olive oil spray.
3. Blend tofu with all the ingredients into a chunky mixture.
4. Divide this prepared batter into the muffin cups and bake for 30 minutes.
5. Serve warm.

The Plant Based Cookbook For Beginners
650 Easy, Quick, & Simple Plant Based Vegan Diet Recipes With A 31 Day Meal Plan To Lose Weight & Live A Long Healthy Life

243

Mango Smoothie Bowl

SERVINGS | PREPARATION TIME | COOKING TIME
2 | 5 minutes | 0 minutes

Nutritional Values Per Serving

Calories	221
Total Fat	4.7g
Saturated Fat	2.5g
Cholesterol	1mg
Sodium	87mg
Total Carbohydrate	21.7g
Dietary Fiber	4.2g
Total Sugars	17.7g
Protein	4.6g

Ingredients:

- 2 ripe bananas, peeled and frozen
- 1 cup frozen mango chunks
- 1 tablespoon lemon juice
- 1 tablespoon hemp seeds
- ½ cup coconut milk

Toppings

- Almonds
- Berries
- Banana slices
- Chia seeds

Instructions:

1. Blend banana with mango, lemon juice, milk and hemp seeds in a blender until smooth.

2. Garnish with berries, almonds, chia seeds and bananas.

3. Serve.

Roasted Tomato Hummus Toast

SERVINGS	PREPARATION TIME	COOKING TIME
4	10 minutes	20 minutes

Nutritional Values Per Serving	
Calories	278
Total Fat	2.7g
Saturated Fat	0.5g
Cholesterol	0mg
Sodium	157mg
Total Carbohydrate	24.4g
Dietary Fiber	4.5g
Total Sugars	5.8g
Protein	5.6g

Ingredients:

- 4 vines cherry tomatoes, stems removed
- 1 cup kale, chopped
- 2 garlic cloves, minced
- 2 tablespoons balsamic vinegar
- 2 tablespoons olive oil
- 4 tablespoons hummus
- 4 toasted sourdough bread slices
- Salt and black pepper, to taste

Instructions:

1. At 375 degrees, preheat your oven.
2. Mix tomatoes with kale, olive oil, balsamic vinegar and garlic in a baking tray.
3. Sprinkle black pepper and salt on top then bake for 20 minutes.
4. Spread the hummus over the toasted bread slices.
5. Divide the roasted tomatoes mixture on top of the hummus bread.
6. Serve.

The Plant Based Cookbook For Beginners
650 Easy, Quick, & Simple Plant Based Vegan Diet Recipes With A 31 Day Meal Plan To Lose Weight & Live A Long Healthy Life

245

French Toast

SERVINGS	PREPARATION TIME	COOKING TIME
6	10 minutes	7 minutes

Nutritional Values Per Serving

Calories	214
Total Fat	4.9g
Saturated Fat	0.7g
Cholesterol	0mg
Sodium	240mg
Total Carbohydrate	23.1g
Dietary Fiber	14.3g
Total Sugars	13.1g
Protein	10.1g

Ingredients:

- 3 tablespoons flour
- 1 cup almond milk
- 1 tablespoon brown sugar
- 1 teaspoon vanilla extract
- ½ teaspoon cinnamon
- ⅛ teaspoons salt
- 6 whole-wheat bread slices

Serve

- Maple syrup

Instructions:

1. Mix flour and all the batter ingredients in a bowl.
2. Dip the bread slices in this batter for 30 seconds, then transfer to a plate.
3. Set a griddle over medium heat.
4. Sear the bread slices for 3 minutes per side.
5. Serve with maple syrup.

246

The Plant Based Cookbook For Beginners
650 Easy, Quick, & Simple Plant Based Vegan Diet Recipes With A 31 Day Meal Plan To Lose Weight & Live A Long Healthy Life

Breakfast Sausage

SERVINGS
5

PREPARATION TIME
15 minutes

COOKING TIME
45 minutes

Nutritional Values Per Serving	
Calories	280
Total Fat	2.4g
Saturated Fat	0g
Cholesterol	0mg
Sodium	99mg
Total Carbohydrate	21.7g
Dietary Fiber	10.2g
Total Sugars	49.7g
Protein	2.3g

Ingredients:

- ½ cup chickpeas, cooked
- ½ cup vegetable stock
- 2 tablespoons maple syrup
- 2 tablespoons soy sauce
- 1 cup vital wheat gluten
- ⅓ cup nutritional yeast
- 2 teaspoons garlic powder
- 1 teaspoon sage
- 1 teaspoon paprika
- 1 teaspoon onion powder
- ½ teaspoon fennel seeds
- ½ teaspoon thyme leaves
- ½ teaspoon red pepper flakes
- ¼ teaspoons garlic cloves
- 1 pinch of black pepper
- sausage casings

Instructions:

1. Blend the chickpeas and stock with the rest of the ingredients in a food processor until well combined.
2. Divide this dough into 10 pieces, then roll each piece into a sausage link.
3. Wrap the sausage casing around the sausage links.
4. Set a large saucepan, filled half with water, over medium heat.
5. Place a steamer basket in this pan for steaming.
6. Add these sausages to the steamer, cover and steam them for 45 minutes.
7. Serve.

The Plant Based Cookbook For Beginners
650 Easy, Quick, & Simple Plant Based Vegan Diet Recipes With A 31 Day Meal Plan To Lose Weight & Live A Long Healthy Life

247

Potato Vegan Quiche

SERVINGS	PREPARATION TIME	COOKING TIME
4	10 minutes	51 minutes

Nutritional Values Per Serving

Calories	278
Total Fat	2.4g
Saturated Fat	0.1g
Cholesterol	0mg
Sodium	291mg
Total Carbohydrate	29.4g
Dietary Fiber	3.7g
Total Sugars	13.2g
Protein	6.4g

Ingredients:

- 1 (14 oz.) package firm tofu, drained
- 2 tablespoons nutritional yeast flakes
- 2 tablespoons soy sauce
- 1 tablespoon lemon juice
- ¼ teaspoon turmeric
- 1 tablespoon soy milk
- 1 tablespoon olive oil
- 1 cup russet potato, diced
- Salt and black pepper to taste
- 1 medium leek, chopped
- 2 garlic cloves, minced

Instructions:

1. Blend tofu with turmeric, soy milk, lemon juice, soy sauce and yeast in a blender until smooth.
2. Sauté potatoes with oil, black pepper and salt in a skillet for 10 minutes.
3. Stir in leeks and sauté for 5 minutes.
4. Now add garlic and sauté for 1 minute.
5. Stir in tofu mixture, mix well and spread it in a baking dish.
6. At 375 degrees F, preheat your oven.
7. Bake this quiche for 35 minutes in the oven.
8. Allow it cool, then slice.
9. Serve.

248

The Plant Based Cookbook For Beginners
650 Easy, Quick, & Simple Plant Based Vegan Diet Recipes With A 31 Day Meal Plan To Lose Weight & Live A Long Healthy Life

Buckwheat Crepes

SERVINGS	PREPARATION TIME	COOKING TIME
4	10 minutes	8 minutes

Nutritional Values Per Serving

Calories	139
Total Fat	1.1g
Saturated Fat	0.3g
Cholesterol	0mg
Sodium	16mg
Total Carbohydrate	29.4g
Dietary Fiber	5g
Total Sugars	3.2g
Protein	4.5g

Serving Suggestion:

Enjoy these crepes wrapped around guacamole and fresh vegetables in the middle.

Ingredients:

- 1 cup raw buckwheat flour
- ¾ tablespoons flaxseed meal
- 1 ¾ cups light canned coconut milk
- 1 pinch salt
- 1 tablespoon avocado oil
- ⅛ teaspoons cinnamon

Instructions:

1. Mix flour with flaxseed meals, coconut milk, salt, oil and cinnamon in a bowl.
2. Set a skillet over medium heat and grease it with a cooking spray.
3. Add a dollop of the batter, spread it around and cook for 2 minutes per side.
4. Make more crepes in the same way.
5. Serve warm.

The Plant Based Cookbook For Beginners
650 Easy, Quick, & Simple Plant Based Vegan Diet Recipes With A 31 Day Meal Plan To Lose Weight & Live A Long Healthy Life

249

Avocado Banana Smoothie

SERVINGS	PREPARATION TIME	COOKING TIME
2	5 minutes	0 minutes

Nutritional Values Per Serving

Calories	106
Total Fat	0.1g
Saturated Fat	0g
Cholesterol	0mg
Sodium	176mg
Total Carbohydrate	13.6g
Dietary Fiber	3.5g
Total Sugars	1.3g
Protein	3.6g

Serving Suggestion:

Garnish this smoothie with hemp seeds, maca, berries, or sliced bananas.

Ingredients:

- 1 large banana, peeled and sliced
- ½ medium ripe avocado
- 1 scoop vanilla protein powder
- 1 large handful of greens
- 1 cup almond milk

Instructions:

1. Blend avocado with the rest of the ingredients in a blender until smooth.
2. Serve.

250

The Plant Based Cookbook For Beginners
650 Easy, Quick, & Simple Plant Based Vegan Diet Recipes With A 31 Day Meal Plan To Lose Weight & Live A Long Healthy Life

Tempeh Sausage Patties

SERVINGS
5

PREPARATION TIME
10 minutes

COOKING TIME
16 minutes

Nutritional Values Per Serving

Calories	201
Total Fat	2.4g
Saturated Fat	0.7g
Cholesterol	0mg
Sodium	303mg
Total Carbohydrate	10.8g
Dietary Fiber	5.8g
Total Sugars	12.7g
Protein	5g

Ingredients:

- 8 oz. tempeh
- ¼ white onion, diced
- 4 garlic cloves, minced
- 1 teaspoon coconut sugar
- ½ teaspoon salt
- 1 teaspoon black pepper
- 1½ teaspoon dried sage
- 1 red bell pepper, chopped
- 1½ teaspoon dried thyme
- 1½ teaspoon smoked paprika
- 2 tablespoons fresh rosemary, chopped
- ⅛ teaspoons nutmeg
- ¼ teaspoon cayenne pepper
- ¼ teaspoon red pepper flake
- 2 tablespoons vegan Worcestershire sauce
- 1 tablespoon avocado oil
- 1 pinch allspice
- ½ teaspoon dried marjoram

Instructions:

1. Crumble tempeh by blending in a food processor.
2. Add rest of the ingredients, then blend until evenly mixed.
3. Divide the mixture into 5 portions and shape each into a sausage patty.
4. Sear each sausage in a skillet, greased with oil, for 4 minutes per side.
5. Serve with ketchup.

The Plant Based Cookbook For Beginners
650 Easy, Quick, & Simple Plant Based Vegan Diet Recipes With A 31 Day Meal Plan To Lose Weight & Live A Long Healthy Life

251

Eggplant Bacon

SERVINGS	PREPARATION TIME	COOKING TIME
6	15 minutes	30 minutes

Nutritional Values Per Serving

Calories	256
Total Fat	13.6g
Saturated Fat	9.1g
Cholesterol	0mg
Sodium	420mg
Total Carbohydrate	7.6g
Dietary Fiber	7.1g
Total Sugars	19.9g
Protein	7g

Ingredients:

- 1 medium eggplant, sliced thinly
- 1 tablespoon avocado oil
- 1½ tablespoons tamari
- 1 tablespoon vegan Worcestershire
- 1 tablespoon maple syrup
- 2 teaspoons liquid smoke
- 1 teaspoon smoked paprika
- 1 pinch salt
- 1 pinch garlic powder
- ½ teaspoon black pepper

Instructions:

1. At 250 degrees F, preheat your oven.
2. Mix all the spices, oil, tamari, maple syrup, liquid smoke and Worcestershire in a bowl.
3. Abundantly brush this mixture over the eggplant slices.
4. Place these slices in a baking sheet lined with wax paper.
5. Bake the eggplant slices for 30 minutes in the oven.
6. Flip them once cooked halfway through.
7. Serve.

252

The Plant Based Cookbook For Beginners
650 Easy, Quick, & Simple Plant Based Vegan Diet Recipes With A 31 Day Meal Plan To Lose Weight & Live A Long Healthy Life

CHAPTER 04

DRESSING AND DIPS RECIPES

Vegan Nacho Cheese

SERVINGS | PREPARATION TIME | COOKING TIME
8 | 10 minutes | 15 minutes

Nutritional Values Per Serving

Calories	145
Total Fat	3.5g
Saturated Fat	0.4g
Cholesterol	0mg
Sodium	159mg
Total Carbohydrate	22.9g
Dietary Fiber	6.6g
Total Sugars	6.2g
Protein	7.2g

Serving Suggestion:

Enjoy this nacho cheese with toasted tortilla chips.

Ingredients:

- 1 ¼ cup potatoes, peeled and cubed
- ⅓ cup carrots, peeled and cubed
- 1 ¼ cup almond milk
- ¼ cup nutritional yeast
- 1 tablespoon lime juice
- 1 tablespoon tomato paste
- 3 teaspoons cornstarch
- 2 teaspoons chili powder
- 1 teaspoon garlic powder
- 1 teaspoon onion powder
- ½ teaspoon paprika
- ½ teaspoon cumin
- ½ teaspoon salt
- ⅛ teaspoon cayenne pepper

Instructions:

1. Boil carrots and potatoes in a cooking pot filled with water for 10 minutes.

2. Drain and blend them with the rest of the ingredients in a blender until smooth.

3. Transfer this cheese to a cooking pot and cook on medium-low heat until it thickens.

4. Serve.

Spinach Dip

SERVINGS
8

PREPARATION TIME
15 minutes

COOKING TIME
10 minutes

Nutritional Values Per Serving

Calories	266
Total Fat	12g
Saturated Fat	0.5g
Cholesterol	0mg
Sodium	802mg
Total Carbohydrate	22g
Dietary Fiber	4.3g
Total Sugars	4.8g
Protein	10.7g

Serving Suggestion:

Try this spinach dip with toasted whole wheat bread slices.

Ingredients:

- 2 teaspoons olive oil
- 1 small onion, chopped
- 5 garlic cloves, minced
- 6 oz fresh baby spinach, chopped
- 1 ½ cup coconut cream
- ½ cup vegan mayo
- ¼ teaspoon paprika
- Salt to taste
- Black pepper to taste

Instructions:

1. In a suitable pan, heat the olive oil on medium heat.
2. Add in the chopped onion and sauté until translucent.
3. Stir in the garlic and sauté for 1 minute.
4. Stir in spinach then sauté for 1 minute.
5. Transfer to a bowl and add rest of the ingredients.
6. Mix well and serve.

The Plant Based Cookbook For Beginners
650 Easy, Quick, & Simple Plant Based Vegan Diet Recipes With A 31 Day Meal Plan To Lose Weight & Live A Long Healthy Life

255

Ranch Dressing

SERVINGS	PREPARATION TIME	COOKING TIME
6	5 minutes	0 minutes

Nutritional Values Per Serving

Calories	126
Total Fat	20.4g
Saturated Fat	3.7g
Cholesterol	0mg
Sodium	173mg
Total Carbohydrate	19g
Dietary Fiber	8g
Total Sugars	10.4g
Protein	11.3g

Ingredients:

- 1 ½ cup vegan mayo
- ½ cup almond milk
- 1 ½ teaspoon apple cider vinegar
- 3 garlic cloves, crushed
- ½ tablespoon dried parsley
- 1 teaspoon dried dill
- 1 teaspoon onion powder
- ¼ teaspoon paprika
- ¼ teaspoon black pepper
- Salt, to taste

Instructions:

1. Add mayo, milk and the rest of the ingredients to a small bowl.
2. Mix all the ingredients together until smooth.
3. Serve.

256

The Plant Based Cookbook For Beginners
650 Easy, Quick, & Simple Plant Based Vegan Diet Recipes With A 31 Day Meal Plan To Lose Weight & Live A Long Healthy Life

Vegan Queso

SERVINGS
6

PREPARATION TIME
10 minutes

COOKING TIME
0 minutes

Nutritional Values Per Serving

Calories	193
Total Fat	4.5g
Saturated Fat	0.8g
Cholesterol	1mg
Sodium	42mg
Total Carbohydrate	31g
Dietary Fiber	4.8g
Total Sugars	1.7g
Protein	8.6g

Serving Suggestion:

Try this queso with toasted tortilla chips.

Ingredients:

- 1 cup raw cashews
- ¾ cup almond milk
- 1 can (4 ½ oz) diced green chilis
- 2 tablespoon nutritional yeast
- ½ teaspoon red pepper flakes
- Salt to taste

Instructions:

1. Add cashews with the rest of the ingredients to a small blender.
2. Puree the ingredients together until smooth.
3. Serve.

The Plant Based Cookbook For Beginners
650 Easy, Quick, & Simple Plant Based Vegan Diet Recipes With A 31 Day Meal Plan To Lose Weight & Live A Long Healthy Life

257

Buffalo Dip

SERVINGS	PREPARATION TIME	COOKING TIME
8	10 minutes	0 minutes

Nutritional Values Per Serving

Calories	180
Total Fat	14.7g
Saturated Fat	12.8g
Cholesterol	0mg
Sodium	12mg
Total Carbohydrate	15.1g
Dietary Fiber	3g
Total Sugars	5.7g
Protein	4.9g

Serving Suggestion:

Enjoy this buffalo dip with crispy tortilla chips.

Ingredients:

- 1 cup cauliflower, shredded
- 1 (8oz) coconut cream
- ½ cup vegan ranch
- ½ cup cayenne pepper hot sauce
- ½ cup vegan melted cheese

Instructions:

1. Add coconut cream and ranch, hot sauce and cheese to a blender.
2. Puree the ingredients together until smooth.
3. Stir in shredded cauliflower and mix with a spoon
4. Serve.

258

The Plant Based Cookbook For Beginners
650 Easy, Quick, & Simple Plant Based Vegan Diet Recipes With A 31 Day Meal Plan To Lose Weight & Live A Long Healthy Life

Oil-Free Hummus

SERVINGS
8

PREPARATION TIME
5 minutes

COOKING TIME
0 minutes

Nutritional Values Per Serving

Calories	167
Total Fat	27.4g
Saturated Fat	23.3g
Cholesterol	0mg
Sodium	19mg
Total Carbohydrate	12.8g
Dietary Fiber	4.9g
Total Sugars	26g
Protein	3.3g

Serving Suggestion:

Try this hummus with crispy eggplant chips.

Ingredients:

- 1 can chickpeas, drained
- ¼ cup aquafaba
- 3 garlic cloves
- 1 tablespoon tahini
- 2 tablespoons lemon juice
- ¼ teaspoons paprika
- Salt to taste

Instructions:

1. Blend chickpeas with the rest of the ingredients in a bowl until smooth.
2. Serve.

The Plant Based Cookbook For Beginners
650 Easy, Quick, & Simple Plant Based Vegan Diet Recipes With A 31 Day Meal Plan To Lose Weight & Live A Long Healthy Life

259

Hot Broccoli Dip

SERVINGS	PREPARATION TIME	COOKING TIME
8	10 minutes	25 minutes

Nutritional Values Per Serving

Calories	138
Total Fat	5.8g
Saturated Fat	1.1g
Cholesterol	0mg
Sodium	270mg
Total Carbohydrate	20.2g
Dietary Fiber	4.6g
Total Sugars	2.7g
Protein	5.8g

Serving Suggestion:

Enjoy this dip with roasted broccoli florets on the side.

Ingredients:

- 1 cup white beans, drained
- 1 cup cashews, soaked
- 1 tablespoon lemon juice
- 1 tablespoon tapioca starch
- 2 tablespoons nutritional yeast
- 1 teaspoon garlic powder
- 1 teaspoon onion powder
- ½ teaspoon paprika
- Salt, to taste
- 1 pinch red pepper flakes
- 1¼ cup almond milk
- 1½ cups fresh broccoli, florets

Instructions:

1. At 375 degrees F, preheat your oven.
2. Spread broccoli in a baking sheet.
3. Blend rest of the dip ingredients in a blender until smooth.
4. Spread this mixture over the broccoli and bake for 25 minutes.
5. After baking, transfer the mixture to a blender and puree until smooth.
6. Serve.

260

The Plant Based Cookbook For Beginners
650 Easy, Quick, & Simple Plant Based Vegan Diet Recipes With A 31 Day Meal Plan To Lose Weight & Live A Long Healthy Life

Roasted Cauliflower Dip

SERVINGS	PREPARATION TIME	COOKING TIME
12	10 minutes	20 minutes

Nutritional Values Per Serving

Calories	111
Total Fat	1.8g
Saturated Fat	0.2g
Cholesterol	0mg
Sodium	9mg
Total Carbohydrate	17.9g
Dietary Fiber	5.7g
Total Sugars	2.8g
Protein	7.2g

Serving Suggestion:

Try this dip with crispy cauliflower florets.

Ingredients:

Roasting

- 4 cups cauliflower florets
- 2 jalapeños, sliced
- 2 teaspoons curry powder
- 2 tablespoons olive oil

Blending

- ⅓ cup olive oil
- 1 tablespoon lemon juice
- 2 garlic cloves
- ½ teaspoon dried cilantro
- ½ teaspoon salt
- ¼ teaspoon black pepper

Instructions:

1. At 400 degrees F, preheat your oven.
2. Toss cauliflower with jalapenos and 2 tablespoons olive oil on a baking sheet.
3. Sprinkle curry powder on top and bake for 20 minutes in the oven.
4. After baking, puree the cauliflower mixture with the rest of the ingredients in a blender.
5. Serve.

The Plant Based Cookbook For Beginners
650 Easy, Quick, & Simple Plant Based Vegan Diet Recipes With A 31 Day Meal Plan To Lose Weight & Live A Long Healthy Life

261

White Bean Spinach Dip

SERVINGS	PREPARATION TIME	COOKING TIME
8	15 minutes	45 minutes

Nutritional Values Per Serving

Calories	141
Total Fat	4.8g
Saturated Fat	0.3g
Cholesterol	0mg
Sodium	165mg
Total Carbohydrate	12.6g
Dietary Fiber	4.1g
Total Sugars	15.1g
Protein	3.5g

Serving Suggestion:

Try this dip with toasted pita.

Ingredients:

- 1 garlic head
- 3 ½ tablespoon of olive oil
- 1 (15 oz.) can white beans, drained
- 2 tablespoons lemon juice
- ½ teaspoon cumin
- 1 ½ cups fresh spinach
- Salt and black pepper to taste

Instructions:

1. At 350 degrees F, preheat your oven.
2. Chop of the top of the garlic head and place in a baking sheet.
3. Drizzle ½ tbs olive oil on and cover with a tin foil.
4. Bake the garlic for 45 minutes in the oven and allow it to cool then peel.
5. Puree roasted garlic cloves with the rest of the ingredients in a blender until smooth.
6. Serve.

Spicy Eggplant Dip

SERVINGS	PREPARATION TIME	COOKING TIME
12	5 minutes	10 minutes

Nutritional Values Per Serving

Calories	121
Total Fat	2.3g
Saturated Fat	0.4g
Cholesterol	20mg
Sodium	128mg
Total Carbohydrate	12.5g
Dietary Fiber	4.9g
Total Sugars	24.6g
Protein	10g

Serving Suggestion:

Try this dip with crispy eggplant chips.

Ingredients:

- 2 eggplants, sliced
- 3 tablespoons olive oil
- 3 tablespoons roasted tahini
- 2 garlic cloves, chopped
- ½ teaspoon ground cumin
- Juice of 1 lemon
- Salt and cayenne pepper to taste
- 1 tablespoon parsley, chopped

Instructions:

1. Slice and rub the eggplant with olive oil.
2. Grill these eggplant slices for 5 minutes per side.
3. Peel and puree the eggplant slices in the blender.
4. Add rest of the ingredients then blend again.
5. Serve.

The Plant Based Cookbook For Beginners
650 Easy, Quick, & Simple Plant Based Vegan Diet Recipes With A 31 Day Meal Plan To Lose Weight & Live A Long Healthy Life

263

Tofu Ranch Dressing

SERVINGS	PREPARATION TIME	COOKING TIME
12	5 minutes	0 minutes

Nutritional Values Per Serving

Calories	166
Total Fat	3.4g
Saturated Fat	0.3g
Cholesterol	0mg
Sodium	224mg
Total Carbohydrate	11.4g
Dietary Fiber	2.5g
Total Sugars	3.2g
Protein	3.3g

Serving Suggestion:

Try this dressing with kale fennel salad.

Ingredients:

- 1 (12-oz.) pkg. soft silken tofu
- 3 tablespoons almond milk
- 2 teaspoons onion powder
- 1 ½ teaspoon white wine vinegar
- 1 ½ teaspoon garlic powder
- Salt and black pepper, to taste
- 2 teaspoons fresh parsley, chopped
- 2 teaspoons fresh dill, chopped
- 2 teaspoons fresh chives, chopped

Instructions:

1. Add tofu with the rest of the ingredients to a small blender.
2. Puree the ingredients together until smooth.
3. Serve.

264

The Plant Based Cookbook For Beginners
650 Easy, Quick, & Simple Plant Based Vegan Diet Recipes With A 31 Day Meal Plan To Lose Weight & Live A Long Healthy Life

Corn Dressing with Dill

SERVINGS	PREPARATION TIME	COOKING TIME
8	10 minutes	0 minutes

Nutritional Values Per Serving

Calories	110
Total Fat	5.1g
Saturated Fat	1.6g
Cholesterol	1mg
Sodium	89mg
Total Carbohydrate	7.3g
Dietary Fiber	3.4g
Total Sugars	13.6g
Protein	5.6g

Serving Suggestion:

Add this dressing to a spinach lettuce salad.

Ingredients:

- 1 (10-oz.) pkg. frozen golden corn
- 2 tablespoons lemon juice
- 1 tablespoon fresh dill, chopped
- 1 teaspoon fresh chives, chopped
- 1 teaspoon Dijon-style mustard
- ⅛ teaspoon garlic powder
- ⅛ teaspoon black salt
- Black pepper, to taste

Instructions:

1. Add corn with the rest of the ingredients to a small blender.
2. Puree the ingredients together until smooth.
3. Pass this mixture through fine mesh sieve into a suitable bowl.
4. Discard the solid and keep the liquid.
5. Serve.

The Plant Based Cookbook For Beginners
650 Easy, Quick, & Simple Plant Based Vegan Diet Recipes With A 31 Day Meal Plan To Lose Weight & Live A Long Healthy Life

265

Vegan Italian Dressing

SERVINGS	PREPARATION TIME	COOKING TIME
8	5 minutes	0 minutes

Nutritional Values Per Serving

Calories	190
Total Fat	20.3g
Saturated Fat	1.4g
Cholesterol	0mg
Sodium	68mg
Total Carbohydrate	6.6g
Dietary Fiber	8.3g
Total Sugars	19.7g
Protein	12.3g

Serving Suggestion:

Add this Italian dressing to a chickpea kale salad.

Ingredients:

- ½ cup cooked chickpeas
- ½ cup almond milk
- 2 tablespoons lemon juice
- 1 tablespoon nutritional yeast
- 1 teaspoon yellow mustard
- ½ teaspoon dried Italian seasoning, crushed

Instructions:

1. Add chickpea with the rest of the ingredients to a small blender.
2. Puree the ingredients together until smooth.
3. Serve.

266

The Plant Based Cookbook For Beginners
650 Easy, Quick, & Simple Plant Based Vegan Diet Recipes With A 31 Day Meal Plan To Lose Weight & Live A Long Healthy Life

Wasabi Orange Sauce

SERVINGS	PREPARATION TIME	COOKING TIME
6	5 minutes	0 minutes

Nutritional Values Per Serving

Calories	131
Total Fat	1.7g
Saturated Fat	0.2g
Cholesterol	0mg
Sodium	75mg
Total Carbohydrate	9.5g
Dietary Fiber	3.4g
Total Sugars	18.2g
Protein	1.8g

Serving Suggestion:

Enjoy this dressing with an orange spinach salad.

Ingredients:

- 3 medium oranges, peeled and seeded
- 2 small dates, pitted
- 3 tablespoons peanut butter
- 2 ¼ teaspoons tamari
- ¾ teaspoon wasabi paste

Instructions:

1. Add oranges, dates, peanut butter, tamari and wasabi to a small blender.
2. Puree the ingredients together until smooth.
3. Serve.

The Plant Based Cookbook For Beginners
650 Easy, Quick, & Simple Plant Based Vegan Diet Recipes With A 31 Day Meal Plan To Lose Weight & Live A Long Healthy Life

267

Date Mustard Dressing

SERVINGS | PREPARATION TIME | COOKING TIME
8 | 5 minutes | 0 minutes

Nutritional Values Per Serving

Calories	148
Total Fat	15.6g
Saturated Fat	12.9g
Cholesterol	0mg
Sodium	17mg
Total Carbohydrate	8.6g
Dietary Fiber	5.6g
Total Sugars	9.2g
Protein	3g

Serving Suggestion:

Add this dressing to a mixed carrot and cabbage salad.

Ingredients:

- ½ cup unsweetened applesauce
- 2 tablespoons date paste
- 2 tablespoons mustard
- 1 tablespoon lemon juice
- Black pepper, to taste

Instructions:

1. Add apple sauce with date paste, mustard, lemon juice, black pepper and salt to a small blender.
2. Puree the ingredients together until smooth.
3. Serve.

268

The Plant Based Cookbook For Beginners
650 Easy, Quick, & Simple Plant Based Vegan Diet Recipes With A 31 Day Meal Plan To Lose Weight & Live A Long Healthy Life

Tahini Sauce

SERVINGS	PREPARATION TIME	COOKING TIME
8	**5 minutes**	**0 minutes**

Nutritional Values Per Serving

Calories	114
Total Fat	1.8g
Saturated Fat	0.5g
Cholesterol	10mg
Sodium	54mg
Total Carbohydrate	8g
Dietary Fiber	4.8g
Total Sugars	7.9g
Protein	7.3g

Serving Suggestion:

Try this dip with crispy eggplant chips.

Ingredients:

- ½ cup tahini
- 1 cup water
- ¼ cup lemon juice
- 3 garlic cloves, minced
- Salt and black pepper, to taste

Instructions:

1. Add tahini with water and the rest of the ingredients to a small blender.
2. Puree the ingredients together until smooth.
3. Serve.

The Plant Based Cookbook For Beginners
650 Easy, Quick, & Simple Plant Based Vegan Diet Recipes With A 31 Day Meal Plan To Lose Weight & Live A Long Healthy Life

269

French Onion Dip

SERVINGS | PREPARATION TIME | COOKING TIME
12 | 10 minutes | 30 minutes

Nutritional Values Per Serving

Calories	134
Total Fat	10g
Saturated Fat	1.7g
Cholesterol	0mg
Sodium	81mg
Total Carbohydrate	7.5g
Dietary Fiber	0.8g
Total Sugars	2.9g
Protein	4.4g

Serving Suggestion:

Try this dip with fresh veggies.

Ingredients:

- 1 medium yellow onion, diced
- 1 tablespoon olive oil
- 1 ¼ cups vegan sour cream
- 1 teaspoon vegan Worcestershire sauce
- ½ teaspoon garlic powder
- ½ teaspoon onion powder
- Salt, to taste
- Chopped parsley to serve

Instructions:

1. Sauté onions with oil in a suitable skillet for 15 minutes.

2. Add a splash of water and cook for another 15 minutes until the onion is caramelized.

3. Transfer this onion along with the rest of the ingredients to a blender.

4. Puree the ingredients together until smooth.

5. Serve.

Romesco Oat Sauce

SERVINGS
8

PREPARATION TIME
5 minutes

COOKING TIME
0 minutes

Nutritional Values Per Serving

Calories	162
Total Fat	10.1g
Saturated Fat	2.1g
Cholesterol	0mg
Sodium	23mg
Total Carbohydrate	8.9g
Dietary Fiber	5.2g
Total Sugars	7.9g
Protein	2.3g

Serving Suggestion:

Add this dressing to a quinoa tofu salad.

Ingredients:

- ½ cup toasted rolled oats
- 1 ¼ cups roasted red pepper
- 1 medium garlic clove
- ½ cup toasted almonds
- ½ teaspoon salt
- Black pepper to taste
- 1 ½ tablespoon red wine vinegar
- ⅛ teaspoons smoked paprika
- 5 tablespoons water

Instructions:

1. Add rolled oats and the rest of the ingredients to a blender.
2. Puree the ingredients together until smooth.
3. Serve.

The Plant Based Cookbook For Beginners
650 Easy, Quick, & Simple Plant Based Vegan Diet Recipes With A 31 Day Meal Plan To Lose Weight & Live A Long Healthy Life

271

Applesauce Vinaigrette

SERVINGS	PREPARATION TIME	COOKING TIME
8	5 minutes	0 minutes

Nutritional Values Per Serving

Calories	138
Total Fat	13.5g
Saturated Fat	2.8g
Cholesterol	0mg
Sodium	472mg
Total Carbohydrate	5.8g
Dietary Fiber	13.9g
Total Sugars	5.7g
Protein	14.2g

Serving Suggestion:

Add this dressing to a kale apple salad.

Ingredients:

- ¼ cup unsweetened applesauce
- 1 teaspoon mild miso
- ¼ teaspoon cumin
- ⅛ teaspoon cinnamon
- 2 tablespoons apple cider vinegar
- 1 tablespoon balsamic vinegar
- 1 teaspoon Dijon mustard
- 1 tablespoon pure maple syrup
- ¼ teaspoon salt
- Black pepper, to taste

Instructions:

1. Add applesauce, miso, cumin and the rest of the ingredients to a small bowl.
2. Mix the ingredients together until smooth.
3. Serve.

Caesar Dressing

SERVINGS	PREPARATION TIME	COOKING TIME
8	5 minutes	0 minutes

Nutritional Values Per Serving

Calories	116
Total Fat	0.5g
Saturated Fat	0.1g
Cholesterol	0mg
Sodium	37mg
Total Carbohydrate	9.5g
Dietary Fiber	5g
Total Sugars	22.4g
Protein	2g

Serving Suggestion:

Add this dressing to a kale tofu salad.

Ingredients:

- ⅓ cup raw cashews, soaked and drained
- 2 tablespoons nutritional yeast
- 1 teaspoon whole chia seeds
- ½ teaspoon salt
- ½ teaspoon kelp granules
- ½ teaspoon capers
- 1 garlic clove, chopped
- Black pepper to taste
- ½ cup almond milk
- 2 tablespoons lemon juice
- 1½ teaspoon pure maple syrup

Instructions:

1. Add cashews, capers and the rest of the ingredients to a blender.
2. Puree the ingredients together until smooth.
3. Serve.

The Plant Based Cookbook For Beginners
650 Easy, Quick, & Simple Plant Based Vegan Diet Recipes With A 31 Day Meal Plan To Lose Weight & Live A Long Healthy Life

273

Carrots Dressing

SERVINGS	PREPARATION TIME	COOKING TIME
8	5 minutes	0 minutes

Nutritional Values Per Serving

Calories	166
Total Fat	18.5g
Saturated Fat	13g
Cholesterol	0mg
Sodium	486mg
Total Carbohydrate	7g
Dietary Fiber	4.5g
Total Sugars	15.2g
Protein	5.8g

Serving Suggestion:

Add this dressing to a kale carrot salad.

Ingredients:

- ½ cup carrot, cut into chunks
- ⅓ cup of water
- 1 ½ tablespoons red wine vinegar
- 1 tablespoons tahini
- 1 tablespoon pure maple syrup
- ½ tablespoons chickpea miso
- ½ teaspoon fresh ginger, chopped
- ¼ teaspoons salt

Instructions:

1. Add all ingredients to a small blender.
2. Puree the ingredients together until smooth.
3. Serve.

Cilantro-Garlic Dressing

SERVINGS	PREPARATION TIME	COOKING TIME
6	5 minutes	0 minutes

Nutritional Values Per Serving

Calories	163
Total Fat	11.1g
Saturated Fat	3.8g
Cholesterol	0mg
Sodium	250mg
Total Carbohydrate	8.5g
Dietary Fiber	2.5g
Total Sugars	15.6g
Protein	3.5g

Serving Suggestion:

Add this dressing to a sweet potato salad.

Ingredients:

- 1 package (12 oz.) silken tofu, drained
- ½ cup of rice wine vinegar
- ¼ cup of soy sauce
- 3 garlic cloves, crushed
- ½ bunch fresh cilantro, chopped

Instructions:

1. Add tofu with vinegar, soy sauce, garlic and cilantro to a small blender.
2. Puree the ingredients together until smooth.
3. Serve.

The Plant Based Cookbook For Beginners
650 Easy, Quick, & Simple Plant Based Vegan Diet Recipes With A 31 Day Meal Plan To Lose Weight & Live A Long Healthy Life

275

Balsamic Dressing

SERVINGS	PREPARATION TIME	COOKING TIME
6	5 minutes	0 minutes

Nutritional Values Per Serving

Calories	118
Total Fat	6.6g
Saturated Fat	1.9g
Cholesterol	1mg
Sodium	97mg
Total Carbohydrate	15.1g
Dietary Fiber	8.2g
Total Sugars	10.5g
Protein	9g

Serving Suggestion:

Add this dressing to a lettuce apple salad.

Ingredients:

- 2 teaspoons balsamic vinegar
- 1 teaspoon Dijon mustard
- 1 teaspoon nutritional yeast
- ¼ teaspoon dried basil
- Salt and black pepper, to taste

Instructions:

1. Add vinegar with mustard, yeast, basil, black pepper and salt to a small bowl.
2. Mix well for 30 seconds with a spoon.
3. Serve.

276

The Plant Based Cookbook For Beginners
650 Easy, Quick, & Simple Plant Based Vegan Diet Recipes With A 31 Day Meal Plan To Lose Weight & Live A Long Healthy Life

Cilantro Cashew Dressing

SERVINGS	PREPARATION TIME	COOKING TIME
8	5 minutes	0 minutes

Nutritional Values Per Serving

Calories	150
Total Fat	7.8g
Saturated Fat	4.1g
Cholesterol	0mg
Sodium	150mg
Total Carbohydrate	10g
Dietary Fiber	5.2g
Total Sugars	12.8g
Protein	6g

Serving Suggestion:

Add this dressing to a kale cucumber salad.

Ingredients:

- ½ cup cashews
- 1 cup fresh cilantro leaves
- 3 tablespoons lemon juice
- ½-inch serrano pepper piece, seeded
- 3 garlic cloves
- 1 teaspoon hot sauce
- Salt, to taste

Instructions:

1. Blend cashews with cilantro and the rest of the ingredients in a blender until smooth.
2. Serve.

The Plant Based Cookbook For Beginners
650 Easy, Quick, & Simple Plant Based Vegan Diet Recipes With A 31 Day Meal Plan To Lose Weight & Live A Long Healthy Life

277

Tamari Vinaigrette

SERVINGS	PREPARATION TIME	COOKING TIME
4	5 minutes	0 minutes

Nutritional Values Per Serving

Calories	115
Total Fat	0.7g
Saturated Fat	0.1g
Cholesterol	0mg
Sodium	6mg
Total Carbohydrate	8.7g
Dietary Fiber	5.2g
Total Sugars	3.3g
Protein	5.1g

Ingredients:

- ¼ cup tamari
- ¼ cup balsamic vinegar
- 2 teaspoons Dijon mustard

Instructions:

1. Mix tamari with balsamic vinegar and mustard in a bowl.
2. Serve.

(278)

The Plant Based Cookbook For Beginners
650 Easy, Quick, & Simple Plant Based Vegan Diet Recipes With A 31 Day Meal Plan To Lose Weight & Live A Long Healthy Life

CHAPTER 05

SOUPS AND SALADS RECIPES

Beet Soup

SERVINGS	PREPARATION TIME	COOKING TIME
6	10 minutes	26 minutes

Nutritional Values Per Serving

Calories	276
Total Fat	6.6g
Saturated Fat	1.9g
Cholesterol	1mg
Sodium	97mg
Total Carbohydrate	30g
Dietary Fiber	8.2g
Total Sugars	4g
Protein	9g

Ingredients:

- 3 tablespoons olive oil
- 1 medium onion, chopped
- 3 cloves garlic, chopped
- 6 medium beets, peeled and chopped
- 2 cups vegetable stock
- Salt and black pepper, to taste

Garnish

- Chopped parsley

Instructions:

1. Sauté onion with olive oil in a deep pan for 5 minutes.
2. Stir in garlic and cook for 30 seconds.
3. Add beets, vegetable stock, black pepper and salt.
4. Cook on a simmer for 20 minutes until beets are soft.
5. Puree this soup with a hand blender until smooth.
6. Garnish with parsley.
7. Serve warm.

280

The Plant Based Cookbook For Beginners
650 Easy, Quick, & Simple Plant Based Vegan Diet Recipes With A 31 Day Meal Plan To Lose Weight & Live A Long Healthy Life

Fennel Walnut Soup

SERVINGS
4

PREPARATION TIME
15 minutes

COOKING TIME
29 minutes

Nutritional Values Per Serving

Calories	284
Total Fat	11.9g
Saturated Fat	2g
Cholesterol	0mg
Sodium	456mg
Total Carbohydrate	19.4g
Dietary Fiber	6.1g
Total Sugars	30.7g
Protein	6.5g

Ingredients:

Soup

- 2 tablespoons olive oil
- 3 leeks, chopped
- 2 teaspoons fresh thyme leaves, chopped
- 1 fennel bulb, cored and chopped
- 1 apple, peeled, cored and chopped
- 1 teaspoon turmeric
- ½ cup walnut halves, toasted
- Salt and black pepper, to taste
- 4 cups vegetable stock

Garnish

- Black pepper
- Chopped fennel fronds
- Toasted walnuts chopped

Instructions:

1. Sauté leeks with oil and thyme in a soup pot over medium heat for 4 minutes.
2. Stir in apples and fennel then sauté for 30 seconds.
3. Add turmeric and sauté for 4 minutes.
4. Stir in vegetable stock, black pepper, salt and walnuts.
5. Cover and cook this soup for 15 minutes.
6. Puree the cooked soup with a hand blender until smooth.
7. Garnish with walnuts, fennel fronds, and black pepper.
8. Serve warm.

The Plant Based Cookbook For Beginners
650 Easy, Quick, & Simple Plant Based Vegan Diet Recipes With A 31 Day Meal Plan To Lose Weight & Live A Long Healthy Life

281

Coconut Green Soup

SERVINGS | **PREPARATION TIME** | **COOKING TIME**
6 | 15 minutes | 20 minutes

Nutritional Values Per Serving

Calories	315
Total Fat	7.1g
Saturated Fat	2.6g
Cholesterol	1mg
Sodium	97mg
Total Carbohydrate	10.3g
Dietary Fiber	10.9g
Total Sugars	34.3g
Protein	6.6g

Serving Suggestion:

Enjoy this soup with toasted croutons and kale salad.

Ingredients:

Soup

- 1 teaspoon whole cumin seeds
- 1 teaspoon whole coriander seeds
- 2 teaspoons coconut oil
- 1 large shallot, chopped
- 1 medium zucchini, chopped
- 1 small bunch celery, chopped
- 1 medium apple, peeled, cored and chopped
- 3 inches of ginger, peeled and chopped
- 6 cups vegetable stock
- Salt and black pepper, to taste
- 4 cups greens, chopped
- 1 (14-oz.) can full fat coconut milk
- 2 tablespoons lime juice

Garnish

- Cooked brown rice
- Cooked lentils or chickpeas
- Sliced ripe avocado
- Coconut milk
- Chili-infused olive oil
- Chopped basil

Instructions:

1. Roast coriander seeds and cumin in a skillet for 1 minute then transfer to a grinder and grind.
2. Sauté shallots with coconut oil in a saucepan for 3 minutes.
3. Stir in apple, celery, zucchini, ginger, coriander powder and cumin powder.
4. Sauté for 3 minutes, then add vegetable stock, black pepper and salt.
5. Boil, reduce its heat and cook for 10 minutes.
6. Stir in coconut milk, and chopped greens, then cook for 3 minutes.
7. Puree this soup with a hand blender until smooth.
8. Add lime juice and mix well.
9. Serve warm.

282

The Plant Based Cookbook For Beginners
650 Easy, Quick, & Simple Plant Based Vegan Diet Recipes With A 31 Day Meal Plan To Lose Weight & Live A Long Healthy Life

Roasted Cauliflower Soup

SERVINGS
6

PREPARATION TIME
15 minutes

COOKING TIME
65 minutes

Nutritional Values Per Serving

Calories	294
Total Fat	9.3g
Saturated Fat	1.6g
Cholesterol	0mg
Sodium	255mg
Total Carbohydrate	19.8g
Dietary Fiber	1.7g
Total Sugars	2.1g
Protein	9.4g

Serving Suggestion:

Enjoy this soup with toasted croutons and fennel cucumber

Ingredients:

Soup

- 1 cauliflower head, cut into florets
- 1 lb Yukon gold potatoes, scrubbed
- 2 yellow onions, skin removed
- 2 tablespoons rosemary leaves
- 2 tablespoons olive oil
- Salt and black pepper, to taste
- 1 tablespoon fresh lemon juice
- 6 cups vegetable stock

Garnish

- Olive oil
- Croutons
- Toasted and chopped nuts
- Chopped leafy herbs
- Balsamic reduction
- Squeezes of lemon
- Black pepper
- Roasted garlic chips

Instructions:

1. At 400 degrees F, preheat your oven.

2. Spread the cauliflower florets, onion and potatoes in a baking sheet.

3. Sprinkle oil, black pepper, salt and rosemary on top, then toss well.

4. Roast these veggies for 1 hour and toss them after every 10 minutes.

5. Puree veggies with lemon juice and vegetable stock in a blender.

6. Transfer this blend to a saucepan and cook to a boil.

7. Add more stock or water if needed.

8. Serve warm with recommended garnishes on top.

The Plant Based Cookbook For Beginners
650 Easy, Quick, & Simple Plant Based Vegan Diet Recipes With A 31 Day Meal Plan To Lose Weight & Live A Long Healthy Life

283

Squash and Chestnut Soup

SERVINGS   **PREPARATION TIME**   **COOKING TIME**
4   20 minutes   55 minutes

Nutritional Values Per Serving	
Calories	213
Total Fat	4.9g
Saturated Fat	1.1g
Cholesterol	0mg
Sodium	248mg
Total Carbohydrate	28.3g
Dietary Fiber	3.7g
Total Sugars	16g
Protein	6.6g

Serving Suggestion:

Enjoy this soup with toasted bread and spinach salad.

Ingredients:

Soup

- 1 lb. chestnuts
- 2 tablespoons olive oil
- 1 onion, chopped
- 4 garlic cloves, chopped
- 1 teaspoon salt
- 7 cups water
- 1 large sage sprig
- 3 bay leaves
- 2 teaspoons tamari soy sauce
- 1 kabocha squash, peeled, seeded and diced
- Black pepper, to taste

Kale Sesame Crisps

- 1 bunch Lacinato kale, leaves separated
- 2 teaspoons olive oil
- 1 teaspoon maple syrup
- Salt and black pepper, to taste
- 2 tablespoons sesame seeds

Instructions:

1. At 425 degrees F, preheat your oven.
2. Make a slit on top of each chestnut and add them to a saucepan.
3. Pour enough water to cover them, and cook to a boil then drain.
4. Spread these chestnuts in a baking sheet and roast for 20 minutes.
5. Allow them to cool then peel off their shells.
6. Reduce the oven's heat to 400 degrees F.
7. Toss kale leaves with black pepper, salt, 2 teaspoons olive oil and maple syrup in a baking sheet.
8. Sprinkle sesame seeds on top and bake for 8 minutes and take out the oven to cool.
9. Sauté onion with olive oil in a soup pan over medium heat for 6 minutes.
10. Add garlic and sauté for 30 seconds.
11. Stir in bay leaves, sage, water, chestnuts, squash, and salt then cook to a boil.
12. Reduce its heat and cook for 20 minutes.
13. Puree this soup with a blender in batches then return to the pot.
14. Stir in black pepper, salt and tamari and boil again.
15. Garnish with kale chips.
16. Serve warm.

284

The Plant Based Cookbook For Beginners
650 Easy, Quick, & Simple Plant Based Vegan Diet Recipes With A 31 Day Meal Plan To Lose Weight & Live A Long Healthy Life

Shiitake Tortilla Soup

SERVINGS
6

PREPARATION TIME
15 minutes

COOKING TIME
57 minutes

Nutritional Values Per Serving

Calories	246
Total Fat	0.8g
Saturated Fat	0g
Cholesterol	0mg
Sodium	1mg
Total Carbohydrate	31.1g
Dietary Fiber	1.7g
Total Sugars	59.3g
Protein	0.8g

Serving Suggestion:

Enjoy this soup with toasted tortilla chips.

Ingredients:

Soup

- 6 (6-inch) corn tortillas
- 2 tablespoons avocado oil
- 1 (15-oz) can crushed tomatoes
- 4 cups vegetable stock
- 1 small white onion, diced
- 4 garlic cloves, minced
- 1 jalapeño, minced
- ½ teaspoon dried Mexican oregano
- 1 teaspoon cumin
- 1 teaspoon chipotle powder
- ¾ lb shiitake mushrooms, sliced
- 1 (15-oz) can black beans, drained
- 1 cup corn kernels
- Salt and black pepper, to taste

Garnish

- Coconut cream
- Tortilla chips
- Cilantro, chopped
- Lime wedges

Instructions:

1. Cut each tortilla into thin strips and spread them in a baking sheet.
2. Bake these tortillas strips for 12 minutes in the oven at 350 degrees.
3. Toss them once cooked halfway and then allow them to cool when cooked.
4. Blend crushed tomatoes with half of the tortilla strips, and 1 cup stock until smooth.
5. Sauté onion with avocado oil in a cooking pot over medium heat for 3 minutes.
6. Stir in chipotle powder, cumin, oregano, jalapeno, and garlic then cook for 30 seconds.
7. Stir in mushrooms and cook for 2 minutes.
8. Add vegetable stock, corn, black beans, black pepper and salt.
9. Stir in blended tomato mixture then cook to a boil.
10. Now, reduce its heat and cook for 10 minutes.
11. Garnish with remaining tortillas strips, cilantro, lime wedges, and coconut cream.
12. Serve warm.

The Plant Based Cookbook For Beginners
650 Easy, Quick, & Simple Plant Based Vegan Diet Recipes With A 31 Day Meal Plan To Lose Weight & Live A Long Healthy Life

285

Vegan Tomato Soup

SERVINGS	PREPARATION TIME	COOKING TIME
6	15 minutes	70 minutes

Nutritional Values Per Serving

Calories	191
Total Fat	6.9g
Saturated Fat	0.7g
Cholesterol	0mg
Sodium	70mg
Total Carbohydrate	19.9g
Dietary Fiber	5.2g
Total Sugars	10.8g
Protein	4.9g

Serving Suggestion:

Enjoy this soup with toasted croutons and kale salad.

Ingredients:

- 4 lbs tomatoes
- 3 shallots, peeled
- 5 garlic cloves, peeled
- 2 tablespoons olive oil
- Salt and black pepper, to taste
- ½ cup raw cashews, soaked and drained
- 1 tablespoon tomato paste
- ½ cup basil leaves, packed
- 3 cups vegetable stock
- 1 tablespoon balsamic vinegar

Instructions:

1. At 350 degrees F, preheat your oven. Layer a baking sheet with parchment paper.

2. Spread the tomato pieces in the baking sheet add garlic cloves on top.

3. Add shallots around the tomato pieces.

4. Drizzle olive oil, black pepper and salt over the veggies.

5. Roast these veggies for 1 hour, then allow them to cool.

6. Blend the roasted tomatoes with cashews, tomato paste, basil, and vegetable stock in a blender until smooth.

7. Transfer this soup to a cooking pan and cook to a boil.

8. Stir in vinegar and garnish with basil and olive oil.

9. Serve warm.

286

The Plant Based Cookbook For Beginners
650 Easy, Quick, & Simple Plant Based Vegan Diet Recipes With A 31 Day Meal Plan To Lose Weight & Live A Long Healthy Life

Chickpea Salad

SERVINGS
6

PREPARATION TIME
5 minutes

COOKING TIME
0 minutes

Nutritional Values Per Serving

Calories	240
Total Fat	6.4g
Saturated Fat	1.2g
Cholesterol	0mg
Sodium	359mg
Total Carbohydrate	28.9g
Dietary Fiber	4.1g
Total Sugars	3g
Protein	5.3g

Ingredients:

- 3 cups cooked garbanzo beans
- 1 red bell pepper, diced
- 1 onion, chopped
- 1 cup vine tomatoes, chopped
- 1 cup cucumber, peeled and chopped
- 5 green onions, sliced
- 1 cup fresh mint, chopped
- 1 cup Italian parsley, chopped
- 1 garlic clove, minced
- Salt and black pepper, to taste
- ½ cup olive oil
- zest of 1 lemon
- ¼ cup lemon juice
- 1 teaspoon sumac
- ½ teaspoon cayenne chili flakes
- Black olives, to serve

Instructions:

1. Mix beans with bell pepper, cucumber and the rest of the ingredients in a salad bowl.
2. Garnish with black olives.
3. Serve.

The Plant Based Cookbook For Beginners
650 Easy, Quick, & Simple Plant Based Vegan Diet Recipes With A 31 Day Meal Plan To Lose Weight & Live A Long Healthy Life

287

Cabbage Mango Slaw

SERVINGS	PREPARATION TIME	COOKING TIME
6	10 minutes	0 minutes

Nutritional Values Per Serving

Calories	288
Total Fat	13g
Saturated Fat	2.8g
Cholesterol	0mg
Sodium	751mg
Total Carbohydrate	12.1g
Dietary Fiber	3.8g
Total Sugars	0.4g
Protein	3.2g

Serving Suggestion:

Enjoy this salad alongside with warming bowl of sweet potato soup.

Ingredients:

- 3 cups red cabbage, shredded
- 1 large mango, pitted and cubed
- ½ cup cilantro, chopped
- ¼ cup red onion, diced
- 1 jalapeno, chopped
- 2 teaspoons olive oil
- 1 orange, zest and juice
- 1 lime juice
- ½ teaspoon salt

Instructions:

1. Mix shredded cabbage with mango and the rest of the ingredients in a salad bowl.
2. Serve.

288

The Plant Based Cookbook For Beginners
650 Easy, Quick, & Simple Plant Based Vegan Diet Recipes With A 31 Day Meal Plan To Lose Weight & Live A Long Healthy Life

Quinoa Crunch Salad

SERVINGS **6**

PREPARATION TIME **10 minutes**

COOKING TIME **0 minutes**

Nutritional Values Per Serving

Calories	172
Total Fat	0.3g
Saturated Fat	0g
Cholesterol	0mg
Sodium	2mg
Total Carbohydrate	28g
Dietary Fiber	2.3g
Total Sugars	14.6g
Protein	0.8g

Ingredients:

- 4 cups cooked quinoa
- 1 cup pomegranate seeds
- 1 cup baby spinach leaves
- ½ orange, zest and juice
- ⅓ cup olive oil
- ½ radishes, sliced
- ½ teaspoon salt
- ¼ teaspoon cracked black pepper
- ¼ teaspoon cinnamon
- ¼ teaspoon allspice

Instructions:

1. Mix quinoa with spinach, and the rest of the ingredients in a salad bowl.
2. Serve fresh.

The Plant Based Cookbook For Beginners
650 Easy, Quick, & Simple Plant Based Vegan Diet Recipes With A 31 Day Meal Plan To Lose Weight & Live A Long Healthy Life

289

Roasted Root Veggies

SERVINGS	PREPARATION TIME	COOKING TIME
4	15 minutes	68 minutes

Nutritional Values Per Serving

Calories	314
Total Fat	18g
Saturated Fat	3g
Cholesterol	10mg
Sodium	54mg
Total Carbohydrate	28g
Dietary Fiber	4.8g
Total Sugars	1.9g
Protein	13g

Ingredients:

- 6 ½ lbs. Maris Piper potatoes, peeled and diced
- 16 carrots, peeled and diced
- 12 parsnips, peeled and diced
- 1 bulb of garlic, cloves separated
- 1 tablespoon olive oil
- Salt, to taste
- ½ a bunch of fresh rosemary
- ½ tablespoon red wine vinegar

Instructions:

1. At 375 degrees F, preheat your oven.
2. Add potatoes, parsnips and carrots to boiling salted water in a cooking pot for 8 minutes.
3. Drain and leave the veggies in a colander.
4. Toss garlic cloves with oil, and 1 tsp salt in two baking sheets. Spread rosemary sprigs on top.
5. Spread the veggies around and pour the red wine vinegar on top.
6. Roast these veggies for 40 minutes, squeeze the garlic flesh out and return to the roasting trays then mix well.
7. Continue cooking for 20 minutes until golden and crispy.
8. Serve.

290

The Plant Based Cookbook For Beginners
650 Easy, Quick, & Simple Plant Based Vegan Diet Recipes With A 31 Day Meal Plan To Lose Weight & Live A Long Healthy Life

Fennel Salad with Cucumber

SERVINGS	PREPARATION TIME	COOKING TIME
4	10 minutes	15 minutes

Nutritional Values Per Serving

Calories	161
Total Fat	14.7g
Saturated Fat	12.8g
Cholesterol	0mg
Sodium	161mg
Total Carbohydrate	10.3g
Dietary Fiber	2.7g
Total Sugars	2.6g
Protein	4.8g

Ingredients:

- 2 fennel bulbs, cored and sliced
- 3 Persian cucumbers, diced
- ½ cup fresh dill, chopped
- ¼ cup white onion, sliced
- ⅓ cup olive oil
- 3 tablespoons lemon juice
- Salt to taste
- Black pepper to taste

Instructions:

1. Mix fennel with the rest of the ingredients in a salad bowl.
2. Cover and refrigerate this salad for 15 minutes.
3. Serve.

The Plant Based Cookbook For Beginners
650 Easy, Quick, & Simple Plant Based Vegan Diet Recipes With A 31 Day Meal Plan To Lose Weight & Live A Long Healthy Life

291

Curry Tofu Salad

SERVINGS	PREPARATION TIME	COOKING TIME
4	10 minutes	10 minutes

Nutritional Values Per Serving	
Calories	255
Total Fat	2.5g
Saturated Fat	1.2g
Cholesterol	0mg
Sodium	340mg
Total Carbohydrate	19.7g
Dietary Fiber	1.7g
Total Sugars	3.1g
Protein	3.7g

Ingredients:

- 8 oz. tofu, cubed
- 1 tablespoon olive oil
- ¼ teaspoon salt
- 1 pinch black pepper
- ¼ cup cashews, chopped
- ½ cup celery, chopped
- ¼ cup red onion, diced
- ½ cup apple, diced
- ¼ cup cilantro, chopped
- ½ teaspoon cayenne pepper
- 3 teaspoons curry powder
- 3 tablespoons vegan mayo
- 1 tablespoon agave
- 1 tablespoon apple cider vinegar

Instructions:

1. Pat dry the tofu block and dice it into cubes.
2. Sauté these tofu cubes with oil, black pepper and salt in a skillet until golden brown.
3. Mix cilantro, cashews, celery, apple, and onions in a salad bowl.
4. Whisk vinegar, agave, mayo and spices in a bowl and add to the salad.
5. Mix well and toss in golden brown tofu.
6. Serve.

292

The Plant Based Cookbook For Beginners
650 Easy, Quick, & Simple Plant Based Vegan Diet Recipes With A 31 Day Meal Plan To Lose Weight & Live A Long Healthy Life

Farro Tabbouleh Salad

SERVINGS | **PREPARATION TIME** | **COOKING TIME**
4 | 10 minutes | 0 minutes

Nutritional Values Per Serving

Calories	238
Total Fat	3.7g
Saturated Fat	1.2g
Cholesterol	0mg
Sodium	19mg
Total Carbohydrate	25g
Dietary Fiber	3g
Total Sugars	7.4g
Protein	4g

Serving Suggestion:

Enjoy this salad alongside with warming bowl of tomato soup.

Ingredients:

- 4 cups cooked farro
- 1 bunch Italian parsley, chopped
- ¼ cup mint, chopped
- 1 English cucumber, diced
- ½ cup cherry tomatoes, cut in half
- ⅓ cup red onion, diced
- ¼ cup olive oil
- ⅛ cup lemon juice
- ¾ teaspoon kosher salt

Instructions:

1. Mix farro and the rest of the ingredients in a salad bowl.
2. Serve fresh.

The Plant Based Cookbook For Beginners
650 Easy, Quick, & Simple Plant Based Vegan Diet Recipes With A 31 Day Meal Plan To Lose Weight & Live A Long Healthy Life

293

Kohlrabi Slaw with Cilantro

SERVINGS	PREPARATION TIME	COOKING TIME
6	10 minutes	0 minutes

Nutritional Values Per Serving

Calories	182
Total Fat	4.2g
Saturated Fat	1.9g
Cholesterol	0mg
Sodium	91mg
Total Carbohydrate	14.4g
Dietary Fiber	3.5g
Total Sugars	25.6g
Protein	4.5g

Serving Suggestion:

Enjoy this salad alongside with warming bowl of broccoli soup.

Ingredients:

- 4 cups kohlrabi, cut into matchsticks
- 2 cup shredded cabbage
- 1 cucumber diced
- ½ cup cilantro, chopped
- ½ jalapeno, minced
- ¼ cup green onions, chopped
- Zest and juice from 1 orange
- Zest and juice from 1 lime

Citrus Dressing

- ¼ cup olive oil
- ¼ cup orange juice
- ⅛ cup lime juice
- ¼ cup agave
- ½ teaspoon kosher salt
- 1 tablespoon rice wine vinegar

Instructions:

1. Mix all the citrus dressing ingredients in a salad bowl.
2. Toss in kohlrabi and the rest of the ingredients, then mix well.
3. Serve.

294

The Plant Based Cookbook For Beginners
650 Easy, Quick, & Simple Plant Based Vegan Diet Recipes With A 31 Day Meal Plan To Lose Weight & Live A Long Healthy Life

Blackened Carrots

SERVINGS	PREPARATION TIME	COOKING TIME
6	15 minutes	25 minutes

Nutritional Values Per Serving	
Calories	197
Total Fat	16.8g
Saturated Fat	2.4g
Cholesterol	0mg
Sodium	71mg
Total Carbohydrate	12.6g
Dietary Fiber	1.6g
Total Sugars	8.3g
Protein	0.6g

Ingredients:

- 5 large carrots, peeled and sliced
- 2 garlic cloves, sliced
- 1 sprig of thyme
- 1½ cups olive oil
- Kosher salt, to taste
- 3 tablespoons pomegranate juice
- 3 tablespoons red wine vinegar

Garnish

- Chopped parsley leaves

Instructions:

1. At 300 degrees F, preheat your oven.
2. Toss carrots with a pinch salt, oil, pomegranate juice, vinegar, thyme, and garlic in a baking dish.
3. Cover the carrots with foil and bake for 20 minutes.
4. Uncover and bake for 5 minutes in the oven.
5. Garnish with chopped parsley.
6. Serve.

The Plant Based Cookbook For Beginners
650 Easy, Quick, & Simple Plant Based Vegan Diet Recipes With A 31 Day Meal Plan To Lose Weight & Live A Long Healthy Life

295

Thai Noodle Salad

SERVINGS	PREPARATION TIME	COOKING TIME
6	10 minutes	10 minutes

Nutritional Values Per Serving

Calories	240
Total Fat	4g
Saturated Fat	0.8g
Cholesterol	0mg
Sodium	650mg
Total Carbohydrate	19.2g
Dietary Fiber	6.5g
Total Sugars	7.7g
Protein	10.9g

Ingredients:

- 6 oz. dry rice noodles
- 4 cups mix of carrots, cabbage and radish, shredded
- 1 red bell pepper, sliced
- 3 green onions, sliced
- ½ bunch cilantro, chopped
- 1 tablespoon jalapeño, chopped
- ½ cup crushed peanuts, roasted

Thai Peanut Sauce

- 3 ginger slices
- 1 garlic clove, chopped
- ¼ cup peanut butter
- ¼ cup fresh orange juice
- 3 tablespoons fresh lime juice
- 2 tablespoons soy sauce
- 3 tablespoons agave
- 3 tablespoons toasted sesame oil
- 1 teaspoon cayenne pepper

Instructions:

1. Boil pasta as per the package's instructions, then drain.
2. For the peanut sauce, blend all the ingredients in a blender until smooth.
3. Toss pasta with all the veggies and peanut sauce in a salad bowl and mix well.
4. Serve.

296

The Plant Based Cookbook For Beginners
650 Easy, Quick, & Simple Plant Based Vegan Diet Recipes With A 31 Day Meal Plan To Lose Weight & Live A Long Healthy Life

Winter Kale Salad

SERVINGS	PREPARATION TIME	COOKING TIME
6	10 minutes	10 minutes

Nutritional Values Per Serving	
Calories	285
Total Fat	4.8g
Saturated Fat	1.3g
Cholesterol	1mg
Sodium	168mg
Total Carbohydrate	32.9g
Dietary Fiber	3.7g
Total Sugars	13.4g
Protein	4.9g

Ingredients:

- 3 cups cooked quinoa
- 1 tablespoon fennel seeds
- 1 tablespoon coriander seeds
- 1 bunch Lacinato kale, chopped
- 2 teaspoons olive oil
- 1 pinch of salt
- 1 bunch Italian parsley, chopped
- 1 large apple, chopped
- 2 green onions, chopped
- 1½ cup chickpeas
- ⅓ cup dried currants
- 1½ teaspoon lemon zest

Vinaigrette

- ⅛ cup lemon juice
- ⅛ cup apple cider vinegar
- 1 tablespoon agave
- 1 teaspoon miso paste
- ¼ teaspoon smoked paprika
- 1 teaspoon salt
- ¼ teaspoon black pepper
- ⅛ cup olive oil

Instructions:

1. Boil quinoa as per the package's instruction, drain and allow it to cool.
2. Mix all the vinaigrette ingredients in a salad bowl.
3. Toss in the rest of the ingredients for the salad then mix well.
4. Serve.

The Plant Based Cookbook For Beginners
650 Easy, Quick, & Simple Plant Based Vegan Diet Recipes With A 31 Day Meal Plan To Lose Weight & Live A Long Healthy Life

297

Pasta Salad with Asparagus

SERVINGS	PREPARATION TIME	COOKING TIME
6	10 minutes	20 minutes

Nutritional Values Per Serving

Calories	242
Total Fat	1.3g
Saturated Fat	0.1g
Cholesterol	0mg
Sodium	281mg
Total Carbohydrate	27g
Dietary Fiber	6.7g
Total Sugars	30.6g
Protein	5.3g

Ingredients:

- 8 oz. pasta
- 2 tablespoon olive oil
- 1 shallot, chopped
- 1 bunch asparagus, chopped
- Salt and black pepper, to taste
- 1 bunch Italian Parsley, chopped
- 5 green onions, chopped

Dressing

- Zest of one lemon
- 2 tablespoons lemon juice.
- 4 tablespoons olive oil
- 1 garlic clove, minced
- ¾ teaspoon salt
- Black pepper, to taste

Instructions:

1. Boil pasta as per the package's instructions then drain.
2. Sauté shallots with 2 tablespoons oil in a skillet for 3 minutes.
3. Add asparagus then cook until soft and bright green.
4. Transfer these ingredients to a salad bowl then add pasta, parsley, green onions, black pepper and salt.
5. Mix lemon zest, lemon juice and the rest of the dressing ingredients in a small bowl.
6. Pour this prepared dressing over the salad and mix well.
7. Serve.

298

The Plant Based Cookbook For Beginners
650 Easy, Quick, & Simple Plant Based Vegan Diet Recipes With A 31 Day Meal Plan To Lose Weight & Live A Long Healthy Life

Beet Salad

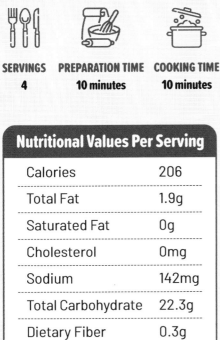

SERVINGS	PREPARATION TIME	COOKING TIME
4	10 minutes	10 minutes

Nutritional Values Per Serving

Calories	206
Total Fat	1.9g
Saturated Fat	0g
Cholesterol	0mg
Sodium	142mg
Total Carbohydrate	22.3g
Dietary Fiber	0.3g
Total Sugars	17.9g
Protein	1.1g

Ingredients:

- ⅓ cup red onion, chopped
- 1½ lbs. red beets, cooked, peeled and shredded
- 1 garlic clove, minced
- 4 tablespoons olive oil
- 2 tablespoons red wine vinegar
- 2 tablespoons orange zest
- 4 tablespoons orange juice
- 1 cup craisins
- ½ teaspoon salt
- ½ teaspoon black pepper
- 1 cup cilantro, chopped
- 1 cup walnut, chopped

Instructions:

1. Boil beets in a pan filled with boiling water until tender then drain.
2. Transfer boiled beets to a salad bowl.
3. Stir in diced onions and the rest of the ingredients then mix well.
4. Serve.

The Plant Based Cookbook For Beginners
650 Easy, Quick, & Simple Plant Based Vegan Diet Recipes With A 31 Day Meal Plan To Lose Weight & Live A Long Healthy Life

299

Curry Chickpea Salad

SERVINGS
4

PREPARATION TIME
15 minutes

COOKING TIME
5 minutes

Nutritional Values Per Serving

Calories	219
Total Fat	5.1g
Saturated Fat	1.1g
Cholesterol	0mg
Sodium	244mg
Total Carbohydrate	21.9g
Dietary Fiber	7.5g
Total Sugars	25.5g
Protein	7.2g

Ingredients:

- ½ cup shredded coconut, toasted
- ⅓ cup cashews, toasted
- 1 (14 oz.) can chickpeas, drained
- 1 cup celery, diced
- ½ cup apple, chopped
- ¼ cup red onion, diced
- ¼ cup cilantro, chopped
- 1 tablespoon orange zest
- 4 tablespoons vegan mayo
- 1 tablespoon maple syrup
- 2 teaspoons apple cider vinegar
- 3 teaspoons yellow curry powder
- ¼ teaspoon salt
- ¼ teaspoon black pepper

Instructions:

1. Toast coconut and cashews in a skillet on low heat until golden.

2. Mix chickpeas with cilantro, zest, onion, apple and celery in a bowl.

3. Stir in vinegar, maple, mayo, curry powder, black pepper and salt then mix well.

4. Add cashews and coconut then mix well.

5. Serve.

300

The Plant Based Cookbook For Beginners
650 Easy, Quick, & Simple Plant Based Vegan Diet Recipes With A 31 Day Meal Plan To Lose Weight & Live A Long Healthy Life

Fennel Asparagus Salad

SERVINGS
4

PREPARATION TIME
15 minutes

COOKING TIME
6 minutes

Nutritional Values Per Serving

Calories	160
Total Fat	2.9g
Saturated Fat	0.3g
Cholesterol	0mg
Sodium	229mg
Total Carbohydrate	12.1g
Dietary Fiber	3.8g
Total Sugars	10.6g
Protein	11.7g

Ingredients:

- 1 leek, sliced
- ⅓ cup olive oil
- 1 fennel bulb, sliced
- 6 asparagus stalks, chopped
- 1 tablespoon lemon thyme
- 2 tablespoons lemon juice
- ¾ teaspoon salt
- ½ teaspoon black pepper
- 1 teaspoon coriander
- ¼ cup toasted almonds, crushed

Instructions:

1. Sauté olive oil and leek in a skillet for 6 minutes.
2. Sprinkle salt on top, mix well and transfer to a salad bowl.
3. Toss in the rest of the ingredients and mix well.
4. Serve.

The Plant Based Cookbook For Beginners
650 Easy, Quick, & Simple Plant Based Vegan Diet Recipes With A 31 Day Meal Plan To Lose Weight & Live A Long Healthy Life

301

Poke Beets Salad

SERVINGS	PREPARATION TIME	COOKING TIME
6	10 minutes	20 minutes

Nutritional Values Per Serving

Calories	178
Total Fat	0.9g
Saturated Fat	0.1g
Cholesterol	0mg
Sodium	5mg
Total Carbohydrate	23.8g
Dietary Fiber	4.1g
Total Sugars	32.7g
Protein	2.1g

Ingredients:

- 3 cups beets, peeled and halved
- ½ teaspoon salt
- 1 cup of water
- 3 green onions, chopped
- ¼ cup cilantro, chopped
- 2 tablespoons sesame seeds, toasted

Poke Marinade

- 1 tablespoon tamari sauce
- 1 ½ tablespoon sesame oil
- 1 tablespoon rice vinegar
- 1 ½ teaspoon ginger, grated
- 2 teaspoon lime
- 3 teaspoons maple syrup
- ¼ teaspoon chili flakes

Instructions:

1. Add beet cubes, salt and water to a saucepan and cook for 20 minutes on a simmer.
2. Drain the beet cubes and transfer them to a salad bowl.
3. Toss in the rest of the ingredients and mix well.
4. Serve fresh.

302

The Plant Based Cookbook For Beginners
650 Easy, Quick, & Simple Plant Based Vegan Diet Recipes With A 31 Day Meal Plan To Lose Weight & Live A Long Healthy Life

Citrus Salad with Dates

SERVINGS	PREPARATION TIME	COOKING TIME
6	**15 minutes**	**10 minutes**

Nutritional Values Per Serving

Calories	185
Total Fat	8.2g
Saturated Fat	1.5g
Cholesterol	0mg
Sodium	72mg
Total Carbohydrate	23.6g
Dietary Fiber	4.5g
Total Sugars	51.5g
Protein	5.9g

Ingredients:

Citrus Vinaigrette

- 4 tablespoons olive oil
- 2 tablespoons vinegar
- 2 tablespoons orange juice
- 1 tablespoon lemon juice
- 1 tablespoon shallot, chopped
- ¼ teaspoon salt
- ¼ teaspoon black pepper

Orange Salad

- ¼ cup red onion, sliced
- 5 oranges, peeled and sliced
- 3 handfuls of baby arugula
- ¼ cup Medjool dates, chopped
- ¼ cup pistachios, sliced
- Mint or parsley, chopped

Instructions:

1. Mix orange juice, black pepper and rest of the citrus vinaigrette ingredients in a small bowl.
2. Toast the coconut shreds in a suitable skillet until golden brown.
3. Soak red onions in a bowl, filled with salted water then drain.
4. Toss all the veggies, dates, nuts, and oranges in a bowl.
5. Add in citrus vinaigrette then give it a mix.
6. Serve fresh.

The Plant Based Cookbook For Beginners
650 Easy, Quick, & Simple Plant Based Vegan Diet Recipes With A 31 Day Meal Plan To Lose Weight & Live A Long Healthy Life

303

Creamy Broccoli Salad

SERVINGS	PREPARATION TIME	COOKING TIME
4	15 minutes	0 minutes

Nutritional Values Per Serving

Calories	180
Total Fat	5.4g
Saturated Fat	0.6g
Cholesterol	0mg
Sodium	93mg
Total Carbohydrate	10.9g
Dietary Fiber	6.7g
Total Sugars	16.1g
Protein	9.1g

Serving Suggestion:

Try this salad with toasted whole wheat bread slices.

Ingredients:

Dressing

- 1 cup hemp seeds
- ½ cup water
- 2 tablespoons olive oil
- 4 tablespoons lemon juice
- 2 tablespoon apple cider vinegar
- 4 garlic cloves
- 1 teaspoon salt
- 2 tablespoons nutritional yeast
- ½ cup fresh parsley

Broccoli Salad

- 8 oz. broccoli, chopped
- 1 cup purple cabbage, shredded
- ¼ cup red onion, sliced
- ½ cup radishes, sliced
- 1 cup turnips, sliced

Garnish

- Sunflower seeds

Instructions:

1. Blend all the dressing ingredients in a blender until smooth.
2. Toss broccoli with cabbage, onion, radishes, and turnips in a bowl.
3. Pour the prepared dressing over the salad and mix well.
4. Garnish with seeds.
5. Serve.

304

The Plant Based Cookbook For Beginners
650 Easy, Quick, & Simple Plant Based Vegan Diet Recipes With A 31 Day Meal Plan To Lose Weight & Live A Long Healthy Life

Kale Farro Salad

SERVINGS	PREPARATION TIME	COOKING TIME
4	10 minutes	42 minutes

Nutritional Values Per Serving

Calories	137
Total Fat	14.9g
Saturated Fat	4.7g
Cholesterol	194mg
Sodium	607mg
Total Carbohydrate	20.7g
Dietary Fiber	1.4g
Total Sugars	3.3g
Protein	6.4g

Serving Suggestion:

Enjoy this salad with some cooked potatoes on the side.

Ingredients:

- 1 cup cooked farro
- 1 bunch kale chopped
- 4 tablespoons olive oil
- 1 garlic clove, minced
- 1 tablespoon lemon zest
- ½ teaspoon salt
- 1 bunch flat leaf parsley, chopped
- ¼ cup red onion, chopped
- 1 cup pomegranate seeds
- 1½ cup toasted almonds, chopped
- 1 tablespoon lemon juice
- ½ teaspoon allspice
- ½ teaspoon cinnamon

Instructions:

1. Add farro to a cooking pot, filled with salted water. And cook for 30-40 minutes.

2. Drain and transfer the farro to a salad bowl.

3. Sauté kale with oil, garlic, and lemon zest in a skillet for 2 minutes.

4. Transfer this kale to the farro and add rest of the ingredients.

5. Mix well and serve fresh.

The Plant Based Cookbook For Beginners
650 Easy, Quick, & Simple Plant Based Vegan Diet Recipes With A 31 Day Meal Plan To Lose Weight & Live A Long Healthy Life

305

Chickpea Quinoa Salad

SERVINGS	PREPARATION TIME	COOKING TIME
4	10 minutes	20 minutes

Nutritional Values Per Serving

Calories	139
Total Fat	0.2g
Saturated Fat	0.1g
Cholesterol	0mg
Sodium	568mg
Total Carbohydrate	33.6g
Dietary Fiber	2g
Total Sugars	33.6g
Protein	0.6g

Ingredients:

- ¼ cup preserved lemons, chopped
- ¼ cup olive oil
- ¼ cup lemon juice
- 2 garlic cloves, minced
- ½ teaspoon salt
- ½ teaspoon black pepper
- ½ teaspoon sumac

Chickpea Quinoa Salad

- ¾ cup quinoa, dry
- 1 ½ cups water
- 1 (15-oz.) can chickpeas, drained
- ½ cup red onion, chopped
- 1 English cucumber, diced
- 1 bell pepper, diced
- 1 cup cherry tomatoes, halved
- ¼ cup kalamata olives, chopped
- ½ cup parsley, chopped
- ¼ cup dill, chopped

Instructions:

1. Add quinoa, a pinch of salt and water to a medium-sized pot, cover and cook for 15-20 minutes until quinoa is done.
2. Remove its lid and fluff the quinoa.
3. Mix all the veggies, chickpeas and quinoa in a salad bowl.
4. Stir in the rest of the ingredients then mix well.
5. Serve warm.

CHAPTER 06

SMOOTHIES AND BEVERAGES

Turmeric Eggnog

SERVINGS	PREPARATION TIME	COOKING TIME
2	5 minutes	0 minutes

Nutritional Values Per Serving

Calories	145
Total Fat	7.1g
Saturated Fat	6g
Cholesterol	0mg
Sodium	21mg
Total Carbohydrate	21.8g
Dietary Fiber	3.7g
Total Sugars	16.7g
Protein	1.1g

Serving Suggestion:

Enjoy this eggnog with pumpkin muffins.

Ingredients:

- 1 can (13 ½ oz.) coconut milk
- 1 ½ cups water
- 3 pitted dates
- 1 teaspoon ground turmeric
- 1 teaspoon ground cinnamon
- ¼ teaspoons ground nutmeg
- ⅛ teaspoons ground allspice
- ⅛ teaspoons black pepper
- 1 tablespoon coconut oil
- 1 tablespoon maple syrup
- Coconut cream for garnish

Instructions:

1. Blend dates, water and the rest of the ingredients in a blender for 3 minutes.

2. Pour the eggnog into a saucepan and cook until it's warm.

3. Garnish with coconut cream and serve.

Pina Colada

SERVINGS	PREPARATION TIME	COOKING TIME
2	5 minutes	0 minutes

Nutritional Values Per Serving

Calories	279
Total Fat	10.8g
Saturated Fat	8.7g
Cholesterol	0mg
Sodium	26mg
Total Carbohydrate	42.2g
Dietary Fiber	0.5g
Total Sugars	29g
Protein	2.2g

Ingredients:

- 2 cups fresh pineapple juice
- 1 cup coconut cream
- 1 cup ice
- 2 tablespoons coconut sugar

Instructions:

1. Blend pineapple juice and the rest of the ingredients in a blender jug until creamy.
2. Pour into a glass and garnish with pineapple slices.
3. Serve.

The Plant Based Cookbook For Beginners
650 Easy, Quick, & Simple Plant Based Vegan Diet Recipes With A 31 Day Meal Plan To Lose Weight & Live A Long Healthy Life

309

Cashew Milk

SERVINGS	PREPARATION TIME	COOKING TIME
2	8 minutes	0 minutes

Nutritional Values Per Serving

Calories	100
Total Fat	3.1g
Saturated Fat	0.5g
Cholesterol	0mg
Sodium	5mg
Total Carbohydrate	16.2g
Dietary Fiber	0.6g
Total Sugars	12.2g
Protein	1.3g

Ingredients:

- ½ cup cashews raw
- 2 tablespoons raw maple syrup
- ½ teaspoon cinnamon
- ¾ cup water
- 1 teaspoon organic vanilla

Instructions:

1. Add cashews to a large bowl with water, and soak overnight.
2. Transfer the cashews and their liquid to a blender and add the remaining ingredients.
3. Blend well until creamy and smooth.
4. Serve.

310

The Plant Based Cookbook For Beginners
650 Easy, Quick, & Simple Plant Based Vegan Diet Recipes With A 31 Day Meal Plan To Lose Weight & Live A Long Healthy Life

Cherry Moon Milk

SERVINGS
2

PREPARATION TIME
10 minutes

COOKING TIME
5 minutes

Nutritional Values Per Serving

Calories	211
Total Fat	10.2g
Saturated Fat	2.4g
Cholesterol	0mg
Sodium	258mg
Total Carbohydrate	27.2g
Dietary Fiber	2g
Total Sugars	16.5g
Protein	4.5g

Ingredients:

- 2 cups almond milk
- ¼ cup rolled oats
- ¼ cup sweet cherries fresh
- 2 tablespoons raw walnuts
- ½ teaspoon dried lavender buds
- ¼ teaspoons ground ginger
- ¼ teaspoons ground nutmeg
- ¼ teaspoons ground turmeric
- ⅛ teaspoons sea salt
- 1 tablespoon raw maple syrup
- 1 teaspoon coconut oil

Garnish

- Lavender buds
- Turmeric
- Sliced cherries

Instructions:

1. Blend milk with oats, cherries, walnuts, lavender buds, ginger, nutmeg, turmeric and salt in a blender.

2. Transfer this mixture to a bowl and leave it for 30 minutes.

3. Strain the prepared milk and transfer it to a saucepan.

4. Place it over medium-low heat and heat until frothy.

5. Add maple syrup and coconut oil, then mix well.

6. Divide into cups and garnish with cherries, turmeric and lavender.

7. Serve.

The Plant Based Cookbook For Beginners
650 Easy, Quick, & Simple Plant Based Vegan Diet Recipes With A 31 Day Meal Plan To Lose Weight & Live A Long Healthy Life

311

Mango Lassi

SERVINGS	PREPARATION TIME	COOKING TIME
2	5 minutes	0 minutes

Nutritional Values Per Serving

Calories	181
Total Fat	3.9g
Saturated Fat	0.6g
Cholesterol	0mg
Sodium	26mg
Total Carbohydrate	32g
Dietary Fiber	3g
Total Sugars	25.5g
Protein	6.9g

Serving Suggestion:

Enjoy this lassi with mango slices and berries.

Ingredients:

- 1 cup soy yogurt
- 1 cup frozen mango chunks
- ¼ cup soy milk
- 2 Medjool dates, pitted

Instructions:

1. Blend soy yogurt with mango, milk and dates in a blender until smooth.
2. Serve.

Spiced Chai

SERVINGS	PREPARATION TIME	COOKING TIME
2	5 minutes	5 minutes

Nutritional Values Per Serving

Calories	135
Total Fat	2.2g
Saturated Fat	0.3g
Cholesterol	0mg
Sodium	64mg
Total Carbohydrate	25.5g
Dietary Fiber	1g
Total Sugars	22.3g
Protein	4.1g

Serving Suggestion:

Enjoy this spiced chia with a pumpkin muffin.

Ingredients:

- 1 cup soymilk
- 1 black tea bag
- 2 tablespoons agave
- ½ teaspoon vanilla
- ⅛ teaspoons cardamom
- ⅛ teaspoons ground cinnamon
- ⅛ teaspoons ginger
- 1 pinch of ground cloves
- 1 pinch of black pepper

Instructions:

1. Add milk, agave, vanilla, cardamom, cinnamon, ginger, cloves and black pepper in a saucepan.

2. Cook this mixture for 5 minutes on medium-high heat, then remove from the heat.

3. Add the tea bag to the milk and leave it for 10 minutes.

4. Strain the mixture and serve warm.

The Plant Based Cookbook For Beginners
650 Easy, Quick, & Simple Plant Based Vegan Diet Recipes With A 31 Day Meal Plan To Lose Weight & Live A Long Healthy Life

313

White Russian

SERVINGS	PREPARATION TIME	COOKING TIME
3	4 hours 5 minutes	0 minutes

Nutritional Values Per Serving

Calories	334
Total Fat	21.2g
Saturated Fat	4.2g
Cholesterol	0mg
Sodium	14mg
Total Carbohydrate	27.3g
Dietary Fiber	1.4g
Total Sugars	13.6g
Protein	7g

Ingredients:

Cashew Cream

- 1 cup raw cashews
- 2 cups water
- 2 tablespoons raw maple syrup
- 2 teaspoons vanilla extract

Cocktail

- 1-ounce vodka
- 1-ounce Kahlua
- 2 ounces cashew cream

Instructions:

1. Firstly, soak cashews in a large bowl filled with water for 2-4 hours, then rinse and drain.
2. Blend cashews with 1 cup water in a blender until smooth and creamy.
3. Stir in vanilla extract, raw maple syrup and 1 cup water, then blend well.
4. Add vodka, Kahlua and ice to a short cocktail glass.
5. Pour the cashew cream on top.
6. Serve.

314

The Plant Based Cookbook For Beginners
650 Easy, Quick, & Simple Plant Based Vegan Diet Recipes With A 31 Day Meal Plan To Lose Weight & Live A Long Healthy Life

Spiced Almond Milk

SERVINGS
2

PREPARATION TIME
5 minutes

COOKING TIME
3 minutes

Nutritional Values Per Serving	
Calories	344
Total Fat	33.2g
Saturated Fat	25.7g
Cholesterol	0mg
Sodium	19mg
Total Carbohydrate	13g
Dietary Fiber	3.6g
Total Sugars	8.4g
Protein	4.5g

Ingredients:

- 1 cup almond milk
- ¼ teaspoon cinnamon
- A pinch of ground ginger
- 2 teaspoons raw maple syrup
- 1 tablespoon almond butter

Instructions:

1. Mix almond milk with almond butter and the rest of the ingredients in a saucepan.
2. Cook this mixture to a boil, then remove it from the heat.
3. Pour into the serving mug.
4. Serve.

The Plant Based Cookbook For Beginners
650 Easy, Quick, & Simple Plant Based Vegan Diet Recipes With A 31 Day Meal Plan To Lose Weight & Live A Long Healthy Life

315

Coconut Orange Chai

SERVINGS	PREPARATION TIME	COOKING TIME
2	10 minutes	7 minutes

Nutritional Values Per Serving	
Calories	158
Total Fat	6.3g
Saturated Fat	3.3g
Cholesterol	0mg
Sodium	158mg
Total Carbohydrate	23.9g
Dietary Fiber	1.8g
Total Sugars	15.6g
Protein	2.8g

Ingredients:

- 2 cups almond milk
- 1 ½ cups lite coconut milk
- 4 orange slices
- 4 cinnamon sticks
- 6 cardamom pods
- 2-star anise
- 4 black peppercorns
- 6 whole cloves
- 4-5 slices of fresh ginger
- 2 tablespoons unsweetened cocoa powder
- 1 ½ tablespoon raw maple syrup
- 2 teaspoons vanilla extract

Instructions:

1. Add almond milk, 2 orange slices, spices and coconut milk to a saucepan.
2. Cook this mixture to a boil, reduce its heat and let it simmer for 5 minutes.
3. Add maple syrup, vanilla and cocoa powder to the saucepan, then cook for 2 minutes.
4. Strain out the liquid with a strainer.
5. Pour the hot chocolate into the serving mugs.
6. Garnish the drink with more orange slices and cinnamon sticks.
7. Serve warm.

Tahini Hot Chocolate

SERVINGS
2

PREPARATION TIME
5 minutes

COOKING TIME
5 minutes

Nutritional Values Per Serving

Calories	260
Total Fat	15.4g
Saturated Fat	2.1g
Cholesterol	0mg
Sodium	246mg
Total Carbohydrate	29.2g
Dietary Fiber	3.7g
Total Sugars	18.2g
Protein	5.8g

Ingredients:

- 2 cups almond milk
- 3 tablespoons tahini
- 2 tablespoons cocoa powder
- 2 tablespoons raw maple syrup
- ¼ teaspoon vanilla extract
- 1 pinch of salt

Garnish

- 3 tablespoons dark chocolate chips
- Vegan marshmallows
- Tahini

Instructions:

1. Mix almond milk with the rest of the ingredients in a saucepan and cook for 5 minutes on a simmer.

2. Pour into serving mugs and garnish with marshmallows, tahini and chocolate chips.

3. Serve.

The Plant Based Cookbook For Beginners
650 Easy, Quick, & Simple Plant Based Vegan Diet Recipes With A 31 Day Meal Plan To Lose Weight & Live A Long Healthy Life

317

Coconut Milk Hot Chocolate

SERVINGS	PREPARATION TIME	COOKING TIME
2	5 minutes	5 minutes

Nutritional Values Per Serving	
Calories	244
Total Fat	20.7g
Saturated Fat	17.6g
Cholesterol	0mg
Sodium	42mg
Total Carbohydrate	18.5g
Dietary Fiber	2g
Total Sugars	8.6g
Protein	4.2g

Serving Suggestion:

Enjoy this hot chocolate with banana bread.

Ingredients:

- 1 (15 oz.) can lite coconut milk
- ½ cup almond milk
- ⅓ cup dark chocolate chips
- 2 tablespoons cocoa powder
- ½ teaspoon vanilla extract
- 1 small pinch of salt, to taste

(Optional) Topping

- Coconut cream, coconut milk

Instructions:

1. Boil almond and coconut milk in a saucepan.
2. Stir in vanilla, cacao powder, and chocolate chips.
3. Mix well and cook for 5 minutes on a simmer.
4. Pour into the serving mugs and garnish with cream.
5. Serve.

318

The Plant Based Cookbook For Beginners
650 Easy, Quick, & Simple Plant Based Vegan Diet Recipes With A 31 Day Meal Plan To Lose Weight & Live A Long Healthy Life

Pumpkin Spice Drink

SERVINGS
2

PREPARATION TIME
5 minutes

COOKING TIME
5 minutes

Nutritional Values Per Serving

Calories	161
Total Fat	3.2g
Saturated Fat	0.4g
Cholesterol	0mg
Sodium	152mg
Total Carbohydrate	32.6g
Dietary Fiber	5.5g
Total Sugars	20.9g
Protein	3.1g

Serving Suggestion:

Enjoy this spiced drink with a pumpkin muffin.

Ingredients:

- 2 cups almond milk
- 1 ½ cups pumpkin puree
- 2 tablespoons brown sugar
- 1 ½ teaspoon pumpkin spice
- Coconut cream, for topping
- Pumpkin spice, for sprinkling

Instructions:

1. Add milk, pumpkin spice and the rest of the ingredients to a saucepan.
2. Cook this mixture to a boil, then pour into the serving cups.
3. Garnish with pumpkin spice and cream.
4. Serve.

The Plant Based Cookbook For Beginners
650 Easy, Quick, & Simple Plant Based Vegan Diet Recipes With A 31 Day Meal Plan To Lose Weight & Live A Long Healthy Life

319

Cranberry Apple Cider

SERVINGS	PREPARATION TIME	COOKING TIME
4	5 minutes	2 hours

Nutritional Values Per Serving

Calories	42
Total Fat	1g
Saturated Fat	1g
Cholesterol	0mg
Sodium	7mg
Total Carbohydrate	11g
Dietary Fiber	2g
Total Sugars	8g
Protein	1g

Ingredients:

- 64 ounces Cran-Apple Juice
- 2 cinnamon sticks
- 5 whole cloves
- 2-star anise pods
- 2 Gala apples, sliced
- ½ cup fresh cranberries

Instructions:

1. Add apple juice, cinnamon sticks, cloves, anise pods, apples and cranberries to a slow cooker.

2. Cook on High setting for 2 hours.

3. Strain and serve warm.

320

The Plant Based Cookbook For Beginners
650 Easy, Quick, & Simple Plant Based Vegan Diet Recipes With A 31 Day Meal Plan To Lose Weight & Live A Long Healthy Life

Lavender London Fog

SERVINGS
2

PREPARATION TIME
10 minutes

COOKING TIME
5 minutes

Nutritional Values Per Serving

Calories	182
Total Fat	5g
Saturated Fat	0.4g
Cholesterol	0mg
Sodium	162mg
Total Carbohydrate	17.2g
Dietary Fiber	10.7g
Total Sugars	12.3g
Protein	4.2g

Serving Suggestion:

Enjoy this London fog drink with chia seed muffins.

Ingredients:

- ¾ cup almond milk
- ½ teaspoon culinary lavender
- ¼ teaspoon pure vanilla extract
- ½ cup water
- 2 Earl grey teabags
- Raw maple syrup, to taste

Instructions:

1. Add ½ cup almond milk and lavender pods to a saucepan, cook to a boil, then leave for 5 minutes.

2. Mix ¼ cup almond milk with ½ cup water in a saucepan, cook to a boil, then add grey teabags.

3. Let this tea steep in the water for 4 minutes, then strain.

4. Pour the grey tea into the almond milk and stir in the rest of the ingredients.

5. Pour into a serving mug and enjoy.

The Plant Based Cookbook For Beginners
650 Easy, Quick, & Simple Plant Based Vegan Diet Recipes With A 31 Day Meal Plan To Lose Weight & Live A Long Healthy Life

321

Turmeric Latte

SERVINGS	PREPARATION TIME	COOKING TIME
2	5 minutes	0 minutes

Nutritional Values Per Serving

Calories	142
Total Fat	4.4g
Saturated Fat	0.1g
Cholesterol	0mg
Sodium	33mg
Total Carbohydrate	13g
Dietary Fiber	5.1g
Total Sugars	8.9g
Protein	1.9g

Serving Suggestion:

Try this latte with pumpkin muffins.

Ingredients:

- 2 cups almond milk
- 1 teaspoon turmeric powder
- ½ teaspoon ground cinnamon
- 2 tablespoons raw maple syrup

Instructions:

1. Boil almond milk in a saucepan, then add turmeric, cinnamon and raw maple syrup.

2. Mix well and cook to a boil, then froth this mixture with a milk frother.

3. Serve warm.

322

The Plant Based Cookbook For Beginners
650 Easy, Quick, & Simple Plant Based Vegan Diet Recipes With A 31 Day Meal Plan To Lose Weight & Live A Long Healthy Life

Choco Banana Chai Latte

SERVINGS
2

PREPARATION TIME
5 minutes

COOKING TIME
0 minutes

Nutritional Values Per Serving

Calories	269
Total Fat	2.8g
Saturated Fat	0.8g
Cholesterol	0mg
Sodium	75mg
Total Carbohydrate	65.2g
Dietary Fiber	5.4g
Total Sugars	45.6g
Protein	3.2g

Ingredients:

- 3 small bananas, peeled
- 1 cup almond milk
- 1 cup hot water
- 1 tea bag
- 2 tablespoons cacao powder
- 4 tablespoons coconut sugar
- ¼ teaspoons vanilla extract

Instructions:

1. Add tea bag to hot water in a bowl and leave for 10 minutes.

2. Blend bananas with the rest of the ingredients in a blender.

3. Mix all ingredients together.

4. Serve in a mug.

The Plant Based Cookbook For Beginners
650 Easy, Quick, & Simple Plant Based Vegan Diet Recipes With A 31 Day Meal Plan To Lose Weight & Live A Long Healthy Life

323

Blackberry Mulled Cider

SERVINGS	PREPARATION TIME	COOKING TIME
2	5 minutes	5 minutes

Nutritional Values Per Serving	
Calories	177
Total Fat	0.9g
Saturated Fat	0.1g
Cholesterol	0mg
Sodium	9mg
Total Carbohydrate	43g
Dietary Fiber	6.3g
Total Sugars	35.4g
Protein	1.7g

Serving Suggestion:

Enjoy this mulled cider with orange slices.

Ingredients:

- 1 ½ cups fresh blackberries
- ½ tablespoon coconut sugar
- ½ teaspoon ground cinnamon
- ¼ teaspoons ground nutmeg
- 2 cups apple cider
- 3 sprigs fresh thyme

Instructions:

1. Add blackberries, sugar, cinnamon and the rest of the ingredients to a saucepan.
2. Cook this berry mixture for 5 minutes on low heat.
3. Strain and serve.

324

The Plant Based Cookbook For Beginners
650 Easy, Quick, & Simple Plant Based Vegan Diet Recipes With A 31 Day Meal Plan To Lose Weight & Live A Long Healthy Life

White Hot Chocolate

SERVINGS
2

PREPARATION TIME
5 minutes

COOKING TIME
0 minutes

Nutritional Values Per Serving

Calories	349
Total Fat	30.2g
Saturated Fat	18.4g
Cholesterol	0mg
Sodium	149mg
Total Carbohydrate	20.1g
Dietary Fiber	0.3g
Total Sugars	12.5g
Protein	3g

Ingredients:

- 1 ½ cups coconut milk
- 1 tablespoon raw cashew butter
- 3 tablespoons shaved cocoa butter
- 2 tablespoons pure raw maple syrup
- ½ teaspoon vanilla extract
- ⅛ teaspoon sea salt, if needed
- Coconut cream, nutmeg, cinnamon

Instructions:

1. Blend coconut milk with butter, cocoa butter, raw maple syrup, and vanilla extract in a blender until smooth.
2. Garnish with cream, cinnamon, and nutmeg.
3. Serve.

The Plant Based Cookbook For Beginners
650 Easy, Quick, & Simple Plant Based Vegan Diet Recipes With A 31 Day Meal Plan To Lose Weight & Live A Long Healthy Life

325

Peppermint Hot Chocolate

SERVINGS	PREPARATION TIME	COOKING TIME
2	5 minutes	4 minutes

Nutritional Values Per Serving

Calories	285
Total Fat	15g
Saturated Fat	8.7g
Cholesterol	10mg
Sodium	173mg
Total Carbohydrate	33g
Dietary Fiber	1.4g
Total Sugars	27.6g
Protein	4.2g

Ingredients:

- 2 cups almond milk
- ½ cup dark chocolate
- 6 drops peppermint extract
- Whipped coconut cream for topping

Instructions:

1. Add almond milk, dark chocolate, peppermint extract to a saucepan.

2. Cook this mixture to a boil then reduce its heat for 4 minutes.

3. Transfer to a mug and garnish with whipped coconut cream.

4. Serve warm.

326

The Plant Based Cookbook For Beginners
650 Easy, Quick, & Simple Plant Based Vegan Diet Recipes With A 31 Day Meal Plan To Lose Weight & Live A Long Healthy Life

Matcha Latte

SERVINGS	PREPARATION TIME	COOKING TIME
2	5 minutes	0 minutes

Nutritional Values Per Serving	
Calories	157
Total Fat	14.3g
Saturated Fat	12.7g
Cholesterol	0mg
Sodium	52mg
Total Carbohydrate	8.1g
Dietary Fiber	2.3g
Total Sugars	4.5g
Protein	1.4g

Ingredients:

- 1 teaspoon matcha powder
- ¾ cup hot water
- ½ cup almond milk
- 1-2 teaspoons raw maple syrup

Instructions:

1. Blend matcha powder with hot water, almond milk and raw maple syrup in a blender.
2. Serve.

The Plant Based Cookbook For Beginners
650 Easy, Quick, & Simple Plant Based Vegan Diet Recipes With A 31 Day Meal Plan To Lose Weight & Live A Long Healthy Life

327

Boba Tea

SERVINGS	PREPARATION TIME	COOKING TIME
1	10 minutes	10 minutes

Nutritional Values Per Serving

Calories	260
Total Fat	2.5g
Saturated Fat	0g
Cholesterol	0mg
Sodium	155mg
Total Carbohydrate	58.5g
Dietary Fiber	0.3g
Total Sugars	7.3g
Protein	1.1g

Ingredients:

- ¼ cup Boba tapioca pearls
- 1 tablespoon agave syrup
- 1 tea bag
- 1 cup almond milk

Garnish

- Lemon slices, mint, fruit slices

Instructions:

1. Boil tapioca pearls in boiling water in a saucepan as per the package's directions.
2. Strain the tapioca balls and allow them to cool.
3. Heat almond milk in a saucepan to a boil and add agave syrup and tea bag.
4. Simmer this mixture for 10 minutes, then strain.
5. Stir in tapioca pearls and mix well.
6. Garnish with mint, lemon slices and fruit slices.
7. Serve.

Beetroot Latte

SERVINGS	PREPARATION TIME	COOKING TIME
2	5 minutes	0 minutes

Nutritional Values Per Serving

Calories	144
Total Fat	2.6g
Saturated Fat	0g
Cholesterol	0mg
Sodium	143mg
Total Carbohydrate	28.4g
Dietary Fiber	0g
Total Sugars	24.1g
Protein	1g

Ingredients:

- 1 tablespoon of beetroot powder
- 2 cups of almond milk
- 3 tablespoons of raw maple syrup
- 1 teaspoon of vanilla

Instructions:

1. Cook almond milk in a saucepan on medium heat for 5 minutes.
2. Add raw maple syrup, beetroot powder, and vanilla.
3. Mix well and serve.

The Plant Based Cookbook For Beginners
650 Easy, Quick, & Simple Plant Based Vegan Diet Recipes With A 31 Day Meal Plan To Lose Weight & Live A Long Healthy Life

329

Ginger Pineapple Smoothie

SERVINGS	PREPARATION TIME	COOKING TIME
2	5 minutes	0 minutes

Nutritional Values Per Serving

Calories	303
Total Fat	23g
Saturated Fat	19.8g
Cholesterol	5mg
Sodium	45mg
Total Carbohydrate	25.1g
Dietary Fiber	3.6g
Total Sugars	17.7g
Protein	3.9g

Serving Suggestion:

Enjoy this pineapple smoothie with pineapple slices.

Ingredients:

- ½ cup frozen peaches
- ½ cup frozen pineapple
- ½ cup frozen mango
- juice of 1 whole, lemon
- ½ tablespoon lemon zest
- ¾ cup unsweetened coconut milk
- 1 tablespoon grated ginger
- ½ tablespoon agave syrup

Instructions:

1. Blend peaches with pineapple and the rest of the ingredients in a blender.
2. Serve.

330

The Plant Based Cookbook For Beginners
650 Easy, Quick, & Simple Plant Based Vegan Diet Recipes With A 31 Day Meal Plan To Lose Weight & Live A Long Healthy Life

Cranberry Smoothie

SERVINGS	PREPARATION TIME	COOKING TIME
3	5 minutes	0 minutes

Nutritional Values Per Serving	
Calories	168
Total Fat	3.1g
Saturated Fat	0.2g
Cholesterol	0mg
Sodium	33mg
Total Carbohydrate	30.8g
Dietary Fiber	6.5g
Total Sugars	18.9g
Protein	2.5g

Ingredients:

- 2 cups frozen cranberries
- 2 ripe pears, cored and diced
- 2 tablespoons hemp seeds
- ¾ teaspoon fresh ginger, grated
- 1 teaspoon ground cinnamon
- 1 tablespoon pure raw maple syrup
- ¾ cup pure orange juice
- ½ cup unsweetened almond milk

Instructions:

1. Blend cranberries with pears and the rest of the ingredients in a blender.
2. Serve.

The Plant Based Cookbook For Beginners
650 Easy, Quick, & Simple Plant Based Vegan Diet Recipes With A 31 Day Meal Plan To Lose Weight & Live A Long Healthy Life

331

Raspberry Apple Smoothie

SERVINGS	PREPARATION TIME	COOKING TIME
2	5 minutes	0 minutes

Nutritional Values Per Serving

Calories	221
Total Fat	4.6g
Saturated Fat	0.4g
Cholesterol	0mg
Sodium	92mg
Total Carbohydrate	44.8g
Dietary Fiber	10g
Total Sugars	33.5g
Protein	3.1g

Ingredients:

- 1 cup frozen raspberries
- ½ apple, cored
- 1 teaspoon ground cinnamon
- 2 tablespoons whole flaxseed
- 1 cup unsweetened almond milk
- 5 drops liquid stevia

Instructions:

1. Blend raspberries with apple, cinnamon, flaxseeds, almond milk and stevia in a blender until smooth.
2. Serve.

CHAPTER 07

LUNCH RECIPES

Pita Pizzas

SERVINGS	PREPARATION TIME	COOKING TIME
6	15 minutes	35 minutes

Nutritional Values Per Serving

Calories	413
Total Fat	6.5g
Saturated Fat	1.4g
Cholesterol	0mg
Sodium	232mg
Total Carbohydrate	71.6g
Dietary Fiber	14.7g
Total Sugars	4.6g
Protein	19.9g

Ingredients:

- 1 cup onion, chopped
- 1 cup bell pepper, chopped
- 2 garlic cloves, minced
- ½ teaspoon ground cumin
- 1 (15-ounce) can black beans, rinsed
- 1 cup fresh corn kernels
- 6 (6-inch) whole-wheat pita rounds
- 1 cup avocado, pitted, peeled and chopped
- 1 cup oil-free salsa
- ¼ cup vegan cheddar, shredded
- 2 tablespoons fresh cilantro, snipped

Instructions:

1. At 350 degrees F, preheat your oven.
2. Layer 2 baking sheets with parchment paper.
3. Boil ¼ cup water in a saucepan then stir in cumin, garlic, bell pepper and onion.
4. Cook on medium-low heat for 10 minutes then add corn and beans then cook for 5 minutes.
5. Mix and lightly mash this bean mixture with a fork.
6. Place the pita round in the baking sheets and bake them for 15 minutes.
7. Add the salsa over the pita bread.
8. Spread the bean mixture and avocado on top of the pita bread.
9. Garnish with vegan cheddar, and cilantro.
10. Serve.

334

The Plant Based Cookbook For Beginners
650 Easy, Quick, & Simple Plant Based Vegan Diet Recipes With A 31 Day Meal Plan To Lose Weight & Live A Long Healthy Life

Onigiri

SERVINGS	PREPARATION TIME	COOKING TIME
4	10 minutes	0 minutes

Nutritional Values Per Serving	
Calories	391
Total Fat	1.9g
Saturated Fat	0.3g
Cholesterol	0mg
Sodium	46mg
Total Carbohydrate	33.4g
Dietary Fiber	18.7g
Total Sugars	24.8g
Protein	16.2g

Ingredients:

- 2 Cucumbers, cut into ¼-inch pieces
- Kosher salt, to taste
- 4 cups cooked sushi rice
- Toasted sesame seeds, a drizzle
- Furikake seasoning, to taste
- 2 toasted nori sheets, sliced

Instructions:

1. Mix cucumbers with salt in a bowl, rinse and drain.
2. Wet your hands and take ½ cup sticky rice to roll into a ball.
3. Flatten the ball a bit, sprinkle sesame seeds, and furikake on top.
4. Make a well at the center of the balls with your thumb and add 1 tablespoon cucumber.
5. Again, roll the rice into a ball to cover the filling then shape into a triangle.
6. Wrap a strip of nori sheet around the rice and repeat the same with the remaining rice, cucumber and nori sheet.
7. Serve.

The Plant Based Cookbook For Beginners
650 Easy, Quick, & Simple Plant Based Vegan Diet Recipes With A 31 Day Meal Plan To Lose Weight & Live A Long Healthy Life

335

Roasted Beets with Citrus

SERVINGS	PREPARATION TIME	COOKING TIME
4	10 minutes	60 minutes

Nutritional Values Per Serving

Calories	365
Total Fat	11.3g
Saturated Fat	0.6g
Cholesterol	0mg
Sodium	192mg
Total Carbohydrate	24.7g
Dietary Fiber	6.6g
Total Sugars	6.2g
Protein	7.2g

Ingredients:

- 8 medium red beets
- 1 tablespoon olive oil
- ½ cup orange juice
- ½ orange, sliced cut in half
- 1 teaspoon sherry vinegar
- Juice of ½ lemon
- 1 pinch salt
- 1 pinch black pepper
- 1 avocado, sliced

Garnish

- 2 tablespoon chopped mixed nuts

Instructions:

1. At 400 degrees F, preheat your oven.
2. Place each beet on a foil sheet piece and sprinkle salt and olive oil on top.
3. Wrap these beets and roast for 60 minutes.
4. Allow the beets to cool, uncover and peel.
5. Cut the beets into 1-inch wedges and transfer them to a bowl.
6. Mix orange juice, black pepper, lemon juice, and vinegar in a bowl.
7. Spread the beets with avocado and orange segments on a plate.
8. Drizzle orange juice mixture and chopped nuts on top.
9. Serve.

336

The Plant Based Cookbook For Beginners
650 Easy, Quick, & Simple Plant Based Vegan Diet Recipes With A 31 Day Meal Plan To Lose Weight & Live A Long Healthy Life

Hummus Quesadillas

SERVINGS	PREPARATION TIME	COOKING TIME
1	15 minutes	4 minutes

Nutritional Values Per Serving

Calories	257
Total Fat	9.5g
Saturated Fat	1g
Cholesterol	0mg
Sodium	16mg
Total Carbohydrate	20g
Dietary Fiber	9.4g
Total Sugars	48g
Protein	9.4g

Ingredients:

- 1 (8-inch) whole-grain tortilla
- ⅓ cup hummus
- Olive oil, for brushing

Serving

- Vegan sour cream
- Hot sauce
- Pesto

Instructions:

1. Divide the hummus on top of the tortilla and fold in half, then press together.
2. Set a suitable skillet over medium heat and add olive oil to heat.
3. Sear the folded tortillas for 2 minutes per side until golden brown.
4. Serve with vegan sour cream, hot sauce or pesto.

The Plant Based Cookbook For Beginners
650 Easy, Quick, & Simple Plant Based Vegan Diet Recipes With A 31 Day Meal Plan To Lose Weight & Live A Long Healthy Life

337

Tofu Spring Rolls

SERVINGS	PREPARATION TIME	COOKING TIME
10	20 minutes	10 minutes

Nutritional Values Per Serving

Calories	319
Total Fat	10.6g
Saturated Fat	3.1g
Cholesterol	131mg
Sodium	834mg
Total Carbohydrate	31.4g
Dietary Fiber	0.2g
Total Sugars	0.3g
Protein	4.6g

Serving Suggestion:

Try the rolls with sweet chili sauce and crushed peanuts.

Ingredients:

- 1 (14-ounces) block firm tofu
- 3 tablespoons vegetable oil
- v cup peanut-tamarind Sauce
- 1 large carrot, peeled and julienned
- 4 ounces pea greens
- 2 cups lettuce leaves
- 1 tablespoon toasted peanuts, Chopped
- 20 dried spring roll rice paper wrappers

Instructions:

1. Soak tofu in boiling water and strain in the colander for 1 minute.
2. Place a nonstick skillet over medium heat and add vegetable oil.
3. Pat dry the tofu and slice into 2-inch-long thick sticks.
4. Add the tofu to the hot oil and sear the tofu for 10 minutes until golden brown from all the sides.
5. Toss the seared tofu with peanut tamarind sauce in a large bowl.
6. Mix the tofu with carrots, pea greens, and peanuts in a large bowl.
7. Spread the rice wrappers on a working surface and top them with lettuce leaves.
8. Divide the tofu filling into the wrappers.
9. Wrap the rice paper around the tofu filling.
10. Serve.

No-Tuna Salad Sandwich

SERVINGS	PREPARATION TIME	COOKING TIME
4	15 minutes	4 minutes

Nutritional Values Per Serving	
Calories	307
Total Fat	7.4g
Saturated Fat	1g
Cholesterol	0mg
Sodium	255mg
Total Carbohydrate	47.3g
Dietary Fiber	11.9g
Total Sugars	9g
Protein	15g

Ingredients:

- 1 (15-ounce) can chickpeas, rinsed and drained
- 3 tablespoons tahini
- 1 teaspoon Dijon or spicy brown mustard
- 1 tablespoon raw maple syrup
- ¼ cup diced red onion
- ¼ cup diced celery
- ¼ cup diced pickle
- 1 teaspoon capers, drained and chopped
- 1 pinch sea salt
- 1 pinch black pepper
- 1 tablespoon roasted sunflower seeds

Serving

- Dijon or spicy brown mustard
- Tomato, sliced
- Whole wheat bread slices

Instructions:

1. Mash chickpeas in a mixing bowl with a fork.

2. Stir in sunflower seeds, black pepper, salt, capers, pickle, celery, red onion, raw maple syrup, mustard and tahini then mix well.

3. Divide the chickpeas mixture on top of half of the bread slices.

4. Place the tomato slices and mustard on the other two bread slices on top and press.

5. Serve.

The Plant Based Cookbook For Beginners
650 Easy, Quick, & Simple Plant Based Vegan Diet Recipes With A 31 Day Meal Plan To Lose Weight & Live A Long Healthy Life

339

Avocado Bean Salad Wraps

SERVINGS | **PREPARATION TIME** | **COOKING TIME**
8 | 5 minutes | 10 minutes

Nutritional Values Per Serving

Calories	105
Total Fat	5.5g
Saturated Fat	0.8g
Cholesterol	0mg
Sodium	277mg
Total Carbohydrate	13.5g
Dietary Fiber	6.2g
Total Sugars	1.3g
Protein	4.7g

Ingredients:

- 1½ cups cooked northern beans
- 1 tablespoon liquid aminos
- 1 tablespoon white balsamic vinegar
- 1 large avocado, pitted and mashed
- 2 tablespoons lime juice
- 2 tablespoons parsley
- 1 tablespoon diced canned green chiles
- 1 teaspoon garlic powder
- 1 teaspoon smoked paprika
- ½ teaspoon onion powder
- Salt, to taste
- Black pepper, to taste
- 2 Roma tomatoes, sliced
- 2 handfuls of baby spinach
- Tortilla wraps

Instructions:

1. Sauté beans in a suitable skillet for 2 minutes.
2. Stir in liquid aminos and cook until the liquid is absorbed.
3. Add vinegar then mix well then remove from the heat.
4. Mash avocado flesh in a large bowl
5. Stir in mashed beans, onion powder, paprika, garlic powder, green chiles, parsley, black pepper, salt and lime juice.
6. Mix well and spread the mixture over tortillas.
7. Add spinach and tomatoes on top and roll the tortillas tightly.
8. Serve.

 340

The Plant Based Cookbook For Beginners
650 Easy, Quick, & Simple Plant Based Vegan Diet Recipes With A 31 Day Meal Plan To Lose Weight & Live A Long Healthy Life

Black Bean Burgers

SERVINGS	PREPARATION TIME	COOKING TIME
6	15 minutes	15 minutes

Nutritional Values Per Serving

Calories	389
Total Fat	2.2g
Saturated Fat	0.5g
Cholesterol	0mg
Sodium	42mg
Total Carbohydrate	75.2g
Dietary Fiber	12.8g
Total Sugars	2.4g
Protein	18.6g

Serving Suggestion:

Enjoy these patties with whole-wheat buns, grilled onion rings and tomato slices.

Ingredients:

- 1 cup cooked brown rice
- 1 (15-ounce) can black beans
- ½ onion, diced
- ¼ cup corn
- 1 teaspoon cumin
- 1 teaspoon garlic powder
- ¼ teaspoon chili powder
- ¼ cup cornmeal
- 2 tablespoons salsa

Instructions:

1. At 350 degrees F, preheat your oven.
2. Sauté onion in a skillet until soft then stir in spices and corn.
3. Toss in salsa, rice and cornmeal then mix well.
4. Add rice and beans to the food processor and blend for 1-2 minutes.
5. Stir in the salsa mixture then mix for 2 minutes.
6. Layer a baking sheet with wax paper.
7. Make 4-6 patties out of this mixture and place on a baking sheet lined with parchment paper.
8. Bake the patties for 15 minutes in the preheated oven.
9. Serve warm.

The Plant Based Cookbook For Beginners
650 Easy, Quick, & Simple Plant Based Vegan Diet Recipes With A 31 Day Meal Plan To Lose Weight & Live A Long Healthy Life

341

Spinach-Potato Tacos

SERVINGS	PREPARATION TIME	COOKING TIME
12	10 minutes	33 minutes

Nutritional Values Per Serving

Calories	143
Total Fat	5.8g
Saturated Fat	4.4g
Cholesterol	0mg
Sodium	39mg
Total Carbohydrate	20.8g
Dietary Fiber	3.9g
Total Sugars	1.9g
Protein	4.6g

Serving Suggestion:

Try these tacos with avocado guacamole on top.

Ingredients:

- 2 Yukon gold potatoes, diced
- 1 (10-ounce) package spinach
- 1 large onion, diced
- 1 medium poblano pepper, seeded and diced
- 2 garlic cloves, minced
- 2 teaspoons ground cumin
- 3 tablespoons nutritional yeast
- Salt and black pepper, to taste
- 12 corn tortillas

Instructions:

1. Add potatoes and water to a saucepan and cook for 12 minutes until soft.
2. Drain and keep the potatoes aside.
3. Sauté onion with poblano pepper and 2 tablespoons water in a skillet for 7 minutes.
4. Stir in cumin and garlic then cook for 1 minute.
5. Add potatoes, spinach, yeast, black pepper and salt then cook for 3 minutes.
6. Then remove the cooked mixture from the heat and mash this mixture a little.
7. Sear the corn tortillas in a skillet for 3-5 minutes per side.
8. Divide the potato mixture on top of the corn tortillas.
9. Roll the tortillas.
10. Serve with cilantro.

342

The Plant Based Cookbook For Beginners
650 Easy, Quick, & Simple Plant Based Vegan Diet Recipes With A 31 Day Meal Plan To Lose Weight & Live A Long Healthy Life

Sweet Potato Quesadillas

SERVINGS	PREPARATION TIME	COOKING TIME
8	15 minutes	51 minutes

Nutritional Values Per Serving

Calories	324
Total Fat	4.4g
Saturated Fat	0.7g
Cholesterol	0mg
Sodium	394mg
Total Carbohydrate	59.3g
Dietary Fiber	8.1g
Total Sugars	7.3g
Protein	13.6g

Serving Suggestion:

Try these quesadillas with avocado guacamole.

Ingredients:

- 1 large sweet potato
- 1 cup brown rice, cooked
- 8 ounces re-fried beans
- 1 cup of salsa
- 1 cup fresh spinach
- 8 ounces black beans, drained and rinsed
- ¼ teaspoon onion powder
- ¼ teaspoon chili powder
- ¼ teaspoon cumin
- 1 jalapeño pepper, diced
- 8 whole-wheat tortillas

Instructions:

1. At 375 degrees F, preheat your oven.
2. Layer a sheet pan with parchment paper.
3. Peel and dice all the sweet potatoes into quarters.
4. Spread the sweet potato wedges on a baking sheet and bake for 45 minutes.
5. Add rice to a rice cooker and cook as per the package's instructions.
6. Mix the sweet potatoes with spinach, rice and salsa in a saucepan.
7. Stir in refried beans, black beans, chili powder, jalapeno pepper, cumin and onion powder.
8. Divide the sweet potatoes and black beans on only half of the tortilla and fold them.
9. Sear the tortillas roll in a greased skillet for 3 minutes per side.
10. Cut in half and garnish with salsa.
11. Repeat process for all tortillas.
12. Serve.

The Plant Based Cookbook For Beginners
650 Easy, Quick, & Simple Plant Based Vegan Diet Recipes With A 31 Day Meal Plan To Lose Weight & Live A Long Healthy Life

343

Slow-Cooker Chili

SERVINGS	PREPARATION TIME	COOKING TIME
6	10 minutes	5 hr. 15 minutes

Nutritional Values Per Serving

Calories	268
Total Fat	1.2g
Saturated Fat	0.2g
Cholesterol	0mg
Sodium	111mg
Total Carbohydrate	49.7g
Dietary Fiber	12g
Total Sugars	4.3g
Protein	15.5g

Ingredients:

- 2 cups pinto beans, rinsed
- 1 (14 ½-ounce) can fire-roasted diced tomatoes, undrained
- 1 cup red onion, chopped
- 1 (1-ounce) vegetarian chili seasoning
- 6 garlic cloves, minced
- 4 cups vegetable stock
- 2 cups water
- 1 cup fresh whole kernel corn

Toppings

- Tortilla chips

Instructions:

1. Add beans and all other ingredients, except corn to a slow cooker.
2. Cover and cook this bean chili for 5 hours on high heat.
3. Stir in corn then cook for 15 minutes and mix well.
4. Garnish with bell pepper, cilantro, and green onions.
5. Serve warm.

344

The Plant Based Cookbook For Beginners
650 Easy, Quick, & Simple Plant Based Vegan Diet Recipes With A 31 Day Meal Plan To Lose Weight & Live A Long Healthy Life

Sweet Potato Chili with Kale

SERVINGS
4

PREPARATION TIME
10 minutes

COOKING TIME
43 minutes

Nutritional Values Per Serving

Calories	391
Total Fat	1.9g
Saturated Fat	0.3g
Cholesterol	0mg
Sodium	46mg
Total Carbohydrate	83.4g
Dietary Fiber	18.7g
Total Sugars	24.8g
Protein	16.2g

Ingredients:

- 2 medium sweet potatoes, diced
- 1 large red onion, chopped
- 2 (15 ounce) cans beans
- 2 red bell peppers, seeded and diced
- 2 pounds fresh tomatoes, diced
- 1 tablespoon chili powder
- 2 teaspoons smoked paprika
- ¼ teaspoon chipotle powder
- 2 cups Lacinato kale, shredded
- 4 cups vegetable stock
- 1 cup of orange juice

Instructions:

1. Sauté onion with bell pepper and orange juice in a pot for 10 minutes.
2. Stir in the rest of the ingredients, reserving the kale and cook for 30 minutes on medium heat.
3. Mash the cooked mixture a little then add kale.
4. Cook for 3 minutes then serve warm.

The Plant Based Cookbook For Beginners
650 Easy, Quick, & Simple Plant Based Vegan Diet Recipes With A 31 Day Meal Plan To Lose Weight & Live A Long Healthy Life

345

Potato-Cauliflower Curry

SERVINGS	PREPARATION TIME	COOKING TIME
4	15 minutes	39 minutes

Nutritional Values Per Serving

Calories	505
Total Fat	6.6g
Saturated Fat	1.1g
Cholesterol	0mg
Sodium	130mg
Total Carbohydrate	94.9g
Dietary Fiber	17.7g
Total Sugars	18.7g
Protein	20.7g

Ingredients:

- 4 cups cauliflower florets
- 2 cups potato pieces, cubed
- 1 jalapeno, cubed
- ¼ cup tomato, chopped
- 1 cup onion wedges
- ¼ cup tomato paste
- 1 tablespoon mild curry powder
- 1½ teaspoon fresh ginger, grated
- 1 teaspoon cumin seeds
- 1 garlic clove, minced
- ¼ cup raw cashews, ground
- 2 tablespoons lime juice
- Cayenne pepper, to taste
- Sea salt, to taste
- 1 tablespoon fresh cilantro, snipped

Instructions:

1. Add cauliflower to a steamer basket, cover and cook for 5 minutes.

2. Transfer the cauliflower to a bowl.

3. Add potato pieces to the steamer and cook for 10 minutes.

4. Transfer these potatoes to the cauliflower then mix well.

5. Blend onion wedges with garlic, cumin seeds, ginger, curry powder, and tomato paste in a blender.

6. Pour this mixture into a skillet along with 1 cup water and cook for 7 minutes.

7. Reduce its heat to medium-low heat and cook for 10 minutes until the sauce thickens.

8. Add potatoes, bell peppers, cauliflower and the rest of the ingredients.

9. Mix well and cook for 7 minutes.

10. Garnish and serve warm.

(346)

The Plant Based Cookbook For Beginners
650 Easy, Quick, & Simple Plant Based Vegan Diet Recipes With A 31 Day Meal Plan To Lose Weight & Live A Long Healthy Life

Zucchini and Chickpea Sauté

SERVINGS
6

PREPARATION TIME
10 minutes

COOKING TIME
25 minutes

Nutritional Values Per Serving

Calories	317
Total Fat	5.6g
Saturated Fat	0.5g
Cholesterol	0mg
Sodium	209mg
Total Carbohydrate	54g
Dietary Fiber	14.9g
Total Sugars	13.1g
Protein	15.5g

Serving Suggestion:

Enjoy this chickpea saute with rice.

Ingredients:

- 1 onion, chopped
- 1 large red bell pepper, chopped
- 6 garlic cloves, minced
- 1 teaspoon dried oregano
- ½ teaspoon dried thyme
- 1 cup oil-free marinara sauce
- 1 tablespoon white wine vinegar
- Salt and black pepper, to taste
- 3 medium zucchinis, halved lengthwise and sliced
- 1 15-ounces can chickpeas, rinsed and drained
- 10 fresh basil leaves, chopped

Instructions:

1. Sauté onion, bell pepper, garlic, oregano, and thyme in a greased skillet for 10 minutes.
2. Stir in zucchini and cook for 10 minutes.
3. Stir in vinegar, marinara sauce, black pepper, salt and chickpeas.
4. Cook the mixture for 5 minutes then garnish with basil.
5. Serve warm.

The Plant Based Cookbook For Beginners
650 Easy, Quick, & Simple Plant Based Vegan Diet Recipes With A 31 Day Meal Plan To Lose Weight & Live A Long Healthy Life

347

Gazpacho Soup

SERVINGS	PREPARATION TIME	COOKING TIME
6	10 minutes	0 minutes

Nutritional Values Per Serving

Calories	215
Total Fat	3.2g
Saturated Fat	0.1g
Cholesterol	0mg
Sodium	310mg
Total Carbohydrate	20.9g
Dietary Fiber	2.8g
Total Sugars	29g
Protein	6.8g

Serving Suggestion:

Enjoy this soup with sprouts on top.

Ingredients:

- 1 cup red onion, diced
- 1 cucumber, peeled, seeded, and diced
- 6 vine-ripened tomatoes, peeled and seeded
- 1 red bell pepper, seeded and diced
- 2 garlic cloves, minced
- 2 cups tomato juice
- 5 drops hot sauce
- 3 teaspoons balsamic vinegar
- 2 teaspoons vegan Worcestershire sauce
- ¼ cup olive oil
- salt and black pepper to taste

Instructions:

1. Blend ¼ cucumbers with red peppers and red onions in a food processor.
2. Stir in the rest of the ingredients and blend until pureed.
3. Serve.

348

The Plant Based Cookbook For Beginners
650 Easy, Quick, & Simple Plant Based Vegan Diet Recipes With A 31 Day Meal Plan To Lose Weight & Live A Long Healthy Life

Mushroom Asada Tacos

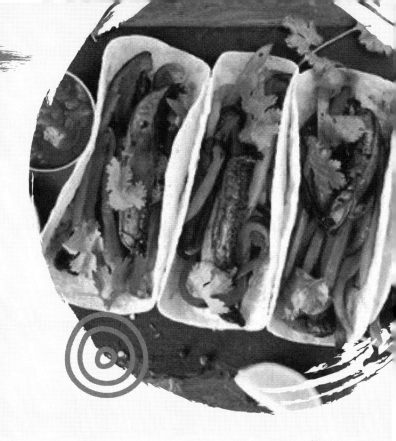

SERVINGS
12

PREPARATION TIME
15 minutes

COOKING TIME
22 minutes

Nutritional Values Per Serving

Calories	194
Total Fat	19.3g
Saturated Fat	14g
Cholesterol	0mg
Sodium	22mg
Total Carbohydrate	21.5g
Dietary Fiber	3.7g
Total Sugars	10.3g
Protein	13.1g

Serving Suggestion:

Enjoy these tacos with avocado and guacamole.

Ingredients:

- 6 tablespoons of orange juice
- ¼ cup cilantro, chopped
- 2 tablespoons soy sauce
- 1 ½ teaspoon ground cumin
- 1 ½ teaspoon smoked paprika
- ¼ large white onion, chopped
- 3 garlic cloves, minced
- 1 chipotle chile canned in adobo sauce
- 1 jalapeño, chopped
- Juice of ½ lemon
- 6 tablespoons olive oil
- 1 lb cremini mushrooms, stemmed and sliced
- 12 (6-inch) corn tortillas
- 2 cups mixed bell peppers, julienned
- 3 limes, quartered
- Cilantro, to garnish

Instructions:

1. Blend the first 11 ingredients in a food processor.
2. Pour this marinade over the mushrooms in a bowl and leave for 30 minutes.
3. At 350 degrees F, preheat your oven.
4. Sauté mushrooms with oil in a suitable skillet for 7 minutes.
5. Cover the tortillas with foil and warm in the oven for 15 minutes.
6. Spread the tortillas on the working surface and divide the bell peppers and mushrooms on top.
7. Garnish with lime wedges and cilantro.
8. Serve.

The Plant Based Cookbook For Beginners
650 Easy, Quick, & Simple Plant Based Vegan Diet Recipes With A 31 Day Meal Plan To Lose Weight & Live A Long Healthy Life

349

Mediterranean Pinwheels

SERVINGS
8

PREPARATION TIME
10 minutes

COOKING TIME
0 minutes

Nutritional Values Per Serving

Calories	233
Total Fat	7.6g
Saturated Fat	18g
Cholesterol	0mg
Sodium	130mg
Total Carbohydrate	21.6g
Dietary Fiber	12.9g
Total Sugars	16.2g
Protein	14.4g

Ingredients:

Tahini Sauce

- 3 tablespoons tahini paste
- 3 tablespoons lemon juice
- 4 tablespoons white vinegar
- ½ cup water
- 1 garlic clove
- Salt and black pepper to taste

Pinwheels

- 2 tablespoons olives sliced
- 4 Cherry tomatoes, sliced
- 1 cup Artichokes in a jar
- 2 lettuce leaves
- 2 whole wheat Tortillas

Instructions:

1. Blend all the tahini sauce ingredients in a blender until creamy.
2. Spread tahini sauce over the tortillas and top it with tomatoes, artichokes, lettuces and olives.
3. Roll the tortillas and cut into pinwheels.
4. Slice and serve.

350

The Plant Based Cookbook For Beginners
650 Easy, Quick, & Simple Plant Based Vegan Diet Recipes With A 31 Day Meal Plan To Lose Weight & Live A Long Healthy Life

Raw Collard Wraps

SERVINGS
4

PREPARATION TIME
10 minutes

COOKING TIME
0 minutes

Nutritional Values Per Serving

Calories	293
Total Fat	5.2g
Saturated Fat	1g
Cholesterol	0mg
Sodium	413mg
Total Carbohydrate	13.2g
Dietary Fiber	5.3g
Total Sugars	8.1g
Protein	6g

Serving Suggestion:

Try these wraps with sprouts on top.

Ingredients:

- 4 large collard leaves
- 1 red bell pepper, julienned
- 1 avocado. sliced
- 3 ounces alfalfa sprouts
- ½ lime, juiced
- 1 cup raw pecans, chopped
- 1 tablespoon tamari
- ½ teaspoon garlic, minced
- ½ teaspoon ginger, grated
- 1 teaspoon olive oil

Instructions:

1. Soak the collard leaves in warm water for 10 minutes then drain.
2. Puree pecans with olive oil, ginger, garlic, and tamari and in a blender.
3. Spread the collard leaf on the working surface and top them with the pecan's mixture.
4. Divide the avocado slices, red pepper slices and alfalfa sprouts on top.
5. Drizzle the lime juice on top and roll the leaves.
6. Cut the roll in half and serve.

The Plant Based Cookbook For Beginners
650 Easy, Quick, & Simple Plant Based Vegan Diet Recipes With A 31 Day Meal Plan To Lose Weight & Live A Long Healthy Life

351

Tofu Lettuce Cups

SERVINGS	PREPARATION TIME	COOKING TIME
4	10 minutes	6 minutes

Nutritional Values Per Serving	
Calories	302
Total Fat	11.5g
Saturated Fat	1g
Cholesterol	0mg
Sodium	16mg
Total Carbohydrate	26g
Dietary Fiber	9.4g
Total Sugars	27g
Protein	9.4g

Ingredients:

- 2 ounces thin rice noodles
- ¼ cup water
- 5 teaspoons vegan fish sauce
- 2 tablespoons lime juice
- 1 tablespoon sugar
- ½-1 teaspoon crushed red pepper
- 8 ounces firm tofu, cut into triangle slices.
- ½ cup mushrooms, sliced
- ½ cup carrot, chopped
- ¼ cup chopped fresh basil
- ¼ cup chopped fresh mint
- 8 large leaves green-leaf lettuce

Instructions:

1. Boil rice noodles with water in a pan until soft then drain.
2. Mix lime juice, fish sauce, sugar and red pepper to a bowl.
3. Place the tofu slices in this mixture and rub well to coat.
4. Transfer the tofu to a plate.
5. Add mushrooms, carrots and remaining marinade to a pan and cook for 2-3 minutes.
6. Stir in noodles, basil and mint then mix well.
7. Divide the noodle mixture in the lettuce leaves.
8. Top each lettuce leave with 2-3 tofu triangles.
9. Serve.

352

The Plant Based Cookbook For Beginners
650 Easy, Quick, & Simple Plant Based Vegan Diet Recipes With A 31 Day Meal Plan To Lose Weight & Live A Long Healthy Life

Pita Pockets with Roasted Veggies

SERVINGS
4

PREPARATION TIME
10 minutes

COOKING TIME
35 minutes

Nutritional Values Per Serving

Calories	210
Total Fat	2.8g
Saturated Fat	0½g
Cholesterol	0mg
Sodium	109mg
Total Carbohydrate	22.9g
Dietary Fiber	5.9g
Total Sugars	14.4g
Protein	4.9g

Ingredients:

Pita Pockets

- 1 eggplant, cut into sticks
- 2 carrots, julienned
- 1 red bell pepper, julienned
- 1 teaspoon Ras-el-Hanout
- 1 teaspoon turmeric
- ½ teaspoon sweet paprika
- ¼ teaspoon black pepper
- ¼ teaspoon salt
- 4 whole grain pita bread
- 1 cup hummus
- 1 handful baby spinach
- Vegan Feta cheese, crumbled
- Chopped parsley, to garnish

Hummus

- 1 cup cooked chickpeas
- juice of ½ lemon
- 1½ tablespoon tahini paste
- 1 small garlic clove
- 3 tablespoons olive oil
- ½ teaspoon ground cumin
- ½ teaspoon Ras-el-Hanout
- ½ teaspoon turmeric
- ¼ teaspoon sweet paprika
- a dash of chili flakes
- 2 tablespoons water
- Salt and black pepper to taste

Instructions:

1. At 400 degrees F, preheat your oven.

2. Toss eggplant with bell peppers and carrots on a baking sheet and add black pepper, spices, and salt then bake for 25 minutes.

3. Blend all the ingredients for hummus in a blender until smooth.

4. Place the pita breads on a baking sheet and bake as per package's instruction.

5. Stuff each pita pocket with 2 tablespoons hummus, spinach and roasted veggies.

6. Garnish with parsley, and crumbled vegan cheese.

7. Serve.

The Plant Based Cookbook For Beginners
650 Easy, Quick, & Simple Plant Based Vegan Diet Recipes With A 31 Day Meal Plan To Lose Weight & Live A Long Healthy Life

353

Spinach Pepper Wraps

SERVINGS	PREPARATION TIME	COOKING TIME
2	10 minutes	5 minutes

Nutritional Values Per Serving

Calories	311
Total Fat	11g
Saturated Fat	0.9g
Cholesterol	0mg
Sodium	8mg
Total Carbohydrate	24g
Dietary Fiber	9.1g
Total Sugars	10.4g
Protein	14g

Ingredients:

- 1 cup mixed bell peppers, julienned
- 1 cup spinach
- 1 cup tofu cubes
- 2 tortilla wraps
- 2 tablespoons olive oil.
- Salt and black pepper to taste

Instructions:

1. Sauté tofu cubes with black pepper, salt and oil in a skillet for 5 minutes.
2. Spread the tortillas on a working surface.
3. Top the tortilla with spinach leaves.
4. Divide the bell peppers and tofu on top.
5. Roll the tortilla and cut in half.
6. Serve.

Veggie Sushi Rolls

SERVINGS	PREPARATION TIME	COOKING TIME
6	**10 minutes**	**10 minutes**

Nutritional Values Per Serving

Calories	221
Total Fat	4.7g
Saturated Fat	2½g
Cholesterol	1mg
Sodium	87mg
Total Carbohydrate	21.7g
Dietary Fiber	4.2g
Total Sugars	17.7g
Protein	4.6g

Serving Suggestion:

Enjoy these sushi rolls with tamari sauce.

Ingredients:

- ¼ cup white rice
- ¼ teaspoon apple cider vinegar
- ¼ cup cabbage, chopped
- ¼ cup kale, chopped
- ¼ cup radish, julienned
- 2 tablespoons jalapeno, finely chopped
- ¼ cup red pepper, julienned
- ¼ cup jicama, julienned
- ¼ cup cucumber, julienned
- ¼ cup avocado, julienned
- 1 pack of seaweed wraps
- 1 small bowl of water for wrappers

Instructions:

1. Prepare the rice as per the package's instructions.
2. Mix ¼ cup rice with ¼ teaspoons apple cider vinegar.
3. Place the seaweed rectangles on the working surface.
4. Divide the rice and veggies over the seaweed.
5. Roll the seaweed carefully and wet the edges with water.
6. Seal the roll edges and serve.

The Plant Based Cookbook For Beginners
650 Easy, Quick, & Simple Plant Based Vegan Diet Recipes With A 31 Day Meal Plan To Lose Weight & Live A Long Healthy Life

355

Butternut Squash Lasagna

SERVINGS	PREPARATION TIME	COOKING TIME
6	15 minutes	1 hr. 36 minutes

Nutritional Values Per Serving

Calories	278
Total Fat	2.7g
Saturated Fat	0½g
Cholesterol	0mg
Sodium	157mg
Total Carbohydrate	24.4g
Dietary Fiber	4g
Total Sugars	5.8g
Protein	5.6g

Ingredients:

- 2 tablespoons olive oil
- 2 pounds butternut squash, cubed
- ½ cup water
- 4 amaretti cookies, crumbled
- 8 ounces shiitake mushrooms, sliced
- ¼ cup vegan butter
- ¼ cup whole-wheat flour
- 3 ½ cups almond milk
- ½ teaspoon ground nutmeg
- 1 cup fresh basil leaves
- 13 ounces DeLillo no-boil lasagna noodles
- 3 cups vegan cheese, shredded
- Salt and black pepper, to taste

Instructions:

1. At 375 degrees F, preheat your oven.
2. Sauté squash with black pepper, salt and oil in a skillet for 5 minutes.
3. Add water to the squash, cover and cook for about 20 minutes on medium heat.
4. Blend the squash with amaretti in a blender until smooth.
5. Sauté mushrooms with oil and ¼ teaspoons salt in a skillet for 10 minutes.
6. Mix butter with flour in a skillet for 1 minute.
7. Pour in milk, mix well until lump-free then boil the mixture.
8. Stir in black pepper, nutmeg and ¼ teaspoons salt.
9. Mix well then cook for about 5 minutes until the sauce thickens.
10. Add basil and blend the sauce with a blender.
11. Grease a 13x9 inch baking dish with vegan butter.
12. Spread ¾ cup sauce in the baking dish.
13. Arrange the lasagna noodles at the bottom of this dish.
14. Top the noodles with 1/3 squash puree and add 1/3 mushrooms on top.
15. Sprinkle 1 cup vegan cheese on top.
16. Repeat all the layers and cover this dish with a last layer of noodles and cheese then cover with a foil sheet.
17. Bake the prepared lasagna for 40 minutes in the oven.
18. Remove the tin foil from the top and bake for another 15 minutes.
19. Serve warm.

356

The Plant Based Cookbook For Beginners
650 Easy, Quick, & Simple Plant Based Vegan Diet Recipes With A 31 Day Meal Plan To Lose Weight & Live A Long Healthy Life

Vegetarian Pancit Bihon

SERVINGS
6

PREPARATION TIME
10 minutes

COOKING TIME
10 minutes

Nutritional Values Per Serving

Calories	214
Total Fat	4.9g
Saturated Fat	0.7g
Cholesterol	0mg
Sodium	240mg
Total Carbohydrate	23.1g
Dietary Fiber	14.3g
Total Sugars	13.1g
Protein	10.1g

Ingredients:

- 4 cups vegetable stock
- 8 ounces Bihon noodles
- 2 tablespoons canola oil
- 1 medium onion, diced
- 3 garlic cloves, crushed
- 1 red bell pepper, julienned
- 6 ounces firm tofu, sliced
- 3 tablespoons soy sauce
- 1 tablespoon vegan fish sauce
- Black pepper, to taste
- 1 ½ Chinese cabbage, shredded
- 3 carrots julienne cut
- 2 stalks of celery, sliced
- 1 cup green beans
- Cilantro, for garnish
- Lemon wedges, for garnish

Instructions:

1. Boil noodles with stock in a large pot for 3 minutes.
2. Drain the noodles and allow them to cool.
3. Sauté garlic and onion with oil in a skillet until soft.
4. Stir in tofu, black pepper, fish sauce, soy sauce and all the vegetables.
5. Sauté until the veggies are soft then add noodles and cook for 5 minutes.
6. Garnish with lemon juice and cilantro.
7. Serve warm.

The Plant Based Cookbook For Beginners
650 Easy, Quick, & Simple Plant Based Vegan Diet Recipes With A 31 Day Meal Plan To Lose Weight & Live A Long Healthy Life

357

Spiralized Vegetable Lo Mein

SERVINGS	PREPARATION TIME	COOKING TIME
4	15 minutes	10 minutes

Nutritional Values Per Serving

Calories	280
Total Fat	2.4g
Saturated Fat	0g
Cholesterol	0mg
Sodium	99mg
Total Carbohydrate	21.7g
Dietary Fiber	10.2g
Total Sugars	49.7g
Protein	2.3g

Ingredients:

- 2 tablespoons soy sauce
- 1 teaspoon sesame oil
- 1" peeled ginger, minced
- 2 teaspoons agave
- ¼ teaspoon red pepper flakes
- 1 tablespoon olive oil
- 2 garlic cloves, minced
- ½ cup snow peas
- 1 red bell pepper, julienned
- 1 large carrot, spiralized
- 4 medium zucchinis, spiralized
- 3 cups baby spinach
- 1 tablespoon arrowroot powder
- Sesame seeds, to garnish
- Crushed peanuts, to garnish

Instructions:

1. Mix red pepper flakes, agave, ginger, sesame oil, soy sauce in a small bowl.
2. Sauté zucchini noodles, carrot noodles, bell pepper, snow peas and garlic with olive oil in a skillet for 5 minutes.
3. Stir in spinach and soy sauce mixture, then cook for 3 minutes.
4. Mix arrowroot powder with 2 tablespoons water and pour into the noodles.
5. Mix well and cook for 2 minutes until the mixture thickens.
6. Garnish with sesame seeds and crushed peanuts.
7. Serve warm.

358

The Plant Based Cookbook For Beginners
650 Easy, Quick, & Simple Plant Based Vegan Diet Recipes With A 31 Day Meal Plan To Lose Weight & Live A Long Healthy Life

Kimchi Cauliflower Rice

SERVINGS
4

PREPARATION TIME
10 minutes

COOKING TIME
9 minutes

Nutritional Values Per Serving

Calories	278
Total Fat	2.4g
Saturated Fat	0.1g
Cholesterol	0mg
Sodium	291mg
Total Carbohydrate	29.4g
Dietary Fiber	3.7g
Total Sugars	13.2g
Protein	6.4g

Serving Suggestion:

Try the rice with roasted tofu slices on top.

Ingredients:

- 3 green onions, sliced
- 1 ½ cup kimchi, chopped
- 1 tablespoon kimchi juice from jar
- 3 ¼ cup cauliflower rice
- ¾ cup cooked edamame
- 2 teaspoons soy sauce
- 2 teaspoons sesame oil

Instructions:

1. Sauté green onion in a suitable skillet for 2 minutes.
2. Stir in kimchi juice and kimchi then sauté for 2 minutes.
3. Then add cauliflower rice and cook for 2 minutes.
4. Stir in sesame oil, soy sauce and edamame then cook for 3 minutes.
5. Add green onion and serve.

The Plant Based Cookbook For Beginners
650 Easy, Quick, & Simple Plant Based Vegan Diet Recipes With A 31 Day Meal Plan To Lose Weight & Live A Long Healthy Life

359

Eggplant Parmesan

SERVINGS	PREPARATION TIME	COOKING TIME
4	15 minutes	30 minutes

Nutritional Values Per Serving

Calories	339
Total Fat	1.1g
Saturated Fat	0.3g
Cholesterol	0mg
Sodium	16mg
Total Carbohydrate	29.4g
Dietary Fiber	5g
Total Sugars	3.2g
Protein	14g

Ingredients:

- 1 medium eggplant
- ¼ cup whole-wheat flour
- 1 cup panko bread crumbs
- 2 tablespoons vegan parmesan, shredded
- 1 teaspoon dried oregano
- ¼ teaspoons sea salt
- ½ cup almond milk
- 1 teaspoon cornstarch
- Vegan cheese, shredded

Sauce

- 2 cups marinara sauce

Instructions:

1. Cut the eggplant into ½ inch thick slices and place them in a colander and rinse.
2. Sprinkle salt over the eggplant and leave them for 15 minutes.
3. At 400 degrees F, preheat your oven.
4. Layer a baking sheet with foil sheet.
5. Mix cornstarch with almond milk in a bowl.
6. Whisk breadcrumbs with vegan parmesan, oregano and salt in a bowl.
7. First dip the eggplant slice in the flour, then coat with the almond milk mixture and finally coat with the breadcrumbs.
8. Place the eggplant slices in the baking sheet and bake for 30 minutes.
9. Flip the eggplant slices once cooked halfway through.
10. Spread the marinara sauce in a baking and place the eggplant slices on top.
11. Sprinkle cheese on top and bake for 5 minutes.
12. Serve warm.

Thai Coconut Cauliflower

SERVINGS
4

PREPARATION TIME
10 minutes

COOKING TIME
40 minutes

Nutritional Values Per Serving

Calories	306
Total Fat	0.1g
Saturated Fat	0g
Cholesterol	0mg
Sodium	176mg
Total Carbohydrate	13.6g
Dietary Fiber	3½g
Total Sugars	1.3g
Protein	3.6g

Serving Suggestion:

Enjoy the curry with warmed tortillas or boiled white rice.

Ingredients:

- 2 cauliflower heads, cut into floret
- 1 can coconut milk
- 2 tablespoons vegan fish sauce
- 2 tablespoons sweet mirin
- 3 tablespoons shredded coconut
- Zest of 1 lime
- Coriander, to garnish

Instructions:

1. Mix sweet mirin, fish sauce, coconut milk and cauliflower in a large saucepan.
2. Cook this mixture to a boil then reduce its heat and cook for 20 minutes.
3. Stir in shredded coconut then cook for 15 minutes.
4. Garnish with lime zest and coriander.
5. Serve warm.

The Plant Based Cookbook For Beginners
650 Easy, Quick, & Simple Plant Based Vegan Diet Recipes With A 31 Day Meal Plan To Lose Weight & Live A Long Healthy Life

361

Grilled Zucchini with Pine Nuts

SERVINGS	PREPARATION TIME	COOKING TIME
4	10 minutes	6 minutes

Nutritional Values Per Serving

Calories	201
Total Fat	2.4g
Saturated Fat	0.7g
Cholesterol	0mg
Sodium	303mg
Total Carbohydrate	10.8g
Dietary Fiber	5.8g
Total Sugars	12.7g
Protein	5g

Ingredients:

- 4 medium zucchinis
- Olive oil, to taste
- ½ teaspoon salt and black pepper
- Zest of ½ lemon
- Juice of ½ lime
- 3 ounces coconut shavings
- ¼ cup toasted pine nuts
- ⅛ cup parsley leaves, chopped

Instructions:

1. Set the grill over medium heat.
2. Cut the zucchini into ¼ inch thick strips.
3. Mix the zucchini with black pepper, salt and oil.
4. Sauté pine nuts with oil in a skillet for 4 minutes then transfer to a plate.
5. Grill the zucchini for 3 minutes per side.
6. Place the grilled zucchini in a plate and top it with pine nuts, lemon zest, lime juice, olive oil, coconut shavings and parsley.
7. Enjoy.

Chickpea Salad Bites

SERVINGS
4

PREPARATION TIME
15 minutes

COOKING TIME
0 minutes

Nutritional Values Per Serving

Calories	356
Total Fat	13.6g
Saturated Fat	9.1g
Cholesterol	0mg
Sodium	420mg
Total Carbohydrate	37.6g
Dietary Fiber	7.1g
Total Sugars	19.9g
Protein	7g

Ingredients:

Bread

- 1 ½ cups whole grain rye bread, crumbled
- ⅓ cup of raisins
- 1 small chili pepper
- 2 tablespoons fresh parsley, chopped
- 2 tablespoons balsamic vinegar
- ½ tablespoon raw maple syrup
- 1 teaspoon garlic powder
- ½ teaspoon smoked paprika
- ½ teaspoon cayenne pepper
- Salt and black pepper, to taste

Salad

- 1 can of chickpeas
- 2 green onions, chopped
- ⅓ cup of pickles, chopped
- ⅓ cup of soy yogurt
- 1 teaspoon mustard
- 1 garlic clove, minced
- 1 lemon, juice
- 2 tablespoons fresh chives, chopped
- Salt and black pepper, to taste

Instructions:

1. Mix raisins with crumbled bread, mustard, spices, raw maple syrup, vinegar, parsley, and chili pepper in a food processor and blend.

2. Divide the mixture into 4-6 equal portions and shape them into a thick bread slice.

3. Mix chickpeas with pickles, chives, and garlic in a large bowl.

4. Stir in black pepper, salt, lemon juice, yogurt and green onions.

5. Mix well and divide on top of the bread slices.

6. Serve.

The Plant Based Cookbook For Beginners
650 Easy, Quick, & Simple Plant Based Vegan Diet Recipes With A 31 Day Meal Plan To Lose Weight & Live A Long Healthy Life

363

Rainbow Taco Boats

SERVINGS	PREPARATION TIME	COOKING TIME
4	10 minutes	0 minutes

Nutritional Values Per Serving

Calories	223
Total Fat	1.4g
Saturated Fat	0.4g
Cholesterol	0mg
Sodium	159mg
Total Carbohydrate	26g
Dietary Fiber	6.6g
Total Sugars	6.2g
Protein	7.2g

Ingredients:

- 1 head romaine lettuce, leaves separated

Filling

- ½ cup hummus
- ½ cup halved cherry tomatoes
- ½ cup boiled quinoa
- 1 cup carrots, chopped
- ¾ cup cabbage, chopped
- ½ onion, chopped
- 1 green onion, chopped
- Sweet chili sauce

Instructions:

1. Arrange the lettuce boats in the serving plate.
2. Spread the hummus in the lettuce boats.
3. Mix quinoa and rest of the veggies in a bowl.
4. Divide the veggies mixture in the boats.
5. Serve with sweet chili sauce.

364

The Plant Based Cookbook For Beginners
650 Easy, Quick, & Simple Plant Based Vegan Diet Recipes With A 31 Day Meal Plan To Lose Weight & Live A Long Healthy Life

Instant Pot Mujadara

SERVINGS
4

PREPARATION TIME
1 hr. 15 minutes

COOKING TIME
18 minutes

Nutritional Values Per Serving

Calories	266
Total Fat	12g
Saturated Fat	0½g
Cholesterol	0mg
Sodium	802mg
Total Carbohydrate	22g
Dietary Fiber	4.3g
Total Sugars	4.8g
Protein	10.7g

Ingredients:

- 1 cup brown lentils
- 1 ½ tablespoon olive oil
- 3 shallots, sliced
- 4 garlic cloves, chopped
- 2 teaspoons cumin
- 1 teaspoon coriander
- 1 teaspoon allspice
- ½ teaspoon cinnamon
- ½ teaspoon turmeric
- ¼ teaspoon ground ginger
- 1 ½ teaspoon salt
- 1 teaspoon dried mint
- Zest from 1 small lemon
- 3 cups water
- 1 cup brown basmati rice

Instructions:

1. Soak lentils in tap water for 1 hour then drain.
2. Sauté shallots with oil in the Instant Pot for 5 minutes on Sauté mode.
3. Stir in garlic and sauté for 2 minutes.
4. Add water and the rest of the ingredients and then stir well.
5. Cover and seal the Instant Pot then cook for 11 minutes on a high pressure.
6. Once done, release the pressure naturally then remove the lid.
7. Fluff the cooked mujadara and divide in the bowl.
8. Garnish with olive oil, avocado and the rest of the ingredients of your desire.
9. Serve.

The Plant Based Cookbook For Beginners
650 Easy, Quick, & Simple Plant Based Vegan Diet Recipes With A 31 Day Meal Plan To Lose Weight & Live A Long Healthy Life

365

Szechuan Tofu and Veggies

SERVINGS	PREPARATION TIME	COOKING TIME
4	10 minutes	20 minutes

Nutritional Values Per Serving	
Calories	226
Total Fat	20.4g
Saturated Fat	3.7g
Cholesterol	0mg
Sodium	173mg
Total Carbohydrate	19g
Dietary Fiber	8g
Total Sugars	10.4g
Protein	11.3g

Serving Suggestion:

Enjoy this tofu meal with fried rice.

Ingredients:

- 12 ounces tofu, dry and cubed
- 2 tablespoons peanut oil
- 1 pinch salt and black pepper
- ½ cup onion, sliced
- 4 ounces mushrooms, sliced
- 2 cups cabbage, shredded
- 1 cup carrots, shredded
- ½ red bell pepper, sliced
- 1 cup asparagus, chopped
- 8 small dried red Chinese chilies
- ¼ cup Szechuan sauce

Garnish

- Green onions
- Sesame seeds
- Chili flakes

Instructions:

1. Sear tofu with oil, black pepper and salt in a suitable skillet until golden brown from both the sides.
2. Transfer the tofu slices to a serving plate.
3. Add mushrooms, and onion to the skillet then sauté for 3 minutes.
4. Stir in dried chilies and the remaining veggies then sauté for 5 minutes.
5. Add Szechuan sauce and cook for 2 minutes with occasional stirring.
6. Return the tofu to the skillet and mix well.
7. Divide the mixture in the serving bowls and garnish with green onions, chili flakes and sesame seeds.
8. Serve warm.

366

The Plant Based Cookbook For Beginners
650 Easy, Quick, & Simple Plant Based Vegan Diet Recipes With A 31 Day Meal Plan To Lose Weight & Live A Long Healthy Life

Warm Lentils with Roasted Beets

SERVINGS
4

PREPARATION TIME
15 minutes

COOKING TIME
73 minutes

Nutritional Values Per Serving

Calories	393
Total Fat	4½g
Saturated Fat	0.8g
Cholesterol	1mg
Sodium	42mg
Total Carbohydrate	31g
Dietary Fiber	4.8g
Total Sugars	1.7g
Protein	8.6g

Ingredients:

- 4 beets
- 2 cups cooked lentils
- 2 tablespoons olive oil
- ½ a red onion, diced
- 3 garlic cloves, chopped
- 4 cups swiss chard, chopped
- Salt and black pepper to taste
- 1 tablespoon balsamic vinegar
- ¼ cup vegan cheese, crumbled
- 3 tablespoons almonds

Instructions:

1. At 425 degrees F, preheat your oven.
2. Scrub the beets and cut into wedges and then toss with oil on a baking sheet.
3. Roast the beets for 30 minutes in the oven.
4. Boil lentils with water and a pinch of salt in a saucepan then boil.
5. Cover and cook these lentils for 30 minutes then drain and leave on the side.
6. Sauté onion with oil in a skillet for 4 minutes.
7. Stir in garlic then sauté for 2 minutes.
8. Reduce its heat and add chard, black pepper and salt then cook for 3 minutes.
9. Add cooked lentils and adjust the seasoning with black pepper and salt.
10. Stir in 1 tablespoon balsamic vinegar, and beets then cook for 5 minutes.
11. Garnish with almonds, herbs and serve warm.

The Plant Based Cookbook For Beginners
650 Easy, Quick, & Simple Plant Based Vegan Diet Recipes With A 31 Day Meal Plan To Lose Weight & Live A Long Healthy Life

367

Spaghetti Squash with Eggplant Puttanesca

SERVINGS	PREPARATION TIME	COOKING TIME
4	15 minutes	67 minutes

Nutritional Values Per Serving

Calories	380
Total Fat	14.7g
Saturated Fat	12.8g
Cholesterol	0mg
Sodium	12mg
Total Carbohydrate	15.1g
Dietary Fiber	3g
Total Sugars	5.7g
Protein	4.9

Ingredients:

- 3 pounds Spaghetti Squash
- 4 tablespoon olive oil
- 1 medium eggplant, diced
- 1 red onion, diced
- 6 garlic cloves, chopped
- 1 red bell pepper, diced
- 14 ounce can crush tomatoes
- 1 tablespoon dry Italian herb
- 1 teaspoon salt
- ¼ teaspoon red chili flakes
- Splash of red wine
- 2 tablespoons capers
- 3 tablespoons sliced olives

Garnish

- Italian parsley, grated vegan cheese, or a drizzle of olive oil

Instructions:

1. At 425 degrees F, preheat your oven.
2. Cut the squash in half and remove its seeds.
3. Place the squash in a baking sheet and roast for 40 minutes.
4. Sauté onion with eggplant and olive oil in a Dutch oven for 5 minutes.
5. Stir in bell pepper and garlic then cook for 12 minutes.
6. Add Italian herbs, black pepper, salt, chili flakes, wine and tomatoes then cook for 10 minutes.
7. Stir in olives and capers then mix well.
8. Shred the spaghetti squash using a fold and mix its shreds with olive oil, black pepper and salt.
9. Divide the spaghetti squash in the serving bowl.
10. Top it with eggplant sauce, vegan cheese, parsley and olive oil.
11. Serve warm.

368

The Plant Based Cookbook For Beginners
650 Easy, Quick, & Simple Plant Based Vegan Diet Recipes With A 31 Day Meal Plan To Lose Weight & Live A Long Healthy Life

Jade Noodles

SERVINGS
4

PREPARATION TIME
10 minutes

COOKING TIME
10 minutes

Nutritional Values Per Serving	
Calories	267
Total Fat	27.4g
Saturated Fat	23.3g
Cholesterol	0mg
Sodium	19mg
Total Carbohydrate	12.8g
Dietary Fiber	4.9g
Total Sugars	26g
Protein	3.3g

Ingredients:

- 8 ounces dry soba noodles
- 1 (8 oz.) small bunch asparagus
- 4 ounces snow peas
- 1 small bunch broccolini
- 16 ounces edamame, shelled
- 8 ounces baked tofu
- 3 handfuls baby spinach
- 3 green onions, sliced

Sesame Ginger Dressing

- ⅓ cup olive oil
- 2 tablespoons sesame oil
- ⅓ cup soy sauce
- ¼ cup rice wine vinegar
- 3 tablespoons coconut sugar
- 1 tablespoon chili sauce
- 2 tablespoons ginger, chopped
- 3 garlic cloves, minced

Garnishes

- Baked tofu, optional

Instructions:

1. Blend all the ingredients for sesame ginger dressing in a blender and keep it aside.
2. Boil the noodles in salted water until tender then drain.
3. Add veggies to boiling water for 2 minutes then drain.
4. Mix all these veggies with the sesame dressing in a salad bowl.
5. Top them with baked tofu.
6. Serve warm.

The Plant Based Cookbook For Beginners
650 Easy, Quick, & Simple Plant Based Vegan Diet Recipes With A 31 Day Meal Plan To Lose Weight & Live A Long Healthy Life

369

Garlic Tofu with Broccolini

SERVINGS | **PREPARATION TIME** | **COOKING TIME**
4 | 10 minutes | 12 minutes

Nutritional Values Per Serving

Calories	138
Total Fat	5.8g
Saturated Fat	1.1g
Cholesterol	0mg
Sodium	270mg
Total Carbohydrate	20.2g
Dietary Fiber	4.6g
Total Sugars	2.7g
Protein	5.8g

Serving Suggestion:

Enjoy this tofu meal with brown rice on the side.

Ingredients:

- 12 ounces extra firm tofu
- 2 tablespoons peanut oil
- ½ teaspoon salt
- ½ teaspoon cracked peppercorns
- 4 smashed garlic cloves
- 8 ounces broccolini
- 1 tablespoon chili garlic sauce
- 2 tablespoons seaweed strips
- 1 ½ teaspoon liquid aminos

Instructions:

1. Drain and pat dry the tofu with a paper towel then cut into thick pieces.
2. Sauté garlic with oil, peppercorns and salt in a skillet for 2 minutes.
3. Add tofu and cook for 5 minutes.
4. Place a steamer basket over boiling water in a pot and add broccolini.
5. Cover and steam the broccolini for 5 minutes then transfer to the tofu.
6. Stir in soy sauce, chili sauce and seaweed strips.
7. Serve warm.

Sweet Roasted Moroccan Carrots

SERVINGS
4

PREPARATION TIME
10 minutes

COOKING TIME
34 minutes

Nutritional Values Per Serving	
Calories	211
Total Fat	1.8g
Saturated Fat	0.2g
Cholesterol	0mg
Sodium	9mg
Total Carbohydrate	17.9g
Dietary Fiber	5.7g
Total Sugars	2.8g
Protein	7.2g

Ingredients:

- 1 ½ lbs whole carrots, peeled and julienned
- 2 tablespoons olive oil
- 1 tablespoon brown sugar
- ½ teaspoon salt
- ½ teaspoon black pepper
- 2 tablespoons orange juice
- ½ teaspoon Aleppo chili pepper
- ¼ teaspoon cumin
- ⅛ teaspoon cinnamon
- ¼ cup parsley, chopped
- orange zest, to taste

Instructions:

1. At 450 degrees F, preheat your oven.
2. Mix sugar with black pepper, oil and salt in a baking dish.
3. Stir in carrots, cover with a foil sheet and bake for 12 minutes.
4. Remove the foil and roast for 22 minutes.
5. Mix cinnamon, cumin, Aleppo chili pepper and orange juice in a bowl.
6. Pour this dressing over carrots.
7. Mix well and garnish with orange zest and parsley.
8. Serve warm.

The Plant Based Cookbook For Beginners
650 Easy, Quick, & Simple Plant Based Vegan Diet Recipes With A 31 Day Meal Plan To Lose Weight & Live A Long Healthy Life

371

Tofu Stir-Fry with Broccoli

SERVINGS **PREPARATION TIME** **COOKING TIME**
4 15 minutes 20 minutes

Nutritional Values Per Serving	
Calories	241
Total Fat	4.8g
Saturated Fat	0.3g
Cholesterol	0mg
Sodium	165mg
Total Carbohydrate	12.6g
Dietary Fiber	4.1g
Total Sugars	15.1g
Protein	3g

Serving Suggestion:

Try this tofu stir-fry with rice or noodles.

Ingredients:

- 8 ounces broccoli
- 10 ounces tofu, patted dry and cubed
- 1 shallot, sliced
- 5 garlic cloves, chopped
- 8 ounces shiitake mushrooms, sliced
- 2 tablespoons coconut oil
- Salt and black pepper, to taste
- 5 chilies de arbol
- 2 tablespoons peanuts, chopped
- 2 tablespoons black vinegar
- 2 tablespoons soy sauce
- 2 tablespoons water
- Chopped red chilies, to garnish

Instructions:

1. Add water to a suitable cooking pot and set the steamer basket over it.
2. Boil this water, add broccoli to the basket, cover and cook for 5 minutes.
3. Sear tofu with black pepper, salt and coconut oil in a skillet for 6 minutes per side.
4. Transfer the tofu slices to a serving plate.
5. Add garlic and shallots to the cooking pan then sauté for 2 minutes.
6. Stir in sliced mushrooms, nuts and chilies de arbol then sauté for 1 minute.
7. Add water, soy, vinegar, broccoli, tofu and salt.
8. Divide into the serving bowl and garnish with red chilies.
9. Serve warm.

Roasted Sunchoke Barley Bowl

SERVINGS	PREPARATION TIME	COOKING TIME
4	15 minutes	31 minutes

Nutritional Values Per Serving

Calories	321
Total Fat	2.3g
Saturated Fat	0.4g
Cholesterol	20mg
Sodium	128mg
Total Carbohydrate	22g
Dietary Fiber	4.9g
Total Sugars	24.6g
Protein	10g

Serving Suggestion:

Enjoy this bowl with boiled rice or warmed bread.

Ingredients:

- 4 cups cooked whole barley
- 12 ounces sunchokes
- ½ lb mushrooms, cut in half
- 2 large parsnips, diced
- 2 teaspoon olive oil
- 1 bunch Lacinato kale, sliced
- 1 medium onion, sliced

Zaatar tahini sauce

- ¼ cup tahini paste
- ⅓ cup warm water
- 2 teaspoons lemon juice
- 1 garlic clove, minced
- 1 ½ teaspoon zaatar spice
- ⅛ teaspoon cayenne
- ½ teaspoon salt
- Black pepper to taste

Instructions:

1. At 450 degrees F, preheat your oven.
2. Scrub the sunchokes and cut them into bite-sized pieces.
3. Peel and dice the parsnips into cubes.
4. Slice all the mushrooms in half.
5. Toss mushrooms, parsnips, and sunchokes with black pepper, salt and 1 teaspoon olive oil in a bowl.
6. Spread the veggies on a baking sheet, lined with parchment paper.
7. Bake for 10 minutes then remove the mushrooms and continue baking the rest for 10 minutes.
8. Sauté onion with 1 teaspoon olive oil in a skillet for 3 minutes on high heat.
9. Reduce its heat and sauté for 5 minutes.
10. Stir in kale and barley, cook for 3 minutes then adjust seasoning with black pepper and salt.
11. Add the baked veggies to the mixture.
12. Blend all the tahini sauce ingredients in a blender.
13. Pour this sauce over the salad and serve.

The Plant Based Cookbook For Beginners
650 Easy, Quick, & Simple Plant Based Vegan Diet Recipes With A 31 Day Meal Plan To Lose Weight & Live A Long Healthy Life

373

Spicy Black Beans Stew

SERVINGS
6

PREPARATION TIME
10 minutes

COOKING TIME
1 hour 42 minutes

Nutritional Values Per Serving	
Calories	366
Total Fat	3.4g
Saturated Fat	0.3g
Cholesterol	0mg
Sodium	224mg
Total Carbohydrate	34g
Dietary Fiber	2½g
Total Sugars	3.2g
Protein	13g

Serving Suggestion:

Try this stew with warmed whole wheat tortillas.

Ingredients:

- 4 cups water
- 1½ cups dried black beans, soaked and drained
- ½ teaspoon ground turmeric
- 3 tablespoons olive oil
- 1 small onion, chopped
- 1 green chili, chopped
- 1 (1-inch) piece fresh ginger, minced
- 2 garlic cloves minced
- 1½ tablespoon ground coriander
- 1 teaspoon ground cumin
- ½ teaspoon cayenne pepper
- Sea salt, to taste
- 2 medium tomatoes, chopped
- ½ cup fresh cilantro, chopped

Instructions:

1. In a large pan, add water, black beans and turmeric and bring to a boil on high heat.
2. Reduce its heat to low and simmer, covered for about 1 hour or until desired tenderness of beans.
3. Meanwhile, in a skillet, heat the oil over medium heat and sauté the onion for about 4-5 minutes.
4. Add the green chili, ginger, garlic, spices and salt and sauté for about 1-2 minutes.
5. Stir in the tomatoes and cook, occasionally stirring for about 10 minutes.
6. Transfer the tomato mixture into the pan with black beans and stir to combine.
7. Reduce its heat to medium-low and simmer for about 15-20 minutes.
8. Stir in the cilantro and simmer for about 5 minutes.
9. Serve hot.

374

The Plant Based Cookbook For Beginners
650 Easy, Quick, & Simple Plant Based Vegan Diet Recipes With A 31 Day Meal Plan To Lose Weight & Live A Long Healthy Life

Pinto Beans with Salsa

SERVINGS	PREPARATION TIME	COOKING TIME
4	10 minutes	11 minutes

Nutritional Values Per Serving

Calories	310
Total Fat	5.1g
Saturated Fat	1.6g
Cholesterol	1mg
Sodium	89mg
Total Carbohydrate	23g
Dietary Fiber	3.4g
Total Sugars	13.6g
Protein	5.6g

Serving Suggestion:

Enjoy these beans with rice.

Ingredients:

- 1 tablespoon canola oil
- 1 small onion, chopped
- 1 garlic clove, minced
- 2 teaspoons fresh cilantro, minced
- 2 (15-ounce) cans pinto beans, drained
- ⅔ cup red bell pepper, chopped

Instructions:

1. In a suitable skillet, heat the oil over medium heat and sauté the onion for about 4-5 minutes.
2. Add the garlic and cilantro and sauté for about 1 minute.
3. Stir in the beans and red bell pepper and cook for about 4-5 minutes or until heated completely.
4. Serve hot.

The Plant Based Cookbook For Beginners
650 Easy, Quick, & Simple Plant Based Vegan Diet Recipes With A 31 Day Meal Plan To Lose Weight & Live A Long Healthy Life

375

Vegetable Couscous Pilaf

SERVINGS	PREPARATION TIME	COOKING TIME
4	10 minutes	22 minutes

Nutritional Values Per Serving

Calories	290
Total Fat	10.3g
Saturated Fat	1.4g
Cholesterol	0mg
Sodium	68mg
Total Carbohydrate	26g
Dietary Fiber	8.3g
Total Sugars	19.7g
Protein	12.3g

Ingredients:

- 3 tablespoons vegetable oil
- 1 medium onion, chopped
- 1 medium parsnip, peeled and diced
- 1 medium carrot, peeled and diced
- 1 medium zucchini, chopped
- 1 medium yellow squash, chopped
- 2 garlic cloves, minced
- 1 teaspoon ground cumin
- ½ teaspoon red pepper flakes, crushed
- ½ teaspoon smoked paprika
- 1½ cups couscous
- Salt and black pepper, to taste
- ½ cup dried apricots, chopped
- 2¼ cups vegetable broth
- ¼ cup fresh cilantro, chopped
- ½ cup almonds, toasted and chopped
- Vegan feta, crumbled, to garnish

Instructions:

1. In a suitable iron skillet, heat the oil over medium-high heat and sauté the onion for about 4-5 minutes.

2. Add the parsnip and carrot and sauté for about 4-5 minutes.

3. Add the zucchini, yellow squash, garlic, cloves and spices and sauté for about 4-5 minutes.

4. Stir in the couscous and cook for about 2 minutes, stirring occasionally.

5. Stir in the apricots and broth and cook, covered for about 5 minutes or until all the liquid is absorbed.

6. Remove from the heat and with a fork, fluff the couscous completely.

7. Stir in the cilantro and almonds and garnish with vegan feta.

8. serve.

Black-Eyed Peas Curry

SERVINGS	PREPARATION TIME	COOKING TIME
6	10 minutes	12 minutes

Nutritional Values Per Serving

Calories	331
Total Fat	17g
Saturated Fat	12g
Cholesterol	20mg
Sodium	275mg
Total Carbohydrate	29g
Dietary Fiber	3.4g
Total Sugars	8.2g
Protein	18g

Serving Suggestion:

Enjoy this curry with rice.

Ingredients:

- 1 teaspoon canola oil
- 1 red bell pepper, seeded and chopped
- ¼ cup shallot, chopped
- 2 teaspoons fresh ginger, minced
- 3 garlic cloves, minced
- 1 fresh green chili, chopped
- 1 tablespoon fresh thyme, chopped
- 2 bay leaves
- 2 teaspoons curry powder
- ½ teaspoon ground cumin
- ¾ cup water
- ¾ cup coconut milk
- 1 teaspoon unsweetened applesauce
- 1 tablespoon fresh lime juice
- Salt and black pepper, to taste
- 1 (16-ounce) can black-eyed peas, drained and rinsed
- 2 tablespoons fresh parsley, chopped

Instructions:

1. In a pan, heat the oil over medium heat and sauté the bell pepper and shallot for about 4-5 minutes.

2. Add the ginger, garlic, green chili, thyme, bay leaves, curry powder and cumin and sauté for about 1 minute.

3. Add the black-eyed peas, water, coconut milk and applesauce and bring to a boil.

4. Cover and cook for about 5 minutes.

5. Stir in the salt, lime juice, and black pepper and cook or about 1 minute.

6. Remove this curry from the heat and discard the bay leaves.

7. Serve hot and garnish with parsley.

The Plant Based Cookbook For Beginners
650 Easy, Quick, & Simple Plant Based Vegan Diet Recipes With A 31 Day Meal Plan To Lose Weight & Live A Long Healthy Life

377

Okra Stir Fry

SERVINGS 4 **PREPARATION TIME** 10 minutes **COOKING TIME** 13 minutes

Nutritional Values Per Serving

Calories	248
Total Fat	5.6g
Saturated Fat	2.9g
Cholesterol	0mg
Sodium	17mg
Total Carbohydrate	26g
Dietary Fiber	5.6g
Total Sugars	9.2g
Protein	3g

Ingredients:

- 1 tablespoon olive oil
- ¾ pound okra pods, cut into 2-inch pieces
- ½ teaspoon curry powder
- ½ teaspoon red chili powder
- 1 teaspoon ground coriander
- ½ teaspoon ground cumin
- Salt and black pepper, to taste

Instructions:

1. In a suitable skillet, heat the oil over medium heat and stir fry the okra for about 2 minutes.

2. Reduce its heat to low and cook covered for about 6-8 minutes, stirring occasionally.

3. Uncover and increase the heat to medium.

4. Stir in the spices and cook for about 2-3 minutes more.

5. Season with salt and pepper then remove from heat.

6. Serve hot.

378

The Plant Based Cookbook For Beginners
650 Easy, Quick, & Simple Plant Based Vegan Diet Recipes With A 31 Day Meal Plan To Lose Weight & Live A Long Healthy Life

Green Beans Mushrooms Stir Fry

SERVINGS
4

PREPARATION TIME
10 minutes

COOKING TIME
18 minutes

Nutritional Values Per Serving

Calories	314
Total Fat	18g
Saturated Fat	3g
Cholesterol	10mg
Sodium	54mg
Total Carbohydrate	28g
Dietary Fiber	4.8g
Total Sugars	1.9g
Protein	13g

Ingredients:

- 2 tablespoons olive oil
- 2 tablespoons yellow onion, minced
- ½ teaspoon garlic, minced
- 8-ounce white mushrooms, sliced
- 1 cup frozen green beans
- Salt and black pepper, to taste

Instructions:

1. In a suitable skillet, heat the oil over medium heat and sauté the onion and garlic for about 1 minute.

2. Add the mushrooms and cook for about 6-7 minutes.

3. Stir in the green beans and cook for about 5-10 minutes or until desired tenderness.

4. Serve hot and garnish with salt and pepper.

The Plant Based Cookbook For Beginners
650 Easy, Quick, & Simple Plant Based Vegan Diet Recipes With A 31 Day Meal Plan To Lose Weight & Live A Long Healthy Life

379

Yellow Squash Stir Fry

SERVINGS | PREPARATION TIME | COOKING TIME
4 | 10 minutes | 25 minutes

Nutritional Values Per Serving

Calories	334
Total Fat	20g
Saturated Fat	17g
Cholesterol	41mg
Sodium	381mg
Total Carbohydrate	14g
Dietary Fiber	0.8g
Total Sugars	2.9g
Protein	4.4g

Ingredients:

- 1 tablespoon canola oil
- ½ cup onion, sliced
- ½ cup red bell pepper, julienned
- ½ cup green bell pepper, julienned
- 3 cups yellow squash, peeled and diced
- 1 ½ teaspoon garlic, minced
- ¼ cup water
- Salt and black pepper, to taste

Instructions:

1. Set a large cooking pot filled with water over medium high heat.

2. Stir in yellow squash and cook for 15 minutes until tender then drain.

3. In a suitable skillet, heat the oil over medium-high heat and sauté the onion, bell peppers and squash cubes for about 4-5 minutes.

4. Add the garlic and sauté for about 1 minute.

5. Add the remaining ingredients and stir to combine.

6. Reduce its heat to medium and cook for about 3-4 minutes, stirring occasionally.

7. Serve hot.

380

The Plant Based Cookbook For Beginners
650 Easy, Quick, & Simple Plant Based Vegan Diet Recipes With A 31 Day Meal Plan To Lose Weight & Live A Long Healthy Life

Mushrooms Cashew Curry

SERVINGS
6

PREPARATION TIME
10 minutes

COOKING TIME
19 minutes

Nutritional Values Per Serving

Calories	362
Total Fat	11g
Saturated Fat	21g
Cholesterol	10mg
Sodium	133mg
Total Carbohydrate	21g
Dietary Fiber	5.2g
Total Sugars	1.9g
Protein	13g

Serving Suggestion:

Enjoy this curry with rice.

Ingredients:

- 2 cups tomatoes, chopped
- 1 green chili, chopped
- 1 teaspoon fresh ginger, chopped
- ¼ cup cashews
- 2 tablespoons canola oil
- ½ teaspoon cumin seeds
- ¼ teaspoon ground coriander
- ¼ teaspoon ground turmeric
- ¼ teaspoon red chili powder
- 1½ cups fresh shiitake mushrooms, sliced
- 1½ cups fresh button mushrooms, sliced
- 1 cup frozen corn kernels
- 1¼ cups water
- ¼ cup coconut milk
- Salt and black pepper, to taste

Instructions:

1. In a food processor, add the tomatoes, green chili, ginger and cashews and pulse until a smooth paste is formed.

2. In a pan, heat the oil over medium heat and sauté the cumin seeds for about 1 minute.

3. Add the spices and sauté for about 1 minute.

4. Add the blended tomato sauce and cook for about 5 minutes.

5. Stir in the mushrooms, corns, water and coconut milk and bring to a boil.

6. Cook for about 10-12 minutes, stirring occasionally.

7. Season with the black pepper and salt then remove from the heat.

8. Serve hot.

The Plant Based Cookbook For Beginners
650 Easy, Quick, & Simple Plant Based Vegan Diet Recipes With A 31 Day Meal Plan To Lose Weight & Live A Long Healthy Life

381

Butternut Squash Curry

SERVINGS	PREPARATION TIME	COOKING TIME
4	10 minutes	35 minutes

Nutritional Values Per Serving	
Calories	338
Total Fat	15g
Saturated Fat	8g
Cholesterol	0mg
Sodium	232mg
Total Carbohydrate	28g
Dietary Fiber	13.9g
Total Sugars	5.7g
Protein	14.2g

Serving Suggestion:

Try this curry with rice.

Ingredients:

- 1 tablespoon coconut oil
- 2 onions, chopped
- 3 tablespoons curry paste
- 4 cups coconut milk
- 1 cup kale chopped
- Salt and black pepper, to taste
- 2 pounds butternut squash, peeled and cubed
- ¼ cup fresh basil, chopped

Instructions:

1. In a suitable skillet, heat the oil over medium heat and sauté the onion for about 5 minutes until tender.

2. Add the curry paste and cook for about 1 minute.

3. Add the butternut squash and stir to combine.

4. Add the coconut milk, kale, salt, and pepper and cook to a boil.

5. Then reduce its heat to medium and cook, covered for about 20-25 minutes or until the desired thickness of sauce.

6. Serve hot and garnish with basil.

382

The Plant Based Cookbook For Beginners
650 Easy, Quick, & Simple Plant Based Vegan Diet Recipes With A 31 Day Meal Plan To Lose Weight & Live A Long Healthy Life

Vegetable Noodles

SERVINGS **PREPARATION TIME** **COOKING TIME**
4 10 minutes 13 minutes

Nutritional Values Per Serving	
Calories	287
Total Fat	7g
Saturated Fat	2.1g
Cholesterol	10mg
Sodium	327mg
Total Carbohydrate	26g
Dietary Fiber	8g
Total Sugars	2.4g
Protein	9g

Ingredients:

- 1 ½ tablespoon sunflower oil
- ¼ cup onion, chopped
- 2 garlic cloves, minced
- 1 jalapeño pepper, seeded and chopped
- 1 large carrot, peeled and spiralized
- 1 large zucchini, spiralized
- 1 large yellow squash, spiralized
- 2 tablespoons fresh lime juice
- Salt and black pepper, to taste
- ½ cup green onions, chopped

Instructions:

1. In a suitable skillet, heat the oil over medium heat and sauté the onion for about 4-5 minutes.
2. Add the garlic and jalapeño pepper and sauté for about 1 minute.
3. Add the carrot noodles and cook for about 2-3 minutes.
4. Add the squash and zucchini noodles and cook for about 3-4 minutes.
5. Stir in the salt, lime juice, and black pepper and remove from the heat.
6. Serve immediately and garnish with the topping of green onions.

The Plant Based Cookbook For Beginners
650 Easy, Quick, & Simple Plant Based Vegan Diet Recipes With A 31 Day Meal Plan To Lose Weight & Live A Long Healthy Life

383

Tempeh in Tomato Sauce

SERVINGS	PREPARATION TIME	COOKING TIME
4	15 minutes	37 minutes

Nutritional Values Per Serving

Calories	366
Total Fat	8.6g
Saturated Fat	3g
Cholesterol	21mg
Sodium	146mg
Total Carbohydrate	24g
Dietary Fiber	4g
Total Sugars	15.2g
Protein	5.8g

Serving Suggestion:

Enjoy this tempeh with rice.

Ingredients:

- ½ cup vegetable oil
- 2 (8-ounce) packages tempeh, cubed
- 1 large onion, chopped
- 3 garlic cloves, minced
- 1 teaspoon dried oregano, crushed
- 1 teaspoon dried thyme, crushed
- 1 teaspoon red chili powder
- 1 teaspoon paprika
- 2 large green bell peppers, sliced

Red Sauce

- 4 cups tomatoes, chopped
- 1 teaspoon balsamic vinegar
- 1 tablespoon raw maple syrup

Instructions:

1. At 350 degrees F, preheat your oven.
2. Mix tempeh cubes with 2 tablespoons oil in a large bowl.
3. Set a skillet over medium-high heat and add ¼ cup oil to heat.
4. Sear the tempeh cubes in this oil for 7 minutes per side.
5. Transfer the seared tempeh to a plate, lined with a paper towel.
6. Sauté onion, garlic, spices and herbs in the same skillet for 10 minutes.
7. Stir in bell pepper then sauté for 10 minutes approximately.
8. Then add the rest of the red sauce ingredients to the mixture and mix well until combined.
9. Spread the tempeh cubes to a large casserole dish.
10. Top these cubes with red tomato sauce.
11. Cover with a foil sheet and bake for 1 hour.
12. Serve warm.

384

The Plant Based Cookbook For Beginners
650 Easy, Quick, & Simple Plant Based Vegan Diet Recipes With A 31 Day Meal Plan To Lose Weight & Live A Long Healthy Life

Sweet Potato Cauliflower Lentil

SERVINGS	PREPARATION TIME	COOKING TIME
6	20 minutes	60 minutes

Nutritional Values Per Serving

Calories	363
Total Fat	11.1g
Saturated Fat	3.8g
Cholesterol	0mg
Sodium	650mg
Total Carbohydrate	23g
Dietary Fiber	2g
Total Sugars	1.6g
Protein	7g

Ingredients:

- 1 large sweet potato, scrubbed and cut into chunks
- 1 cauliflower, florets, diced
- 1 tablespoon garam masala
- 3 tablespoons groundnut oil
- 2 garlic cloves
- 7 ounces puy lentils
- 1 thumb-sized ginger piece, grated
- 1 teaspoon Dijon mustard
- 1 tablespoon lime juice

Instructions:

1. At 425 degrees F, preheat your oven.
2. Toss cauliflower with garam masala, oil, and sweet potatoes in a bowl.
3. Spread the mixture in a roasting tray and add garlic on top.
4. Roast the sweet potatoes for 35 minutes.
5. Boil lentils with 40ml water in a saucepan then cook for 25 minutes on a simmer.
6. Drain and keep the lentils aside.
7. Remove the garlic from the roasting pan and squeeze the garlic out.
8. Mix garlic with the remaining oil, ginger, mustard, 1 pinch sugar, mustard and ⅓ lime juice in a bowl.
9. Add this mixture, sweet potatoes and cauliflower to the lentils then mix well.
10. Puree the soup with a hand blender and serve warm.

The Plant Based Cookbook For Beginners
650 Easy, Quick, & Simple Plant Based Vegan Diet Recipes With A 31 Day Meal Plan To Lose Weight & Live A Long Healthy Life

385

Sesame Parsnip with Wild Rice

SERVINGS	PREPARATION TIME	COOKING TIME
6	20 minutes	55 minutes

Nutritional Values Per Serving

Calories	348
Total Fat	6.6g
Saturated Fat	1.9g
Cholesterol	1mg
Sodium	97mg
Total Carbohydrate	35.1g
Dietary Fiber	8.2g
Total Sugars	4g
Protein	9g

Ingredients:

- 5 parsnips, peeled and cut into chunks
- 2 ½ tablespoon rapeseed oil
- 1 teaspoon ground turmeric
- 2 teaspoons ground coriander
- 2 tablespoons sesame seeds
- 4 ½ ounces wild rice
- 2 red onions, sliced
- 2 tablespoons white wine vinegar
- 3 tablespoons tahini
- 1 small pack mint, leaves chopped
- 1 small pack coriander, chopped
- 2 tablespoons pomegranate seeds

Instructions:

1. At 360 degrees F, preheat your oven.
2. Toss parsnips with coriander, turmeric, 1 ½ tablespoon oil and sesame seeds in a bowl.
3. Spread the parsnip on a baking sheet and roast for 30 minutes.
4. Cook the wild rice as per the package's instruction.
5. Sauté onion with 1 tablespoon oil and 3 tablespoons water in a cooking pan for 15 minutes.
6. Stir in 1 tablespoon vinegar, then mix well.
7. Mix the remaining vinegar with tahini and a tablespoon of warm water in a bowl.
8. Drain the cooked wild rice and mix with chopped herbs and onion mixture.
9. Divide the wild rice in the serving bowls.
10. Serve with parsnips, pomegranate seeds and the remaining herbs on top.
11. Drizzle tahini dressing on top and serve.

386

The Plant Based Cookbook For Beginners
650 Easy, Quick, & Simple Plant Based Vegan Diet Recipes With A 31 Day Meal Plan To Lose Weight & Live A Long Healthy Life

Cauliflower Steaks with Salsa

SERVINGS	PREPARATION TIME	COOKING TIME
2	15 minutes	20 minutes

Nutritional Values Per Serving

Calories	250
Total Fat	7.8g
Saturated Fat	4.1g
Cholesterol	0mg
Sodium	150mg
Total Carbohydrate	20g
Dietary Fiber	5.2g
Total Sugars	12.8g
Protein	6g

Ingredients:

- 1 cauliflower
- ½ teaspoon smoked paprika
- 2 tablespoons olive oil
- 1 roasted red pepper
- 4 black olives, pitted
- 1 small handful parsley
- 1 teaspoon capers
- ½ tablespoon red wine vinegar
- 2 tablespoons toasted almonds flakes

Instructions:

1. At 425 degrees F, preheat your oven.
2. Layer a baking tray with wax paper.
3. Cut the cauliflower into two steaks,
4. Mix ½ tablespoon oil with paprika, and rub over the cauliflower slices.
5. Place the steaks in the baking tray and roast for 20 minutes.
6. Meanwhile, mix chopped capers, parsley, olives and pepper in a bowl.
7. Stir in vinegar and the remaining oil then mix well.
8. Serve the steaks with sauce mixture and almonds on top.
9. Enjoy.

The Plant Based Cookbook For Beginners
650 Easy, Quick, & Simple Plant Based Vegan Diet Recipes With A 31 Day Meal Plan To Lose Weight & Live A Long Healthy Life

387

Artichoke Eggplant Rice

SERVINGS	PREPARATION TIME	COOKING TIME
4	20 minutes	55 minutes

Nutritional Values Per Serving

Calories	315
Total Fat	17g
Saturated Fat	6g
Cholesterol	23mg
Sodium	116mg
Total Carbohydrate	28g
Dietary Fiber	4.1g
Total Sugars	1.3g
Protein	8g

Ingredients:

- ¼ cup olive oil
- 2 eggplant, cut into chunks
- 1 large onion, chopped
- 2 garlic cloves, crushed
- 1 small pack parsley, leaves chopped
- 2 teaspoons smoked paprika
- 2 teaspoons turmeric
- 14 ounces paella rice, cooked
- 2 tomatoes, chopped
- 2 cups vegetable stock
- 2 x 6 ounces packs chargrilled artichokes
- 1 lemon, juiced

Instructions:

1. Sear eggplant with 2 tablespoons oil in a deep skillet until golden brown from both sides.
2. Transfer the eggplant to a plate.
3. Stir in 1 tablespoon oil and onion then sauté for 3 minutes.
4. Stir in parsley stalks and garlic then sauté for 1 minute.
5. Add rice and spices then sauté for 2 minutes.
6. Stir in half of the stock and cook for 20 minutes on medium heat.
7. Add artichokes, tomatoes, eggplant and the remaining stock then cook for 20 minutes.
8. Drizzle lemon juice and parsley leaves on top.
9. Serve and enjoy.

388

The Plant Based Cookbook For Beginners
650 Easy, Quick, & Simple Plant Based Vegan Diet Recipes With A 31 Day Meal Plan To Lose Weight & Live A Long Healthy Life

Spinach Sweet Potato Lentil

SERVINGS	PREPARATION TIME	COOKING TIME
4	15 minutes	40 minutes

Nutritional Values Per Serving

Calories	384
Total Fat	19g
Saturated Fat	20g
Cholesterol	13mg
Sodium	556mg
Total Carbohydrate	29g
Dietary Fiber	6.1g
Total Sugars	7g
Protein	14g

Ingredients:

- 1 tablespoon sesame oil
- 1 red onion, chopped
- 1 garlic clove, crushed
- 1 thumb-sized piece ginger, peeled and chopped
- 1 red chili, chopped
- 1 ½ teaspoon ground turmeric
- 1 ½ teaspoon ground cumin
- 1 tomato, chopped
- 2 sweet potatoes, cut into chunks
- 9 ounces red split lentils
- 2 ½ cups vegetable stock
- 3 ounces bag of spinach
- Green onions, sliced
- Thai basil leaves

Instructions:

1. Sauté red onion with 1 tablespoon sesame oil in a suitable skillet for 10 minutes on low heat.

2. Stir in 1 crushed garlic clove, ginger, red chili, and sauté for 1 minute.

3. Add cumin and turmeric then sauté for 1 minute.

4. Toss in sweet potatoes then increase it heat to sauté for 5 minutes.

5. Add red lentils, stocks, tomato and then let the mixture boil.

6. Then reduce its heat, cover and cook for 20 minutes.

7. Stir in spinach and cook for 3 minutes, then garnish with sliced green onions and basil leaves.

8. Serve warm.

The Plant Based Cookbook For Beginners
650 Easy, Quick, & Simple Plant Based Vegan Diet Recipes With A 31 Day Meal Plan To Lose Weight & Live A Long Healthy Life

389

Mushroom Barley Pilaf

SERVINGS	PREPARATION TIME	COOKING TIME
4	15 minutes	66 minutes

Nutritional Values Per Serving

Calories	371
Total Fat	11g
Saturated Fat	6g
Cholesterol	12mg
Sodium	417mg
Total Carbohydrate	30.3g
Dietary Fiber	9g
Total Sugars	4.3g
Protein	12g

Ingredients:

- 1-ounce dried porcini mushrooms
- 1 cup boiling water
- 2 teaspoon olive oil
- 1 leek, trimmed, sliced
- 2 celery sticks, chopped
- 2 garlic cloves, crushed
- 1 cup pearl barley, rinsed
- 2 cups vegetable liquid stock
- ½ cup water
- 3 ounces kale, stems removed, chopped
- 12 ounces mixed mushrooms, quartered
- 2 tablespoons walnuts, toasted, chopped

Instructions:

1. At 360 degrees F, preheat your oven.
2. Soak porcini mushrooms in a bowl filled with boiling water for 10 minutes and drain but reserve ½ cup of mushroom liquid and keep aside.
3. Chop the soaked mushroom and keep them aside.
4. Sauté celery, with leek and oil in a skillet for 5 minutes.
5. Stir in garlic and sauté for 1 minute.
6. Add porcini mushrooms, water, mushroom liquid, stock, and barley then cook to a boil.
7. Reduce its heat, cover and cook for 35 minutes.
8. Place mixed mushrooms on a baking sheet and roast for 15 minutes.
9. Add kale and mixed mushrooms to the barley mixture.
10. Cook for 3 minutes and garnish with walnuts.
11. Serve warm.

390

The Plant Based Cookbook For Beginners
650 Easy, Quick, & Simple Plant Based Vegan Diet Recipes With A 31 Day Meal Plan To Lose Weight & Live A Long Healthy Life

Creamy Primavera Pasta

SERVINGS	PREPARATION TIME	COOKING TIME
4	1 hour 15 minutes	20 minutes

Nutritional Values Per Serving

Calories	394
Total Fat	9g
Saturated Fat	1.6g
Cholesterol	0mg
Sodium	455mg
Total Carbohydrate	31g
Dietary Fiber	1.7g
Total Sugars	2.1g
Protein	6g

Ingredients:

- 1 ½ cups raw cashews
- 1 cup warm water
- 7 ½ ounces penne pasta
- 1 bunch asparagus, cut into thirds
- 1 tablespoon olive oil
- 1 leek, trimmed, sliced
- 2 garlic cloves, chopped
- 2 zucchinis, cut into noodles
- Black pepper, to serve
- Fresh basil leaves, to serve
- Vegan parmesan cheese, to serve

Instructions:

1. Soak cashews in a bowl filled with boiling water for 1 hour.
2. Drain the cashews and transfer them to a food processor.
3. Add 1 cup warm water then blend well until smooth.
4. Boil the pasta as per the package's instruction then remove the pasta from the pan and keep the pasta liquid on the heat.
5. Add asparagus to the pasta liquid and cook for 3 minutes.
6. Drain and keep them aside. Reserve ½ cup cooking liquid.
7. Sauté leek, garlic with oil in a skillet for 3 minutes.
8. Stir in zucchini and sauté for 3 minutes.
9. Add pasta, cashew mixture and reserved ½ cooking liquid.
10. Mix well and sprinkle black pepper on top.
11. Garnish with basil, and vegan parmesan cheese.
12. Serve warm.

The Plant Based Cookbook For Beginners
650 Easy, Quick, & Simple Plant Based Vegan Diet Recipes With A 31 Day Meal Plan To Lose Weight & Live A Long Healthy Life

391

Teriyaki Tofu Kebabs

SERVINGS 4

PREPARATION TIME 10 minutes

COOKING TIME 10 minutes

Nutritional Values Per Serving	
Calories	330
Total Fat	4.9g
Saturated Fat	1.1g
Cholesterol	0mg
Sodium	248mg
Total Carbohydrate	18.3g
Dietary Fiber	3.7g
Total Sugars	16g
Protein	6g

Ingredients:

- 4 bell peppers, cubed
- 2 zucchinis, cut into 2cm pieces
- 10 ½ ounces firm tofu, cut into cubes
- ⅔ cups teriyaki marinade

Teriyaki Marinade

- ½ cup soy sauce
- ¼ cup brown sugar
- 1 ½ teaspoons fresh ginger, minced
- 1 teaspoon garlic, minced
- 1 tablespoon agave
- 1 teaspoon sesame oil
- 3 tablespoons mirin
- ¼ cup water mixed with 3 teaspoons cornstarch

Instructions:

1. Mix teriyaki marinade ingredients in a saucepan and cook for 4 minutes on a simmer.
2. Mix well and allow the marinade to cool.
3. Thread tofu, zucchini and bell peppers on the bamboo skewers.
4. Place the skewers in a baking dish and pour the teriyaki sauce on top.
5. Cover and refrigerate these skewers for 20 minutes for marination.
6. Set the suitable pan over medium heat greased with cooking oil and sear the skewers for 5 minutes per side.
7. Serve warm.

392

The Plant Based Cookbook For Beginners
650 Easy, Quick, & Simple Plant Based Vegan Diet Recipes With A 31 Day Meal Plan To Lose Weight & Live A Long Healthy Life

Sweet Potato Noodles with Kale

SERVINGS
4

PREPARATION TIME
15 minutes

COOKING TIME
25 minutes

Nutritional Values Per Serving	
Calories	246
Total Fat	0.8g
Saturated Fat	0g
Cholesterol	0mg
Sodium	1mg
Total Carbohydrate	31.1g
Dietary Fiber	1.7g
Total Sugars	59.3g
Protein	0.8g

Ingredients:

- 1 bunch kale, leaves torn
- 2 tablespoons sesame seeds
- ¼ cup olive oil
- 2 large garlic cloves, crushed
- 2 teaspoons chili flakes
- 1 lemon, rind grated
- 24 ounces sweet potato, peeled, cut into noodles using a spiralizer

Instructions:

1. At 325 degrees F, preheat your oven.
2. Toss the kales leaves with oil in one of two baking sheets and bake for 12 minutes until crispy.
3. Spread pine nuts in the other baking tray and roast for 5 minutes.
4. Mix lemon rind with garlic, oil and chili in a deep skillet.
5. Sauté for 3 minutes then stir in sweet potato noodles.
6. Stir and cook for 5 minutes then add kale.
7. Mix well and garnish with sesame seeds.
8. Serve warm.

The Plant Based Cookbook For Beginners
650 Easy, Quick, & Simple Plant Based Vegan Diet Recipes With A 31 Day Meal Plan To Lose Weight & Live A Long Healthy Life

393

Toasted Buckwheat with Artichokes

SERVINGS	PREPARATION TIME	COOKING TIME
4	15 minutes	26 minutes

Nutritional Values Per Serving	
Calories	391
Total Fat	12g
Saturated Fat	0.7g
Cholesterol	0mg
Sodium	70mg
Total Carbohydrate	19g
Dietary Fiber	5.2g
Total Sugars	1.8g
Protein	9g

Serving Suggestion:

Enjoy this buckwheat with sauteed zucchini.

Ingredients:

- 1 cup raw buckwheat
- 1 tablespoon olive oil
- 1 brown onion, chopped
- 2 garlic cloves, sliced
- 4 sprigs fresh thyme
- 14 ounces can artichokes in brine, drained, rinsed
- 2 cups vegetable stock
- 1 teaspoon grated lemon rind
- 1 tablespoon lemon juice
- ¼ cup parsley leaves, chopped
- Lemon wedges, to serve

Instructions:

1. Toast buckwheat in a saucepan over medium heat for 5 minutes then transfer to a bowl.
2. Sauté onion with oil in a suitable skillet for 5 minutes.
3. Stir in thyme and garlic then cook for 1 minute.
4. Drain the artichokes and cut then in half.
5. Add the artichokes and buckwheat to the skillet.
6. Stir in lemon rind and stock then boil.
7. Reduce its heat, cover and cook for 15 minutes.
8. Remove the mixture from the heat.
9. Garnish with parsley, lemon juice, thyme and lemon wedges.
10. Enjoy.

394

The Plant Based Cookbook For Beginners
650 Easy, Quick, & Simple Plant Based Vegan Diet Recipes With A 31 Day Meal Plan To Lose Weight & Live A Long Healthy Life

Quinoa and Chickpea Balls

SERVINGS **6** | PREPARATION TIME **25 minutes** | COOKING TIME **35 minutes**

Nutritional Values Per Serving

Calories	340
Total Fat	14g
Saturated Fat	1.2g
Cholesterol	10mg
Sodium	359mg
Total Carbohydrate	28.2g
Dietary Fiber	4.1g
Total Sugars	3g
Protein	13g

Ingredients:

- ⅓ cup white quinoa, rinsed
- 9 ounces cauliflower florets
- 14 ounces can chickpeas, drained but reserve liquid
- 1 garlic clove, crushed
- ½ cup fresh mint leaves
- ½ cup parsley leaves
- ¼ cup coriander leaves
- 2 green onions, thinly sliced
- 1 lemon, zested
- Vegetable oil, to shallow fry
- ¼ cup tahini
- 2 tablespoons lemon juice
- ½ teaspoon raw maple syrup
- Sliced green onion, to serve
- Mint leaves, to serve

Instructions:

1. Boil quinoa with ⅔ cup water in a saucepan, reduce its heat to low then cook for 15 minutes.
2. Cover the quinoa and leave it for 10 minutes, then allow it to cool.
3. Chop coriander, parsley, garlic, mint, chickpeas and cauliflower in a food processor.
4. Add this cauliflower mixture to the quinoa along with lemon zest and green onion.
5. Beat ¼ cup chickpea liquid in a bowl then add the quinoa mixture.
6. Mix well and make 20 equal sized balls out of this mixture.
7. Place these prepared balls on a baking sheet, lined with parchment paper.
8. Allow the ball to cool and refrigerate for 1 hour.
9. Set a deep skillet over medium heat and add oil to heat.
10. Sear the balls for 5 minutes per side then transfer to a plate.
11. Mix tahini with raw maple syrup, lemon juice and 2 tablespoons water in a bowl.
12. Divide seared balls in serving plates and garnish with tahini dressing.
13. Garnish with mint and green onion.
14. Serve warm.

The Plant Based Cookbook For Beginners
650 Easy, Quick, & Simple Plant Based Vegan Diet Recipes With A 31 Day Meal Plan To Lose Weight & Live A Long Healthy Life

395

Beetroot Pumpkin Curry

SERVINGS	PREPARATION TIME	COOKING TIME
4	20 minutes	85 minutes

Nutritional Values Per Serving

Calories	316
Total Fat	13g
Saturated Fat	2.8g
Cholesterol	0mg
Sodium	751mg
Total Carbohydrate	32g
Dietary Fiber	3.8g
Total Sugars	0.4g
Protein	12g

Serving Suggestion:

Enjoy this curry with white boiled rice or warmed flatbreads.

Ingredients:

- 2 pounds baby beetroot, stalks trimmed, scrubbed
- 14 ounces butternut pumpkin, peeled, cut into 2cm pieces
- 1 onion, halved, thinly sliced
- 2 garlic cloves, crushed
- 1 long red chili, thinly sliced
- 2 tablespoons tomato paste
- 1 teaspoon ground turmeric
- 2 teaspoons ground cumin
- ½ teaspoon chili powder
- ¼ cup baby spinach leaves
- 1 tablespoon sunflower oil
- 2 tablespoons raw unsalted cashews
- Fried curry leaves, to serve
- Soy Yogurt, to serve

Instructions:

1. Add beetroot and enough water to cover them, to a saucepan and cook for 60 minutes on a simmer.

2. Strain the beetroots and keep 2 cups of the beetroot liquid.

3. Pour the reserved cooking liquid to a saucepan.

4. Add chili powder, cumin, turmeric, tomato paste, chili, garlic, onion and pumpkin to the liquid.

5. Cook for 15 minutes on a low heat with occasional stirring.

6. Peel the beetroot gently then puree 5-6 ounces of beetroot it in a food processor.

7. Dice the remaining beetroot and transfer to the pumpkin.

8. Stir in beetroot puree and cook for 5 minutes.

9. Add spinach and cook for 2 minutes then remove from the heat.

10. Sauté cashews with oil in a skillet for 3 minutes then allow them to cool

11. Chop the roasted cashews.

12. Garnish the curry with yogurt, cashews and curry leaves.

13. Enjoy.

396

The Plant Based Cookbook For Beginners
650 Easy, Quick, & Simple Plant Based Vegan Diet Recipes With A 31 Day Meal Plan To Lose Weight & Live A Long Healthy Life

Chili-Roasted Pumpkin

SERVINGS
8

PREPARATION TIME
10 minutes

COOKING TIME
35 minutes

Nutritional Values Per Serving

Calories	372
Total Fat	0.3g
Saturated Fat	0g
Cholesterol	0mg
Sodium	2mg
Total Carbohydrate	46g
Dietary Fiber	2.3g
Total Sugars	6g
Protein	12.1g

Ingredients:

- 4 ½ pounds butternut pumpkin, peeled, seeded, diced
- ¼ cup olive oil
- 2 tablespoons lemon juice
- 1 tablespoon fresh rosemary, chopped
- 4 long red chilies, seeded, sliced
- ⅓ cup olive oil
- 1 teaspoon salt
- ⅓ cup pumpkin seeds, toasted
- 1 tablespoon shallot, chopped
- 1 tablespoon lemon zest, grated

Instructions:

1. At 450 degrees F, preheat your oven.
2. Mix pumpkin with lemon juice, ¼ cup oil, salt and rosemary in a large bowl.
3. Spread the pumpkin mixture on a baking sheet and roast for 25 minutes.
4. Stir in chili then roast for another 10 minutes.
5. Mix pumpkin seeds with ⅓ cup oil, lemon zest, and shallot in a bowl.
6. Drizzle this mixture over the roasted pumpkin.
7. Serve warm.

The Plant Based Cookbook For Beginners
650 Easy, Quick, & Simple Plant Based Vegan Diet Recipes With A 31 Day Meal Plan To Lose Weight & Live A Long Healthy Life

397

Kale Pumpkin Pilaf

SERVINGS	PREPARATION TIME	COOKING TIME
4	15 minutes	61 minutes

Nutritional Values Per Serving

Calories	361
Total Fat	14.7g
Saturated Fat	12.8g
Cholesterol	0mg
Sodium	161mg
Total Carbohydrate	23g
Dietary Fiber	2.7g
Total Sugars	2.6g
Protein	8g

Ingredients:

- 2 pounds pumpkin, peeled, seeded, cut into 1 ½cm cubes
- Spray olive oil
- 1 tablespoon olive oil
- 1 onion, chopped
- 2 garlic cloves, crushed
- 1 teaspoon grated ginger
- 1 teaspoon ground coriander
- ½ teaspoon ground turmeric
- 1 cup quinoa, rinsed, drained
- 3 ½ ounces chopped Kale
- ¼ cup pepitas
- Salt and black pepper, to season

Instructions:

1. At 400 degrees F, preheat your oven.
2. Layer a baking sheet with parchment paper.
3. Toss pumpkin with olive oil spray in the baking sheet then roast for 40 minutes.
4. Sauté onion with oil in a saucepan for 5 minutes over medium heat.
5. Stir in ginger, garlic, coriander and turmeric then cook for 1 minute.
6. Add 2 cups water and quinoa, cook to a boil then reduce its heat to low.
7. Cover and cook the mixture on a simmer for 15 minutes.
8. Stir in kale and cook the mixture until kale is wilted.
9. Add roasted pumpkin, salt, black pepper and pepitas.
10. Serve warm.

Kumara Rice Risotto

SERVINGS
4

PREPARATION TIME
10 minutes

COOKING TIME
85 minutes

Nutritional Values Per Serving

Calories	350
Total Fat	11g
Saturated Fat	12g
Cholesterol	23mg
Sodium	340mg
Total Carbohydrate	20g
Dietary Fiber	1.7g
Total Sugars	3.1g
Protein	7g

Ingredients:

- 1 (21 oz.) kumara, skin on, halved lengthways
- 6 teaspoons olive oil
- 1 bunch baby carrots
- 2 parsnips, quartered
- 1 cup (7 oz.) brown rice
- 5 green onions, chopped
- 7 oz. vegetable liquid stock
- 1 teaspoon ground cumin
- 2 tablespoons parsley leaves, chopped

Instructions:

1. At 400 degrees F, preheat your oven.
2. Mix kumara with 2 teaspoons oil on a baking sheet and roast for 30 minutes.
3. Toss parsnip with carrots and 2 teaspoons oil on a baking sheet then roast for 45 minutes.
4. Remove the kumara flesh with a scoop then transfer the flesh to a bowl.
5. Boil and cook the brown rice as per the package's instructions.
6. Sauté rice with the remaining 2 teaspoons of oil and green onion in a deep pan for 1 minute.
7. Stir in cumin and stock then cook to a simmer.
8. Add parsley and kumara flesh then cook for 4 minutes.
9. Serve warm with roasted carrots and parsnip.

The Plant Based Cookbook For Beginners
650 Easy, Quick, & Simple Plant Based Vegan Diet Recipes With A 31 Day Meal Plan To Lose Weight & Live A Long Healthy Life

399

Marrakesh Eggplants

SERVINGS	PREPARATION TIME	COOKING TIME
4	10 minutes	22 minutes

Nutritional Values Per Serving

Calories	238
Total Fat	3.7g
Saturated Fat	1.2g
Cholesterol	0mg
Sodium	19mg
Total Carbohydrate	25g
Dietary Fiber	3g
Total Sugars	7.4g
Protein	4g

Serving Suggestion:

Enjoy this eggplant meal alongside warming bowl of brown rice.

Ingredients:

- 2 pounds eggplants, cut into 1cm-thick slices
- ½ cup olive oil
- ⅓ cup tomato paste
- ½ teaspoon packed saffron threads
- 1 cup verjuice
- 1 red onion, chopped
- 1 garlic clove, crushed
- 1 teaspoon ground cumin
- ¼ teaspoon smoked paprika
- Salt and black pepper, to taste
- 7 ounces grape tomatoes, halved
- 9 ounces cherry truss tomatoes, cut into small bunches
- ¼ cup pine nuts, roasted

Instructions:

1. Mix eggplant slices with black pepper, oil and salt in a large bowl.
2. Add tomato paste then mix and rub over eggplants.
3. Sear the eggplant slices in a skillet for 4 minutes per side.
4. Transfer the eggplant to a flat dish.
5. Mix verjuice with saffron in a small bowl.
6. Sauté onion with garlic and 1 tablespoon salt in the same skillet for 5 minutes.
7. Stir in paprika and cumin then sauté for 1 minute.
8. Add grape tomatoes then mix well.
9. Stir in truss tomatoes, cover and cook for 8 minutes.
10. Add verjuice mixture then cook to a simmer with occasional stirring.
11. Spread this mixture over the eggplant slices and garnish with pine nuts.
12. Serve warm.

400

The Plant Based Cookbook For Beginners
650 Easy, Quick, & Simple Plant Based Vegan Diet Recipes With A 31 Day Meal Plan To Lose Weight & Live A Long Healthy Life

Indian Chickpea Curry

SERVINGS
4

PREPARATION TIME
10 minutes

COOKING TIME
24 minutes

Nutritional Values Per Serving

Calories	327
Total Fat	12g
Saturated Fat	1.9g
Cholesterol	0mg
Sodium	91mg
Total Carbohydrate	25g
Dietary Fiber	3g
Total Sugars	5.6g
Protein	10g

Ingredients:

- 1 tablespoon vegetable oil
- 1 brown onion, cut into thin wedges
- 1/4 cup korma curry paste
- 1 (10 ½ oz.) small eggplant, cubed
- 17 ½ ounces butternut pumpkin, peeled, cubed
- ½ (14 oz.) cauliflower, cut into florets
- 1 ½ cups vegetable liquid stock
- 15 ½ ounces can crushed tomatoes
- 15 ½ ounces can chickpeas, drained, rinsed
- ½ cup frozen peas
- Steamed Basmati rice, to serve
- Spinach salad, to serve

Instructions:

1. Sauté onion with oil in a skillet over medium-high heat for 3 minutes.
2. Stir in curry paste then cook for 1 minute.
3. Add tomatoes, stock, cauliflower, pumpkin and eggplant then cook to a boil.
4. Reduce its heat and cook for 15 minutes on a simmer.
5. Add peas and chickpeas then cook for 5 minutes.
6. Serve warm with rice and a spinach salad.
7. Enjoy.

The Plant Based Cookbook For Beginners
650 Easy, Quick, & Simple Plant Based Vegan Diet Recipes With A 31 Day Meal Plan To Lose Weight & Live A Long Healthy Life

401

Tofu Snow Pea Stir-Fry

SERVINGS	PREPARATION TIME	COOKING TIME
6	10 minutes	6 minutes

Nutritional Values Per Serving

Calories	340
Total Fat	14g
Saturated Fat	8g
Cholesterol	17mg
Sodium	310mg
Total Carbohydrate	22g
Dietary Fiber	4g
Total Sugars	7g
Protein	19g

Ingredients:

- 16 ounces firm tofu, squeezed and cubed
- ¼ cup peanut oil
- 8 ounces snow peas, halved diagonally
- 1 onion, chopped
- ¼ cup kecap manis
- ¼ cup cashews
- ½ cup vegetable liquid stock

Instructions:

1. Sauté tofu cubes with oil in a skillet for 3 minutes.
2. Transfer to a plate, lined with a paper towel.
3. Add snow peas and onion to the same skillet and sauté for 1 minute.
4. Stir in kecap manis, cashews and stock then cook for 2 minutes.
5. Strain excess liquid and transfer to a plate.
6. Serve warm.

402

The Plant Based Cookbook For Beginners
650 Easy, Quick, & Simple Plant Based Vegan Diet Recipes With A 31 Day Meal Plan To Lose Weight & Live A Long Healthy Life

Stir-Fried Tofu and Broccoli

SERVINGS
4

PREPARATION TIME
15 minutes

COOKING TIME
7 minutes

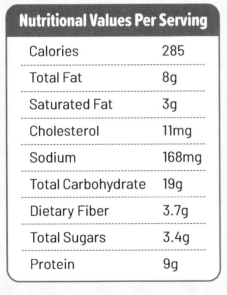

Nutritional Values Per Serving

Calories	285
Total Fat	8g
Saturated Fat	3g
Cholesterol	11mg
Sodium	168mg
Total Carbohydrate	19g
Dietary Fiber	3.7g
Total Sugars	3.4g
Protein	9g

Ingredients:

- ¼ cup 1 teaspoon corn flour
- 1 teaspoon sea salt
- 12 ounces firm tofu, cut into pieces
- 1 ½ tablespoon vegetable oil
- 2 tablespoons dry sherry
- 2 tablespoons soy sauce
- 2 teaspoons caster sugar
- 1 brown onion, cut into thin wedges
- 14 ounces broccoli, trimmed, cut into florets
- 1 long fresh red chili, halved, deseeded, chopped
- Brown rice, cooked

Instructions:

1. Mix ¼ cup corn flour with salt in a large bowl then add tofu and coat well.
2. Shake off the excess corn flour and keep it aside.
3. Set a deep skillet with 1 tablespoon oil over medium heat.
4. Sear the coated tofu slices in the oil for 1 minute per side until golden brown.
5. Mix 1 teaspoon corn flour with sugar, soy sauce and sherry in a small bowl.
6. Stir together soy sauce mixture and mix well until sugar is dissolved.
7. Sauté onion with the remaining oil in a deep skillet for 1 minute.
8. Stir in broccoli and red chili then sauté for 2 minutes.
9. Add sherry mixture and seared tofu to the skillet and cook for 2 minutes.
10. Serve warm with brown rice.

The Plant Based Cookbook For Beginners
650 Easy, Quick, & Simple Plant Based Vegan Diet Recipes With A 31 Day Meal Plan To Lose Weight & Live A Long Healthy Life

403

Vegetable Ratatouille

SERVINGS
6

PREPARATION TIME
10 minutes

COOKING TIME
23 minutes

Nutritional Values Per Serving

Calories	242
Total Fat	3g
Saturated Fat	10g
Cholesterol	12mg
Sodium	281mg
Total Carbohydrate	21g
Dietary Fiber	3.7g
Total Sugars	1.6g
Protein	13g

Ingredients:

- 2 teaspoons olive oil
- 3 zucchinis, sliced
- 3 Lebanese eggplants, sliced
- 1 red capsicum, halved, deseeded, chopped
- 1 brown onion, halved, sliced
- 1 garlic clove, crushed
- 2 x 14 ounces cans tomatoes, chopped
- 2 tablespoons tomato paste
- 3 ½ ounces green beans, topped, chopped
- ¼ cup fresh basil, shredded
- Creamy polenta, to serve

Instructions:

1. Sauté eggplant, onion, capsicum, garlic, and zucchini with oil in a deep skillet for 3 minutes.
2. Reduce its heat and add tomato paste and tomato.
3. Cook for 15 minutes with occasional stirring.
4. Stir in beans and cook for 5 minutes then remove from the heat.
5. Add basil, mix and serve with polenta.

404

The Plant Based Cookbook For Beginners
650 Easy, Quick, & Simple Plant Based Vegan Diet Recipes With A 31 Day Meal Plan To Lose Weight & Live A Long Healthy Life

Angel Hair Pasta with Watercress

SERVINGS
4

PREPARATION TIME
10 minutes

COOKING TIME
13 minutes

Nutritional Values Per Serving

Calories	246
Total Fat	9g
Saturated Fat	10g
Cholesterol	12mg
Sodium	312mg
Total Carbohydrate	22g
Dietary Fiber	0.3g
Total Sugars	7.9g
Protein	8g

Ingredients:

- 12 ounces angel hair pasta
- 2 tablespoons olive oil
- 2 garlic cloves, sliced
- 2 carrots, sliced
- 1 large bunch watercress, trimmed
- ⅓ cup lemon juice
- 2 teaspoons sumac

Instructions:

1. Boil and cook pasta as per the package's instructions until tender then drain and reserve its cooking liquid.

2. Return the pasta to the pan and reserve 1 tablespoon cooking liquid aside.

3. Sauté carrots and garlic with oil in a skillet for 3 minutes.

4. Add boiled pasta, watercress, cooking liquid, sumac and lemon juices.

5. Mix well and serve warm.

The Plant Based Cookbook For Beginners
650 Easy, Quick, & Simple Plant Based Vegan Diet Recipes With A 31 Day Meal Plan To Lose Weight & Live A Long Healthy Life

405

Pumpkin Green Bean Pilaf

SERVINGS	PREPARATION TIME	COOKING TIME
4	10 minutes	30 minutes

Nutritional Values Per Serving

Calories	319
Total Fat	5g
Saturated Fat	3.1g
Cholesterol	14mg
Sodium	354mg
Total Carbohydrate	29g
Dietary Fiber	7g
Total Sugars	5g
Protein	7g

Serving Suggestion:

Enjoy this pilaf with a side of baked tofu.

Ingredients:

- 1 ½ cups white long-grain rice
- 4 cups vegetable liquid stock
- 18 ounces butternut pumpkin, peeled, diced
- 1 teaspoon ground cumin
- 7 ounces green beans, topped, cut into 6cm pieces
- ¼ cup pine nuts
- 1 tablespoon olive oil
- 1 red onion, sliced
- ¼ cup loosely packed parsley leaves

Instructions:

1. Mix rice, cumin, stock and pumpkin in a large saucepan.
2. Cover the rice and cook to a boil then reduce its heat.
3. Cover and cook for 12 minutes on a simmer.
4. Stir in beans and cook for 2 minutes then remove from the heat.
5. Leave the rice for 5 minutes.
6. Roast pine nuts in a skillet for 2 minutes then transfer to a bowl.
7. Sauté onion with oil in a skillet for 6 minutes.
8. Garnish with rice pilaf with pine nuts, fried onions and parsley.
9. Serve warm.

406

The Plant Based Cookbook For Beginners
650 Easy, Quick, & Simple Plant Based Vegan Diet Recipes With A 31 Day Meal Plan To Lose Weight & Live A Long Healthy Life

Pumpkin tofu Skewers

SERVINGS
4

PREPARATION TIME
10 minutes

COOKING TIME
10 minutes

Nutritional Values Per Serving

Calories	386
Total Fat	9g
Saturated Fat	10.3g
Cholesterol	14mg
Sodium	322mg
Total Carbohydrate	32g
Dietary Fiber	3.8g
Total Sugars	4.6g
Protein	17g

Ingredients:

- 21-ounce butternut pumpkin, peeled, cubed, steamed
- 17 ½ ounces firm tofu, drained, cubed
- 1 (7 oz.) red capsicum, cut into 2cm pieces
- 2 tablespoons peanut oil
- 3 cm piece fresh ginger, peeled, grated
- ⅓ cup soy sauce
- 1 small red chili, thinly sliced

Instructions:

1. Thread capsicum, tofu and pumpkin cubes, alternately, over 8 skewers.
2. Place the skewers on a baking sheet.
3. Mix ginger with peanut oil in a bowl and brush over the skewers liberally.
4. Set a barbecue grill over medium heat and grill the skewers for 5 minutes per side until golden brown.
5. Drizzle soy sauce, and sliced red chili over the skewers.
6. Serve warm.

The Plant Based Cookbook For Beginners
650 Easy, Quick, & Simple Plant Based Vegan Diet Recipes With A 31 Day Meal Plan To Lose Weight & Live A Long Healthy Life

407

Tofu Asparagus Stir-Fry

SERVINGS	PREPARATION TIME	COOKING TIME
4	10 minutes	8 minutes

Nutritional Values Per Serving

Calories	378
Total Fat	9g
Saturated Fat	11g
Cholesterol	13mg
Sodium	5mg
Total Carbohydrate	23g
Dietary Fiber	4.1g
Total Sugars	2.7g
Protein	12g

Serving Suggestion:

Enjoy this tofu stir fry with rice.

Ingredients:

- 1 tablespoon peanut oil
- 2 garlic cloves, crushed
- 1 teaspoon grated ginger
- 12 ounces firm tofu, cut into 5mm-thick slices
- 7 ounces snake beans, cut into pieces
- 2 bunches asparagus, cut into chunks
- 3 tablespoons hoisin sauce
- ¼ cup soy sauce
- Toasted cashews, for serving
- Parsley, for serving

Instructions:

1. Sauté garlic and ginger with peanut oil in a deep-frying pan over medium heat for 1 minute.
2. Add tofu and cook until golden brown.
3. Add asparagus and beans, then cover and cook for 3 minutes.
4. Stir in soy sauce and hoisin then cook for 2 minutes on a simmer.
5. Serve warm with cashews and parsley on top.

Red Bean Pumpkin Curry

SERVINGS	PREPARATION TIME	COOKING TIME
4	10 minutes	23 minutes

Nutritional Values Per Serving

Calories	385
Total Fat	8g
Saturated Fat	3g
Cholesterol	23mg
Sodium	132mg
Total Carbohydrate	26g
Dietary Fiber	4g
Total Sugars	3g
Protein	11g

Serving Suggestion:

Try this bean curry with cauliflower rice.

Ingredients:

- 2 tablespoons olive oil
- 1 medium onion, chopped
- 2 garlic cloves, crushed
- 22 ounces butternut pumpkin, peeled, cubed
- 1 tablespoon Madras curry powder
- 28 ounces can tomato
- 15 ½ ounces can red kidney beans, drained
- 5 ounces baby spinach leaves
- Vegan coconut cream, to garnish

Instructions:

1. Sauté onion and garlic with olive oil in a cooking pan for 4 minutes over medium-high heat.
2. Stir in pumpkin then cook for 3 minutes.
3. Add curry powder then sauté for 1 minute.
4. Stir in tomatoes, kidney beans and cook it to boil.
5. Cover and cook these beans over medium heat for 10 minutes.
6. Remove the lid and continue cooking for 2 minutes.
7. Stir in spinach and cook for 3 minutes.
8. Garnish with coconut cream.
9. Serve warm.

The Plant Based Cookbook For Beginners
650 Easy, Quick, & Simple Plant Based Vegan Diet Recipes With A 31 Day Meal Plan To Lose Weight & Live A Long Healthy Life

409

Lentil Ragu with Zucchini

SERVINGS	PREPARATION TIME	COOKING TIME
4	10 minutes	40 minutes

Nutritional Values Per Serving

Calories	380
Total Fat	14g
Saturated Fat	6g
Cholesterol	12mg
Sodium	155mg
Total Carbohydrate	19g
Dietary Fiber	1.7g
Total Sugars	1.1g
Protein	9g

Ingredients:

- 2 tablespoons rapeseed oil
- 3 celery sticks, chopped
- 2 carrots, chopped
- 4 garlic cloves, chopped
- 2 onions, chopped
- 5 ounces button mushrooms, quartered
- 17 ½ ounces pack dried red lentils
- 17 ½ ounces pack passata
- 4 cups vegetable stock
- 1 teaspoon dried oregano
- 2 tablespoons balsamic vinegar
- 2 large zucchinis, spiralized

Instructions:

1. Sauté onions, garlic, carrots and celery with 2 tablespoons oil in a skillet for 5 minutes.
2. Stir in mushrooms then sauté for 2 minutes.
3. Add balsamic vinegar, oregano, vegetable stock, passata and lentils.
4. Cover and cook this mixture for 30 minutes with occasional stirring.
5. Serve the lentils mixture on top of the zucchini.
6. Enjoy.

410

The Plant Based Cookbook For Beginners
650 Easy, Quick, & Simple Plant Based Vegan Diet Recipes With A 31 Day Meal Plan To Lose Weight & Live A Long Healthy Life

Vegetable Jambalaya

SERVINGS	PREPARATION TIME	COOKING TIME
6	10 minutes	30 minutes

Nutritional Values Per Serving

Calories	247
Total Fat	4.9g
Saturated Fat	14g
Cholesterol	194mg
Sodium	407mg
Total Carbohydrate	27g
Dietary Fiber	4g
Total Sugars	1.3g
Protein	16g

Ingredients:

- 2 tablespoons olive oil
- 1 large onion, chopped
- 4 celery sticks, chopped
- 1 red bell pepper, chopped
- ½ cup chopped carrot
- 2 teaspoons smoked paprika
- ½ teaspoon chili flakes
- ½ teaspoon dried oregano
- 3 ½ ounces brown basmati rice
- 14 ounces can tomato, chopped
- 2 garlic cloves, grated
- 14 ounces butter beans, drained and rinsed
- 2 teaspoons vegetable bouillon powder
- 1 large handful of parsley, chopped

Instructions:

1. Sauté bell pepper, celery, and onion with oil in a suitable skillet for 5 minutes over high heat.
2. Add rice, spices, carrots, tomatoes, a cup of water, garlic, bouillon and beans.
3. Cover and cook this mixture on a simmer for 25 minutes until liquid is absorbed.
4. Garnish with parsley.
5. Serve warm.

The Plant Based Cookbook For Beginners
650 Easy, Quick, & Simple Plant Based Vegan Diet Recipes With A 31 Day Meal Plan To Lose Weight & Live A Long Healthy Life

411

Lentil Lasagna

SERVINGS	PREPARATION TIME	COOKING TIME
6	20 minutes	1 hour 35 minutes

Nutritional Values Per Serving	
Calories	439
Total Fat	12g
Saturated Fat	10g
Cholesterol	23mg
Sodium	318mg
Total Carbohydrate	36g
Dietary Fiber	12g
Total Sugars	3.6g
Protein	18g

Ingredients:

- 1 tablespoon olive oil
- 1 onion, chopped
- 1 carrot, chopped
- 1 celery stick, chopped
- 1 garlic clove, crushed
- 2 x 14 ounces cans lentils, drained, rinsed
- 1 tablespoon corn flour
- 14 ounces can tomato, chopped
- 1 teaspoon mushroom ketchup
- 1 teaspoon oregano, chopped
- 1 teaspoon vegetable stock powder
- 2 cauliflower heads, florets
- 2 tablespoons soya milk
- 1 pinch of nutmeg, grated
- 9 dried egg-free lasagna sheets
- ½ cup vegan cheese

Instructions:

1. Sauté celery, carrots and onion with oil in a skillet for 15 minutes.
2. Stir in garlic, lentils and corn flour then mix well.
3. Stir in tomatoes and a cup of water along with stock powder, oregano and mushroom ketchup.
4. Cook for 15 minutes on a simmer with occasional stirring.
5. Meanwhile, boil cauliflower in a pan filled with water for 10 minutes until soft.
6. Drain and puree the cauliflower with soy milk and nutmeg in a blender.
7. At 360 degrees F, preheat your oven.
8. Spread ⅓ lentil mixture in a 20x30 cm baking dish and top it with ⅓ cauliflower puree.
9. Add a single layer of lasagna sheets on top and top them with ⅓ lentil mixture.
10. Add cauliflower puree on top and spread another layer of lasagna on top.
11. Spread another ⅓ lentil mixture on to and top with cauliflower mixture.
12. Lay vegan cheese on top of the lasagna.
13. Cover with a foil sheet and bake for 45 minutes.
14. Remove the foil sheet and bake for 10 minutes.
15. Serve warm.

412

The Plant Based Cookbook For Beginners
650 Easy, Quick, & Simple Plant Based Vegan Diet Recipes With A 31 Day Meal Plan To Lose Weight & Live A Long Healthy Life

Tofu Vegetable Stir-Fry

SERVINGS
4

PREPARATION TIME
10 minutes

COOKING TIME
9 minutes

Nutritional Values Per Serving

Calories	345
Total Fat	21g
Saturated Fat	6g
Cholesterol	0mg
Sodium	21mg
Total Carbohydrate	21.8g
Dietary Fiber	3.7g
Total Sugars	16.7g
Protein	11g

Ingredients:

- 1-inch piece ginger
- ¼ cup soy sauce
- 2 tablespoons garlic chili sauce
- 1 tablespoon toasted sesame oil
- 12 ounces baked tofu
- 3 tablespoons canola oil
- 1 (3 ½-ounce) package shiitake mushrooms, sliced
- Salt, to taste
- 1 green onion, chopped
- ½ cup cashew, roasted and salted, halves and pieces

Instructions:

1. Mix ginger with sesame oil, garlic chili sauce and soy sauce in a bowl.
2. Stir in tofu chunks, then mix well to coat.
3. Sauté mushrooms with canola oil in a suitable skillet for 2 minutes.
4. Add a pinch of salt, then sauté for 5 minutes.
5. Add 2 tablespoons water, green onion, marinated tofu and cook for 2 minutes.
6. Garnish with cashews and serve warm.

The Plant Based Cookbook For Beginners
650 Easy, Quick, & Simple Plant Based Vegan Diet Recipes With A 31 Day Meal Plan To Lose Weight & Live A Long Healthy Life

413

Pulled Jackfruit Sandwiches

SERVINGS	PREPARATION TIME	COOKING TIME
8	10 minutes	60 minutes

Nutritional Values Per Serving

Calories	319
Total Fat	10.8g
Saturated Fat	8.7g
Cholesterol	0mg
Sodium	26mg
Total Carbohydrate	42.2g
Dietary Fiber	0.5g
Total Sugars	29g
Protein	12g

Ingredients:

- 1 (8-ounce) bag coleslaw mix
- 4 teaspoons apple cider vinegar
- Salt and black pepper, to taste
- 2 (20-ounce) cans jackfruit in brine, rinsed and patted dry
- 2 teaspoon chili powder
- 2 tablespoons vegetable oil
- ¾ cup barbecue sauce
- 2 tablespoons coconut sugar
- 8 large potato buns

Instructions:

1. Mix coleslaw mix with black pepper, salt, and vinegar in a bowl.

2. Cover and refrigerate this coleslaw until ready to serve.

3. Mix jackfruits with black pepper, salt and chili powder in a bowl.

4. Sauté this jackfruit with 2 tablespoons oil in a skillet for 3 minutes.

5. Stir in barbecue sauce, 3 cups water and cover to cook on low heat for 50 minutes.

6. Uncover and cook the jackfruits for 5 minutes, then mix well.

7. Remove from heat and shred the cooked jackfruits with a fork.

8. Mix this jackfruit with black pepper, coconut sugar and salt.

9. Divide the pulled jackfruit in the buns and serve with coleslaw.

10. Enjoy.

414

The Plant Based Cookbook For Beginners
650 Easy, Quick, & Simple Plant Based Vegan Diet Recipes With A 31 Day Meal Plan To Lose Weight & Live A Long Healthy Life

Lentil Chili

SERVINGS
6

PREPARATION TIME
10 minutes

COOKING TIME
30 minutes

Nutritional Values Per Serving

Calories	300
Total Fat	3.1g
Saturated Fat	0.5g
Cholesterol	0mg
Sodium	5mg
Total Carbohydrate	26.2g
Dietary Fiber	0.6g
Total Sugars	12.2g
Protein	13g

Ingredients:

- 2 tablespoons olive oil
- 1 bunch green onions, sliced
- 1 red bell pepper, diced
- 1 orange bell pepper, diced
- Salt and black pepper, to taste
- ¼ cup tomato paste
- 3 garlic cloves, minced
- 1 tablespoon ancho chile powder
- 1 tablespoon ground cumin
- ½ teaspoon ground cinnamon
- 2 (14 ½-ounces) cans diced tomatoes
- 1 cup dried red lentils
- 2 (14 ½-ounces) cans kidney beans, rinsed
- 2 cups butternut squash, diced
- 1 tablespoon agave syrup

Serving

- Sliced radish and jalapeno
- Cubed avocado and pepitas

Instructions:

1. Sauté green onions, salt, black pepper and bell peppers in a skillet with oil for 5 minutes.
2. Stir in cinnamon, cumin, ancho chile powder, garlic and tomato paste, then sauté for 1 minute.
3. Stir in tomatoes, 2 cups water, and lentils, then cook to a boil.
4. Reduce its heat and cook on a simmer for 15 minutes.
5. Stir in butternut squash, kidney beans and agave syrup.
6. Continue cooking for 2 minutes with occasional stirring.
7. Optional: Garnish with green onions, pepitas, avocado, jalapeno and radish.
8. Serve warm.

The Plant Based Cookbook For Beginners
650 Easy, Quick, & Simple Plant Based Vegan Diet Recipes With A 31 Day Meal Plan To Lose Weight & Live A Long Healthy Life

415

Scalloped Potatoes

SERVINGS	PREPARATION TIME	COOKING TIME
6	15 minutes	71 minutes

Nutritional Values Per Serving

Calories	411
Total Fat	10.2g
Saturated Fat	2.4g
Cholesterol	0mg
Sodium	258mg
Total Carbohydrate	27.2g
Dietary Fiber	2g
Total Sugars	16.5g
Protein	4.5g

Ingredients:

- 3 tablespoons olive oil
- 8 ounces silken tofu
- 2 tablespoons blanched almonds, sliced
- 2 tablespoons nutritional yeast
- 2 tablespoons lemon juice
- 1 garlic clove, minced
- Salt and black pepper, to taste
- 1 medium onion, chopped
- ½ cup parsley leaves, chopped
- 1 tablespoon fresh thyme leaves, chopped
- 2 pounds large yellow new potatoes, peeled and sliced
- 1½ cups almond milk

Instructions:

1. Set the oven's rack in the middle and preheat it at 375 degrees F.
2. Grease a 2-quart baking dish with oil.
3. Blend tofu with black pepper, salt, garlic, lemon juice, yeast, almonds and 2 tablespoons oil in a food processor.
4. Sauté onions with 1 tablespoon oil in a suitable skillet for 8 minutes until golden brown.
5. Transfer to a bowl, then add thyme and parsley, then mix well.
6. Mix potatoes with salt, water and almond milk in a skillet over medium heat.
7. Cook the potatoes for 18 minutes until soft, then spread half of this mixture in the baking dish.
8. Top these potatoes with ½ tofu mixture and then½ onion mixture.
9. Add the remaining potatoes on top, repeat the tofu and onion layer.
10. Cover this potato dish with a foil sheet and bake for 30 minutes.
11. Uncover and bake for 15 minutes.
12. Garnish with parsley leaves.
13. Serve warm.

416

The Plant Based Cookbook For Beginners
650 Easy, Quick, & Simple Plant Based Vegan Diet Recipes With A 31 Day Meal Plan To Lose Weight & Live A Long Healthy Life

Wild-Rice-Stuffed Squash

SERVINGS **4** PREPARATION TIME **15 minutes** COOKING TIME **1 hour 50 minutes**

Nutritional Values Per Serving

Calories	481
Total Fat	19g
Saturated Fat	0.6g
Cholesterol	0mg
Sodium	26mg
Total Carbohydrate	32g
Dietary Fiber	3g
Total Sugars	5.5g
Protein	6.9g

Ingredients:

- 2 medium butternut squash
- 3 tablespoons apple cider vinegar
- 2 tablespoons pure maple syrup
- 4 tablespoons olive oil
- Salt and black pepper, to taste
- 1 small onion, chopped
- ½ cup wild rice
- ½ teaspoon mild curry powder
- ½ teaspoon ground cinnamon
- ½ cup crumbled tofu
- ¼ teaspoon cayenne pepper
- 1 cup parsley leaves, chopped
- 1 tablespoon fresh sage, chopped
- ¼ cup walnuts, chopped

Instructions:

1. Set the oven's rack in the middle position and preheat it for 400 degrees F.
2. Slice the squash in half and remove its seeds.
3. Place the halved squash in a suitable baking dish with the skin side down.
4. Mix 2 tablespoons oil, maple syrup and vinegar in a bowl.
5. Brush this mixture over the squash and seasoning with black pepper and salt.
6. Roast the squash for 40 minutes, then allow it to cool.
7. Scoop out the flesh and leave ¼ inch border.
8. Cut the squash flesh into small pieces and keep them aside.
9. Sauté onion with 1 tablespoon oil in a suitable skillet for 6 minutes until golden.
10. Stir in salt, cayenne, cinnamon, curry powder, and rice, then cook for 1 minute.
11. Add 2 cups water and cover to cook on a simmer for 40 minutes.
12. Stir in butternut squash, crumbled tofu, maple marinade, black pepper, salt, sage and parsley.
13. Mix well and divide the mixture in the squash skin and bake for another 30 minutes.
14. Garnish with parsley and walnuts.
15. Serve warm.

The Plant Based Cookbook For Beginners
650 Easy, Quick, & Simple Plant Based Vegan Diet Recipes With A 31 Day Meal Plan To Lose Weight & Live A Long Healthy Life

417

Lentil Burgers

SERVINGS	PREPARATION TIME	COOKING TIME
6	10 minutes	45 minutes

Nutritional Values Per Serving

Calories	235
Total Fat	2.2g
Saturated Fat	0.3g
Cholesterol	0mg
Sodium	64mg
Total Carbohydrate	25.5g
Dietary Fiber	1g
Total Sugars	22.3g
Protein	4.1g

Ingredients:

- ¾ cup brown lentils, rinsed
- 1 ¾ cups and 1 tablespoon vegetable broth
- 2 teaspoons olive oil
- 1 large red onion, chopped
- Juice of ½ lemon
- Salt, to taste
- 8 ounces fresh baby spinach
- 2 large garlic cloves, minced
- Black pepper, to taste
- ½ teaspoon ground cumin
- 1 cup whole-wheat breadcrumbs
- ½ cup walnuts, toasted and chopped
- Cooking spray
- 6 whole-grain vegan hamburger buns

Serving

- Baby arugula
- Roasted red bell peppers
- Basil
- Spicy mustard

Instructions:

1. Add 1 ¾ cup broth and lentils to a cooking pot and cook to a boil.
2. Reduce it heat, cover and cook for 30 minutes.
3. Mix the lentils with 1 tablespoon broth in a bowl and mash with a potato masher.
4. Sauté onion, salt and lemon juice in a skillet for 6 minutes.
5. Stir in cumin, black pepper, garlic and spinach, then cook for 3 minutes.
6. Transfer this mixture to the lentils along with walnuts and breadcrumbs.
7. Cover and refrigerate the lentil mixture for 30 minutes.
8. Set a grill over medium-high heat.
9. Make 6 (4 inch) patties out of this mixture.
10. Grease the grilling grates and grill for 3 minutes per side.
11. Place the patties in the serving buns and the rest of the serving ingredients.
12. Serve warm.

418

The Plant Based Cookbook For Beginners
650 Easy, Quick, & Simple Plant Based Vegan Diet Recipes With A 31 Day Meal Plan To Lose Weight & Live A Long Healthy Life

Broccoli Stir-fry

SERVINGS
4

PREPARATION TIME
10 minutes

COOKING TIME
50 minutes

Nutritional Values Per Serving

Calories	234
Total Fat	21.2g
Saturated Fat	4.2g
Cholesterol	0mg
Sodium	14mg
Total Carbohydrate	7.3g
Dietary Fiber	1.4g
Total Sugars	13.6g
Protein	7g

Ingredients:

- 1 ½ pounds broccoli
- 2 tablespoons soy sauce
- 1 tablespoon cornstarch
- 1 teaspoon sugar
- 2 tablespoons 1 teaspoon vegetable oil
- 1 green onion, chopped
- 2 to 3 garlic cloves, chopped
- 1-inch piece ginger, peeled and chopped
- Pinch to ¼ teaspoon crushed red pepper flakes
- ¼ teaspoon toasted sesame oil
- Brown rice, cooked, for serving

Instructions:

1. Mix sugar, cornstarch, soy sauce and ½ cup water in a small bowl.
2. Sauté broccoli florets with 2 tablespoons oil in a suitable skillet for 2 minutes.
3. Add 2 tablespoons water, then cook for 2 minutes.
4. Make a large well at the center, and add 1 teaspoon oil, pepper flakes, ginger, garlic and green onions.
5. Then sauté for 45 minutes, then stir in soy mixture.
6. Mix and cook the broccoli for 30 seconds.
7. Garnish with sesame oil, then serve warm with rice.
8. Enjoy.

The Plant Based Cookbook For Beginners
650 Easy, Quick, & Simple Plant Based Vegan Diet Recipes With A 31 Day Meal Plan To Lose Weight & Live A Long Healthy Life

419

Harissa Roast Cauliflower

SERVINGS | **PREPARATION TIME** | **COOKING TIME**
4 | 10 minutes | 1 hour 3 minutes

Nutritional Values Per Serving

Calories	344
Total Fat	33.2g
Saturated Fat	25.7g
Cholesterol	0mg
Sodium	19mg
Total Carbohydrate	13g
Dietary Fiber	3.6g
Total Sugars	8.4g
Protein	4.5g

Ingredients:

- 5 dried New Mexico chiles
- 4 dried guajillo chiles
- 2 cups boiling water
- ¼ teaspoon whole coriander seeds
- ¼ teaspoon whole cumin seeds
- 2 tablespoons vegetable oil
- 3 garlic cloves, chopped
- Juice of ½ lemon
- Salt and black pepper, to taste
- 1 large head cauliflower, cut into florets
- ¼ cup cilantro leaves

Instructions:

1. Add chiles to a bowl filled with 2 cups boiling water, then leave for minutes 20 minutes.

2. Sauté cumin seeds and coriander in a skillet for 3 minutes.

3. Remove from heat and blend the cumin seeds with 2 teaspoons salt, lemon juice, 1 tbsp oil and garlic in a blender until smooth.

4. Add chiles and ½ cup soaking liquid to the blender, then blend well.

5. At 450 degrees F, preheat your oven.

6. Cut the cauliflower into florets and place them on a baking sheet.

7. Drizzle 1 tbsp oil over the cauliflower and roast for 40 minutes.

8. Drizzle the harissa over the cauliflower.

9. Garnish with cilantro.

10. Serve warm.

Crispy Tofu

SERVINGS
4

PREPARATION TIME
10 minutes

COOKING TIME
12 minutes

Nutritional Values Per Serving

Calories	358
Total Fat	6.3g
Saturated Fat	3.3g
Cholesterol	0mg
Sodium	158mg
Total Carbohydrate	23.9g
Dietary Fiber	1.8g
Total Sugars	15.6g
Protein	28g

Serving Suggestion:

Enjoy this tofu with rice.

Ingredients:

- 1 (14-ounces) block firm tofu, drained
- 2 tablespoons soy sauce
- Juice of 1 lime
- 2 teaspoons agave syrup
- 2 green onions, minced
- ½ teaspoon sriracha
- ½ cup panko
- 1 tablespoon cornstarch
- 1 teaspoon garlic salt
- 1 teaspoon onion powder
- Salt and black pepper, to taste
- 3 tablespoons olive oil

Instructions:

1. Pat dry the tofu block with a paper towel and slice into planks.
2. Mix sriracha, green onion whites, agave syrup, lime juice and soy sauce in a small bowl.
3. Mix panko with onion powder, salt, black pepper, garlic salt, and cornstarch in another bowl.
4. Coat the tofu with the panko mixture.
5. Sear the tofu in a skillet with oil for 5 minutes per side over high heat.
6. Pour in soy sauce mixture and cook for 2 minutes on medium-low heat.
7. Garnish with rest of the green onions.
8. Serve warm.

The Plant Based Cookbook For Beginners
650 Easy, Quick, & Simple Plant Based Vegan Diet Recipes With A 31 Day Meal Plan To Lose Weight & Live A Long Healthy Life

421

Mushroom Sliders

SERVINGS	PREPARATION TIME	COOKING TIME
12	15 minutes	65 minutes

Nutritional Values Per Serving

Calories	346
Total Fat	14g
Saturated Fat	2.1g
Cholesterol	0mg
Sodium	246mg
Total Carbohydrate	25.2g
Dietary Fiber	2.1g
Total Sugars	18.2g
Protein	8g

Ingredients:

- 6 tablespoons vegetable oil
- 1-pound portobello mushrooms, cleaned and sliced
- 2 tablespoons soy sauce
- 1 tablespoon molasses
- 1 tablespoon coconut sugar
- ¾ teaspoon smoked paprika
- ½ teaspoon garlic powder
- Salt and black pepper, to taste
- Vegan cheese

Serving

- Slider buns
- Pickle slices
- Tomato slices
- Lettuce leaves

Instructions:

1. At 300 degrees F, preheat your oven.
2. Layer two baking sheets with parchment paper.
3. Grease these baking sheets with 1 tablespoon oil and spread the mushroom slices.
4. Bake these mushrooms for 30 minutes, flip and continue baking for 30 minutes.
5. Mix garlic powder, paprika, coconut sugar, molasses, and soy sauce in a suitable bowl.
6. Toss in baked mushrooms and mix well.
7. Spread these mushrooms on the baking sheet, sprinkle salt, black pepper, and vegan cheese on top, then bake for 5 minutes.
8. Divide the mushrooms, lettuce leaves, and tomato slices in the buns.
9. Serve.

422

The Plant Based Cookbook For Beginners
650 Easy, Quick, & Simple Plant Based Vegan Diet Recipes With A 31 Day Meal Plan To Lose Weight & Live A Long Healthy Life

Curried Vegetable Chowder

SERVINGS	PREPARATION TIME	COOKING TIME
6	10 minutes	36 minutes

Nutritional Values Per Serving

Calories	344
Total Fat	20.7g
Saturated Fat	17.6g
Cholesterol	0mg
Sodium	42mg
Total Carbohydrate	18.5g
Dietary Fiber	2g
Total Sugars	8.6g
Protein	4.2g

Ingredients:

- 2 tablespoons olive oil
- 2 medium leeks, sliced
- 2 large carrots, chopped
- 1 pound Yukon Gold potatoes, peeled and diced
- 1 teaspoon salt, to taste
- 3 garlic cloves, chopped
- 1 tablespoon fresh ginger, chopped
- 2 tablespoons curry powder
- ¼ teaspoon cayenne pepper
- 1 (13 ½-ounces) can coconut milk
- 4 cups vegetable broth
- Zest and juice of 1 lime
- ½ small head cauliflower, cut into small florets
- 1 (15 ½-ounces) can chickpeas, rinsed
- ½ cup cilantro leaves, coarsely chopped

Instructions:

1. Sauté potatoes, carrots and leeks with olive oil and 1 teaspoon salt in a skillet for 5 minutes.

2. Stir in cayenne, curry, ginger and garlic, then sauté for 1 minute.

3. Pour in 4 cups water, salt to taste, vegetable broth, coconut milk, and lime juice, then cook the mixture on a simmer for 10 minutes.

4. Stir in chickpeas and cauliflower, then cook for 20 minutes.

5. Garnish with cilantro and lime zest.

6. Serve warm.

The Plant Based Cookbook For Beginners
650 Easy, Quick, & Simple Plant Based Vegan Diet Recipes With A 31 Day Meal Plan To Lose Weight & Live A Long Healthy Life

423

Cauliflower Rice

SERVINGS	PREPARATION TIME	COOKING TIME
2	5 minutes	13 minutes

Nutritional Values Per Serving

Calories	161
Total Fat	3.2g
Saturated Fat	0.4g
Cholesterol	0mg
Sodium	152mg
Total Carbohydrate	2.6g
Dietary Fiber	5.5g
Total Sugars	20.9g
Protein	3.1g

Ingredients:

- 1 large head cauliflower, grated
- 3 tablespoons olive oil
- 1 medium onion, diced
- Salt, to taste
- 2 tablespoons parsley leaves, chopped
- Juice of ½ lemon

Instructions:

1. Sauté onion with oil in a suitable skillet for 8 minutes.
2. Stir in cauliflower, and salt then cook for 5 minutes.
3. Garnish with lemon juice and parsley.
4. Serve warm.

424

The Plant Based Cookbook For Beginners
650 Easy, Quick, & Simple Plant Based Vegan Diet Recipes With A 31 Day Meal Plan To Lose Weight & Live A Long Healthy Life

Spicy Sloppy Joes

SERVINGS	PREPARATION TIME	COOKING TIME
6	**15 minutes**	**15 minutes**

Nutritional Values Per Serving

Calories	442
Total Fat	1g
Saturated Fat	1g
Cholesterol	0mg
Sodium	7mg
Total Carbohydrate	31g
Dietary Fiber	2g
Total Sugars	8g
Protein	10g

Ingredients:

- 1-pound cremini mushrooms, chopped
- 1 tablespoon olive oil
- 1 large sweet onion, diced
- 1 ¾ cups light beer
- Salt, to taste
- ⅓ cup walnuts, chopped
- 1 green bell pepper, seeded and diced
- Black pepper, to taste
- ½ teaspoon chipotle chile powder
- ¼ cup ketchup
- 3 tablespoons tomato paste
- 6 whole grain hamburger buns

Instructions:

1. Sauté onions with ¼ teaspoons salt, oil and 1 tablespoon beer in a suitable skillet for 5 minutes.
2. Stir in bell peppers and walnuts then sauté for 3 minutes.
3. Add mushrooms, chipotle powder and ¾ teaspoons black pepper then sauté for 5 minutes.
4. Add ketchup, remaining beer, tomato paste and ⅛ teaspoons salt.
5. Sauté for 2 minutes then divide the mixture into the serving buns.
6. Add desired toppings then serve.

The Plant Based Cookbook For Beginners
650 Easy, Quick, & Simple Plant Based Vegan Diet Recipes With A 31 Day Meal Plan To Lose Weight & Live A Long Healthy Life

425

Tofu and Spinach Scramble

SERVINGS	PREPARATION TIME	COOKING TIME
4	10 minutes	8 minutes

Nutritional Values Per Serving

Calories	382
Total Fat	5g
Saturated Fat	0.4g
Cholesterol	0mg
Sodium	162mg
Total Carbohydrate	17.2g
Dietary Fiber	10.7g
Total Sugars	12.3g
Protein	22g

Ingredients:

- 1 (14-ounces) package firm tofu, crumbled
- ½ teaspoon ground turmeric
- Salt and black pepper, to taste
- ⅛ teaspoon ground cayenne pepper
- 2 tablespoons olive oil
- 3 green onions, sliced
- 5 ounces fresh spinach, chopped
- 1 to 2 teaspoons fresh lemon juice
- 1 cup tomatoes, chopped
- ½ cup fresh basil, chopped

Instructions:

1. Mix tofu with ½ teaspoons black pepper, ¼ teaspoons salt, cayenne and turmeric in a bowl.
2. Sauté green onion whites with oil in a skillet over medium heat for 1 minute.
3. Stir in tofu mixture and cook for 5 minutes.
4. Add ½ teaspoons salt, lemon juice and spinach then cook for 1 minute.
5. Stir in green onions and tomatoes then cook for 1 minute.
6. Garnish with basil.
7. Serve warm.

426

The Plant Based Cookbook For Beginners
650 Easy, Quick, & Simple Plant Based Vegan Diet Recipes With A 31 Day Meal Plan To Lose Weight & Live A Long Healthy Life

Mushroom Bacon

SERVINGS	PREPARATION TIME	COOKING TIME
4	10 minutes	80 minutes

Nutritional Values Per Serving

Calories	142
Total Fat	4.4g
Saturated Fat	0.1g
Cholesterol	0mg
Sodium	33mg
Total Carbohydrate	13g
Dietary Fiber	5.1g
Total Sugars	8.9g
Protein	9g

Ingredients:

- 6 tablespoons vegetable oil
- 1-pound portobello mushrooms, sliced into ⅛-inch slices
- 2 tablespoons molasses
- 2 tablespoons soy sauce
- 2 tablespoons coconut sugar
- ½ teaspoon garlic powder
- ¾ teaspoon smoked paprika
- Salt and black pepper, to taste
- Applewood chips for smoking

Instructions:

1. At 300 degrees F, preheat your oven.
2. Layer two baking sheets with parchment paper then grease with a tablespoon of oil.
3. Mix mushrooms with oil and spread in the baking sheet.
4. Bake these mushrooms for 30 minutes then flip the slices and bake for 35 minutes.
5. Mix paprika, garlic powder, coconut sugar, soy sauce and molasses in a bowl.
6. Add mushroom slices to the molasses mixture.
7. Add two chunks of applewood chips to a cooking pot lined with foil sheet.
8. Set a steamer basket above them and add mushrooms to the basket.
9. Cover and smoke the mushrooms for 10 minutes.
10. Return the mushrooms to the baking sheets and bake for 5 minutes.
11. Serve.

The Plant Based Cookbook For Beginners
650 Easy, Quick, & Simple Plant Based Vegan Diet Recipes With A 31 Day Meal Plan To Lose Weight & Live A Long Healthy Life

427

Marinated White Beans

SERVINGS	PREPARATION TIME	COOKING TIME
4	15 minutes	12 minutes

Nutritional Values Per Serving

Calories	369
Total Fat	2.8g
Saturated Fat	0.8g
Cholesterol	0mg
Sodium	75mg
Total Carbohydrate	65.2g
Dietary Fiber	5.4g
Total Sugars	45.6g
Protein	12g

Ingredients:

- 2 garlic cloves, chopped
- 3 tablespoons olive oil
- 1 tablespoon capers, drained
- 1 teaspoon grated lemon zest
- 1 tablespoon lemon juice
- 1 teaspoon chopped fresh rosemary
- ¼ teaspoon crushed red pepper flakes
- Salt, to taste
- 1 (15 ½-ounces) can white beans, rinsed
- 2 tablespoons parsley, chopped

Instructions:

1. Sauté garlic with oil in a suitable skillet over low heat for 2 minutes.
2. Stir in capers, salt, red pepper flakes, rosemary, lemon juice and lemon zest then cook for 5 minutes.
3. Mix well then stir in parsley, and beans then cook for 5 minutes.
4. Serve warm.

Lentil-Mushroom Meatballs

SERVINGS	PREPARATION TIME	COOKING TIME
6	20 minutes	1 hour 32 minutes

Nutritional Values Per Serving

Calories	377
Total Fat	0.9g
Saturated Fat	0.1g
Cholesterol	0mg
Sodium	9mg
Total Carbohydrate	43g
Dietary Fiber	6.3g
Total Sugars	5.4g
Protein	17g

Serving Suggestion:

Enjoy the meatballs with zucchini noodles and marinara sauce.

Ingredients:

Meatballs

- 3 tablespoons olive oil
- 1 cup brown lentils, rinsed
- ⅓ cup wheat berries
- 1 small yellow onion, chopped
- 4 ounces shiitake mushrooms, chopped
- 5 garlic cloves, chopped
- Salt and black pepper, to taste
- 3 tablespoons tomato paste
- 3 tablespoons soy sauce
- 2 tablespoons red wine vinegar
- 4 teaspoons nutritional yeast
- ½ cup fresh parsley leaves
- 2 slices white bread bun, torn into small piece

Sauce

- 2 tablespoons olive oil
- 4 garlic cloves, sliced
- 1 (28-ounces) can whole peeled tomatoes
- 1 handful basil leaves, torn
- Salt, to taste

Instructions:

1. Sauté garlic with olive oil in a suitable skillet for 4 minutes.
2. Stir in tomatoes and ½ cup water then cook to a simmer.
3. Add basil leaves and salt then cook for 25 minutes then remove from heat.
4. Meanwhile, at 400 degrees F, preheat your oven.
5. Layer a suitable baking sheet with parchment paper and grease it with cooking oil.
6. Boil wheat berries with water in a suitable cooking pan for 30 minutes.
7. Drain and keep these berries aside.
8. Add 2 ½ cups water and lentils in a medium saucepan then cook to a boil.
9. Reduce it heat and cook for 15 minutes then remove from the heat.
10. Sauté garlic, mushrooms, onion and 1 tsp. salt and black pepper then cook for 6 minutes.
11. Stir in yeast, vinegar, soy sauce, and tomato paste then cook for 2 minutes.
12. Blend this mushroom mixture with lentils, parsley, and wheat berries.
13. Soak bread in ¼ cup water and leave for 5 minutes then mash it into a paste.
14. Add the bread mixture to the lentil and mix well.
15. Make 18 meatballs out of this mixture and place them in the baking sheet.
16. Bake the meatballs for 30 minutes until golden brown then flip once cooked halfway through.
17. Add the meatballs to a bowl and pour the sauce over them.
18. Garnish with parsley and serve warm.

The Plant Based Cookbook For Beginners
650 Easy, Quick, & Simple Plant Based Vegan Diet Recipes With A 31 Day Meal Plan To Lose Weight & Live A Long Healthy Life

429

Green Bean Casserole

SERVINGS
6

PREPARATION TIME
15 minutes

COOKING TIME
31 minutes

Nutritional Values Per Serving

Calories	349
Total Fat	30.2g
Saturated Fat	18.4g
Cholesterol	0mg
Sodium	149mg
Total Carbohydrate	20.1g
Dietary Fiber	0.3g
Total Sugars	12.5g
Protein	3g

Ingredients:

- 3 tablespoons olive oil
- 1 ¼ pounds green beans, cut into 2-inch pieces
- Salt, to taste
- 8 ounces cremini mushrooms, sliced
- Black pepper, to taste
- 1 medium onion, diced
- 2 garlic cloves, minced
- 1 tablespoon fresh thyme leaves
- ¾ cup vegetable broth
- 3 tablespoons whole wheat flour
- 1 cup almond milk
- ⅓ cup vegan sour cream
- 1 teaspoon soy sauce
- 2 cups crispy fried onions

Instructions:

1. At 400 degrees F, preheat your oven.
2. Boil water with a pinch of salt in a cooking pan and add green beans then cook for 5 minutes.
3. Drain and set the green beans on the side.
4. Sauté mushrooms with oil in a suitable skillet for 4 minutes.
5. Stir in black pepper, salt, thyme, garlic and onion then sauté for 2 minutes.
6. Pour ¼ cup broth and cook for 1 minute on a simmer.
7. Stir in flour, mix then add almond milk and remaining broth.
8. Mix and cook for 4 minutes with occasional stirring until it thickens.
9. Stir in soy sauce, sour cream, and green beans then mix well.
10. Spread the green bean mixture in a baking pan and top with fried onions.
11. Bake the casserole for 15 minutes.
12. Serve warm.

430

The Plant Based Cookbook For Beginners
650 Easy, Quick, & Simple Plant Based Vegan Diet Recipes With A 31 Day Meal Plan To Lose Weight & Live A Long Healthy Life

Indian Spicy Eggplant

SERVINGS
6

PREPARATION TIME
10 minutes

COOKING TIME
40 minutes

Nutritional Values Per Serving

Calories	285
Total Fat	15g
Saturated Fat	8.7g
Cholesterol	10mg
Sodium	173mg
Total Carbohydrate	33g
Dietary Fiber	1.4g
Total Sugars	27.6g
Protein	4.2g

Ingredients:

- 1 large eggplant
- 2 tablespoons vegetable oil
- 1 teaspoon curry powder
- 1 teaspoon cumin powder
- ½ teaspoon ground turmeric
- 1 small onion, diced
- 1 tablespoon ginger, minced
- 2 garlic cloves, minced
- 3 plum tomatoes, diced
- Salt, to taste
- 1 cup frozen peas, thawed
- Cooked basmati rice, for serving
- 1 tablespoon fresh cilantro leaves, chopped
- 1 tablespoon fresh mint leaves, chopped

Instructions:

1. Poke the eggplant with a knife then place on a rack in a 6-quart instant Pot.
2. Add 1 cup water, secure the lid and pressure cook for 20 minutes.
3. Release the pressure completely then remove the lid.
4. Empty the Instant pot and switch it to the Sauté mode.
5. Add oil, cumin, curry powder and turmeric to the Instant Pot.
6. Sauté for 30 seconds then add onions and sauté for 8 minutes.
7. Stir in garlic and ginger then sauté for 2 minutes.
8. Add tomatoes and sauté for 7 minutes.
9. Cut the eggplant into chunks and add them to the tomatoes.
10. Stir in 1 teaspoon salt and peas then sauté for 3 minutes.
11. Garnish with mint and cilantro.
12. Serve warm with basmati rice.

The Plant Based Cookbook For Beginners
650 Easy, Quick, & Simple Plant Based Vegan Diet Recipes With A 31 Day Meal Plan To Lose Weight & Live A Long Healthy Life

431

Spinach and Mushroom Lasagna

SERVINGS	PREPARATION TIME	COOKING TIME
6	20 minutes	82 minutes

Nutritional Values Per Serving

Calories	357
Total Fat	14.3g
Saturated Fat	12.7g
Cholesterol	0mg
Sodium	52mg
Total Carbohydrate	21g
Dietary Fiber	2.3g
Total Sugars	4.5g
Protein	1.4g

Ingredients:

- 3 tablespoons olive oil
- 3 garlic cloves, sliced
- 1 teaspoon fennel seeds
- 1 pinch crushed red pepper flakes
- 1-pound white mushrooms, sliced
- 1 (28-ounces) can crushed tomatoes
- Salt, to taste
- 1 (12-ounces) package firm tofu, strained
- 1 (10-ounces) package frozen spinach, thawed and squeezed
- 1 (8-ounces) package vegan cream cheese
- ½ cup fresh basil leaves
- 3 tablespoons nutritional yeast
- ½ teaspoon freshly nutmeg, grated
- 12 vegan lasagna noodles
- ½ cup vegan mozzarella cheese, shredded

Instructions:

1. At 350 degrees F, preheat your oven.
2. Layer a 9-inch baking dish with cooking spray.
3. Sauté ½ of the garlic slices with oil, red pepper flakes, nutmeg and fennel seeds in a suitable skillet for 1 minute.
4. Stir in mushrooms then sauté for 7 minutes with occasional.
5. Add tomatoes, 1 tsp. salt and 1 cup water then cook for 15 minutes.
6. Blend tofu with spinach, 1 teaspoon salt, remaining garlic slices, yeast, basil and vegan cream cheese in a food processor.
7. Spread the ½ mushroom sauce in the baking dish and top it with noodles in a single layer.
8. Top the noodles with ½ of the tofu mixture and with 1/3 sauce.
9. Repeat the noodle, spinach mixture and tofu mixture layers.
10. Cover the lasagna with a foil sheet and bake for 45 minutes.
11. Sprinkle vegan cheese on top and bake for 15 minutes.
12. Serve warm.

432

The Plant Based Cookbook For Beginners
650 Easy, Quick, & Simple Plant Based Vegan Diet Recipes With A 31 Day Meal Plan To Lose Weight & Live A Long Healthy Life

Quinoa with Roasted Squash

SERVINGS
4

PREPARATION TIME
15 minutes

COOKING TIME
44 minutes

Nutritional Values Per Serving

Calories	260
Total Fat	2.5g
Saturated Fat	0g
Cholesterol	0mg
Sodium	155mg
Total Carbohydrate	28.5g
Dietary Fiber	0.3g
Total Sugars	7.3g
Protein	1.1g

Ingredients:

- 2-pounds butternut squash, seeded, and cut into chunks
- 5 tablespoons olive oil
- 2 teaspoons thyme leaves, chopped
- Salt and black pepper, to taste 1 ½ cups quinoa
- 4 cups vegetable broth
- ¼ cup dried cranberries
- 1 tablespoon white wine vinegar
- 3 ounces baby kale

Instructions:

1. At 400 degrees F, preheat your oven.
2. Layer a rimmed baking sheet with a foil sheet.
3. Toss squash with thyme, 1 tsp salt and black pepper and 3 tablespoons oil in a large bowl.
4. Spread the squash in the baking sheet and bake for 30 minutes.
5. Rinse the quinoa and boil with vegetable broth in a pot for 9 minutes.
6. Drain and mix quinoa with black pepper and salt to taste, vinegar, cranberries and roasted pistachios in a bowl.
7. Add squash and baby kale to the quinoa bowl then mix well.
8. Serve.

The Plant Based Cookbook For Beginners
650 Easy, Quick, & Simple Plant Based Vegan Diet Recipes With A 31 Day Meal Plan To Lose Weight & Live A Long Healthy Life

433

Quinoa-Cranberry Stuffed Acorn Squash

SERVINGS	PREPARATION TIME	COOKING TIME
4	15 minutes	95 minutes

Nutritional Values Per Serving

Calories	314
Total Fat	2.6g
Saturated Fat	0g
Cholesterol	0mg
Sodium	143mg
Total Carbohydrate	28.4g
Dietary Fiber	0g
Total Sugars	24.1g
Protein	1g

Ingredients:

- 2 medium acorn squash
- 3 tablespoons apple cider vinegar
- 3 tablespoons olive oil
- 2 tablespoons pure maple syrup
- Salt and black pepper, to taste
- 1 small onion, chopped
- 1 cup red quinoa, rinsed
- 2 cups water
- 1 teaspoon mild curry powder
- ½ teaspoon ground cinnamon
- ¼ teaspoon cayenne pepper
- 1 cup parsley leaves, chopped
- ¼ cup roasted pistachios, chopped

Instructions:

1. Set the oven rack in the middle portion and preheat it at 400 degrees F.
2. Slice the squash in half and remove it seeds. Place the halved squash in a large baking dish.
3. Mix maple syrup, 2 tablespoons oil, ¼ teaspoons salt, black pepper and vinegar in a bowl.
4. Brush this mixture over the squash skin and flesh then roast for 60 minutes.
5. Sauté onions with 1 teaspoon oil in a suitable skillet for 6 minutes.
6. Stir in quinoa, 1 teaspoon salt, cinnamon, and curry powder then sauté for 1 minute.
7. Add water to quinoa, cover and cook on low heat for 24 minutes.
8. Uncover and cook for 5 minutes.
9. Stir in maple mixture, parsley, and pistachios.
10. Divide this mixture in the roasted squash.
11. Serve warm.

434

The Plant Based Cookbook For Beginners
650 Easy, Quick, & Simple Plant Based Vegan Diet Recipes With A 31 Day Meal Plan To Lose Weight & Live A Long Healthy Life

Vegan Bread Stuffing

SERVINGS	PREPARATION TIME	COOKING TIME
4	15 minutes	60 minutes

Nutritional Values Per Serving

Calories	303
Total Fat	23g
Saturated Fat	19.8g
Cholesterol	5mg
Sodium	45mg
Total Carbohydrate	25.1g
Dietary Fiber	3.6g
Total Sugars	17.7g
Protein	3.9g

Ingredients:

- 4 tablespoons olive oil
- 2 bags green tea
- 1 large onion, chopped
- 2 stalks celery, chopped
- 8 ounces sliced mushrooms
- 1 tablespoon fresh sage, chopped
- 1 tablespoon fresh thyme, chopped
- Salt and black pepper, to taste
- 16 cups white bread, 1-inch cubed
- ¼ cup fresh parsley, chopped

Instructions:

1. At 375 degrees F, preheat your oven.
2. Grease a 9x13 inch baking dish with olive oil.
3. Steep tea bags in 2 cup boiling water for 5 minutes then remove the bags from the liquid and keep this tea aside.
4. Sauté onions and celery with 3 tablespoons oil in a suitable skillet for 6 minutes.
5. Stir in black pepper, salt, thyme, sage and mushrooms then sauté for 4 minutes.
6. Add green tea, cook to a simmer then remove it from the heat.
7. Stir in bread chunks, and parsley, and leave for 10 minutes.
8. Spread the prepared bread mixture in the baking dish and drizzle 1 teaspoon oil on top.
9. Cover them with a foil sheet and bake for 30 minutes.
10. Uncover and cook again for 15 minutes.
11. Serve warm.

The Plant Based Cookbook For Beginners
650 Easy, Quick, & Simple Plant Based Vegan Diet Recipes With A 31 Day Meal Plan To Lose Weight & Live A Long Healthy Life

435

Okra Carrot Stew

SERVINGS	PREPARATION TIME	COOKING TIME
4	10 minutes	15 minutes

Nutritional Values Per Serving

Calories	289
Total Fat	4.1g
Saturated Fat	0.2g
Cholesterol	0mg
Sodium	33mg
Total Carbohydrate	19g
Dietary Fiber	6.5g
Total Sugars	18.9g
Protein	2.5g

Serving Suggestion:

Enjoy the stew with rice.

Ingredients:

- 1-pound okra, trimmed and halved
- 1 onion, chopped
- 1 tablespoon vegetable oil
- 14-ounces carrots, diced
- ½ cup tomatoes
- ¼ cup water
- 2 teaspoons garam masala
- Salt and black pepper, to taste

Instructions:

1. Sauté onion with oil in a suitable skillet for 5 minutes.
2. Toss in okra and carrots and sauté for 5 minutes
3. Stir in tomatoes, water, garam masala, black pepper, and salt.
4. Partially cover and cook for 5 minutes on a simmer.
5. Serve warm.

436

The Plant Based Cookbook For Beginners
650 Easy, Quick, & Simple Plant Based Vegan Diet Recipes With A 31 Day Meal Plan To Lose Weight & Live A Long Healthy Life

Tofu Tacos

SERVINGS
8

PREPARATION TIME
15 minutes

COOKING TIME
17 minutes

Nutritional Values Per Serving

Calories	421
Total Fat	4.6g
Saturated Fat	0.4g
Cholesterol	0mg
Sodium	92mg
Total Carbohydrate	44.8g
Dietary Fiber	10g
Total Sugars	33.5g
Protein	3.1g

Serving Suggestion:

Enjoy the tacos with guacamole.

Ingredients:

- 1 tablespoon chili powder
- 1 teaspoon ground cumin
- ½ teaspoon dried oregano
- ½ teaspoon salt
- ¼ teaspoon black pepper
- ⅛ teaspoon ground cinnamon
- 1 (16 ounces) block tofu (firm tofu), cut into chunks
- 3 tablespoons olive oil
- ½ cup onion, chopped
- 2 large garlic cloves, minced
- 1 (15-ounces) can black beans, rinsed
- 2 teaspoons cider vinegar
- ½ cup cilantro, chopped
- 8 corn tortillas, warmed
- ¼ cup cabbage, Shredded
- Pico de Gallo and guacamole
- Vegan sour cream, to garnish

Instructions:

1. Mix cinnamon, black pepper, salt, oregano, cumin and chili powder in a bowl.
2. Toss in tofu then mix well.
3. Sauté onion with olive oil in a suitable skillet for 3 minutes.
4. Stir in garlic and sauté for 1 minute.
5. Add tofu then cook for 10 minutes.
6. Stir in beans then sauté for 3 minutes then stir in vinegar and cilantro.
7. Divide the beans mixture over the tortillas and top it with Pico de Gallo, cabbage and vegan sour cream.
8. Roll the tortillas and serve.

The Plant Based Cookbook For Beginners
650 Easy, Quick, & Simple Plant Based Vegan Diet Recipes With A 31 Day Meal Plan To Lose Weight & Live A Long Healthy Life

437

Zucchini-Chickpea Burgers

SERVINGS	PREPARATION TIME	COOKING TIME
8	15 minutes	17 minutes

Nutritional Values Per Serving

Calories	313
Total Fat	6.5g
Saturated Fat	1.4g
Cholesterol	0mg
Sodium	232mg
Total Carbohydrate	16g
Dietary Fiber	1.7g
Total Sugars	4.6g
Protein	19.9g

Ingredients:

- 4 tablespoons tahini
- 1 tablespoon lemon juice
- 3 teaspoons white miso
- 1¼ teaspoons onion powder
- 1¼ teaspoons garlic powder
- 1¼ teaspoons black pepper
- 2 tablespoons water
- 1 teaspoon fresh chives, chopped
- 1 (15-ounces) can chickpeas, rinsed
- 1 teaspoon ground cumin
- ¼ teaspoon salt
- ¼ cup fresh parsley leaves
- ½ cup zucchini, shredded
- ⅓ cup old-fashioned rolled oats
- 1 tablespoon olive oil
- 4 whole-grain hamburger buns, toasted
- 1 cup packed fresh arugula
- 4 tomato slices

Instructions:

1. Mix ¼ teaspoons black pepper, ¼ teaspoons garlic powder, ½ teaspoons onion powder, 1 teaspoon miso, 2 tablespoons tahini and lemon juice in a small bowl.
2. Stir in water and chives then mix well.
3. Blend chickpeas with ¾ teaspoons onion powder, 1 teaspoon black pepper, 1 teaspoon garlic powder, 2 teaspoons miso, 2 tablespoons tahini, salt, and cumin in a food processor.
4. Add chives and parsley then blend again.
5. Squeeze the grated zucchini and mix it with chickpea mixture and oat in a bowl.
6. Make 4 patties out of this zucchini mixture.
7. Sear these patties in a skillet, greased with oil, for 5 minutes per side.
8. Serve these burgers with buns, tahini sauce, tomato slices and arugula.
9. Enjoy.

438

The Plant Based Cookbook For Beginners
650 Easy, Quick, & Simple Plant Based Vegan Diet Recipes With A 31 Day Meal Plan To Lose Weight & Live A Long Healthy Life

Cucumber Sushi Rolls

SERVINGS
8

PREPARATION TIME
10 minutes

COOKING TIME
10 minutes

Nutritional Values Per Serving

Calories	277
Total Fat	3.4g
Saturated Fat	0.2g
Cholesterol	0mg
Sodium	145mg
Total Carbohydrate	13g
Dietary Fiber	1.9g
Total Sugars	2g
Protein	1.5g

Ingredients:

- 2 large English cucumbers
- 4 ounces vegan cream cheese
- 1 teaspoon sriracha
- ½ daikon radish, cut into matchsticks
- ¼ teaspoon ginger powder
- 2 carrot sticks cut into matchsticks
- 1 red pepper cut into matchsticks
- 1 avocado thinly sliced

Instructions:

1. Cut the cucumbers into long thin slices.
2. Spread the cucumber slices on a working surface.
3. Brush them with vegan cream cheese, and sriracha.
4. Add ginger powder, carrot, daikon radish, red pepper and avocado on top.
5. Roll the cucumber slices and seal with a toothpick.
6. Serve.

The Plant Based Cookbook For Beginners
650 Easy, Quick, & Simple Plant Based Vegan Diet Recipes With A 31 Day Meal Plan To Lose Weight & Live A Long Healthy Life

439

Potatoes Jacket

SERVINGS	PREPARATION TIME	COOKING TIME
4	10 minutes	60 minutes

Nutritional Values Per Serving

Calories	276
Total Fat	5.5g
Saturated Fat	0.8g
Cholesterol	0mg
Sodium	277mg
Total Carbohydrate	25.8g
Dietary Fiber	5.2g
Total Sugars	1.3g
Protein	3.2g

Serving Suggestion:

Try these potatoes with sautéed carrots on the side.

Ingredients:

- 4 medium russet potatoes
- 4 teaspoon parsley, chopped
- Salt and black pepper, to taste

Instructions:

1. Poke the potatoes with a fork and bake in a baking sheet for 1 hour at 425 degrees F.
2. Carve 1 deep slit on top of the potatoes vertically.
3. Lightly mash the potato flesh with a fork.
4. Add parsley, black pepper and salt to each potato jacket.
5. Serve warm.

440

The Plant Based Cookbook For Beginners
650 Easy, Quick, & Simple Plant Based Vegan Diet Recipes With A 31 Day Meal Plan To Lose Weight & Live A Long Healthy Life

Rice Noodle Bowls with Tofu

SERVINGS	PREPARATION TIME	COOKING TIME
4	15 minutes	58 minutes

Nutritional Values Per Serving

Calories	389
Total Fat	2.2g
Saturated Fat	0.5g
Cholesterol	0mg
Sodium	42mg
Total Carbohydrate	75.2g
Dietary Fiber	12.8g
Total Sugars	2.4g
Protein	18.6g

Ingredients:

- 3 tablespoons avocado oil
- 1 tablespoon lemongrass, minced
- 3 teaspoons garlic, minced
- 1 cup rice noodles
- 1 (15-ounces) can light coconut milk
- ⅓ cup water
- ¾ teaspoon salt
- 2 tablespoons toasted sesame oil
- 2 tablespoons tamari
- 1 tablespoon packed coconut sugar
- ¼ teaspoon crushed red pepper
- 1 (14 ounces) package extra-firm water-packed tofu
- 1 tablespoon peeled fresh ginger, grated
- 1 tablespoon lime juice
- 3 green onions, sliced

Instructions:

1. Sauté garlic and lemon grass with 1 tablespoon avocado oil in a saucepan for 30 seconds.

2. Stir in rice noodles, water, coconut milk and ½ teaspoons salt.

3. Cook this mixture to a simmer, cover and cook for 10 minutes.

4. Mix coconut sugar, red pepper, tamari and sesame oil in a small bowl.

5. Slice the tofu in slabs and pat them dry.

6. Sear tofu with 2 tbsp. avocado oil in skillet for 5 minutes per side.

7. Transfer the tofu to a plate and sauté garlic, green onion and ginger in the same pan for 3 minutes.

8. Stir in prepared sauce, and lime juice, then mix gently.

9. Serve warm.

The Plant Based Cookbook For Beginners
650 Easy, Quick, & Simple Plant Based Vegan Diet Recipes With A 31 Day Meal Plan To Lose Weight & Live A Long Healthy Life

441

Spinach Penne Pasta

SERVINGS	PREPARATION TIME	COOKING TIME
4	10 minutes	20 minutes

Nutritional Values Per Serving

Calories	343
Total Fat	5.8g
Saturated Fat	4.4g
Cholesterol	0mg
Sodium	39mg
Total Carbohydrate	20.8g
Dietary Fiber	3.9g
Total Sugars	1.9g
Protein	16g

Ingredients:

- 12 ounces whole-wheat penne
- ¼ cup olive oil
- 3 large garlic cloves, sliced
- 1 (16 ounces) jar roasted red peppers, chopped
- 1 (10 ounce) package baby spinach
- ½ teaspoon salt
- ½ teaspoon black pepper
- ¼ cup vegan cheese, crumbled

Instructions:

1. Boil penne pasta in water as per the package's instruction then drain.
2. Sauté garlic with oil in suitable skillet until golden brown.
3. Stir in spinach, black pepper, red peppers and salt then sauté for 4 minutes.
4. Stir in penne and garnish with vegan cheese.
5. Serve.

442

The Plant Based Cookbook For Beginners
650 Easy, Quick, & Simple Plant Based Vegan Diet Recipes With A 31 Day Meal Plan To Lose Weight & Live A Long Healthy Life

Ramen Noodles with Mushrooms

SERVINGS	PREPARATION TIME	COOKING TIME
4	15 minutes	20 minutes

Nutritional Values Per Serving

Calories	324
Total Fat	4.4g
Saturated Fat	0.7g
Cholesterol	0mg
Sodium	394mg
Total Carbohydrate	59.3g
Dietary Fiber	8.1g
Total Sugars	7.3g
Protein	13.6g

Ingredients:

- 4 ounces Ramen noodles
- 1 tablespoon canola oil
- 1½ tablespoons fresh garlic, minced
- 1 tablespoon fresh ginger, grated
- 1 serrano pepper, seeded and minced
- 1 (32 fluid ounces) vegetable broth
- 1 tablespoon mirin
- 1 tablespoon soy sauce
- 2 cups cremini mushrooms, sliced
- 1 cup broccoli, diced
- 2 teaspoons white miso
- 2 baby bok choy heads, cut into 1-inch pieces
- ¼ cup warm water
- 1 (14 ounces) package tofu, cubed
- ½ cup green onions, sliced
- 4 teaspoons toasted sesame oil

Instructions:

1. Boil and cook noodles as per the package's instructions then drain.
2. Sauté ginger, garlic and serrano with oil in a suitable skillet for 1 minute.
3. Stir in 1 tablespoon soy sauce, mirin and broth then cook to a simmer.
4. Add broccoli and mushrooms then cook for 6 minutes.
5. Toss in bok choy and cook for 2 minutes.
6. Mix miso with warm water in a bowl then add to broth.
7. Stir in tofu and cook for 1 minute.
8. Add green onions and mix well.
9. Divide the noodles in the serving bowls and top them with the broth and vegetables.
10. Garnish with soy sauce and sesame oil.
11. Enjoy.

The Plant Based Cookbook For Beginners
650 Easy, Quick, & Simple Plant Based Vegan Diet Recipes With A 31 Day Meal Plan To Lose Weight & Live A Long Healthy Life

443

Zucchini Enchilada Casserole

SERVINGS	PREPARATION TIME	COOKING TIME
6	15 minutes	40 minutes

Nutritional Values Per Serving

Calories	268
Total Fat	1.2g
Saturated Fat	0.2g
Cholesterol	0mg
Sodium	111mg
Total Carbohydrate	49.7g
Dietary Fiber	12g
Total Sugars	4.3g
Protein	15.5g

Ingredients:

- 2 tablespoons olive oil
- 1 cup onion, chopped
- ¾ cup poblano peppers, chopped
- 6 garlic cloves, minced
- 1 medium yellow squash, halved and sliced
- 1 medium zucchini, halved and sliced
- 1 cup fresh corn kernels
- 1 cup Pico de Gallo
- ½ teaspoon salt
- 1 (15-ounces) can pinto beans, rinsed
- 1 (15-ounces) can black beans, rinsed
- 8 6-inch corn tortillas
- 1½ cups vegan cheese, shredded
- 1 avocado, diced
- ½ cup green onions
- ½ cup vegan sour cream

Instructions:

1. At 350 degrees F, preheat your oven.
2. Sauté onion, garlic and poblanos with oil in a suitable skillet for 4 minutes.
3. Stir in salt, Pico de Gallo, corn, zucchini and squash then sauté for 6 minutes.
4. Mix and cook for 2 minutes then add black beans and pinto beans.
5. Grease a 9x13 inch baking dish with cooking spray.
6. Spread ⅓ of the beans mixture in the dish and top it with 4 tortillas.
7. Repeat these layers and top them with cheese.
8. Bake the casserole for 30 minutes in the oven.
9. Garnish with green onions, avocado and sour cream.
10. Serve warm.

444

The Plant Based Cookbook For Beginners
650 Easy, Quick, & Simple Plant Based Vegan Diet Recipes With A 31 Day Meal Plan To Lose Weight & Live A Long Healthy Life

Black Bean-Cauliflower Rice

SERVINGS
4

PREPARATION TIME
10 minutes

COOKING TIME
13 minutes

Nutritional Values Per Serving

Calories	391
Total Fat	1.9g
Saturated Fat	0.3g
Cholesterol	0mg
Sodium	46mg
Total Carbohydrate	83.4g
Dietary Fiber	18.7g
Total Sugars	24.8g
Protein	16.2g

Ingredients:

- Olive oil
- 1 cup frozen cauliflower rice
- ⅛ teaspoon salt
- 2 tablespoons onion, chopped
- 2 tablespoons green onion, chopped
- ½ teaspoon chili powder
- ½ teaspoon ground cumin
- ¼ teaspoon dried oregano
- ⅔ cup canned black beans, rinsed
- 2 tablespoons roasted red pepper, chopped
- ¼ cup water
- 1 tablespoon lime juice
- ¼ cup vegan cheese, shredded
- 1 medium tomato, chopped
- 1 tablespoon fresh cilantro, chopped

Instructions:

1. Sauté cauliflower rice, with 1 tablespoon oil and salt in a skillet for 5 minutes then transfer to a small bowl.

2. Sauté onion, with 2 teaspoons oil, cumin, oregano, cumin, chili powder and green onion in the same skillet then sauté for 3 minutes.

3. Stir in red pepper, beans, and water and cook for 5 minutes.

4. Add lime juice, mix and divide the mixture over cauliflower rice.

5. Garnish with tomatoes, cilantro and vegan cheese.

6. Enjoy.

The Plant Based Cookbook For Beginners
650 Easy, Quick, & Simple Plant Based Vegan Diet Recipes With A 31 Day Meal Plan To Lose Weight & Live A Long Healthy Life

445

Zucchini Noodle Primavera

SERVINGS | PREPARATION TIME | COOKING TIME
4 | **15 minutes** | **10 minutes**

Nutritional Values Per Serving

Calories	505
Total Fat	6.6g
Saturated Fat	1.1g
Cholesterol	0mg
Sodium	130mg
Total Carbohydrate	94.9g
Dietary Fiber	17.7g
Total Sugars	18.7g
Protein	20.7g

Ingredients:

- 2 tablespoons vegan butter
- 2 tablespoons whole wheat flour
- 1 cup almond milk
- 3 tablespoons basil pesto
- 1 tablespoon olive oil
- 2 cups cherry tomatoes, halved
- 4 garlic cloves, sliced
- ¼ teaspoon salt
- 2 cups broccoli florets
- 1 cup green bell pepper, sliced
- 2 (10 ounces) packages spiralized zucchini noodles
- 2 tablespoons fresh basil, chopped

Instructions:

1. Sauté flour with butter in a suitable cooking pot over medium high heat.
2. Stir in almond milk and cook until the mixture thickens.
3. Add pesto, mix well and leave the mixture aside.
4. Sauté garlic and tomatoes with olive oil in a suitable skillet over medium high heat for 3 minutes.
5. Add pesto mixture, salt, bell pepper and broccoli then cook for 4 minutes.
6. Stir in zucchini noodles then mix well.
7. Cook for 2 minutes then garnish with basil.
8. Serve warm.

446

The Plant Based Cookbook For Beginners
650 Easy, Quick, & Simple Plant Based Vegan Diet Recipes With A 31 Day Meal Plan To Lose Weight & Live A Long Healthy Life

Vegetarian Gumbo

SERVINGS | PREPARATION TIME | COOKING TIME
6 | 10 minutes | 27 minutes

Nutritional Values Per Serving	
Calories	317
Total Fat	5.6g
Saturated Fat	0.5g
Cholesterol	0mg
Sodium	209mg
Total Carbohydrate	54g
Dietary Fiber	14.9g
Total Sugars	13.1g
Protein	15.5g

Ingredients:

- ½ cup whole wheat flour
- ⅓ cup olive oil
- 1 butternut squash, peeled, seeded and cubed
- 2 cups yellow onions, chopped
- 2 cups poblano peppers, chopped
- 1 cup celery, chopped
- 8 cups vegetable broth
- 1 (28 ounces) can plum tomatoes, drained and crushed
- 1¾ teaspoons salt
- 3 cups fresh okra, trimmed and sliced
- 3 cups zucchini, chopped
- 2 (15 ounces) cans pinto beans, rinsed
- 2 tablespoons hot sauce
- 1 tablespoon red-wine vinegar
- ½ teaspoon black pepper
- 4 cups brown rice, cooked, warmed

Instructions:

1. Mix flour with oil in a 7-quart pot and sauté for 12 minutes.
2. Stir in celery, poblanos, onions and squash then sauté for 5 minutes.
3. Add salt, tomatoes and broth then cook over high heat to a boil.
4. Add okra, reduce the heat and cook for 5 minutes.
5. Stir in beans and zucchini and cook for 5 minutes.
6. Add black pepper, vinegar and hot sauce.
7. Mix well and serve warm with rice.

The Plant Based Cookbook For Beginners
650 Easy, Quick, & Simple Plant Based Vegan Diet Recipes With A 31 Day Meal Plan To Lose Weight & Live A Long Healthy Life

447

Lo Mein with Shiitakes

SERVINGS	PREPARATION TIME	COOKING TIME
6	10 minutes	15 minutes

Nutritional Values Per Serving

Calories	415
Total Fat	3.2g
Saturated Fat	0.1g
Cholesterol	0mg
Sodium	310mg
Total Carbohydrate	20.9g
Dietary Fiber	2.8g
Total Sugars	29g
Protein	6.8g

Ingredients:

- 8 ounces fresh lo Mein noodles
- 2 teaspoons toasted sesame oil
- 3 tablespoons soy sauce
- 2 teaspoons Sriracha
- 2 tablespoons vegetable oil
- 2 tablespoons garlic, minced
- 1 large carrot, halved and cut into half-moon slices
- 1 cup shredded purple cabbage
- 2 cups bell peppers, julienned
- 3 tablespoons fresh cilantro, chopped

Instructions:

1. Boil noodles with water in a suitable pot as per the package's instruction then drain.
2. Mix noodles with sesame oil, sriracha and soy sauce in a bowl.
3. Sauté garlic with 1 tablespoon oil in a skillet for 10 seconds.
4. Stir in cabbage, and carrot then sauté for 1 minute.
5. Stir in remaining oil, noodles, bell peppers then cook for 2 minutes.
6. Garnish with cilantro.
7. Serve warm.

448

The Plant Based Cookbook For Beginners
650 Easy, Quick, & Simple Plant Based Vegan Diet Recipes With A 31 Day Meal Plan To Lose Weight & Live A Long Healthy Life

Eggplant Pizza Slices

SERVINGS	PREPARATION TIME	COOKING TIME
2	15 minutes	25 minutes

Nutritional Values Per Serving

Calories	232
Total Fat	13.3g
Saturated Fat	4.3g
Cholesterol	8mg
Sodium	1394mg
Total Carbohydrate	24.5g
Dietary Fiber	10g
Total Sugars	10.3g
Protein	8g

Ingredients:

- 1 large eggplant, cut into 2-3 slices
- 1 tablespoon olive oil
- 1 cup vegan mozzarella cheese, shredded
- 1 cup vegan cheddar cheese, shredded
- 1 cup cherry tomatoes, sliced
- ¼ cup fresh basil (10 g)
- 1 tablespoon garlic powder
- 1 teaspoon salt
- 1 teaspoon pepper
- ½ teaspoon red pepper flakes

Instructions:

1. At 350 degrees F, preheat your oven.
2. Layer a baking sheet with a foil sheet and grease it with 1 tbsp oil.
3. Place the eggplant slices on the foil sheet.
4. Sprinkle garlic powder, red pepper flakes, and black pepper on top.
5. Divide the tomato slices, and vegan cheese on top of the eggplant slices.
6. Bake the eggplant pizzas for 25 minutes in the preheated oven.
7. Drizzle basil leaves on top of the eggplant slices.
8. Serve.

The Plant Based Cookbook For Beginners
650 Easy, Quick, & Simple Plant Based Vegan Diet Recipes With A 31 Day Meal Plan To Lose Weight & Live A Long Healthy Life

449

Vegan Pizza

SERVINGS	PREPARATION TIME	COOKING TIME
8	10 minutes	15 minutes

Nutritional Values Per Serving

Calories	233
Total Fat	7.6g
Saturated Fat	18g
Cholesterol	0mg
Sodium	130mg
Total Carbohydrate	21.6g
Dietary Fiber	12.9g
Total Sugars	16.2g
Protein	14.4g

Ingredients:

- 1 tablespoon cornmeal
- 1-pound whole-wheat pizza dough
- 2 tablespoons olive oil
- 2 garlic cloves, sliced
- ¼ teaspoon kosher salt
- ⅛ teaspoon crushed red pepper
- 2 cups cherry tomatoes
- 1 cup rocket leaves
- 1 teaspoon lemon zest
- 2 tablespoons lemon juice
- 1 ½ cups vegan mozzarella, cut into chunks
- ¼ teaspoon black pepper
- Shiso leaves

Instructions:

1. Set the oven's rack in the middle position and preheat it at 450 degrees F.
2. Dust a baking sheet with cornmeal.
3. Roll the dough into a 12-inch oval and place it in the baking sheet.
4. Top it with 1 tablespoon oil, garlic, ⅛ teaspoons salt, and crushed red pepper.
5. Bake this pizza for 15 minutes in the oven.
6. Mix rocket leaves, tomatoes with lemon juice, lemon zest, pepper, oil, salt, and black pepper in a bowl.
7. Spread the veggies, shiso, and mozzarella chunks over the pizza.
8. Serve warm.

450

The Plant Based Cookbook For Beginners
650 Easy, Quick, & Simple Plant Based Vegan Diet Recipes With A 31 Day Meal Plan To Lose Weight & Live A Long Healthy Life

BBQ Tofu Bowl

SERVINGS
4

PREPARATION TIME
15 minutes

COOKING TIME
18 minutes

Nutritional Values Per Serving

Calories	293
Total Fat	5.2g
Saturated Fat	1g
Cholesterol	0mg
Sodium	413mg
Total Carbohydrate	13.2g
Dietary Fiber	5.3g
Total Sugars	8.1g
Protein	6g

Ingredients:

- ½ cup water
- 5 tablespoons rice vinegar
- 4 tablespoons tamari
- 4 tablespoons coconut sugar
- 2 cups napa cabbage, sliced
- 1 cup radishes, sliced
- 1 tablespoon gochujang
- 3 garlic cloves, minced
- 1 teaspoon peeled fresh ginger, grated
- 1 tablespoon cornstarch
- 8 ounces Tofu, cut into 16 pieces
- 2 cups brown rice, cooked
- ¼ cup fresh cilantro

Instructions:

1. At 425 degrees F, preheat your oven.
2. Layer a rimmed baking sheet with cooking spray.
3. Mix 1 tablespoon coconut sugar, 1 tablespoon tamari, 4 tablespoons vinegar and ¼ cup water in a medium bowl.
4. Stir in radishes and cabbage then toss well.
5. Mix remaining vinegar, coconut sugar, vinegar, tamari, ginger, garlic and gochujang in a saucepan.
6. Cook this mixture on a simmer for 2 minutes.
7. Mix cornstarch with ¼ cup water in a bowl and pour into the pan then cook for 1 minute.
8. Pour this sauce over the tofu in a large bowl then mix well to coat.
9. Spread the tofu on the baking sheet and bake for 15 minutes.
10. Flip the tofu once when cooked half way through.
11. Divide the rice and veggies in a serving bowl.
12. Top the rice with tempeh and garnish with cilantro.
13. Serve warm.

The Plant Based Cookbook For Beginners
650 Easy, Quick, & Simple Plant Based Vegan Diet Recipes With A 31 Day Meal Plan To Lose Weight & Live A Long Healthy Life

451

Chile Cauliflower Quesadillas

SERVINGS	PREPARATION TIME	COOKING TIME
4	15 minutes	16 minutes

Nutritional Values Per Serving

Calories	257
Total Fat	9.5g
Saturated Fat	1g
Cholesterol	0mg
Sodium	16mg
Total Carbohydrate	20g
Dietary Fiber	9.4g
Total Sugars	48g
Protein	9.4g

Serving Suggestion:

Enjoy the quesadillas with avocado, Pico de Gallo and tortilla chips on the side.

Ingredients:

- 2 tablespoons corn oil
- 1 tablespoon chili-lime seasoning
- 2 cups chopped cauliflower
- 1 cup poblano peppers, chopped
- 8 (6 inch) whole-wheat tortillas, warmed
- ½ cup refried black beans
- ¾ cup vegan cheese, shredded
- Salsa for serving

Instructions:

1. Set the oven's rack in the middle position and preheat its broiler at high heat.
2. Layer a baking sheet with a foil sheet.
3. Mix seasoning, cauliflower, poblanos, and 1 tablespoon oil in a bowl.
4. Spread the cauliflower in a baking sheet and bake for 8 minutes.
5. Reduce its temperature to 200 degrees F.
6. Top each tortilla with 1 tablespoon beans, cheese and cauliflower mixture.
7. Fold the tortillas in half and press gently.
8. Set a tablespoons oil to a cooking pan and sear the quesadillas for 4 minutes per side.
9. Serve with salsa.

452

The Plant Based Cookbook For Beginners
650 Easy, Quick, & Simple Plant Based Vegan Diet Recipes With A 31 Day Meal Plan To Lose Weight & Live A Long Healthy Life

Eggplant Lasagna

SERVINGS	PREPARATION TIME	COOKING TIME
6	15 minutes	75 minutes

Nutritional Values Per Serving

Calories	410
Total Fat	12.8g
Saturated Fat	0½g
Cholesterol	0mg
Sodium	109mg
Total Carbohydrate	22.9g
Dietary Fiber	5.9g
Total Sugars	14.4g
Protein	14.9g

Ingredients:

- 2 large eggplants, cut into ¼-inch-thick slices
- 2 tablespoons olive oil
- 1 cup onion, chopped
- 2 garlic cloves, minced
- 1 (28 ounces) can crushed tomatoes
- ¼ cup dry red wine
- 1 teaspoon dried basil
- 1 teaspoon dried oregano
- ¾ teaspoon salt
- ¼ teaspoon black pepper
- 1 (16 ounces) package firm tofu, crumbled and patted dry
- 2 teaspoons nutritional yeast
- 1 cup vegan mozzarella-cheese, shredded
- Chopped fresh basil for garnish

Instructions:

1. At 400 degrees F, preheat your oven.
2. Layer 2 baking sheets with cooking spray.
3. Spread the eggplant slices in the baking sheets and bake for 20 minutes.
4. Flip the eggplant once cooked halfway through.
5. Sauté onion with 1 tablespoon oil in a suitable skillet for 4 minutes.
6. Stir in garlic then sauté for 1 minute.
7. Add black pepper, salt, oregano, basil, wine and tomatoes.
8. Cook this mixture on a simmer for 10 minutes with occasional stirring.
9. Mix tofu with 1 tablespoon oil and yeast in a bowl.
10. Spread about 1 cup tomato mixture in a 9x13 inch baking dish.
11. Add ⅓ eggplant slices in the sauce and top them with ⅓ tofu mixture and add 1/3 cheese on top.
12. Repeat these layers while finishing off with cheese.
13. Bake the eggplant lasagna for 40 minutes in the oven.
14. Garnish with basil then serve warm.

The Plant Based Cookbook For Beginners
650 Easy, Quick, & Simple Plant Based Vegan Diet Recipes With A 31 Day Meal Plan To Lose Weight & Live A Long Healthy Life

453

Cauliflower Curry

SERVINGS	PREPARATION TIME	COOKING TIME
4	10 minutes	22 minutes

Nutritional Values Per Serving

Calories	388
Total Fat	7g
Saturated Fat	0.9g
Cholesterol	0mg
Sodium	8mg
Total Carbohydrate	28g
Dietary Fiber	9.1g
Total Sugars	10.4g
Protein	8g

Ingredients:

- 1 yellow onion, chopped
- 1-pound sweet potato, chopped
- 1 head cauliflower, chopped
- 2 tablespoons olive oil
- 1 teaspoon kosher salt
- 2 tablespoons curry powder
- 1 tablespoon garam masala
- 1 teaspoon cumin
- ¼ teaspoon cayenne
- 1 (28-ounces) can diced tomatoes
- 1 (15-ounces) can coconut milk
- 1 (15-ounces) can chickpeas
- 4 cups spinach leaves
- Cilantro, for garnish
- Brown rice, for serving

Instructions:

1. Sauté onion with 2 tablespoons oil in a suitable skillet for 2 minutes.
2. Stir in sweet potato then sauté for 3 minutes.
3. Toss in cauliflower and salt then sauté for 5 minutes.
4. Stir in ¼ teaspoons cayenne, 1 teaspoon cumin, 1 tablespoon garam masala, 2 tablespoons curry powder.
5. Mix well then add coconut milk and tomatoes then cook to a boil.
6. Cover, reduce its heat and cook for 10 minutes on a simmer.
7. Drain the canned chickpeas then add them to the veggies.
8. Stir in spinach and cook for 2 minutes.
9. Garnish with chopped cilantro and serve warm with rice.

454

The Plant Based Cookbook For Beginners
650 Easy, Quick, & Simple Plant Based Vegan Diet Recipes With A 31 Day Meal Plan To Lose Weight & Live A Long Healthy Life

BBQ Bean Tacos

SERVINGS	PREPARATION TIME	COOKING TIME
6	10 minutes	10 minutes

Nutritional Values Per Serving

Calories	321
Total Fat	4.7g
Saturated Fat	2½g
Cholesterol	1mg
Sodium	87mg
Total Carbohydrate	21.7g
Dietary Fiber	4.2g
Total Sugars	17.7g
Protein	4.6g

Serving Suggestion:

Enjoy these tacos with fresh guacamole and rice on the side.

Ingredients:

- 2 (15-ounces) cans black beans
- 2 tablespoons Dijon mustard
- 1 tablespoon maple syrup
- ¾ cup organic ketchup
- ½ teaspoon garlic powder
- ½ teaspoon chili powder
- ¾ teaspoon salt
- ¼ cup red onion, minced
- ¼ cup cilantro, chopped
- 1 small green cabbage, sliced
- 3 radishes, sliced
- 1 lime wedge
- Tortillas, for serving
- Vegan cheese

Instructions:

1. Drain the beans and rinse then transfer to a saucepan.
2. Stir in ½ teaspoons salt, chili powder, garlic powder, ketchup, maple syrup, and mustard.
3. Mix well and cook the beans on low heat until the mixture thickens.
4. Mix ¼ teaspoons salt, red onion and cilantro in a bowl.
5. Divide the beans on the tortillas and top them with radishes, cabbage and rest of the veggies.
6. Wrap and serve with vegan cheese and lime juice.

The Plant Based Cookbook For Beginners
650 Easy, Quick, & Simple Plant Based Vegan Diet Recipes With A 31 Day Meal Plan To Lose Weight & Live A Long Healthy Life

455

Sweet Potatoes with Peanut Butter Sauce

SERVINGS	PREPARATION TIME	COOKING TIME
4	15 minutes	35 minutes

Nutritional Values Per Serving

Calories	378
Total Fat	2.7g
Saturated Fat	0½g
Cholesterol	0mg
Sodium	157mg
Total Carbohydrate	24.4g
Dietary Fiber	4g
Total Sugars	5.8g
Protein	5.6g

Ingredients:

Sweet potatoes

- 4 medium sweet potatoes
- 1 cup broccoli florets

Thai peanut butter sauce

- ⅓ cup peanut butter
- 2 tablespoons soy sauce
- 2 tablespoons lime juice
- 1 teaspoon maple syrup
- 2 tablespoons water

Instructions:

1. Rub the sweet potatoes with oil and place them in a baking sheet.
2. Roast the potatoes for 35 minutes in the oven at 350 degrees F.
3. Blend all the Thai peanut butter sauce in a bowl.
4. Cut all the sweet potatoes in half, horizontally and top each sweet potato half with Thai peanuts butter sauce.
5. Garnish with broccoli florets.
6. Serve.

456

The Plant Based Cookbook For Beginners
650 Easy, Quick, & Simple Plant Based Vegan Diet Recipes With A 31 Day Meal Plan To Lose Weight & Live A Long Healthy Life

Moroccan Stew with Sweet Potatoes

SERVINGS
4

PREPARATION TIME
10 minutes

COOKING TIME
50 minutes

Nutritional Values Per Serving

Calories	414
Total Fat	14.9g
Saturated Fat	0.7g
Cholesterol	0mg
Sodium	240mg
Total Carbohydrate	23.1g
Dietary Fiber	14.3g
Total Sugars	13.1g
Protein	10.1g

Ingredients:

- 2 cups uncooked quinoa
- 1 large onion
- 3 garlic cloves
- 2 large sweet potatoes
- 2 tablespoons olive oil
- 1 teaspoon paprika
- 1 teaspoon ground cumin
- ½ teaspoon ground coriander
- ½ teaspoon turmeric
- ½ teaspoon ground ginger
- ¼ teaspoon ground cinnamon
- ½ teaspoon salt
- ½ teaspoon ground black pepper
- 2 pinches cayenne pepper
- 1 (15-ounces) can diced tomatoes
- 2 cups vegetable broth
- 1 (15 ounces) can chickpeas, drained
- 3 cups spinach
- 2 tablespoons fresh cilantro, chopped
- 1 lemon, for garnish
- 1 cup coconut yogurt

Instructions:

1. Boil the quinoa in a cooking pot as per the package's instruction then drain.
2. Sauté onion with 2 tablespoons oil in a suitable pot for 5 minutes.
3. Stir in garlic and sauté for 1 minute.
4. Add 2 pinches cayenne pepper, black pepper, salt, cinnamon, ginger, turmeric, coriander, cumin and paprika then sauté 3 minutes.
5. Stir in tomatoes and vegetable broth then cook to a boil.
6. Add chickpeas, and sweet potatoes then cook on a simmer for 30 minutes.
7. Stir in spinach then cook for 2 minutes.
8. Garnish with lemon juice, cilantro and yogurt.
9. Serve warm.

The Plant Based Cookbook For Beginners
650 Easy, Quick, & Simple Plant Based Vegan Diet Recipes With A 31 Day Meal Plan To Lose Weight & Live A Long Healthy Life

457

Mediterranean Couscous

SERVINGS
4

PREPARATION TIME
10 minutes

COOKING TIME
10 minutes

Nutritional Values Per Serving

Calories	280
Total Fat	2.4g
Saturated Fat	0g
Cholesterol	0mg
Sodium	99mg
Total Carbohydrate	21.7g
Dietary Fiber	10.2g
Total Sugars	49.7g
Protein	2.3

Ingredients:

Chickpeas Lentils

- 1 (15-ounces) can chickpeas
- 1 tablespoon olive oil
- ½ teaspoon cumin
- ½ teaspoon kosher salt

Couscous

- 1 cup whole wheat couscous
- ¾ teaspoon kosher salt
- 1 tablespoon olive oil
- 2 tablespoons parsley, chopped

Bowl

- 1 small cucumber
- 1-pint cherry tomatoes
- 8 cups salad greens

Instructions:

1. Mix chickpeas with salt, oil and cumin in a bowl.
2. Boil couscous with salt and 1¼ cups water in a cooking pot.
3. Cover and leave for 5 minutes then stir in parsley, and salt.
4. Mix couscous with chickpeas and rest of the veggies in a bowl.
5. Serve.

458

The Plant Based Cookbook For Beginners
650 Easy, Quick, & Simple Plant Based Vegan Diet Recipes With A 31 Day Meal Plan To Lose Weight & Live A Long Healthy Life

Chana Masala

SERVINGS	PREPARATION TIME	COOKING TIME
4	15 minutes	41 minutes

Nutritional Values Per Serving	
Calories	278
Total Fat	2.4g
Saturated Fat	0.1g
Cholesterol	0mg
Sodium	291mg
Total Carbohydrate	29.4g
Dietary Fiber	3.7g
Total Sugars	13.2g
Protein	6.4g

Ingredients:

- 1 ½ cups chickpeas, soaked and drained
- 3 tablespoons vegan butter
- 2 bay leaves
- 2 teaspoons cumin seeds whole
- 1 teaspoon fennel seeds
- 2 onions, diced
- 4 garlic cloves, chopped
- 1 jalapeno, diced
- 1 tablespoon fresh ginger, minced
- 1 teaspoon garam masala
- 1 teaspoon ground cumin
- 1 teaspoon ground coriander
- ½ teaspoon chili powder
- 1 teaspoon dried fenugreek leaves
- ½ teaspoon ground turmeric
- 2 medium tomatoes
- 1 ½ teaspoons salt
- 2 cups water

Instructions:

1. Sauté cumin seeds with fennel seeds and bay leaves with vegan butter in an Instant pot for 3 minutes on Sauté mode.
2. Stir in onions then sauté for 7 minutes until golden brown.
3. Add jalapeno, ginger and garlic then sauté for 3 minutes.
4. Stir in chili powder, turmeric, fenugreek, coriander, cumin and garam masala.
5. Mix well then add tomatoes then sauté for 3 minutes.
6. Stir in chickpeas and water then secure the lid.
7. Cook the chickpeas for 25 minutes at High pressure.
8. Once done, release the pressure completely then remove the lid.
9. Serve warm.

The Plant Based Cookbook For Beginners
650 Easy, Quick, & Simple Plant Based Vegan Diet Recipes With A 31 Day Meal Plan To Lose Weight & Live A Long Healthy Life

459

Sweet Potato and Wild Rice Burgers

SERVINGS	PREPARATION TIME	COOKING TIME
6	15 minutes	1 hour 44 minutes

Nutritional Values Per Serving

Calories	339
Total Fat	1.1g
Saturated Fat	0.3g
Cholesterol	0mg
Sodium	16mg
Total Carbohydrate	29.4g
Dietary Fiber	5g
Total Sugars	3.2g
Protein	14g

Ingredients:

- 1 large sweet potato
- ½ cup uncooked wild rice blend
- 1 (15 ounces) can chickpeas, rinsed
- 1 teaspoon curry powder
- 1 ½ teaspoons cumin
- ¼ teaspoon garlic powder
- Salt and black pepper to taste
- ½ cup breadcrumbs
- 2 teaspoons coconut oil
- ¼ cup chopped pecans

Garnish

- Avocado
- Arugula
- Red onion

Instructions:

1. At 400 degrees F, preheat your oven.
2. Poke a large sweet potato with a fork and place in baking pan lined with foil sheet.
3. Bake the sweet potato then roast for 45 minutes.
4. Boil wild rice with 1 cup water in a saucepan, cover and cook on medium low heat for 40 minutes.
5. Mash sweet potato with chicken peas in a bowl.
6. Stir in rest of the ingredients and mix well.
7. Bake six equal patties out of this mixture.
8. Set a suitable skillet, over medium heat and add coconut oil to heat.
9. Sear the patties for 9 minutes per side.
10. Serve warm and enjoy the burgers with buns, avocado, arugula, red onions, and condiments.

460

The Plant Based Cookbook For Beginners
650 Easy, Quick, & Simple Plant Based Vegan Diet Recipes With A 31 Day Meal Plan To Lose Weight & Live A Long Healthy Life

Calabacita Quesadillas

SERVINGS 4

PREPARATION TIME 10 minutes

COOKING TIME 6 minutes

Nutritional Values Per Serving

Calories	306
Total Fat	0.1g
Saturated Fat	0g
Cholesterol	0mg
Sodium	176mg
Total Carbohydrate	13.6g
Dietary Fiber	3½g
Total Sugars	1.3g
Protein	3.6g

Ingredients:

- 1 teaspoon olive oil
- 2 garlic cloves, minced
- ½ yellow onion, diced
- 1 jalapeno, seeded and diced
- 1 small zucchini, quartered
- Kernels from 1 ear of corn
- ¼ teaspoon cumin
- Salt and black pepper, to taste
- 2 large whole wheat tortillas
- ½ cup vegan Mexican cheese Shreds
- Vegan mayo, to garnish

Instructions:

1. Sauté corn, zucchini, jalapeno, onion and garlic with oil in a suitable skillet for 6 minutes.
2. Stir in black pepper, salt and cumin then mix well.
3. Sear a wheat tortilla in a flat pan and divide the Calabacita mixture over the tortillas.
4. Top the corn mixture with the cheese and place another tortilla on top.
5. Cut into 4 equal pieces and garnish with vegan mayo.
6. Serve warm.

The Plant Based Cookbook For Beginners
650 Easy, Quick, & Simple Plant Based Vegan Diet Recipes With A 31 Day Meal Plan To Lose Weight & Live A Long Healthy Life

461

Macadamia Coconut Tofu

SERVINGS	PREPARATION TIME	COOKING TIME
4	10 minutes	68 minutes

Nutritional Values Per Serving

Calories	381
Total Fat	2.4g
Saturated Fat	0.7g
Cholesterol	0mg
Sodium	303mg
Total Carbohydrate	10.8g
Dietary Fiber	5.8g
Total Sugars	12.7g
Protein	5g

Ingredients:

Brown rice

- 1 cup short grain brown rice
- 2 cups water
- Pinch of salt

Tofu

- 1 package tofu
- 2 tablespoons coconut flour
- ½ teaspoon salt
- ½ teaspoon cumin
- ¼ teaspoon cayenne pepper
- 2 tablespoons coconut oil

Sweet potato mixture

- 1 (15 oz) can light coconut milk
- 1 sweet potato, diced
- 1 red pepper, cut into large chunks
- ½ teaspoon ground turmeric
- ½ teaspoon salt
- Black pepper, to taste

Assemble

- 1 (5 oz) package baby spinach
- ¼ cup macadamia nuts, chopped
- Freshly cilantro, chopped

Instructions:

1. Boil rice with a pinch of salt and water in a cooking pot over high heat.
2. Reduce its heat and cook for 45 minutes then fluff.
3. Pat dry the tofu gently then cut into cubes.
4. Mix tofu, coconut flour with cayenne, cumin and salt in a bowl.
5. Set a skillet with coconut oil over medium high heat.
6. Sear the tofu for 4 minutes per side until golden brown then transfer to a plate.
7. Mix coconut milk, salt, black pepper, turmeric, bell pepper and sweet potato in a cooking pot.
8. Cook for 15 minutes on a simmer until soft.
9. Divide the rice in the serving bowl.
10. Top the rice with potato curry, spinach, tofu, macadamia nuts and cilantro.
11. Serve warm.

462

The Plant Based Cookbook For Beginners
650 Easy, Quick, & Simple Plant Based Vegan Diet Recipes With A 31 Day Meal Plan To Lose Weight & Live A Long Healthy Life

CHAPTER 08

DINNER RECIPES

Creamy Farfelle Pasta

SERVINGS	PREPARATION TIME	COOKING TIME
4	10 minutes	15 minutes

Nutritional Values Per Serving

Calories	356
Total Fat	13.6g
Saturated Fat	9.1g
Cholesterol	0mg
Sodium	420mg
Total Carbohydrate	37.6g
Dietary Fiber	7.1g
Total Sugars	19.9g
Protein	7g

Ingredients:

Sauce

- ½ cup cashews
- 1 roasted potato, peeled
- ⅔ cup water
- 2 garlic cloves
- 1 chipotle pepper
- ⅛ teaspoon nutmeg
- ½ teaspoon sea salt
- Black pepper, to taste

Pasta

- 3 cups of farfelle

Mushrooms

- ½ tablespoon olive oil
- 1 cup baby bella mushrooms, sliced
- ¼ teaspoon garlic powder
- Salt and black pepper, to taste

Assemble

- Parsley, chopped

Instructions:

1. Soak cashews in 4 cups water in a bowl for 2 hours then drain.
2. Blend cashews with black pepper, salt, nutmeg, chipotle pepper, garlic, water, and potato in a blender until smooth.
3. Boil pasta in a boiling water in a cooking pot as per the package's instructions.
4. Drain the pasta and transfer to the pot.
5. Sauté mushrooms with oil, black pepper, salt and garlic powder in a skillet for 5 minutes.
6. Add the potato cashew sauce and pasta then mix well.
7. Garnish with parsley.
8. Serve warm.

464

The Plant Based Cookbook For Beginners
650 Easy, Quick, & Simple Plant Based Vegan Diet Recipes With A 31 Day Meal Plan To Lose Weight & Live A Long Healthy Life

Roasted Butternut Squash Pasta

SERVINGS	PREPARATION TIME	COOKING TIME
4	10 minutes	40 minutes

Nutritional Values Per Serving

Calories	335
Total Fat	12.1g
Saturated Fat	0.2g
Cholesterol	0mg
Sodium	131mg
Total Carbohydrate	19.3g
Dietary Fiber	4.4g
Total Sugars	6.2g
Protein	7.2g

Ingredients:

- ½ tablespoon olive oil
- 4 cups butternut squash, cubed
- 2 garlic cloves, unpeeled
- Salt and black pepper, to taste
- 8 ounces brown rice pasta
- Vegan Parmesan cheese, shredded, to garnish
- Cilantro, to garnish

Instructions:

1. At 400 degrees F, preheat your oven.
2. Toss butternut squash with oil, garlic, black pepper and salt in a baking pan and roast for 30 minutes.
3. Cook the pasta as per the package's instruction then drain.
4. Mix squash with the pasta in a bowl and garnish with vegan cheese and cilantro.
5. Serve.

The Plant Based Cookbook For Beginners
650 Easy, Quick, & Simple Plant Based Vegan Diet Recipes With A 31 Day Meal Plan To Lose Weight & Live A Long Healthy Life

465

Mushroom Stuffed Poblano

SERVINGS	PREPARATION TIME	COOKING TIME
4	10 minutes	12 minutes

Nutritional Values Per Serving

Calories	218
Total Fat	7g
Saturated Fat	0.9g
Cholesterol	0mg
Sodium	8mg
Total Carbohydrate	28g
Dietary Fiber	9.1g
Total Sugars	10.4g
Protein	8g

Ingredients:

- 10 poblano peppers, cut in half and seeded
- 2 teaspoons garlic, minced
- ¼ cup canned corn, drained
- ¼ cup canned black beans
- 8 ounces mushrooms, chopped
- ¼ cup cooked quinoa
- ½ cup cilantro, chopped
- 1 white onion, chopped
- 1 tablespoon olive oil
- Salt and black pepper to taste
- 1 cup breadcrumbs, toasted

Instructions:

1. Place a nonstick pan over medium heat and add oil.
2. Stir in mushrooms and onion, sauté for 5 minutes.
3. Add salt, black pepper, quinoa, black beans, corn, cilantro and garlic.
4. Stir while cooking for 2 additional minutes, then take it off the heat.
5. Divide this mixture into the poblano peppers and stuff them neatly then place them in a baking sheet.
6. Spread and coat the breadcrumbs evenly over the stuffed peppers.
7. At 350 degreed F, preheat your oven.
8. Bake the peppers for 5 minutes in the oven until golden brown.
9. Enjoy.

466

The Plant Based Cookbook For Beginners
650 Easy, Quick, & Simple Plant Based Vegan Diet Recipes With A 31 Day Meal Plan To Lose Weight & Live A Long Healthy Life

Mushroom Stuffed Tomatoes

SERVINGS	PREPARATION TIME	COOKING TIME
6	10 minutes	12 minutes

Nutritional Values Per Serving

Calories	221
Total Fat	4.7g
Saturated Fat	2½g
Cholesterol	1mg
Sodium	87mg
Total Carbohydrate	21.7g
Dietary Fiber	4.2g
Total Sugars	17.7g
Protein	4.6g

Ingredients:

- 4 tomatoes
- 1 yellow onion, chopped
- ½ cup mushrooms, chopped
- 1 tablespoon bread crumbs, crumbled
- 1 tablespoon vegan butter
- ¼ teaspoon caraway seeds
- 1 tablespoon parsley, chopped
- 2 tablespoons celery, chopped
- 1 cup vegan cheese, shredded
- Salt and black pepper to the taste

Instructions:

1. Cut the top of the tomatoes and remove their seeds and pulp from inside to make tomato cups.
2. Chop up the tomato pulp and keep it aside.
3. Place a pan over medium heat, add butter.
4. When it melts, add onion and celery then sauté for 3 minutes.
5. Stir in mushrooms and tomato pulp.
6. Cook for 1 minute, then add crumbled bread, pepper, salt, cheese, parsley, and caraway seeds.
7. Cook while stirring for 4 minutes, then remove from the heat.
8. After cooling the mixture, stuff it equally in the tomatoes.
9. Place the stuffed tomatoes and their top portions in a baking sheet.
10. Broil them for 5 minutes in the oven at 350 degrees F.
11. Enjoy.

The Plant Based Cookbook For Beginners
650 Easy, Quick, & Simple Plant Based Vegan Diet Recipes With A 31 Day Meal Plan To Lose Weight & Live A Long Healthy Life

467

Spinach Stuffed Portobello

SERVINGS	PREPARATION TIME	COOKING TIME
4	15 minutes	12 minutes

Nutritional Values Per Serving

Calories	278
Total Fat	2.7g
Saturated Fat	0½g
Cholesterol	0mg
Sodium	157mg
Total Carbohydrate	24.4g
Dietary Fiber	4g
Total Sugars	5.8g
Protein	5.6g

Ingredients:

- 4 portobello mushrooms, chopped
- 10 basil leaves
- 1 tablespoon parsley
- ¼ cup olive oil
- 8 cherry tomatoes, halved
- 1 cup baby spinach
- 3 garlic cloves, chopped
- 1 cup almonds, chopped
- 2 tablespoons vegan parmesan, shredded
- Salt and black pepper to the taste

Instructions:

1. Add all ingredients except mushrooms to a food processor.
2. Blend it all well until smooth, then stuff each mushroom cap with the mixture.
3. Place the prepared stuffed mushrooms in a greased roasting pan.
4. Sprinkle vegan parmesan on top.
5. Cook them for 12 minutes at 350 degrees F in the preheated oven.
6. Enjoy.

468

The Plant Based Cookbook For Beginners
650 Easy, Quick, & Simple Plant Based Vegan Diet Recipes With A 31 Day Meal Plan To Lose Weight & Live A Long Healthy Life

Butternut Squash Lasagna

SERVINGS	PREPARATION TIME	COOKING TIME
4	15 minutes	80 minutes

Nutritional Values Per Serving

Calories	366
Total Fat	12g
Saturated Fat	1g
Cholesterol	0mg
Sodium	802mg
Total Carbohydrate	22g
Dietary Fiber	4.3g
Total Sugars	4.8g
Protein	10.7g

Ingredients:

Butternut squash sauce

- 1 large butternut squash
- 1 cup almond milk
- ½ tablespoon olive oil
- 1 tablespoon pure maple syrup
- ¾ teaspoon salt
- ½ teaspoon cinnamon
- ¼ teaspoon nutmeg
- ¼ teaspoon allspice
- Black pepper, to taste

Noodles

- 8 lasagna noodles, gluten free if desired

Tahini cream sauce

- 1 package Tofu, drained
- 3 garlic cloves
- ½ cup warm water
- 3 tablespoons tahini
- 1 tablespoon lemon juice
- ¾ teaspoon salt
- Black pepper, to taste

Veggies

- 1 tablespoon olive oil
- 1 (6 ounces) bag spinach
- Salt and black pepper, to taste

Instructions:

1. At 375 degrees F, preheat your oven.
2. Cut the butternut squash and remove the seeds.
3. Drizzle ½ tbsp oil, ¼ tsp black pepper and ¼ tsp salt over the squash then place them in a baking sheet.
4. Roast the squash for 45 minutes in the oven.
5. Allow the squash to cool, and transfer the roasted flesh to a food processor.
6. Add milk, black pepper, allspice, nutmeg, cinnamon, salt, and maple syrup then blend.
7. Blend the tofu mixture and keep it aside.
8. Add the tofu tahini cream sauce to a blender and blend until smooth.
9. Boil noodles in a cooking pot filled with salted water as per the package's instruction then drain.
10. Sauté spinach with olive oil, black pepper and salt in a skillet for 3 minutes.
11. Spread ¾ butternut squash mixture in the baking dish and top it with 4 noodle strips.
12. Add 1 cup tofu sauce on top and add ½ of the spinach.
13. Spread 1 cup butternut squash sauce and repeat the layers.
14. Cover this lasagna with a foil then bake for 30 minutes at 375 degrees F.
15. Serve warm.

The Plant Based Cookbook For Beginners
650 Easy, Quick, & Simple Plant Based Vegan Diet Recipes With A 31 Day Meal Plan To Lose Weight & Live A Long Healthy Life

469

Cashew Mac and Cheese

SERVINGS	PREPARATION TIME	COOKING TIME
4	2 hours 10 minutes	10 minutes

Nutritional Values Per Serving

Calories	326
Total Fat	20.4g
Saturated Fat	3.7g
Cholesterol	0mg
Sodium	173mg
Total Carbohydrate	29g
Dietary Fiber	8g
Total Sugars	10.4g
Protein	11.3g

Ingredients:

- 1 ½ cups raw cashews
- 2 garlic cloves
- ½ cup nutritional yeast
- 1 ¼ cups almond milk
- 1 jalapeño, chopped
- ¾ teaspoon ground turmeric
- ¾ teaspoon paprika
- ½ teaspoon onion powder
- 1 teaspoon Dijon mustard
- 1 teaspoon salt
- Black pepper, to taste
- 1-pound shell Conchiglie pasta

Instructions:

1. Soak cashews in 4 cups water in a bowl for 2 hours then drain.

2. Drain and blend the cashews with black pepper, salt, mustard, onion powder, paprika, turmeric, jalapeno, almond milk, yeast, and garlic in a blender until smooth.

3. Cook the noodles as per the package's instructions then drain.

4. Mix the noodles with the cashews sauce in a bowl.

5. Garnish with black pepper.

6. Serve warm.

470

The Plant Based Cookbook For Beginners
650 Easy, Quick, & Simple Plant Based Vegan Diet Recipes With A 31 Day Meal Plan To Lose Weight & Live A Long Healthy Life

Taco Pasta with Sweet Corn

SERVINGS	PREPARATION TIME	COOKING TIME
4	2 hours 10 minutes	10 minutes

Nutritional Values Per Serving

Calories	393
Total Fat	4½g
Saturated Fat	0.8g
Cholesterol	1mg
Sodium	42mg
Total Carbohydrate	31g
Dietary Fiber	4.8g
Total Sugars	1.7g
Protein	8.6g

Ingredients:

Pasta cheese sauce

- ¾ cup cashews
- ½ cup water
- 1 garlic clove
- 2 tablespoons lime juice
- 2 ½ teaspoons cumin
- 2 teaspoons chili powder
- 1 teaspoon dried oregano
- ½ teaspoon paprika
- ⅛ teaspoon cayenne pepper
- ¾ teaspoon salt

Pasta

- 8 ounces large elbow noodles
- 1 (15-ounces) can black beans, rinsed
- 1 ¼ cups Birds Eye Sweet Corn, cooked
- ¾ cup chunky salsa

Serving

- 1 jalapeno, sliced
- Cilantro
- Salsa
- Diced Avocado
- Hot sauce
- Vegan yogurt

Instructions:

1. Soak cashews in 2 cups water for 2 hours then drain.
2. Blend cashews with cayenne pepper, salt, paprika, oregano, chili powder, cumin, lime juice, garlic, and ½ cup water.
3. Boil the pasta as per the package's instruction then drain.
4. Return the pasta to a cooking pot then add cashew sauce, corn, salsa and beans.
5. Mix well and garnish with all the toppings.
6. Serve warm.

The Plant Based Cookbook For Beginners
650 Easy, Quick, & Simple Plant Based Vegan Diet Recipes With A 31 Day Meal Plan To Lose Weight & Live A Long Healthy Life

471

Chickpea with Sweet Potato Crust

SERVINGS	PREPARATION TIME	COOKING TIME
4	15 minutes	45 minutes

Nutritional Values Per Serving

Calories	380
Total Fat	14.7g
Saturated Fat	12.8g
Cholesterol	0mg
Sodium	12mg
Total Carbohydrate	15.1g
Dietary Fiber	3g
Total Sugars	5.7g
Protein	4.9g

Ingredients:

Curry

- 2 teaspoons coconut oil
- 3 garlic cloves, minced
- 1 jalapeno, seeded and diced
- 1 medium white onion, chopped
- 1 cup carrots, sliced
- 1 tablespoon ginger, minced
- 1 tablespoon medium yellow curry powder
- ½ teaspoon turmeric
- 1 (15-ounces) can full-fat coconut milk
- 1 (15-ounces) can chickpeas, rinsed
- 1 red bell pepper, chopped
- 1 cup frozen peas
- 1 tablespoon soy sauce
- ½ teaspoon salt
- ¼ teaspoon cayenne pepper
- 1 tablespoon cornstarch

Sweet potato crust

- 2 medium sweet potatoes, sliced
- Olive oil

Garnish

- Vegan feta, crumbled
- Cilantro
- Green onion
- Hot sauce
- Vegan sour cream

Instructions:

1. Sauté garlic, jalapeno, carrots, ginger and onion with oil in a cooking pot for 5 minutes.
2. Stir in turmeric and curry powder then sauté for 20 seconds.
3. Add cayenne pepper, salt, soy sauce, bell pepper, chickpeas and coconut milk.
4. Cook this mixture to a boil then cook on low heat for 5 minutes.
5. Stir in peas and cornstarch the cook until the mixture thickens.
6. At 375 degrees F, preheat your oven.
7. Spread the sweet potatoes over the chickpea curry in a baking sheet and drizzle oil, black pepper and salt on top.
8. Bake the prepared sweet potatoes for 30 minutes in the preheated oven.
9. Garnish with vegan feta, vegan sour cream and cilantro.
10. Serve warm.

472

The Plant Based Cookbook For Beginners
650 Easy, Quick, & Simple Plant Based Vegan Diet Recipes With A 31 Day Meal Plan To Lose Weight & Live A Long Healthy Life

Vegetarian Lentil Loaf

SERVINGS	PREPARATION TIME	COOKING TIME
6	15 minutes	53 minutes

Nutritional Values Per Serving

Calories	367
Total Fat	27.4g
Saturated Fat	23.3g
Cholesterol	0mg
Sodium	19mg
Total Carbohydrate	22.8g
Dietary Fiber	4.9g
Total Sugars	26g
Protein	3.3g

Ingredients:

- 1 cup dry green lentils
- 4 cups water
- 3 tablespoons flaxseed meal
- ⅓ cup water
- ½ tablespoon olive oil
- 4 garlic cloves, minced
- 1 small white or yellow onion, diced
- 1 red bell pepper, diced
- 1 carrot, diced
- 1 jalapeño, seeded and diced
- 2 teaspoons cumin
- 1 teaspoon chili powder
- ½ teaspoon paprika
- ½ teaspoon garlic powder
- ½ teaspoon onion powder
- ¼ teaspoon coriander
- ½ cup gluten free rolled oats
- ½ cup gluten free oat flour
- ½ cup fresh cilantro, chopped
- 1 teaspoon salt
- Black pepper, to taste

Glaze

- ½ cup ketchup
- ½ teaspoon yellow mustard
- ½ teaspoon apple cider vinegar
- ¼ teaspoon chipotle chili powder

Instructions:

1. Rinse and add lentils to a cooking pot with 4 cups water.
2. Add a dash of salt and cook for 30 minutes on a simmer then drain.
3. Mix ⅓ cup water and flaxseed meal in a bowl.
4. At 350 degrees F, preheat your oven.
5. Grease a loaf pan with cooking spray.
6. Sauté garlic, jalapeno, cilantro, carrot, bell pepper, onion with oil in a suitable skillet for 7 minutes.
7. Stir in spices and cook for 30 seconds.
8. Blend the 2 cups of cooked lentils in a blender until smooth.
9. Return the lentils to the cooking pot and add the veggies.
10. Stir in rest of the ingredients then mix well.
11. Prepare the glaze by mixing of its ingredients in a bowl.
12. Spread the meatloaf mixture in a pan then brush the glaze over the meatloaf and bake for 45 minutes.
13. Allow it to cool then slice.
14. Serve warm.

The Plant Based Cookbook For Beginners
650 Easy, Quick, & Simple Plant Based Vegan Diet Recipes With A 31 Day Meal Plan To Lose Weight & Live A Long Healthy Life

473

Black Bean Loaf

SERVINGS	PREPARATION TIME	COOKING TIME
6	15 minutes	42 minutes

Nutritional Values Per Serving

Calories	338
Total Fat	5.8g
Saturated Fat	1.1g
Cholesterol	0mg
Sodium	270mg
Total Carbohydrate	30.2g
Dietary Fiber	4.6g
Total Sugars	2.7g
Protein	18g

Ingredients:

- 3 tablespoons flaxseed meal
- ½ cup water
- 1 teaspoon olive oil
- 1 small yellow onion
- 3 garlic cloves, minced
- 1 red bell pepper, diced
- 1 carrot, shredded
- 1 jalapeno, seeded and diced
- 2 teaspoons cumin
- 1 tablespoon chili powder
- 1 teaspoon dried oregano
- ¼ teaspoon cayenne pepper
- ¼ cup cilantro, diced
- 2 (15 oz) cans black beans, rinsed
- 3/4 cup sweet corn organic
- ½ cup gluten free oats
- ½ cup gluten free oat flour
- Salt and black pepper, to taste

Instructions:

1. At 350 degrees F, preheat your oven.
2. Layer a 9-inch loaf pan with cooking spray.
3. Mix ½ cup water with flaxseed meal in a bowl then leave for 10 minutes.
4. Sauté garlic, jalapeno, carrot, bell pepper, and onion with 1 teaspoon oil in a skillet for 7 minutes.
5. Blend beans with sautéed veggies, black pepper, salt and rest of the ingredients along with flaxseeds.
6. Spread this meatloaf mixture in the pan and bake for 35 minutes in the oven.
7. Allow the meatloaf to cool then slice.
8. Serve warm.

474

The Plant Based Cookbook For Beginners
650 Easy, Quick, & Simple Plant Based Vegan Diet Recipes With A 31 Day Meal Plan To Lose Weight & Live A Long Healthy Life

Pineapple Tofu Kabobs

SERVINGS	PREPARATION TIME	COOKING TIME
4	10 minutes	10 minutes

Nutritional Values Per Serving

Calories	311
Total Fat	1.8g
Saturated Fat	0.2g
Cholesterol	0mg
Sodium	9mg
Total Carbohydrate	37.9g
Dietary Fiber	5.7g
Total Sugars	2.8g
Protein	12g

Ingredients:

- 2 tablespoons tamari
- 1 teaspoon apple cider vinegar
- 2 tablespoons fresh pineapple juice
- 2 teaspoon ginger, grated
- 2 garlic cloves, minced
- ½ teaspoon ground turmeric
- 1 (14 oz.) package Nagoya extra firm tofu
- 2 cups fresh pineapple, cubed

Garnish

- Fresh chopped cilantro

Instructions:

1. Pat dry the tofu block with a paper towel and cut into cubes.
2. Mix tamari, turmeric, garlic, ginger, pineapple juice, and apple cider vinegar in a large bowl.
3. Toss in tofu cubes then mix well and cover to marinate for 30 minutes.
4. Set a grill over medium high heat and grease its grilling grates.
5. Thread tofu and pineapple on the skewers and grill the skewers for 5 minutes per side.
6. Garnish with cilantro.
7. Serve warm.

The Plant Based Cookbook For Beginners
650 Easy, Quick, & Simple Plant Based Vegan Diet Recipes With A 31 Day Meal Plan To Lose Weight & Live A Long Healthy Life

475

Butternut Squash Enchiladas

SERVINGS	PREPARATION TIME	COOKING TIME
6	2 hours 20 minutes	40 minutes

Nutritional Values Per Serving

Calories	241
Total Fat	4.8g
Saturated Fat	0.3g
Cholesterol	0mg
Sodium	165mg
Total Carbohydrate	22.6g
Dietary Fiber	4.1g
Total Sugars	15.1g
Protein	3g

Serving Suggestion:

Enjoy the enchiladas with avocado slices, jalapenos, and hot sauce.

Ingredients:

Cashew crema

- ½ cup raw cashews
- 1 garlic clove
- ½ jalapeno
- 2 tablespoons cilantro, chopped
- ⅓ cup filtered water
- ¼ teaspoon salt

Garnish

- Fresh cilantro

Enchiladas

- 1 tablespoon olive oil
- 2 garlic cloves, minced
- 1 small red onion, chopped
- 4 cups butternut squash, cubed
- 1 teaspoon chili powder
- ½ teaspoon cumin
- ¼ teaspoon salt
- Salt and black pepper, to taste
- 1 (15-ounces) can black beans, rinsed
- 12 (6 inch) corn tortillas
- Vegan cheese

Enchilada sauce

- 1 (15-ounces) can tomato sauce
- 2 tablespoons tomato paste
- ⅔ cup water
- ½ teaspoon apple cider vinegar
- 3 garlic cloves, minced
- 2 ½ tablespoons chili powder
- 1 ½ teaspoons cumin
- 1 teaspoon dried oregano
- ¼ teaspoon cayenne pepper
- ¼ teaspoon salt

Instructions:

1. At 350 degrees F, preheat your oven.
2. Layer a 9x13 inch baking pan with cooking spray.
3. Soak cashews in 2 cups boiling water in a bowl for 2 hours then drain.
4. Prepare the enchiladas sauce in a cooking pot and add all its ingredients.
5. Mix well, cook for 5 minutes on a simmer and keep the sauce aside.
6. For the enchiladas sauté onions and garlic with oil in a large skillet for 30 seconds.
7. Stir in salt, cumin, chili powder, and butternut squash then mix well and cover to cook for 8 minutes.
8. Stir in 1 cup enchiladas sauce and black beans then mix well.
9. Spread ⅔ cup enchilada sauce in the prepared pan and place tortilla in the pan and top it with ⅓ cup butternut squash filling and roll it. Make more rolls as in the same way.
10. Place these rolls in the pan and pour the remaining enchiladas sauce and vegan cheese on top.
11. Bake the enchiladas for 30 minutes.
12. Blend cashews with water, salt, cilantro, garlic and jalapenos in a blender.
13. Pour this cashew sauce over enchiladas then garnish with cilantro
14. Serve.

476

The Plant Based Cookbook For Beginners
650 Easy, Quick, & Simple Plant Based Vegan Diet Recipes With A 31 Day Meal Plan To Lose Weight & Live A Long Healthy Life

Lentil Sloppy Joes with Spaghetti

SERVINGS	PREPARATION TIME	COOKING TIME
4	15 minutes	4 hours

Nutritional Values Per Serving

Calories	321
Total Fat	2.3g
Saturated Fat	0.4g
Cholesterol	20mg
Sodium	128mg
Total Carbohydrate	22g
Dietary Fiber	4.9g
Total Sugars	24.6g
Protein	10g

Ingredients:

- 1¼ cups uncooked green lentils, rinsed
- 1 white onion, diced
- 1 red pepper, diced
- 1 carrot, sliced
- 3 garlic cloves, minced
- 1½ tablespoons chili powder
- 1 teaspoon cumin
- ½ teaspoon onion powder
- ¼ teaspoon cayenne pepper
- 1 (15 oz) can tomato sauce
- 1 (15 oz) can diced tomatoes
- 1½ cups water
- 2 tablespoons organic ketchup
- 1 teaspoon yellow mustard
- 2 cups spaghetti noodles
- 1 teaspoon gluten free soy sauce
- Salt and black pepper, to taste
- 1 tablespoon grated vegan parmesan cheese, to garnish

Instructions:

1. Add all the ingredients except spaghetti to a slow cooker.
2. Cover and slow-cook on high for 4 hours on High heat.
3. Boil the spaghetti noodles, as per the package's instructions then drain.
4. Transfer the spaghetti to a serving plate and then top it with lentils mixture.
5. Garnish with vegan parmesan cheese and serve warm.

The Plant Based Cookbook For Beginners
650 Easy, Quick, & Simple Plant Based Vegan Diet Recipes With A 31 Day Meal Plan To Lose Weight & Live A Long Healthy Life

477

Sesame-Orange Chickpea Stir-Fry

SERVINGS	PREPARATION TIME	COOKING TIME
4	15 minutes	20 minutes

Nutritional Values Per Serving

Calories	366
Total Fat	3.4g
Saturated Fat	0.3g
Cholesterol	0mg
Sodium	224mg
Total Carbohydrate	34g
Dietary Fiber	2½g
Total Sugars	3.2g
Protein	13g

Ingredients:

Sauce

- ¾ cup orange juice
- 1 tablespoon agave
- 2 tablespoons soy sauce
- 1 teaspoon ginger, grated
- 1 tablespoon cornstarch organic
- Zest of 1 orange

Garnish

- 1 tablespoon green onion
- 1 tablespoon chopped greens
- 1 teaspoon red pepper flakes

Stir-fry

- 1½ tablespoon toasted sesame oil
- 1 (15 oz) can chickpeas, rinsed
- ½ red onion, chopped
- 3 garlic cloves, minced
- 1 large red bell pepper, sliced
- 8 ounces artichoke, halved
- 2 ounces boiled couscous

Instructions:

1. Mix orange zest, cornstarch, ginger, soy sauce, agave, and orange juice in a large bowl.
2. Set a suitable skillet with 1 tablespoon sesame oil over medium-high heat.
3. Stir in chickpeas then sauté for 5 minutes.
4. Mix well and transfer the chickpeas to a plate.
5. Sauté onion with ½ tablespoons oil in a skillet over medium heat for 4 minutes.
6. Stir in bell pepper and garlic then sauté for 3 minutes.
7. Add artichoke then sauté for 4 minutes.
8. Pour in the prepared sauce then mix and cook until the sauce thickens.
9. Add chickpeas and cook on low heat for 4 minutes.
10. Stir in couscous and rest of the ingredients.
11. Garnish with green onion, chopped greens and red pepper flakes.
12. Serve warm.

478

The Plant Based Cookbook For Beginners
650 Easy, Quick, & Simple Plant Based Vegan Diet Recipes With A 31 Day Meal Plan To Lose Weight & Live A Long Healthy Life

Sweet Potato Zoodles

SERVINGS
4

PREPARATION TIME
15 minutes

COOKING TIME
21 minutes

Nutritional Values Per Serving

Calories	310
Total Fat	5.1g
Saturated Fat	1.6g
Cholesterol	1mg
Sodium	89mg
Total Carbohydrate	23g
Dietary Fiber	3.4g
Total Sugars	13.6g
Protein	5.6g

Ingredients:

- 1 teaspoon coconut oil
- 3 garlic cloves, minced
- 2 teaspoons fresh grated ginger
- 1 small white onion, diced
- 1 red pepper, diced
- 2 medium sweet potato, peeled and diced
- 1 ¼ teaspoon ground turmeric
- ½ teaspoon salt
- Black pepper, to taste
- 1 (15 oz) can light coconut milk
- 2 tablespoons creamy peanut butter
- 2 medium zucchinis, spiralized
- Spinach leaves, to garnish

Instructions:

1. Sauté ginger, and garlic with oil in a suitable skillet for 30 seconds.
2. Stir in sweet potatoes cubes, onion and red pepper then cook for 5 minutes.
3. Add turmeric, coconut milk, black pepper, salt and peanut butter then cook to a boil.
4. Reduce its heat, and cook for 15 minutes.
5. Puree this sweet potato mixture until smooth.
6. Add zucchini noodles to a bowl then mix with the sweet potato mixture.
7. Garnish with spinach leaves.
8. Serve warm.

The Plant Based Cookbook For Beginners
650 Easy, Quick, & Simple Plant Based Vegan Diet Recipes With A 31 Day Meal Plan To Lose Weight & Live A Long Healthy Life

479

Butternut Squash Chickpea Stew

SERVINGS
4

PREPARATION TIME
10 minutes

COOKING TIME
26 minutes

Nutritional Values Per Serving

Calories	290
Total Fat	10.3g
Saturated Fat	1.4g
Cholesterol	0mg
Sodium	68mg
Total Carbohydrate	26g
Dietary Fiber	8.3g
Total Sugars	19.7g
Protein	12.3g

Serving Suggestion:

Try this stew with brown rice.

Ingredients:

- 1 tablespoon olive oil
- 1 medium white onion, chopped
- 6 garlic cloves, minced
- 2 teaspoons cumin
- 1 teaspoon cinnamon
- 1 teaspoon ground turmeric
- ¼ teaspoon cayenne pepper
- 1 (28 ounces) can crushed tomatoes
- 2 ½ cups vegetable broth
- 1 (15-ounces) can chickpeas, rinsed
- 4 cups butternut squash, cubed
- 1 cup green lentils, rinsed
- ½ teaspoon salt
- Black pepper, to taste
- fresh juice of ½ a lemon
- ⅓ cup cilantro, chopped
- 1 tablespoon basil leaves, chopped

Instructions:

1. Sauté garlic and onion with oil in a suitable pot over medium high heat for 5 minutes.
2. Stir in cayenne, turmeric, cinnamon and cumin then sauté for 30 seconds.
3. Add black pepper, salt, lentils, butternut squash, chickpeas, broth and tomatoes.
4. Cook to a boil, reduce its heat then cover and cook for 20 minutes.
5. Add basil, cilantro and lemon juice.
6. Serve warm.

480

The Plant Based Cookbook For Beginners
650 Easy, Quick, & Simple Plant Based Vegan Diet Recipes With A 31 Day Meal Plan To Lose Weight & Live A Long Healthy Life

Tofu Tikka Masala

SERVINGS
4

PREPARATION TIME
10 minutes

COOKING TIME
7 hours 10 minutes

Nutritional Values Per Serving

Calories	331
Total Fat	17g
Saturated Fat	12g
Cholesterol	20mg
Sodium	275mg
Total Carbohydrate	29g
Dietary Fiber	3.4g
Total Sugars	8.2g
Protein	18g

Serving Suggestion:

Enjoy this tofu masala with white rice.

Ingredients:

- 1 (16 ounce) package tofu, cubed
- 3 garlic cloves, minced
- 1 white onion, diced
- 1 red bell pepper, cut into chunks
- 2 medium carrots, sliced
- 1 ½ cups gold potatoes, diced
- 2 cups cauliflower florets
- 1 (15-ounces) can tomato sauce
- 1 (15-ounces) can lite coconut milk
- ½ tablespoon pure maple syrup
- ½ tablespoon ginger, grated
- 1 tablespoon garam masala
- 1 ½ teaspoons cumin
- 1 teaspoon coriander
- ½ teaspoon ground turmeric
- ¼ teaspoon paprika
- ¼ teaspoon cayenne pepper
- ½ teaspoon salt
- Black pepper, to taste
- ¾ cup frozen peas

Garnish

- Chopped green onions

Instructions:

1. Add tofu, garlic and rest of the ingredients except peas to a slow cooker.
2. Mix gently, cover and cook for 7 hours on High heat settings.
3. Stir in peas and cook for 10 minutes.
4. Serve warm and garnish with green onions.

The Plant Based Cookbook For Beginners
650 Easy, Quick, & Simple Plant Based Vegan Diet Recipes With A 31 Day Meal Plan To Lose Weight & Live A Long Healthy Life

481

Puerto Rican Rice and Beans

SERVINGS	PREPARATION TIME	COOKING TIME
4	8 hours 15 minutes	3 hours 13 minutes

Nutritional Values Per Serving

Calories	248
Total Fat	5.6g
Saturated Fat	2.9g
Cholesterol	0mg
Sodium	17mg
Total Carbohydrate	26g
Dietary Fiber	5.6g
Total Sugars	9.2g
Protein	13g

Ingredients:

Beans

- 1-pound kidney beans
- 8 cups water
- 2 bay leaves

Sofrito For The Beans

- 2 teaspoons olive oil
- ½ cup yellow onion, diced
- ½ cup green bell pepper, diced
- ¼ cup cilantro, chopped
- 3 garlic cloves, minced
- 1 cup tomato sauce
- 3 teaspoons 2 packets sazon

Rice

- 2 teaspoons olive oil
- ⅓ cup yellow onion, diced
- ⅓ cup green bell pepper, chopped
- ¼ cup cilantro, chopped
- 2 garlic cloves, minced
- ½ cup tomato sauce
- 3 teaspoons 2 packets sazon
- ⅛ teaspoon adobo
- 1 (15 oz.) can Pigeon peas
- 3 cups water
- 2 cups basmati white rice

Instructions:

1. Soak beans in 8 cup water in a bowl for 8 hours then drain.
2. Boil beans with water in a cooking pot for 2 minutes then reduce the heat and cook for 2 hours.
3. Drain the beans and keep them aside.
4. Sauté onion, garlic, cilantro, green pepper with oil in a suitable pan for 5 minutes.
5. Reduce the heat and add sazon and tomato sauce then cook for 3 minutes.
6. Stir in beans and cook for 30 minutes.
7. Meanwhile, cook rice and sauté onion, bay leaf, garlic, cilantro, and green bell pepper with oil in a suitable pan for 5 minutes.
8. Stir in adobo, pigeon peas, sazon and tomato sauce then cook for 2 minutes.
9. Add rice and 3 cups water then cook for 30 minutes.
10. Serve the rice with the beans.
11. Enjoy warm.

482

The Plant Based Cookbook For Beginners
650 Easy, Quick, & Simple Plant Based Vegan Diet Recipes With A 31 Day Meal Plan To Lose Weight & Live A Long Healthy Life

Curried Brown Rice with Tofu

SERVINGS | PREPARATION TIME | COOKING TIME
4 | **24 hours 15 minutes** | **66 minutes**

Nutritional Values Per Serving

Calories	314
Total Fat	18g
Saturated Fat	3g
Cholesterol	10mg
Sodium	54mg
Total Carbohydrate	28g
Dietary Fiber	4.8g
Total Sugars	1.9g
Protein	13g

Ingredients:

Rice & Veggies

- ½ tablespoon olive oil
- 3 garlic cloves, minced
- 8 ounces baby bella mushrooms, sliced
- 1 white onion, diced
- 1 red bell pepper, diced
- 2 large carrots, sliced
- 2 cups jasmine brown rice
- 1 can (15 oz) light coconut milk
- 2 cups water
- 1 cup frozen peas
- 1 tablespoon yellow curry powder
- ½ teaspoon ground turmeric
- ¾ teaspoon salt
- Black pepper, to taste

Tofu Marinade

- 1 package extra firm tofu, cubed
- ½ tablespoon olive oil
- 1 teaspoon yellow curry powder
- ½ teaspoon coconut sugar
- ½ teaspoon garlic powder
- 1 pinch of cayenne pepper
- ¼ teaspoon salt
- Black pepper, to taste

Instructions:

1. Mix all ingredients for tofu marinade in a bowl then add tofu.
2. Toss, cover and refrigerate for 24 hours.
3. Sauté tofu with oil in a suitable skillet for 6 minutes per side.
4. Sauté mushrooms, carrots, bell pepper, onion, and garlic with ½ tablespoons olive oil in another pan for 5 minutes.
5. Add brown rice, coconut milk and rest of the ingredients then cook for 45 minutes on a simmer.
6. Add tofu to the rice and serve warm.
7. Enjoy.

The Plant Based Cookbook For Beginners
650 Easy, Quick, & Simple Plant Based Vegan Diet Recipes With A 31 Day Meal Plan To Lose Weight & Live A Long Healthy Life

483

Chickpeas in Sofrito

SERVINGS	PREPARATION TIME	COOKING TIME
4	20 minutes	43 minutes

Nutritional Values Per Serving

Calories	334
Total Fat	20g
Saturated Fat	17g
Cholesterol	41mg
Sodium	381mg
Total Carbohydrate	34g
Dietary Fiber	0.8g
Total Sugars	2.9g
Protein	4.4g

Ingredients:

Sofrito for the chickpeas

- 2 teaspoons olive oil
- ½ cup yellow onion, chopped
- ½ cup green bell pepper, chopped
- ⅓ cup cilantro, chopped
- 3 garlic cloves, minced
- 1 cup tomato sauce
- 3 teaspoons sazon
- 2 (15 ounces) cans Garbanzo Beans, drained
- 2 ½ cups vegetable broth

Rice

- 2 teaspoons olive oil, chopped
- ⅓ cup yellow onion, chopped
- ⅓ cup green bell pepper, chopped
- ¼ cup cilantro, chopped
- 2 garlic cloves, minced
- ½ cup tomato sauce
- 3 teaspoons sazon
- 1 (15 oz) can green pigeon peas
- 3 cups water
- 2 cups basmati white rice

Instructions:

1. Sauté cilantro, garlic, bell pepper, onion with oil in a suitable pan for 4 minutes.
2. Stir in tomato sauce and sazon then cook for 3 minutes on a simmer.
3. Add broth and chickpeas beans then cook for 10 minutes.
4. Sauté garlic, cilantro, green pepper and onion with oil in another pot for 4 minutes.
5. Stir in tomato sauce and sazon then cook for 2 minutes.
6. Add rice, 3 cups water and pigeon peas then cook for 20 minutes on a simmer.
7. Divide the rice and beans in the serving bowl.
8. Garnish and serve warm.

484

The Plant Based Cookbook For Beginners
650 Easy, Quick, & Simple Plant Based Vegan Diet Recipes With A 31 Day Meal Plan To Lose Weight & Live A Long Healthy Life

Sweet Potato Buddha Bowl

SERVINGS	PREPARATION TIME	COOKING TIME
2	20 minutes	84 minutes

Nutritional Values Per Serving

Calories	362
Total Fat	11g
Saturated Fat	21g
Cholesterol	10mg
Sodium	133mg
Total Carbohydrate	21g
Dietary Fiber	5.2g
Total Sugars	1.9g
Protein	13g

Ingredients:

Roasted Veggies

- 1 cup brussel sprouts, quartered
- 2 medium sweet potatoes, diced
- 2 garlic cloves, minced
- 1 tablespoon toasted sesame oil
- Salt and black pepper, to taste

Mango Coconut Rice

- 2 teaspoons unrefined coconut oil
- 1 cup coconut milk
- 1 cup water
- 1 cup brown rice, cooked
- 3 tablespoons mango, minced

Almond Butter Dressing

- ¼ cup almond butter
- 4 tablespoons orange juice
- 2 teaspoons pure maple syrup
- ½ teaspoon apple cider vinegar
- 1 teaspoon toasted sesame oil

Instructions:

1. Sauté brown rice with coconut oil in a suitable pan for 5 minutes.
2. Stir in coconut milk, mango and water and cook to a boil, then reduce the heat and cook for 45 minutes on a simmer.
3. At 375 degrees F, preheat your oven.
4. Layer a baking sheet with wax paper.
5. Heat sweet potatoes in a bowl for 4 minutes in the microwave.
6. Toss the sweet potatoes, with salt, black pepper, garlic and broccoli in a baking sheet.
7. Drizzle sesame oil on top and bake for 30 minutes.
8. Mix sesame oil, cider vinegar, maple syrup, orange juice and almond butter in a bowl.
9. Divide the rice in the serving bowl.
10. Top the rice with veggies and the dressing.
11. Serve warm.

The Plant Based Cookbook For Beginners
650 Easy, Quick, & Simple Plant Based Vegan Diet Recipes With A 31 Day Meal Plan To Lose Weight & Live A Long Healthy Life

485

Potato Stuffed Peppers

SERVINGS	PREPARATION TIME	COOKING TIME
4	10 minutes	16 minutes

Nutritional Values Per Serving

Calories	338
Total Fat	15g
Saturated Fat	8g
Cholesterol	0mg
Sodium	232mg
Total Carbohydrate	18g
Dietary Fiber	13.9g
Total Sugars	5.7g
Protein	14.2g

Ingredients:

- 10 medium red peppers
- 1 lb potatoes, chopped
- 2 onions chopped
- 4 tablespoons olive oil
- 1 teaspoon black pepper
- 2 teaspoons paprika
- 1 teaspoon garlic powder
- 1 teaspoon dried savory
- Salt to taste

Instructions:

1. Chop the top of the bell peppers and remove their seeds to hollow them.
2. Sauté onion with oil in suitable skillet until soft.
3. Stir in potatoes, and rest of the seasonings then sauté for 6 minutes.
4. Divide the potatoes into the bell peppers.
5. Place the bell pepper tops on top.
6. Serve warm.

486

The Plant Based Cookbook For Beginners
650 Easy, Quick, & Simple Plant Based Vegan Diet Recipes With A 31 Day Meal Plan To Lose Weight & Live A Long Healthy Life

Tofu Hummus Buddha

SERVINGS	PREPARATION TIME	COOKING TIME
4	10 minutes	17 minutes

Nutritional Values Per Serving

Calories	287
Total Fat	7g
Saturated Fat	2.1g
Cholesterol	10mg
Sodium	327mg
Total Carbohydrate	26g
Dietary Fiber	8g
Total Sugars	2.4g
Protein	9g

Ingredients:

- ½ teaspoons turmeric
- ½ cup basmati rice
- ½ teaspoon red pepper flakes
- 1 cup water
- 10 ounces smoked tofu
- 2 teaspoons olive oil
- 4 tablespoons hummus
- 1 tablespoon lemon juice
- 1 tablespoon water
- ½ teaspoons salt

Instructions:

1. Add rice, water, turmeric and salt to a cooking pot then cook for 10 minutes.
2. Sauté tofu with oil and red pepper flakes in a skillet for 7 minutes until golden brown.
3. Mix hummus with water and lemon juice in a bowl.
4. Divide the rice in the serving bowls.
5. Top them with tofu and hummus dressing.
6. Enjoy.

The Plant Based Cookbook For Beginners
650 Easy, Quick, & Simple Plant Based Vegan Diet Recipes With A 31 Day Meal Plan To Lose Weight & Live A Long Healthy Life

487

Zucchini Corn Fritters

SERVINGS	PREPARATION TIME	COOKING TIME
4	15 minutes	6 minutes

Nutritional Values Per Serving

Calories	366
Total Fat	8.6g
Saturated Fat	3g
Cholesterol	21mg
Sodium	146mg
Total Carbohydrate	24g
Dietary Fiber	4g
Total Sugars	15.2g
Protein	5.8g

Ingredients:

- 1 cup whole wheat flour
- 2 teaspoons baking powder
- ½ teaspoons salt
- ¼ teaspoons black pepper
- 1 tablespoon chia seeds
- 3 tablespoons water
- ½ cup almond milk
- 1 tablespoon olive oil
- 1 ½ cup grated zucchini
- 1 cup corn kernels
- ½ jalapeño pepper, chopped
- 3 garlic cloves, minced
- 3 green onions, diced
- ⅓ cup parsley, chopped
- 1 tablespoon lime juice
- 2 tablespoons olive oil

Instructions:

1. Place the zucchini in a colander and sprinkle salt on top and leave for 10 minutes then rinse.
2. Squeeze the zucchini and mix with rest of the ingredients in a bowl.
3. Set a cooking pan with 2 tablespoons oil over medium heat.
4. Take 2 tablespoons of the zucchini batter, make it into patties, and place in the pan.
5. Sear the fritter for 2-3 minutes per side and cook more fritters in the same way.
6. Serve warm.

488

The Plant Based Cookbook For Beginners
650 Easy, Quick, & Simple Plant Based Vegan Diet Recipes With A 31 Day Meal Plan To Lose Weight & Live A Long Healthy Life

Vegan Burrito

SERVINGS	PREPARATION TIME	COOKING TIME
4	10 minutes	15 minutes

Nutritional Values Per Serving

Calories	363
Total Fat	11.1g
Saturated Fat	3.8g
Cholesterol	0mg
Sodium	650mg
Total Carbohydrate	23g
Dietary Fiber	2g
Total Sugars	1.6g
Protein	7g

Ingredients:

- 7 ounces smoked tofu, diced
- 1 onion, chopped
- 1 bell pepper, green, chopped
- 1 tablespoon olive oil
- 1 cup chopped tomatoes
- 1 avocado, sliced
- 4 tortilla wraps
- Salt and black pepper to taste
- 1 teaspoon tabasco
- 1 tablespoon cilantro
- 1 tablespoon soy yogurt

Instructions:

1. Sauté onion, pepper and tofu with oil in a suitable skillet for 15 minutes.
2. Mix avocado flesh with tomatoes, black pepper and salt in a bowl.
3. Spread the tofu on the tortillas wraps and top it with avocado mash.
4. Add black pepper, salt, tabasco and yogurt on top.
5. Roll the wraps and serve.

The Plant Based Cookbook For Beginners
650 Easy, Quick, & Simple Plant Based Vegan Diet Recipes With A 31 Day Meal Plan To Lose Weight & Live A Long Healthy Life

489

Herb Pasta Salad

SERVINGS	PREPARATION TIME	COOKING TIME
4	10 minutes	10 minutes

Nutritional Values Per Serving

Calories	348
Total Fat	6.6g
Saturated Fat	1.9g
Cholesterol	1mg
Sodium	97mg
Total Carbohydrate	35.1g
Dietary Fiber	8.2g
Total Sugars	4g
Protein	9g

Serving Suggestion:

Enjoy this pasta salad with sprouts on top.

Ingredients:

Lemon Herb Vinaigrette

- 1 cup olive oil
- 2 tablespoons fresh lemon juice
- 1 tablespoon lemon zest
- 2 tablespoons red wine vinegar
- 2 teaspoons fresh garlic minced
- 2 teaspoons dried oregano
- 1 teaspoon dried parsley
- 1 teaspoon dried basil
- 2 teaspoons fresh chives chopped
- 2 teaspoons fresh dill chopped
- ½ teaspoons salt
- ½ teaspoons black pepper

Pasta Salad

- 1 box 12 ounces gluten-free pasta
- 1 large English cucumber, chopped
- 2 large bell peppers, sliced
- 1 ½ cup cherry tomatoes, sliced
- ½ large red onion, sliced

Garnish

- Alfalfa sprouts

Instructions:

1. Boil pasta as per the package's instruction then drain.
2. Mix all the lemon herb dressing ingredients in a bowl.
3. Toss pasta with the dressing and veggies in a salad bowl.
4. Garnish with sprouts and serve.

490

The Plant Based Cookbook For Beginners
650 Easy, Quick, & Simple Plant Based Vegan Diet Recipes With A 31 Day Meal Plan To Lose Weight & Live A Long Healthy Life

Buffalo Tofu

SERVINGS
6

PREPARATION TIME
25 minutes

COOKING TIME
30 minutes

Nutritional Values Per Serving

Calories	250
Total Fat	7.8g
Saturated Fat	4.1g
Cholesterol	0mg
Sodium	150mg
Total Carbohydrate	20g
Dietary Fiber	5.2g
Total Sugars	12.8g
Protein	6g

Serving Suggestion:

Enjoy the tofu with rice on the side.

Ingredients:

- 1 (14-ounce) block tofu, drained
- 1 cup rolled oats
- 2 tablespoons avocado oil
- ½ teaspoon smoked paprika
- 1 teaspoon dried oregano
- ½ teaspoon salt
- ¼ teaspoon black pepper
- 6 tablespoons cornstarch
- ⅓ cup unsweetened oat milk
- 1 tablespoon vegan butter
- ¾ cup buffalo sauce
- Green onions, to garnish

Instructions:

1. At 425 degrees F, preheat your oven.
2. Layer a baking sheet with wax paper.
3. Cut the tofu in cubes and place them in a large bowl.
4. Blend black pepper, salt, oregano, paprika, avocado oil, and oats in food processor.
5. Mix milk with cornstarch in another bowl.
6. Dip the tofu in milk mixture then coat with the oat's crumbs and place in the baking sheet.
7. Bake these tofu rectangles for 30 minutes, and flip once cooked halfway through.
8. Meanwhile, mix buffalo sauce with butter in a cooking pot and cook for 3-5 minutes then pour this sauce over the tofu.
9. Garnish with green onions.
10. Serve warm.

The Plant Based Cookbook For Beginners
650 Easy, Quick, & Simple Plant Based Vegan Diet Recipes With A 31 Day Meal Plan To Lose Weight & Live A Long Healthy Life

491

Peruvian Sandwich

SERVINGS	PREPARATION TIME	COOKING TIME
4	15 minutes	15 minutes

Nutritional Values Per Serving

Calories	315
Total Fat	17g
Saturated Fat	6g
Cholesterol	23mg
Sodium	116mg
Total Carbohydrate	28g
Dietary Fiber	4.1g
Total Sugars	1.3g
Protein	8g

Serving Suggestion:

Enjoy the sandwich with fries on the side.

Ingredients:

- 1 tablespoon oil
- 2 teaspoon garlic powder
- 2 teaspoon ground cumin
- 2 teaspoons paprika
- 1 teaspoon dried oregano
- ½ teaspoon black pepper
- ½ teaspoon salt
- 1 red bell pepper, cut into strips
- 6 mushrooms, sliced

Pickled Red Onions

- 1 red onion sliced
- Juice of 1 lime
- 2 tablespoon white vinegar

Serve

- 2 Rolls
- 2 tomato, sliced

Instructions:

1. At 400 degrees F, preheat your oven.
2. Mix black pepper, salt, spices and oil in a large bowl.
3. Stir in mushrooms, and pepper then mix well.
4. Spread these veggies in a baking tray and bake for 15 minutes.
5. Prepare the pickled onions and mix its ingredients in a bowl then leave for 10 minutes.
6. Cut the rolls in half, add veggies to the rolls and top them with pickled onions, tomato slices and roasted vegetables.
7. Serve warm.

492

The Plant Based Cookbook For Beginners
650 Easy, Quick, & Simple Plant Based Vegan Diet Recipes With A 31 Day Meal Plan To Lose Weight & Live A Long Healthy Life

Peanut Noodles with Tofu

SERVINGS **PREPARATION TIME** **COOKING TIME**
4   15 minutes   42 minutes

Nutritional Values Per Serving

Calories	384
Total Fat	19g
Saturated Fat	20g
Cholesterol	13mg
Sodium	556mg
Total Carbohydrate	29g
Dietary Fiber	6.1g
Total Sugars	7g
Protein	14g

Ingredients:

Tofu

- 8 ounces extra firm tofu, pressed
- 1 tablespoon soy sauce
- ½ teaspoon garlic powder
- ½ teaspoon onion powder

Peanut sauce

- 1 tablespoon peanut butter
- 1 tablespoon tamari
- ½ teaspoon garlic powder
- 2 teaspoon maple syrup
- 1 teaspoon rice vinegar
- 1 teaspoon sesame oil

Noodles

- 4 ounces noodles
- ½ red bell pepper, julienned
- 1 tablespoon olive oil
- ½ carrot, julienned
- ½ small red onion, diced
- 2 garlic cloves, minced
- 1 handful of bean sprouts
- Chopped green onions, to garnish

Instructions:

1. Mix soy sauce, garlic powder and onion powder in a bowl and soak the tofu in the marinade for 20 minutes.
2. At 400 degrees F, preheat your oven.
3. Spread the tofu in a baking sheet and bake for 20 minutes.
4. Cook the noodles as per the package's instructions then drain.
5. Prepare the peanut sauce by mixing all its ingredients in a bowl.
6. Sauté onion with olive oil in a skillet until brown.
7. Stir in garlic then cook for 2 minutes.
8. Stir in carrot and red pepper then cook for 10 minutes.
9. Add noodles, peanut sauce, tofu and bean sprout then mix well.
10. Garnish with green onions then serve warm.

The Plant Based Cookbook For Beginners
650 Easy, Quick, & Simple Plant Based Vegan Diet Recipes With A 31 Day Meal Plan To Lose Weight & Live A Long Healthy Life

493

Vegan Egg Salad

SERVINGS	PREPARATION TIME	COOKING TIME
4	5 minutes	0 minutes

Nutritional Values Per Serving

Calories	371
Total Fat	11g
Saturated Fat	6g
Cholesterol	12mg
Sodium	417mg
Total Carbohydrate	30.3g
Dietary Fiber	9g
Total Sugars	4.3g
Protein	12g

Ingredients:

- 16 ounces firm tofu, water-packed
- 3 tablespoons chives, chopped
- ½ cup vegan mayo
- 1 tablespoon nutritional yeast flakes
- 1 teaspoon onion powder
- 1 teaspoon yellow mustard
- 1 teaspoon Himalayan black salt
- ⅛ teaspoon turmeric

Instructions:

1. Mix tofu with rest of the ingredients in a salad bowl.
2. Serve.

494

The Plant Based Cookbook For Beginners
650 Easy, Quick, & Simple Plant Based Vegan Diet Recipes With A 31 Day Meal Plan To Lose Weight & Live A Long Healthy Life

Red Pesto Pasta

SERVINGS
4

PREPARATION TIME
10 minutes

COOKING TIME
15 minutes

Nutritional Values Per Serving

Calories	394
Total Fat	9g
Saturated Fat	1.6g
Cholesterol	0mg
Sodium	455mg
Total Carbohydrate	31g
Dietary Fiber	1.7g
Total Sugars	2.1g
Protein	6g

Ingredients:

- 7 ounces wholegrain pasta
- 1 onion
- 1 tablespoon olive oil
- 3-4 tablespoons red pesto
- 1 handful spinach
- 1 handful cherry tomatoes

Garnish

- Sunflower seeds

Instructions:

1. Boil the whole grain pasta as per the package's instructions then drain.
2. Sauté onion with oil in a suitable skillet until soft.
3. Stir in red pesto, spinach, cherry tomatoes and cook for 2 minutes.
4. Add pasta then mix well.
5. Garnish with sunflower seeds.
6. Serve warm.

The Plant Based Cookbook For Beginners
650 Easy, Quick, & Simple Plant Based Vegan Diet Recipes With A 31 Day Meal Plan To Lose Weight & Live A Long Healthy Life

495

Broccoli Pesto Pasta

SERVINGS	PREPARATION TIME	COOKING TIME
4	10 minutes	12 minutes

Nutritional Values Per Serving

Calories	330
Total Fat	4.9g
Saturated Fat	1.1g
Cholesterol	0mg
Sodium	248mg
Total Carbohydrate	18.3g
Dietary Fiber	3.7g
Total Sugars	16g
Protein	6g

Ingredients:

- 12 ounces conchigelie pasta

Broccoli pesto sauce

- 1 lb. broccoli
- 1 cup fresh basil
- 1 cup baby spinach
- ½ ounces garlic cloves
- ¼ cup pine nuts
- 3 tablespoons nutritional yeast
- 1 cup olive oil
- Zest from ½ lemon
- 2 tablespoons lemon juice
- Salt and black pepper to taste

Instructions:

1. Boil the whole grain pasta as per the package's instructions then drain.
2. Sauté onion with oil in a suitable skillet until soft.
3. Stir in red pesto, spinach, cherry tomatoes and cook for 2 minutes.
4. Add pasta then mix well.
5. Garnish with sunflower seeds.
6. Serve warm.

496

The Plant Based Cookbook For Beginners
650 Easy, Quick, & Simple Plant Based Vegan Diet Recipes With A 31 Day Meal Plan To Lose Weight & Live A Long Healthy Life

Pesto Zoodles

SERVINGS	PREPARATION TIME	COOKING TIME
4	5 minutes	8 minutes

Nutritional Values Per Serving	
Calories	246
Total Fat	0.4g
Saturated Fat	0g
Cholesterol	0mg
Sodium	1mg
Total Carbohydrate	31.1g
Dietary Fiber	1.7g
Total Sugars	59.3g
Protein	0.4g

Ingredients:

- 1 medium zucchini
- 1 cup basil, fresh
- 1 tablespoon pesto
- 1 handful cherry tomatoes
- 1 teaspoon olive oil
- Salt and black pepper to taste

Instructions:

1. Pass the zucchini through a spiralizer to get zoodles.
2. Sauté tomatoes with oil, basil, black pepper and salt in a suitable skillet for 8 minutes.
3. Stir in pesto and zoodles then cook for 3 minutes.
4. Serve warm.

The Plant Based Cookbook For Beginners
650 Easy, Quick, & Simple Plant Based Vegan Diet Recipes With A 31 Day Meal Plan To Lose Weight & Live A Long Healthy Life

497

Chickpea Falafel Wrap

SERVINGS	PREPARATION TIME	COOKING TIME
4	10 minutes	8 minutes

Nutritional Values Per Serving

Calories	388
Total Fat	21g
Saturated Fat	0.7g
Cholesterol	0mg
Sodium	240mg
Total Carbohydrate	19g
Dietary Fiber	5.2g
Total Sugars	1.8g
Protein	8g

Ingredients:

- 1 ½ cup boiled chickpeas
- 2 teaspoon cumin powder
- Salt, to taste
- 2 cloves garlic, minced
- 3 tablespoon parsley, chopped
- Black pepper, to taste
- 2 tablespoon refined oil
- 1 avocado
- 5 tortillas
- 1 cup ice berg lettuce
- 2 tablespoon vegan mayonnaise
- 1 ½ red onion, sliced

Instructions:

1. Mix chickpeas in a bowl, and stir in cumin powder, black pepper, parsley, salt and garlic.
2. Mix well and make 4-inch-long sausages out of this chickpea mixture.
3. Set a pan with oil over medium heat and sear the chickpea falafels for 3-4 minutes per side.
4. Spread the tortillas and top them with lettuce leaves.
5. Add one falafel and remaining ingredients in top.
6. Roll the tortillas and serve.

498

The Plant Based Cookbook For Beginners
650 Easy, Quick, & Simple Plant Based Vegan Diet Recipes With A 31 Day Meal Plan To Lose Weight & Live A Long Healthy Life

Sesame Broccolini

SERVINGS
6

PREPARATION TIME
10 minutes

COOKING TIME
10 minutes

Nutritional Values Per Serving	
Calories	340
Total Fat	14g
Saturated Fat	1.2g
Cholesterol	10mg
Sodium	359mg
Total Carbohydrate	28.2g
Dietary Fiber	4.1g
Total Sugars	3g
Protein	13g

Ingredients:

- 3 cups broccolini
- 1 tablespoon olive oil
- 1 tablespoon sesame seeds
- 2 tablespoons peanuts
- 2 green onions, sliced
- 2-3 tablespoons water
- Salt to taste
- ⅛ cup water
- 2 tablespoons soy sauce dark
- 1 tablespoon sweet chili sauce
- 1 tablespoon vinegar lemon juice is also fine
- 1 teaspoon corn starch

Instructions:

1. Mix broccolini and water in a cooking pot and cook for 3 minutes.
2. Drain and keep the broccolini aside.
3. Mix soy sauce with vinegar, chili sauce, olive oil and a little bit of water in a cooking pot.
4. Whisk cornstarch with 3 tbsp water in a small bowl and pour into the sauce.
5. Cook this mixture until it thickens then add green onions, peanuts, sesame seeds and broccoli.
6. Adjust seasoning with vinegar and salt then mix well.
7. Serve warm.

The Plant Based Cookbook For Beginners
650 Easy, Quick, & Simple Plant Based Vegan Diet Recipes With A 31 Day Meal Plan To Lose Weight & Live A Long Healthy Life

499

Chinese Sesame Tofu

SERVINGS	PREPARATION TIME	COOKING TIME
4	10 minutes	20 minutes

Nutritional Values Per Serving

Calories	316
Total Fat	13g
Saturated Fat	2.8g
Cholesterol	0mg
Sodium	751mg
Total Carbohydrate	32g
Dietary Fiber	3.8g
Total Sugars	0.4g
Protein	12g

Serving Suggestion:

Enjoy this tofu curry with white rice and steamed broccoli on the side.

Ingredients:

Sauce

- 4 ounces light soy sauce
- 1-ounce hoisin sauce
- 3 ounces sugar
- 6 ounces pineapple juice
- 4 ounces water
- 7 medium pieces of ginger, smashed
- 7 garlic cloves, smashed

Tofu

- 1 broccoli head, cut into florets, boiled
- 1 block tofu, cubed
- Sesame seeds, lightly toasted
- 1 teaspoon dry chilies, chopped
- 1 teaspoon seasame oil
- 1 tablespoon water
- 1 tablespoon corn starch

Instructions:

1. Mix all the sauce ingredients in a cooking pan and cook on a simmer for 10 minutes.
2. Then drain the ginger sauce and keep it aside.
3. Sauté tofu cubes with oil in a suitable pan for 5 minutes per side.
4. Stir in the sauce, sesame seeds, chilis and the broccoli.
5. Mix cornstarch with 1 tbsp water and pour into the tofu.
6. Stir and cook until the mixture thickens.
7. Serve warm.

Hummus Pasta

SERVINGS	PREPARATION TIME	COOKING TIME
4	10 minutes	15 minutes

Nutritional Values Per Serving

Calories	372
Total Fat	0.3g
Saturated Fat	0g
Cholesterol	0mg
Sodium	2mg
Total Carbohydrate	46g
Dietary Fiber	2.3g
Total Sugars	6g
Protein	12.1g

Ingredients:

- 1 ¾ cups penne pasta
- 1 cup vegan hummus
- 2 handfuls spinach, chopped
- 8 sun-dried tomatoes, chopped
- 4 cherry tomatoes, halved
- 20 pitted black olives, sliced
- Salt, to taste

Instructions:

1. Cook and boil the pasta as per the package's instructions then drain.
2. Drain and mix the pasta with hummus in a cooking pot then cook for 2 minutes.
3. Stir in black olives, sun dried tomatoes and spinach then sauté for 3 minutes.
4. Serve warm and garnish with salt for tasting.

The Plant Based Cookbook For Beginners
650 Easy, Quick, & Simple Plant Based Vegan Diet Recipes With A 31 Day Meal Plan To Lose Weight & Live A Long Healthy Life

501

Wraps with Cauliflower Rice

SERVINGS	PREPARATION TIME	COOKING TIME
8	10 minutes	10 minutes

Nutritional Values Per Serving

Calories	361
Total Fat	14.7g
Saturated Fat	12.8g
Cholesterol	0mg
Sodium	161mg
Total Carbohydrate	23g
Dietary Fiber	2.7g
Total Sugars	2.6g
Protein	8g

Ingredients:

- 1 teaspoon coconut oil
- 4 cups riced cauliflower
- 1 green bell pepper, chopped
- ½ teaspoons sea salt
- ¼ cup cilantro, chopped
- 8 (10 inch) tortilla wraps

Dressing

- 4 cups slaw mixture
- 2 tablespoons olive oil
- 2 tablespoons peanut butter
- 3 tablespoons tamari
- 2 tablespoons rice vinegar
- ½ lime, squeezed
- 1 tablespoon maple syrup
- ½ teaspoons sriracha
- ½ teaspoons garlic powder

Instructions:

1. Grate cauliflower in a food processor into cauliflower rice.
2. Sauté cauliflower rice with bell pepper, oil and salt in a suitable skillet for 10 minutes.
3. Meanwhile, mix all the slaw and dressing ingredients in a bowl.
4. Divide the cauliflower rice on top of 4 tortilla wraps and top them with slaw mixture.
5. Place the remaining tortillas on top and press them gently.
6. Cut them in four pieces and grill each piece for 2-3 minutes per side.
7. Garnish with cilantro and serve.

502

The Plant Based Cookbook For Beginners
650 Easy, Quick, & Simple Plant Based Vegan Diet Recipes With A 31 Day Meal Plan To Lose Weight & Live A Long Healthy Life

Moroccan Lentils

SERVINGS
4

PREPARATION TIME
10 minutes

COOKING TIME
40 minutes

Nutritional Values Per Serving

Calories	350
Total Fat	11g
Saturated Fat	12g
Cholesterol	23mg
Sodium	340mg
Total Carbohydrate	20g
Dietary Fiber	1.7g
Total Sugars	3.1g
Protein	7g

Serving Suggestion:

Enjoy these lentils with rice alongside a spinach apple salad.

Ingredients:

- 2 cups brown lentils
- 3 tomatoes grated
- 1 medium onion, chopped
- 5 garlic cloves, chopped
- 4 tablespoons parsley
- 2 ½ teaspoons cumin
- 2 ½ teaspoons paprika
- 1 ½ teaspoons ginger
- ½ teaspoon black pepper
- 1 teaspoon cayenne pepper
- 2 teaspoons salt

Garnish

- Croutons
- Vegan feta cheese
- Green onions

Instructions:

1. Add lentils, cumin and rest of the ingredients along with 2 quarts water to a pressure cooker.

2. Cover and secure the lid then pressure cook on medium heat for 40 minutes.

3. Once done, release the pressure completely then remove the lid.

4. Mix well and garnish with green onions, croutons, and vegan feta cheese.

5. Serve warm.

The Plant Based Cookbook For Beginners
650 Easy, Quick, & Simple Plant Based Vegan Diet Recipes With A 31 Day Meal Plan To Lose Weight & Live A Long Healthy Life

503

Simple Pea Potato Curry

SERVINGS	PREPARATION TIME	COOKING TIME
4	10 minutes	14 minutes

Nutritional Values Per Serving

Calories	317
Total Fat	3.7g
Saturated Fat	1.2g
Cholesterol	0mg
Sodium	19mg
Total Carbohydrate	31g
Dietary Fiber	3g
Total Sugars	7.4g
Protein	4g

Ingredients:

- 2 tomatoes, chopped
- 1 teaspoon salt
- ½ teaspoon garam masala
- ½ teaspoon cumin powder
- ½ teaspoon chili powder
- ¼ teaspoon cayenne pepper
- 1 tablespoon safflower oil
- ½ cup vegetable broth
- ½ cup coconut milk
- ¼ cup peas
- ½ onion, chopped
- 2 garlic cloves, minced
- 2 potatoes, quartered
- 1 splash lemon juice

Garnish

- Chopped cilantro

Instructions:

1. Mash 2 tomatoes with salt, chili powder, cayenne pepper, cumin and garam masala in a bowl.
2. Sauté onions, potatoes and garlic with safflower oil in a suitable skillet for 3 minutes.
3. Stir in broth and coconut milk then cook to a boil
4. Add spices and tomato mixture and cook for 15 minutes.
5. Stir in peas and lemon juice and cook for 5 minutes.
6. Garnish with cilantro.
7. Serve warm.

504

The Plant Based Cookbook For Beginners
650 Easy, Quick, & Simple Plant Based Vegan Diet Recipes With A 31 Day Meal Plan To Lose Weight & Live A Long Healthy Life

Stuffed Chili Rellenos

SERVINGS	PREPARATION TIME	COOKING TIME
6	10 minutes	24 minutes

Nutritional Values Per Serving

Calories	327
Total Fat	12g
Saturated Fat	1.9g
Cholesterol	0mg
Sodium	91mg
Total Carbohydrate	25g
Dietary Fiber	3g
Total Sugars	5.6g
Protein	10g

Ingredients:

- 6 large poblano chiles
- 2 tablespoons olive oil
- 1 medium onion, chopped
- 2 garlic cloves, chopped
- 2 jalapenos, seeded and chopped
- ½ red bell pepper, chopped
- ½ cup fresh cilantro, chopped
- 1 teaspoon ground cumin
- 1 (28 oz.) can baked beans, drained
- 3 teaspoons hot sauce
- 12 ounces vegan cheese, grated
- Salt, to taste
- Black pepper, to taste, to taste

Instructions:

1. At 350 degrees F, preheat your oven.
2. Slice the poblano chiles in half and remove their seeds.
3. Sauté onion, jalapenos, bell pepper, cumin, cilantro and garlic with 2 tablespoons oil in a suitable skillet for 4 minutes.
4. Remove this onion mixture from the heat and add beans, hot sauce, black pepper, salt and cheese then mix well.
5. Divide this mixture in the hollow chiles.
6. Set the chilies in a baking sheet and bake for 20 minutes until golden brown.
7. Serve warm.

The Plant Based Cookbook For Beginners
650 Easy, Quick, & Simple Plant Based Vegan Diet Recipes With A 31 Day Meal Plan To Lose Weight & Live A Long Healthy Life

505

Grilled Eggplant Pizza

SERVINGS	PREPARATION TIME	COOKING TIME
6	10 minutes	25 minutes

Nutritional Values Per Serving

Calories	340
Total Fat	14g
Saturated Fat	8g
Cholesterol	17mg
Sodium	310mg
Total Carbohydrate	22g
Dietary Fiber	4g
Total Sugars	7g
Protein	19g

Ingredients:

- ¼ cup olive oil
- 1 small eggplant
- 1 whole wheat pizza dough
- 2 teaspoons dried basil
- ⅓ cup pizza sauce
- ⅔ cup vegan cheese, grated

Instructions:

1. Preheat your broiler at 350 degrees F.
2. Cut the eggplant into thin slices and rub them with olive oil.
3. Broil the eggplants in a baking sheet for 10 minutes.
4. Spread ⅓ cup pizza sauce on top of the pizza dough.
5. Set the grilled eggplant slices on top and add the remaining ingredients on top.
6. Bake this pizza for 15 minutes in the oven.
7. Serve warm.

Pasta E Fagioli With White Beans

SERVINGS	PREPARATION TIME	COOKING TIME
4	10 minutes	20 minutes

Nutritional Values Per Serving

Calories	285
Total Fat	8g
Saturated Fat	3g
Cholesterol	11mg
Sodium	168mg
Total Carbohydrate	19g
Dietary Fiber	3.7g
Total Sugars	3.4g
Protein	9g

Ingredients:

- 4 cups water
- 1 ½ teaspoons salt
- 1 ½ cups small shell pasta
- 2 cans great northern beans
- 3 tablespoons olive oil
- 1 onion, diced
- 3 garlic cloves, minced
- 2 teaspoons fresh basil, chopped
- 1 teaspoon dried oregano
- ½ teaspoons black pepper
- 1 ½ tablespoons paprika
- 1 cup tomato sauce

Garnish

- Vegan cheddar cheese

Instructions:

1. Boil the pasta in salted water in a cooking pan as per the package's instruction and drain.

2. Drain and reserve ⅓ cup cooking water.

3. Add beans and reserved water to a cooking pot.

4. Sauté onions, basil, oregano, salt, black pepper and garlic in a suitable skillet with oil for 5 minutes.

5. Transfer this mixture to the beans along with pasta then cook on low heat.

6. Add tomato sauce, and paprika then cook for 5 minutes.

7. Garnish with vegan cheddar cheese and serve warm.

The Plant Based Cookbook For Beginners
650 Easy, Quick, & Simple Plant Based Vegan Diet Recipes With A 31 Day Meal Plan To Lose Weight & Live A Long Healthy Life

507

Couscous Stuffed Bell Peppers

SERVINGS	PREPARATION TIME	COOKING TIME
6	10 minutes	45 minutes

Nutritional Values Per Serving

Calories	242
Total Fat	3g
Saturated Fat	10g
Cholesterol	12mg
Sodium	281mg
Total Carbohydrate	21g
Dietary Fiber	3.7g
Total Sugars	1.6g
Protein	13g

Ingredients:

- ½ cup couscous uncooked
- 1 cup water
- 6 whole bell peppers
- 2 yellow bell peppers, diced
- 6 green onions, sliced
- 2 tablespoons fresh lemon juice
- 2 tablespoons olive oil
- ¼ cup fresh parsley chopped
- Salt and black pepper to taste

Instructions:

1. Boil couscous with 1 cup water in a cooking pot and simmer for 10 minutes then fluff.

2. At 350 degrees F, preheat your oven.

3. Cut bell peppers in half and remove their cores.

4. Mix couscous with chopped yellow bell peppers, green onions in a bowl.

5. Whisk olive oil, lemon juice, black pepper, salt and parsley and pour over the couscous.

6. Mix well and divide the couscous in the bell peppers.

7. Roast the bell peppers in a baking sheet for 35 minutes in the oven.

8. Serve warm.

508

The Plant Based Cookbook For Beginners
650 Easy, Quick, & Simple Plant Based Vegan Diet Recipes With A 31 Day Meal Plan To Lose Weight & Live A Long Healthy Life

Thai Pineapple Fried Rice

SERVINGS
4

PREPARATION TIME
10 minutes

COOKING TIME
12 minutes

Nutritional Values Per Serving

Calories	446
Total Fat	9g
Saturated Fat	10g
Cholesterol	12mg
Sodium	312mg
Total Carbohydrate	32g
Dietary Fiber	0.3g
Total Sugars	7.9g
Protein	8g

Ingredients:

- 3 cups cooked rice
- 3 tablespoons oil
- 3 tablespoons soy sauce
- 2 teaspoons curry powder
- 2 shallots, chopped
- 3 garlic cloves, chopped
- 1 red or green chile, sliced
- ½ cup vegetable stock
- ¼ cup carrot, grated
- ½ cup frozen peas
- 1 small can pineapple chunks, drained
- ¼ cup currants
- ½ cup roasted cashews
- Lime juice, to taste

Garnish

- ⅓ cup cilantro leaves
- 3 green onions, chopped

Serve

- Pineapple shell

Instructions:

1. Mix rice with 1 tablespoon oil in a bowl.
2. Mix curry powder with soy sauce in another bowl.
3. Sauté garlic, chile and shallots with remaining oil in a suitable skillet for 1 minutes.
4. Stir in vegetable stock and cook for 1 minute.
5. Add peas, lime juice and carrots then sauté for 2 minutes.
6. Toss in cashews, currants, pineapple chunks, soy sauce mixture and rice then cook for 8 minutes.
7. Serve warm in a pineapple shell and garnish with green onions and cilantro.

The Plant Based Cookbook For Beginners
650 Easy, Quick, & Simple Plant Based Vegan Diet Recipes With A 31 Day Meal Plan To Lose Weight & Live A Long Healthy Life

509

Spinach and Mushroom Strudel

SERVINGS	PREPARATION TIME	COOKING TIME
4	15 minutes	52 minutes

Nutritional Values Per Serving

Calories	319
Total Fat	5g
Saturated Fat	3.1g
Cholesterol	14mg
Sodium	354mg
Total Carbohydrate	29g
Dietary Fiber	7g
Total Sugars	5g
Protein	7g

Ingredients:

- 5 sweet onion, sliced
- ½ cup mushroom broth
- 10 ounces mushrooms, sliced
- 3 cups spinach fresh, chopped
- 1 silken tofu extra-firm, drained
- 5 tablespoons vegan cream cheese
- 1 teaspoon olive oil
- 2 teaspoons tahini
- Salt to taste
- Black pepper to taste
- 1 package vegan puff pastry

Instructions:

1. At 375 degrees F, preheat your oven.
2. Cook onions with mushroom broth in a cooking pot for 10 minutes.
3. Stir in mushrooms, black pepper and salt then cook for 1 minute.
4. Add spinach and cook for 45 seconds.
5. Crumble the tofu and blend it with cream cheese, black pepper, salt, tahini and olive oi in a food processor.
6. Add sautéed mushrooms it the tofu mixture and mix evenly with a spatula.
7. Roll out the packaged puff pastry into a square.
8. Add half of the filling along with one border of the dough while leaving 2-inch border.
9. Starting rolling the dough from this end and pinch the edges to seal.
10. Repeat the same steps with remaining dough and filling.
11. Place the prepared rolls in a baking sheet and score the top with a knife.
12. Bake them for almost 40 minutes until golden brown.
13. Slice and serve warm.

510

The Plant Based Cookbook For Beginners
650 Easy, Quick, & Simple Plant Based Vegan Diet Recipes With A 31 Day Meal Plan To Lose Weight & Live A Long Healthy Life

Pumpkin Risotto

SERVINGS
4

PREPARATION TIME
10 minutes

COOKING TIME
10 minutes

Nutritional Values Per Serving

Calories	386
Total Fat	9g
Saturated Fat	10.3g
Cholesterol	14mg
Sodium	322mg
Total Carbohydrate	32g
Dietary Fiber	3.8g
Total Sugars	4.6g
Protein	17g

Ingredients:

- 1 onion, diced
- 1 tablespoon olive oil
- 2 cups arborio risotto rice
- 1 cup white wine
- 4 cups vegetable broth
- 1 cup canned pumpkin cubes
- 1 teaspoon ginger, grated
- 1 teaspoon nutmeg
- 1 tablespoon basil, chopped
- 1 tablespoon vegan butter
- Salt and black pepper, to taste

Instructions:

1. Sauté onions with olive oil in a suitable skillet for 5 minutes.
2. Stir in rice and sauté for 3 minutes.
3. Add white wine, vegetable broth and cook until the liquid is absorbed.
4. Stir in pumpkin, butter, basil, nutmeg, ginger, black pepper and salt.
5. Mix well and cook for 2 minutes.
6. Serve warm.

The Plant Based Cookbook For Beginners
650 Easy, Quick, & Simple Plant Based Vegan Diet Recipes With A 31 Day Meal Plan To Lose Weight & Live A Long Healthy Life

511

Spinach Peas Risotto

SERVINGS	PREPARATION TIME	COOKING TIME
2	10 minutes	40 minutes

Nutritional Values Per Serving

Calories	295
Total Fat	3g
Saturated Fat	11g
Cholesterol	13mg
Sodium	5mg
Total Carbohydrate	23g
Dietary Fiber	4.1g
Total Sugars	2.7g
Protein	7g

Ingredients:

- 1 ½ cups rice, uncooked and rinsed
- 2 cups water
- 1 handful fresh spinach
- ¼ cup vegetarian pesto
- ½ teaspoon lemon juice
- Salt to taste
- Black pepper to taste

Instructions:

1. Boil rice in water, in a cooking pot, cover and cook for 30 minutes on a simmer.
2. Add spinach and peas to the rice then cook for 10 minutes.
3. Add lime juice, black pepper and salt then transfer to a plate.
4. Serve.

512

The Plant Based Cookbook For Beginners
650 Easy, Quick, & Simple Plant Based Vegan Diet Recipes With A 31 Day Meal Plan To Lose Weight & Live A Long Healthy Life

Artichoke Tomato Pasta

SERVINGS
4

PREPARATION TIME
10 minutes

COOKING TIME
17 minutes

Nutritional Values Per Serving

Calories	385
Total Fat	8g
Saturated Fat	3g
Cholesterol	23mg
Sodium	132mg
Total Carbohydrate	26g
Dietary Fiber	4g
Total Sugars	3g
Protein	11g

Ingredients:

- 1 (12-ounces) box pasta
- 2 tablespoons olive oil
- 3 garlic cloves, minced
- ½ red pepper, diced
- 1 jar sun-dried tomatoes drained
- 1 cup artichoke hearts, drained and chopped
- ⅓ cup black olives, sliced
- ⅓ cup basil fresh, chopped
- Vegan feta cheese, shaved

Instructions:

1. Boil rice in water, in a cooking pot, cover and cook for 30 minutes on a simmer.
2. Add spinach and peas to the rice then cook for 10 minutes.
3. Add lime juice, black pepper and salt then transfer to a plate.
4. Serve.

The Plant Based Cookbook For Beginners
650 Easy, Quick, & Simple Plant Based Vegan Diet Recipes With A 31 Day Meal Plan To Lose Weight & Live A Long Healthy Life

513

Chickpea Tacos with Cauliflower

SERVINGS	PREPARATION TIME	COOKING TIME
4	10 minutes	51 minutes

Nutritional Values Per Serving

Calories	380
Total Fat	14g
Saturated Fat	6g
Cholesterol	12mg
Sodium	155mg
Total Carbohydrate	19g
Dietary Fiber	1.7g
Total Sugars	1.1g
Protein	9g

Serving Suggestion:

Try these tacos with guacamole and salsa.

Ingredients:

- 2 pounds cauliflower, florets
- 2 tablespoons olive oil
- ½ teaspoons salt
- 1 can 15 ounces chickpeas, drained
- 1 tablespoon olive oil
- ½ teaspoons salt
- ¼ teaspoons chili powder
- ¼ teaspoons ground cumin
- ¼ teaspoons ground oregano
- 2 cups fresh cilantro leaves

Pepita Pesto

- ⅓ cup pepitas
- 1 garlic clove, halved
- 2 tablespoons jalapeño chiles, chopped
- 2 tablespoons lime juice
- ½ teaspoons salt
- ¼ cup olive oil

Serving

- 8 gluten-free white corn tortillas
- 2 cups vegan cheddar, shredded

Instructions:

1. At 425 degrees F, preheat your oven.
2. Toss and mix the cauliflower florets with 2 tablespoons oil and ½ tsp. salt in a bowl.
3. Spread these florets in a baking sheet and bake for 15 minutes.
4. Meanwhile, mix chickpeas with oregano, cumin, chili powder, salt and olive oil in a bowl.
5. Spread these chickpeas in a baking sheet and bake for 30 minutes while tossing halfway through.
6. Blend all the pepita pesto ingredients in a blender.
7. Spread a tablespoons pesto on top of the tortillas.
8. Top each with ½ cup cauliflower, ¼ cup vegan cheese and 1 tablespoon chickpeas then fold over.
9. Sear the wraps in a hot skillet for 2-3 minutes per side.
10. Roll and serve.

514

The Plant Based Cookbook For Beginners
650 Easy, Quick, & Simple Plant Based Vegan Diet Recipes With A 31 Day Meal Plan To Lose Weight & Live A Long Healthy Life

Vegan Mushroom Pasta

SERVINGS	PREPARATION TIME	COOKING TIME
4	10 minutes	12 minutes

Nutritional Values Per Serving

Calories	247
Total Fat	4.9g
Saturated Fat	14g
Cholesterol	194mg
Sodium	407mg
Total Carbohydrate	27g
Dietary Fiber	4g
Total Sugars	1.3g
Protein	16g

Ingredients:

- 1-pound long noodle pasta
- ¼ cup soy margarine
- 2 garlic cloves, minced
- 16 ounces cremini mushrooms, halved
- 1 tablespoon whole wheat flour
- 1 cup plain soy milk
- ¼ cup vegan sour cream
- ¼ teaspoon salt
- Black pepper, to taste

Garnish

- Fresh parsley

Instructions:

1. Boil pasta in a pot filled with salted water as per the package's instruction then drain.
2. Sauté garlic and mushrooms with 1 tbsp margarine in a suitable skillet for 4 minutes.
3. Transfer this mixture to a bowl.
4. Sauté flour with remaining margarine in the same skillet for 1 minute.
5. Stir in soy milk, and mix until smooth.
6. Add black pepper, salt, and sour cream then add the mushrooms.
7. Mix well and cook for 2 minutes.
8. Stir in boiled pasta and mix well.
9. Garnish with parsley and serve warm.

The Plant Based Cookbook For Beginners
650 Easy, Quick, & Simple Plant Based Vegan Diet Recipes With A 31 Day Meal Plan To Lose Weight & Live A Long Healthy Life

515

Bang-Bang Cauliflower

SERVINGS	PREPARATION TIME	COOKING TIME
4	10 minutes	20 minutes

Nutritional Values Per Serving

Calories	288
Total Fat	12g
Saturated Fat	6g
Cholesterol	13mg
Sodium	208mg
Total Carbohydrate	21g
Dietary Fiber	2g
Total Sugars	2.1g
Protein	8g

Ingredients:

- 4 cups cauliflower florets
- 2 flaxseed eggs
- 2 cups panko breadcrumbs
- Salt and black pepper, to taste

Bang Bang Sauce

- 2 tablespoons sweet chili sauce
- 2 teaspoons Sriracha hot sauce
- ½ cup mayonnaise
- ½ cup coconut yogurt

Garnish

- Parsley, chopped
- Green onions, sliced

Instructions:

1. At 425 degrees F, preheat your oven.
2. Beat flaxseed eggs with black pepper and salt in a suitable bow.
3. Dip the cauliflower florets in the eggs and coat well.
4. Coat the cauliflower in the breadcrumbs and shake off the excess.
5. Spread the coated cauliflower florets in a baking lined with wax paper.
6. Spray the florets with cooking spray and bake for 20 minutes.
7. Meanwhile, prepare the bang bang sauce by mixing all its ingredients in a bowl.
8. Pour the sauce over the cauliflower florets.
9. Garnish with parsley and green onions, then serve warm.

516

The Plant Based Cookbook For Beginners
650 Easy, Quick, & Simple Plant Based Vegan Diet Recipes With A 31 Day Meal Plan To Lose Weight & Live A Long Healthy Life

Grilled Asparagus and Shiitake Tacos

SERVINGS	PREPARATION TIME	COOKING TIME
8	10 minutes	11 minutes

Nutritional Values Per Serving

Calories	361
Total Fat	25g
Saturated Fat	12g
Cholesterol	0mg
Sodium	445mg
Total Carbohydrate	32g
Dietary Fiber	1.7g
Total Sugars	6.7g
Protein	6g

Ingredients:

- 3 tablespoons canola oil
- 4 garlic cloves, crushed
- 1 teaspoon ground chipotle chile
- ½ teaspoons Kosher salt, to taste
- 8 ounces shiitake mushrooms, stems discarded
- 1 bunch green onions, trimmed
- 1 bundle asparagus, cut into pieces
- 8 corn tortillas, warmed
- 1 avocado, sliced

Avocado Sauce

- 1 large, ripe avocado, peeled and pitted
- ⅓ cup coconut cream
- ½ small clove of garlic
- Juice of ½ lemon
- 2 tbsp olive oil
- ½ cup coriander, roughly chopped
- Salt and black pepper to taste

Instructions:

1. Toss asparagus with green onions, shiitakes, oil, garlic, salt and chipotle in a bowl.

2. Set a grill over medium heat and grill the asparagus for 6 minutes while turning occasionally.

3. Grill green onion and shiitake mushrooms for 5 minutes.

4. Chop the grilled green onions, and asparagus then slice the shiitakes.

5. Add the grilled veggies on top of the tortillas.

6. Top them with avocado slices.

7. Blend coconut cream and rest of the avocado sauce ingredients in a blender until smooth.

8. Serve the tacos with the avocado sauce.

9. Serve.

The Plant Based Cookbook For Beginners
650 Easy, Quick, & Simple Plant Based Vegan Diet Recipes With A 31 Day Meal Plan To Lose Weight & Live A Long Healthy Life

517

Tofu Pad Thai

SERVINGS	PREPARATION TIME	COOKING TIME
6	10 minutes	22 minutes

Nutritional Values Per Serving

Calories	440
Total Fat	10g
Saturated Fat	8.7g
Cholesterol	0mg
Sodium	620mg
Total Carbohydrate	73g
Dietary Fiber	5g
Total Sugars	19g
Protein	16g

Ingredients:

- 14 ounces extra-firm tofu, drained
- 2 tablespoons cornstarch
- 8 ounces rice noodles
- ¼ cup soy sauce
- 2 tablespoons brown sugar
- 2 teaspoons sweet chili sauce
- Juice of 1 lime
- 1 garlic clove, grated
- 1 tablespoon oil
- 1 red pepper, sliced
- 2 cups mung bean sprouts
- 2 green onions, sliced

Garnish

- Peanuts, chopped

Instructions:

1. Cut the tofu into ½ inch thick slices. Pat them dry with a paper towel.
2. Dice the tofu into cubes and toss with cornstarch in a bowl.
3. Boil the noodles as per the package's instructions and rinse.
4. Mix soy sauce, garlic, lime juice, chili sauce, and sugar in a small bowl.
5. Sauté pepper with 1 tablespoon oil in a suitable skillet for 5 minutes.
6. Stir in tofu and sauté for 5 minutes.
7. Add prepared sauce and noodles then mix well.
8. Stir in sprouts and green onions then sauté for 2 minutes.
9. Garnish with chopped peanuts and serve warm.

518

The Plant Based Cookbook For Beginners
650 Easy, Quick, & Simple Plant Based Vegan Diet Recipes With A 31 Day Meal Plan To Lose Weight & Live A Long Healthy Life

Creamy Avocado Linguine

SERVINGS	PREPARATION TIME	COOKING TIME
6	10 minutes	15 minutes

Nutritional Values Per Serving

Calories	300
Total Fat	3.1g
Saturated Fat	0.5g
Cholesterol	0mg
Sodium	5mg
Total Carbohydrate	26.2g
Dietary Fiber	0.6g
Total Sugars	12.2g
Protein	13g

Ingredients:

- 8 ounces linguine
- 2 ripe avocados
- 3 tablespoons lemon juice
- 3 tablespoons olive oil
- ¾ teaspoons kosher salt, to taste
- ¼ teaspoons white pepper
- 2 whole garlic cloves
- 1 handful arugula
- 1 teaspoon lemon zest

Garnish

- Toasted pine nuts
- Basil ribbons
- Vegan parmesan cheese

Instructions:

1. Boil linguine pasta in salted water as per the package's instruction then drain.
2. Blend avocados, lemon juice, white pepper, olive oil, salt, garlic and salt in a blender.
3. Transfer the avocado puree to a bowl.
4. Stir in pasta, lemon zest, arugula and garnish with basil ribbons and pine nuts.
5. Garnish with cheese and serve.

The Plant Based Cookbook For Beginners
650 Easy, Quick, & Simple Plant Based Vegan Diet Recipes With A 31 Day Meal Plan To Lose Weight & Live A Long Healthy Life

519

Spaghetti Squash with Mushrooms

SERVINGS	PREPARATION TIME	COOKING TIME
4	15 minutes	64 minutes

Nutritional Values Per Serving

Calories	411
Total Fat	10.2g
Saturated Fat	2.4g
Cholesterol	0mg
Sodium	258mg
Total Carbohydrate	27.2g
Dietary Fiber	2g
Total Sugars	16.5g
Protein	4.5g

Ingredients:

- 1 small spaghetti squash
- 1 tablespoon butter
- 2 tablespoon olive oil
- ½ onion, chopped
- 16 ounces mushrooms, sliced
- 6 garlic cloves, chopped
- ½ cup kale, chopped
- 3 tablespoons fresh torn sage
- Salt and black pepper, to taste
- 1 pinch nutmeg

Garnish

- Vegan parmesan cheese
- Truffle oil
- Pine nuts

Instructions:

1. At 400 degrees F, preheat your oven.
2. Cut the spaghetti squash in half, then place it in baking pan lined with wax paper.
3. Bake the squash for 50 minutes.
4. Sauté onions with oil and butter in a large skillet for 3 minutes.
5. Stir in mushrooms, then sauté for 7 minutes.
6. Add sage, kale, garlic, nutmeg, black pepper and salt, then sauté for 4 minutes.
7. Scrape the spaghetti squash flesh with a fork and transfer it to the mushrooms.
8. Mix well and garnish with cheese, truffle oil and pine nuts on top.
9. Serve.

520

The Plant Based Cookbook For Beginners
650 Easy, Quick, & Simple Plant Based Vegan Diet Recipes With A 31 Day Meal Plan To Lose Weight & Live A Long Healthy Life

Pad Thai With Tofu

SERVINGS	PREPARATION TIME	COOKING TIME
4	15 minutes	25 minutes

Nutritional Values Per Serving

Calories	481
Total Fat	19g
Saturated Fat	0.6g
Cholesterol	0mg
Sodium	26mg
Total Carbohydrate	32g
Dietary Fiber	3g
Total Sugars	5.5g
Protein	6.9g

Ingredients:

- 24 ounces dry pad Thai noodles
- Boiling water, as required
- 1 large shallot, diced
- 4 garlic cloves, chopped
- 1 teaspoon ginger, chopped
- 2 flaxseed eggs, whisked
- 8 ounces tofu, diced
- Salt and black pepper, to taste
- 2 tablespoons peanut oil

Pad Thai Sauce

- 3 tablespoons vegan fish sauce
- 3 tablespoons brown sugar
- 3 tablespoons of rice wine vinegar
- 1 teaspoon soy sauce

Garnish

- Lime wedges
- Fresh bean sprouts
- Chopped green onions
- Chili flakes
- Roasted peanuts

Instructions:

1. Boil the noodles as per the package's instructions.
2. Beat two flaxseed eggs with 3 pinch salt in a bowl.
3. Mix soy sauce, brown sugar, rice vinegar and fish sauce in a bowl.
4. Dice the tofu, and toss with and salt.
5. Sauté this tofu with cooking oil in a suitable pan until golden brown, then transfer to a bowl.
6. Sauté shallots, ginger and garlic in a pan with 2 tablespoons peanut oil until golden.
7. Make well then create a hole in the center and pour flaxseed eggs in it.
8. Stir in noodles and sauté for 4 minutes.
9. Add the prepared sauce and cook for 1 minute.
10. Stir in crispy tofu, peanuts, bean sprouts, chili flakes, green onions, lime juice and salt.
11. Mix well and enjoy.

The Plant Based Cookbook For Beginners
650 Easy, Quick, & Simple Plant Based Vegan Diet Recipes With A 31 Day Meal Plan To Lose Weight & Live A Long Healthy Life

521

Cauliflower Tacos with Cashew Crema

SERVINGS
12

PREPARATION TIME
10 minutes

COOKING TIME
40 minutes

Nutritional Values Per Serving

Calories	235
Total Fat	2.2g
Saturated Fat	0.3g
Cholesterol	0mg
Sodium	64mg
Total Carbohydrate	25.5g
Dietary Fiber	1g
Total Sugars	22.3g
Protein	4.1g

Ingredients:

Sauce

- 1 green chile, grated
- 1 garlic clove, grated
- ¼ cup cashew butter
- 3 tablespoons lime juice
- Kosher salt, to taste

Serving

- Sliced avocado
- sliced radishes
- cilantro leaves
- lime wedges
- 1 small white onion, sliced
- ¼ cup corn

Assemble

- 3 garlic cloves, grated
- ¼ cup grapeseed oil
- 2 teaspoons ground cumin
- 2 teaspoons smoked paprika
- 2 medium cauliflower heads, florets
- Kosher salt, to taste
- 12 6"-diameter corn tortillas

Instructions:

1. Mix 3 tbs water, lime juice, cashew butter, garlic, salt and chile in a bowl.

2. At 450 degrees F, preheat your oven.

3. Mix paprika, cumin, oil and garlic in a bowl.

4. Spread the cauliflower in a rimmed baking sheet and pour half of the sauces over the cauliflower.

5. Roast the cauliflower for 20 minutes, flip and roast for another 20 minutes.

6. Toast tortillas in a large skillet for 1 minute per side.

7. Spread the cauliflower on the tortillas and pour the remaining sauces on top.

8. Garnish with cilantro, corn, radishes, avocado, onion and lime wedges.

9. Serve.

522

The Plant Based Cookbook For Beginners
650 Easy, Quick, & Simple Plant Based Vegan Diet Recipes With A 31 Day Meal Plan To Lose Weight & Live A Long Healthy Life

Tofu and Vegetable Curry

SERVINGS	PREPARATION TIME	COOKING TIME
4	10 minutes	20 minutes

Nutritional Values Per Serving

Calories	234
Total Fat	21.2g
Saturated Fat	4.2g
Cholesterol	0mg
Sodium	14mg
Total Carbohydrate	17g
Dietary Fiber	1.4g
Total Sugars	13.6g
Protein	7g

Ingredients:

- 4 tablespoons coconut oil
- 1 14-ounces package tofu, cut into cubes
- Kosher salt, to taste
- 2 medium onions, chopped
- ⅓ cup red curry paste
- 2 large zucchinis, cut into cubes
- 1 large Japanese eggplant, cut into cubes
- 8 ounces green beans, trimmed, chopped
- ½ red bell pepper, chopped
- 1 (13 ½-ounces) can unsweetened coconut milk

Serving

- Lime wedges
- Cilantro leaves
- Roasted peanuts

Instructions:

1. Sauté tofu with 2 tablespoons oil in a suitable skillet for 4 minutes.
2. Sprinkle salt to adjust the seasoning and transfer to a plate lined with wax paper.
3. Sauté onions with 2 tablespoons oil and a pinch of salt in the same skillet for 4 minutes.
4. Stir in curry paste and sauté for 2 minutes.
5. Add green beans, eggplant, and zucchini then sauté for 7 minutes.
6. Pour in ½ cup water and coconut milk then cook to a simmer.
7. Stir in tofu and bell pepper then cook for 3 minutes.
8. Garnish with peanuts, cilantro and lime juice.
9. Serve warm.

The Plant Based Cookbook For Beginners
650 Easy, Quick, & Simple Plant Based Vegan Diet Recipes With A 31 Day Meal Plan To Lose Weight & Live A Long Healthy Life

523

Caramelized Cabbage

SERVINGS	PREPARATION TIME	COOKING TIME
4	10 minutes	58 minutes

Nutritional Values Per Serving

Calories	344
Total Fat	33.2g
Saturated Fat	25.7g
Cholesterol	0mg
Sodium	19mg
Total Carbohydrate	13g
Dietary Fiber	3.6g
Total Sugars	8.4g
Protein	4.5g

Ingredients:

- ¼ cup tomato paste
- 3 garlic cloves, grated
- 1½ teaspoons ground coriander
- 1½ teaspoons ground cumin
- 1 teaspoon crushed red pepper flakes
- 1 medium head green cabbage
- ½ cup olive oil
- Kosher salt, to taste
- 3 tablespoons dill, chopped
- Coconut yogurt, to serve

Instructions:

1. At 350 degrees F, preheat your oven.
2. Mix tomato paste, red pepper flakes, cumin, garlic and coriander in a small bowl.
3. Cut the cabbage into 4 wedges after removing the core.
4. Sauté cabbage with ¼ cup oil in a suitable skillet for 4 minutes per side.
5. Transfer the cabbage to a plate.
6. Add remaining ¼ cup oil and tomato paste mixture to the same skillet.
7. Sauté for 3 minutes, then stir in 1½ cups water, salt and cook to a simmer.
8. Return the cabbage to the skillet and mix well, then bake for 50 minutes.
9. Serve with coconut yogurt and herbs on top.

524

The Plant Based Cookbook For Beginners
650 Easy, Quick, & Simple Plant Based Vegan Diet Recipes With A 31 Day Meal Plan To Lose Weight & Live A Long Healthy Life

Pantry Pasta with Cream Sauce

SERVINGS	PREPARATION TIME	COOKING TIME
4	10 minutes	22 minutes

Nutritional Values Per Serving

Calories	386
Total Fat	12.2g
Saturated Fat	3.3g
Cholesterol	0mg
Sodium	158mg
Total Carbohydrate	31g
Dietary Fiber	1.8g
Total Sugars	15.6g
Protein	29.4g

Ingredients:

- ½ cup 2 tablespoons olive oil
- 1 cup walnuts, chopped
- ½ teaspoons crushed red pepper flakes
- 4 garlic cloves sliced
- 2 sprigs rosemary
- 2 (15.5-ounces) cans cannellini beans, rinsed
- ¼ cup coconut cream
- 12 ounces paccheri pasta
- Kosher salt, to taste
- 1 lemon, juiced
- 2 tablespoons chopped parsley
- Black pepper, to taste

Instructions:

1. Sauté red pepper flakes, garlic and walnuts with ¼ cup oil in a large Dutch oven for 5 minutes.
2. Stir in rosemary, coconut cream and beans then cook for 5 minutes then puree this mixture in a blender.
3. Return this sauce to the Dutch oven.
4. Boil pasta as per the package's instructions then drain and reserve pasta liquid.
5. Add pasta, 2 tablespoons oil and 1 cup pasta liquid to the bean sauce.
6. Cook the mixture to a simmer and cook for 2 minutes.
7. Stir in the rest of the ingredients in the Dutch oven and serve warm.

The Plant Based Cookbook For Beginners
650 Easy, Quick, & Simple Plant Based Vegan Diet Recipes With A 31 Day Meal Plan To Lose Weight & Live A Long Healthy Life

525

Soy-Glazed Tofu and Mushrooms

SERVINGS	PREPARATION TIME	COOKING TIME
4	15 minutes	15 minutes

Nutritional Values Per Serving

Calories	360
Total Fat	15.4g
Saturated Fat	2.1g
Cholesterol	0mg
Sodium	246mg
Total Carbohydrate	29.2g
Dietary Fiber	3.7g
Total Sugars	18.2g
Protein	8g

Ingredients:

- 1 (14-ounces) block tofu, drained and diced
- 3 tablespoons vegetable oil
- 12 ounces mixed mushrooms, chopped
- 2"-piece ginger, peeled, sliced
- 3 tablespoons soy sauce
- 1 teaspoon toasted sesame oil
- Kosher salt, to taste
- 1 teaspoon sesame seeds, to garnish
- 2 cups pasta, to serve

Instructions:

1. Boil pasta as per the package's instructions then drain.
2. Pat dry the tofu slices with a paper towel.
3. Sear tofu with 2 tablespoons of oil in a skillet for 4 minutes.
4. Flip and sear the tofu for 4 minutes, then transfer to a plate lined with a paper towel and pat dry.
5. Sauté mushrooms with 1 tablespoon oil in the same skillet for 4 minutes.
6. Return the tofu and add sesame oil, salt, soy sauce, and ginger then cook for 3 minutes.
7. Serve warm on top of noodles in a bowl.
8. Sprinkle sesame seeds on top and serve.

526

The Plant Based Cookbook For Beginners
650 Easy, Quick, & Simple Plant Based Vegan Diet Recipes With A 31 Day Meal Plan To Lose Weight & Live A Long Healthy Life

Tofu and Bok Choy

SERVINGS
6

PREPARATION TIME
10 minutes

COOKING TIME
15 minutes

Nutritional Values Per Serving

Calories	344
Total Fat	20.7g
Saturated Fat	17.6g
Cholesterol	0mg
Sodium	42mg
Total Carbohydrate	18.5g
Dietary Fiber	2g
Total Sugars	8.6g
Protein	4.2g

Ingredients:

- 1 (14-ounces) package tofu, drained
- 2 garlic cloves, grated
- 1 ½" piece ginger, peeled, grated
- 1 tablespoon cornstarch
- ½ teaspoons Kosher salt, to taste
- 3 tablespoons olive oil
- 4 tablespoon vegetable broth
- 1 small yellow onion, diced
- 1 lb. bok choy, diced
- ¼ teaspoon cracker black pepper
- ⅓ cup soy sauce
- 1 tablespoon sugar
- 1 teaspoon unseasoned rice vinegar

Serving

- Cooked white rice

Instructions:

1. Pat dry the tofu with a paper towel.
2. Dice the tofu into cubes with cornstarch and salt in a bowl.
3. Remove tofu from heat.
4. Sauté tofu with oil in a suitable skillet for 8 minutes.
5. Stir in cracked pepper and sauté for 2 minutes.
6. Stir in onion, bok choy and sauté for 1 minute.
7. Add ginger and garlic, then cook for 1 minute.
8. Return the tofu to the pan and increase the heat to medium-high heat.
9. Stir in sugar, broth and soy sauce and cook for 3 minutes.
10. Remove from the heat and stir in vinegar.
11. Serve warm with rice.

The Plant Based Cookbook For Beginners
650 Easy, Quick, & Simple Plant Based Vegan Diet Recipes With A 31 Day Meal Plan To Lose Weight & Live A Long Healthy Life

527

Collard Greens Salad

SERVINGS **PREPARATION TIME** **COOKING TIME**
4 5 minutes 0 minutes

Nutritional Values Per Serving	
Calories	161
Total Fat	3.2g
Saturated Fat	0.4g
Cholesterol	0mg
Sodium	152mg
Total Carbohydrate	26g
Dietary Fiber	5.5g
Total Sugars	20.9g
Protein	3.1g

Ingredients:

- ¼ cup olive oil
- 3 tablespoons sherry vinegar
- 2 tablespoons fresh lime juice
- 2 tablespoons sumac
- 1 tablespoon Dijon mustard
- 1 tablespoon mild-flavored molasses
- 1 bunch collard greens, stems removed, leaves sliced
- 1 fennel bulb, fronds reserved, bulb sliced
- 1 large shallot, sliced

Instructions:

1. Mix olive oil, molasses, mustard, sumac, lime juice, and vinegar in a bowl.
2. Toss in fennel bulb, shallots and collard green, then mix well and let it sit for 10 minutes.
3. Garnish with fennel fronds.

528

The Plant Based Cookbook For Beginners
650 Easy, Quick, & Simple Plant Based Vegan Diet Recipes With A 31 Day Meal Plan To Lose Weight & Live A Long Healthy Life

Lentil-Greens with Country Bread

SERVINGS
4

PREPARATION TIME
10 minutes

COOKING TIME
32 minutes

Nutritional Values Per Serving

Calories	382
Total Fat	5g
Saturated Fat	0.4g
Cholesterol	0mg
Sodium	162mg
Total Carbohydrate	17.2g
Dietary Fiber	10.7g
Total Sugars	12.3g
Protein	22g

Ingredients:

- ⅔ cup 2 tablespoons olive oil
- 1 medium onion, chopped
- 1 fennel bulb, chopped
- 2 celery stalks, chopped
- 10 garlic cloves, smashed
- ¾ teaspoons crushed red pepper flakes
- 1½ teaspoons smoked paprika
- ¼ cup tomatoes, chopped
- 1 teaspoon Kosher salt
- ½ cup red split lentils
- 2 bunches of hardy greens
- 1 lemon
- ½ country-style bread loaf, to serve

Instructions:

1. Sauté onion, garlic, celery, and fennel with ⅔ cup oil in a Dutch oven for 10 minutes.
2. Stir in salt, paprika and red pepper flakes then mix well.
3. Add 1¼ cup water, tomatoes, and lentil then place the greens on top.
4. Cover and cook for 15 minutes on low heat.
5. Uncover and cook for 2 minutes with occasional stirring.
6. Stir in lemon juice.
7. Serve the lentil greens with country style bread.
8. Enjoy.

The Plant Based Cookbook For Beginners
650 Easy, Quick, & Simple Plant Based Vegan Diet Recipes With A 31 Day Meal Plan To Lose Weight & Live A Long Healthy Life

529

Chickpea Kale Pancakes

SERVINGS	PREPARATION TIME	COOKING TIME
4	10 minutes	19 minutes

Nutritional Values Per Serving

Calories	142
Total Fat	4.4g
Saturated Fat	0.1g
Cholesterol	0mg
Sodium	33mg
Total Carbohydrate	13g
Dietary Fiber	5.1g
Total Sugars	8.9g
Protein	9g

Ingredients:

- ½ cup chickpea flour
- 6 tablespoons olive oil
- Kosher salt, to taste
- 3 garlic cloves, grated
- 1 (15-ounces) can chickpeas, mashed
- 1 tablespoons za'atar
- 1 small bunch Tuscan kale, leaves torn
- 1 small fennel bulb, sliced crosswise
- ¼ cup tahini
- 2 tablespoons fresh lemon juice

Instructions:

1. Mix ½ cup water, 1 pinch of salt, 1 tablespoon oil and chickpea flour in a bowl and leave for 10 minutes.
2. Sauté 2 garlic cloves with 2 tbsp oil in a skillet for 3 minutes.
3. Stir in chickpeas and cook for 8 minutes then mash a little.
4. Stir in Za'atar, salt and kale then sauté for 2 minutes.
5. Stir in fennel, grated garlic, tahini, lemon juice, 2 tablespoons water, salt and 2 tablespoons oil.
6. Transfer this mixture to the flour batter in the bowl then mix well.
7. Pour the chickpea kale batter into the same skillet, greased with 1 ½ teaspoons oil.
8. Bake this chickpea batter for 10 minutes in the oven.
9. Serve.

530

The Plant Based Cookbook For Beginners
650 Easy, Quick, & Simple Plant Based Vegan Diet Recipes With A 31 Day Meal Plan To Lose Weight & Live A Long Healthy Life

Eggplant Grain Bowls

SERVINGS
4

PREPARATION TIME
15 minutes

COOKING TIME
33 minutes

Nutritional Values Per Serving	
Calories	369
Total Fat	2.8g
Saturated Fat	0.8g
Cholesterol	0mg
Sodium	75mg
Total Carbohydrate	65.2g
Dietary Fiber	5.4g
Total Sugars	45.6g
Protein	12g

Ingredients:

- 4 small eggplants, halved
- 6 tablespoons olive oil
- Kosher salt, to taste
- 1½" piece ginger, peeled, grated
- ¼ cup white miso
- 2 tablespoons 1½ teaspoons tamari sauce
- 2 tablespoons rice vinegar
- 2 teaspoons sugar
- 2 tablespoons lime juice
- 1 cup roasted tomatoes, chopped
- 4 green onions, sliced
- 1½ cups mixed cooked whole grains
- 1 cup basil leaves

Instructions:

1. Set the oven rack in the upper third portion of the oven.
2. At 400 degrees F, preheat your oven.
3. Score the eggplants and rub with 2 tablespoons oil and salt.
4. Place them in a rimmed baking sheet and roast for 28 minutes.
5. Mix 4 tablespoons oil, sugar, vinegar, lime juice, tamari, miso and ginger in a medium bowl.
6. Increase the oven's temperature to 450 degrees F.
7. Cut the eggplants in half and return to the baking sheet.
8. Pour half of the glaze over the eggplants and roast for 15 minutes.
9. Mix remaining glaze with basil, grains, green onions and tomatoes in a bowl.
10. Stuff the eggplant halves with the grain tomato mixture.
11. Serve.

The Plant Based Cookbook For Beginners
650 Easy, Quick, & Simple Plant Based Vegan Diet Recipes With A 31 Day Meal Plan To Lose Weight & Live A Long Healthy Life

531

Cold Udon with Ponzu

SERVINGS	PREPARATION TIME	COOKING TIME
4	20 minutes	22 minutes

Nutritional Values Per Serving

Calories	377
Total Fat	0.9g
Saturated Fat	0.1g
Cholesterol	0mg
Sodium	9mg
Total Carbohydrate	43g
Dietary Fiber	6.3g
Total Sugars	5.4g
Protein	17g

Ingredients:

- 1 grapefruit, squeezed and juiced
- 1 lemon, squeezed and juiced
- 1 red chile, seeds removed, chopped
- 2"-piece ginger, peeled, grated
- ⅓ cup unseasoned rice vinegar
- 3 tablespoons soy sauce
- 1 teaspoon sugar
- 2 pints cherry tomatoes
- 1 garlic clove, grated
- 1 tablespoon olive oil
- A pinch of Kosher salt
- 18 ounces frozen Udon noodles
- 2 Persian cucumbers, peeled, sliced

For serving

- Cilantro sprigs
- Crumbled nori
- Toasted sesame seeds

Instructions:

1. At medium heat, preheat the broiler.
2. Mix lemon and grapefruit juice with sugar, soy sauce, vinegar, ginger and chile in a bowl.
3. Cover and refrigerate this ponzu until noodles are ready.
4. Toss tomatoes with salt, oil, and garlic in a rimmed baking sheet.
5. Broil these tomatoes for 12 minutes in the broiler.
6. Boil the noodles as per the package's instruction, then drain and rinse.
7. Divide the noodles into the serving bowls.
8. Top the noodles with ponzu, tomatoes, cucumbers, nori, cilantro and sesame seeds.
9. Serve.

532

The Plant Based Cookbook For Beginners
650 Easy, Quick, & Simple Plant Based Vegan Diet Recipes With A 31 Day Meal Plan To Lose Weight & Live A Long Healthy Life

Miso-Tahini Noodles with Asparagus

SERVINGS	PREPARATION TIME	COOKING TIME
4	15 minutes	21 minutes

Nutritional Values Per Serving

Calories	349
Total Fat	30.2g
Saturated Fat	18.4g
Cholesterol	0mg
Sodium	149mg
Total Carbohydrate	20.1g
Dietary Fiber	0.3g
Total Sugars	12.5g
Protein	3g

Ingredients:

- ⅓ cup raw cashews
- 2"-piece ginger, peeled, sliced
- garlic clove, crushed
- ⅓ cup soy sauce
- ¼ cup mirin
- ¼ cup tahini
- ¼ cup unseasoned rice vinegar
- 1 tablespoon mellow white miso
- 1 lb. asparagus, trimmed, sliced
- 12 ounces fresh noodles
- 3 green onions, sliced on a bias
- 2 Persian cucumbers, sliced
- 1½ cup torn mixed herbs
- Kosher salt, to taste

Instructions:

1. At 350 degrees F, preheat your oven.
2. Toss cashews in a rimmed baking sheet and roast for 8 minutes.
3. Chop the roasted cashews and keep them aside.
4. Blend ginger, miso, vinegar, tahini, mirin, soy sauce and garlic in a blender until smooth.
5. Add asparagus to a pot filled with boiling water for 3 minutes then drain.
6. Boil noodles as per the package's instructions then drain.
7. Toss asparagus with noodles, prepared tahini sauce, cucumbers, herbs, green onions and salt in a bowl.
8. Garnish with cashews and serve.

The Plant Based Cookbook For Beginners
650 Easy, Quick, & Simple Plant Based Vegan Diet Recipes With A 31 Day Meal Plan To Lose Weight & Live A Long Healthy Life

533

Honeynet Squash with Apples

SERVINGS	PREPARATION TIME	COOKING TIME
4	10 minutes	41 minutes

Nutritional Values Per Serving

Calories	285
Total Fat	15g
Saturated Fat	8.7g
Cholesterol	10mg
Sodium	173mg
Total Carbohydrate	33g
Dietary Fiber	1.4g
Total Sugars	27.6g
Protein	4.2g

Ingredients:

- 1 cup kale leaves
- Kosher salt, to taste
- 3 honeynet squash, seeded, cut into wedges
- 5 tablespoons olive oil
- ⅓ cup almonds, chopped
- 1 garlic clove, chopped
- 1 tablespoon white miso
- 2 tablespoons apple cider vinegar
- 1 tablespoon chives, sliced
- ½ cup raisins
- 1 Granny Smith apple, sliced

Instructions:

1. At 425 degrees F, preheat your oven.
2. Toss squash with 1 tablespoon oil and salt in a rimmed baking sheet and roast for 20 minutes.
3. Sauté almonds with 4 tablespoons oil in a saucepan for 5 minutes then remove from the heat.
4. Stir miso, garlic, vinegar, salt and 1 tablespoon chives in a bowl.
5. Add 1 tablespoon of this dressing to the kale and mix well.
6. Toss apple with the remaining 2 tablespoons of dressing and raisin in a medium bowl.
7. Spread the kale on the serving plate and top it with squash and apple salad.
8. Drizzle remaining dressing on top and garnish with chopped almonds.
9. Serve.

534

The Plant Based Cookbook For Beginners
650 Easy, Quick, & Simple Plant Based Vegan Diet Recipes With A 31 Day Meal Plan To Lose Weight & Live A Long Healthy Life

Loaded Sweet Potatoes

SERVINGS | PREPARATION TIME | COOKING TIME
4 | 1 hour 20 minutes | 2 hours 15 minutes

Nutritional Values Per Serving

Calories	357
Total Fat	14.3g
Saturated Fat	12.7g
Cholesterol	0mg
Sodium	52mg
Total Carbohydrate	21g
Dietary Fiber	2.3g
Total Sugars	4.5g
Protein	1.4g

Ingredients:

- 2 small sweet potatoes
- 5 tablespoons olive oil
- Kosher salt, to taste
- 1 small onion, chopped
- ½ cup black beans
- ¼ cup canned corn, drained
- ½ teaspoons crushed red pepper flakes
- 1 tablespoon fresh lemon juice
- Lime segments, chopped
- Cilantro leaves with tender stems
- Avocado sauce, to serve

Avocado Sauce

- 1 large, ripe avocado, peeled and pitted
- ⅓ cup coconut cream
- ½ small clove of garlic
- Juice of ½ lemon
- 2 tbsp olive oil
- ½ cup coriander, roughly chopped
- Salt and black pepper to taste

Instructions:

1. Blend coconut cream, garlic, avocado and rest of the avocado sauce ingredients in a blender until smooth.

2. At 400 degrees F, preheat your oven.

3. Place the sweet potatoes in baking sheet and bake for 45 minutes.

4. Smash these potatoes a little using a heavy spatula and drizzle salt and 1 tablespoon oil on top.

5. Continue roasting them for another 15 minutes.

6. Boil black beans in a pot with salted boiling water for 60 minutes, then drain.

7. Mix the beans with salt and 1 tablespoon oil in a bowl.

8. Sauté onion with 3 tablespoons oil in a suitable skillet for 2 minutes.

9. Remove it from the heat and add lemon juice, salt and red pepper, then mix well.

10. Divide the black beans, onion, lime, corn and dressing on top of the roasted potatoes.

11. Garnish with cilantro and avocado sauce on top.

12. Serve warm.

The Plant Based Cookbook For Beginners
650 Easy, Quick, & Simple Plant Based Vegan Diet Recipes With A 31 Day Meal Plan To Lose Weight & Live A Long Healthy Life

535

Spaghetti Aglio e Olio with Kale

SERVINGS	PREPARATION TIME	COOKING TIME
4	15 minutes	15 minutes

Nutritional Values Per Serving

Calories	260
Total Fat	2.5g
Saturated Fat	0g
Cholesterol	0mg
Sodium	155mg
Total Carbohydrate	28.5g
Dietary Fiber	0.3g
Total Sugars	7.3g
Protein	1.1g

Ingredients:

- Kosher salt, to taste
- 3 large bunches kale, chopped
- 5 garlic cloves
- ¼ cup olive oil
- Black pepper, to taste
- 12 ounces spaghetti
- Vegan parmesan and crushed red pepper flakes for serving
- Flaky sea salt

Instructions:

1. Boil the kale in salted boiling water for 2 minutes, then drain.
2. Sauté garlic with ¼ cup oil in a heavy pot for 3 minutes.
3. Stir in, salt and kale them sauté for 8 minutes.
4. Boil pasta as per the package's instruction, then drain.
5. Add pasta to the kale and cook for 2 minutes.
6. Drizzle parmesan, salt, black pepper, and red pepper flakes on top.
7. Serve.

536

The Plant Based Cookbook For Beginners
650 Easy, Quick, & Simple Plant Based Vegan Diet Recipes With A 31 Day Meal Plan To Lose Weight & Live A Long Healthy Life

Cauliflower Sabzi with Cashews

SERVINGS	PREPARATION TIME	COOKING TIME
4	15 minutes	15 minutes

Nutritional Values Per Serving

Calories	314
Total Fat	2.6g
Saturated Fat	0g
Cholesterol	0mg
Sodium	143mg
Total Carbohydrate	28.4g
Dietary Fiber	0g
Total Sugars	24.1g
Protein	1g

Ingredients:

- 1 cup raw cashews
- 1 large fennel bulb, plus ½ cup fennel fronds
- ⅓ cup coconut oil, melted
- 1 tablespoon whole black mustard seeds
- 6 green onions, sliced
- 2 medium sweet potatoes, cut into ¾-inch pieces
- 1 medium cauliflower head, cut into florets
- 2 green chiles, chopped
- 1 teaspoon ground turmeric
- 1 teaspoon garam masala
- ½ cup cilantro leaves, chopped

Instructions:

1. At 350 degrees F, preheat your oven.
2. Spread cashews in a rimmed baking sheet and roast for 10 minutes, then chop.
3. Sauté mustard seeds with oil in a suitable pan for 1 minute.
4. Stir in sweet potatoes, green onions and fennel fronds, and bulb, then cook for 4 minutes.
5. Stir in turmeric, chiles, cauliflower and 3 tbsp water, then cook for 8 minutes.
6. Add cashews, cilantro, and garam masala, then cook for 2 minutes.
7. Serve warm.

The Plant Based Cookbook For Beginners
650 Easy, Quick, & Simple Plant Based Vegan Diet Recipes With A 31 Day Meal Plan To Lose Weight & Live A Long Healthy Life

537

Ginger Scallion Ramen Noodles

SERVINGS	PREPARATION TIME	COOKING TIME
4	15 minutes	15 minutes

Nutritional Values Per Serving

Calories	303
Total Fat	23g
Saturated Fat	19.8g
Cholesterol	5mg
Sodium	45mg
Total Carbohydrate	25.1g
Dietary Fiber	3.6g
Total Sugars	17.7g
Protein	3.9g

Ingredients:

- 1 (5-inch) piece ginger, peeled, chopped
- 4 garlic cloves, chopped
- 1 large bunch of green onions, sliced
- 2 cups vegetable broth
- ½ cup grapeseed oil
- 2 tablespoons soy sauce
- 1 tablespoon rice vinegar
- 1 teaspoon black pepper
- 1 teaspoon toasted sesame oil
- ½ teaspoon sugar
- Kosher salt, to taste
- 4 5-ounce packages of ramen noodles
- 1 tablespoon seaweed, chopped
- Toasted sesame seeds and chili oil for serving

Instructions:

1. Mix ⅔ green onions, garlic and ginger in a bowl.

2. Sauté green onion mixture with grapeseed oil in a skillet for 2 minutes.

3. Remove from the heat, then add remaining green onions, vegetable broth, sugar, salt, sesame oil, pepper, vinegar, and soy sauce, mix well and leave for 15 minutes.

4. Boil noodles as per the package's instructions, then drain.

5. Add the noodles to the green onion broth and mix well.

6. Garnish with seaweed, sesame seeds and chili oil.

7. Serve.

538

The Plant Based Cookbook For Beginners
650 Easy, Quick, & Simple Plant Based Vegan Diet Recipes With A 31 Day Meal Plan To Lose Weight & Live A Long Healthy Life

Roasted Winter Squash with Kale

SERVINGS **4** PREPARATION TIME **10 minutes** COOKING TIME **53 minutes**

Nutritional Values Per Serving

Calories	368
Total Fat	3.1g
Saturated Fat	0.2g
Cholesterol	0mg
Sodium	33mg
Total Carbohydrate	30.8g
Dietary Fiber	6.5g
Total Sugars	18.9g
Protein	2.5g

Ingredients:

- 1 cup raw pumpkin seeds
- 3 lb. mixed winter squash pieces, diced
- 3 tablespoons olive oil
- Kosher salt, to taste
- ¼ white onion, sliced
- 3 garlic cloves, crushed
- 8 ounces tomatillos, husks removed, rinsed
- 1 small bunch kale, stems removed, leaves torn
- 2 small serrano chiles, charred

Serving

- Cilantro leaves
- Lime wedges

Instructions:

1. At 350 degrees F, preheat your oven.
2. Spread pumpkin seeds on a baking sheet and roast for 8 minutes.
3. Increase the temperature to 425 degrees F.
4. Toss squash with oil and salt on a baking sheet and bake for 40 minutes.
5. Boil tomatillos, garlic and onion with 2 cups water in a pan for 5 minutes, then add kale.
6. Cook for 1 minute, then allow the kale mixture to cool.
7. Drain and keep its liquid aside.
8. Transfer the kale mixture, chilies, and ¾ cup pumpkin seeds to a blender and puree them.
9. Divide the squash in the serving plates and sprinkle salt, the rest of the pumpkin seeds and cilantro on top.
10. Garnish with lime juice.
11. Serve.

The Plant Based Cookbook For Beginners
650 Easy, Quick, & Simple Plant Based Vegan Diet Recipes With A 31 Day Meal Plan To Lose Weight & Live A Long Healthy Life

539

Stellar Quinoa Burger

SERVINGS	PREPARATION TIME	COOKING TIME
4	15 minutes	60 minutes

Nutritional Values Per Serving

Calories	421
Total Fat	4.6g
Saturated Fat	0.4g
Cholesterol	0mg
Sodium	92mg
Total Carbohydrate	44.8g
Dietary Fiber	10g
Total Sugars	33.5g
Protein	3.1g

Serving Suggestion:

Place one patty in a bun and top it with guacamole, sprouts and condiments.

Ingredients:

- 1 small sweet potato
- 4 tablespoons olive oil
- Kosher salt and black pepper, to taste
- 1 portobello mushroom, chopped
- ½ small zucchini, grated
- 1 small shallot, chopped
- ¼ teaspoon crushed red pepper flakes
- 1 cup cooked quinoa
- ¾ cup dried breadcrumbs
- 1 ½ teaspoons fresh lemon juice
- 4 burger buns toasted

Serving

- Guacamole
- Tomato chutney
- Sprouts

Instructions:

1. At 350 degrees F, preheat your oven.
2. Score the sweet potato with a fork and rub with salt, 1 tablespoon oil and then place in a baking sheet.
3. Roast them for 45 minutes, allow them to cool and peel.
4. Mash the peeled sweet potatoes in a bowl with a fork.
5. Sauté shallots and red pepper flakes with 1 tablespoon oil in a medium skillet for 2 minutes.
6. Stir in zucchini and mushrooms, then sauté for 2 minutes.
7. Remove from the heat and mix this mixture with quinoa and salt in a bowl.
8. Mix ¼ cup mashed potatoes, lemon juice and breadcrumbs and add to the quinoa.
9. Mix well and make 4 patties out of this mixture.
10. Set a skillet with 2 tablespoons oil in a skillet and sear the patties in it for 2 minutes per side.
11. Serve.

540

The Plant Based Cookbook For Beginners
650 Easy, Quick, & Simple Plant Based Vegan Diet Recipes With A 31 Day Meal Plan To Lose Weight & Live A Long Healthy Life

Tofu with Miso-Mustard Dressing

SERVINGS	PREPARATION TIME	COOKING TIME
4	15 minutes	10 minutes

Nutritional Values Per Serving

Calories	313
Total Fat	6.5g
Saturated Fat	1.4g
Cholesterol	0mg
Sodium	232mg
Total Carbohydrate	16g
Dietary Fiber	1.7g
Total Sugars	4.6g
Protein	19.9g

Ingredients:

Tofu & Soba

- 8 ounces dried soba noodles
- Kosher salt, to taste
- 3 green onions, sliced diagonal
- 8 ounces braised tofu, cut into matchsticks
- 2 cups pea shoots
- 1 cup sugar snap peas, sliced
- 1 cup radish, sliced
- 2 toasted nori sheets, crumbled

Miso Mustard Dressing

- 3 tablespoons fresh lemon juice
- 3 tablespoons white miso
- 1 tablespoon Dijon mustard
- 1 teaspoon pure maple syrup
- 1 garlic clove, grated
- ½ cup olive oil

Garnish

- Parsley
- Chili pepper

Instructions:

1. For the dressing, mix 1 tablespoon water, garlic, maple syrup, mustard, miso and lemon juice in a bowl.
2. Pour in oil slowly and mix until emulsified.
3. Boil the soba noodles in salted water as per the package's instructions.
4. Drain and rinse the noodles, then transfer to a bowl.
5. Stir in the rest of the ingredients and the prepared mustard dressing.
6. Mix well and garnish with parsley and chili pepper.
7. Serve and enjoy.

The Plant Based Cookbook For Beginners
650 Easy, Quick, & Simple Plant Based Vegan Diet Recipes With A 31 Day Meal Plan To Lose Weight & Live A Long Healthy Life

541

Sweet Potato Curry

SERVINGS	PREPARATION TIME	COOKING TIME
4	10 minutes	73 minutes

Nutritional Values Per Serving

Calories	307
Total Fat	7.4g
Saturated Fat	1g
Cholesterol	0mg
Sodium	255mg
Total Carbohydrate	47.3g
Dietary Fiber	11.9g
Total Sugars	9g
Protein	15g

Ingredients:

- 1 lemongrass stalk, chopped
- 2" piece ginger, peeled, chopped
- 4 garlic cloves
- 2 tablespoons vegetable oil
- Kosher salt, to taste
- ¼ cup red curry paste
- 2 tablespoons tomato paste
- 1 (14.5-ounces) can crushed tomatoes
- 2 (13.5-ounces) cans coconut milk
- 1½ pound sweet potatoes, peeled, cut into 1" pieces
- ¾ pound small carrots, peeled, cut into 2" pieces
- 6 medium shallots, peeled, quartered
- 1 red Thai chile, sliced
- 1 tablespoon lime juice
- 2 tablespoons water

Serving

- Steamed jasmine rice
- Basil
- Green onions
- Cilantro
- Lime wedges

Instructions:

1. Blend lemongrass with garlic and ginger in a food processor until chopped finely.
2. Sauté this mixture with oil in a heavy pot for 5 minutes.
3. Stir in salt, tomato and curry paste then cook for 3 minutes.
4. Add tomatoes and cook for 5 minutes with stirring.
5. Pour in coconut milk, boil then reduce it heat and cook for 25 minutes.
6. Add carrots, sweet potatoes and water, cover and cook for 15 minutes.
7. Stir in shallots and cook for 20 minutes.
8. Stir in chiles, and lime juice.
9. Garnish with basil, green onions, cilantro and lime wedges.
10. Serve warm.

542

The Plant Based Cookbook For Beginners
650 Easy, Quick, & Simple Plant Based Vegan Diet Recipes With A 31 Day Meal Plan To Lose Weight & Live A Long Healthy Life

Bejeweled Rice

SERVINGS
4

PREPARATION TIME
10 minutes

COOKING TIME
39 minutes

Nutritional Values Per Serving

Calories	405
Total Fat	5.5g
Saturated Fat	0.8g
Cholesterol	0mg
Sodium	277mg
Total Carbohydrate	33.5g
Dietary Fiber	6.2g
Total Sugars	1.3g
Protein	4.7g

Ingredients:

- ⅓ cup unsalted shelled pistachios
- ⅓ cup slivered almonds
- 4 tablespoons olive oil
- 2 large carrots, peeled, sliced
- 2 teaspoons sugar
- Kosher salt, to taste
- 8 green onions, sliced
- 3 garlic cloves, sliced
- 3 cups long-grain rice, rinsed
- ¾ teaspoon crushed red pepper flakes
- ¾ teaspoon ground cardamom
- ¾ teaspoon ground cinnamon
- ¾ teaspoon ground turmeric
- 4 tablespoons vegan butter
- 2 teaspoons orange zest, grated

Instructions:

1. At 350 degrees F, preheat your oven.
2. Add almonds to one side of the baking sheet and pistachios to the other side.
3. Roast these nuts for 8 minutes, then allow them to cool. Chop the nuts.
4. Sauté carrots with 1 tablespoon oil in a heavy pot for 10 minutes.
5. Stir in a pinch of salt and sugar, then cook for 1 minute and transfer to a bowl.
6. Sauté green onions and garlic with 3 tablespoons oil in the same pot for 6 minutes.
7. Stir in the turmeric, cinnamon, cardamom, red pepper flakes and rice, then cook for 3 minutes.
8. Stir in 1 tablespoon salt and 3 ¾ cups water, then cook to a boil.
9. Reduce its heat, cover and cook for 18 minutes.
10. Remove the rice from the heat and add orange zest and butter.
11. Cover and leave the rice to steam for 10 minutes.
12. Spread the pilaf on the serving plate.
13. Add green onions, carrots, pistachios, and almonds on top.
14. Serve.

The Plant Based Cookbook For Beginners
650 Easy, Quick, & Simple Plant Based Vegan Diet Recipes With A 31 Day Meal Plan To Lose Weight & Live A Long Healthy Life

543

Roasted Cauliflower with Chickpea Curry

SERVINGS	PREPARATION TIME	COOKING TIME
4	15 minutes	62 minutes

Nutritional Values Per Serving

Calories	389
Total Fat	2.2g
Saturated Fat	0.5g
Cholesterol	0mg
Sodium	42mg
Total Carbohydrate	75.2g
Dietary Fiber	12.8g
Total Sugars	2.4g
Protein	18.6g

Ingredients:

- 2 Fresno chiles, sliced
- ¼ cup Champagne vinegar
- ¼ teaspoon sugar
- 1½ teaspoons Kosher salt
- 1 cauliflower head, cut into florets
- ¼ cup olive oil
- 2 tablespoons vadouvan powder
- 2 shallots, sliced
- ¾ cup vegetable oil
- 1 (15.5-ounces) can chickpeas, rinsed, patted dry
- 1 medium onion, chopped
- 1 (1-inch piece) ginger, peeled, grated
- 1 garlic clove, grated
- 1 teaspoon lemongrass, grated
- 2 teaspoons tomato paste
- 1 teaspoon harissa paste
- 1 (13.5-ounces) can unsweetened coconut milk
- 1 tablespoon cilantro stems, chopped
- Steamed basmati rice, for serving

Instructions:

1. Mix chiles with ¼ cup water, ½ teaspoons salt, sugar and vinegar in a bowl.
2. At 450 degrees F, preheat your oven.
3. Toss cauliflower with 1 teaspoon salt, vadouvan, and olive oil in a rimmed baking sheet and roast for 35 minutes.
4. Sauté shallots with ½ cup oil and salt in a saucepan for 10 minutes then transfer to a plate.
5. Sauté remaining oil with onion in the same pan for 7 minutes.
6. Stir in garlic, ginger and lemongrass then sauté for 1 minute.
7. Add harissa paste, and tomato paste, then cook for 2 minutes.
8. Pour in coconut milk and cook for 7 minutes until it thickens.
9. Add ¼ cup water and chickpeas, then boil again.
10. Remove it from the heat and add cilantro and salt for seasoning.
11. Serve warm with rice and top the curry with reserved chiles, roasted cauliflower, cilantro and fried shallots.

544

The Plant Based Cookbook For Beginners
650 Easy, Quick, & Simple Plant Based Vegan Diet Recipes With A 31 Day Meal Plan To Lose Weight & Live A Long Healthy Life

Grilled Cauliflower Steaks

SERVINGS **4**

PREPARATION TIME **10 minutes**

COOKING TIME **20 minutes**

Nutritional Values Per Serving

Calories	343
Total Fat	5.8g
Saturated Fat	4.4g
Cholesterol	0mg
Sodium	39mg
Total Carbohydrate	20.8g
Dietary Fiber	3.9g
Total Sugars	1.9g
Protein	16g

Ingredients:

- 1 large head cauliflower
- 6 tablespoons vegetable oil
- 1 bunch green onions, trimmed
- Kosher salt and black pepper, to taste
- 1 (1-inch piece) ginger, peeled, grated
- 1 garlic clove
- ½ cup fresh cilantro leaves
- 2 tablespoons fresh lime juice

Serving

- Hummus
- Arugula
- Sesame oil
- Sesame seeds

Instructions:

1. Slice the cauliflower head into four- ½ inch thick steaks.
2. Set a grill over medium-high heat and grease the grilling grate with oil.
3. Sprinkle salt and 4 tablespoons of oil over the cauliflower steaks.
4. Grill these steaks for 10 minutes per side.
5. Blend lime juice, cilantro, garlic, ginger, salt and the remaining 2 tablespoons oil in a blender until smooth.
6. Place the cauliflower steak and green onions on the serving plate and pour the cilantro sauce on top.
7. Garnish with hummus, sesame oil, arugula, and sesame seeds.
8. Serve.

The Plant Based Cookbook For Beginners
650 Easy, Quick, & Simple Plant Based Vegan Diet Recipes With A 31 Day Meal Plan To Lose Weight & Live A Long Healthy Life

545

Seared Radicchio and Roasted Beets

SERVINGS	PREPARATION TIME	COOKING TIME
6	15 minutes	59 minutes

Nutritional Values Per Serving	
Calories	324
Total Fat	4.4g
Saturated Fat	0.7g
Cholesterol	0mg
Sodium	394mg
Total Carbohydrate	59.3g
Dietary Fiber	8.1g
Total Sugars	7.3g
Protein	13.6g

Ingredients:

- 6 medium beets, scrubbed
- 5 tablespoons olive oil
- Kosher salt, to taste
- 2 small radicchio heads, cut into wedges
- 1 cup pomegranate juice
- 2 tablespoons red wine vinegar
- ½ cup pomegranate seeds
- Flaky sea salt, for serving

Instructions:

1. At 450 degrees F, preheat your oven.
2. Toss beets with 1 tablespoon oil and salt in a baking sheet lined with a foil sheet.
3. Roast the beets for 50 minutes, then allow them to cool.
4. Cook radicchio with 2 tablespoons oil in a suitable skillet for 2 minutes per side, then transfer to a plate.
5. Add pomegranate juice to the same skillet, boil and cook for 5 minutes until thickens.
6. Stir in salt and vinegar, then mix well.
7. Shred the roasted beets and place them with radicchio in a bowl.
8. Drizzle the prepared dressing on top and garnish with pomegranate seeds, salt, and remaining oil.
9. Serve.

546

The Plant Based Cookbook For Beginners
650 Easy, Quick, & Simple Plant Based Vegan Diet Recipes With A 31 Day Meal Plan To Lose Weight & Live A Long Healthy Life

Tofu Sloppy Joes

SERVINGS | PREPARATION TIME | COOKING TIME
4 | **15 minutes** | **30 minutes**

Nutritional Values Per Serving

Calories	268
Total Fat	1.2g
Saturated Fat	0.2g
Cholesterol	0mg
Sodium	111mg
Total Carbohydrate	19.7g
Dietary Fiber	12g
Total Sugars	4.3g
Protein	15.5g

Ingredients:

- 2 tablespoons olive oil
- 1 medium onion, chopped
- 1 Fresno chile, chopped
- 4 garlic cloves, sliced
- 8 ounces cremini mushrooms, grated
- 8 ounces firm tofu, drained
- 2 tablespoons chili powder
- 1 teaspoon smoked paprika
- 1 (15-ounce) can tomato purée
- ½ cup chopped walnuts
- 2 tablespoons apple cider vinegar
- 2 tablespoons ketchup
- 1 tablespoon soy sauce
- Kosher salt, to taste
- 4 hamburger buns, toasted

Instructions:

1. Sauté onion, garlic and chiles with oil in a skillet for 10 minutes.

2. Stir in tofu, chili powder, mushrooms, and paprika then sauté for 5 minutes.

3. Add tomato puree, apple cider vinegar, soy sauce, ketchup, and walnuts, then cook for 15 minutes.

4. Adjust seasoning with salt and divide in the buns.

5. Serve warm.

The Plant Based Cookbook For Beginners
650 Easy, Quick, & Simple Plant Based Vegan Diet Recipes With A 31 Day Meal Plan To Lose Weight & Live A Long Healthy Life

547

Green Curry with Rice Noodles

SERVINGS	PREPARATION TIME	COOKING TIME
4	15 minutes	47 minutes

Nutritional Values Per Serving

Calories	505
Total Fat	6.6g
Saturated Fat	1.1g
Cholesterol	0mg
Sodium	130mg
Total Carbohydrate	94.9g
Dietary Fiber	17.7g
Total Sugars	18.7g
Protein	20.7g

Ingredients:

- 4 green onions, chopped
- 4 garlic cloves, smashed
- 3 green Thai chiles, chopped
- 2-inch piece ginger, peeled, chopped
- 2 teaspoons green peppercorns in brine
- ½ teaspoon ground turmeric
- 2 cups cilantro leaves
- ⅓ cup mint leaves
- ¼ cup coconut oil, melted
- 2 (13.5-ounces) cans of unsweetened coconut milk
- 1 tablespoon fresh lime juice
- 1 lemongrass stalk, chopped
- 4 cups Swiss chard leaves, chopped
- 1 tablespoon coconut sugar
- Kosher salt, to taste
- 8 ounces dried thin brown rice noodles

Garnish

- Lime wedges
- Mint
- Cilantro

Instructions:

1. Blend 2 tablespoons water, cup mint, cilantro, turmeric, green peppercorns, ginger, chiles, garlic and green onions in a blender.
2. Stir in coconut oil and mix well.
3. Sauté this mixture in a cooking pan for 5 minutes.
4. Stir in 3 cups water, lime juice, and coconut milk, then cook to a boil.
5. Add lemongrass, reduce its heat and cook for 30 minutes on a simmer with occasional stirring.
6. Stir in Swiss chard and cook for 2 minutes.
7. Add salt and coconut sugar.
8. Cook the rice noodles as per the package's instruction, then drain.
9. Divide the noodles in the serving bowls and top them with curry.
10. Garnish with mint, cilantro and lime wedges.
11. Serve.

548

The Plant Based Cookbook For Beginners
650 Easy, Quick, & Simple Plant Based Vegan Diet Recipes With A 31 Day Meal Plan To Lose Weight & Live A Long Healthy Life

Noodle Bowl with Escarole

SERVINGS
6

PREPARATION TIME
10 minutes

COOKING TIME
10 minutes

Nutritional Values Per Serving

Calories	317
Total Fat	5.6g
Saturated Fat	0.5g
Cholesterol	0mg
Sodium	209mg
Total Carbohydrate	54g
Dietary Fiber	14.9g
Total Sugars	13.1g
Protein	15.5g

Ingredients:

- 2 (5.5-ounce) dried somen noodles
- 3 ½ cups torn escarole, chopped
- 3 tablespoons roasted garlic chili sauce
- kosher salt, to taste
- 4 pickled green onions, chopped
- ½ cup mushrooms, sliced
- ½ cup kale, chopped

Serving

- Sliced radish
- Chopped peanuts

Instructions:

1. Boil the noodles as per the package's instructions, then remove them from the water.
2. Add escarole, mushrooms and kale to the boiling water for 1 minute, then drain.
3. Mix noodles with chili sauce and escarole, kale and mushrooms in a bowl.
4. Adjust seasoning with salt, then divide in the serving bowls.
5. Top each bowl chopped peanuts, and green onions.
6. Serve.

The Plant Based Cookbook For Beginners
650 Easy, Quick, & Simple Plant Based Vegan Diet Recipes With A 31 Day Meal Plan To Lose Weight & Live A Long Healthy Life

549

Chilled Ramen with Soy Milk

SERVINGS	PREPARATION TIME	COOKING TIME
4	10 minutes	16 minutes

Nutritional Values Per Serving

Calories	409
Total Fat	3.2g
Saturated Fat	0.1g
Cholesterol	0mg
Sodium	310mg
Total Carbohydrate	19.3g
Dietary Fiber	2.8g
Total Sugars	29g
Protein	6.8g

Ingredients:

Sichuan Chili Paste

- 1 (1-inch piece) ginger, peeled, chopped
- ¼ cup toasted sesame oil
- ¼ cup vegetable oil
- 4 ½ teaspoons crushed red pepper flakes
- 1 tablespoon paprika
- 4 teaspoons toasted sesame seeds
- 1 tablespoon mirin
- 1 tablespoon raw sugar
- 1 tablespoon red miso
- 1 tablespoon sake
- 1 tablespoon Sichuan peppercorns

Chili Oil

- ¼ cup vegetable oil
- 2 green onions, sliced
- 1 teaspoon paprika
- Kosher salt, to taste

Miso Tare

- 2 green onions, sliced
- 1½-inch piece ginger, peeled, grated
- 1 apple wedge, peeled, grated
- 2 garlic cloves, grated
- ⅔ cup white or red miso
- 1 tablespoon mirin
- 1 tablespoon sake
- 1½ teaspoons toban djan (chili bean paste)
- ½ teaspoon crushed red pepper flakes

Noodles & Assembly

- 20 ounces ramen noodles
- Kosher salt, to taste
- ½ cup chopped greens onions
- ½ cup mushrooms, diced
- ¼ cup sliced basil
- 4 cups soy milk
- 3x1-inch strip grapefruit zest, sliced
- 2 tablespoons white or regular soy sauce
- Seaweed flakes, to garnish

Instructions:

1. Mix ginger, paprika, red pepper flakes, vegetable and sesame oil in a saucepan for 30 seconds.
2. Stir in Sichuan peppercorns, sake, miso, raw sugar, mirin, sesame seeds.
3. Mix well until sugar is dissolved, then remove from the heat.
4. Mix red pepper flakes, toban djan, sake, mirin, miso, garlic, apple, ginger and green onions in a saucepan and cook for 5 minutes.
5. Sauté green onions with oil, salt and paprika in a skillet for 2 minutes, then transfer to a plate.
6. Boil the noodles as per the package's instruction, then drain.
7. Mix mushrooms, basil, salt, and 3 tablespoons Sichuan chili pasta in a small bowl.
8. Mix milk, soy sauce, grapefruit zest and miso tare in a medium bowl
9. Divide noodles, vegetables and milk mixture into the serving bowls.
10. Garnish with seaweed and green onions on top.
11. Serve.

550

The Plant Based Cookbook For Beginners
650 Easy, Quick, & Simple Plant Based Vegan Diet Recipes With A 31 Day Meal Plan To Lose Weight & Live A Long Healthy Life

Snap Pea and Carrot Noodles

SERVINGS **4** PREPARATION TIME **15 minutes** COOKING TIME **20 minutes**

Nutritional Values Per Serving

Calories	220
Total Fat	29.3g
Saturated Fat	5.5 g
Cholesterol	0mg
Sodium	21mg
Total Carbohydrate	5.2g
Dietary Fiber	3.7g
Total Sugars	10.3g
Protein	13.1g

Ingredients:

- 6 ounces soba noodles
- 2 cups organic edamame
- 10 ounces (3 cups) snap peas
- 6 medium-sized carrots, peeled and julienned
- ½ cup fresh cilantro, chopped
- ¼ cup sesame seeds
- ½ cup baby spinach

Ginger Sesame Sauce

- ¼ cup tamari sauce
- 2 tablespoons peanut oil
- 1 small lime, juiced
- 1 tablespoon toasted sesame oil
- 1 tablespoon agave
- 1 tablespoon white miso
- 2 teaspoons ginger, grated
- 1 teaspoon chili garlic sauce

Instructions:

1. Mix all the sesame sauce ingredients in a bowl.
2. Toast sesame seeds in a skillet for 5 minutes, then transfer to a plate.
3. Boil soba noodles as per the package's instruction, then drain.
4. Add edamame to boiling water for 20 seconds, then drain.
5. Mix soba noodles with spinach, carrots, snap peas, and edamame in a bowl.
6. Pour the prepared sauce on top and mix well.
7. Garnish with sesame seeds and cilantro.
8. Serve.

The Plant Based Cookbook For Beginners
650 Easy, Quick, & Simple Plant Based Vegan Diet Recipes With A 31 Day Meal Plan To Lose Weight & Live A Long Healthy Life

551

Vegetable Paella

SERVINGS	PREPARATION TIME	COOKING TIME
6	10 minutes	1 hour 59 minutes

Nutritional Values Per Serving

Calories	233
Total Fat	7.6g
Saturated Fat	18g
Cholesterol	0mg
Sodium	130mg
Total Carbohydrate	21.6g
Dietary Fiber	12.9g
Total Sugars	16.2g
Protein	14.4g

Ingredients:

- 3 tablespoons olive oil
- 1 medium yellow onion, chopped
- 1 ½ teaspoons sea salt
- 6 garlic cloves, pressed
- 2 teaspoons smoked paprika
- 1 can (15 ounces) diced tomatoes
- 2 cups short-grain brown rice
- 1 can (15 ounces) chickpeas, rinsed
- 3 cups vegetable broth
- ⅓ cup dry white wine
- ½ teaspoon saffron threads, crumbled
- 1 can (14 ounces) quartered artichokes
- 2 red bell peppers, seeded and sliced
- ½ cup Kalamata olives, pitted and halved
- Black pepper, to taste
- ¼ cup parsley, chopped
- 2 tablespoons lemon juice
- ½ cup frozen peas

Garnish

- Green olives
- Parsley
- Lemon wedges

Instructions:

1. Place the oven rack in the upper and lower third portion to make space for a Dutch oven.
2. At 350 degrees F, preheat your oven.
3. Sauté onion with 2 tablespoons oil and salt in a Dutch oven for 5 minutes.
4. Stir in paprika and garlic then sauté for 30 seconds.
5. Add tomatoes and cook for 2 minutes until thickens.
6. Stir in rice and sauté for 1 minute.
7. Add saffron, 1 teaspoon salt, wine, broth, and chickpeas then cook to a boil.
8. Then cover this Dutch oven and transfer to the oven for 55 minutes.
9. Layer a rimmed baking sheet with wax paper and toss artichokes with ½ teaspoons salt, 1 tablespoon olive oil, chopped olives, and peppers in the baking sheet.
10. Roast for 45 minutes in the oven.
11. Add lemon juice and parsley to the veggies.
12. Transfer the Dutch oven to medium-high heat, add peas and cook for 5 minutes.
13. Add the roasted veggies on top of the rice.
14. Cover and leave for 5 minutes.
15. Garnish with green olives, parsley and lemon wedges.
16. Serve warm.

552

The Plant Based Cookbook For Beginners
650 Easy, Quick, & Simple Plant Based Vegan Diet Recipes With A 31 Day Meal Plan To Lose Weight & Live A Long Healthy Life

Sweet Potato and Rice Bowls

SERVINGS	PREPARATION TIME	COOKING TIME
4	15 minutes	1 hour 35 minutes

Nutritional Values Per Serving

Calories	275
Total Fat	5.2g
Saturated Fat	1g
Cholesterol	0mg
Sodium	413mg
Total Carbohydrate	13.2g
Dietary Fiber	5.3g
Total Sugars	8.1g
Protein	6g

Ingredients:

- 3 tablespoons olive oil
- 1½ cups long-grain brown rice
- 3 cups vegetable broth
- 1½ cup green beans
- ½ cup cilantro
- 1 jalapeño pepper, seeded, chopped
- 1 medium shallot, peeled and chopped
- 1 garlic clove, peeled, chopped
- ¼ teaspoon salt, more to taste
- 1 cup peas, thawed

Sweet Potatoes

- 2 pounds sweet potatoes, peeled and sliced
- 2 tablespoons olive oil
- ½ teaspoon smoked paprika
- ¼ teaspoon sea salt

Instructions:

1. At 425 degrees F, preheat your oven.
2. Layer a rimmed baking sheet with wax paper.
3. Sauté rice with oil in a heavy pot until golden.
4. Stir in peas and the rest of the rice ingredients.
5. Cook the rice to a boil, cover and cook on a simmer for 40 minutes.
6. Toss sweet potatoes with olive oil, salt and smoked paprika in a bowl.
7. Spread them in the prepared baking sheet and bake for 40 minutes, then toss halfway through.
8. Remove the cooked rice from the heat and leave for 10 minutes.
9. Fluff the cooked rice and divide it into the serving bowls.
10. Toss in sweet potatoes and mix well.
11. Serve.

The Plant Based Cookbook For Beginners
650 Easy, Quick, & Simple Plant Based Vegan Diet Recipes With A 31 Day Meal Plan To Lose Weight & Live A Long Healthy Life

553

Spaghetti Alla Puttanesca

SERVINGS	PREPARATION TIME	COOKING TIME
6	15 minutes	30 minutes

Nutritional Values Per Serving

Calories	410
Total Fat	12.8g
Saturated Fat	0½g
Cholesterol	0mg
Sodium	109mg
Total Carbohydrate	22.9g
Dietary Fiber	5.9g
Total Sugars	14.4g
Protein	14.9g

Ingredients:

- 1 large (28 ounces) can of tomato sauce
- ⅓ cup chopped Kalamata olives
- ⅓ cup capers
- 1 tablespoon Kalamata olive brine
- 1 tablespoon caper brine
- 3 garlic cloves, pressed
- ¼ teaspoon red pepper flakes

- 1 tablespoon olive oil
- ½ cup fresh parsley leaves, chopped
- Black pepper, to taste
- Salt, to taste
- 8 ounces whole-grain spaghetti

Garnish

- Parsley

Instructions:

1. Add tomato sauce, red pepper flakes, garlic, caper brine, olive brine, capers, and olives to a saucepan and cook for 20 minutes.

2. Remove the sauce from the heat and add olive oil, parsley, salt and black pepper.

3. Boil the spaghetti in salted water as per the package's instruction then drain.

4. Serve the spaghetti with Puttanesca sauce on top then garnish with parsley leaves.

554

The Plant Based Cookbook For Beginners
650 Easy, Quick, & Simple Plant Based Vegan Diet Recipes With A 31 Day Meal Plan To Lose Weight & Live A Long Healthy Life

Thai Red Curry with Vegetables

SERVINGS
4

PREPARATION TIME
10 minutes

COOKING TIME
60 minutes

Nutritional Values Per Serving

Calories	388
Total Fat	7g
Saturated Fat	0.9g
Cholesterol	0mg
Sodium	8mg
Total Carbohydrate	28g
Dietary Fiber	9.1g
Total Sugars	10.4g
Protein	8g

Ingredients:

- 1 ¼ cups brown jasmine rice
- 1 tablespoon coconut oil
- 1 small white onion, chopped
- 1 pinch of salt
- 1 tablespoon ginger, grated
- 2 garlic cloves, pressed or minced
- 1 red bell pepper, sliced
- 1 yellow, orange bell pepper, sliced
- 3 carrots, peeled and sliced
- 2 tablespoons Thai red curry paste
- 1 can (14 ounces) regular coconut milk
- ½ cup water
- 1 ½ cups packed kale, sliced
- 1 ½ teaspoon coconut sugar
- 1 tablespoon tamari
- 2 teaspoons rice vinegar

Garnish

- Fresh basil
- Red pepper flakes
- Lime wedges

Instructions:

1. Boil rice in salted water for 30 minutes in a cooking pot, drain and leave them covered in a pan.
2. Sauté onion with oil and salt in a suitable pan for 5 minutes.
3. Stir in garlic and ginger, then sauté for 30 seconds.
4. Add carrots and bell peppers, then sauté for 5 minutes.
5. Stir in curry paste, then sauté for 2 minutes.
6. Add sugar, kale, water, and coconut milk, then cook to a simmer.
7. Cook for 10 minutes with occasional stirring.
8. Remove this pot from the heat and add rice vinegar and tamari.
9. Divide the rice in the serving bowls and top them with curry.
10. Garnish with cilantro, red pepper flakes and lime wedges.
11. Serve warm.

The Plant Based Cookbook For Beginners
650 Easy, Quick, & Simple Plant Based Vegan Diet Recipes With A 31 Day Meal Plan To Lose Weight & Live A Long Healthy Life

555

Butternut Squash Stuffed Shells

SERVINGS	PREPARATION TIME	COOKING TIME
6	10 minutes	40 minutes

Nutritional Values Per Serving

Calories	321
Total Fat	4.7g
Saturated Fat	2½g
Cholesterol	1mg
Sodium	87mg
Total Carbohydrate	21.7g
Dietary Fiber	4.2g
Total Sugars	17.7g
Protein	4.6g

Ingredients:

- 1 ½ cups butternut squash, cubed
- olive oil, for drizzling
- 16 jumbo shells
- Salt, to taste

Cashew Cream

- 1 ½ cups raw cashews
- 1 cup water
- 1 garlic clove
- 3 ½ tablespoons lemon juice
- ½ teaspoon sea salt

Filling

- 4 cups fresh baby spinach
- ½ tablespoon olive oil
- 1 cup crumbled firm tofu
- 1 teaspoon dried oregano
- ½ teaspoon lemon zest
- 1 pinch of red pepper flakes
- 1 cup cashew cream
- Salt and Black pepper, to taste

Instructions:

1. At 350 degrees F, preheat your oven.
2. Layer a baking sheet with parchment paper.
3. Toss squash with oil and salt then sauté for 25 minutes.
4. Blend cashews with salt, lemon juice, garlic and water in a blender until smooth.
5. Sauté spinach with oil in a skillet until soft and transfer to a bowl
6. Stir in ¼ teaspoons salt, 1 cup cashew cream, red pepper flakes, lemon zest, oregano, and crumbled tofu.
7. Mix well and keep this mixture aside.
8. Boil the jumbo shells in salted water in a pan as per the package's instructions, then drain.
9. Spread ¼ cup cashew cream in an 11x7 inch baking dish.
10. Fill each jumbo shell with spinach filling and squash cubes.
11. Place these shells in the baking dish, drizzle olive oil on top, cover with foil and bake for 15 minutes.
12. Pour the remaining cashew cream on top.
13. Serve.

556

The Plant Based Cookbook For Beginners
650 Easy, Quick, & Simple Plant Based Vegan Diet Recipes With A 31 Day Meal Plan To Lose Weight & Live A Long Healthy Life

Spaghetti Bolognese

SERVINGS
4

PREPARATION TIME
15 minutes

COOKING TIME
39 minutes

Nutritional Values Per Serving

Calories	378
Total Fat	2.7g
Saturated Fat	0½g
Cholesterol	0mg
Sodium	157mg
Total Carbohydrate	24.4g
Dietary Fiber	4g
Total Sugars	5.8g
Protein	5.6g

Ingredients:

- 2 tablespoons olive oil
- ½ yellow onion, diced
- 1 medium carrot, diced
- 4 cups cremini mushrooms, chopped
- 1 tablespoon rosemary, chopped
- ½ cup walnuts, crushed
- 2 garlic cloves, minced
- 1 tablespoon balsamic vinegar
- 1 tablespoon tamari
- 1 (14-ounce) can fire roasted diced tomatoes
- 1½ cups brown lentils, cooked
- 1 tablespoon tomato paste
- 1 teaspoon dried sage
- 1 cup cherry tomatoes, halved
- 8 ounces spaghetti
- Salt and black pepper, to taste

Garnish

- Fresh basil
- Toasted pine nuts
- Red pepper flakes

Instructions:

1. Sauté carrots and onion with oil and salt in a suitable pot for 3 minutes.
2. Stir in mushrooms and sauté for 8 minutes.
3. Add rosemary and walnuts then sauté for 30 seconds.
4. Add garlic, tamari, balsamic vinegar, tomatoes, sage, cherry tomatoes, lentils, and tomato paste.
5. Reduce its heat, and cook for 30 minutes with occasional stirring.
6. Boil pasta in salted water as per the package's instruction.
7. Drain the pasta and divide it into the serving bowls.
8. Top this pasta with the lentil sauce.
9. Garnish with basil, red pepper flakes and pine nuts.
10. Serve.

The Plant Based Cookbook For Beginners
650 Easy, Quick, & Simple Plant Based Vegan Diet Recipes With A 31 Day Meal Plan To Lose Weight & Live A Long Healthy Life

557

Pasta Pomodoro

SERVINGS	PREPARATION TIME	COOKING TIME
4	10 minutes	42 minutes

Nutritional Values Per Serving

Calories	414
Total Fat	14.9g
Saturated Fat	0.7g
Cholesterol	0mg
Sodium	240mg
Total Carbohydrate	21g
Dietary Fiber	11.3g
Total Sugars	13.1g
Protein	10.1g

Ingredients:

Marinara

- 1 tablespoon olive oil
- 3 tablespoons minced shallot
- 1 large garlic clove, minced
- ¼ teaspoon sea salt
- 1 (14-ounce) can chopped tomatoes
- 1 teaspoon balsamic vinegar
- ⅛ teaspoon cane sugar
- Pinch of dried oregano
- Pinch of crushed red pepper flakes

Garnish

- Basil
- Parsley

Creamy Tomato Sauce

- ¼ cup raw cashews
- ½ tablespoon tomato paste
- ¼ cup water
- ½ teaspoon sea salt

Pasta

- 10 ounces pasta
- 1 tablespoon olive oil
- 2 tablespoons thyme leaves
- 2 (14-ounce) cans Mutti Cherry Tomatoes, drained
- 6 cups spinach
- Sea salt and black pepper, to taste

Instructions:

1. Sauté garlic, and shallots with oil, and salt in a suitable pot for 3 minutes.

2. Stir in tomatoes with their juice, cane sugar, red pepper flakes, oregano, and balsamic vinegar, then cover and cook on a simmer for 20 minutes.

3. Blend cashews with water, salt, and tomato paste in a blender until smooth.

4. Boil the pasta in salted water as per the package's instructions, then drain.

5. Sauté tomatoes with oil, salt and thyme in a suitable pan for 6 minutes.

6. Add spinach and cook until wilted.

7. Divide the pasta into the serving bowls.

8. Top them with cream sauce and zucchini mixture.

9. Garnish with basil and parsley.

10. Serve.

558

The Plant Based Cookbook For Beginners
650 Easy, Quick, & Simple Plant Based Vegan Diet Recipes With A 31 Day Meal Plan To Lose Weight & Live A Long Healthy Life

Vegan Broccoli Pizza

SERVINGS	PREPARATION TIME	COOKING TIME
4	10 minutes	15 minutes

Nutritional Values Per Serving

Calories	280
Total Fat	2.4g
Saturated Fat	0g
Cholesterol	0mg
Sodium	99mg
Total Carbohydrate	21.7g
Dietary Fiber	10.2g
Total Sugars	49.7g
Protein	2.3g

Ingredients:

- 1 small head broccoli, florets chopped
- 4 oil-packed sun-dried tomatoes, diced
- olive oil for drizzling and brushing
- 1 tablespoon olive oil
- 1 (16-ounce) ball of pizza dough

Garnish

- ½ cup fresh basil leaves
- 2 tablespoons fresh thyme leaves
- 1 pinch of red pepper flakes
- Salt and black pepper, to taste
- 1 cup coconut Cream, to spread
- 1 garlic head, to garnish
- ½ cup baked kale, to garnish

Instructions:

1. At 400 degrees F, preheat your oven.
2. Chop of the top of the garlic head and wrap it in a foil sheet.
3. Place the wrapped garlic head in a baking sheet and roast it for 30 minutes in the oven.
4. After 25 minutes, spread the kale leaves around the garlic head and bake for 5 minutes.
5. Unwrap the garlic head, peel the cloves and keep them aside along with baked kale.
6. Toss broccoli with olive oil, and sun-dried tomatoes in a bowl.
7. Spread the pizza dough in a 14-inch pizza pan.
8. Brush the edges of the pizza dough with olive oil and spread ⅔ of the coconut cream at the center.
9. Spread the vegetable mixture over the dough and bake for 15 minutes.
10. Garnish with remaining coconut cream, baked kale, roasted garlic, red pepper flakes, thyme and basil.
11. Serve.

The Plant Based Cookbook For Beginners
650 Easy, Quick, & Simple Plant Based Vegan Diet Recipes With A 31 Day Meal Plan To Lose Weight & Live A Long Healthy Life

559

Jamaican Jerk Tacos

SERVINGS	PREPARATION TIME	COOKING TIME
4	15 minutes	24 minutes

Nutritional Values Per Serving

Calories	278
Total Fat	2.4g
Saturated Fat	0.1g
Cholesterol	0mg
Sodium	291mg
Total Carbohydrate	29.4g
Dietary Fiber	3.7g
Total Sugars	13.2g
Protein	6.4g

Ingredients:

Mango Avocado Salsa

- 2 cups mango, peeled and diced
- 1 medium ripe avocado, diced
- ¾ cup red onion, diced
- ½ cup cucumber, diced
- 3 tablespoons orange juice
- 3 tablespoons lime juice
- ½ cup cilantro, chopped
- Sea salt, to taste

Jackfruit

- 2 (20-ounce) cans jackfruit in brine
- 2 tablespoons olive oil
- 6 green onions, sliced
- 4 garlic cloves, minced
- 1½-inch piece fresh ginger, grated

Jamaican Jerk Seasoning

- 1½ teaspoons onion powder
- 1 teaspoon sweet or hot paprika
- 1 teaspoon black pepper, to taste
- 1 teaspoon dried thyme
- ½ teaspoon ground allspice
- ½ teaspoon ground cumin
- ¼ teaspoon cayenne pepper
- ¼ teaspoon ground cinnamon
- ¼ teaspoon nutmeg

- 1 habanero pepper, minced
- 2 tablespoons coconut sugar
- 2 tablespoons tomato paste
- ¼ cup tamari
- 3 tablespoons fresh lime juice
- 12 corn tortillas, charred

Instructions:

1. Mix mango with cilantro, salt, lime juice, orange juice, cucumber, onion and avocado in a bowl.
2. Mix all the ingredients for Jamaican jerk seasoning in a bowl.
3. Drain the jackfruits and rinse under water, then shred with a fork.
4. Sauté green onions with oil in a skillet for 2 minutes.
5. Stir in habanero pepper, ginger, and garlic, then sauté for 1 minute.
6. Add Jamaican jerk seasoning, then sauté for 30 seconds.
7. Stir in shredded jackfruit, lime juice, tamari, tomato paste, and coconut sugar.
8. Stir in ½ cup water, mix well, cover and cook for 20 minutes with occasional stirring.
9. Divide the jackfruit over the tortillas and top it with mango avocado salsa.
10. Serve.

560

The Plant Based Cookbook For Beginners
650 Easy, Quick, & Simple Plant Based Vegan Diet Recipes With A 31 Day Meal Plan To Lose Weight & Live A Long Healthy Life

Chipotle Cauliflower Nachos

SERVINGS	PREPARATION TIME	COOKING TIME
4	15 minutes	10 minutes

Nutritional Values Per Serving

Calories	339
Total Fat	1.1g
Saturated Fat	0.3g
Cholesterol	0mg
Sodium	16mg
Total Carbohydrate	29.4g
Dietary Fiber	5g
Total Sugars	3.2g
Protein	14g

Ingredients:

Chipotle Cauliflower Sauce

- 1 cup cauliflower, chopped
- 1 cup Yukon gold potato, peeled and cubed
- ¼ cup raw cashews
- 3 tablespoons water
- 2 tablespoons apple cider vinegar
- 2 tablespoons olive oil
- 1 chipotle pepper
- 1 garlic clove
- ½ teaspoon onion powder
- ½ teaspoon sea salt

Nachos

- Tortilla chips
- 1 cup salsa
- ¼ cup red onions, diced
- ¼ cup tomatoes, diced
- 1 jalapeno, sliced
- ¼ cup cilantro, chopped

Instructions:

1. Boil potatoes and cauliflower to a pan filled with cold water.
2. Add one pinch of salt, cover and cook for 10 minutes.
3. Drain and blend with cashews, water, salt, onion powder, garlic, chipotle pepper, olive oil, and apple cider vinegar until smooth.
4. Spread the chips in the platter and top them with cilantro, tomatoes, red onions, and salsa.
5. Pour the cauliflower sauce on top and garnish with jalapeno.
6. Serve.

The Plant Based Cookbook For Beginners
650 Easy, Quick, & Simple Plant Based Vegan Diet Recipes With A 31 Day Meal Plan To Lose Weight & Live A Long Healthy Life

561

Maki Sushi

SERVINGS	PREPARATION TIME	COOKING TIME
6	10 minutes	1 hour 15 minutes

Nutritional Values Per Serving

Calories	306
Total Fat	0.1g
Saturated Fat	0g
Cholesterol	0mg
Sodium	176mg
Total Carbohydrate	13.6g
Dietary Fiber	3½g
Total Sugars	1.3g
Protein	3.6g

Ingredients:

Roasted Shiitakes
- 6 ounces shiitake mushrooms
- 1 tablespoon olive oil
- 1 tablespoon tamari

Rolls
- 3 nori sheets
- 3 long thin cucumber strips
- 1 large carrots, julienned
- ½ avocado, sliced

Garnish
- Sesame seeds
- Tamari
- Pickled ginger
- Carrot ginger sauce

Carrot Ginger Sauce
- ½ cup carrots, chopped
- ⅓ to ½ cup water
- ¼ cup olive oil
- 2 tablespoons rice vinegar
- 2 teaspoons minced ginger
- ¼ teaspoon sea salt

Sushi Rice
- 1 cup brown rice, rinsed
- 2 cups water
- 1 teaspoon olive oil
- 2 tablespoons rice vinegar
- 1 tablespoon cane sugar
- 1 teaspoon sea salt

Instructions:

1. At 400 degrees F, preheat your oven.
2. Layer a baking sheet with wax paper.
3. Toss mushrooms with tamari and olive oil on the baking sheet.
4. Roast the mushrooms for 30 minutes.
5. Blend carrots with salt, ginger, rice vinegar, olive oil and water in a blender until smooth then transfer to a bowl.
6. Boil rice with olive oil and water in a pan, cover and cook on a simmer for 45 minutes.
7. Leave the rice for 10 minutes, then add salt, sugar, and rice vinegar.
8. Mix well and leave them covered until ready to use.
9. Place one nori sheet strip on the working surface and add a handful of rice on top of the lower 2/3 portion.
10. Top the rice with cucumber strips, carrot strips, sliced avocado, roll and place the sushi aside.
11. Repeat the same steps with the remaining sushi ingredients.
12. Garnish with sesame seeds and serve with pickled ginger, tamari and dipping sauce.
13. Serve.

562

The Plant Based Cookbook For Beginners
650 Easy, Quick, & Simple Plant Based Vegan Diet Recipes With A 31 Day Meal Plan To Lose Weight & Live A Long Healthy Life

Bok Choy Stir Fry

SERVINGS
4

PREPARATION TIME
10 minutes

COOKING TIME
14 minutes

Nutritional Values Per Serving

Calories	359
Total Fat	2.4g
Saturated Fat	0.7g
Cholesterol	0mg
Sodium	303mg
Total Carbohydrate	10.8g
Dietary Fiber	5.8g
Total Sugars	12.7g
Protein	12g

Ingredients:

Stir Fry

- 1 tablespoon sunflower oil
- 4 ounces shiitake mushrooms, sliced
- 1 cup tofu, sliced
- 2 green onions, chopped
- 2 baby bok choy, chopped
- ½ cup edamame
- 1 green onion, julienned
- 4 ounces brown rice pasta
- 1 teapoon lime juice

Sauce

- 1 ½ tablespoons tamari
- 2 tablespoons rice vinegar
- 1 teaspoon lime juice
- ½ teaspoon agave
- ½ teaspoon ginger, minced
- 1 small garlic clove, minced
- ½ teaspoon sesame oil

Instructions:

1. Mix sesame oil, garlic, ginger, agave, lime juice, rice vinegar, and tamari in a bowl.
2. Boil pasta as per the package's instructions, then drain.
3. Sauté tofu and mushrooms with oil in a large skillet for 2 minutes.
4. Stir in edamame, bok choy, and green onions, then sauté for 2 minutes.
5. Add noodles, green onion, prepared sauce, and lime juice.
6. Serve.

The Plant Based Cookbook For Beginners
650 Easy, Quick, & Simple Plant Based Vegan Diet Recipes With A 31 Day Meal Plan To Lose Weight & Live A Long Healthy Life

563

Risotto with Butternut Squash

SERVINGS	PREPARATION TIME	COOKING TIME
4	15 minutes	22 minutes

Nutritional Values Per Serving

Calories	366
Total Fat	12g
Saturated Fat	1g
Cholesterol	0mg
Sodium	802mg
Total Carbohydrate	22g
Dietary Fiber	4.3g
Total Sugars	4.8g
Protein	10.7g

Ingredients:

- 2 tablespoons vegan butter
- 1 shallot, chopped
- ½ yellow onion, chopped
- ½ teaspoon sea salt
- 1 cup arborio rice
- ½ butternut squash, peeled and cubed
- 2 cups vegetable broth
- ¼ cup cashew cream
- Fresh sage leaves, chopped
- 3 tablespoons olive oil

Cashew cream

- 1 cup raw cashews
- ½ cup water
- 1½ tablespoons lemon juice
- 1 tablespoon nutritional yeast
- 1 tablespoon olive oil
- ½ teaspoon sea salt

Instructions:

1. Set the Instant Pot on sauté mode and add vegan butter to melt.
2. Stir in onion, shallots, and ½ teaspoons salt then sauté for 3 minutes.
3. Add rice, then sauté for 2 minutes and stir in broth and squash.
4. Cover and seal the lid, then cook for 6 minutes on high pressure.
5. Boil cashews with water in a pan for 10 minutes.
6. Blend these cashews with lemon juice, water, yeast, salt and olive oil in a blender until smooth.
7. Add ¼ cup cashew cream to the rice.
8. Sauté sage with oil in a small skillet for 30 seconds, then remove the leaves to a plate lined with a paper towel.
9. Garnish the risotto with sage leaves.
10. Serve.

564

The Plant Based Cookbook For Beginners
650 Easy, Quick, & Simple Plant Based Vegan Diet Recipes With A 31 Day Meal Plan To Lose Weight & Live A Long Healthy Life

Roasted Squash Pasta with Kale

SERVINGS	PREPARATION TIME	COOKING TIME
4	10 minutes	41 minutes

Nutritional Values Per Serving

Calories	326
Total Fat	20.4g
Saturated Fat	3.7g
Cholesterol	0mg
Sodium	173mg
Total Carbohydrate	29g
Dietary Fiber	8g
Total Sugars	10.4g
Protein	11.3g

Ingredients:

Pasta

- 8 ounces gnocchi pasta
- 1 teaspoon olive oil
- 2 leeks, chopped
- 2 tablespoons vegan butter
- 2 large garlic cloves, chopped
- ½ teaspoon salt
- 2 packed cups of kale leaves, chopped

Roasted delicata squash

- 1 delicata squash
- 2 teaspoons olive oil
- ½ teaspoon salt

Garnish

- Shredded vegan parmesan

Instructions:

1. At 400 degrees F, preheat your oven.
2. Cut the squash in half, remove the seeds and cut the squash into ½ inch wide half-moon slices.
3. Toss the squash pieces with salt and 2 teaspoons olive oil in a baking sheet.
4. Roast the squash for 10 minutes, flip and cook for 12 more minutes.
5. Boil pasta in salted water as per the package's instruction, then drain.
6. Mix cooked pasta with 1 teaspoon olive oil in a bowl.
7. Sauté leek with vegan butter and salt in a skillet for 3 minutes.
8. Stir in garlic and kale, then sauté for 1 minute.
9. Add pasta and mix well.
10. Mix kale with pasta in a bowl.
11. Add roasted squash and garnish with vegan parmesan cheese.
12. Serve and enjoy.

The Plant Based Cookbook For Beginners
650 Easy, Quick, & Simple Plant Based Vegan Diet Recipes With A 31 Day Meal Plan To Lose Weight & Live A Long Healthy Life

565

Green Curry with Tofu

SERVINGS	PREPARATION TIME	COOKING TIME
4	10 minutes	25 minutes

Nutritional Values Per Serving

Calories	393
Total Fat	4½g
Saturated Fat	0.8g
Cholesterol	1mg
Sodium	42mg
Total Carbohydrate	31g
Dietary Fiber	4.8g
Total Sugars	1.7g
Protein	8.6g

Ingredients:

Coconut Green Curry Sauce

- 2 tablespoons coconut oil
- 1 large jalapeño, seeds removed and diced
- 1 large shallot, diced
- 3 garlic cloves, minced
- 1 inch of ginger, peeled and minced
- ½ teaspoon salt
- ½ teaspoon ground coriander
- ½ teaspoon ground cumin
- 1 (15-ounces) can coconut milk
- ½ cup fresh basil leaves
- 2 handfuls of baby spinach
- 2 tablespoons lime juice
- ¼ teaspoon lemon zest
- 1 teaspoon soy sauce

Tofu

- 1 package tofu, drained, cut into cubes
- 2 teaspoons curry powder
- 2 cups broccoli, chopped into florets
- 1 red bell pepper, sliced

Serving

- Green onion, sliced
- Cooked rice for serving
- Cashews or peanuts, chopped
- Fresh Basil

Instructions:

1. Sauté cumin, coriander, salt, ginger, garlic, shallot and jalapeno with 1 tablespoon coconut oil in a skillet for 5 minutes.
2. Stir in coconut milk and cook for 10 minutes.
3. Blend this mixture with soy sauce, lemon zest, lime juice, basil and spinach in a blender.
4. Sauté tofu with remaining coconut oil in a skillet for 5 minutes.
5. Flip and sprinkle curry powder for seasoning. Cook for another 5 minutes.
6. Pour the prepared green curry sauce over the tofu.
7. Add bell pepper and broccoli to the tofu.
8. Garnish with green onions, basil and nuts.
9. Serve warm with rice.

566

The Plant Based Cookbook For Beginners
650 Easy, Quick, & Simple Plant Based Vegan Diet Recipes With A 31 Day Meal Plan To Lose Weight & Live A Long Healthy Life

Butternut Squash Wellington

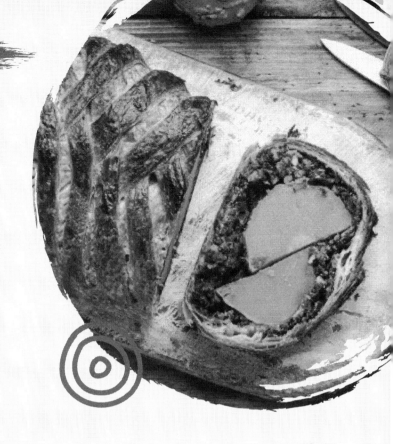

SERVINGS	PREPARATION TIME	COOKING TIME
4	15 minutes	1 hour 20 minutes

Nutritional Values Per Serving

Calories	380
Total Fat	14.7g
Saturated Fat	12.8g
Cholesterol	0mg
Sodium	12mg
Total Carbohydrate	15.1g
Dietary Fiber	3g
Total Sugars	5.7g
Protein	4.9g

Serving Suggestion:

Enjoy this wellington with some mushroom gravy.

Ingredients:

- ½ butternut squash, peeled and diced
- 3 cups brussels sprouts, quartered
- 2 shallots, chopped
- 1 cup chopped mushrooms
- 1 tablespoon olive oil
- Pinch of salt
- ½ cup French lentils
- 1½ cups vegetable broth
- ½ teaspoon soy sauce
- 1 teaspoon maple syrup
- Pinch of paprika
- ½ cup raw walnuts, chopped
- 1 tablespoon fresh thyme leaves
- 1 tablespoon fresh rosemary, chopped
- 1½ tablespoons whole wheat flour
- 2 puff pastry sheets, thawed

Instructions:

1. At 400 degrees F, preheat your oven.
2. Toss butternuts squash with shallots and brussels sprouts with salt and olive oil on a baking sheet.
3. Roast these veggies for 30 minutes until caramelized.
4. BOil lentils with vegetable broth in a saucepan, cover and cook on a simmer for 20 minutes.
5. Mix paprika, maple syrup and soy sauce in a small bowl.
6. Strain the lentils and transfer them to a bowl.
7. Stir in mushrooms, walnuts, herbs, roasted veggies and prepared sauce.
8. Sprinkle some flour on top and mix well.
9. Unwrap and roll out one puff pastry sheet into a 12x15 inch rectangle sheet.
10. Add half of the lentil filling at the center of the rectangle, leaving 2-inch-wide borders on both sides.
11. Cut both sides into 1-inch diagonal slits.
12. Fold the top and bottom edges of the rectangle over the filling and start folding the diagonal slit over the filling.
13. Place the wellington in a baking sheet and brush with olive oil and thyme leaves.
14. Repeat the same steps with the remaining puff pastry and lentil filling.
15. Bake the wellingtons for 30 minutes.
16. Serve warm.

The Plant Based Cookbook For Beginners
650 Easy, Quick, & Simple Plant Based Vegan Diet Recipes With A 31 Day Meal Plan To Lose Weight & Live A Long Healthy Life

567

Pumpkin Pasta with Apple

SERVINGS	PREPARATION TIME	COOKING TIME
6	15 minutes	36 minutes

Nutritional Values Per Serving

Calories	367
Total Fat	27.4g
Saturated Fat	23.3g
Cholesterol	0mg
Sodium	19mg
Total Carbohydrate	22.8g
Dietary Fiber	4.9g
Total Sugars	26g
Protein	3.3g

Ingredients:

- 8 ounces rigatoni
- 1 tablespoon olive oil
- ½ yellow onion, diced
- 4 garlic cloves, minced
- 1 small apple, diced
- 4 sage leaves, chopped
- ½ teaspoon cinnamon
- ¼ teaspoon nutmeg
- 1 (15-ounces) can pumpkin puree
- 1 cup vegetable broth
- ½ cup full fat coconut milk
- ¾ teaspoon salt

Tempeh

- 1 tablespoon soy sauce
- 1 teaspoon apple cider vinegar
- 1 teaspoon maple syrup
- 1 teaspoon paprika
- ½ teaspoon garlic powder
- Pinch of red pepper flakes
- 2 teaspoons olive oil
- 1 (8-ounces) block of tempeh, crumbled

Garnish

- Vegan parmesan

Instructions:

1. Boil pasta as per the package's instructions, then drain.
2. Sauté garlic and onion with oil in a large skillet for 3 minutes.
3. Stir in nutmeg, cinnamon, sage, and apple, then sauté for 30 seconds.
4. Add coconut milk, vegetable broth, salt and pumpkin puree.
5. Cook for 15 minutes on a simmer, then remove from the heat.
6. Mix red pepper flakes, garlic powder, paprika, maple syrup, apple cider vinegar and soy sauce in a bowl.
7. Sauté crumbled tempeh with olive oil in a skillet for 7 minutes.
8. Stir in soy sauce mixture and mix well to coat.
9. Add cooked pasta and pumpkin sauce.
10. Garnish with vegan parmesan.
11. Serve warm.

568

The Plant Based Cookbook For Beginners
650 Easy, Quick, & Simple Plant Based Vegan Diet Recipes With A 31 Day Meal Plan To Lose Weight & Live A Long Healthy Life

Tofu Mushroom Pasta

SERVINGS
6

PREPARATION TIME
15 minutes

COOKING TIME
36 minutes

Nutritional Values Per Serving

Calories	338
Total Fat	5.8g
Saturated Fat	1.1g
Cholesterol	0mg
Sodium	270mg
Total Carbohydrate	30.2g
Dietary Fiber	4.6g
Total Sugars	2.7g
Protein	18g

Ingredients:

- 2 teaspoons of olive oil
- 6 garlic cloves, minced
- 1 ¼ cups dry white wine
- 1 package tofu lite firm
- ¼ cup nutritional yeast
- 1 teaspoon salt
- 1 large shallot, minced
- 1 pound of crimini mushrooms, sliced
- 1 pinch of salt
- 1 tablespoon fresh thyme leaves
- 1 pound of dry pasta

Garnish

- Sliced zucchini

Instructions:

1. Sauté minced garlic with 1 teaspoon olive oil in a large skillet for 4 minutes.
2. Stir in 1 cup white wine and cook for 10 minutes on a simmer, with occasional stirring.
3. Blend tofu with salt and yeast in a blender.
4. Stir in cooked wine and blend until smooth.
5. Pour this sauce into the skillet and add ¼ cup white wine.
6. Cook for 4 minutes on low heat.
7. Boil the dry pasta as per the package's instructions, then rinse and drain.
8. Sauté shallots with oil in a deep skillet for 3 minutes.
9. Stir in mushrooms and salt, then sauté for 8 minutes.
10. Add thyme and cook for 1 minute.
11. Stir in pasta and mix well.
12. Pour in the tofu sauce and mix again.
13. Garnish with sliced zucchini.
14. Serve warm.

The Plant Based Cookbook For Beginners
650 Easy, Quick, & Simple Plant Based Vegan Diet Recipes With A 31 Day Meal Plan To Lose Weight & Live A Long Healthy Life

569

Beet Linguine

SERVINGS	PREPARATION TIME	COOKING TIME
4	10 minutes	40 minutes

Nutritional Values Per Serving

Calories	311
Total Fat	1.8g
Saturated Fat	0.2g
Cholesterol	0mg
Sodium	9mg
Total Carbohydrate	37.9g
Dietary Fiber	5.7g
Total Sugars	2.8g
Protein	12g

Ingredients:

- 8 ounces beets, trimmed and sliced
- ½ cup raw cashews
- 1¼ cups of water
- ½ teaspoons salt
- 1 tablespoon olive oil
- 2 garlic cloves, minced
- 2 tablespoons lemon juice
- 8 ounces spaghetti pasta

Garnish

- Lemon zest
- Fresh parsley

Instructions:

1. Boil water in a suitable pot and set a steamer basket on top.

2. Set the beets in the steamer basket, cover and cook for 20 minutes.

3. Boil cashews with 1¼ cups of water in a saucepan for 10 minutes.

4. Blend the cashews with cooking water in a blender.

5. Peel the steamed beets and add them to the blender along with lemon juice, garlic, olive oil and salt then blend until smooth.

6. Boil pasta as per the package's instruction, then drain.

7. Add pasta to the beet sauce and mix well.

8. Garnish with parsley and lemon zest.

9. Serve warm.

Mexican Lasagna

SERVINGS	PREPARATION TIME	COOKING TIME
6	20 minutes	31 minutes

Nutritional Values Per Serving

Calories	241
Total Fat	4.8g
Saturated Fat	0.3g
Cholesterol	0mg
Sodium	165mg
Total Carbohydrate	22.6g
Dietary Fiber	4.1g
Total Sugars	15.1g
Protein	3g

Ingredients:

- 1 tablespoon olive oil
- 1 cup yellow onion, diced
- 3 garlic cloves, minced
- 1 teaspoon paprika
- ½ tablespoons cumin
- tablespoon chili powder
- ½ teaspoons sea salt
- 1 (15-ounces) can refried beans
- 1 15-ounces can of black beans, drained and rinsed
- 1 (14.5-ounces) can diced tomatoes, drained
- 1 15-ounces can of corn, drained
- 1 4-ounces can dice green chiles
- ¾ cup enchilada sauce
- 4 green onions, chopped
- 12 taco-sized tortillas
- 1 cup vegan cheese

Garnish

- Fresh cilantro, chopped
- Avocado, sliced
- Green onion, chopped

Instructions:

1. At 350 degrees F, preheat your oven.
2. Sauté onion and garlic with olive oil in a deep skillet for 5 minutes.
3. Stir in chili powder, paprika, salt and cumin then sauté for 30 seconds.
4. Stir in refried beans, tomatoes, 1 cup corn, green onion, black beans, green chiles and enchilada sauce.
5. Mix well, then remove from the heat.
6. Grease a 9x13 inch baking dish with oil and set two tortillas in it.
7. Add some of the bean mixture on top of the tortillas and then repeat the layers.
8. Sprinkle vegan cheese on top and cover with a foil sheet.
9. Bake this lasagna for 25 minutes in the oven.
10. Add green onion, remaining corn, cilantro and avocado on top.
11. Serve.

The Plant Based Cookbook For Beginners
650 Easy, Quick, & Simple Plant Based Vegan Diet Recipes With A 31 Day Meal Plan To Lose Weight & Live A Long Healthy Life

571

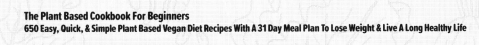

Flatbread with Asparagus

SERVINGS	PREPARATION TIME	COOKING TIME
4	15 minutes	20 minutes

Nutritional Values Per Serving

Calories	321
Total Fat	2.3g
Saturated Fat	0.4g
Cholesterol	20mg
Sodium	128mg
Total Carbohydrate	22g
Dietary Fiber	4.9g
Total Sugars	24.6g
Protein	10g

Ingredients:

- 4 (6-inch) pita
- 1 tablespoon olive oil
- 1 cup white bean puree
- 2 ounces of asparagus, sliced
- Pinch of sea salt

Garnish

- Vegan feta cheese
- Frish dill or basil
- Lemon zest

White Bean Puree

- 1 (15-ounces) can great northern beans, rinsed
- 2 tablespoons olive oil
- 2 tablespoons water
- 2 tablespoons lemon juice
- 3 garlic cloves, minced
- ½ teaspoons salt

Instructions:

1. At 400 degrees F, preheat your oven.
2. Divide pita into two baking sheets and brush them with olive oil.
3. Bake the flatbreads for 10 minutes.
4. Blend beans with salt, garlic, lemon juice, water and olive oil in a blender until smooth.
5. Spread the white beans on top of the flatbreads.
6. Add asparagus on top and sprinkle and salt.
7. Bake these pizzas for 5 minutes.
8. Add lemon zest, herbs, and vegan feta cheese on top of the pizzas.
9. Serve.

(572)

The Plant Based Cookbook For Beginners
650 Easy, Quick, & Simple Plant Based Vegan Diet Recipes With A 31 Day Meal Plan To Lose Weight & Live A Long Healthy Life

Tempeh Kabobs

SERVINGS	PREPARATION TIME	COOKING TIME
4	2 hours 15 minutes	6 minutes

Nutritional Values Per Serving

Calories	366
Total Fat	3.4g
Saturated Fat	0.3g
Cholesterol	0mg
Sodium	224mg
Total Carbohydrate	34g
Dietary Fiber	2½g
Total Sugars	3.2g
Protein	13g

Ingredients:

- 8 ounces tempeh, cut into chunks
- 1 cup barbecue sauce
- ½ green bell pepper, cut into pieces
- ½ red bell pepper, cut into pieces
- ½ red onion, cut into pieces
- 2 cups zucchini, diced
- 2 tablespoons olive oil
- ½ cup green onion, sliced
- Cooked quinoa for serving

Instructions:

1. Boil water in a cooking pot, place the steamer basket in it and add tempeh pieces, then cover.
2. Remove pot from the heat and leave for 5 minutes to steam.
3. Drain and spread the tempeh pieces in a shallow dish.
4. Pour ½ cup BBQ sauce over tempeh and coat well.
5. Cover and refrigerate the tempeh for 2 hours.
6. Set a grill on medium heat and grease its grilling grates.
7. Thread tempeh, red pepper, onion, zucchini and green pepper on each skewer.
8. Grill these tempeh kabobs for 3 minutes per side and brush them with the remaining BBQ sauce.
9. Garnish with green onion and serve with quinoa on the side.

The Plant Based Cookbook For Beginners
650 Easy, Quick, & Simple Plant Based Vegan Diet Recipes With A 31 Day Meal Plan To Lose Weight & Live A Long Healthy Life

573

Greek Cauliflower Stew

SERVINGS	PREPARATION TIME	COOKING TIME
4	1 hour 15 minutes	25 minutes

Nutritional Values Per Serving

Calories	310
Total Fat	5.1g
Saturated Fat	1.6g
Cholesterol	1mg
Sodium	89mg
Total Carbohydrate	23g
Dietary Fiber	3.4g
Total Sugars	13.6g
Protein	5.6g

Ingredients:

- 1 lemon, juiced
- 1 tablespoon olive oil
- 1 bulb of garlic, peeled and chopped
- 2 red onions, petals separated
- 10 ½ ounces new potatoes, sliced
- ½ a bunch of fresh oregano
- Salt, to taste
- ¼ cup water
- 10 large ripe plum tomatoes, chopped
- 1 cauliflower head, cut into florets
- 7 ounces fresh peas

Instructions:

1. At 400 degrees F, preheat your oven.
2. Add garlic, oil, onions, potatoes, and oregano to a suitable pan for 5 minutes on medium high heat.
3. Stir in tomatoes, salt, and water and cook to a boil.
4. Stir in cauliflower then cook for 15 minutes until the veggies are soft.
5. Add peas and beans to the stew and cook for 5 minutes.
6. Add lemon juice to the stew.
7. Mix well and serve.

574

The Plant Based Cookbook For Beginners
650 Easy, Quick, & Simple Plant Based Vegan Diet Recipes With A 31 Day Meal Plan To Lose Weight & Live A Long Healthy Life

Pumpkin Rice with Okra Beans

SERVINGS	PREPARATION TIME	COOKING TIME
4	10 minutes	25 minutes

Nutritional Values Per Serving

Calories	290
Total Fat	10.3g
Saturated Fat	1.4g
Cholesterol	0mg
Sodium	68mg
Total Carbohydrate	26g
Dietary Fiber	8.3g
Total Sugars	19.7g
Protein	12.3g

Ingredients:

- 14 ounces pumpkin, peeled and diced
- 3 ½ ounces coconut cream
- 4 allspice berries
- 3 ½ cups water
- 4 green onions, chopped
- ½ a bunch of fresh thyme
- 2 Scotch bonnet chilis, chopped
- ½ a pointed cabbage, chopped
- 14 ½ ounces basmati rice
- 2 garlic cloves, chopped
- 1 onion, chopped
- 2 tablespoons olive oil
- 7 ounces ripe cherry tomatoes
- 7 ounces okra, sliced
- 24 ounce jar of butter beans

Instructions:

1. Add coconut cream and water to a large pan over medium heat and boil it.

2. Stir in allspice berries, pumpkin, green onions, thyme, scotch bonnet chilis, cabbage, and ½ tsp salt, then cover.

3. Cook for 10, then add rice.

4. Put on the lid, then cook for about 12 minutes on low heat until water is absorbed.

5. Remove the heat and allow the rice to steam.

6. Sauté onion and garlic with 2 tbsp oil in a saucepan for 5 minutes.

7. Stir in tomatoes, thyme, beans and okra, then sauté for 8 minutes.

8. Add the pumpkin rice to the okra beans and mix evenly.

9. Enjoy.

The Plant Based Cookbook For Beginners
650 Easy, Quick, & Simple Plant Based Vegan Diet Recipes With A 31 Day Meal Plan To Lose Weight & Live A Long Healthy Life

575

Vegan Tagine

SERVINGS	PREPARATION TIME	COOKING TIME
4	10 minutes	51 minutes

Nutritional Values Per Serving

Calories	331
Total Fat	17g
Saturated Fat	12g
Cholesterol	20mg
Sodium	275mg
Total Carbohydrate	29g
Dietary Fiber	3.4g
Total Sugars	8.2g
Protein	18g

Ingredients:

- 1 pinch of saffron
- 4 garlic cloves, peeled and sliced
- 4 cm piece of ginger, peeled and sliced
- 1 tablespoon olive oil, for cooking
- 1 teaspoon ground cumin
- Salt and black pepper, to taste
- ½ teaspoon ground cinnamon
- 1 teaspoon Ras El Hanout
- 1 tablespoon sun-dried tomato paste
- 1 x 14 ounces tin of chickpeas
- ½ cup spinach
- 1/cup sun dried tomatoes
- 3 ½ ounces dried apricots
- 1 preserved lemon
- 10 ½ ounces couscous
- 3 cups water

Instructions:

1. Soak saffron in 2 cups hot water in a bowl, and leave for 10 minutes.
2. Sauté ginger and garlic with oil, cumin, Ras El Hanout and cinnamon in a pan for 30 seconds.
3. Stir in tomato paste and cook for 5 minutes, then pour in saffron water.
4. Stir in chickpeas, spinach, tomatoes, apricots, lemon, and salt, then cook to a boil.
5. Cover and reduce its heat and cook for 45 minutes on a simmer with occasional stirring.
6. Meanwhile, boil couscous in water with a pinch of salt and black pepper in a saucepan until soft then drain.
7. Serve the tagine curry over couscous and garnish with herbs and almonds.
8. Enjoy.

576

The Plant Based Cookbook For Beginners
650 Easy, Quick, & Simple Plant Based Vegan Diet Recipes With A 31 Day Meal Plan To Lose Weight & Live A Long Healthy Life

Stuffed Curried Eggplant

SERVINGS	PREPARATION TIME	COOKING TIME
4	15 minutes	51 minutes

Nutritional Values Per Serving

Calories	248
Total Fat	5.6g
Saturated Fat	2.9g
Cholesterol	0mg
Sodium	17mg
Total Carbohydrate	26g
Dietary Fiber	5.6g
Total Sugars	9.2g
Protein	13g

Ingredients:

- 1 onion, chopped
- 4 garlic cloves, chopped
- 4 cm piece of ginger, chopped
- ½ a bunch of fresh coriander, chopped
- 2 fresh red chilies, chopped
- 1 teaspoon cumin seeds
- 1 teaspoon mustard seeds
- 1 teaspoon ground turmeric
- 1 teaspoon garam masala
- 1 teaspoon fenugreek seeds
- 1 big handful of fresh curry leaves
- Groundnut oil, for cooking
- Salt, to taste
- 2 tablespoons peanut butter
- 2 tablespoons tamarind paste
- 12 finger eggplant
- 1 x 14 ounces tin of light coconut milk
- 9 ounces ripe mixed cherry tomatoes

Instructions:

1. At 375 degrees F, preheat your oven.
2. Blend onion, ginger, garlic, chilies and coriander until smooth.
3. Sauté curry leaves, fenugreek seeds, garam masala, turmeric, mustard seeds, and cumin seeds with 2 tbsp oil in a deep-frying pan for 1 minute.
4. Stir in coriander paste and cook for 5 minutes.
5. Stir in tamarind paste, peanut butter and salt to taste.
6. Mix well and transfer to a bowl.
7. Cut the eggplant into quarters and rub them with the mango paste over the eggplant.
8. Place the eggplants in the roasting tray and sauté for 5 minutes and flip halfway through.
9. Add eggplants, coconut milk, tamarind mixture, black pepper, salt, and tomatoes to a cooking pot then cook to a boil.
10. Cover with the tin foil and roast this stew for 40 minutes.
11. Serve warm with rice on the side.

The Plant Based Cookbook For Beginners
650 Easy, Quick, & Simple Plant Based Vegan Diet Recipes With A 31 Day Meal Plan To Lose Weight & Live A Long Healthy Life

577

Dumpling Soup

SERVINGS	PREPARATION TIME	COOKING TIME
4	20 minutes	10 minutes

Nutritional Values Per Serving

Calories	311
Total Fat	14g
Saturated Fat	12g
Cholesterol	11mg
Sodium	344mg
Total Carbohydrate	26g
Dietary Fiber	0.8g
Total Sugars	2.9g
Protein	7.4g

Ingredients:

- 2 tbsp olive oil
- 2 shallots diced
- 1½ tsp fresh thyme chopped
- ½ tsp salt
- 1 bay leaf
- 6 cups vegetable broth
- 3 tbsp balsamic vinegar
- 1 cup all-purpose flour

- 1 tsp salt
- ½ tsp garlic powder
- 2 tsp baking powder
- 1 tbsp olive oil

Garnish

- Fresh parsley

Instructions:

1. Sauté shallots with olive oil in a suitable stock pot for 5 minutes.
2. Stir in thyme, salt, bay leaf, broth and vinegar.
3. Cook this mixture to a boil on medium high heat.
4. Meanwhile, mix flour with salt, garlic powder, baking powder, olive oil and enough water to make a smooth dough.
5. Make 2-inch round dumplings out of this dough.
6. Drop the dumplings into the broth and cook on medium high heat.
7. Garnish with parsley.
8. Serve warm.

578

The Plant Based Cookbook For Beginners
650 Easy, Quick, & Simple Plant Based Vegan Diet Recipes With A 31 Day Meal Plan To Lose Weight & Live A Long Healthy Life

Eggplant Penne Arrabbiata

SERVINGS	PREPARATION TIME	COOKING TIME
4	20 minutes	25 minutes

Nutritional Values Per Serving

Calories	362
Total Fat	11g
Saturated Fat	21g
Cholesterol	10mg
Sodium	133mg
Total Carbohydrate	21g
Dietary Fiber	5.2g
Total Sugars	1.9g
Protein	13g

Ingredients:

- 12 fresh mixed-color chilies
- 2 eggplant
- 1 tablespoon olive oil
- 10 ½ ounces dried whole-wheat penne
- 4 garlic cloves
- 1 (14 ounces) can plum tomatoes

Garnish

- Fresh basil

Instructions:

1. Sauté chilies with olive oil in a suitable skillet on medium-low heat for 30 seconds, then leave.

2. Boil the penne pasta in salted water as per the package's instructions, then drain.

3. Blanch the eggplant in hot water, cover and leave for 5 minutes, then drain.

4. Remove the chilies from the oil and add 2 tbsp chili oil to another pan.

5. Chop the eggplant and toss it with salt.

6. Add them to the pan and add garlic, then sauté for 2 minutes.

7. Stir in tomatoes and fill half of the tomato can tin with water then add to the pan and cook on a simmer until soft.

8. Drain the pasta and add them to the sauce then mix well.

9. Garnish with fresh basil and serve.

The Plant Based Cookbook For Beginners
650 Easy, Quick, & Simple Plant Based Vegan Diet Recipes With A 31 Day Meal Plan To Lose Weight & Live A Long Healthy Life

579

Sicilian Eggplant Stew

SERVINGS	PREPARATION TIME	COOKING TIME
4	10 minutes	34 minutes

Nutritional Values Per Serving

Calories	338
Total Fat	15g
Saturated Fat	8g
Cholesterol	0mg
Sodium	232mg
Total Carbohydrate	18g
Dietary Fiber	13.9g
Total Sugars	5.7g
Protein	14.2g

Ingredients:

- 1 large eggplant, peeled and diced
- 1 tablespoon olive oil
- ½ teaspoon dried oregano
- 1 small red onion, chopped
- 1 garlic clove, chopped
- ½ bunch flat-leaf parsley
- 2 large tomatoes, chopped
- 1 tablespoon baby capers
- 8 green olives, pitted
- 1 tablespoon red wine vinegar
- Salt, to taste
- 4 oz. whole-wheat couscous

Garnish

- 1 tablespoon flaked almonds
- Fresh Parsley

Instructions:

1. Toss eggplant with oil, salt to taste, and oregano in a pan and sauté for 5 minutes.
2. Stir in garlic, onion and parsley then sauté for 2 minutes.
3. Add olives, vinegar, and capers, and cook until vinegar is evaporated.
4. Stir in tomatoes then cook for 15 minutes on a simmer.
5. Prepare the couscous as per the package's instructions.
6. Toast almonds in another skillet for 2 minutes then keep them aside.
7. Serve the eggplant stew with couscous and garnish with almonds and parsley

580

The Plant Based Cookbook For Beginners
650 Easy, Quick, & Simple Plant Based Vegan Diet Recipes With A 31 Day Meal Plan To Lose Weight & Live A Long Healthy Life

Cauliflower Dhal

SERVINGS	PREPARATION TIME	COOKING TIME
4	10 minutes	42 minutes

Nutritional Values Per Serving

Calories	287
Total Fat	7g
Saturated Fat	2.1g
Cholesterol	10mg
Sodium	327mg
Total Carbohydrate	26g
Dietary Fiber	8g
Total Sugars	2.4g
Protein	9g

Ingredients:

- 4 shallots, sliced
- 1 garlic clove, peeled and sliced
- 1 small cauliflower, florets
- 1 tablespoon groundnut oil, to cook
- 1 small handful of curry leaves
- 2 teaspoons mustard seeds
- ½ a dried red chili
- 1 cup water
- 10 ½ ounces yellow split peas
- 2 x 14 ounces tins coconut milk

Instructions:

1. Sauté shallots and garlic with oil, mustard seeds, curry leaves, and chili in a suitable pan for 2 minutes.
2. Stir in split peas, coconut milk, cauliflower, and water, then cook to a boil.
3. Cook on a simmer for 40 minutes with occasional stirring.
4. Serve.

The Plant Based Cookbook For Beginners
650 Easy, Quick, & Simple Plant Based Vegan Diet Recipes With A 31 Day Meal Plan To Lose Weight & Live A Long Healthy Life

581

Grilled Red Chili Cauliflower

SERVINGS	PREPARATION TIME	COOKING TIME
4	15 minutes	28 minutes

Nutritional Values Per Serving

Calories	366
Total Fat	8.6g
Saturated Fat	3g
Cholesterol	21mg
Sodium	146mg
Total Carbohydrate	24g
Dietary Fiber	4g
Total Sugars	15.2g
Protein	5.8g

Ingredients:

- 3 banana shallots, chopped
- 1 tablespoon olive oil
- 1 large cauliflower, cut into steaks
- 1 teaspoon ground dried red chili
- 2 x 14 ounces tins cannellini beans
- Salt, to taste
- Arugula, chopped

Instructions:

1. Sauté shallots with ½ tbsp oil in a deep skillet for 15 minutes until golden, then transfer to a plate.
2. Cook cauliflower in boiling salted water for 3 minutes, then drain.
3. Transfer to a bowl, then toss in ½ tbsp oil, salt to taste and chili.
4. Add beans and 4 tbsp of bean liquid to a pan and cook for 10 minutes.
5. Mash them lightly, then keep it aside.
6. Set a suitable griddle pan over high heat and grill the cauliflower for 8 minutes until golden brown.
7. Divide the bean mash into four serving plates and top them with cauliflower.
8. Garnish with arugula, shallots and herb oil.
9. Serve warm.

582

The Plant Based Cookbook For Beginners
650 Easy, Quick, & Simple Plant Based Vegan Diet Recipes With A 31 Day Meal Plan To Lose Weight & Live A Long Healthy Life

Beetroot Carpaccio

SERVINGS	PREPARATION TIME	COOKING TIME
4	10 minutes	42 minutes

Nutritional Values Per Serving	
Calories	363
Total Fat	11.1g
Saturated Fat	3.8g
Cholesterol	0mg
Sodium	650mg
Total Carbohydrate	23g
Dietary Fiber	2g
Total Sugars	1.6g
Protein	7g

Ingredients:

- 8 medium beetroots
- 2 limes, juiced
- ½ a bunch of fresh dill, chopped
- 1 red onion, chopped
- 2 teaspoons caster sugar
- 2 tablespoons olive oil
- 1 tablespoon capers , drained and rinsed
- Salt, to taste

Instructions:

1. Cook beets in a large saucepan with water to a boil, reduce its heat, cover and cook for 40 minutes, then drain.
2. Peel and slice into thin rounds.
3. Sauté onion with oil, sugar, lime juice, dill, caper, and salt to taste in a pan until soft.
4. Stir in beetroots and sauté for 2 minutes.
5. Serve.

The Plant Based Cookbook For Beginners
650 Easy, Quick, & Simple Plant Based Vegan Diet Recipes With A 31 Day Meal Plan To Lose Weight & Live A Long Healthy Life

583

Vegan Mushroom Pie

SERVINGS	PREPARATION TIME	COOKING TIME
6	25 minutes	54 minutes

Nutritional Values Per Serving

Calories	450
Total Fat	7.8g
Saturated Fat	4.1g
Cholesterol	0mg
Sodium	150mg
Total Carbohydrate	30g
Dietary Fiber	5.2g
Total Sugars	12.8g
Protein	16g

Ingredients:

- 21 ounces potatoes, peeled and chopped
- 21 ounces sweet potatoes, peeled and chopped
- Vegan margarine for cooking
- 1 onion, chopped
- 2 carrots, chopped
- 3 garlic cloves, chopped
- 2 sticks of celery, chopped
- 1 tablespoon coriander seeds
- 2 tablespoons olive oil
- ½ a bunch of fresh thyme, chopped
- 11 ounces chestnut mushrooms, chopped
- 2 tablespoons balsamic vinegar
- ¼ cup organic vegetable stock
- 14 ounces can of lentils
- 14 ounces can of chickpeas
- 5 sprigs of fresh flat-leaf parsley
- 2 sprigs of fresh rosemary
- 1 lemon, for zest
- Salt, to taste
- 1 ounces fresh breadcrumbs

Instructions:

1. At 400 degrees F, preheat your oven.
2. Add chopped potatoes to a pan with salted water and cook for 15 minutes on a simmer.
3. Stir in sweet potatoes, and mushrooms then cook for 5 minutes.
4. Drain and mash the potatoes with 1 tbsp vegan margarine and salt to taste in a bowl.
5. Sauté coriander seeds with 1 tbsp oil and thyme in a pan for 1 minute.
6. Stir in onion, celery, carrots, and garlic then sauté for 10 minutes.
7. Stir in chickpeas, stock and lentils then cook for 5 minutes.
8. Spread this mixture in a baking dish, add cilantro and spread the potato mash on top.
9. Mix breadcrumbs with 1 tbsp oil, lemon zest and rosemary in a bowl and spread over the potato mash.
10. Bake the pie for 10 minutes in the oven and broil for 3 minutes.
11. Serve warm.

584

The Plant Based Cookbook For Beginners
650 Easy, Quick, & Simple Plant Based Vegan Diet Recipes With A 31 Day Meal Plan To Lose Weight & Live A Long Healthy Life

Turkish-Style Couscous

SERVINGS | PREPARATION TIME | COOKING TIME
4 | 15 minutes | 10 minutes

Nutritional Values Per Serving

Calories	315
Total Fat	17g
Saturated Fat	6g
Cholesterol	23mg
Sodium	116mg
Total Carbohydrate	28g
Dietary Fiber	4.1g
Total Sugars	1.3g
Protein	8g

Ingredients:

- 9 ounces couscous
- 18 ounces boiling water
- 1 teaspoon ground cumin
- 1 teaspoon smoked paprika
- Pinch of sea salt
- Black pepper, to taste
- 1 medium red onion, peeled and chopped
- 1 medium cucumber, chopped
- 2 ripe tomatoes, chopped
- 1 fresh red chili, chopped
- 1 bunch of fresh mint, chopped
- ½ bunch of fresh coriander, chopped
- 1 bunch parsley, chopped
- 1 tablespoon tomato purée
- 2 tablespoons olive oil
- ½ lemon, zest and juice

Instructions:

1. Mix couscous with cumin, a pinch of salt and paprika in a bowl.
2. Pour in boiling water to cover the couscous and leave for 10 minutes.
3. Drain the cooked couscous and leave it for 10 minutes in a strainer.
4. Mix couscous with tomato puree and the rest of the ingredients in a bowl.
5. Serve.

The Plant Based Cookbook For Beginners
650 Easy, Quick, & Simple Plant Based Vegan Diet Recipes With A 31 Day Meal Plan To Lose Weight & Live A Long Healthy Life

585

Briam

SERVINGS	PREPARATION TIME	COOKING TIME
4	15 minutes	72 minutes

Nutritional Values Per Serving

Calories	384
Total Fat	19g
Saturated Fat	20g
Cholesterol	13mg
Sodium	556mg
Total Carbohydrate	29g
Dietary Fiber	6.1g
Total Sugars	7g
Protein	14g

Ingredients:

- ½ cup olive oil
- 1 large eggplant, sliced
- 1 large onion, chopped
- 3 garlic cloves, chopped
- 28 ounces large potatoes, peeled, chopped
- 6 medium tomatoes, chopped
- 12 cherry tomatoes, chopped
- 5 zucchinis, sliced
- 10 ½ ounces tomato passata
- 1 tablespoon dried oregano
- ½ a bunch of fresh flat-leaf parsley, chopped

Instructions:

1. At 425 degrees F, preheat your oven.
2. Sauté eggplant with olive oil in a deep pan for 7 minutes until golden brown.
3. Transfer them to a plate and keep them aside.
4. Sauté onion and garlic with oil in a skillet for 5 minutes, then add to the eggplant.
5. Add 1 cup water, passata, zucchinis, parsley, salt, oregano, tomatoes and potato to the pan.
6. Stir in the eggplant mixture and bake for 30 minutes.
7. Reduce the oven's heat to 400 degrees F and then continue baking for 30 minutes.
8. Serve warm.

586

The Plant Based Cookbook For Beginners
650 Easy, Quick, & Simple Plant Based Vegan Diet Recipes With A 31 Day Meal Plan To Lose Weight & Live A Long Healthy Life

Crunchy Carrot Pittas

SERVINGS
4

PREPARATION TIME
5 minutes

COOKING TIME
4 minutes

Nutritional Values Per Serving

Calories	371
Total Fat	11g
Saturated Fat	6g
Cholesterol	12mg
Sodium	417mg
Total Carbohydrate	30.3g
Dietary Fiber	9g
Total Sugars	4.3g
Protein	12g

Ingredients:

- 6 whole meal pittas
- 6 medium carrots, julienned
- a bunch of fresh coriander, chopped
- 2 tablespoons sesame seeds
- 1 tablespoon poppy seeds
- 1 orange, zest
- 1 teaspoon olive oil
- 2 lemons, zest and juice
- 1 cucumber, sliced
- Sea salt, to taste
- Black pepper, to taste

Instructions:

1. At 250 degrees F, preheat your oven.
2. Sauté poppy seeds with oil in a pan for 4 minutes.
3. Mix carrots with seeds and the rest of the ingredients except pittas.
4. Open the pittas from one side and add the carrots and cucumber to stuff the pittas.
5. Serve.

The Plant Based Cookbook For Beginners
650 Easy, Quick, & Simple Plant Based Vegan Diet Recipes With A 31 Day Meal Plan To Lose Weight & Live A Long Healthy Life

587

Mushrooms with Posh Vinegar

SERVINGS	PREPARATION TIME	COOKING TIME
4	10 minutes	4 minutes

Nutritional Values Per Serving

Calories	394
Total Fat	9g
Saturated Fat	1.6g
Cholesterol	0mg
Sodium	455mg
Total Carbohydrate	31g
Dietary Fiber	1.7g
Total Sugars	2.1g
Protein	6g

Ingredients:

- 4 sprigs fresh tarragon
- 2 sprigs fresh thyme
- 6 white peppercorns
- 2 garlic cloves, peeled and sliced
- 2 cups white wine vinegar
- 1-litre olive oil
- 3 ½ ounces plain flour
- 1 teaspoon sea salt, or to taste
- ½ teaspoon black pepper, or to taste
- 1 lemon, zest
- 4 large handfuls of mixed mushrooms
- 1 small bunch of fresh flat-leaf parsley

Instructions:

1. Mix thyme, mushrooms, garlic, peppercorns, tarragon and vinegar in a bowl, cover and leave for 1 hour.

2. Drain the marinated mushrooms and keep them in a colander for 10 minutes.

3. Mix flour, black pepper, salt, mushrooms and lemon zest in a bowl to coat well.

4. Add oil to a deep skillet and fry the mushrooms for 4 minutes.

5. Serve.

588

The Plant Based Cookbook For Beginners
650 Easy, Quick, & Simple Plant Based Vegan Diet Recipes With A 31 Day Meal Plan To Lose Weight & Live A Long Healthy Life

Tray-Baked Artichokes

SERVINGS	PREPARATION TIME	COOKING TIME
4	10 minutes	30 minutes

Nutritional Values Per Serving

Calories	330
Total Fat	4.9g
Saturated Fat	1.1g
Cholesterol	0mg
Sodium	248mg
Total Carbohydrate	18.3g
Dietary Fiber	3.7g
Total Sugars	16g
Protein	6g

Ingredients:

- 8 medium-sized globe artichokes
- 1 lemon, zest and juiced
- 2 garlic cloves, chopped
- 1 handful whole almonds, chopped
- 2 handfuls coarse breadcrumbs
- 1 handful fresh mint, chopped
- 1 handful fresh parsley, chopped
- ½ teaspoon sea salt, or to taste
- ½ teaspoon black pepper, or to taste

Instructions:

1. Rub the artichokes with lemon juice.
2. At 400 degrees F, preheat your oven.
3. Toss herbs, breadcrumbs, almonds, olive oil, salt, pepper, and garlic in a bowl.
4. Stuff the artichokes with this breadcrumb mixture and place them on a baking sheet.
5. Bake them for 30 minutes in the oven.
6. Serve warm.

The Plant Based Cookbook For Beginners
650 Easy, Quick, & Simple Plant Based Vegan Diet Recipes With A 31 Day Meal Plan To Lose Weight & Live A Long Healthy Life

589

Tempeh Skewers

SERVINGS	PREPARATION TIME	COOKING TIME
4	1 hour 5 minutes	8 minutes

Nutritional Values Per Serving

Calories	246
Total Fat	0.8g
Saturated Fat	0g
Cholesterol	0mg
Sodium	1mg
Total Carbohydrate	31.1g
Dietary Fiber	1.7g
Total Sugars	59.3g
Protein	0.8g

Ingredients:

- 1 ½ tablespoons tamari
- 1 tablespoon olive oil
- 1 tablespoon brown sugar
- 2 teaspoons lime juice
- 1 teaspoon onion powder
- 1 teaspoon chili powder
- ½ teaspoon black pepper
- ½ teaspoon dried oregano
- ½ teaspoon ground cumin
- Pinch of salt, optional
- 8 ounces tempeh, cubed
- 8 ounces button mushrooms, cut in half
- 1 ½ cups red bell pepper, chopped
- 1 small zucchini, chopped
- 1 cup yellow onion, chopped

Instructions:

1. Mix all the veggies, tempeh, spices, oil, sugar, lime juice and tamari in a bowl.
2. Cover and refrigerate the mixture for 1 hour.
3. At 375 degrees F, preheat a grill.
4. Thread the veggies and tempeh on the skewers alternately.
5. Grill the tempeh skewers for 5 minutes per side.
6. Serve warm.

590

The Plant Based Cookbook For Beginners
650 Easy, Quick, & Simple Plant Based Vegan Diet Recipes With A 31 Day Meal Plan To Lose Weight & Live A Long Healthy Life

Ginger Tempeh

SERVINGS	PREPARATION TIME	COOKING TIME
4	10 minutes	24 minutes

Nutritional Values Per Serving

Calories	391
Total Fat	12g
Saturated Fat	0.7g
Cholesterol	0mg
Sodium	70mg
Total Carbohydrate	19g
Dietary Fiber	5.2g
Total Sugars	1.8g
Protein	9g

Ingredients:

- 8 ounces of tempeh, cubed
- 2 tablespoons ginger paste
- 2 tablespoons garlic paste
- 1 tablespoon sesame oil
- 1 tablespoon rice vinegar
- 4 tablespoons soy sauce
- 3 tablespoons maple syrup
- 1 tablespoon cornstarch
- 1 tablespoon peanut butter
- 3 tablespoons olive oil
- 2 cups of green beans, trimmed and chopped
- 2 green chilies, chopped
- 2 red chilies, chopped

Instructions:

1. Blend peanut butter, cornstarch, maple syrup, soy sauce, rice vinegar, sesame oil, garlic and ginger in a blender.

2. Sear the tempeh in olive oil in a large skillet for 8 minutes per side.

3. Stir in 2 tbsp of prepared sauce and mix well to coat.

4. Transfer the tempeh to a plate.

5. Sauté chilies and green beans with remaining oil in a skillet for 5 minutes.

6. Stir in the remaining sauce and cook for 3 minutes.

7. Add this mixture to the tempeh and mix well.

8. Serve warm.

The Plant Based Cookbook For Beginners
650 Easy, Quick, & Simple Plant Based Vegan Diet Recipes With A 31 Day Meal Plan To Lose Weight & Live A Long Healthy Life

591

Enchilada Zucchini Boats

SERVINGS	PREPARATION TIME	COOKING TIME
6	10 minutes	45 minutes

Nutritional Values Per Serving

Calories	340
Total Fat	14g
Saturated Fat	1.2g
Cholesterol	10mg
Sodium	359mg
Total Carbohydrate	28.2g
Dietary Fiber	4.1g
Total Sugars	3g
Protein	13g

Ingredients:

- 1 tablespoon of oil
- ½ of a sweet onion
- ½ red bell pepper
- 3 garlic cloves, minced
- ¼ teaspoon of cumin
- ¼ teaspoon of dried oregano
- ¼ teaspoon of paprika
- ¼ teaspoon of salt
- 1 (15 ounces) can black beans, rinsed
- 3 medium zucchinis
- 1 cup of enchilada sauce
- 1 cup of vegan cheese, shredded

Enchilada sauce

- 3 tablespoons olive oil
- 3 tablespoons flour
- 1 tablespoon ground chili powder
- 1 teaspoon ground cumin
- ½ teaspoon garlic powder
- ¼ teaspoon dried oregano
- ¼ teaspoon salt, to taste
- Pinch of cinnamon
- 2 tablespoons tomato paste
- 2 cups vegetable broth
- 1 teaspoon apple cider vinegar
- Freshly ground black pepper, to taste

Instructions:

1. Blend all the ingredients for enchilada sauce in a high-speed blender until smooth.
2. Pour this sauce into a saucepan and cook on a simmer for 7 minutes.
3. Remove this enchilada sauce from the heat and allow it to cool.
4. At 400 degrees F, preheat your oven.
5. Prepare a baking dish with parchment paper.
6. Cut the zucchinis in half and scoop out some flesh from the center to make boats.
7. Sauté onion and bell pepper with oil in a skillet for 5 minutes.
8. Stir in spices and garlic, then sauté for 2 minutes.
9. Add black beans and cook for 3 minutes.
10. Divide the beans mixture in the zucchini boats and place them in the baking dish.
11. Pour the enchilada sauce on top and sprinkle vegan cheese on top.
12. Bake these boats for 35 minutes in the oven.
13. Serve warm.

592

The Plant Based Cookbook For Beginners
650 Easy, Quick, & Simple Plant Based Vegan Diet Recipes With A 31 Day Meal Plan To Lose Weight & Live A Long Healthy Life

Spinach Gnocchi

SERVINGS
6

PREPARATION TIME
10 minutes

COOKING TIME
5 minutes

Nutritional Values Per Serving

Calories	216
Total Fat	3g
Saturated Fat	2.8g
Cholesterol	0mg
Sodium	751mg
Total Carbohydrate	32g
Dietary Fiber	3.8g
Total Sugars	0.4g
Protein	12g

Ingredients:

- 2 pounds of golden potatoes
- 3 ounces of fresh spinach
- ½ teaspoon of salt
- 1 ¼ cups of whole wheat flour
- Shredded vegan parmesan, to garnish

Instructions:

1. At 400 degrees F, preheat your oven.
2. Place the potatoes in a baking sheet, lined with a foil sheet and bake for 60 minutes.
3. Peel the cooked potatoes and mash them in a bowl.
4. Boil spinach in water in a pan for 3 minutes, then drain and puree the spinach in a blender.
5. Add this spinach, salt and flour to the potato mash, then mix well.
6. Divide the dough into 8 pieces and roll each piece into ½ inch thick log.
7. Cut each log into 1-inch pieces and keep them aside.
8. Add salted water to a cooking pot and boil it.
9. Stir in prepared gnocchi and cook for 30 seconds– 1 minutes.
10. Then use a slotted spoon to transfer the green gnocchi to a plate.
11. Garnish with shredded vegan parmesan cheese.
12. Serve.

The Plant Based Cookbook For Beginners
650 Easy, Quick, & Simple Plant Based Vegan Diet Recipes With A 31 Day Meal Plan To Lose Weight & Live A Long Healthy Life

593

Tempeh Fajitas

SERVINGS | **PREPARATION TIME** | **COOKING TIME**
4 | 40 minutes | 20 minutes

Nutritional Values Per Serving

Calories	372
Total Fat	0.3g
Saturated Fat	0g
Cholesterol	0mg
Sodium	2mg
Total Carbohydrate	46g
Dietary Fiber	2.3g
Total Sugars	6g
Protein	12.1g

Ingredients:

Tempeh Marinade

- 1 tablespoon lime juice
- 2 tablespoons olive oil
- 1 garlic clove, minced
- ½ teaspoon salt
- ½ teaspoon ground cumin
- ½ teaspoon chili powder
- ½ teaspoon of onion powder
- ¼ teaspoon of paprika

Fajitas

- 8-ounce package of tempeh, sliced into triangles
- 1 teaspoon olive oil
- 2 bell peppers, diced
- ½ white onion, sliced
- 4 tortillas, warmed

Instructions:

1. Mix all the tempeh marinade ingredients in a medium-sized bowl.
2. Add tempeh slices to this marinade, mix, cover and leave for 30 minutes.
3. Sauté bell peppers and onion with oil in a large skillet over medium heat for 10 minutes.
4. Add tempeh, black pepper and salt and cook it for 5 minutes per side.
5. Divide the marinade, tempeh, and bell pepper slices on top each tortilla and roll them to serve.
6. Serve warm.

594

The Plant Based Cookbook For Beginners
650 Easy, Quick, & Simple Plant Based Vegan Diet Recipes With A 31 Day Meal Plan To Lose Weight & Live A Long Healthy Life

Burrito Stuffed Peppers

SERVINGS	PREPARATION TIME	COOKING TIME
4	10 minutes	30 minutes

Nutritional Values Per Serving

Calories	361
Total Fat	14.7g
Saturated Fat	12.8g
Cholesterol	0mg
Sodium	161mg
Total Carbohydrate	23g
Dietary Fiber	2.7g
Total Sugars	2.6g
Protein	8g

Ingredients:

- 1 can of black beans
- 1 ½ cups of uncooked brown rice
- 1 cup of sweet corn
- 4 bell peppers
- 1 teaspoon salt, or to taste
- 1 cup vegan cheese, shredded

Serving

- Cilantro
- Salsa
- Vegan sour cream

Instructions:

1. At 350 degrees F, preheat your oven.
2. Prepare a baking tray with foil around it.
3. Boil the rice as per the package's instruction.
4. Add beans, corn, black pepper and salt to the rice in a bowl and mix.
5. Cut the bell peppers in half, then remove their seeds.
6. Stuff each of these peppers with a rice mixture and place them in a baking dish.
7. Sprinkle vegan cheese on top and bake for 10 minutes.
8. Garnish with salsa, sour cream and cilantro.
9. Enjoy.

The Plant Based Cookbook For Beginners
650 Easy, Quick, & Simple Plant Based Vegan Diet Recipes With A 31 Day Meal Plan To Lose Weight & Live A Long Healthy Life

595

Tofu Banh Mi Sandwich

SERVINGS	PREPARATION TIME	COOKING TIME
2	1 hour 10 minutes	10 minutes

Nutritional Values Per Serving

Calories	350
Total Fat	11g
Saturated Fat	12g
Cholesterol	23mg
Sodium	340mg
Total Carbohydrate	20g
Dietary Fiber	1.7g
Total Sugars	3.1g
Protein	7g

Ingredients:

Pickled Vegetables

- 3 carrots, peeled and julienned
- 1 English cucumber, sliced
- 1 teaspoon of salt
- ½ cup of rice vinegar
- ½ cup apple cider vinegar
- ½ cup of water
- 2 tablespoons of sugar

Tofu

- 1 inch of ginger, peeled and minced
- 1 garlic clove, minced
- 2 tablespoons of soy sauce
- ½ tablespoon of sesame oil
- ½ package of tofu, sliced
- 1 tablespoon of sesame seeds

Sandwich

- 1 handful of parsley, chopped
- 1 carrot, julienned
- 2 tablespoons of mayo
- 1 tablespoon of sriracha sauce
- 2 pieces of fresh French bread

Instructions:

1. Add all the pickled veggies ingredients to a mason jar, cover and refrigerate for 1 hour.
2. Mix tofu with sesame oil, soy sauce, garlic and ginger in a bowl, cover and marinate for 10 minutes.
3. Add tofu with its sesame oil marinade to a large skillet and cook the tofu for 5 minutes per side.
4. Sprinkle sesame seeds on top.
5. Toast the bread slices in a pan and top them with sriracha sauce and mayo.
6. Add pickled veggies and tofu on top of half of the bread slices.
7. Add carrots and parsley on top.
8. Place the remaining bread slices on top.
9. Serve.

596

The Plant Based Cookbook For Beginners
650 Easy, Quick, & Simple Plant Based Vegan Diet Recipes With A 31 Day Meal Plan To Lose Weight & Live A Long Healthy Life

Spinach Stuffed Shells

SERVINGS	PREPARATION TIME	COOKING TIME
4	10 minutes	35 minutes

Nutritional Values Per Serving

Calories	340
Total Fat	14g
Saturated Fat	8g
Cholesterol	17mg
Sodium	310mg
Total Carbohydrate	22g
Dietary Fiber	4g
Total Sugars	7g
Protein	19g

Ingredients:

- 12 ounces of jumbo shells
- 10 ounces of spinach
- 1 batch of vegan ricotta
- ½ teaspoon of dried oregano
- 1 ½ cups of marinara sauce

Instructions:

1. At 350 degrees F, preheat your oven.
2. Grease a baking dish with cooking spray.
3. Boil the pasta shells as per the package's instruction until soft then drain.
4. Mix vegan ricotta with spinach and oregano in a bowl.
5. Spread half of the marinara sauce in a baking dish.
6. Stuff the vegan ricotta mixture and place them in the baking dish.
7. Pour the remaining marinara sauce over the stuffed shells and bake for 25 minutes.
8. Garnish with some more cheese on top and serve warm.

The Plant Based Cookbook For Beginners
650 Easy, Quick, & Simple Plant Based Vegan Diet Recipes With A 31 Day Meal Plan To Lose Weight & Live A Long Healthy Life

597

Smoked Tomato Pasta

SERVINGS	PREPARATION TIME	COOKING TIME
4	10 minutes	10 minutes

Nutritional Values Per Serving

Calories	285
Total Fat	8g
Saturated Fat	3g
Cholesterol	11mg
Sodium	168mg
Total Carbohydrate	19g
Dietary Fiber	3.7g
Total Sugars	3.4g
Protein	9g

Ingredients:

- 1 lb. of pasta
- ¾ cup of cashews, soaked
- 1½ cups of vegetable broth
- 1 can of tomato sauce
- ¾ cup of sun-dried tomatoes
- ½ teaspoon of salt
- Pinch of pepper
- ¼ teaspoon of garlic powder
- ¼ cup of nutritional yeast

Instructions:

1. Boil the dry pasta in salted water as per the package's instructions.
2. Blend cashews with vegetable broth in a blender for 2 minutes.
3. Add tomato sauce, tomatoes, yeast, garlic powder, black pepper and salt then blend again.
4. Mix this sauce with pasta in a bowl.
5. Serve.

598

The Plant Based Cookbook For Beginners
650 Easy, Quick, & Simple Plant Based Vegan Diet Recipes With A 31 Day Meal Plan To Lose Weight & Live A Long Healthy Life

Spinach Artichoke Pasta

SERVINGS	PREPARATION TIME	COOKING TIME
6	10 minutes	25 minutes

Nutritional Values Per Serving	
Calories	242
Total Fat	3g
Saturated Fat	10g
Cholesterol	12mg
Sodium	281mg
Total Carbohydrate	21g
Dietary Fiber	3.7g
Total Sugars	1.6g
Protein	13g

Ingredients:

- 12 ounces box of gluten-free penne
- 4 cups spinach
- 1 (12 ounces) jar of artichoke hearts, chopped
- ½ cup sweet onion, chopped
- 2 teaspoons olive oil
- 1 teaspoon garlic, minced
- 8 ounces vegan cream cheese
- ¼ teaspoon black pepper, or to taste
- ½ cup unsweetened coconut yogurt
- 1 teaspoon lemon juice
- ½ cup vegan mozzarella shreds
- ¼ cup homemade vegan parmesan cheese

Instructions:

1. At 375 degrees F, preheat your oven.

2. Boil the pasta as per the package's instruction, then drain.

3. Sauté artichokes with garlic, black pepper, onion, spinach and oil in a skillet until soft.

4. Mix coconut yogurt with lemon juice in a bowl.

5. Add vegan cream cheese, yogurt mixture and vegan mozzarella cheese to the artichokes.

6. Stir in cooked pasta, mix well and bake for 15 minutes in a baking dish.

7. Serve warm.

The Plant Based Cookbook For Beginners
650 Easy, Quick, & Simple Plant Based Vegan Diet Recipes With A 31 Day Meal Plan To Lose Weight & Live A Long Healthy Life

599

Butternut Squash Au Gratin

SERVINGS	PREPARATION TIME	COOKING TIME
6	10 minutes	50 minutes

Nutritional Values Per Serving

Calories	446
Total Fat	9g
Saturated Fat	10g
Cholesterol	12mg
Sodium	312mg
Total Carbohydrate	32g
Dietary Fiber	0.3g
Total Sugars	7.9g
Protein	8g

Ingredients:

- 2 medium butternut squash, sliced
- 1 large onion, sliced
- 1 cup grated vegan parmesan
- 1 green chili, chopped
- handful of fresh sage, chopped
- 1 cup of almond milk
- 3 tablespoons of vegetable stock
- ½ tablespoon of garlic powder
- 1 teaspoon black pepper
- 1 teaspoon salt
- ¼ cup breadcrumbs

Instructions:

1. At 400 degrees F, preheat your oven.
2. Toss butternut squash with onion, green chili, black pepper and salt in a baking pan.
3. Mix veggie stock and almond milk in a bowl and pour over the squash.
4. Mix breadcrumbs with parmesan, sage, and garlic powder then sprinkle over the veggies.
5. Bake the veggie mixture for 50 minutes in the oven.
6. Serve warm.

600

The Plant Based Cookbook For Beginners
650 Easy, Quick, & Simple Plant Based Vegan Diet Recipes With A 31 Day Meal Plan To Lose Weight & Live A Long Healthy Life

Artichoke Bruschetta

SERVINGS	PREPARATION TIME	COOKING TIME
4	15 minutes	10 minutes

Nutritional Values Per Serving

Calories	319
Total Fat	5g
Saturated Fat	3.1g
Cholesterol	14mg
Sodium	354mg
Total Carbohydrate	29g
Dietary Fiber	7g
Total Sugars	5g
Protein	7g

Serving Suggestion:

Enjoy the bruschetta alongside baked tofu.

Ingredients:

- 8 baby artichokes
- 1 avocado
- 4 garlic cloves, sliced
- 1 white onion, sliced
- 1 lemon, juiced
- Olive oil
- 1 pinch of salt, or to taste
- 1 bunch of fresh mint, chopped

Bruschetta

- 1 large loaf, sliced
- 1 garlic clove, sliced
- Olive oil, to grease

Garnish

- Baby spinach leaves
- Black pepper

Instructions:

1. Sauté artichokes with onion, garlic and 3 tbsp of oil in a skillet for 4 minutes.

2. Stir in mint, lemon juice and salt then mix well.

3. Mash the artichoke and avocado with a potato masher in a bowl and set aside.

4. Rub the bread slices with garlic and oil then sear them for 3 minutes per side in a pan until golden brown.

5. Spread the mashed artichokes and avocado over the bread slices.

6. Garnish with spinach and black pepper.

7. Serve.

The Plant Based Cookbook For Beginners
650 Easy, Quick, & Simple Plant Based Vegan Diet Recipes With A 31 Day Meal Plan To Lose Weight & Live A Long Healthy Life

601

Tofu Wrapped in Collard Leaves

SERVINGS	PREPARATION TIME	COOKING TIME
4	10 minutes	20 minutes

Nutritional Values Per Serving

Calories	386
Total Fat	9g
Saturated Fat	10.3g
Cholesterol	14mg
Sodium	322mg
Total Carbohydrate	32g
Dietary Fiber	3.8g
Total Sugars	4.6g
Protein	17g

Ingredients:

Jerk Marinade

- 1 cup yellow onion, chopped
- 3 green onions, sliced
- 1 tablespoon fresh ginger, minced
- 1 tablespoon garlic, minced
- 2 tablespoons muscovado sugar
- 1 tablespoon ground allspice
- 1 teaspoon nutmeg, grated
- 1 tablespoon black pepper
- 1 pinch of cayenne pepper
- 2 Scotch bonnet chiles, seeded, and minced
- 2 tablespoons lime juice
- 2 tablespoons apple cider vinegar
- 6 tablespoons shoyu
- ¼ cup coconut oil
- 2 tablespoons fresh thyme, minced
- 1 teaspoon sea salt, or to taste

Garlic Oil

- ¾ cup olive oil
- 16 large garlic cloves, sliced

Cilantro Sauce

- 2 garlic cloves, minced
- 3 tablespoons olive oil
- ¼ teaspoon ground coriander
- ¼ teaspoon sea salt
- 1 cup fresh cilantro leaves

Dish

- 2 (16-ounce) blocks tofu, sliced
- 2 cups Jerk Marinade
- 1 carrot, sliced
- 1 cucumber, julienned
- 1 tablespoon 2 teaspoons sea salt
- 16 collard green leaves, stem removed
- 1 cup arrowroot powder
- ¼ cup garlic chips

Instructions:

1. Blend all the jerk marinade ingredients in a blender and keep it aside.
2. Sauté garlic with oil in a skillet for 10 minutes then strain from the oil.
3. Keep the garlic oil and garlic chips aside.
4. Sauté garlic with oil, salt and coriander in a small skillet for 1½ minute, then remove from the heat.
5. Blend this mixture with jalapeno, ¼ cup water, lemon juice and cilantro in a blender until smooth to make a cilantro sauce.
6. Drain the tofu liquid and cut it into four pieces.
7. Place the tofu pieces in a baking dish and pour the jerk marinade on top.
8. Cover and refrigerate for 8 hours, then remove the tofu from the marinade.
9. Boil collard leaves in 2 quarts of water with 1 tbsp salt in a cooking pot for 30 seconds, then drain.
10. Mix arrowroot with the remaining 2 tsp salt and coat the tofu with this mixture.
11. Sear the tofu in 1 tbsp peanut oil in a skillet for 3 minutes per side.
12. Place the two green leaves overlapping on the working surface.
13. Add 2 tbsp cilantro sauce, one tofu slice, cucumber, carrot slices, ¼ garlic oil, 1 tsp garlic chips and wrap the leaves around to make a roll.
14. Repeat the same steps with the remaining leaves and fillings.
15. Serve.

602

The Plant Based Cookbook For Beginners
650 Easy, Quick, & Simple Plant Based Vegan Diet Recipes With A 31 Day Meal Plan To Lose Weight & Live A Long Healthy Life

Piri Piri Vegetable Bake

SERVINGS
4

PREPARATION TIME
10 minutes

COOKING TIME
30 minutes

Nutritional Values Per Serving

Calories	378
Total Fat	9g
Saturated Fat	11g
Cholesterol	13mg
Sodium	5mg
Total Carbohydrate	23g
Dietary Fiber	4.1g
Total Sugars	2.7g
Protein	12g

Ingredients:

Bake

- 2 sweet potatoes, peeled and cubed
- 1 tablespoon olive oil, to cook
- 1 lemon, juiced
- 1 red bell pepper, diced
- 1 green bell pepper, diced
- 1 yellow bell pepper, diced
- 3 garlic cloves, chopped
- 7 oounces canned tomatoes, chopped
- ¾ ounces cilantro, chopped
- ½ teaspoon salt, or to taste
- ½ teaspoon black pepper, or to taste

Piri Piri Sauce

- 1 red onion, chopped
- 4 garlic cloves, chopped
- 1 red bell pepper, chopped
- 2 red chiles, chopped
- 2 tablespoons smoked paprika
- 1 teaspoon dried oregano
- 2 tablespoons red wine vinegar
- 1 large bunch of fresh basil, chopped
- 1 lemon, juiced

Instructions:

1. At 350 degrees F, preheat your oven.

2. Toss potatoes with garlic, peppers, lemon juice, oil, black pepper and salt in a baking sheet.

3. Roast these veggies for 15 minutes in the oven.

4. Blend all the Piri piri sauce ingredients in a blender until smooth.

5. Add tomatoes and piri-piri sauce to the veggies. Mix well and roast for 15 minutes.

6. Serve warm.

The Plant Based Cookbook For Beginners
650 Easy, Quick, & Simple Plant Based Vegan Diet Recipes With A 31 Day Meal Plan To Lose Weight & Live A Long Healthy Life

603

Cuban Rice and Beans

SERVINGS	PREPARATION TIME	COOKING TIME
4	10 minutes	45 minutes

Nutritional Values Per Serving

Calories	385
Total Fat	8g
Saturated Fat	3g
Cholesterol	23mg
Sodium	132mg
Total Carbohydrate	26g
Dietary Fiber	4g
Total Sugars	3g
Protein	11g

Ingredients:

- 1 red bell pepper, diced
- 1 large onion, halved and sliced
- 1 tomato, chopped
- 3 garlic cloves, sliced
- 1 tablespoon olive oil
- 1 teaspoon salt
- 1 cup long-grain white rice
- 2 (15-ounce) cans black beans, rinsed
- 1 teaspoon ground cumin
- 1 teaspoon dried oregano
- ½ teaspoon ground fennel
- ½ teaspoon ground coriander

Instructions:

1. At 400 degrees F, preheat your oven.
2. Grease a sheet pan with cooking spray.
3. Toss onion with garlic, ¼ tsp salt, oil and bell peppers in a medium bowl.
4. Spread this mixture in a pan and roast for 15 minutes.
5. Mix rice, 2 ½ cups water, ¾ tsp salt, tomato, coriander, fennel, oregano, cumin and beans in a bowl.
6. Add this mixture to the pan, mix well, and cover with a foil and bake again for 30 minutes.
7. Serve warm.

604

The Plant Based Cookbook For Beginners
650 Easy, Quick, & Simple Plant Based Vegan Diet Recipes With A 31 Day Meal Plan To Lose Weight & Live A Long Healthy Life

Carrot Curry

SERVINGS	PREPARATION TIME	COOKING TIME
4	10 minutes	70 minutes

Nutritional Values Per Serving

Calories	380
Total Fat	14g
Saturated Fat	6g
Cholesterol	12mg
Sodium	155mg
Total Carbohydrate	19g
Dietary Fiber	1.7g
Total Sugars	1.1g
Protein	9g

Ingredients:

- 10-star anise pods
- 8 cardamom pods
- 2 cinnamon sticks
- 1½ tablespoons garam masala
- 2 pounds pureed tomatoes
- 2 tablespoons canola oil
- 6 shallots, minced
- 4 cups carrot juice
- ¼ cup fresh lime juice
- Pinch of saffron threads
- 1⅓ cups unsweetened coconut milk
- Kosher salt, to taste
- 8 carrots, peeled and diced

Garnish

- Cilantro leaves
- Lime juice and zest
- Rice

Instructions:

1. Toast garam masala, cinnamon sticks, cardamom and star anise in a skillet for 30 seconds on medium-high heat then transfer to a plate.
2. Sauté shallots with oil in a skillet for 3 minutes.
3. Stir in toasted whole spices, tomato puree, lime juice and carrot juice then cook on a simmer for 30 minutes.
4. Stir in saffron then cook for 1 minute.
5. Add coconut milk and remove it from the heat and discard the toasted whole spice.
6. Puree this mixture until smooth with a hand blender.
7. Stir in carrots, cover and cook for 35 minutes until soft.
8. Garnish with lime zest, cilantro and lime juice.
9. Serve warm with rice.

The Plant Based Cookbook For Beginners
650 Easy, Quick, & Simple Plant Based Vegan Diet Recipes With A 31 Day Meal Plan To Lose Weight & Live A Long Healthy Life

605

Falafel Mushroom Loaf

SERVINGS	PREPARATION TIME	COOKING TIME
6	10 minutes	96 minutes

Nutritional Values Per Serving

Calories	247
Total Fat	4.9g
Saturated Fat	14g
Cholesterol	194mg
Sodium	407mg
Total Carbohydrate	27g
Dietary Fiber	4g
Total Sugars	1.3g
Protein	16g

Ingredients:

Meatloaf

- 2 ½ pounds mixed wild mushrooms, trimmed
- 1 medium onion, chopped
- 1 garlic clove, peeled, smashed
- 1 teaspoon ground coriander
- 1 teaspoon ground cumin
- ½ teaspoon ground cardamom
- 2 tablespoons vegetable oil
- 1 (15-ounce) can chickpeas, rinsed, drained
- 1 tablespoon flaxseed
- 1 tablespoon water
- ¾ cup chickpea flour
- ¾ cup cilantro, chopped
- ½ cup parsley, chopped
- 2 teaspoons salt, to taste

Tahini Sauce

- 1 garlic clove, peeled
- ½ cup tahini
- 1 tablespoon dried herbs
- 5 tablespoons lemon juice
- 1 teaspoon salt, to taste

Instructions:

1. Mix flaxseed with water in a bowl and leave for 5 minutes
2. At 350 degrees F, preheat your oven. Grease an 8 ½ x 4 ½ inch loaf pan with cooking spray.
3. Blend mushrooms with cumin, cardamom, coriander, garlic and onion in a food processor for 45 seconds.
4. Sauté this mushroom mixture with oil in a skillet for 5 minutes.
5. Blend chickpeas with mushroom mixture, flaxseed mixture, chickpea flour, parsley, salt and cilantro in a food processor.
6. Spread this meatloaf mixture in the loaf pan and bake for 90 minutes.
7. Allow the meatloaf to cool.
8. Blend the tahini sauce ingredients in a blender until smooth.
9. Slice the meatloaf and top each slice with tahini sauce.
10. Serve warm.

 606

The Plant Based Cookbook For Beginners
650 Easy, Quick, & Simple Plant Based Vegan Diet Recipes With A 31 Day Meal Plan To Lose Weight & Live A Long Healthy Life

Tofu in Shiitake Broth

SERVINGS	PREPARATION TIME	COOKING TIME
4	10 minutes	39 minutes

Nutritional Values Per Serving

Calories	288
Total Fat	12g
Saturated Fat	6g
Cholesterol	13mg
Sodium	208mg
Total Carbohydrate	31g
Dietary Fiber	2g
Total Sugars	2.1g
Protein	18g

Serving Suggestion:

Serve the tofu bowl with vegetable lo-Mein or boiled rice.

Ingredients:

- ¼ cup 2 tablespoons soy sauce
- 1 tablespoon light brown sugar
- 1 (12-ounce) package firm tofu, drained
- 3 green onions, chopped
- 4 tablespoons red Thai curry paste
- 12 shiitake mushrooms, rinsed, chopped
- 2 (4x3-inch) pieces dried kombu
- 1 (3-inch) piece ginger, peeled, sliced
- 4 garlic cloves, chopped
- 2 tablespoons vegetable oil
- Kosher salt, to taste
- 4 baby bok choy, halved lengthwise
- 2 medium carrots, peeled, sliced
- 1 small radish, trimmed, sliced
- Toasted sesame oil, for serving

Instructions:

1. Mix ¼ cup soy sauce with brown sugar in a bowl.
2. Toss in tofu and leave for 20 minutes.
3. Add kombu, mushrooms, garlic and ginger to 8 cups water to a saucepan.
4. Cover and cook for 10 minutes then discard the kombi.
5. Strain the broth and discard the solids.
6. Sauté tofu with oil and salt in a deep skillet for 3 minutes per side then transfer to a plate.
7. Boil carrots and bok choy with broth in a pan for 3 minutes.
8. Stir in the red Thai curry paste, remaining 2 tbsp soy sauce and salt.
9. Divide this mixture into the serving bowl.
10. Add tofu, green onions, radishes and sesame oil.
11. Serve warm.

The Plant Based Cookbook For Beginners
650 Easy, Quick, & Simple Plant Based Vegan Diet Recipes With A 31 Day Meal Plan To Lose Weight & Live A Long Healthy Life

607

CHAPTER 09

SNACKS AND DESSERTS

Spicy Peanuts

SERVINGS
8

PREPARATION TIME
10 minutes

COOKING TIME
10 minutes

Nutritional Values Per Serving	
Calories	171
Total Fat	15g
Saturated Fat	17g
Cholesterol	0mg
Sodium	235mg
Total Carbohydrate	22g
Dietary Fiber	1.7g
Total Sugars	2.7g
Protein	7g

Ingredients:

- 2 cups peeled peanuts
- 1 tablespoon chili powder
- ½ teaspoon ground cinnamon
- ½ teaspoon ground cumin
- ½ teaspoon ground coriander
- Salt and black pepper, to taste
- 1 tablespoon olive oil

Instructions:

1. At 350 degrees F, preheat your oven.
2. Line a suitable baking pan with parchment paper.
3. Toss peanuts with all the spices and oil.
4. Spread the peanuts mixture into the prepared baking dish in a single layer.
5. Roast for about 10 minutes, flipping twice.
6. Remove from the oven and let it cool completely before serving.

The Plant Based Cookbook For Beginners
650 Easy, Quick, & Simple Plant Based Vegan Diet Recipes With A 31 Day Meal Plan To Lose Weight & Live A Long Healthy Life

609

Roasted Chickpeas

SERVINGS	PREPARATION TIME	COOKING TIME
8	10 minutes	30 minutes

Nutritional Values Per Serving

Calories	240
Total Fat	10g
Saturated Fat	8.7g
Cholesterol	0mg
Sodium	620mg
Total Carbohydrate	51g
Dietary Fiber	5g
Total Sugars	19g
Protein	6g

Ingredients:

- 2 cups canned chickpeas, rinsed and drained
- 1 tablespoon olive oil
- 1 teaspoon dried marjoram, crushed
- 1 teaspoon ground cumin
- ½ teaspoon cayenne pepper
- ¼ teaspoon ground allspice
- Salt, to taste

Instructions:

1. At 450 degrees F, preheat your oven.
2. Arrange a rack in the upper third of the oven.
3. With paper towels, pat dry the chickpeas.
4. In a bowl, add the chickpeas and remaining ingredients and toss to coat well.
5. Spread the chickpeas onto a rimmed baking sheet.
6. Bake for about 25-30 minutes, stirring once halfway through.
7. Serve.

610

The Plant Based Cookbook For Beginners
650 Easy, Quick, & Simple Plant Based Vegan Diet Recipes With A 31 Day Meal Plan To Lose Weight & Live A Long Healthy Life

Rosemary Focaccia Bread

SERVINGS	PREPARATION TIME	COOKING TIME
4	10 minutes	20 minutes

Nutritional Values Per Serving

Calories	356
Total Fat	13.6g
Saturated Fat	9.1g
Cholesterol	0mg
Sodium	420mg
Total Carbohydrate	37.6g
Dietary Fiber	7.1g
Total Sugars	19.9g
Protein	7g

Ingredients:

- 1 ¾ cups warm water
- 1 (¼-ounce) package active dry yeast
- 1 tablespoon cane sugar
- 3 ½ cups all-purpose flour
- 1 ½ cups whole wheat flour
- 1 tablespoon sea salt
- ½ cup olive oil
- 1 roasted bulb garlic
- 2 tablespoons rosemary, chopped
- ½ teaspoon red pepper flakes

Instructions:

1. Mix yeast, sugar, and water in a suitable bowl and leave for 5 minutes.
2. Mix flours with ¼ cup olive oil, yeast mixture, and salt in the mixing bowl of the stand mixer for 6 minutes.
3. Knead the dough on the floured surface and transfer it to a greased bowl.
4. Cover and leave for 50 minutes.
5. Grease a 10x15 inch rimmed baking sheet with the remaining oil.
6. Knead the dough and spread it on the baking sheet, cover and leave for 40 minutes.
7. At 425 degrees F, preheat your oven.
8. Cut the garlic cloves in half and push them into the dough.
9. Sprinkle red pepper flakes and rosemary on top.
10. Bake this bread for 20 minutes until golden brown.
11. Serve.

The Plant Based Cookbook For Beginners
650 Easy, Quick, & Simple Plant Based Vegan Diet Recipes With A 31 Day Meal Plan To Lose Weight & Live A Long Healthy Life

611

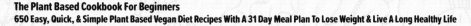

Kale Chips

SERVINGS	PREPARATION TIME	COOKING TIME
6	10 minutes	15 minutes

Nutritional Values Per Serving

Calories	201
Total Fat	3.1g
Saturated Fat	0.5g
Cholesterol	0mg
Sodium	5mg
Total Carbohydrate	16.2g
Dietary Fiber	0.6g
Total Sugars	12.2g
Protein	13g

Ingredients:

- 1-pound fresh kale leaves stemmed and torn
- ¼ teaspoon cayenne pepper
- Salt, to taste
- 1 tablespoon olive oil

Instructions:

1. At 350 degrees F, preheat your oven.
2. Line a suitable baking sheet with parchment paper.
3. Arrange the kale pieces onto the prepared baking sheet in a single layer.
4. Sprinkle the kale with cayenne pepper and salt and drizzle with oil.
5. Bake for about 10-15 minutes then allow them to cool.
6. Serve.

612

The Plant Based Cookbook For Beginners
650 Easy, Quick, & Simple Plant Based Vegan Diet Recipes With A 31 Day Meal Plan To Lose Weight & Live A Long Healthy Life

Cauliflower Nashville

SERVINGS	PREPARATION TIME	COOKING TIME
4	10 minutes	10 minutes

Nutritional Values Per Serving

Calories	238
Total Fat	3.7g
Saturated Fat	1.2g
Cholesterol	0mg
Sodium	19mg
Total Carbohydrate	25g
Dietary Fiber	3g
Total Sugars	7.4g
Protein	4g

Ingredients:

- 1 cauliflower head, chopped
- 4 flax eggs
- ½ cup of almond milk
- 2 tablespoons hot sauce
- 1 cup flour
- ½ cup cornstarch
- 1 tablespoon baking powder
- 2 teaspoons salt
- Oil for frying

Instructions:

1. Mix hot sauce, almond milk, and flax eggs in a shallow bowl.
2. Whisk salt, baking powder, cornstarch and flour in another shallow bowl.
3. Set a pan with oil over medium heat.
4. Dip the cauliflower pieces in the almond milk mixture and coat with the flour mixture.
5. Fry the cauliflower for 5 minutes per side, then transfer to a plate.
6. Serve.

The Plant Based Cookbook For Beginners
650 Easy, Quick, & Simple Plant Based Vegan Diet Recipes With A 31 Day Meal Plan To Lose Weight & Live A Long Healthy Life

613

Hasselback Potatoes

SERVINGS	PREPARATION TIME	COOKING TIME
4	10 minutes	25 minutes

Nutritional Values Per Serving

Calories	301
Total Fat	12g
Saturated Fat	1.9g
Cholesterol	0mg
Sodium	91mg
Total Carbohydrate	20g
Dietary Fiber	3g
Total Sugars	5.6g
Protein	1.4g

Ingredients:

- 4 small potatoes
- 1 tablespoon olive oil
- 1 teaspoon sea salt
- Chopped parsley, to serve

Instructions:

1. At 400 degrees F, preheat your oven.
2. Line a baking sheet with a foil sheet.
3. Make several cuts on top of the potatoes with ½ inch gaps in between.
4. Place these potatoes in the baking sheet and rub them with olive oil, and salt.
5. Bake these potatoes for 20-25 minutes in the oven.
6. Garnish with parsley.
7. Serve warm.

614

The Plant Based Cookbook For Beginners
650 Easy, Quick, & Simple Plant Based Vegan Diet Recipes With A 31 Day Meal Plan To Lose Weight & Live A Long Healthy Life

Carrot Chips

SERVINGS	PREPARATION TIME	COOKING TIME
6	15 minutes	30 minutes

Nutritional Values Per Serving

Calories	141
Total Fat	10.2g
Saturated Fat	2.4g
Cholesterol	0mg
Sodium	258mg
Total Carbohydrate	7.2g
Dietary Fiber	2g
Total Sugars	16.5g
Protein	4.5g

Ingredients:

- 2 medium carrots, peeled and sliced
- 1 tablespoon canola oil
- Salt, to taste

Instructions:

1. At 350 degrees F, preheat your oven.
2. Line a suitable baking sheet with parchment paper.
3. In a large bowl, add the carrot slices, salt, and oil and toss to coat well.
4. Arrange the carrot slices onto the prepared baking sheets in a single layer.
5. Bake for about 20-30 minutes then allow them to cool.
6. Serve.

The Plant Based Cookbook For Beginners
650 Easy, Quick, & Simple Plant Based Vegan Diet Recipes With A 31 Day Meal Plan To Lose Weight & Live A Long Healthy Life

615

Zucchini Chips

SERVINGS | PREPARATION TIME | COOKING TIME
4 | **15 minutes** | **15 minutes**

Nutritional Values Per Serving	
Calories	181
Total Fat	19g
Saturated Fat	0.6g
Cholesterol	0mg
Sodium	26mg
Total Carbohydrate	9g
Dietary Fiber	3g
Total Sugars	5.5g
Protein	6.9g

Ingredients:

- 1 medium zucchini, cut into thin slices
- ⅛ teaspoon ground turmeric
- ⅛ teaspoon ground cumin
- Salt, to taste
- 2 teaspoons olive oil

Instructions:

1. At 400 degrees F, preheat your oven.
2. Line a baking sheet with parchment papers.
3. Toss zucchini slices with spices and oil in a bowl.
4. Transfer the zucchini mixture onto the prepared baking sheet in a single layer.
5. Bake for about 10-15 minutes.
6. Serve immediately.

616

The Plant Based Cookbook For Beginners
650 Easy, Quick, & Simple Plant Based Vegan Diet Recipes With A 31 Day Meal Plan To Lose Weight & Live A Long Healthy Life

Banana Chips

SERVINGS	PREPARATION TIME	COOKING TIME
6	10 minutes	60 minutes

Nutritional Values Per Serving	
Calories	159
Total Fat	2.2g
Saturated Fat	0.3g
Cholesterol	0mg
Sodium	64mg
Total Carbohydrate	25.5g
Dietary Fiber	1g
Total Sugars	2.3g
Protein	4.1g

Ingredients:

- 2 large bananas, peeled and cut into ¼-inch thick slices
- ½ teaspoon ground cinnamon

Instructions:

1. At 250 degrees F, preheat your oven.
2. Line a suitable baking sheet with parchment paper.
3. Place the banana slices onto a prepared baking sheet and sprinkle cinnamon on top.
4. Bake for about 1 hour.
5. Remove the banana chips from the oven and set aside to cool.
6. Serve.

The Plant Based Cookbook For Beginners
650 Easy, Quick, & Simple Plant Based Vegan Diet Recipes With A 31 Day Meal Plan To Lose Weight & Live A Long Healthy Life

617

Apple Leather

SERVINGS	PREPARATION TIME	COOKING TIME
4	10 minutes	12 hours 25 minutes

Nutritional Values Per Serving

Calories	234
Total Fat	21.2g
Saturated Fat	4.2g
Cholesterol	0mg
Sodium	14mg
Total Carbohydrate	17g
Dietary Fiber	1.4g
Total Sugars	13.6g
Protein	7g

Ingredients:

- 1 cup water
- 8 cups apples, peeled, cored and chopped
- 1 tablespoon ground cinnamon
- 2 tablespoons fresh lemon juice

Instructions:

1. In a large pan, add water and apples over medium-low heat and simmer for about 10-15 minutes, stirring occasionally.
2. Remove from heat and set aside to cool slightly.
3. In a blender, add apple mixture and pulse until smooth.
4. Return the mixture into the pan over medium-low heat.
5. Stir in cinnamon and lemon juice and simmer for about 10 minutes.
6. Transfer the mixture onto dehydrator trays and with the back of the spoon, smooth the top.
7. Set the dehydrator at 135 degrees F.
8. Dehydrate for about 10-12 hours.
9. Cut the apple leather into equal-sized rectangles.
10. Now, roll each rectangle to make fruit rolls.

618

The Plant Based Cookbook For Beginners
650 Easy, Quick, & Simple Plant Based Vegan Diet Recipes With A 31 Day Meal Plan To Lose Weight & Live A Long Healthy Life

Seeds Crackers

SERVINGS **6** PREPARATION TIME **10 minutes** COOKING TIME **20 minutes**

Nutritional Values Per Serving

Calories	144
Total Fat	13.2g
Saturated Fat	25.7g
Cholesterol	0mg
Sodium	19mg
Total Carbohydrate	23g
Dietary Fiber	3.6g
Total Sugars	8.4g
Protein	4.5g

Ingredients:

- 3 tablespoons water
- 1 tablespoon chia seeds
- 3 tablespoons sunflower seeds
- 1 tablespoon quinoa flour
- 1 teaspoon ground turmeric
- Pinch of ground cinnamon
- Salt, to taste

Instructions:

1. At 345 degrees F, preheat your oven. Line a baking sheet with parchment paper.
2. In a bowl, add the water and chia seeds and set aside for about 15 minutes.
3. After 15 minutes, add the remaining ingredients and mix well.
4. Spread the mixture onto the prepared baking sheet evenly.
5. Bake for about 20 minutes.
6. Remove from the oven and place onto a wire rack to cool completely before serving.
7. Break into pieces and serve.

The Plant Based Cookbook For Beginners
650 Easy, Quick, & Simple Plant Based Vegan Diet Recipes With A 31 Day Meal Plan To Lose Weight & Live A Long Healthy Life

619

Celery Crackers

SERVINGS	PREPARATION TIME	COOKING TIME
5	10 minutes	2 hours

Nutritional Values Per Serving

Calories	218
Total Fat	6.3g
Saturated Fat	3.3g
Cholesterol	0mg
Sodium	158mg
Total Carbohydrate	23.9g
Dietary Fiber	1.8g
Total Sugars	15.6g
Protein	8g

Ingredients:

- 10 celery sticks
- 1 teaspoon fresh rosemary leaves
- 1 teaspoon fresh thyme leaves
- 2 tablespoons apple cider vinegar
- ¼ cup avocado oil
- Sea salt, to taste
- 3 cups flax seeds, ground

Instructions:

1. At 225 degrees F, preheat your oven.
2. Line 2 suitable baking sheets with parchment paper.
3. In a food processor, blend all ingredients except flax seeds.
4. Add the flax seeds and pulse until well combined.
5. Transfer the dough into a bowl and set aside for about 2-3 minutes.
6. Divide the dough into 2 portions.
7. Place each portion onto 1 prepared baking sheet evenly.
8. With the back of a spatula, smooth and press the dough to ¼-inch thickness.
9. Use a pizza cutter to cut the dough into desired shapes.
10. Bake for about 1 hour.
11. Flip the crackers and bake for 1 hour more.
12. Remove from the oven and place onto a wire rack to cool completely before serving.

620

The Plant Based Cookbook For Beginners
650 Easy, Quick, & Simple Plant Based Vegan Diet Recipes With A 31 Day Meal Plan To Lose Weight & Live A Long Healthy Life

Strawberry Gazpacho

SERVINGS
4

PREPARATION TIME
15 minutes

COOKING TIME
0 minutes

Nutritional Values Per Serving	
Calories	160
Total Fat	1.4g
Saturated Fat	2.1g
Cholesterol	0mg
Sodium	246mg
Total Carbohydrate	29.2g
Dietary Fiber	3.7g
Total Sugars	18.2g
Protein	1g

Ingredients:

- 1 ½ pounds fresh strawberries, hulled and sliced
- ½ cup red bell pepper, seeded and chopped
- 1 small cucumber, peeled, seeded and chopped
- ¼ cup onion, chopped
- ¼ cup fresh basil leaves
- 1 small garlic clove, chopped
- ¼ of small jalapeño pepper, seeded and chopped
- 1 tablespoon olive oil
- 3 tablespoons balsamic vinegar

Instructions:

1. In a blender, blend jalapeno and rest of the ingredients.
2. Transfer the gazpacho into a large bowl.
3. Cover and refrigerate to chill completely before serving.

The Plant Based Cookbook For Beginners
650 Easy, Quick, & Simple Plant Based Vegan Diet Recipes With A 31 Day Meal Plan To Lose Weight & Live A Long Healthy Life

621

Tropical Fruit Salsa

SERVINGS	PREPARATION TIME	COOKING TIME
6	10 minutes	0 minutes

Nutritional Values Per Serving

Calories	244
Total Fat	20.7g
Saturated Fat	17.6g
Cholesterol	0mg
Sodium	42mg
Total Carbohydrate	28.5g
Dietary Fiber	2g
Total Sugars	18.6g
Protein	4.2g

Ingredients:

- 1½ cups fresh mango, peeled, pitted and cut into chunks
- 1½ cups fresh pineapple, peeled and cut into chunks
- ¼ cup red onion, chopped
- 2 tablespoons fresh cilantro, chopped
- 2 tablespoons fresh orange juice
- Salt and black pepper, to taste
- 2 tablespoons unsweetened coconut, shredded

Instructions:

1. In a large bowl, add all the ingredients except coconut in and gently toss to coat well.
2. Serve immediately with the topping of coconut.

622

The Plant Based Cookbook For Beginners
650 Easy, Quick, & Simple Plant Based Vegan Diet Recipes With A 31 Day Meal Plan To Lose Weight & Live A Long Healthy Life

Steamed Green Beans

SERVINGS
4

PREPARATION TIME
5 minutes

COOKING TIME
8 minutes

Nutritional Values Per Serving	
Calories	161
Total Fat	3.2g
Saturated Fat	0.4g
Cholesterol	0mg
Sodium	152mg
Total Carbohydrate	16g
Dietary Fiber	5.5g
Total Sugars	2.9g
Protein	3.1g

Ingredients:

- 1 ½ pounds fresh green beans, trimmed
- 1 tablespoon olive oil
- Salt and black pepper, to taste

Instructions:

1. In a large pan of boiling water, arrange a steamer basket.
2. Place green beans in the steamer basket.
3. Cover and steam for about 7-8 minutes or until desired doneness.
4. Drain well and transfer the beans into a bowl.
5. Drizzle with oil and sprinkle with salt and black pepper and toss to coat.
6. Serve immediately.

The Plant Based Cookbook For Beginners
650 Easy, Quick, & Simple Plant Based Vegan Diet Recipes With A 31 Day Meal Plan To Lose Weight & Live A Long Healthy Life

623

Stir-Fried Asparagus

SERVINGS	PREPARATION TIME	COOKING TIME
6	15 minutes	5 minutes

Nutritional Values Per Serving

Calories	142
Total Fat	1g
Saturated Fat	1g
Cholesterol	0mg
Sodium	7mg
Total Carbohydrate	11g
Dietary Fiber	2g
Total Sugars	8g
Protein	1g

Ingredients:

- 1 tablespoon cooking oil
- 1 ½ pounds asparagus, trimmed and chopped
- Salt and black pepper, to taste
- 3 garlic cloves, minced
- 1 tablespoon fresh ginger, grated
- 1 Serrano pepper, chopped

Instructions:

1. In a suitable skillet, heat the oil over medium-high heat and stir fry the asparagus with salt and black pepper for about 2 minutes.
2. Add the garlic, ginger and Serrano pepper and stir-fry for about 2-3 minutes.
3. Serve hot.

Roasted Brussels Sprout

SERVINGS	PREPARATION TIME	COOKING TIME
8	10 minutes	20 minutes

Nutritional Values Per Serving	
Calories	182
Total Fat	5g
Saturated Fat	0.4g
Cholesterol	0mg
Sodium	162mg
Total Carbohydrate	7.2g
Dietary Fiber	10.7g
Total Sugars	12.3g
Protein	2g

Ingredients:

- 2 pounds small-sized Brussels sprouts, trimmed
- 1 tablespoon fresh rosemary, minced
- Salt and black pepper, to taste
- 1 tablespoon olive oil

Instructions:

1. At 425 degrees F, preheat your oven.
2. In a roasting pan, place Brussels sprouts.
3. Sprinkle rosemary, salt, oil and black pepper on top.
4. Roast for about 20 minutes.
5. Remove from the oven and serve hot.

The Plant Based Cookbook For Beginners
650 Easy, Quick, & Simple Plant Based Vegan Diet Recipes With A 31 Day Meal Plan To Lose Weight & Live A Long Healthy Life

625

Stir-Fried Broccoli

SERVINGS	PREPARATION TIME	COOKING TIME
6	10 minutes	8 minutes

Nutritional Values Per Serving

Calories	142
Total Fat	4.4g
Saturated Fat	0.1g
Cholesterol	0mg
Sodium	33mg
Total Carbohydrate	13g
Dietary Fiber	5.1g
Total Sugars	8.9g
Protein	9g

Ingredients:

- 1 tablespoon olive oil
- 1 garlic clove, minced
- 1 fresh red chili, seeded and chopped
- 2 cups broccoli florets
- 2 tablespoons soy sauce

Instructions:

1. In a suitable skillet, heat the oil over medium heat and sauté the garlic and red chili for about 1 minute.

2. Add the broccoli and stir fry for about 2 minutes.

3. Stir in the soy sauce and stir fry for about 4-5 minutes.

4. Serve warm

Sautéed Zucchini

SERVINGS	PREPARATION TIME	COOKING TIME
6	15 minutes	8 minutes

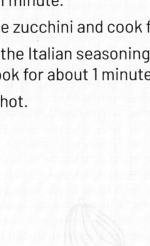

Nutritional Values Per Serving

Calories	169
Total Fat	2.8g
Saturated Fat	0.8g
Cholesterol	0mg
Sodium	75mg
Total Carbohydrate	5.2g
Dietary Fiber	5.4g
Total Sugars	5.6g
Protein	2g

Ingredients:

- 3 tablespoons olive oil
- 1 jalapeño pepper, seeded and minced
- 2 garlic cloves, minced
- 2 pounds zucchini, diced
- 1 teaspoon Italian seasoning
- Salt and black pepper, to taste

Instructions:

1. In a suitable skillet, heat the oil over medium heat
2. Add and sauté the jalapeño pepper and garlic for about 1 minute.
3. Add the zucchini and cook for about 5-6 minutes.
4. Stir in the Italian seasoning, salt and black pepper and cook for about 1 minute.
5. Serve hot.

The Plant Based Cookbook For Beginners
650 Easy, Quick, & Simple Plant Based Vegan Diet Recipes With A 31 Day Meal Plan To Lose Weight & Live A Long Healthy Life

627

Soy Sauce Zucchini Noodles

SERVINGS	PREPARATION TIME	COOKING TIME
4	20 minutes	2 minutes

Nutritional Values Per Serving

Calories	277
Total Fat	0.9g
Saturated Fat	0.1g
Cholesterol	0mg
Sodium	9mg
Total Carbohydrate	10g
Dietary Fiber	6.3g
Total Sugars	5.4g
Protein	1g

Ingredients:

- ½ tablespoon olive oil
- 1 large zucchini, spiralized with Blade C
- Black pepper, to taste
- 1 tablespoon soy sauce
- 1 tablespoon fresh parsley, chopped

Instructions:

1. In a microwave-safe bowl, place the zucchini noodles.
2. Sprinkle with salt and black pepper and microwave on High for about 1 minute.
3. Drizzle with the oil and soy sauce and microwave for about 1 minute more.
4. Transfer zucchini to a large serving plate and serve with the garnishing of parsley.

628

The Plant Based Cookbook For Beginners
650 Easy, Quick, & Simple Plant Based Vegan Diet Recipes With A 31 Day Meal Plan To Lose Weight & Live A Long Healthy Life

Spiced Corn

SERVINGS
6

PREPARATION TIME
15 minutes

COOKING TIME
9 minutes

Nutritional Values Per Serving

Calories	249
Total Fat	10.2g
Saturated Fat	18.4g
Cholesterol	0mg
Sodium	149mg
Total Carbohydrate	20.1g
Dietary Fiber	0.3g
Total Sugars	12.5g
Protein	3g

Ingredients:

- 1 tablespoon vegan butter
- 1 (16-ounce) package frozen corn
- 1 plum tomato, chopped
- 1 tablespoon fresh lime juice
- Salt, to taste
- ½ teaspoon ground cumin
- ⅓ cup fresh cilantro, minced

Instructions:

1. In a suitable cast-iron skillet, melt the butter over medium-high heat.
2. Stir in corn and cook for about 3-5 minutes, with occasional stirring.
3. Add tomato, cilantro, lime juice, cumin and salt and stir to combine.
4. Serve hot.

The Plant Based Cookbook For Beginners
650 Easy, Quick, & Simple Plant Based Vegan Diet Recipes With A 31 Day Meal Plan To Lose Weight & Live A Long Healthy Life

629

Basil Cauliflower

SERVINGS	PREPARATION TIME	COOKING TIME
4	10 minutes	8 minutes

Nutritional Values Per Serving

Calories	285
Total Fat	15g
Saturated Fat	8.7g
Cholesterol	10mg
Sodium	173mg
Total Carbohydrate	13g
Dietary Fiber	1.4g
Total Sugars	27.6g
Protein	4.2g

Serving Suggestion:

Enjoy the cauliflower with tomato sauce.

Ingredients:

- ½ cup vegetable broth
- 4 cups fresh cauliflower florets
- 2 shallots, chopped
- 1 teaspoon dried basil, crushed
- ½ teaspoon seasoned salt
- Black pepper, to taste

Instructions:

1. In a large cast-iron skillet, add all the ingredients and mix well.
2. Place the skillet over medium heat and cook for about 6-8 minutes, stirring occasionally.
3. Serve hot

630

The Plant Based Cookbook For Beginners
650 Easy, Quick, & Simple Plant Based Vegan Diet Recipes With A 31 Day Meal Plan To Lose Weight & Live A Long Healthy Life

Sweet and Sour Kale

SERVINGS	PREPARATION TIME	COOKING TIME
6	20 minutes	20 minutes

Nutritional Values Per Serving	
Calories	157
Total Fat	14.3g
Saturated Fat	12.7g
Cholesterol	0mg
Sodium	52mg
Total Carbohydrate	21g
Dietary Fiber	2.3g
Total Sugars	4.5g
Protein	1.4g

Ingredients:

- 1 tablespoon olive oil
- 1 lemon, seeded and sliced thinly
- 1 onion, chopped
- 3 garlic cloves, minced
- 2-pound fresh kale, trimmed and chopped
- ½ cup green onions, chopped
- 1 tablespoon maple syrup
- Salt and black pepper, to taste

Instructions:

1. In a suitable cast-iron skillet, heat the oil over medium heat and cook the lemon slices for about 5 minutes.

2. With a slotted spoon, remove the lemon slices from the skillet and set them aside.

3. In the same skillet, add the onion and garlic and sauté for about 5 minutes.

4. Add the kale, green onions, maple syrup, salt and pepper and cook for 8-10 minutes.

5. Add the lemon slices and mix until well combined.

6. Serve hot.

The Plant Based Cookbook For Beginners
650 Easy, Quick, & Simple Plant Based Vegan Diet Recipes With A 31 Day Meal Plan To Lose Weight & Live A Long Healthy Life

631

Nutty Spinach

SERVINGS | **PREPARATION TIME** | **COOKING TIME**
4 | 15 minutes | 4 minutes

Nutritional Values Per Serving

Calories	260
Total Fat	2.5g
Saturated Fat	0g
Cholesterol	0mg
Sodium	155mg
Total Carbohydrate	8.5g
Dietary Fiber	0.3g
Total Sugars	7.3g
Protein	1.1g

Ingredients:

- 1 tablespoon olive oil
- 6 cups fresh spinach
- 2 garlic cloves, minced
- Salt, to taste
- 1 tablespoon raisins
- 1 tablespoon roasted pinenuts, peeled

Instructions:

1. In a suitable skillet, heat the oil over medium-high heat and cook the spinach for about 1 minute, stirring continuously.

2. Add the garlic and salt and cook for about 2-3 minutes or until wilted.

3. Garnish with raisins and pine nuts.

4. Serve hot.

632

The Plant Based Cookbook For Beginners
650 Easy, Quick, & Simple Plant Based Vegan Diet Recipes With A 31 Day Meal Plan To Lose Weight & Live A Long Healthy Life

Garlicky Mushrooms

SERVINGS	PREPARATION TIME	COOKING TIME
4	15 minutes	8 minutes

Nutritional Values Per Serving	
Calories	214
Total Fat	2.6g
Saturated Fat	0g
Cholesterol	0mg
Sodium	143mg
Total Carbohydrate	19.4g
Dietary Fiber	0g
Total Sugars	4.1g
Protein	1g

Ingredients:

- ½ tablespoon olive oil
- ½ pound fresh mushrooms, sliced thinly
- 1 teaspoon fresh ginger root, minced
- 1 teaspoon garlic, minced
- 1 tablespoon soy sauce
- Black pepper, to taste
- 1 tablespoon green onions, chopped

Instructions:

1. In a suitable skillet, heat the oil over high heat.
2. Stir fry the mushrooms for about 5-6 minutes.
3. Add the remaining ingredients except for the green onions.
4. Stir fry for about 1-2 minutes.
5. Serve hot with the garnishing of green onions.

The Plant Based Cookbook For Beginners
650 Easy, Quick, & Simple Plant Based Vegan Diet Recipes With A 31 Day Meal Plan To Lose Weight & Live A Long Healthy Life

633

Baked Beans

SERVINGS
8

PREPARATION TIME
15 minutes

COOKING TIME
1 hour

Nutritional Values Per Serving	
Calories	203
Total Fat	23g
Saturated Fat	19.8g
Cholesterol	5mg
Sodium	45mg
Total Carbohydrate	25.1g
Dietary Fiber	3.6g
Total Sugars	17.7g
Protein	3.9g

Serving Suggestion:

Enjoy the baked beans on top of toasted bread slices.

Ingredients:

- ¼ pound dry lima beans, soaked
- ¼ pound white beans, soaked
- 1¼ tablespoons vegetable oil
- 1 small onion, chopped
- 4 garlic cloves, minced
- 1 teaspoon dried thyme, crushed
- ½ teaspoon ground cumin
- ½ teaspoon red pepper flakes, crushed
- ¼ teaspoon paprika
- 1 tablespoon balsamic vinegar
- 1 cup canned tomato sauce
- 1 cup vegetable broth
- Salt and black pepper, to taste
- 2 tablespoons fresh parsley, chopped

Instructions:

1. Add beans and enough water to cover them to a cooking pan and cook them to a boil.
2. Reduce the heat to low and simmer, covered for about 1 hour.
3. Drain the beans from water.
4. At 325 degrees F, preheat your oven.
5. In a large ovenproof pan, heat the oil over medium heat and cook the onion for about 8-9 minutes, stirring frequently.
6. Add the garlic, thyme and red pepper flakes and sauté for about 1 minute.
7. Add the cooked beans and remaining ingredients and immediately remove them from the heat.
8. Cover the pan and transfer it into the oven.
9. Bake for about 1 hour.
10. Serve and enjoy.

634

The Plant Based Cookbook For Beginners
650 Easy, Quick, & Simple Plant Based Vegan Diet Recipes With A 31 Day Meal Plan To Lose Weight & Live A Long Healthy Life

Sweet Potato Mash

SERVINGS
6

PREPARATION TIME
10 minutes

COOKING TIME
20 minutes

Nutritional Values Per Serving

Calories	268
Total Fat	3.1g
Saturated Fat	0.2g
Cholesterol	0mg
Sodium	33mg
Total Carbohydrate	30.8g
Dietary Fiber	6.5g
Total Sugars	18.9g
Protein	2.5g

Serving Suggestion:

Spread the mash on top of bread slices.

Ingredients:

- 3 sweet potatoes, peeled and diced
- ¼ cup unsweetened almond milk
- 1-2 tablespoons maple syrup
- Salt, to taste
- ¼ teaspoon ground cinnamon
- Pinch of ground nutmeg

Instructions:

1. In a large pan of boiling water, arrange a steamer basket.
2. Place the sweet potato chunks in the steamer basket.
3. Cover and steam the sweet potato for about 15-20 minutes or until desired tenderness.
4. Drain well and transfer the sweet potato chunks into a bowl.
5. With a potato masher, mash the chunks.
6. Add the rest of the ingredients and mix until well combined.
7. Serve immediately.

The Plant Based Cookbook For Beginners
650 Easy, Quick, & Simple Plant Based Vegan Diet Recipes With A 31 Day Meal Plan To Lose Weight & Live A Long Healthy Life

635

Cauliflower Mash

SERVINGS	PREPARATION TIME	COOKING TIME
6	15 minutes	12 minutes

Nutritional Values Per Serving

Calories	121
Total Fat	4.6g
Saturated Fat	0.4g
Cholesterol	0mg
Sodium	92mg
Total Carbohydrate	4.8g
Dietary Fiber	10g
Total Sugars	3.5g
Protein	3.1g

Ingredients:

- 1 head cauliflower, chopped
- 2 tablespoons vegetable broth
- 2 garlic cloves, chopped
- 2 tablespoons coconut oil
- Salt, to taste

Instructions:

1. Add the cauliflower and broth to a suitable cooking pot and cook for 10-12 minutes on medium heat.
2. In a food processor, add the cauliflower mixture and remaining ingredients and pulse until smooth.
3. Serve immediately.

636

The Plant Based Cookbook For Beginners
650 Easy, Quick, & Simple Plant Based Vegan Diet Recipes With A 31 Day Meal Plan To Lose Weight & Live A Long Healthy Life

Avocado Yogurt

SERVINGS **6**   PREPARATION TIME **15 minutes**   COOKING TIME **0 minutes**

Nutritional Values Per Serving

Calories	213
Total Fat	6.5g
Saturated Fat	1.4g
Cholesterol	0mg
Sodium	232mg
Total Carbohydrate	16g
Dietary Fiber	1.7g
Total Sugars	4.6g
Protein	9.9g

Ingredients:

- 2 medium avocados, peeled, pitted and chopped
- ½ cup unsweetened almond milk
- ½ cup plain coconut yogurt
- 1 tablespoon maple syrup
- 2 tablespoons fresh lemon juice
- 1 teaspoon vanilla extract
- 1 teaspoon fresh mint leaves

Instructions:

1. Blend almond milk, yogurt, maple syrup, lemon juice, vanilla and avocado in a blender.
2. Transfer this avocado mixture to an airtight container and refrigerate for at least 2-3 hours.
3. Remove from the refrigerator and set aside for at least 10-15 minutes.
4. With a spoon, stir well and serve with a topping of fresh mint leaves.

The Plant Based Cookbook For Beginners
650 Easy, Quick, & Simple Plant Based Vegan Diet Recipes With A 31 Day Meal Plan To Lose Weight & Live A Long Healthy Life

637

Strawberry Ice Cream

SERVINGS	PREPARATION TIME	COOKING TIME
4	4 hours 10 minutes	0 minutes

Nutritional Values Per Serving

Calories	207
Total Fat	7.4g
Saturated Fat	1g
Cholesterol	0mg
Sodium	255mg
Total Carbohydrate	7.3g
Dietary Fiber	11.9g
Total Sugars	9g
Protein	5g

Ingredients:

- 1 cup fresh strawberries, hulled and sliced
- ½ small banana, peeled and sliced
- 2 tablespoon unsweetened coconut, shredded
- ½ cup coconut cream

Instructions:

1. Blend strawberries, coconut cream, banana and coconut in a blender.
2. Transfer the strawberry mixture into an ice cream maker and process it according to the manufacturer's directions.
3. Now, transfer the mixture into an airtight container.
4. Freeze to set for at least 3-4 hours, stirring after every 30 minutes.

638

The Plant Based Cookbook For Beginners
650 Easy, Quick, & Simple Plant Based Vegan Diet Recipes With A 31 Day Meal Plan To Lose Weight & Live A Long Healthy Life

Strawberry Pudding

SERVINGS	PREPARATION TIME	COOKING TIME
4	4 hours 10 minutes	0 minutes

Nutritional Values Per Serving

Calories	205
Total Fat	5.5g
Saturated Fat	0.8g
Cholesterol	0mg
Sodium	277mg
Total Carbohydrate	13.5g
Dietary Fiber	6.2g
Total Sugars	1.3g
Protein	4.7g

Ingredients:

- 1 (16-ounce) package strawberries, hulled and sliced
- 2 cups unsweetened almond milk
- ½ cup chia seeds
- 1 teaspoon vanilla extract
- ¼ cup maple syrup

Instructions:

1. In a blender, add strawberries and almond milk and pulse until smooth.
2. Transfer the mixture into a large bowl.
3. Add the remaining ingredients and stir to combine well.
4. Cover and refrigerate to chill for about 4 hours before serving.

The Plant Based Cookbook For Beginners
650 Easy, Quick, & Simple Plant Based Vegan Diet Recipes With A 31 Day Meal Plan To Lose Weight & Live A Long Healthy Life

639

Banana Mousse

SERVINGS	PREPARATION TIME	COOKING TIME
2	15 minutes	0 minutes

Nutritional Values Per Serving

Calories	289
Total Fat	2.2g
Saturated Fat	0.5g
Cholesterol	0mg
Sodium	42mg
Total Carbohydrate	15.2g
Dietary Fiber	12.8g
Total Sugars	2.4g
Protein	8.6g

Ingredients:

- 2 bananas
- ⅓ cup coconut cream
- 1 teaspoon unsweetened coconut, shredded
- ½ teaspoon ground cinnamon
- 1 tablespoon cocoa powder

Instructions:

1. Blend bananas with cream, cocoa powder, and coconut in a blender.
2. Transfer the mixture into serving bowls.
3. Refrigerate to chill for at least 30 minutes before serving.
4. Sprinkle with cinnamon and serve.

640

The Plant Based Cookbook For Beginners
650 Easy, Quick, & Simple Plant Based Vegan Diet Recipes With A 31 Day Meal Plan To Lose Weight & Live A Long Healthy Life

Chocolate Tofu Mousse

SERVINGS
4

PREPARATION TIME
10 minutes

COOKING TIME
0 minutes

Nutritional Values Per Serving	
Calories	213
Total Fat	5.8g
Saturated Fat	4.4g
Cholesterol	0mg
Sodium	39mg
Total Carbohydrate	20.8g
Dietary Fiber	3.9g
Total Sugars	1.9g
Protein	6g

Ingredients:

- 1-pound firm tofu, drained
- 2 tablespoons unsweetened cocoa powder
- ¼ cup almond milk
- 2 tablespoons maple syrup
- 1 tablespoon vanilla extract

Instructions:

1. Blend tofu with cocoa powder, milk, vanilla and maple syrup in a blender.
2. Transfer the mousse into 4 serving bowls.
3. Refrigerate this mousse to chill for at least 2 hours.

The Plant Based Cookbook For Beginners
650 Easy, Quick, & Simple Plant Based Vegan Diet Recipes With A 31 Day Meal Plan To Lose Weight & Live A Long Healthy Life

641

Banana Cookies

SERVINGS	PREPARATION TIME	COOKING TIME
2	15 minutes	25 minutes

Nutritional Values Per Serving

Calories	224
Total Fat	4.4g
Saturated Fat	0.7g
Cholesterol	0mg
Sodium	394mg
Total Carbohydrate	19.3g
Dietary Fiber	8.1g
Total Sugars	7.3g
Protein	3.6g

Ingredients:

- ¾ cup unsweetened coconut, shredded
- 1 banana, peeled and sliced
- Pinch of ground cinnamon

Instructions:

1. At 350 degrees F, preheat your oven.
2. In a food processor, add banana, cinnamon and coconut and pulse until smooth.
3. Divide this mixture in a cookie mold tray.
4. Gently, press each cookie slightly into the molds.
5. Bake for about 25 minutes or until golden brown.
6. Remove from the oven and transfer the cookies onto a tray to cool for about 5 minutes.
7. Serve.

642

The Plant Based Cookbook For Beginners
650 Easy, Quick, & Simple Plant Based Vegan Diet Recipes With A 31 Day Meal Plan To Lose Weight & Live A Long Healthy Life

Apple Cookies

SERVINGS
6

PREPARATION TIME
15 minutes

COOKING TIME
12 minutes

Nutritional Values Per Serving	
Calories	268
Total Fat	1.2g
Saturated Fat	0.2g
Cholesterol	0mg
Sodium	111mg
Total Carbohydrate	19.7g
Dietary Fiber	12g
Total Sugars	4.3g
Protein	5.5g

Ingredients:

- ¼ cup warm water
- 2 teaspoons chia seeds
- 2 cups oats
- ½ teaspoon baking soda
- ½ teaspoon ground cinnamon
- ¼ teaspoon ground nutmeg
- ¼ teaspoon ground ginger
- ¼ cup golden raisins
- 1 large apple, peeled, cored and chopped
- 4 Medjool dates, pitted and chopped
- 1 teaspoon apple cider vinegar
- 2 tablespoons cold water

Instructions:

1. At 375 degrees F, preheat your oven.
2. Line a large cookie sheet with parchment paper.
3. In a bowl, mix together warm water and chia seeds.
4. Set aside until thickened.
5. In a large food processor, add 1 cup of the oats and pulse until finely ground.
6. Transfer the ground oats to a large bowl.
7. Add the remaining oats, baking soda, spices and raisins and mix well.
8. Now in a blender, add the remaining ingredients and pulse until smooth.
9. Transfer everything to a mixing bowl and mix well.
10. Spoon the cookie mixture onto the prepared cookie sheet in a single layer, and with your finger, flatten each cookie slightly.
11. Bake these apple cookies for about 12 minutes or until golden brown.
12. Remove from oven and place the cookie sheet onto a wire rack to cool for about 5 minutes.
13. Carefully invert the cookies onto wire rack to cool completely before serving.

The Plant Based Cookbook For Beginners
650 Easy, Quick, & Simple Plant Based Vegan Diet Recipes With A 31 Day Meal Plan To Lose Weight & Live A Long Healthy Life

643

Butter Glazed Carrots

SERVINGS
4

PREPARATION TIME
10 minutes

COOKING TIME
10 minutes

Nutritional Values Per Serving

Calories	291
Total Fat	1.9g
Saturated Fat	0.3g
Cholesterol	0mg
Sodium	46mg
Total Carbohydrate	33.4g
Dietary Fiber	18.7g
Total Sugars	24.8g
Protein	6.2g

Ingredients:

- 2 cups baby carrots
- 1 tablespoon brown sugar
- ½ teaspoon dried thyme
- ½ tablespoon vegan butter, melted
- 1 pinch salt
- 1 pinch black pepper

Instructions:

1. Toss carrots with thyme, black pepper, salt, butter and brown sugar in a baking pan.
2. Roast the glazed carrots for 10 minutes at 350 degrees F.
3. Serve.

644

The Plant Based Cookbook For Beginners
650 Easy, Quick, & Simple Plant Based Vegan Diet Recipes With A 31 Day Meal Plan To Lose Weight & Live A Long Healthy Life

Roasted leeks

SERVINGS
4

PREPARATION TIME
15 minutes

COOKING TIME
7 minutes

Nutritional Values Per Serving

Calories	205
Total Fat	2.6g
Saturated Fat	1.1g
Cholesterol	0mg
Sodium	130mg
Total Carbohydrate	14.9g
Dietary Fiber	17.7g
Total Sugars	8.7g
Protein	2.7g

Ingredients:

- 1 tablespoon vegan butter, melted
- 1 tablespoon lemon juice
- 4 leeks, washed and halved
- Salt and black pepper to taste

Instructions:

1. Toss leeks with vegan butter, lemon juice, black pepper and salt on a baking sheet.
2. Roast the leeks for 7 minutes in the oven at 350 degrees F.
3. Serve.

The Plant Based Cookbook For Beginners
650 Easy, Quick, & Simple Plant Based Vegan Diet Recipes With A 31 Day Meal Plan To Lose Weight & Live A Long Healthy Life

645

Air Fried Potatoes

SERVINGS	PREPARATION TIME	COOKING TIME
6	10 minutes	20 minutes

Nutritional Values Per Serving

Calories	217
Total Fat	5.6g
Saturated Fat	0.5g
Cholesterol	0mg
Sodium	209mg
Total Carbohydrate	34g
Dietary Fiber	14.9g
Total Sugars	13.1g
Protein	5.5g

Ingredients:

- 1-pound gold potatoes, quartered
- 2 tablespoons olive oil
- ¼ cup parsley leaves, chopped
- Juice from ½ lemon
- Salt and black pepper to taste

Instructions:

1. Toss potatoes with oil, lemon juice, black pepper, and salt in a bowl
2. Spread these potatoes in the air fryer basket.
3. Cook the potatoes for 10-20 minutes at 350 degrees F until golden brown.
4. Serve warm with parsley.
5. Devour.

646

The Plant Based Cookbook For Beginners
650 Easy, Quick, & Simple Plant Based Vegan Diet Recipes With A 31 Day Meal Plan To Lose Weight & Live A Long Healthy Life

Fried Asparagus

SERVINGS	PREPARATION TIME	COOKING TIME
4	**10 minutes**	**8 minutes**

Nutritional Values Per Serving

Calories	215
Total Fat	13.2g
Saturated Fat	0.1g
Cholesterol	0mg
Sodium	310mg
Total Carbohydrate	10.9g
Dietary Fiber	2.8g
Total Sugars	29g
Protein	6.8g

Ingredients:

- 2 pounds fresh asparagus, trimmed
- ½ teaspoon oregano, dried
- 4 ounces vegan cheese, crumbled
- 4 garlic cloves, minced
- 2 tablespoons parsley, chopped
- ¼ teaspoon red pepper flakes
- ¼ cup olive oil
- Salt and black pepper to the taste
- 1 teaspoon lemon zest
- 1 lemon, juiced

Instructions:

1. Combine lemon zest with oregano, pepper flakes, garlic and oil in a large bowl.
2. Add asparagus, salt, pepper, and cheese to the bowl.
3. Toss well to coat, then place the asparagus on a baking sheet.
4. Roast these asparagus sticks for 8 minutes at 350 degrees F.
5. Garnish with lemon juice, parsley and vegan cheese.
6. Serve warm.

The Plant Based Cookbook For Beginners
650 Easy, Quick, & Simple Plant Based Vegan Diet Recipes With A 31 Day Meal Plan To Lose Weight & Live A Long Healthy Life

647

Balsamic Artichokes

SERVINGS	PREPARATION TIME	COOKING TIME
4	15 minutes	7 minutes

Nutritional Values Per Serving

Calories	220
Total Fat	29.3g
Saturated Fat	5.5 g
Cholesterol	0mg
Sodium	21mg
Total Carbohydrate	5.2g
Dietary Fiber	3.7g
Total Sugars	10.3g
Protein	13.1g

Ingredients:

- 4 big artichokes, trimmed and halved
- ¼ cup olive oil
- 2 garlic cloves, minced
- 2 tablespoons lemon juice
- 2 teaspoons balsamic vinegar
- 1 teaspoon oregano, dried
- Salt and black pepper to the taste

Instructions:

1. Season artichokes liberally with salt and pepper, then rub them with half of the lemon juice and oil.

2. Spread the artichoke on a baking sheet and roast for 7 minutes at 360 degrees F.

3. Whisk remaining lemon juice and oil, vinegar, oregano, garlic, salt and pepper in a bowl.

4. Pour this mixture over the artichokes and mix them well.

5. Enjoy.

648

The Plant Based Cookbook For Beginners
650 Easy, Quick, & Simple Plant Based Vegan Diet Recipes With A 31 Day Meal Plan To Lose Weight & Live A Long Healthy Life

Tomato Kebabs

SERVINGS	PREPARATION TIME	COOKING TIME
4	10 minutes	0 minutes

Nutritional Values Per Serving

Calories	233
Total Fat	17.6g
Saturated Fat	18g
Cholesterol	0mg
Sodium	70mg
Total Carbohydrate	11.6g
Dietary Fiber	12.9g
Total Sugars	16.2g
Protein	4.4g

Ingredients:

- 24 cherry tomatoes
- 24 vegan mozzarella balls
- Basil leaves, to garnish

Instructions:

1. Thread the tomatoes and cheese cubes on the wooden skewers.
2. Garnish with basil.
3. Serve.

The Plant Based Cookbook For Beginners
650 Easy, Quick, & Simple Plant Based Vegan Diet Recipes With A 31 Day Meal Plan To Lose Weight & Live A Long Healthy Life

649

Eggplant Chips

SERVINGS	PREPARATION TIME	COOKING TIME
8	15 minutes	20 minutes

Nutritional Values Per Serving

Calories	293
Total Fat	5.2g
Saturated Fat	1g
Cholesterol	0mg
Sodium	413mg
Total Carbohydrate	13.2g
Dietary Fiber	5.3g
Total Sugars	8.1g
Protein	6g

Serving Suggestion:

Try these chips with garlic aioli.

Ingredients:

- 4 eggplants, sliced
- 2 tablespoons lemon juice
- 1 teaspoon oregano, dried
- 3 tablespoons olive oil
- 1 teaspoon thyme, dried
- Salt and black pepper to taste
- Sesame seeds, to garnish

Instructions:

1. Toss the eggplant slices with lemon juice, oregano, oil, thyme, black pepper and salt on a baking sheet.
2. Roast the eggplant slices for 20 minutes at 360 degrees F until crispy.
3. Garnish with sesame seeds.
4. Serve.

650

The Plant Based Cookbook For Beginners
650 Easy, Quick, & Simple Plant Based Vegan Diet Recipes With A 31 Day Meal Plan To Lose Weight & Live A Long Healthy Life

Sautéed Mustard Greens

SERVINGS
4

PREPARATION TIME
15 minutes

COOKING TIME
11 minutes

Nutritional Values Per Serving

Calories	257
Total Fat	9.5g
Saturated Fat	1g
Cholesterol	0mg
Sodium	16mg
Total Carbohydrate	10g
Dietary Fiber	9.4g
Total Sugars	4g
Protein	9.4g

Ingredients:

- 2 garlic cloves, minced
- 1 tablespoon olive oil
- ½ cup yellow onion, sliced
- 3 tablespoons vegetable stock
- ¼ teaspoon dark sesame oil
- 1-pound mustard greens, torn
- Salt and black pepper to the taste

Instructions:

1. Add olive oil and place it over medium heat and sauté onions in it for 5 minutes.
2. Stir in garlic, greens, salt, pepper, and stock.
3. Cook the mustard greens for 5 minutes.
4. Drizzle sesame oil over the greens.
5. Devour.

The Plant Based Cookbook For Beginners
650 Easy, Quick, & Simple Plant Based Vegan Diet Recipes With A 31 Day Meal Plan To Lose Weight & Live A Long Healthy Life

651

Vegan Parmesan Brussels Sprouts

SERVINGS	PREPARATION TIME	COOKING TIME
6	15 minutes	8 minutes

Nutritional Values Per Serving

Calories	210
Total Fat	12.8g
Saturated Fat	0½g
Cholesterol	0mg
Sodium	109mg
Total Carbohydrate	12.9g
Dietary Fiber	5.9g
Total Sugars	14.4g
Protein	4.9g

Ingredients:

- 1-pound brussels sprouts washed
- 3 tablespoons vegan parmesan, grated
- Juice from 1 lemon
- 2 tablespoons vegan butter
- Salt and black pepper to the taste

Instructions:

1. Spread the washed brussels sprouts on a baking sheet.
2. Roast them for 8 minutes at 350 degrees F in the oven.
3. Place a nonstick pan over medium-high heat and add butter to melt.
4. Stir in pepper, salt, lemon juice, and brussels sprouts.
5. Mix well, then add parmesan.
6. Serve warm.

Seasoned Potatoes

SERVINGS	PREPARATION TIME	COOKING TIME
4	10 minutes	15 minutes

Nutritional Values Per Serving	
Calories	214
Total Fat	14.9g
Saturated Fat	0.7g
Cholesterol	0mg
Sodium	240mg
Total Carbohydrate	43.1g
Dietary Fiber	14.3g
Total Sugars	13.1g
Protein	10.1g

Ingredients:

- 1 tablespoon coriander seeds
- ½ teaspoon turmeric powder
- ½ teaspoon red chili powder
- 1 teaspoon pomegranate powder
- 1 tablespoon pickled mango, minced
- 1 tablespoon cumin seeds
- 2 teaspoons fenugreeks, dried
- 5 potatoes, halved
- Salt and black pepper to the taste
- 2 tablespoons olive oil

Instructions:

1. At 350 degrees F, preheat your oven.
2. Toss potatoes with all ingredients in a suitable bowl.
3. Spread the potatoes in a greased roasting pan.
4. Roast the potatoes for 10-15 minutes in the oven until golden brown.
5. Serve warm.

The Plant Based Cookbook For Beginners
650 Easy, Quick, & Simple Plant Based Vegan Diet Recipes With A 31 Day Meal Plan To Lose Weight & Live A Long Healthy Life

653

Banana Muffins

SERVINGS	PREPARATION TIME	COOKING TIME
4	15 minutes	22 minutes

Nutritional Values Per Serving

Calories	232
Total Fat	8.9g
Saturated Fat	4.5g
Cholesterol	57mg
Sodium	340mg
Total Carbohydrate	24.7g
Dietary Fiber	1.2g
Total Sugars	12.3g
Protein	5.3g

Ingredients:

- 3 ripe bananas, mashed
- ½ cup vanilla almond milk
- 1 cup coconut sugar
- 2 cups whole wheat flour
- 1 teaspoon baking soda
- ½ teaspoon cinnamon
- ¼ teaspoon salt

Instructions:

1. At 350 degrees F, preheat your oven.
2. Separately, whisk together the dry ingredients in one bowl and the wet ingredients in another bowl.
3. Combine and beat the two mixtures together until smooth.
4. Line a muffin tray with muffin cups and evenly divide the muffin batter among the cups.
5. Bake for 22 minutes and serve.

654

The Plant Based Cookbook For Beginners
650 Easy, Quick, & Simple Plant Based Vegan Diet Recipes With A 31 Day Meal Plan To Lose Weight & Live A Long Healthy Life

Cashew Oat Muffins

SERVINGS	PREPARATION TIME	COOKING TIME
6	10 minutes	22 minutes

Nutritional Values Per Serving

Calories	227
Total Fat	31.1g
Saturated Fat	4.2g
Cholesterol	123mg
Sodium	86mg
Total Carbohydrate	29g
Dietary Fiber	12.4g
Total Sugars	19.8g
Protein	3.5g

Ingredients:

- 3 cups rolled oats
- ¾ cup raw cashews, chopped
- ¼ cup maple syrup
- ¼ cup sugar
- 1 teaspoon vanilla extract
- ½ teaspoon salt
- 1½ teaspoon baking soda
- 2 cups water

Instructions:

1. Preheat your oven to 375 degrees F.
2. Grind the rolled oats in a food processor.
3. Separately, whisk together the dry ingredients in one bowl and the wet ingredients in another bowl.
4. Combine and beat the two mixtures together until smooth.
5. Fold in cashews and give it a gentle stir.
6. Line a muffin tray with muffin cups and evenly divide the muffin batter among the cups.
7. Bake for 22 minutes and serve.

The Plant Based Cookbook For Beginners
650 Easy, Quick, & Simple Plant Based Vegan Diet Recipes With A 31 Day Meal Plan To Lose Weight & Live A Long Healthy Life

655

Chocolate Peanut Fat Bombs

SERVINGS	PREPARATION TIME	FREEZE TIME
4	10 minutes	1 hour

Nutritional Values Per Serving

Calories	246
Total Fat	7.4g
Saturated Fat	4.6g
Cholesterol	105mg
Sodium	353mg
Total Carbohydrate	29.4g
Dietary Fiber	6.5g
Total Sugars	2.7g
Protein	7.2g

Ingredients:

- ½ cup coconut butter
- 1 cup and 2 tablespoons peanut butter
- 5 tablespoons cocoa powder
- 2 tablespoon peanuts, chopped
- 2 teaspoons maple syrup

Instructions:

1. In a bowl, combine all the ingredients.
2. Melt this butter mixture in the microwave for 1 minute.
3. Mix well, then divide the mixture into silicone molds.
4. Freeze them for 1 hour to set.
5. Serve.

656

The Plant Based Cookbook For Beginners
650 Easy, Quick, & Simple Plant Based Vegan Diet Recipes With A 31 Day Meal Plan To Lose Weight & Live A Long Healthy Life

Protein Fat Bombs

SERVINGS
4

PREPARATION TIME
15 minutes

FREEZE TIME
1 hour

Nutritional Values Per Serving	
Calories	293
Total Fat	16g
Saturated Fat	2.3g
Cholesterol	75mg
Sodium	386mg
Total Carbohydrate	25.2g
Dietary Fiber	2.6g
Total Sugars	1.9g
Protein	4.2g

Ingredients:

- 1 cup coconut oil
- 1 cup peanut butter, melted
- ½ cup cocoa powder
- ¼ cup plant-based protein powder
- 1 pinch of salt
- 2 cups unsweetened coconut, shredded

Instructions:

1. Mix oil, peanut butter, cocoa powder, protein powder and salt in a suitable bowl.
2. Make small balls out of this mixture and place them into a pan or dish.
3. Freeze for 1 hour to set.
4. Roll the balls in the coconut shreds
5. Serve.

The Plant Based Cookbook For Beginners
650 Easy, Quick, & Simple Plant Based Vegan Diet Recipes With A 31 Day Meal Plan To Lose Weight & Live A Long Healthy Life

657

Mojito Ice Cream

SERVINGS	PREPARATION TIME	FREEZE TIME
2	10 minutes	1 hour

Nutritional Values Per Serving

Calories	209
Total Fat	26g
Saturated Fat	3.1g
Cholesterol	131mg
Sodium	834mg
Total Carbohydrate	11.4g
Dietary Fiber	0.2g
Total Sugars	0.3g
Protein	4.6g

Ingredients:

- 1-2 limes, juiced
- 8 medium mint leaves
- 2 tablespoons maple syrup
- 1 can full fat coconut milk
- 1 small drop green food color
- 1 pinch of sea salt

Instructions:

1. Blend coconut milk with mint leaves, lime juice, food color, maple syrup and salt in a blender until smooth.
2. Freeze this blend for 1 hour to set.
3. Scoop out and serve.

658

The Plant Based Cookbook For Beginners
650 Easy, Quick, & Simple Plant Based Vegan Diet Recipes With A 31 Day Meal Plan To Lose Weight & Live A Long Healthy Life

Apple Pie Bites

SERVINGS
4

PREPARATION TIME
10 minutes

FREEZE TIME
1 hour

Nutritional Values Per Serving

Calories	236
Total Fat	25.5g
Saturated Fat	12.4g
Cholesterol	69mg
Sodium	58mg
Total Carbohydrate	38.3g
Dietary Fiber	0.7g
Total Sugars	10.3g
Protein	1.4g

Ingredients:

- ½ cup walnuts, chopped
- ½ cup dates, pitted
- ½ cup coconut oil
- ¼ cup ground flax seeds
- ½ ounce freeze-dried apples
- 1 teaspoon vanilla extract
- 1 teaspoon cinnamon
- Liquid stevia, to taste

Instructions:

1. In a bowl, add all the ingredients to a food processor and blend for 2 minutes.
2. Mix well, then roll the mixture into small balls.
3. Freeze them for 1 hour to set.
4. Serve.

The Plant Based Cookbook For Beginners
650 Easy, Quick, & Simple Plant Based Vegan Diet Recipes With A 31 Day Meal Plan To Lose Weight & Live A Long Healthy Life

 659

Coconut Fat Bombs

SERVINGS
4

PREPARATION TIME
15 minutes

FREEZE TIME
1 hour

Nutritional Values Per Serving

Calories	119
Total Fat	14g
Saturated Fat	2g
Cholesterol	65mg
Sodium	269mg
Total Carbohydrate	19g
Dietary Fiber	4g
Total Sugars	6g
Protein	5g

Ingredients:

- 1 can coconut milk
- ¾ cup coconut oil
- 1 cup coconut flakes
- 20 drops liquid stevia

Instructions:

1. Melt coconut oil in a suitable bowl for 1 minute by heating in the microwave.

2. Blend the coconut oil with coconut milk, coconut flakes and stevia in a blender.

3. Divide the coconut milk mixture in silicon molds.

4. Freeze them for 1 hour to set and then form balls out of mixture.

5. Serve with some coconut flakes on top.

660

The Plant Based Cookbook For Beginners
650 Easy, Quick, & Simple Plant Based Vegan Diet Recipes With A 31 Day Meal Plan To Lose Weight & Live A Long Healthy Life

Peach Popsicles

SERVINGS	PREPARATION TIME	FREEZE TIME
6	15 minutes	2 hours

Nutritional Values Per Serving

Calories	231
Total Fat	10.1g
Saturated Fat	2.4g
Cholesterol	110mg
Sodium	941mg
Total Carbohydrate	20.1g
Dietary Fiber	0.9g
Total Sugars	1.4g
Protein	4.6g

Ingredients:

- 2 ½ cups peaches, peeled and pitted
- 2 tablespoons agave
- ¾ cup coconut cream

Instructions:

1. Blend peaches with cream and agave in a blender until smooth.
2. Divide the popsicle blend into the popsicle molds.
3. Insert the popsicles sticks and close the molds.
4. Place these molds in the freezer for 2 hours to set.
5. Serve.

The Plant Based Cookbook For Beginners
650 Easy, Quick, & Simple Plant Based Vegan Diet Recipes With A 31 Day Meal Plan To Lose Weight & Live A Long Healthy Life

661

Green Popsicle

SERVINGS	PREPARATION TIME	FREEZE TIME
6	15 minutes	2 hours

Nutritional Values Per Serving

Calories	261
Total Fat	16.3g
Saturated Fat	4.9g
Cholesterol	114mg
Sodium	515mg
Total Carbohydrate	29.3g
Dietary Fiber	0.1g
Total Sugars	8.2g
Protein	3.3g

Ingredients:

- 1 ripe avocado, peeled and pitted
- 1 cup fresh spinach
- 1 can (13.5 ounce) full fat coconut milk
- ¼ cup lime juice
- 2 tablespoons maple syrup
- 1 teaspoon vanilla extract
- ½ teaspoon chia seeds

Instructions:

1. Blend vanilla, maple, lime juice, spinach, chia seeds, coconut milk and avocado in a blender until smooth.
2. Divide the popsicle blend into the popsicle molds.
3. Insert the popsicles sticks and close the molds.
4. Place these molds in the freezer for 2 hours to set.
5. Serve.

662

The Plant Based Cookbook For Beginners
650 Easy, Quick, & Simple Plant Based Vegan Diet Recipes With A 31 Day Meal Plan To Lose Weight & Live A Long Healthy Life

Strawberry Banana Coconut Popsicles

SERVINGS	PREPARATION TIME	FREEZE TIME
4	10 minutes	2 hours

Nutritional Values Per Serving	
Calories	205
Total Fat	22.7g
Saturated Fat	6.1g
Cholesterol	4mg
Sodium	227mg
Total Carbohydrate	26.1g
Dietary Fiber	1.4g
Total Sugars	0.9g
Protein	5.2g

Ingredients:

- 2 medium bananas, sliced
- 1 can coconut milk
- 1 cup strawberries
- 3 tablespoons maple syrup

Instructions:

1. Blend coconut milk, maple syrup, strawberries and bananas in a blender until smooth.
2. Divide the popsicle blend into the popsicle molds.
3. Insert the popsicles sticks and close the molds.
4. Place these molds in the freezer for 2 hours to set.
5. Serve.

The Plant Based Cookbook For Beginners
650 Easy, Quick, & Simple Plant Based Vegan Diet Recipes With A 31 Day Meal Plan To Lose Weight & Live A Long Healthy Life

663

Fudge Popsicles

SERVINGS	PREPARATION TIME	FREEZE TIME
6	20 minutes	2 hours

Nutritional Values Per Serving	
Calories	201
Total Fat	8.9g
Saturated Fat	4.5g
Cholesterol	57mg
Sodium	340mg
Total Carbohydrate	24.7g
Dietary Fiber	1.2g
Total Sugars	1.3g
Protein	5.3g

Ingredients:

- 1 cup almond milk
- 3 ripe bananas
- 3 tablespoon cocoa powder
- 1 tablespoon almond butter

Instructions:

1. Blend almond milk, bananas, cocoa powder and almond butter in a blender until smooth.
2. Divide the popsicle blend into the popsicle molds.
3. Insert the popsicles sticks and close the molds.
4. Place the molds in the freezer for 2 hours to set.
5. Serve.

664

The Plant Based Cookbook For Beginners
650 Easy, Quick, & Simple Plant Based Vegan Diet Recipes With A 31 Day Meal Plan To Lose Weight & Live A Long Healthy Life

Lemon Raspberry Ice Cream

SERVINGS	PREPARATION TIME	FREEZE TIME
4	1 hour 15 minutes	4 hours

Nutritional Values Per Serving	
Calories	208
Total Fat	26g
Saturated Fat	7g
Cholesterol	632mg
Sodium	497mg
Total Carbohydrate	9g
Dietary Fiber	3g
Total Sugars	83g
Protein	9g

Ingredients:

- 1½ cups of boiled water
- 1 cup raw cashews
- 1 cup coconut cream
- ¼ cup of coconut oil
- 2 tablespoons coconut sugar
- ½ teaspoon lemon zest
- 1 tablespoon lemon juice
- 1 cup raspberries

Instructions:

1. Add cashews to boiling water and soak for 1 hour then drain.
2. Blend raspberry with cashews, coconut cream and rest of the ingredients in a food processor until smooth.
3. Freeze this raspberry ice cream for 4 hours in the freezer.
4. Scoop out and serve.

The Plant Based Cookbook For Beginners
650 Easy, Quick, & Simple Plant Based Vegan Diet Recipes With A 31 Day Meal Plan To Lose Weight & Live A Long Healthy Life

665

Crunchy Chocolate Brownies

SERVINGS	PREPARATION TIME	FREEZE TIME
4	1 hour 15 minutes	1 hour

Nutritional Values Per Serving

Calories	232
Total Fat	8.9g
Saturated Fat	4.5g
Cholesterol	57mg
Sodium	340mg
Total Carbohydrate	24.7g
Dietary Fiber	1.2g
Total Sugars	12.3g
Protein	5.3g

Ingredients:

Filling

- 2 cups dates, pitted
- 2 cups walnuts
- ¾ cup raw cacao
- Pinch of sea salt
- 2 tablespoons water

Topping

- 1 dark chocolate bar, chopped
- ½ cup peanut butter
- 1 tablespoon coconut oil

Instructions:

1. Add pitted dates in a bowl with water and soak for 10 minutes, then drain.
2. Add walnuts to a blender and pulse until it forms a crumble.
3. Add in sea salt, cacao powder, dates, and 1 tablespoon water to the blender.
4. Blend again until it forms a thick date dough.
5. Spread this mixture in an 8-inch baking pan lined with a parchment sheet.
6. Press the dough in the pan, then freeze for 1 hour.
7. Meanwhile, melt peanut butter, coconut oil, and chocolate chips in a glass bowl by heating in the microwave.
8. Pour this chocolate melt over the dates batter.
9. Allow it to sit in the fridge for 1 hour then slice.
10. Serve.

666

The Plant Based Cookbook For Beginners
650 Easy, Quick, & Simple Plant Based Vegan Diet Recipes With A 31 Day Meal Plan To Lose Weight & Live A Long Healthy Life

Peanut Butter Chocolate Cups

SERVINGS
4

PREPARATION TIME
30 minutes

FREEZE TIME
1 hour

Nutritional Values Per Serving	
Calories	227
Total Fat	21.1g
Saturated Fat	4.2g
Cholesterol	123mg
Sodium	86mg
Total Carbohydrate	9g
Dietary Fiber	12.4g
Total Sugars	19.8g
Protein	3.5g

Ingredients:

- 1 ½ cups dark chocolate chips
- ¼ cup peanut butter
- 1 cup pecans

Instructions:

1. Melt the chocolate chips in a bowl by heating in the microwave for 2 minutes.
2. Divide this half of the chocolate melt into muffin cups, then freeze the tray for 20 minutes.
3. Add peanut butter to a suitable glass bowl.
4. Melt it by heating it in the microwave for 1 minute.
5. Divide this peanut butter melt into the muffin cups.
6. Add the remaining melted chocolate on top.
7. Place one pecan on top of each cup then freeze for 1 hour.
8. Serve.

The Plant Based Cookbook For Beginners
650 Easy, Quick, & Simple Plant Based Vegan Diet Recipes With A 31 Day Meal Plan To Lose Weight & Live A Long Healthy Life

667

Blueberry Cheesecake Bites

SERVINGS	PREPARATION TIME	FREEZE TIME
4	50 minutes	2 hours

Nutritional Values Per Serving

Calories	300
Total Fat	21.8g
Saturated Fat	5.1g
Cholesterol	200mg
Sodium	272mg
Total Carbohydrate	23.6g
Dietary Fiber	1g
Total Sugars	12.3g
Protein	1.8g

Ingredients:

Crust

- 1 cup graham crackers crumbs
- 6 Medjool dates pitted
- ¼ cup coconut, shredded
- ¼ teaspoon sea salt

Topping

- ½ cup blueberrries

Filling

- 1 cup raw cashews, soaked
- ½ cup blueberries
- ¼ cup coconut milk
- ¼ cup agave nectar
- ¼ cup coconut oil, melted
- 2 tablespoons lemon juice

Instructions:

1. Add dates to warm water in a small bowl and soak them for 10 minutes, then drain.

2. Soak cashews in a bowl with water for 30 minutes then drain.

3. Transfer the dates to a blender along with all other ingredients for the crust.

4. Blend until it forms a crumbly mixture.

5. Line 2- 12 muffin cups with cooking spray.

6. Spread 1 ½ teaspoon of this mixture at the bottom of each muffin cup in a muffin tray.

7. Mix cashews, blueberries, coconut milk, coconut oil, lemon juice, and agave nectar in a blender and blend until smooth.

8. Divide this filling into the muffin cups and freeze for 2 hours.

9. Garnish with blueberries.

10. Serve.

668

The Plant Based Cookbook For Beginners
650 Easy, Quick, & Simple Plant Based Vegan Diet Recipes With A 31 Day Meal Plan To Lose Weight & Live A Long Healthy Life

Chickpea Meringues

SERVINGS
4

PREPARATION TIME
10 minutes

COOKING TIME
2 hours

Nutritional Values Per Serving	
Calories	215
Total Fat	14g
Saturated Fat	7g
Cholesterol	632mg
Sodium	497mg
Total Carbohydrate	26g
Dietary Fiber	3g
Total Sugars	10g
Protein	5g

Ingredients:

- 1 (15 oz) can chickpeas
- ¼ teaspoon cream of tartar
- Kosher salt
- ¾ cup of sugar

Instructions:

1. Layer 2 baking sheet with parchment sheet and preheat the oven at 250 degrees F.
2. Drain the chickpeas and reserve ¾ cup of its liquid.
3. Blend the chickpeas with cream of tartar, sugar, a pinch of salt, and the reserved liquid in the blender.
4. Add this mixture to a piping bag and pipe the mixture drop by drop on the baking sheet.
5. Bake these meringue drops for 2 hours in the preheated oven.
6. Serve.

The Plant Based Cookbook For Beginners
650 Easy, Quick, & Simple Plant Based Vegan Diet Recipes With A 31 Day Meal Plan To Lose Weight & Live A Long Healthy Life

669

Jicama Fries

SERVINGS	PREPARATION TIME	COOKING TIME
4	15 minutes	55 minutes

Nutritional Values Per Serving

Calories	172
Total Fat	11.8g
Saturated Fat	4.4g
Cholesterol	62mg
Sodium	871mg
Total Carbohydrate	15.8g
Dietary Fiber	0.6g
Total Sugars	2.3g
Protein	4g

Serving Suggestion:

Enjoy the fries with ketchup.

Ingredients:

- 1 jicama, peeled and cut into sticks
- 1 tablespoon olive oil
- ½ teaspoon paprika
- ½ teaspoon garlic powder
- ½ teaspoon onion powder
- Pinch of Cayenne pepper
- ½ teaspoon salt

Instructions:

1. At 425 degrees F, preheat your oven.
2. Boil jicama sticks in a pot filled with water for 10 minutes, then drain.
3. Toss the boiled jicama sticks with spices and oil in a bowl.
4. Spread the jicama fries on a baking sheet and bake for 45 minutes.
5. Serve warm.

670

The Plant Based Cookbook For Beginners
650 Easy, Quick, & Simple Plant Based Vegan Diet Recipes With A 31 Day Meal Plan To Lose Weight & Live A Long Healthy Life

Potato Chips with Thyme

SERVINGS	PREPARATION TIME	COOKING TIME
8	**15 minutes**	**13 minutes**

Nutritional Values Per Serving	
Calories	293
Total Fat	16g
Saturated Fat	2.3g
Cholesterol	75mg
Sodium	386mg
Total Carbohydrate	25.2g
Dietary Fiber	2.6g
Total Sugars	1.9g
Protein	4.2g

Ingredients:

- ¼ teaspoon garlic, minced
- 1 teaspoon fresh thyme, minced
- 4 potatoes, sliced thinly
- Kosher salt and black pepper

Instructions:

1. Add dried garlic, salt, pepper, and thyme to a food processor and blend well.
2. Toss the potatoes slices with this mixture on a baking sheet.
3. Bake these slices for 8 minutes at 350 degrees F, then toss them well.
4. Continue baking for another 5 minutes until brown and crispy.
5. Serve.

The Plant Based Cookbook For Beginners
650 Easy, Quick, & Simple Plant Based Vegan Diet Recipes With A 31 Day Meal Plan To Lose Weight & Live A Long Healthy Life

671

Plantain Chips

SERVINGS	PREPARATION TIME	COOKING TIME
2	10 minutes	20 minutes

Nutritional Values Per Serving

Calories	89.3
Total Fat	1.8g
Saturated Fat	0.2g
Cholesterol	0mg
Sodium	150mg
Total Carbohydrate	19.9g
Dietary Fiber	1.5g
Total Sugars	9g
Protein	0.5g

Ingredients:

- 1 green plantain, sliced
- ½ tbsp avocado oil
- Sea salt, to taste

Instructions:

1. At 350 degrees F, preheat your oven.
2. Mix plantain slices with avocado oil and salt.
3. Spread these slices in a baking sheet, lined with parchment paper.
4. Bake the plantain slices for 20 minutes and flip once cooked halfway through.
5. Serve.

672

The Plant Based Cookbook For Beginners
650 Easy, Quick, & Simple Plant Based Vegan Diet Recipes With A 31 Day Meal Plan To Lose Weight & Live A Long Healthy Life

Kiwi Popsicle

SERVINGS
4

PREPARATION TIME
6 hours 10 minutes

COOKING TIME
0 minutes

Nutritional Values Per Serving	
Calories	98
Total Fat	0.5g
Saturated Fat	0g
Cholesterol	0mg
Sodium	4mg
Total Carbohydrate	23.7g
Dietary Fiber	2.5g
Total Sugars	16.7g
Protein	1.2g

Ingredients:

- 4 ripe kiwis
- 1 ½ cups pineapple juice
- ½ teaspoon sugar

Instructions:

1. Blend kiwi with pineapple and sugar in a blender until smooth.
2. Divide the kiwi mixture into the popsicle molds.
3. Insert the popsicles sticks and close the molds.
4. Place these molds in the freezer for 6 hours to set.
5. Serve.

The Plant Based Cookbook For Beginners
650 Easy, Quick, & Simple Plant Based Vegan Diet Recipes With A 31 Day Meal Plan To Lose Weight & Live A Long Healthy Life

673

Butterscotch Tart

SERVINGS	PREPARATION TIME	COOKING TIME	FRIDGE TIME
4	10 minutes	40 minutes	2 hours

Nutritional Values Per Serving

Calories	287
Total Fat	7g
Saturated Fat	2.1g
Cholesterol	10mg
Sodium	327mg
Total Carbohydrate	26g
Dietary Fiber	8g
Total Sugars	2.4g
Protein	9g

Ingredients:

Crust

- ½ cup granulated sugar
- ¼ cup virgin coconut oil
- 1 teaspoon pure vanilla extract
- 2 cups almond flour
- ½ teaspoon salt

Filling

- ⅔ cup packed light brown sugar
- ⅔ cup of canned coconut cream
- ½ cup of coconut oil
- 1 teaspoon kosher salt
- Flaked sea salt, as needed
- 1 Granny Smith apple, sliced

Instructions:

1. Start by setting up the oven at 375 degrees F.

2. Prepare the crust by blending all its ingredients in a blender until smooth.

3. Spread this batter in a 9-inch tart pan evenly.

4. Freeze this batter for 10 minutes, then bake for 15 minutes until golden brown.

5. Now prepare the filling by heating all the ingredients in a saucepan.

6. Cook this mixture for 25 minutes until it thickens, then allow it to cool.

7. Add this filling to the tart, then refrigerate for 2 hours.

8. Serve.

674

The Plant Based Cookbook For Beginners
650 Easy, Quick, & Simple Plant Based Vegan Diet Recipes With A 31 Day Meal Plan To Lose Weight & Live A Long Healthy Life

Date Brownies

SERVINGS
6

PREPARATION TIME
15 minutes

COOKING TIME
15 minutes

Nutritional Values Per Serving

Calories	227
Total Fat	31.1g
Saturated Fat	4.2g
Cholesterol	123mg
Sodium	86mg
Total Carbohydrate	29g
Dietary Fiber	12.4g
Total Sugars	19.8g
Protein	3.5g

Ingredients:

- 2 cups dates, pitted
- ¼ cup of hot water
- ½ cup salted peanut butter
- 2 tablespoons melted coconut oil
- ⅓ cup cocoa powder
- ⅓ cup dark chocolate chips
- ½ cup raw walnuts, chopped

Instructions:

1. Start by setting up the oven at 350 degrees F. Layer a loaf pan with a parchment paper.
2. Blend the pitted dates in the food processor until it turns into a fine mixture.
3. Add hot water to the processor and blend while scraping down from the sides.
4. Now add cacao powder, coconut oil, and peanut butter, then blend again.
5. Fold in walnuts and chocolate chips.
6. Mix well, then spread this mixture in the loaf pan.
7. Bake the dates batter for 15 minutes in the oven.
8. Serve chilled.

The Plant Based Cookbook For Beginners
650 Easy, Quick, & Simple Plant Based Vegan Diet Recipes With A 31 Day Meal Plan To Lose Weight & Live A Long Healthy Life

675

Avocado filling Cake

SERVINGS
6

PREPARATION TIME
10 minutes

FREEZE TIME
**5 hours
or overnight**

Nutritional Values Per Serving

Calories	398
Total Fat	13.8g
Saturated Fat	5.1g
Cholesterol	200mg
Sodium	272mg
Total Carbohydrate	53.6g
Dietary Fiber	1g
Total Sugars	12.3g
Protein	1.8g

Ingredients:

Crust

- 2½ cups pecans
- 1 cup pitted dates
- 2 tablespoons maple syrup

Topping

- 1½ cups plain coconut yogurt
- 1 teaspoon pure vanilla extract
- 3 tablespoons maple syrup
- Coconut shavings

Filling

- 3 cups prepared cauliflower rice
- 3 avocados, halved and pitted
- 1½ cups pineapple, crushed
- ¾ cup maple syrup
- Zest and juice of 1 lemon
- ½ teaspoon pure vanilla extract
- ½ teaspoon lemon extract
- Pinch of cinnamon

Instructions:

1. Layer a 9-inch springform pan with a parchment sheet.
2. Add pecans to a food processor and grind until fine.
3. Stir in maple syrup and dates to the pecans and blend for 1 minute.
4. Spread this crust mixture in the prepared pan.
5. Prepare the filling by blending cauliflower rice with maple syrup, lemon juice, lemon zest, pineapple and avocados in a food processor for 1 minute.
6. Add cinnamon, lemon extract and vanilla extract to the processor.
7. Blend well then spread this filling in the crust.
8. Freeze this cake overnight or 5 hours.
9. Prepare the topping by whisking the yogurt with maple syrup and vanilla extract.
10. Spread this mixture over the cake.
11. Garnish with coconut shavings
12. Slice and serve.

676

The Plant Based Cookbook For Beginners
650 Easy, Quick, & Simple Plant Based Vegan Diet Recipes With A 31 Day Meal Plan To Lose Weight & Live A Long Healthy Life

Baked Potato Fries

SERVINGS
4

PREPARATION TIME
10 minutes

COOKING TIME
25 minutes

Nutritional Values Per Serving

Calories	265
Total Fat	14g
Saturated Fat	7g
Cholesterol	632mg
Sodium	497mg
Total Carbohydrate	26g
Dietary Fiber	3g
Total Sugars	1g
Protein	5g

Serving Suggestion:

Enjoy the fries with ketchup.

Ingredients:

- 1 lb. Yukon gold potatoes, unpeeled, cut into wedges
- 1 tablespoon avocado oil
- 1 tablespoon potato starch
- 1 tablespoon nutritional yeast
- A pinch of salt, to taste
- Black pepper to taste

Instructions:

1. Start by setting up the oven at 425 degrees F. Layer a baking tray with parchment paper.

2. Add the potatoes along with the rest of the ingredients to the baking sheet.

3. Toss and mix well together, then bake for 25 minutes while flipping halfway through.

4. Serve warm.

The Plant Based Cookbook For Beginners
650 Easy, Quick, & Simple Plant Based Vegan Diet Recipes With A 31 Day Meal Plan To Lose Weight & Live A Long Healthy Life

677

Crispy Cauliflower

SERVINGS | PREPARATION TIME | COOKING TIME
6 | 25 minutes | 30 minutes

Nutritional Values Per Serving

Calories	272
Total Fat	11.8g
Saturated Fat	4.4g
Cholesterol	62mg
Sodium	871mg
Total Carbohydrate	15.8g
Dietary Fiber	0.6g
Total Sugars	2.3g
Protein	4g

Ingredients:

- 1 head cauliflower, cut into small bites
- 2 tablespoons potato starch
- ½ teaspoons salt
- ¼ teaspoons black pepper
- ½ teaspoons turmeric
- 1 tablespoon nutritional yeast
- ½ teaspoons chilli powder
- 1 tablespoon avocado oil

Instructions:

1. Start by setting up the oven at 450 degrees F.
2. Grease a baking sheet with a tablespoon of oil.
3. Add cauliflower to the baking sheet and toss in the rest of the ingredients.
4. Mix well, then bake for 30 minutes.
5. Serve.

Breaded Tofu

SERVINGS	PREPARATION TIME	COOKING TIME
4	**15 minutes**	**12 minutes**

Nutritional Values Per Serving

Calories	293
Total Fat	16g
Saturated Fat	2.3g
Cholesterol	75mg
Sodium	386mg
Total Carbohydrate	25.2g
Dietary Fiber	2.6g
Total Sugars	1.9g
Protein	4.2g

Ingredients:

- 1 (14-ounce) package of extra firm tofu
- ½ cup cornstarch
- ½ cup breadcrumbs
- ¼ cup of water
- ¼ cup of vegetable oil
- 2 tablespoons soy sauce
- 1 tablespoon nutritional yeast
- Pinch of salt

Instructions:

1. Drain the tofu, then slice it into finger-length strips.
2. Whisk water, soy sauce and cornstarch in a small bowl.
3. Mix breadcrumbs with salt and yeast in a shallow bowl.
4. Pour vegetable oil into a large pan and heat over medium-high heat.
5. First, dip the tofu in the cornstarch mixture, then coat them with breadcrumbs mixture.
6. Shallow fry the tofu for 3 minutes per side.
7. Serve.

The Plant Based Cookbook For Beginners
650 Easy, Quick, & Simple Plant Based Vegan Diet Recipes With A 31 Day Meal Plan To Lose Weight & Live A Long Healthy Life

679

Raisin Protein Balls

SERVINGS	PREPARATION TIME	COOKING TIME
9	15 minutes	30 minutes

Nutritional Values Per Serving

Calories	269
Total Fat	10.6g
Saturated Fat	3.1g
Cholesterol	131mg
Sodium	834mg
Total Carbohydrate	31.4g
Dietary Fiber	0.2g
Total Sugars	0.3g
Protein	4.6g

Ingredients:

- 1 cup of dry oats
- ½ cup of creamy peanut butter
- ¼ cup of raisins

Instructions:

1. Start by thoroughly mixing all the ingredients in a bowl.

2. Make golf ball size fat bombs out of it.

3. Place them on a baking sheet and freeze for 30 minutes.

4. Serve.

680

The Plant Based Cookbook For Beginners
650 Easy, Quick, & Simple Plant Based Vegan Diet Recipes With A 31 Day Meal Plan To Lose Weight & Live A Long Healthy Life

Cucumber Bites

SERVINGS
8

PREPARATION TIME
5 minutes

COOKING TIME
0 minutes

Nutritional Values Per Serving	
Calories	211
Total Fat	25.5g
Saturated Fat	12.4g
Cholesterol	69mg
Sodium	58mg
Total Carbohydrate	2.4g
Dietary Fiber	0.7g
Total Sugars	0.3g
Protein	1.4g

Ingredients:

- 4 large cucumbers
- 1 cup raw sunflower seeds
- ½ teaspoons salt
- 2 tablespoons raw red onion, chopped
- 1 handful fresh chives, chopped
- 1 clove fresh garlic, chopped
- 1 cup coconut cream
- 2 tablespoons nutritional yeast
- 2 tablespoons fresh lemon juice
- ½ cup water

Instructions:

1. Start by blending sunflower seeds with salt in a food processor for 20 seconds.
2. Toss in remaining ingredients except for the cucumber.
3. Slice the cucumber into 1.5-inch-thick rounds.
4. Pipe the coconut cream mixture on top of each cucumber slice.
5. Serve.

The Plant Based Cookbook For Beginners
650 Easy, Quick, & Simple Plant Based Vegan Diet Recipes With A 31 Day Meal Plan To Lose Weight & Live A Long Healthy Life

681

Jam Granola Bars

SERVINGS | PREPARATION TIME | FREEZE TIME
8 | 10 minutes | 1 hour

Nutritional Values Per Serving

Calories	294
Total Fat	9g
Saturated Fat	1.6g
Cholesterol	0mg
Sodium	455mg
Total Carbohydrate	31g
Dietary Fiber	1.7g
Total Sugars	2.1g
Protein	6g

Ingredients:

- 2 ½ cups oats
- 1 cup puffed rice
- 2 tablespoons oat flour
- ½ cup maple syrup
- ½ cup peanut butter
- 2 tablespoons peanuts
- 1 teaspoon vanilla
- ½ teaspoons cinnamon
- ¼ teaspoons salt
- ½ cup chia jam

Instructions:

1. Mix maple syrup and peanut butter in a suitable bowl.
2. Heat this peanut butter mixture for 20 seconds in the microwave.
3. Stir in the rest of the ingredients except the chia jam, then mix well.
4. Spread half of this granola mixture in an 8x8 inch baking pan lined with parchment paper.
5. Spread the chia jam on top and add the rest of the granola mixture on top.
6. Cover and freeze the granola bar for 1 hour.
7. Cut them into 12 bars and serve.

682

The Plant Based Cookbook For Beginners
650 Easy, Quick, & Simple Plant Based Vegan Diet Recipes With A 31 Day Meal Plan To Lose Weight & Live A Long Healthy Life

Red and Golden Beet Chips

SERVINGS	PREPARATION TIME	COOKING TIME
6	10 minutes	50 minutes

Nutritional Values Per Serving

Calories	230
Total Fat	4.9g
Saturated Fat	1.1g
Cholesterol	0mg
Sodium	248mg
Total Carbohydrate	18.3g
Dietary Fiber	3.7g
Total Sugars	16g
Protein	6g

Ingredients:

- 1 large red beet, thinly sliced
- 1 bunch of small golden beets, thinly sliced
- 2 teaspoons salt
- ¼ ground paprika
- 1 teaspoon chili flakes
- Olive oil
- A handful of fresh dill, chopped

Instructions:

1. At 350 degrees F, preheat your oven.
2. Toss beet slices with salt, chili flakes, oil, dill and paprika in a bowl.
3. Spread these beet slices in a baking tray.
4. Bake these slices for 30 minutes and then toss well.
5. Continue baking the beets for 20 minutes at 250 degrees F.
6. Allow the chips to cool and serve.

The Plant Based Cookbook For Beginners
650 Easy, Quick, & Simple Plant Based Vegan Diet Recipes With A 31 Day Meal Plan To Lose Weight & Live A Long Healthy Life

683

Blueberry Crisp

SERVINGS	PREPARATION TIME	COOKING TIME
8	5 minutes	35 minutes

Nutritional Values Per Serving

Calories	246
Total Fat	0.8g
Saturated Fat	0g
Cholesterol	0mg
Sodium	1mg
Total Carbohydrate	31.1g
Dietary Fiber	1.7g
Total Sugars	59.3g
Protein	0.8g

Serving Suggestion:

Enjoy this crisp with a scoop of vegan ice cream.

Ingredients:

- 7 cups frozen blueberries
- 2 cups oats
- 1 lemon, juice and zest
- 1 cup maple syrup
- 1½ teaspoons sea salt
- 1 cup sliced almonds
- 2 tablespoons flax seed
- 4 tablespoons cinnamon
- ½ cup of water

Instructions:

1. At 375 degrees F, preheat your oven.
2. Mix 7 cups of blueberries with lemon juice in a large baking dish.
3. Blend 1 cup oats with 2 tablespoons cinnamon, 1 teaspoon salt, flaxseed, and ½ cup almonds in a food processor.
4. Mix remaining oats, almond, salt, lemon zest, ½ cup maple syrup, and water in another bowl.
5. Drizzle remaining maple syrup over the berries.
6. Spread blended oat mixture on top of the berries.
7. Add the wet oat mixture, cinnamon and lemon zest on top.
8. Bake the blueberry crisp for 35 minutes.
9. Serve.

684

The Plant Based Cookbook For Beginners
650 Easy, Quick, & Simple Plant Based Vegan Diet Recipes With A 31 Day Meal Plan To Lose Weight & Live A Long Healthy Life

Raspberry Banana Ice Cream

SERVINGS
4

PREPARATION TIME
10 minutes

FREEZE TIME
1 hour

Nutritional Values Per Serving	
Calories	191
Total Fat	12g
Saturated Fat	0.7g
Cholesterol	0mg
Sodium	70mg
Total Carbohydrate	19g
Dietary Fiber	5.2g
Total Sugars	1.8g
Protein	9g

Serving Suggestion:

Enjoy the ice cream with fresh fruit on top.

Ingredients:

- 3 frozen bananas
- ½ cup frozen raspberries
- 2 tablespoons water

Instructions:

1. Blend bananas with water and raspberries in a blender.
2. Add this mixture to a suitable pan, cover and freeze for 1 hour.
3. Scoop out ice cream and add to the serving cups.
4. Garnish with raspberries and bananas.
5. Enjoy.

The Plant Based Cookbook For Beginners
650 Easy, Quick, & Simple Plant Based Vegan Diet Recipes With A 31 Day Meal Plan To Lose Weight & Live A Long Healthy Life

685

Golden Milk Cheesecake

SERVINGS	PREPARATION TIME	COOKING TIME	FRIDGE TIME
6	10 minutes	14 minutes	3 hours

Nutritional Values Per Serving

Calories	340
Total Fat	14g
Saturated Fat	1.2g
Cholesterol	10mg
Sodium	359mg
Total Carbohydrate	28.2g
Dietary Fiber	4.1g
Total Sugars	3g
Protein	13g

Ingredients:

Almond Crust

- 1 tablespoon flax meal
- 1 ½ cups whole almonds
- 3 tablespoons coconut oil
- 2 tablespoons agave

Cheesecake Filling

- 16 ounces vegan cream cheese
- 1 ½ cups vegan powdered sugar
- ¾ cup coconut milk
- 1 teaspoon ground turmeric
- ½ teaspoon ground ginger
- ½ teaspoon ground cinnamon

Instructions:

1. At 375 degrees F, preheat your oven.
2. Mix flax meal with 3 tablespoons water in a medium bowl.
3. Blend almonds in a food processor, then mix with flaxseed mixture, coconut oil and agave in a bowl.
4. Spread this mixture in the spring form pan and bake for 14 minutes.
5. Meanwhile, blend the golden milk cheesecake filling in a food processor.
6. Pour this filling into the prepared baked crust and refrigerate for 3 hours.
7. Serve.

686

The Plant Based Cookbook For Beginners
650 Easy, Quick, & Simple Plant Based Vegan Diet Recipes With A 31 Day Meal Plan To Lose Weight & Live A Long Healthy Life

Mudslide Ice Cream

SERVINGS
4

PREPARATION TIME
10 minutes

COOKING TIME
5 minutes

FREEZE TIME
8 hours

Nutritional Values Per Serving

Calories	216
Total Fat	3g
Saturated Fat	2.8g
Cholesterol	0mg
Sodium	751mg
Total Carbohydrate	32g
Dietary Fiber	3.8g
Total Sugars	0.4g
Protein	12g

Ingredients:

- 1 cup dark chocolate chips
- 3 cans coconut cream, divided
- ¼ cup peanut butter
- ½ cup granulated sugar
- 2 teaspoons vanilla extract
- ¼ teaspoon salt
- ¼ cup graham cracker crumbs

Instructions:

1. Blend salt, vanilla extract, sugar, peanuts butter and ½ cup coconut cream in a blender.

2. Spread ½ cup coconut cream in a saucepan and cook on low heat until warm.

3. Stir in chocolate chips and mix for 5 minutes until melted, then allow it to cool.

4. Transfer the prepared peanut butter coconut cream mixture to an ice cream maker and churn according to the instructions.

5. Spread half of the ice cream in a suitable freezer-safe container.

6. Add half of the chocolate cream ganache and graham cracker crumbs on top.

7. Spread the remaining ice cream on top and drizzle the remaining crumbs and ganache.

8. Cover and freeze the ice-cream layers for 8 hours.

9. Slice and serve.

The Plant Based Cookbook For Beginners
650 Easy, Quick, & Simple Plant Based Vegan Diet Recipes With A 31 Day Meal Plan To Lose Weight & Live A Long Healthy Life

687

Vegan Lemon Muffins

SERVINGS	PREPARATION TIME	COOKING TIME
6	10 minutes	17 minutes

Nutritional Values Per Serving

Calories	261
Total Fat	14.7g
Saturated Fat	12.8g
Cholesterol	0mg
Sodium	161mg
Total Carbohydrate	23g
Dietary Fiber	2.7g
Total Sugars	2.6g
Protein	8g

Ingredients:

- 1 cup almond milk
- 1 teaspoon apple cider vinegar
- 1 ¾ cups whole wheat flour
- ½ cup almond flour
- 2 ½ teaspoons baking powder
- ¼ teaspoon baking soda
- ½ teaspoon sea salt
- ½ cup 2 tablespoons coconut sugar
- ⅓ cup olive oil
- 2 tablespoons lemon zest
- 3 tablespoons lemon juice
- 1 teaspoon pure vanilla extract

Glaze

- ½ cup vegan cream cheese
- 2 tablespoons lemon juice
- 2 tablespoons maple syrup
- 1 teaspoon lemon zest

Garnish

- Lemon zest
- Chia seeds

Instructions:

1. At 375 degrees F, preheat your oven.
2. Grease a suitable 12-cup muffin tray with cooking spray.
3. Mix apple cider vinegar, vanilla, lemon juice, lemon zest, olive oil, sugar and almond milk in a bowl.
4. Mix flours with salt, baking soda and baking powder in another bowl.
5. Pour in almond milk mixture and mix until smooth.
6. Divide this batter into the muffin pan and bake for 17 minutes.
7. Allow these muffins to cool.
8. Meanwhile, blend cream cheese with lemon zest, maple syrup and lemon juice in a blender for 1 minute.
9. Add a dollop of this glaze on top of each muffin and garnish with lemon zest and chia seeds.
10. Serve.

Chocolate Cake

SERVINGS	PREPARATION TIME	COOKING TIME	FRIDGE TIME
6	10 minutes	90 minutes	1 hour

Nutritional Values Per Serving

Calories	350
Total Fat	11g
Saturated Fat	12g
Cholesterol	23mg
Sodium	340mg
Total Carbohydrate	20g
Dietary Fiber	1.7g
Total Sugars	3.1g
Protein	7g

Ingredients:

Sweet Potato Frosting

- 1 large sweet potato, peeled
- ¼ cup 2 tablespoons chocolate chips, dark
- 2 tablespoons unsweetened cocoa powder
- 1 tablespoon melted coconut oil
- pinch of sea salt

Chocolate Cake

- ¾ cups almond flour
- ½ cup whole wheat flour
- ½ cup unsweetened cocoa powder
- 1 teaspoon baking soda
- ½ teaspoon sea salt
- ¼ teaspoon cinnamon
- 1 cup almond milk
- ¾ cups maple syrup
- ¼ cup olive oil
- 1 teaspoon apple cider vinegar
- 1 teaspoon vanilla extract

Instructions:

1. At 425 degrees F, preheat your oven.
2. Use a fork to poke some hole in the sweet potato and place it in a baking sheet lined with a foil sheet.
3. Roast the potato for 60 minutes.
4. Blend this sweet potato with salt, coconut oil, cocoa powder and chocolate chips in a blender.
5. Reduce the heat of your oven to 350 degrees F.
6. Grease a suitable 8x8 inch baking pan with cooking spray.
7. Mix flours with the rest of the cake ingredients in a bowl until smooth.
8. Spread this batter into the prepared pan and bake for 30 minutes.
9. Allow the cake to cool, then spread the sweet potato frosting on top.
10. Cover and refrigerate for 1 hour.
11. Slice and serve.

The Plant Based Cookbook For Beginners
650 Easy, Quick, & Simple Plant Based Vegan Diet Recipes With A 31 Day Meal Plan To Lose Weight & Live A Long Healthy Life

689

Summer Strawberry Crumble

SERVINGS	PREPARATION TIME	COOKING TIME
6	10 minutes	15 minutes

Nutritional Values Per Serving	
Calories	238
Total Fat	3.7g
Saturated Fat	1.2g
Cholesterol	0mg
Sodium	19mg
Total Carbohydrate	25g
Dietary Fiber	3g
Total Sugars	7.4g
Protein	4g

Serving Suggestion:

Enjoy the crumble with some vegan ice cream.

Ingredients:

- 2 ½ cups chopped strawberries
- ½ teaspoon balsamic vinegar
- ⅓ cup whole rolled oats
- ⅓ cup chopped pistachios
- ¼ cup almond flour
- ¼ cup brown coconut sugar
- ½ teaspoon cinnamon
- ⅛ teaspoon sea salt
- 1 tablespoon hardened coconut oil
- 1 tablespoon water

Instructions:

1. Preheat your oven to 350 degrees F.
2. Grease four small ramekins with coconut oil.
3. Grind oats with salt, cinnamon, coconut sugar, flour and pistachios in a food processor.
4. Add coconut oil and water, then blend again until crumbly.
5. Mix strawberries with vinegar in a bowl. Mash and mix then divide them into ramekins.
6. Top the berries with the oat's mixture.
7. Place these ramekins in a baking sheet and bake for 15 minutes.
8. Serve.

690

The Plant Based Cookbook For Beginners
650 Easy, Quick, & Simple Plant Based Vegan Diet Recipes With A 31 Day Meal Plan To Lose Weight & Live A Long Healthy Life

Peach Cobbler

SERVINGS	PREPARATION TIME	COOKING TIME
6	10 minutes	30 minutes

Nutritional Values Per Serving

Calories	327
Total Fat	12g
Saturated Fat	1.9g
Cholesterol	0mg
Sodium	91mg
Total Carbohydrate	25g
Dietary Fiber	3g
Total Sugars	5.6g
Protein	10g

Serving Suggestion:

Enjoy the cobbler with some vegan ice cream.

Ingredients:

- 7 medium peaches, thinly sliced
- 1 ½ teaspoons fresh lemon juice
- ¾ cup almond flour
- ¼ cup coconut sugar
- ¼ teaspoon cinnamon
- ¼ teaspoon baking soda
- ¼ teaspoon salt
- ¼ cup melted coconut oil
- 1 teaspoon vanilla extract

Instructions:

1. At 400 degrees F, preheat your oven.
2. Grease a suitable 9x13 inch baking dish with coconut oil.
3. Spread the peaches at the bottom of this dish.
4. Drizzle lemon juice on top.
5. Mix flour and the rest of the ingredients in a bowl until they make a crumbly mixture.
6. Spread this crumbly mixture over the peaches and bake for 30 minutes.
7. Serve.

The Plant Based Cookbook For Beginners
650 Easy, Quick, & Simple Plant Based Vegan Diet Recipes With A 31 Day Meal Plan To Lose Weight & Live A Long Healthy Life

691

Apple Crisp

SERVINGS	PREPARATION TIME	COOKING TIME
4	10 minutes	35 minutes

Nutritional Values Per Serving

Calories	340
Total Fat	14g
Saturated Fat	8g
Cholesterol	17mg
Sodium	310mg
Total Carbohydrate	22g
Dietary Fiber	4g
Total Sugars	7g
Protein	19g

Ingredients:

Apple Filling

- 4 apples, peeled and diced
- 1 tablespoon apple cider vinegar
- 2 tablespoons water
- 1 teaspoon cinnamon
- ¼ teaspoon cardamom
- ¼ teaspoon ginger
- Pinch of sea salt

Crumble Topping

- ½ cup whole rolled oats
- ½ cup almond flour
- ¼ cup crushed walnuts
- ⅓ cup coconut sugar
- ½ teaspoon cinnamon
- ¼ teaspoon sea salt

Instructions:

1. At 400 degrees F, preheat your oven.
2. Grease 4- 8 ounces ramekins with coconut oil.
3. Mix apples with water, cinnamon, ginger, salt, cardamom and apple cider vinegar in a suitable pan and cook for 15 minutes on low heat.
4. Mix oats with salt, water, cinnamon, sugar, walnuts and almond flour in a bowl until crumbly.
5. Divide the apple filling in the ramekins and top them with the oats crumble.
6. Bake them for 20 minutes in the oven.
7. Allow them to cool, then serve.

692

The Plant Based Cookbook For Beginners
650 Easy, Quick, & Simple Plant Based Vegan Diet Recipes With A 31 Day Meal Plan To Lose Weight & Live A Long Healthy Life

Chocolate Chip Cookie Bars

SERVINGS	PREPARATION TIME	FREEZE TIME
6	10 minutes	15 minutes

Nutritional Values Per Serving

Calories	285
Total Fat	8g
Saturated Fat	3g
Cholesterol	11mg
Sodium	168mg
Total Carbohydrate	29g
Dietary Fiber	3.7g
Total Sugars	3.4g
Protein	9g

Ingredients:

Cookie Layer

- ½ cup 2 tablespoons peanut butter
- ¼ cup 1 tablespoon melted coconut oil
- ¼ cup 1 tablespoon maple syrup
- 2 teaspoons vanilla extract
- ½ teaspoon sea salt
- 2 ½ cups almond flour
- 2 ½ tablespoons maca powder
- 1 cup dark chocolate chips

Cacao Layer

- 1 ½ cups walnuts
- 2 tablespoons cacao powder
- ¼ teaspoon sea salt
- 10 soft Medjool dates
- 2 tablespoons water
- Sea salt for sprinkling on top

Instructions:

1. Layer an 8x8inch baking pan with wax paper.
2. Mix peanut butter with salt, vanilla, coconut oil and maple syrup in a bowl.
3. Stir in maca and almond flour, then mix well.
4. Fold in chocolate chips and mix evenly then spread this layer in the baking pan.
5. Cover and refrigerate the dough in the refrigerator for 30 minutes.
6. Blend walnuts with sea salt and cacao powder in a food processor.
7. Add 2 tablespoons water, dates and sea salt, then blend until smooth.
8. Spread the cookie dough mixture over the refrigerated cacao layer.
9. Freeze the layers for 15 minutes and cut the layers into bars.
10. Serve.

The Plant Based Cookbook For Beginners
650 Easy, Quick, & Simple Plant Based Vegan Diet Recipes With A 31 Day Meal Plan To Lose Weight & Live A Long Healthy Life

693

Tahini Pomegranate Cookies

SERVINGS	PREPARATION TIME	COOKING TIME
6	10 minutes	17 minutes

Nutritional Values Per Serving

Calories	242
Total Fat	3g
Saturated Fat	10g
Cholesterol	12mg
Sodium	281mg
Total Carbohydrate	21g
Dietary Fiber	3.7g
Total Sugars	1.6g
Protein	13g

Ingredients:

- ¾ cup tahini
- ½ cup maple syrup
- ½ teaspoon almond extract
- 2 cups almond flour
- ½ teaspoon cinnamon
- ¼ teaspoon ground cardamom
- ¼ teaspoon ground ginger
- ½ teaspoon baking powder
- ½ teaspoon sea salt
- ½ cup pomegranate arils

Instructions:

1. At 350 degrees F, preheat your oven.
2. Layer a suitable baking sheet with wax paper.
3. Mix almond flour, almond extract, tahini, maple syrup, cinnamon, ginger, baking powder, salt, and cardamom in a bowl.
4. Divide the cookie dough into 2 tablespoons of cookie balls and place them on the baking sheet.
5. Flatten the cookie balls and sprinkle pomegranate arils on top.
6. Press the pomegranate arils into the cookies and bake for 17 minutes.
7. Allow the cookies to cool and serve.

694

The Plant Based Cookbook For Beginners
650 Easy, Quick, & Simple Plant Based Vegan Diet Recipes With A 31 Day Meal Plan To Lose Weight & Live A Long Healthy Life

Pistachio Oat Squares

SERVINGS
6

PREPARATION TIME
10 minutes

COOKING TIME
12 minutes

Nutritional Values Per Serving	
Calories	246
Total Fat	9g
Saturated Fat	10g
Cholesterol	12mg
Sodium	312mg
Total Carbohydrate	32g
Dietary Fiber	0.3g
Total Sugars	7.9g
Protein	8g

Ingredients:

- 1 cup raw shelled pistachios
- 1 cup rolled oats
- ½ teaspoon sea salt
- ¼ cup maple syrup
- 2 tablespoons olive oil
- ⅓ cup unsweetened coconut flakes

Instructions:

1. At 350 degrees F, preheat your oven.
2. Layer an 8-inch baking pan with parchment paper.
3. Blend salt, oats, coconut flakes and pistachios in a food processor.
4. Spread this mixture in the baking pan and drizzle oil and maple syrup on top.
5. Bake the oat squares for 12 minutes in the oven.
6. Cut them into squares and serve.

The Plant Based Cookbook For Beginners
650 Easy, Quick, & Simple Plant Based Vegan Diet Recipes With A 31 Day Meal Plan To Lose Weight & Live A Long Healthy Life

695

Tahini Ice Cream

SERVINGS
4

PREPARATION TIME
10 minutes

FREEZE TIME
12 hours

Nutritional Values Per Serving

Calories	286
Total Fat	9g
Saturated Fat	10.3g
Cholesterol	14mg
Sodium	322mg
Total Carbohydrate	32g
Dietary Fiber	3.8g
Total Sugars	4.6g
Protein	17g

Ingredients:

- 1 (14-ounce) can full fat coconut milk
- ⅓ cup pure maple syrup
- ¼ cup tahini

Instructions:

1. Blend coconut milk with maple syrup and tahini in a blender.

2. Add this mixture to the ice cream maker and churn as per the machine's instructions for 20 minutes.

3. Transfer this ice cream to a freezer-safe container and freeze for 12 hours.

4. Scoop out and enjoy.

696

The Plant Based Cookbook For Beginners
650 Easy, Quick, & Simple Plant Based Vegan Diet Recipes With A 31 Day Meal Plan To Lose Weight & Live A Long Healthy Life

Chocolate Pudding Pops

SERVINGS
4

PREPARATION TIME
10 minutes

FREEZE TIME
9 hours

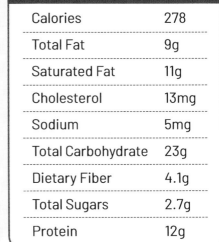

Nutritional Values Per Serving	
Calories	278
Total Fat	9g
Saturated Fat	11g
Cholesterol	13mg
Sodium	5mg
Total Carbohydrate	23g
Dietary Fiber	4.1g
Total Sugars	2.7g
Protein	12g

Ingredients:

- 2 medium ripe avocados
- ¼ cup dark chocolate chips, melted
- 3 tablespoons cacao powder
- 3 tablespoons maple syrup
- 3 tablespoons almond butter
- 1 teaspoon pure vanilla extract
- 2 cups almond milk
- ¼ teaspoon sea salt

Topping

- Crushed nuts

Instructions:

1. Blend salt, almond milk, avocado, vanilla, almond butter, maple syrup, cacao, and chocolate chips in a blender.
2. Divide this mixture into ice pop molds.
3. Insert the popsicles sticks, close the molds and freeze for 9 hours.
4. Garnish the pops with crushed nuts.
5. Serve.

The Plant Based Cookbook For Beginners
650 Easy, Quick, & Simple Plant Based Vegan Diet Recipes With A 31 Day Meal Plan To Lose Weight & Live A Long Healthy Life

697

Creamy Butternut Squash Pudding

SERVINGS	PREPARATION TIME	COOKING TIME	FRIDGE TIME
4	10 minutes	35 minutes	4 hours

Nutritional Values Per Serving	
Calories	285
Total Fat	8g
Saturated Fat	3g
Cholesterol	23mg
Sodium	132mg
Total Carbohydrate	16g
Dietary Fiber	4g
Total Sugars	3g
Protein	11g

Ingredients:

- 1 butternut squash, peeled, and cubed
- 1 tablespoon olive oil
- ½ cup coconut cream
- ¼ cup maple syrup
- 1 tablespoon coconut oil
- 1 teaspoon vanilla
- 1 teaspoon cinnamon
- ¼ teaspoon nutmeg
- ¼ teaspoon ginger
- ⅛ teaspoon sea salt
- 6 tablespoons almond milk

Toppings

- Coconut cream
- Cinnamon

Instructions:

1. At 425 degrees F, preheat your oven.
2. Layer a baking sheet with parchment paper.
3. Toss the squash with olive oil on the baking sheet and bake for 35 minutes.
4. Allow the squash to cool and blend them with ginger and the rest of the ingredients in a blender.
5. Divide the mixture in the ramekins and refrigerate for 4 hours.
6. Garnish the pudding with coconut cream and cinnamon.
7. Serve.

698

The Plant Based Cookbook For Beginners
650 Easy, Quick, & Simple Plant Based Vegan Diet Recipes With A 31 Day Meal Plan To Lose Weight & Live A Long Healthy Life

Raspberry Cheesecake

SERVINGS	PREPARATION TIME	FREEZE TIME
6	10 minutes	2 hours

Nutritional Values Per Serving

Calories	200
Total Fat	24g
Saturated Fat	6g
Cholesterol	12mg
Sodium	155mg
Total Carbohydrate	18.4g
Dietary Fiber	1.7g
Total Sugars	1.1g
Protein	8.8g

Ingredients:

Raspberry Layer

- 1 ½ cup raw cashews, soaked
- ½ cup coconut milk
- ¼ cup 2 tablespoons maple syrup
- ¼ cup fresh lemon juice
- 1 tablespoon lemon zest
- 2 teaspoons vanilla extract
- ½ teaspoon salt
- 1 (12-ounce) bag frozen raspberries, thawed

Walnut Crust

- 1 cup walnuts
- 3 soft Medjool dates, pitted
- ½ tablespoon coconut oil
- heaping ¼ teaspoon sea salt

Instructions:

1. Blend walnuts with salt, oil and dates in a food processor until crumbly.
2. Spread this mixture in an 8x4 inch loaf pan, layered with parchment paper.
3. Drain the cashews and blend with raspberries, lemon juice, zest, vanilla, salt, coconut milk and maple syrup in a blender.
4. Spread this mixture over the crust and freeze for 2 hours.
5. Serve.

The Plant Based Cookbook For Beginners
650 Easy, Quick, & Simple Plant Based Vegan Diet Recipes With A 31 Day Meal Plan To Lose Weight & Live A Long Healthy Life

699

Tart Cherry Mint Sorbet

SERVINGS
4

PREPARATION TIME
10 minutes

FREEZE TIME
3 hours

Nutritional Values Per Serving

Calories	247
Total Fat	4.9g
Saturated Fat	14g
Cholesterol	194mg
Sodium	407mg
Total Carbohydrate	27g
Dietary Fiber	4g
Total Sugars	1.3g
Protein	16g

Ingredients:

- 2 cups frozen tart cherries
- ½ cup maple syrup
- 2 teaspoons lemon juice
- ¼ cup mint leaves
- ¼ cup coconut milk
- ¼ cup water

Instructions:

1. Blend tart cherries with water, milk, mint, lemon juice and maple syrup in a blender.

2. Transfer the mixture to a freeze-safe container and freeze for 3 hours.

3. Scoop out and serve.

700

The Plant Based Cookbook For Beginners
650 Easy, Quick, & Simple Plant Based Vegan Diet Recipes With A 31 Day Meal Plan To Lose Weight & Live A Long Healthy Life

Chocolate Pudding

SERVINGS	PREPARATION TIME	COOKING TIME	FRIDGE TIME
4	10 minutes	2 minutes	2 hours

Nutritional Values Per Serving	
Calories	288
Total Fat	12g
Saturated Fat	6g
Cholesterol	13mg
Sodium	208mg
Total Carbohydrate	31g
Dietary Fiber	2g
Total Sugars	2.1g
Protein	18g

Ingredients:

- ¼ cup cocoa powder
- ¼ cup cornstarch
- ⅓ cup coconut sugar
- 1 pinch salt
- 2 ½ cups plain oat milk
- 3 ounces dark chocolate chips
- ½ tablespoon vanilla extract

Instructions:

1. Mix salt, cornstarch, sugar and cocoa powder in a saucepan.
2. Stir in milk, mix well and cook on a simmer for 2 minutes until it thickens.
3. Add chocolate chips, and vanilla then mix well.
4. Transfer this mixture into a container and allow it to cool.
5. Cover and refrigerate for 2 hours.
6. Scoop out the pudding and serve.

The Plant Based Cookbook For Beginners
650 Easy, Quick, & Simple Plant Based Vegan Diet Recipes With A 31 Day Meal Plan To Lose Weight & Live A Long Healthy Life

701

Cherry Bites

SERVINGS	PREPARATION TIME	COOKING TIME
8	1 hour 10 minutes	1 minute

Nutritional Values Per Serving

Calories	171
Total Fat	15g
Saturated Fat	17g
Cholesterol	0mg
Sodium	235mg
Total Carbohydrate	12g
Dietary Fiber	1.7g
Total Sugars	2.7g
Protein	7g

Ingredients:

Cherry Ripe Filling

- 1 cup dried sour cherries, soaked
- 1½ cup dried cranberries
- 2 tablespoons pure maple syrup
- ¼ teaspoon sea salt
- ¼ cup melted coconut oil
- 2 cup shredded coconut

Chocolate Coating

- ½ cup raw cacao powder
- ½ cup melted cacao butter
- ¼ cup pure maple syrup

Instructions:

1. Blend cherry ripe filling ingredients in a food processor and spread this mixture in a Pyrex dish.
2. Make 1-inch small balls out of this mixture.
3. Transfer these balls to a baking sheet and freeze for 1 hour.
4. Mix the chocolate coating ingredients in a bowl and melt in a microwave by heating in the microwave.
5. Coat the cherry balls with the chocolate melt.
6. Place the coated ball in a baking sheet lined with parchment paper and freeze until set.
7. Serve.

702

The Plant Based Cookbook For Beginners
650 Easy, Quick, & Simple Plant Based Vegan Diet Recipes With A 31 Day Meal Plan To Lose Weight & Live A Long Healthy Life

Caramel Slice

SERVINGS	PREPARATION TIME	COOKING TIME
8	1 hour 10 minutes	2 minutes

Nutritional Values Per Serving

Calories	240
Total Fat	10g
Saturated Fat	8.7g
Cholesterol	0mg
Sodium	620mg
Total Carbohydrate	51g
Dietary Fiber	5g
Total Sugars	19g
Protein	6g

Ingredients:

Base

- ½ cup almonds
- ½ cup Medjool dates, pitted
- 2 tablespoons coconut oil, melted
- ¼ cup raw cacao powder

Chocolate Layer

- 1 cup dark chocolate chips
- ¼ cup coconut oil

Caramel Layer

- 1 cup Medjool dates, pitted
- ½ cup coconut oil, melted
- 4 tablespoons tahini
- 2 tablespoons maple syrup
- 1 teaspoon vanilla

Instructions:

1. Blend almonds Medjool dates, coconut oil and cacao powder in a food processor.
2. Spread this base layer in a baking dish.
3. Blend the caramel layer ingredients in a blender and spread over the crust.
4. Allow the layers to set in the refrigerator for 1 hour.
5. Melt dark chocolate chips with oil in a bowl by heating in the microwave.
6. Mix well and spread over the caramel layer.
7. Allow the chocolate to set.
8. Cut into squares and serve.

The Plant Based Cookbook For Beginners
650 Easy, Quick, & Simple Plant Based Vegan Diet Recipes With A 31 Day Meal Plan To Lose Weight & Live A Long Healthy Life

703

Coconut Lime Cheesecakes

SERVINGS	PREPARATION TIME	FREEZE TIME
6	10 minutes	1 hour

Nutritional Values Per Serving

Calories	201
Total Fat	3.1g
Saturated Fat	0.5g
Cholesterol	0mg
Sodium	5mg
Total Carbohydrate	16.2g
Dietary Fiber	0.6g
Total Sugars	12.2g
Protein	13g

Ingredients:

Base

- ½ cup macadamia nuts
- ½ cup Medjool dates
- 2 tablespoons coconut oil
- 2 tablespoons coconut, shredded

Filling

- 2 cups raw cashews, soaked overnight, drained
- 1 cup coconut cream
- ¼ cup maple syrup
- Juice and zest of 1 lime

Instructions:

1. Blend nuts, Medjool nuts, coconut oil and coconut in a food processor.
2. Spread this mixture at the base of a pie pan.
3. Blend the drained cashews with coconut cream, maple syrup, lime juice and zest in a blender.
4. Divide this mixture over the macadamia crust layer and freeze for 1 hour.
5. Serve.

704

The Plant Based Cookbook For Beginners
650 Easy, Quick, & Simple Plant Based Vegan Diet Recipes With A 31 Day Meal Plan To Lose Weight & Live A Long Healthy Life

Choc-Mint Cups

SERVINGS	PREPARATION TIME	FREEZE TIME
6	40 minutes	30 minutes

Nutritional Values Per Serving

Calories	141
Total Fat	10.2g
Saturated Fat	2.4g
Cholesterol	0mg
Sodium	258mg
Total Carbohydrate	7.2g
Dietary Fiber	2g
Total Sugars	16.5g
Protein	4.5g

Ingredients:

Chocolate Layer

- ½ cup raw cacao powder
- ½ cup coconut oil, melted
- ¼ cup maple syrup
- 1 teaspoon vanilla extract

Peppermint Layer

- 1 cup cashews, soaked overnight
- ¼ cup coconut, shredded
- ¼ cup coconut milk
- ¼ cup coconut oil
- 1 drop of peppermint oil

Instructions:

1. Mix cacao powder, coconut oil, maple and vanilla in a bowl.
2. Spread ½ of this mixture in muffin silicon molds.
3. Blend cashews with coconut, milk, oil, and peppermint in a food processor.
4. Divide this mixture into the mold and add the remaining chocolate mixture on top.
5. Freeze these cups for 30 minutes.
6. Serve.

The Plant Based Cookbook For Beginners
650 Easy, Quick, & Simple Plant Based Vegan Diet Recipes With A 31 Day Meal Plan To Lose Weight & Live A Long Healthy Life

705

Apple Crumble

SERVINGS	PREPARATION TIME	COOKING TIME
6	15 minutes	50 minutes

Nutritional Values Per Serving

Calories	181
Total Fat	19g
Saturated Fat	0.6g
Cholesterol	0mg
Sodium	26mg
Total Carbohydrate	9g
Dietary Fiber	3g
Total Sugars	5.5g
Protein	6.9g

Ingredients:

Filling

- 9 apples, cored and sliced
- ¼ cup coconut sugar
- 2 tablespoons cornstarch
- ½ tablespoons cinnamon
- 1 teaspoon ground ginger
- 1 lemon, squeezed

Crumble

- ½ cup 2 tablespoons almond flour
- 3 tablespoons rolled oats
- ½ cup pecans, chopped
- ½ cup granola
- 1 tablespoon cinnamon
- ⅓ cup coconut oil, melted
- ¼ cup coconut sugar

Instructions:

1. At 350 degrees F, preheat your oven.
2. Mix apples with lemon juice, ginger, cinnamon, cornstarch, and coconut sugar in a mixing bowl.
3. Spread the apple mixture in a 9x12 inch baking pan.
4. Mix all the crumble ingredients in a bowl and spread over the apples.
5. Bake the apple crumble for 50 minutes in the oven.
6. Serve.

Pumpkin Cheesecake

SERVINGS	PREPARATION TIME	FREEZE TIME
6	10 minutes	3 hours

Nutritional Values Per Serving

Calories	159
Total Fat	2.2g
Saturated Fat	0.3g
Cholesterol	0mg
Sodium	64mg
Total Carbohydrate	25.5g
Dietary Fiber	1g
Total Sugars	2.3g
Protein	4.1g

Ingredients:

Graham Cracker Crust

- ½ cup raw pecans
- ½ cup blanched almond flour
- 5 dates, pitted
- 1 tablespoon coconut oil
- 1 teaspoon cinnamon
- ¼ teaspoon salt

Cashew Caramel Sauce

- ¼ cup cashew butter
- 2 tablespoons maple syrup
- 2 tablespoons coconut oil, melted

Cheesecake

- 1 ⅔ cups raw cashews, soaked
- ⅓ cup canned coconut milk
- ⅓ cup pumpkin puree
- ¼ cup coconut oil, melted
- ¼ cup pure maple syrup
- 2 tablespoons molasses
- 1 teaspoon vanilla extract
- 1 teaspoon cinnamon
- ¼ teaspoon nutmeg
- ¼ teaspoon ground ginger
- ⅛ teaspoon ground allspice
- ⅛ teaspoon ground cloves

Instructions:

1. Blend all the cracker crust ingredients in a food processor and spread in a 6-inch baking pan lined with parchment paper.
2. Blend all the cheesecake layer ingredients in a blender.
3. Divide this mixture into the crust.
4. Mix cashew butter with coconut oil and maple syrup in a bowl.
5. Drizzle this mixture over the cheesecake.
6. Freeze the cheesecake in for 3 hours.
7. Slice and serve.

The Plant Based Cookbook For Beginners
650 Easy, Quick, & Simple Plant Based Vegan Diet Recipes With A 31 Day Meal Plan To Lose Weight & Live A Long Healthy Life

707

Banana Cream Pie

SERVINGS	PREPARATION TIME	COOKING TIME
6	10 minutes	26 minutes

Nutritional Values Per Serving

Calories	234
Total Fat	21.2g
Saturated Fat	4.2g
Cholesterol	0mg
Sodium	14mg
Total Carbohydrate	17g
Dietary Fiber	1.4g
Total Sugars	13.6g
Protein	7g

Ingredients:

Crust

- ¾ cup rolled oats
- ¾ cup raw almonds
- ¼ teaspoons sea salt
- 2 tablespoons coconut sugar
- ¼ cup melted coconut oil

Coconut Whip

- 14-ounce can coconut cream
- ½ teaspoon vanilla extract
- 3 tablespoons coconut sugar
- Chopped nuts, to garnish

Filling

- 2 tablespoons cornstarch
- ⅓ cup coconut sugar
- 1 pinch sea salt
- 1½ cups almond milk
- 1 teaspoon pure vanilla extract
- 1 medium just-ripe banana, sliced

Instructions:

1. At 350 degrees F, preheat your oven.
2. Layer an 8x8 inch baking dish with parchment paper.
3. Blend oats with salt, almonds, sugar and coconut oil in a food processor until crumbly.
4. Spread this mixture in the prepared pan and press it down gently.
5. Bake this crust for 15 minutes in the oven, then increase the heat to 375 degrees F.
6. Continue baking for another 5 minutes.
7. Mix all filling ingredients in a saucepan, mix well and cook for 6 minutes until it thickens.
8. Allow the pudding to cool, then spread on the baked crust.
9. Beat all the coconut whip ingredients in a bowl.
10. Spread this mixture over the filling.
11. Garnish with nuts.
12. Slice and serve.

708

The Plant Based Cookbook For Beginners
650 Easy, Quick, & Simple Plant Based Vegan Diet Recipes With A 31 Day Meal Plan To Lose Weight & Live A Long Healthy Life

Chocolate Hazelnut Energy Bites

SERVINGS | PREPARATION TIME | COOKING TIME
6 | 10 minutes | 10 minutes

Nutritional Values Per Serving	
Calories	144
Total Fat	13.2g
Saturated Fat	25.7g
Cholesterol	0mg
Sodium	19mg
Total Carbohydrate	23g
Dietary Fiber	3.6g
Total Sugars	8.4g
Protein	4.5g

Ingredients:

- 1 cup toasted hazelnuts
- 10 Medjool dates
- 2 tablespoons coconut butter
- 2 tablespoons coconut oil
- 3 tablespoons cacao powder

Instructions:

1. Spread hazelnuts in a sheet pan and roast for 10 minutes at 350 degrees F.
2. Toss them once cooked halfway through.
3. Peel the hazelnuts, and grind them with dates in a food processor.
4. Add coconut butter, coconut oil and cacao, then mix well.
5. Make small 1-inch balls out of this mixture.
6. Serve.

The Plant Based Cookbook For Beginners
650 Easy, Quick, & Simple Plant Based Vegan Diet Recipes With A 31 Day Meal Plan To Lose Weight & Live A Long Healthy Life

709

Mango Nice Cream Bars

SERVINGS	PREPARATION TIME	COOKING TIME	FREEZE TIME
6	10 minutes	2 hours	3 hours 20 minutes

Nutritional Values Per Serving

Calories	218
Total Fat	6.3g
Saturated Fat	3.3g
Cholesterol	0mg
Sodium	158mg
Total Carbohydrate	23.9g
Dietary Fiber	1.8g
Total Sugars	15.6g
Protein	8g

Ingredients:

Cardamom Crust

- 1 cup golden raisins
- ¾ cup almond flour
- 1 tbs coconut oil
- ¼ teaspoons ground cardamom

Mango Nice Cream

- 2 frozen bananas
- 1 fresh ripe mango
- 3 tbs coconut oil
- 1 pinch ground turmeric
- 1 pinch ground cinnamon
- 1 tablespoon toasted coconut flakes

Instructions:

1. Blend the cardamom crust ingredients in a food processor until crumbly.
2. Spread this crust in a loaf pan lined with parchment paper.
3. Freeze this crust for 20 minutes.
4. Blend the mango with bananas, cinnamon, turmeric and oil in a blender until smooth.
5. Spread this mango filling in the crust and smooth out the surface.
6. Sprinkle coconut flakes, cover and freeze the layers for 3 hours.
7. Cut into bars and serve immediately.
8. Serve.

710

The Plant Based Cookbook For Beginners
650 Easy, Quick, & Simple Plant Based Vegan Diet Recipes With A 31 Day Meal Plan To Lose Weight & Live A Long Healthy Life

Strawberry Cheesecake Parfaits

SERVINGS
4

PREPARATION TIME
15 minutes

COOKING TIME
1 minute

Nutritional Values Per Serving

Calories	160
Total Fat	1.4g
Saturated Fat	2.1g
Cholesterol	0mg
Sodium	246mg
Total Carbohydrate	29.2g
Dietary Fiber	3.7g
Total Sugars	18.2g
Protein	1g

Ingredients:

- 1 ½ cups raw cashews
- ½ cup lite coconut milk
- ½ cup maple syrup
- ¼ cup coconut oil, melted
- ¼ teaspoon salt
- 3 tablespoons lemon juice
- 1 teaspoon vanilla extract
- Fresh strawberries, diced

Instructions:

1. Blend cashews in a food processor for 1 minute.
2. Stir in coconut milk, maple syrup, oil, salt, vanilla and lemon juice.
3. Blend well until smooth, then divide the mixture in the serving bowls.
4. Top them with the diced strawberries.
5. Serve.

The Plant Based Cookbook For Beginners
650 Easy, Quick, & Simple Plant Based Vegan Diet Recipes With A 31 Day Meal Plan To Lose Weight & Live A Long Healthy Life

711

Gingerbread Freezer Fudge

SERVINGS
6

PREPARATION TIME
5 minutes

FREEZE TIME
4 hours

Nutritional Values Per Serving

Calories	244
Total Fat	20.7g
Saturated Fat	17.6g
Cholesterol	0mg
Sodium	42mg
Total Carbohydrate	28.5g
Dietary Fiber	2g
Total Sugars	18.6g
Protein	4.2g

Ingredients:

- 1 cup almond butter
- ½ cup coconut oil, softened
- ½ cup coconut milk
- 6 tablespoons maple syrup
- 2 tablespoons blackstrap molasses
- 1 teaspoon ground cinnamon
- 1 teaspoon ground ginger
- ½ teaspoon ground nutmeg
- ¼ teaspoon ground cloves
- ¼ teaspoon sea salt

Instructions:

1. Layer a 9x9 inch baking dish with baking paper.
2. Mix almond butter with the rest of the ingredients in a bowl until smooth.
3. Spread this butter mixture in the prepared pan evenly.
4. Freeze this mixture for 4 hours.
5. Cut into bars and serve.

712

The Plant Based Cookbook For Beginners
650 Easy, Quick, & Simple Plant Based Vegan Diet Recipes With A 31 Day Meal Plan To Lose Weight & Live A Long Healthy Life

Chocolate Pomegranate Tart

SERVINGS	PREPARATION TIME	FRIDGE / FREEZER TIME
6	10 minutes	2 hours

Nutritional Values Per Serving

Calories	161
Total Fat	3.2g
Saturated Fat	0.4g
Cholesterol	0mg
Sodium	152mg
Total Carbohydrate	16g
Dietary Fiber	5.5g
Total Sugars	2.9g
Protein	3.1g

Ingredients:

Crust

- 1 cup dates, pitted
- 1 cup walnuts
- 1 pinch of sea salt

Topping

- ⅓ cup pomegranate seeds
- Melted dark chocolate

Filling

- 1 ½ cups raw cacao powder
- 1 cup 2 tablespoons pure maple syrup
- ¾ cup coconut oil, melted
- 1 teaspoon vanilla extract
- 1 pinch of sea salt
- ⅓ cup pomegranate seeds

Instructions:

1. Blend dates with salt and walnuts in a food processor until smooth.
2. Spread this mixture in a 9-inch round tart pan.
3. Freeze this crust in the freezer for 1 hour.
4. Blend cacao powder, maple syrup and the rest of the ingredients in a blender until smooth.
5. Spread this filling in the prepared crust evenly.
6. Add melted chocolate and pomegranate seeds on top.
7. Refrigerate for 1 hour.
8. Slice and serve.

The Plant Based Cookbook For Beginners
650 Easy, Quick, & Simple Plant Based Vegan Diet Recipes With A 31 Day Meal Plan To Lose Weight & Live A Long Healthy Life

713

Watermelon Coconut Sorbet

SERVINGS	PREPARATION TIME	FREEZE TIME
6	10 minutes	6 hours

Nutritional Values Per Serving

Calories	142
Total Fat	1g
Saturated Fat	1g
Cholesterol	0mg
Sodium	7mg
Total Carbohydrate	11g
Dietary Fiber	2g
Total Sugars	8g
Protein	1g

Ingredients:

- 5 cups seedless watermelon, peeled and diced
- 4 cups coconut milk
- ¼ cup coconut syrup
- Juice from ½ lemon

Instructions:

1. Blend watermelon with the rest of the ingredients in a blender until smooth.
2. Spread this mixture in a baking dish and cover it with plastic wrap.
3. Freeze the watermelon mixture for 4 hours.
4. Cut the frozen mixture into cubes and blend in a food processor.
5. Spread this mixture in the baking dish and freeze again for 2 hours.
6. Scoop out and serve.

Vanilla-Maple Ice Cream

SERVINGS	PREPARATION TIME	FREEZE TIME
6	**5 minutes**	**4 hours**

Nutritional Values Per Serving	
Calories	182
Total Fat	5g
Saturated Fat	0.4g
Cholesterol	0mg
Sodium	162mg
Total Carbohydrate	7.2g
Dietary Fiber	10.7g
Total Sugars	12.3g
Protein	2g

Ingredients:

- 3 cups unsweetened oat milk
- ¼ cup rolled oats
- 1 cup raw cashews
- ⅔ cup maple syrup
- 1 tablespoon vanilla extract
- ¼ teaspoon fine sea salt
- 1-ounce gin

Instructions:

1. Blend oats with cashews, maple syrup, vanilla, milk, salt and gin in a blender until smooth.

2. Transfer this mixture to the ice-cream machine and churn as per the machine's instructions.

3. Freeze the ice cream for 4 hours and scoop out to serve.

The Plant Based Cookbook For Beginners
650 Easy, Quick, & Simple Plant Based Vegan Diet Recipes With A 31 Day Meal Plan To Lose Weight & Live A Long Healthy Life

715

Earl Grey Truffles

SERVINGS	PREPARATION TIME	COOKING TIME
6-8	1 hour 20 minutes	3 minute

Nutritional Values Per Serving

Calories	142
Total Fat	4.4g
Saturated Fat	0.1g
Cholesterol	0mg
Sodium	33mg
Total Carbohydrate	13g
Dietary Fiber	5.1g
Total Sugars	8.9g
Protein	9g

Ingredients:

- 5 ounces coconut milk
- 1 ½ tablespoon Earl Grey tea leaves
- 8 ounces dark chocolate chips
- 1 tablespoon coconut oil
- 1 pinch Maldon salt
- Cocoa powder, to roll

Instructions:

1. Cook coconut milk and grey tea leave them in a saucepan for 3 minutes.
2. Stir in salt, coconut oil and chocolate, then mix well.
3. Strain this prepared mixture into a bowl through a fine sieve.
4. Spread this chocolate ganache in a shallow bowl and refrigerate for 45 minutes.
5. Use a scoop to take 2 tablespoons of ganache and make a ball.
6. Make more balls out of this mixture and then place them on a baking sheet.
7. Refrigerate the truffle balls for 30 minutes, then roll with the cocoa powder.
8. Serve.

716

The Plant Based Cookbook For Beginners
650 Easy, Quick, & Simple Plant Based Vegan Diet Recipes With A 31 Day Meal Plan To Lose Weight & Live A Long Healthy Life

Chocolate Mango Candy

SERVINGS
6

PREPARATION TIME
15 minutes

COOKING TIME
1 minute

FREEZE TIME
1 hour

Nutritional Values Per Serving

Calories	295
Total Fat	12.8g
Saturated Fat	1.3g
Cholesterol	10mg
Sodium	151mg
Total Carbohydrate	12g
Dietary Fiber	5.4g
Total Sugars	8.7g
Protein	11g

Ingredients:

- 1 cup unsweetened Mariani dried mango, soaked and drained
- ½ cup roasted unsalted cashews
- ½ cup roasted unsalted walnuts
- 1 cup Medjool dates, pitted
- ⅓ cup dried coconut flakes
- ½ teaspoon Himalayan salt
- 1¼ cup dark chocolate chips
- ¼ teaspoon flaked sea salt

Caramel Sauce

- 1 cup coconut cream
- ¾ cup brown sugar
- 1 tablespoon cornstarch

Instructions:

1. Mix the caramel sauce ingredients in a small saucepan and cook for 7 minutes with occasional stirring.
2. Soak dried mango in warm water in a small bowl for 5 minutes, then drain.
3. Pat dry the mangos, then keep them aside.
4. Blend nuts in a food processor, then transfer to a bowl.
5. Blend drain mango with dates in a food processor.
6. Add the nuts to the mango and add coconut flakes and ½ teaspoon salt, then mix well.
7. Layer a 9x9 inch baking dish with baking paper.
8. Spread the mango mixture in the dish evenly.
9. Now add the caramel sauce on top, cover the pan and freeze for 1 hour.
10. Melt chocolate chips in a bowl by heating them in the microwave.
11. Cut the frozen mango mixture into 2-inches bars.
12. Dip these bars in the melted chocolate and place them on a baking sheet.
13. Sprinkle the remaining salt on top and allow the chocolate to set in the fridge for at least 30 minutes.
14. Serve.

The Plant Based Cookbook For Beginners
650 Easy, Quick, & Simple Plant Based Vegan Diet Recipes With A 31 Day Meal Plan To Lose Weight & Live A Long Healthy Life

717

Coconut Bliss Balls

SERVINGS	PREPARATION TIME	COOKING TIME
6	10 minutes	0 minute

Nutritional Values Per Serving	
Calories	277
Total Fat	0.9g
Saturated Fat	0.1g
Cholesterol	0mg
Sodium	9mg
Total Carbohydrate	10g
Dietary Fiber	6.3g
Total Sugars	5.4g
Protein	1g

Ingredients:

- ½ cup coconut flour
- ¼ cup flaked coconut
- 2 tablespoons maple syrup
- 2 tablespoons coconut oil
- 1 teaspoon vanilla extract
- ½ cup sunflower seeds
- ½ teaspoon sea salt
- ½ teaspoon nutmeg
- 1 tablespoon chia seeds
- 2 tablespoons almond milk
- 2 tablespoons coconut, shredded

Instructions:

1. Soak chia seed in almond milk in a bowl for 5 minutes.
2. Blend flour, maple syrup, oil, coconut flakes, vanilla, sunflower seeds, sea salt, nutmeg and chia seeds mixture in a mixer.
3. Make 1-inch balls out of this mixture and roll them in the shredded coconut to coat.
4. Serve.

718

The Plant Based Cookbook For Beginners
650 Easy, Quick, & Simple Plant Based Vegan Diet Recipes With A 31 Day Meal Plan To Lose Weight & Live A Long Healthy Life

Vegan Panna Cotta

SERVINGS	PREPARATION TIME	COOKING TIME
2	2 hours 15 minutes	20 minutes

Nutritional Values Per Serving

Calories	249
Total Fat	10.2g
Saturated Fat	18.4g
Cholesterol	0mg
Sodium	149mg
Total Carbohydrate	20.1g
Dietary Fiber	0.3g
Total Sugars	12.5g
Protein	3g

Ingredients:

- 1 cup coconut milk
- 1-ounce coconut sugar
- 10 cardamom pods
- 1 teaspoon vanilla extract
- 1 tablespoon agar-agar flakes
- Sliced strawberries
- Mint leaves

Instructions:

1. Add cardamom, sugar, milk, and vanilla extract to a saucepan.

2. Stir and cook this mixture on medium heat until the sugar is dissolved.

3. Stir in agar-agar and cook on medium-high heat for 15 minutes until the mixture thickens with occasional stirring.

4. Remove this panna cotta mixture from the heat and strain this mixture into 2 serving molds through a fine sieve

5. Refrigerate them for 2 hours, then flip the molds onto the serving plates.

6. Garnish with strawberries and mint leaves.

The Plant Based Cookbook For Beginners
650 Easy, Quick, & Simple Plant Based Vegan Diet Recipes With A 31 Day Meal Plan To Lose Weight & Live A Long Healthy Life

719

Kiwi Chia Pudding

SERVINGS	PREPARATION TIME	COOKING TIME
4	1 hour 10 minutes	10 minutes

Nutritional Values Per Serving

Calories	285
Total Fat	15g
Saturated Fat	8.7g
Cholesterol	10mg
Sodium	173mg
Total Carbohydrate	13g
Dietary Fiber	1.4g
Total Sugars	7.6g
Protein	4.2g

Serving Suggestion:

Enjoy this pudding with fresh kiwis on the side.

Ingredients:

Pudding Layer

- 26 ½ ounces coconut water
- 3 ½ ounces tapioca small pearl
- 9 ounces coconut milk
- 3 ½ ounces coconut sugar
- ½ teaspoon coconut extract
- 1 teaspoon chia seeds

Kiwi Jelly Layer

- 1 cup kiwi juice
- 1 tablespoon agar
- 2 drops green food coloring
- Sliced almonds

Instructions:

1. Soak chia seeds in water in a bowl overnight.
2. Soak tapioca in cold water in a bowl for 1 hour.
3. Boil coconut water with sugar in a saucepan.
4. Strain and add the tapioca pearls to the coconut water.
5. Mix and cook for 10 minutes, then add coconut milk.
6. Remove this mixture from the heat and allow it to cool.
7. Stir in soaked chia seeds and mix well.
8. For the kiwi layer, mix kiwi juice, green color and agar in a saucepan.
9. Mix and cook this mixture to a boil.
10. Spread this mixture in a shallow bowl and allow it to cool.
11. Divide the pudding layer in the serving bowls and top them with a jelly mixture.
12. Garnish with sliced almonds.
13. Serve.

720

The Plant Based Cookbook For Beginners
650 Easy, Quick, & Simple Plant Based Vegan Diet Recipes With A 31 Day Meal Plan To Lose Weight & Live A Long Healthy Life

Chocolate Dipped Cherries

SERVINGS	PREPARATION TIME	COOKING TIME	FRIDGE TIME
6	10 minutes	2 minutes	30 minutes

Nutritional Values Per Serving	
Calories	188
Total Fat	14.3g
Saturated Fat	12.7g
Cholesterol	0mg
Sodium	52mg
Total Carbohydrate	26g
Dietary Fiber	2.3g
Total Sugars	4.5g
Protein	1.4g

Ingredients:

- 1 cup cherries with stems
- 1-14 ounces can coconut milk
- 1½ cups dark chocolate chips
- ½ teaspoon vanilla extract
- 1 pinch of Himalayan salt

Instructions:

1. Mix coconut milk and chocolate chips in a saucepan.
2. Cook the cream over low heat until the chocolate is melted.
3. Stir in salt and vanilla, then mix well.
4. Dip the cherries in the melted chocolate.
5. Place these cherries on a baking sheet and refrigerate for 30 minutes.
6. Serve.

The Plant Based Cookbook For Beginners
650 Easy, Quick, & Simple Plant Based Vegan Diet Recipes With A 31 Day Meal Plan To Lose Weight & Live A Long Healthy Life

721

Almond Joys

SERVINGS
6

PREPARATION TIME
5 minutes

FRIDGE TIME
2 hours

Nutritional Values Per Serving

Calories	260
Total Fat	2.5g
Saturated Fat	0g
Cholesterol	0mg
Sodium	155mg
Total Carbohydrate	8.5g
Dietary Fiber	0.3g
Total Sugars	7.3g
Protein	1.1g

Ingredients:

Almond Joy Base

- 2 ⅓ cups of almonds
- 18 organic pitted dates, chopped
- 2 cups unsweetened coconut, shredded
- 1 pinch vanilla bean powder
- 2 tablespoons coconut oil
- 1 pinch pink sea salt

Chocolate Topping

- ½ cup coconut oil
- ½ cup raw cacao powder
- ¼ cup maple syrup

Instructions:

1. Mix 2 cups almonds with dates, shredded coconut, vanilla bean powder, coconut oil and salt in a bowl.
2. Drop this base mixture in a baking pan with baking paper, spoon by spoon
3. Cover and refrigerate the crust for 1 hour.
4. Mix coconut oil with cacao powder and maple syrup in a bowl.
5. Drop this chocolate mixture over the almond clusters.
6. Refrigerate again for 1 hour.
7. Serve.

722

The Plant Based Cookbook For Beginners
650 Easy, Quick, & Simple Plant Based Vegan Diet Recipes With A 31 Day Meal Plan To Lose Weight & Live A Long Healthy Life

Nanaimo Bars

SERVINGS
6

PREPARATION TIME
1 hour 30 minutes

COOKING TIME
2 minutes

Nutritional Values Per Serving

Calories	214
Total Fat	2.6g
Saturated Fat	0g
Cholesterol	0mg
Sodium	143mg
Total Carbohydrate	19.4g
Dietary Fiber	0g
Total Sugars	4.1g
Protein	1g

Ingredients:

Bottom Layer

- 1 cup unsweetened coconut, shredded
- ½ cup pitted dates
- ½ cup dried cranberries
- ½ cup almonds, soaked
- ¼ cup) raw cacao powder

Top Layer

- 1 dark chocolate bar, chopped
- 2 tablespoons coconut oil
- 3 tablespoons cacao nibs

Middle Layer

- 2 cups raw cashews, soaked
- ¼ cup maple syrup
- 2 tablespoons melted coconut oil
- 4 tablespoons lemon juice
- 2 teaspoons vanilla extract

Instructions:

1. Blend coconut and the rest of the bottom layer ingredients in a food processor.

2. Spread this mixture in a suitable sheet pan lined with parchment paper.

3. Refrigerate this layer for 30 minutes.

4. Blend cashews with rest of the middle filling ingredients in a blender for 1 minute.

5. Spread this cashew cream filling over the bottom layer in the pan and refrigerate for 15 minutes.

6. Melt chocolate with coconut oil and cacao nibs in a bowl by heating in the microwave.

7. Mix well and spread over the middle layer.

8. Allow the chocolate to set and refrigerate for 1 hour.

9. Cut into squares and serve.

The Plant Based Cookbook For Beginners
650 Easy, Quick, & Simple Plant Based Vegan Diet Recipes With A 31 Day Meal Plan To Lose Weight & Live A Long Healthy Life

723

Chocolate Praline Truffles

SERVINGS	PREPARATION TIME	COOKING TIME
8	60 minutes	6 minutes

Nutritional Values Per Serving

Calories	203
Total Fat	23g
Saturated Fat	19.8g
Cholesterol	5mg
Sodium	45mg
Total Carbohydrate	25.1g
Dietary Fiber	3.6g
Total Sugars	17.7g
Protein	3.9g

Ingredients:

Praline

- ½ cup coconut sugar
- ½ cup brown sugar
- ⅓ cup canned coconut milk
- 2 tablespoons vegan butter
- 1 teaspoon vanilla

Truffles

- 2 cups dark chocolate chips
- ⅓ cup canned coconut milk
- 1 tablespoon almond butter
- 1 pinch of salt

Instructions:

1. Layer a baking sheet with parchment paper.
2. Mix coconut sugar, brown sugar, coconut milk and butter in a saucepan.
3. Cook and stir this mixture for 6 minutes until it turns golden in color.
4. Stir in vanilla, mix and spread this mixture on the baking sheet.
5. Leave the praline to set for 20 minutes.
6. Break this bark into small chunks and grind in a blender.
7. Melt 1 cup of chocolate chips in a bowl by heating in the microwave for 1 minute.
8. Mix well, then add coconut milk, almond butter, salt and ½ cup praline crumbs.
9. Stir again, cover and refrigerate for 30 minutes.
10. Make 2-inch balls out of this mixture.
11. Melt remaining chocolate chips in a bowl by heating in the microwave.
12. Dip the praline balls in the chocolate and place them on a baking sheet.
13. Allow the truffles to set.
14. Serve.

724

The Plant Based Cookbook For Beginners
650 Easy, Quick, & Simple Plant Based Vegan Diet Recipes With A 31 Day Meal Plan To Lose Weight & Live A Long Healthy Life

Twix Cups

SERVINGS
6

PREPARATION TIME
10 minutes

COOKING TIME
10 minutes

Nutritional Values Per Serving

Calories	268
Total Fat	3.1g
Saturated Fat	0.2g
Cholesterol	0mg
Sodium	33mg
Total Carbohydrate	30.8g
Dietary Fiber	6.5g
Total Sugars	18.9g
Protein	2.5g

Ingredients:

Base

- 1¼ cup coconut flour
- ⅓ cup coconut oil, melted
- ¼ cup maple syrup
- 1 pinch of salt

Chocolate Coating

- 1 cup dark chocolate chips
- 2 tablespoons refined coconut oil
- 1 pinch flaked sea salt

Caramel Layer

- ¾ cup Sun butter Seed Butter
- 4 tablespoons coconut oil, melted
- ⅓ cup maple syrup
- ⅓ cup date paste
- 1 pinch of salt

Instructions:

1. At 350 degrees F, preheat your oven.
2. Layer a mini muffin tray with paper liners.
3. Mix flour, salt, maple syrup and coconut oil in a small bowl.
4. Divide this mixture into the muffin cups and press lightly.
5. Bake the base for 8 minutes, then allow it to cool.
6. Mix all the caramel layer ingredients in a saucepan and cook until melted.
7. Divide this filling in the baked crust.
8. Melt dark chocolate chips with oil in a bowl by heating in the microwave.
9. Divide this chocolate over the caramel filling.
10. Allow the chocolate to set in the fridge and serve.

The Plant Based Cookbook For Beginners
650 Easy, Quick, & Simple Plant Based Vegan Diet Recipes With A 31 Day Meal Plan To Lose Weight & Live A Long Healthy Life

725

Cranberry Almond Clusters

SERVINGS	PREPARATION TIME	COOKING TIME
6	15 minutes	2 minutes

Nutritional Values Per Serving	
Calories	121
Total Fat	4.6g
Saturated Fat	0.4g
Cholesterol	0mg
Sodium	92mg
Total Carbohydrate	4.8g
Dietary Fiber	10g
Total Sugars	3.5g
Protein	3.1g

Ingredients:

- 1 ½ cup dark chocolate chips
- 1 tablespoon coconut oil
- 1 cup fresh cranberries, whole
- ¾ cup raw almonds, toasted

Instructions:

1. Layer a cookie sheet with parchment paper.
2. Toss cranberries with almonds in a bowl.
3. Then melt dark chocolate chips with coconut oil in a bowl by heating in the microwave.
4. Pour this melt over the cranberry mixture, then mix well.
5. Divide this cranberry mixture on a baking sheet into clusters.
6. Allow the chocolate clusters to cool and serve.

726

The Plant Based Cookbook For Beginners
650 Easy, Quick, & Simple Plant Based Vegan Diet Recipes With A 31 Day Meal Plan To Lose Weight & Live A Long Healthy Life

Chocolate Dipped Strawberries

SERVINGS	PREPARATION TIME	COOKING TIME
6	**15 minutes**	**2 minutes**

Nutritional Values Per Serving	
Calories	213
Total Fat	6.5g
Saturated Fat	1.4g
Cholesterol	0mg
Sodium	232mg
Total Carbohydrate	16g
Dietary Fiber	1.7g
Total Sugars	4.6g
Protein	9.9g

Ingredients:

- ½ cup dark chocolate chips
- 12 small strawberries

Instructions:

1. Melt chocolate chips in a bowl by heating them in the microwave.
2. Wash and pat dry the strawberries.
3. Hold each strawberry from the top and dip in the melted chocolate.
4. Place the coated strawberries in a baking sheet lined with baking paper.
5. Allow the chocolate to set in the fridge for 30 minutes, then serve.

The Plant Based Cookbook For Beginners
650 Easy, Quick, & Simple Plant Based Vegan Diet Recipes With A 31 Day Meal Plan To Lose Weight & Live A Long Healthy Life

727

Pumpkin Whipped Cream

SERVINGS	PREPARATION TIME	COOKING TIME
6-8	10 minutes	0 minute

Nutritional Values Per Serving

Calories	207
Total Fat	7.4g
Saturated Fat	1g
Cholesterol	0mg
Sodium	255mg
Total Carbohydrate	7.3g
Dietary Fiber	11.9g
Total Sugars	9g
Protein	5g

Ingredients:

- 1 cup chilled coconut cream
- 4 tablespoons pure pumpkin puree
- 1 ½ teaspoon pumpkin pie spice
- ½ teaspoon vanilla extract
- 1 tablespoon maple syrup
- Coconut cream, to garnish
- Pecan, to garnish

Instructions:

1. Beat coconut cream with pumpkin puree, vanilla, maple and pumpkin pie spices in a bowl with an electric mixture for 1 minute.

2. Garnish with coconut cream and pecans.

3. Serve

728

The Plant Based Cookbook For Beginners
650 Easy, Quick, & Simple Plant Based Vegan Diet Recipes With A 31 Day Meal Plan To Lose Weight & Live A Long Healthy Life

Hermit Cookies

SERVINGS
6

PREPARATION TIME
10 minutes

COOKING TIME
18 minutes

Nutritional Values Per Serving

Calories	205
Total Fat	5.5g
Saturated Fat	0.8g
Cholesterol	0mg
Sodium	277mg
Total Carbohydrate	13.5g
Dietary Fiber	6.2g
Total Sugars	1.3g
Protein	4.7g

Serving Suggestion:

Enjoy the cookies with a dust of powdered sugar on top.

Ingredients:

- ½ cup molasses
- ½ cup vegan butter
- ½ cup organic coconut sugar
- ½ cup coconut palm sugar
- 1 teaspoon baking soda
- ½ cup hot coffee
- 2 tablespoons flaxseeds
- 6 tablespoons water
- 1 cup almond flour
- 2 cup whole wheat flour
- ½ teaspoon salt
- 2 teaspoons cinnamon
- 1 teaspoon cloves
- 1 teaspoon ginger
- 1 cup vegan chocolate chips

Instructions:

1. Mix flaxseeds with 6 tablespoons water in a bowl and leave for 5 minutes.
2. Add flours and the rest of the ingredients except chocolate chips to a mixing bowl.
3. Mix well until smooth.
4. Fold in chocolate chips and mix evenly.
5. Divide this cookie dough into 2-inch round cookies and place them on the cookie sheet.
6. At 350 degrees F, preheat your oven.
7. Layer 2- 8 inch pans with baking paper and spread the cookie dough in these pans.
8. Bake for 18 minutes in the oven, then cut into squares.
9. Serve.

The Plant Based Cookbook For Beginners
650 Easy, Quick, & Simple Plant Based Vegan Diet Recipes With A 31 Day Meal Plan To Lose Weight & Live A Long Healthy Life

729

Vegan Nog Fat Bombs

SERVINGS	PREPARATION TIME	FREEZE TIME
6	10 minutes	1 hour

Nutritional Values Per Serving

Calories	289
Total Fat	2.2g
Saturated Fat	0.5g
Cholesterol	0mg
Sodium	42mg
Total Carbohydrate	15.2g
Dietary Fiber	12.8g
Total Sugars	2.4g
Protein	8.6g

Ingredients:

- ½ cup coconut butter melted
- ½ cup coconut oil melted
- 2 teaspoons vanilla extract
- 1 teaspoon nutmeg
- 1 teaspoon cinnamon
- 16 drops stevia
- 1 pinch of salt

Instructions:

1. Line silicon muffin tray with paper liners.
2. Mix coconut oil and the rest of the ingredients in a bowl.
3. Divide this mixture into the muffin tray and freeze for 1 hour.
4. Serve.

730

The Plant Based Cookbook For Beginners
650 Easy, Quick, & Simple Plant Based Vegan Diet Recipes With A 31 Day Meal Plan To Lose Weight & Live A Long Healthy Life

Chocolate Bean Brownie

SERVINGS	PREPARATION TIME	COOKING TIME
6	60 minutes	25 minutes

Nutritional Values Per Serving	
Calories	213
Total Fat	5.8g
Saturated Fat	4.4g
Cholesterol	0mg
Sodium	39mg
Total Carbohydrate	20.8g
Dietary Fiber	3.9g
Total Sugars	1.9g
Protein	6g

Ingredients:

Brownie Layer

- ½ cup black beans
- ⅓ cup coconut sugar
- ¼ cup cacao powder
- 1 tablespoon chia seed
- 3 tablespoons water
- 1 tablespoon nut butter
- ½ teaspoon vanilla
- ½ teaspoon baking powder
- 2 tablespoons water
- 1 pinch of salt

Coconut Butter Layer

- 2 cups shredded coconut
- ⅓ cup full fat coconut milk
- 2 tablespoons maple syrup

Chocolate Top

- 1 cup dark chocolate chips
- 1 tablespoon avocado oil

Instructions:

1. At 350 degrees F, preheat your oven.
2. Layer a loaf pan with parchment paper.
3. Soak chia seeds in 3 tablespoons of water in a bowl for 10 minutes.
4. Blend all the brownie layer ingredients in a food processor.
5. Spread this brownie mixture in the loaf pan and bake for 25 minutes.
6. Allow this brownie layer to cool.
7. Blend shredded coconut in a blender for around 2-4 minutes..
8. Add coconut milk and maple syrup, then blend well until smooth.
9. Spread this coconut mixture over the brownie layer.
10. Melt chocolate chips with 1 tablespoon oil in a bowl by heating in the microwave.
11. Pour this chocolate over the coconut layer and refrigerate for 30 minutes.
12. Cut into bars and serve.

The Plant Based Cookbook For Beginners
650 Easy, Quick, & Simple Plant Based Vegan Diet Recipes With A 31 Day Meal Plan To Lose Weight & Live A Long Healthy Life

731

Chocolate Popcorn

SERVINGS	PREPARATION TIME	COOKING TIME	FRIDGE TIME
16	15 minutes	5 minutes	30 minutes

Nutritional Values Per Serving

Calories	186
Total Fat	12g
Saturated Fat	2.7g
Cholesterol	0mg
Sodium	164mg
Total Carbohydrate	18.9g
Dietary Fiber	5.1g
Total Sugars	4.3g
Protein	3g

Ingredients:

- 2 quarts popped popcorn
- 1 cup peanuts
- ¾ cup sugar
- ¼ cup corn syrup
- ¼ cup cocoa powder
- ½ cup peanut butter
- 1 teaspoon vanilla

Instructions:

1. Mix peanut butter, vanilla, cocoa powder, corn syrup, and sugar in a saucepan.
2. Stir and cook this mixture for 5 minutes on medium heat.
3. Toss in popcorn and peanuts then mix well.
4. Let it sit the fridge for 30 minutes until chocolate is set.
5. Serve.

732

The Plant Based Cookbook For Beginners
650 Easy, Quick, & Simple Plant Based Vegan Diet Recipes With A 31 Day Meal Plan To Lose Weight & Live A Long Healthy Life

Snickers Chia Pudding

SERVINGS	PREPARATION TIME	COOKING TIME
4	40 minutes	0 minutes

Nutritional Values Per Serving

Calories	268
Total Fat	1.2g
Saturated Fat	0.2g
Cholesterol	0mg
Sodium	111mg
Total Carbohydrate	19.7g
Dietary Fiber	12g
Total Sugars	4.3g
Protein	5.5g

Ingredients:

Chocolate Chia Pudding

- 1 cup almond milk
- 3 tablespoons unsweetened cocoa powder
- 1 tablespoon peanut butter
- 2 tablespoons maple syrup
- 1 teaspoon vanilla
- ¼ cup chia seeds

Sun Butter Mousse

- ¼ cup peanut butter
- 1 tablespoon maple syrup
- 4 tablespoons coconut milk

Garnish

- Chocolate shavings
- Chopped nuts

Instructions:

1. Blend all the chocolate chia pudding ingredients in a bowl and refrigerate for 30 minutes.
2. Blend sun butter mousse in a blender until smooth.
3. Divide the chocolate chia pudding into the serving bowls.
4. Top the pudding with the sun butter mousse.
5. Garnish with chocolate shavings and chopped nuts.
6. Serve.

The Plant Based Cookbook For Beginners
650 Easy, Quick, & Simple Plant Based Vegan Diet Recipes With A 31 Day Meal Plan To Lose Weight & Live A Long Healthy Life

733

Pumpkin Spice Donuts

SERVINGS
6

PREPARATION TIME
5 minutes

COOKING TIME
25 minutes

Nutritional Values Per Serving	
Calories	291
Total Fat	1.9g
Saturated Fat	0.3g
Cholesterol	0mg
Sodium	46mg
Total Carbohydrate	33.4g
Dietary Fiber	18.7g
Total Sugars	24.8g
Protein	6.2g

Ingredients:

- 1 ¾ cup oat flour
- 2 teaspoons baking powder
- 1 teaspoon pumpkin pie spice
- 1 pinch of salt
- ½ cup almond milk
- ½ cups pumpkin purée
- ½ cup coconut sugar
- 1 teaspoon vanilla

Instructions:

1. At 350 degrees F, preheat your oven.
2. Grease the 6 wells of a donut pan.
3. Mix oat flour with salt, pumpkin spice, and baking powder in a bowl.
4. Stir in vanilla, milk, sugar, and pumpkin puree, then mix well until smooth.
5. Divide this mixture into the donut wells and bake for 25 minutes in the oven.
6. Allow the baked donuts to cool.
7. Serve.

734

The Plant Based Cookbook For Beginners
650 Easy, Quick, & Simple Plant Based Vegan Diet Recipes With A 31 Day Meal Plan To Lose Weight & Live A Long Healthy Life

Frosted Cookie Bars

SERVINGS | **PREPARATION TIME** | **COOKING TIME**
6 | 15 minutes | 15 minutes

Nutritional Values Per Serving	
Calories	205
Total Fat	2.6g
Saturated Fat	1.1g
Cholesterol	0mg
Sodium	130mg
Total Carbohydrate	14.9g
Dietary Fiber	17.7g
Total Sugars	8.7g
Protein	2.7g

Serving Suggestion:

Try these bars with sprinkles on top.

Ingredients:

- 3 cups almond flour
- ⅔ cup coconut oil melted
- ⅓ cup maple syrup
- 1 teaspoon vanilla
- 1 pinch of salt

Vanilla Buttercream Frosting

- 1 cup butter unsalted
- 4 ½ cups coconut sugar
- 4 tablespoons almond milk
- 2 teaspoons vanilla
- 1 pinch of salt

Instructions:

1. Mix flour with coconut oil, maple syrup, vanilla, and salt in a bowl.
2. At 350 degrees F, preheat your oven.
3. Prepare an 8x8 inch baking pan and layer with baking paper.
4. Spread the prepared cookie dough in the prepared pan and bake for 15 minutes.
5. Mix the buttercream frosting ingredients in a mixer and combine well.
6. Spread the frosting over the bars.
7. Cut the layers into bars and serve.

The Plant Based Cookbook For Beginners
650 Easy, Quick, & Simple Plant Based Vegan Diet Recipes With A 31 Day Meal Plan To Lose Weight & Live A Long Healthy Life

735

Vanilla Sheet Cake

SERVINGS	PREPARATION TIME	COOKING TIME
6	10 minutes	30 minutes

Nutritional Values Per Serving

Calories	217
Total Fat	5.6g
Saturated Fat	0.5g
Cholesterol	0mg
Sodium	209mg
Total Carbohydrate	34g
Dietary Fiber	14.9g
Total Sugars	13.1g
Protein	5.5g

Ingredients:

- ⅓ cup vegan butter
- 1 cup organic coconut sugar
- 1 cup cold water
- 1 tablespoon apple cider vinegar
- 1 teaspoon vanilla paste
- 2 cups baking flour
- 3 tablespoons corn starch
- ½ teaspoon baking soda
- ½ teaspoon baking powder
- 1 pinch of salt

Instructions:

1. At 350 degrees F, preheat your oven.
2. Layer an 8x8 inch pan with baking paper.
3. Mix baking flour with the rest of the cake ingredients in a mixer until smooth.
4. Spread the prepared batter in this pan.
5. Bake this cake for 30 minutes at 350 degrees F.
6. Take out cake from oven and cool.
7. Slice and serve.

Key Lime Tartlets

SERVINGS	PREPARATION TIME	COOKING TIME
6	15 minutes	15 minutes

Nutritional Values Per Serving

Calories	215
Total Fat	13.2g
Saturated Fat	0.1g
Cholesterol	0mg
Sodium	310mg
Total Carbohydrate	10.9g
Dietary Fiber	2.8g
Total Sugars	29g
Protein	6.8g

Ingredients:

Tart Crust

- 1 ¼ cups almond flour
- ¼ cup coconut butter
- 2 tablespoons maple syrup
- 2 teaspoons lime juice
- 1 tablespoon lime zest
- pinch of sea salt flakes

Tart Filling

- ½ cup cashews, soaked overnight, drained
- 1 avocado, peeled, pitted and chopped
- ¼ cup coconut oil, melted
- ¼ cup lime juice
- 1 tablespoon lemon juice
- 2 tablespoons maple syrup
- 2 tablespoons lime zest

Instructions:

1. Line 12 cup muffin tray with paper liners.
2. Blend the crust ingredients in a food processor.
3. Divide this crust into the paper liners and press down gently.
4. Blend all the tart filling ingredients in a blender and divide them into muffin cups.
5. Freeze the tarts for 30 minutes and serve.

The Plant Based Cookbook For Beginners
650 Easy, Quick, & Simple Plant Based Vegan Diet Recipes With A 31 Day Meal Plan To Lose Weight & Live A Long Healthy Life

737

Trail Mix Energy Bites

SERVINGS	PREPARATION TIME	COOKING TIME
4	40 minutes	0 minutes

Nutritional Values Per Serving

Calories	220
Total Fat	29.3g
Saturated Fat	5.5 g
Cholesterol	0mg
Sodium	21mg
Total Carbohydrate	5.2g
Dietary Fiber	3.7g
Total Sugars	10.3g
Protein	13.1g

Ingredients:

Trail Mix

- ¼ cup pumpkin seeds
- ¼ cup sliced almonds
- ¼ cup chia seeds
- ¼ cup sunflower seeds
- ¼ cup toasted coconut, shredded

Date Energy Balls

- 1½ cups pitted Medjool dates
- 1 cup rolled oats, divided
- 1 cup trail mix mixture
- 2 tablespoons milk of choice
- 1 teaspoon ground cinnamon

Instructions:

1. Grind all the trail mix ingredients in a food processor.
2. Puree dates with milk in a blender.
3. Stir in rolled oats, trail mix and cinnamon.
4. Mix well and transfer to a bowl.
5. Make small balls out of this mixture.
6. Serve.

738

The Plant Based Cookbook For Beginners
650 Easy, Quick, & Simple Plant Based Vegan Diet Recipes With A 31 Day Meal Plan To Lose Weight & Live A Long Healthy Life

Tahini Cashew Clusters

SERVINGS	PREPARATION TIME	COOKING TIME
6	10 minutes	25 minutes

Nutritional Values Per Serving	
Calories	233
Total Fat	17.6g
Saturated Fat	18g
Cholesterol	0mg
Sodium	130mg
Total Carbohydrate	11.6g
Dietary Fiber	12.9g
Total Sugars	16.2g
Protein	4.4g

Ingredients:

- 2 cups raw cashews
- 2 tablespoons tahini
- 2 tablespoons pure maple syrup
- 2 teaspoons sesame seeds
- 1 pinch sea salt

Instructions:

1. At 350 degrees F, preheat your oven.
2. Layer a baking sheet with baking paper.
3. Mix cashews with maple syrup and tahini in a bowl.
4. Divide this mixture into a small cluster on the baking sheet.
5. Sprinkle sesame seeds and sea salt on top.
6. Bake the clusters for 25 minutes until golden brown.
7. Allow the clusters to cool and serve.

The Plant Based Cookbook For Beginners
650 Easy, Quick, & Simple Plant Based Vegan Diet Recipes With A 31 Day Meal Plan To Lose Weight & Live A Long Healthy Life

739

Hummus Energy Bites

SERVINGS	PREPARATION TIME	COOKING TIME
8	15 minutes	0 minutes

Nutritional Values Per Serving

Calories	299
Total Fat	5.2g
Saturated Fat	1g
Cholesterol	0mg
Sodium	413mg
Total Carbohydrate	22g
Dietary Fiber	6.1g
Total Sugars	9.2g
Protein	6.4g

Ingredients:

- 1 ½ cups old-fashioned oats
- ½ cup dates, pitted
- 1 cup toasted pine nut hummus
- 1 tablespoon olive oil
- ¼ cup roasted chickpeas
- ¼ cup sunflower seeds
- ¼ cup pumpkin seeds
- ¼ teaspoon salt
- ¼ teaspoon black pepper
- ¼ teaspoon red pepper flakes
- 1 tablespoon nutritional yeast

Instructions:

1. Mix oats with dates and all other ingredients in a food processor.
2. Make 12 balls out of this mixture.
3. Serve.

740

The Plant Based Cookbook For Beginners
650 Easy, Quick, & Simple Plant Based Vegan Diet Recipes With A 31 Day Meal Plan To Lose Weight & Live A Long Healthy Life

Sweet Potato Balls

SERVINGS	PREPARATION TIME	COOKING TIME
6	10 minutes	0 minutes

Nutritional Values Per Serving	
Calories	257
Total Fat	9.5g
Saturated Fat	1g
Cholesterol	0mg
Sodium	16mg
Total Carbohydrate	10g
Dietary Fiber	9.4g
Total Sugars	4g
Protein	9.4g

Ingredients:

- 12 pitted dates, chopped
- 1 cup pecan pieces, chopped
- 1 cup walnut halves and pieces
- ¼ cup pumpkin seeds
- ½ cup mashed sweet potato
- ¼ cup unsweetened coconut flakes, toasted
- 2 teaspoons ground cinnamon
- 1 teaspoon pumpkin pie spice
- 1 teaspoon vanilla extract
- ½ teaspoon salt

Coating

- 2 tablespoons sesame seeds

Instructions:

1. Blend dates, pecan, walnut, pumpkin seeds, sweet potato, coconut flakes, cinnamon, pumpkin pie spice, vanilla and salt in a food processor until well combined.

2. Make 1-inch balls out of this mixture and roll in the sesame seeds.

3. Serve.

The Plant Based Cookbook For Beginners
650 Easy, Quick, & Simple Plant Based Vegan Diet Recipes With A 31 Day Meal Plan To Lose Weight & Live A Long Healthy Life

741

Raw Oreos

SERVINGS	PREPARATION TIME	FRIDGE TIME
6	15 minutes	1 hour

Nutritional Values Per Serving

Calories	210
Total Fat	12.8g
Saturated Fat	0½g
Cholesterol	0mg
Sodium	109mg
Total Carbohydrate	12.9g
Dietary Fiber	5.9g
Total Sugars	14.4g
Protein	4.9g

Ingredients:

Filling

- 1 cup coconut butter
- ¼ teaspoon vanilla extract
- Organic powdered sweetener, to taste

Cookie

- 1 ½ cups raw almonds
- 6 whole Medjool dates, pitted
- 3 tablespoons melted coconut oil
- 1 tablespoon maple syrup
- ⅓ cup cocoa powder
- 1 pinch sea salt

Instructions:

1. Blend almonds with cookie ingredients in a food processor.
2. Transfer this cookie dough to a bowl.
3. Blend all the coconut filling ingredients in a blender until smooth.
4. Divide the prepared dough into 1-inch balls and press them into flat cookies.
5. Place half of the cookies in a baking sheet lined with baking paper.
6. Top them with the prepared filling and place the remaining cookies on top.
7. Refrigerate these cookies for 1 hour.
8. Serve.

742

The Plant Based Cookbook For Beginners
650 Easy, Quick, & Simple Plant Based Vegan Diet Recipes With A 31 Day Meal Plan To Lose Weight & Live A Long Healthy Life

Pistachio-Stuffed Dates

SERVINGS
5

PREPARATION TIME
10 minutes

COOKING TIME
1 minute

Nutritional Values Per Serving	
Calories	311
Total Fat	10g
Saturated Fat	0.9g
Cholesterol	0mg
Sodium	8mg
Total Carbohydrate	28g
Dietary Fiber	9.1g
Total Sugars	10.4g
Protein	8g

Ingredients:

- 25 whole Medjool dates, pitted
- 4 tablespoons tahini
- 3 tablespoons pistachios, chopped
- 1 pinch sea salt
- 2 tablespoons unsweetened desiccated coconut flake

Instructions:

1. Mix tahini with pistachio, and salt.
2. Stuff the pitted dates with tahini pistachio mixture.
3. Garnish with coconut flakes.
4. Serve.

The Plant Based Cookbook For Beginners
650 Easy, Quick, & Simple Plant Based Vegan Diet Recipes With A 31 Day Meal Plan To Lose Weight & Live A Long Healthy Life

743

Lemon Bars

SERVINGS	PREPARATION TIME	COOKING TIME
6	15 minutes	46 minutes

Nutritional Values Per Serving

Calories	221
Total Fat	4.7g
Saturated Fat	2½g
Cholesterol	1mg
Sodium	87mg
Total Carbohydrate	21.7g
Dietary Fiber	4.2g
Total Sugars	17.7g
Protein	4.6g

Ingredients:

Filling

- 1 cup raw cashews, soaked overnight, drained
- 1 cup coconut cream
- 2 tablespoons arrowroot
- ½ cup lemon juice
- 1 tablespoon lemon zest
- 1 pinch sea salt
- ¼ cup maple syrup
- 2 tablespoons coconut sugar

Crust

- 1 cup gluten-free oats
- 1 cup almonds
- ¼ teaspoons sea salt
- 2 tablespoons coconut sugar
- 1 tablespoon maple syrup
- 5 tablespoons coconut oil, melted

Garnish

- Powdered sugar

Instructions:

1. At 350 degrees F, preheat your oven.
2. Blend oats with the rest of the crust ingredients in a food processor until crumbly.
3. Spread this crust mixture in an 8x8 inch baking dish lined with baking paper.
4. Blend the drained cashews with the rest of the filling ingredients in a blender until smooth.
5. Bake this crust for 15 minutes, then increase the temperature to 375 degrees F, then bake for 8 minutes.
6. Spread this filling over the baked crust, evenly.
7. Bake again for 23 minutes in the oven.
8. Allow it to cool. Garnish with some powdered sugar on top, then slice and serve.

744

The Plant Based Cookbook For Beginners
650 Easy, Quick, & Simple Plant Based Vegan Diet Recipes With A 31 Day Meal Plan To Lose Weight & Live A Long Healthy Life

Macadamia Coconut Truffles

SERVINGS	PREPARATION TIME	COOKING TIME
6	**15 minutes**	**0 minutes**

Nutritional Values Per Serving

Calories	278
Total Fat	2.7g
Saturated Fat	0½g
Cholesterol	0mg
Sodium	157mg
Total Carbohydrate	24.4g
Dietary Fiber	4g
Total Sugars	5.8g
Protein	5.6g

Ingredients:

Truffles

- ½ cup raw macadamia nuts
- 1 ½ cups desiccated unsweetened coconut
- ¼ cup cocoa butter, melted
- 2 tablespoons organic coconut sugar
- ½ teaspoons vanilla extract
- 1 pinch sea salt

Coating

- ¾ cup coconut flakes

Instructions:

1. Blend macadamia nuts with coconut, cocoa butter, sugar, vanilla and salt in a food processor.
2. Make 1-2-inch round balls out of this mixture.
3. Roll these balls in the coconut flakes and serve.

The Plant Based Cookbook For Beginners
650 Easy, Quick, & Simple Plant Based Vegan Diet Recipes With A 31 Day Meal Plan To Lose Weight & Live A Long Healthy Life

745

Pumpkin Ice-Cream

SERVINGS	PREPARATION TIME	FREEZE TIME
6	10 minutes	4 hours

Nutritional Values Per Serving

Calories	214
Total Fat	14.9g
Saturated Fat	0.7g
Cholesterol	0mg
Sodium	240mg
Total Carbohydrate	43.1g
Dietary Fiber	14.3g
Total Sugars	13.1g
Protein	10.1g

Ingredients:

- ¼ cup full fat coconut milk
- 4 ounces vegan cream cheese
- 4 ounces almond butter
- ½ cup pumpkin puree
- ⅓ cup Lakanto Powdered Sweetener
- 2 tablespoons maple syrup
- 1 teaspoon vanilla extract
- 1 tablespoon pumpkin pie spice
- 1 teaspoon cinnamon

Instructions:

1. Blend coconut milk with all ingredients in a blender.
2. Layer a suitable baking tray with parchment sheet and spread this mixture into the tray.
3. Freeze this pumpkin mixture for 4 hours.
4. Scoop out and serve.

746

The Plant Based Cookbook For Beginners
650 Easy, Quick, & Simple Plant Based Vegan Diet Recipes With A 31 Day Meal Plan To Lose Weight & Live A Long Healthy Life

Paleo Lemon Tarts

SERVINGS
6

PREPARATION TIME
10 minutes

COOKING TIME
10 minutes

FRIDGE TIME
1 hour

Nutritional Values Per Serving	
Calories	280
Total Fat	2.4g
Saturated Fat	0g
Cholesterol	0mg
Sodium	99mg
Total Carbohydrate	21.7g
Dietary Fiber	10.2g
Total Sugars	49.7g
Protein	2.3g

Ingredients:

Crust

- 1 ½ cups unsweetened coconut, shredded
- 1 cup almond flour
- 2 tablespoons coconut sugar
- 1 pinch of salt
- ¼ cup 2 tablespoons coconut oil

Filling

- 1 cup raw cashews, soaked overnight
- ½ cup fresh lemon juice
- 2 tablespoons agave nectar
- 1 pinch of turmeric
- Zest of 1 lemon

Instructions:

1. At 350 degrees F, preheat your oven.
2. Prepare a pie dish with parchment paper.
3. Blend almond flour with the rest of the crust ingredients in a food processor.
4. Spread this crust mixture in the pie dish and press down gently.
5. Blend the drained cashews with the rest of the filling ingredients in a blender.
6. Bake the crust for 10 minutes in the preheated oven.
7. Divide this filling in the crust and refrigerate for 1 hour.
8. Serve and enjoy.

The Plant Based Cookbook For Beginners
650 Easy, Quick, & Simple Plant Based Vegan Diet Recipes With A 31 Day Meal Plan To Lose Weight & Live A Long Healthy Life

747

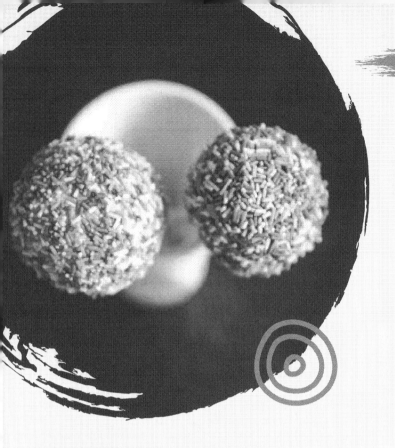

Lemon Cheesecake Pops

SERVINGS	PREPARATION TIME	FREEZE TIME
4	15 minutes	2 hours

Nutritional Values Per Serving

Calories	298
Total Fat	6g
Saturated Fat	7g
Cholesterol	632mg
Sodium	497mg
Total Carbohydrate	31g
Dietary Fiber	3g
Total Sugars	·83g
Protein	2g

Ingredients:

- ½ cup pecan nuts, chopped
- 2 Medjool dates, pitted
- 1 medium lemon, juiced
- 1 cup coconut milk
- ¼ cup canned chickpeas
- 1 cup frozen mango pieces
- ¼ teaspoon ground turmeric
- ¼ teaspoon salt
- ½ teaspoon apple cider vinegar
- 1 tablespoon maple syrup
- Colorful sprinkles, to garnish

Instructions:

1. Blend pecans nuts with 1 pinch of salt and 1 date in a food processor until smooth.
2. Blend chickpeas, milk, lemon juice, date, mango pieces, turmeric, salt, apple cider and maple syrup in a blender.
3. Divide this mixture into the pops molds and top the mixture with a pecan mixture.
4. Insert the ice-pop sticks and coat with sprinkles
5. Shake off the excess and freeze for 2 hours.
6. Serve.

748

The Plant Based Cookbook For Beginners
650 Easy, Quick, & Simple Plant Based Vegan Diet Recipes With A 31 Day Meal Plan To Lose Weight & Live A Long Healthy Life

Lemon Mousse

SERVINGS	PREPARATION TIME	COOKING TIME
6	15 minutes	2 minutes

Nutritional Values Per Serving	
Calories	232
Total Fat	8.9g
Saturated Fat	4.5g
Cholesterol	57mg
Sodium	340mg
Total Carbohydrate	24.7g
Dietary Fiber	1.2g
Total Sugars	12.3g
Protein	5.3g

Ingredients:

Lemon Curd

- ¾ cup lemon juice
- 1 tablespoon lemon zest
- 12 ounces silken tofu
- ½ cup coconut milk
- ½ cup water
- 1 ¼ cup granulated sugar
- 3 ½ tablespoons cornstarch
- 1 pinch salt
- 1 pinch turmeric
- ⅓ cup pistachios, chopped

Aquafaba Whip

- ½ cup aquafaba
- ¼ teaspoons cream of tartar
- 1 teaspoon vanilla extract
- ¾ cup coconut sugar

Instructions:

1. Blend tofu with lemon juice and the rest of the ingredients in a blender.
2. Spread this mixture in a pan and cook over medium heat until the mixture bubbles.
3. Mix well and allow the mousse to cool.
4. Beat the aquafaba with vanilla, sugar, and cream of tartar in a blender until fluffy.
5. Divide the lemon mousse in the serving bowls.
6. Top the mousse with the aquafaba whip on top.
7. Serve.

The Plant Based Cookbook For Beginners
650 Easy, Quick, & Simple Plant Based Vegan Diet Recipes With A 31 Day Meal Plan To Lose Weight & Live A Long Healthy Life

749

Chocolate Strawberry Popsicles

SERVINGS	PREPARATION TIME	COOKING TIME	FREEZE TIME
6	10 minutes	15 minutes	2 hours 30 minutes

Nutritional Values Per Serving	
Calories	227
Total Fat	31.1g
Saturated Fat	4.2g
Cholesterol	123mg
Sodium	86mg
Total Carbohydrate	29g
Dietary Fiber	12.4g
Total Sugars	19.8g
Protein	3.5g

Ingredients:

- 2 cups fresh strawberries, quartered
- 5 Medjool dates, pitted and quartered
- ¼ cup water
- ½ cup coconut cream
- ¼ teaspoon vanilla extract
- ¼ teaspoon lemon juice
- ½ cup fresh strawberries, diced

Chocolate Coating

- 1 cup dark chocolate chips, chopped
- 2 teaspoons coconut oil

Instructions:

1. Mix 2 cups of strawberries with dates and water in a saucepan on a simmer for 10 minutes.
2. Remove from the heat and allow the strawberry mixture to cool.
3. Blend this strawberry mixture with rest of the popsicle ingredients in a blender.
4. Divide this mixture in the popsicle molds, insert a popsicle stick in each mold and freeze for 2 hours.
5. Melt the dark chocolate chips with coconut oil in a bowl, by heating in the microwave.
6. Mix well and dip the frozen popsicles in the chocolate melt.
7. Allow the chocolate to set in the freezer for 30 minutes and serve.

750

The Plant Based Cookbook For Beginners
650 Easy, Quick, & Simple Plant Based Vegan Diet Recipes With A 31 Day Meal Plan To Lose Weight & Live A Long Healthy Life

Orange Popsicles

SERVINGS
8

PREPARATION TIME
10 minutes

FREEZE TIME
6 hours

Nutritional Values Per Serving	
Calories	75
Total Fat	0.1g
Saturated Fat	0g
Cholesterol	0mg
Sodium	20mg
Total Carbohydrate	18.1g
Dietary Fiber	0.1g
Total Sugars	17g
Protein	0.4g

Ingredients:

- 4 tablespoon oragne juice powder
- 1 cup water
- 1 cup orange juice store bought
- 1 cup orange juice freshly squeezed
- 2 teaspoon lemon juice
- ½ tablespoon sugar

Instructions:

1. Blend orange juice powder with water, juices and sugar in a blender until smooth.
2. Divide the orange mixture into the popsicle molds.
3. Insert the popsicles sticks and close the molds.
4. Place these molds in the freezer for 6 hours to set.
5. Serve.

The Plant Based Cookbook For Beginners
650 Easy, Quick, & Simple Plant Based Vegan Diet Recipes With A 31 Day Meal Plan To Lose Weight & Live A Long Healthy Life

751

Conclusion

How was your experience reading this cookbook? Are you planning to incorporate all those easy and practical plant-based recipes into your lifestyle? Well, if you are! Then don't forget to follow the 31-day meal plan from Chapter Two of this cookbook. If you are a beginner and want to start your plant-based diet plan from scratch, then this book has all the right ingredients recommended for you. A detailed guideline discusses the healthy advantages and the Dos and Don'ts of the plant-based diet shared in Chapter One of this cookbook. That chapter will help you prepared your mind for it and get started with it.

Upon moving to the next chapter, you will find a complete 31-day meal plan, which helps all the beginners to get started with their new plant-based diet. Chapter Three is all about the breakfast recipes, which will give you over 100 unique ideas to incorporated plant-based ingredients into your daily morning meals without a hassle. This chapter is followed by an independent section of dressing and dips recipes. Right after this chapter, there is a section for soup and salad recipes. You will be amazed by the variety of smoothies and beverage ideas shared in Chapter Six. Then comes an extensive collection of lunch and dinner recipes perfect for serving your daily caloric needs while living on a plant-based diet. Lastly, there is a complete section sharing snack and dessert recipes. And that sums up our entire collection of 650 easy plant-based recipes for beginners shared in this cookbook.

Getting onto the plant-based dietary approach is difficult for most dieters, as the recipes available in most cookbooks are too complex or too fancy to try daily. Every beginner needs delicious yet simple and easy recipes to incorporate all the plant-based ingredients into his diet without feeling the urge to quit soon. I like the recipes I share in this cookbook because they are relatively simple and easy for all, especially for a novice cook. Plant-based diets aid in reversing most chronic diseases. Health experts and doctors recommend this diet and medications to all those suffering from high blood pressure, cancer, and high cholesterol. By strictly following this approach, most dieters get rid of the medications and their side effects. Here comes a fix to counter all your health problems! This whole food plant-based cookbook is written for all my fellow health-enthusiasts! Eating healthy and delicious food is now possible with my plant-based recipe collection.

There are tons of plant-based cookbooks that can offer you many recipes, but for a beginner, those recipes can be of no use without a well-written meal plan. Having a meal plan helps you keep on the right track and introduces a complete variety to your routine menu. The 31-day meal plan in this cookbook offers you delicious meals for each day of the week. The entire plan is divided into weeks so you could meal-prep and grocery shop easily. All the recipes in this book are provided with a complete nutritional profile, making it easier for you to keep track of your daily caloric intake. Lastly, all the

752

The Plant Based Cookbook For Beginners
650 Easy, Quick, & Simple Plant Based Vegan Diet Recipes With A 31 Day Meal Plan To Lose Weight & Live A Long Healthy Life

ingredients from its recipe collection are listed in an organized index, given at the end of the book, to help you find a recipe with any particular ingredient.

Switching to a new diet plan is always overwhelming. Only a good understanding of the diet can help a beginner garner the true benefits of a dietary approach. And this cookbook will be your key to learn all the basic facts about the plant-based diet plan. Without getting into unnecessary details, I have precisely discussed all the essential facts about the diet. It has all the benefits of the plant-based diet, supported by recent scientific studies. Before that, a comprehensive dietary guide will help you pick the right type of plant-based food to practically incorporate the diet plan into your everyday routine. The 5 main food groups from this dietary approach were discussed in Chapter One. There you have a brief list of the commonly used plant-based ingredients along with a quick list of the plant-based substitutes to support your diet.

I learned from my struggle is that it is crucial to have complete knowledge and understanding of a diet to harness its real benefits. I was lucky that I had the resources to study plant-based nutrition myself; however, not everyone can afford to do so! So, I have written this cookbook to compile the best plant-based recipes I tried and tested and found most useful for all the plant-based diet beginners.

So, if you value your health or suffer from any chronic diseases, then switching to a plant-based diet will greatly help. This cookbook is your calling to a healthy lifestyle. It is here to ease this transition for you with its wide variety of delicious plant-based recipes- all categorized into chapters, to meet your daily needs. Its 31-day meal plan is excellent for all the beginners to get started without having to plan anything. Give it a read, pick out your favorite plant-based meals, try its meal plan and see your health improve quickly!

The Plant Based Cookbook For Beginners
650 Easy, Quick, & Simple Plant Based Vegan Diet Recipes With A 31 Day Meal Plan To Lose Weight & Live A Long Healthy Life

753

Index of Ingredients

A

Active dry yeast 611

Agave 147 165 167 183 208 215 219 240 241 292 294 296 297 313 328 330 358 392 415 421 478 551 563 661 668 686

All-purpose flour 120 129 140 578 611

Allspice 100 124 251 289 305 308 365 469 560 575 602 610 707

Almond butter 106 134 173 183 239 315 487 664 697 712 724 746

Almond flour 106 108 222 674 688 689 690 691 692 693 694 706 707 710 729 735 737 747

Almond milk 96 97 98 99 100 102 103 108 111 113 114 115 118 119 121 122 124 126 127 128 129 131 132 133 134 137 138 139 146 147 148 152 157 159 161 162 163 164 166 167 168 173 175 178 179 187 188 190 192 194 198 199 207 210 214 216 217 218 219 220 222 224 225 226 227 230 233 234 235 240 242 246 250 254 256 257 260 264 266 273 311 315 316 317 318 319 321 322 323 326 327 328 329 331 332 356 360 416 430 446 469 470 488 600 613 635 637 639 641 654 664 688 689 697 698 708 718 733 734 735

Almonds 105 117 121 123 125 176 202 214 234 244 271 301 305 367 376 387 416 468 534 543 576 580 589 684 686 703 708 720 722 723 726 738 742 744

Angel hair pasta 405

Apple 99 100 111 132 147 182 200 203 207 235 281 282 292 297 300 320 332 534 550 568 618 643 659 674 692 706

Apple cider vinegar 97 100 118 119 122 126 129 137 141 169 188 192 256 272 292 297 300 304 355 414 417 434 473 475 476 485 534 547 561 568 592 596 602 620 643 688 679 692 736 748

Apple Juice 141 142 197 200 309 320 475

Apple sauce 98 103 108 114 118 122 137 142 144 146 152 203 221 226 227 268 272 377

Artichoke 513 599

Arugula 303 418 438 460 519 545 582

Asparagus 153 298 301 366 369 391 408 517 533 572 624 647

Avocado 124 136 155 170 171 180 184 231 237 249 250 251 252 282 285 334 336 340 342 343 349 351 355 365 415 439 441 444 452 460 471 476 489 491 498 517 519 522 535 560 562 571 601 620 637 662 672 676 697 737

Avocado oil 249 251 252 285 441 491 620 672 677 678 731

B

Baby carrots 399 644

Baby spinach 170 255 289 340 353 358 369 396 409 418 442 462 468 496 551 556 566 601

Baking powder 97 98 99 100 102 103 106 114 115 118 119 122 124 126 129 135 137 139 141 142 144 146 148 149 151 152 153 157 160 174 175 177 187 188 192 196 198 202 204 205 210 212 218 220 225 226 227 488 578 613 688 694 731 734 736

Baking soda 97 99 100 101 102 103 106 114 122 124 126 135 139 142 151 152 192 204 212 225 226 227 239 242 643 654 655 688 689 691 729 736

Balsamic vinegar 171 186 245 272 276 278 286 340 348 363 367 384 410 557 558 578 584 621 634 648 690

Bananas 96 97 98 99 102 105 107 119 126 128 131 133 135 141 142 143 148 151 157 161 162 166 167 168 170 173 175 177 179 190 192 195 197 202 208 210 212 215 216 217 221 225 229 230 240 244 250 318 323 582 617 638 640 642 654 663 664 685 708 710

Barley 373 390

Basmati rice 365 401 411 431 487 544 575

Bbq sauce 573

Bean sprouts 493 518 521

Beer 425

Beets 280 299 302 336 367 546 570 583 683

Black beans 112 343 374 452 535 731

Black-eyed peas 377

Black salt 120 140 153 243 265 494

Breadcrumbs 360 418 460 466 516 540 584 589 600 679

Broccoli 115 243 260 294 304 372 403 419 443 446 456 485 496 500 559 566 626

Broccolini 369 370 499

Brown lentils 365 418 429 503 557

Brown rice 104 130 164 282 341 343 370 399 400 403 419 447 451 454 462 483 485 552 553 562 595

Brown sugar 100 114 210 211 212 233 246 319 371 392 518 521 590 607 644 674 717 724

Buckwheat flour 98 198 249

Button mushrooms 381 410 590

C

Cabbage 288 294 296 304 355 357 364 366 437 448 451 455 524 575

Cane sugar 558 562 611

Canned chickpeas 259 300 306 339 347 363 395 401 423 438 454 457 458 460 610 748

Canned black beans 146 231 236 285 334 363 341 437 444 445 455 466 471 474 476 472 478 480 530 541 571 584 592 595 604 606 669

Cannellini beans 171 525 582

Canned pumpkin 204 511

Canned green chiles 340

Canned corn 466 535

Canned pumpkin 143 204 511

Canned tomatoes 603

Capers 273 339 368 387 428 554 579 583

Cardamom 163 165 181 194 199 218 226 313 316 543 605 606 692 694 710 719

754

The Plant Based Cookbook For Beginners
650 Easy, Quick, & Simple Plant Based Vegan Diet Recipes With A 31 Day Meal Plan To Lose Weight & Live A Long Healthy Life

Carrots 103 174 180 232 254 274 290 295 296 338 352 353 357 364 366 371 399 405 410 411 412 423 436 440 472 481 483 509 542 543 551 555 557 562 584 587 596 605 607 615 644

Cashew nuts 159 257 260 273 277 286 292 300 310 314 346 381 391 396 402 408 413 464 470 471 476 509 522 533 537 556 558 561 564 566 570 598 655 665 668 699 704 705 707 711 715 717 723 737 739 744 747

Cashew butter 169 325 522 707

Cauliflower 258 261 283 346 361 385 387 395 401 412 420 423 424 452 454 502 514 516 522 537 544 545 561 574 581 582 613 630 636 678

Cauliflower rice 219 359 445 676

Cayenne 110 184 251 254 258 263 287 292 296 346 363 373 374 417 423 426 434 454 457 462 471 472 474 476 477 480 481 483 503 504 560 602 610 612 670

Celery 282 292 300 339 357 390 410 411 412 435 447 467 529 584 620

Cherry tomatoes 155 156 245 293 306 350 364 446 449 450 458 468 490 495 496 497 501 532 557 558 575 577 586 649

Chia seeds 96 113 128 138 158 159 161 167 173 178 202 204 205 209 210 214 218 220 223 234 235 238 242 244 273 488 619 639 643 662 688 718 720 731 733 738

Chickpea flour 101 115 120 140 153 160 530 606

Chickpeas 237 247 266 297 353 498

Chili flakes 287 302 353 366 368 393 411 521 683

Chives 160 196 264 265 363 438 490 494 534 681

Chocolate chips 97 98 118 144 151 164 175 192 202 227 239 317 318 666 667 675 687 689 693 697 701 703 716 717 721 724 725 726 727 729 731 749 750

Cilantro 112 140 231 236 261 275 277 285 288 292 294 296 299 300 302 334 342 344 346 349 357 374 376 420 423 431 437 445 448 451 454 455 457 462 466 471 473 474 476 480 482 484 489 502 504 505 514 537 544 545 548 551 553 560 561 602 603 606 622 629

Cinnamon powder 97 99 100 102 103 104 106 107 108 113 114 124 125 126 130 133 134 135 138 139 141 142 143 144 145 151 159 163 164 165 167 173 174 175 176 181 183 188 192 195 200 203 204 207 209 211 212 218 219 220 221 224 226 229 233 235 239 246 249 272 289 305 308 310 313 315 316 320 322 324 331 332 365 371 415 417 434 437 457 469 479 543 560 568 576 592 606 609 617 618 619 635 640 642 643 664 659 676 682 684 686 689 690 691 692 694 698 706 707 710 712 729 730 738 741 746

Cloves 111 138 313 320 712

Cocoa powder 96 118 129 208 210 217 318 317 318 640 641 656 657 664 675 659 701 716 782 733 742

Coconut cream 255 258 309 517 525 535 559 575 638 640 661 665 681 687 698 704 708 717 728 744 750

Coconut milk 117 158 167 177 178 193 211 212 215 223 244 249 282 308 316 318 325 330 361 377 381 382 423 441 454 462 472 479 481 483 485 504 523 542 544 548 555 566 568 577 581 605 658 660 662 663 668 686 696 699 700 705 707 711 712 714 716 719 720 721 724 731 733 746 749

Coconut oil 106 173 174 188 209 220 224 241 242 282 308 311 372 382 460 462 472 479 485 502 523 537 548 555 566 602 636 657 659 660 665 666 668 674 675 686 689 690 691 692 693 698 699 702 703 704 705 706 707 708 709 710 711 712 713 716 722 723 725 726 730 735 737 742 744 747 750

Coconut shreds 300 361 362 702 718 731

Coconut sugar 119 124 126 129 173 188 202 204 220 225 226 227 251 309 323 324 369 414 422 427 441 451 483 548 555 560 654 665 688 690 691 692 701 706 708 719 720 724 729 731 734 735 736 744 745 747 749

Collard greens 528

Cooked rice 509

Crushed tomatoes 285 401 432 453 480 542

Canned tomatoes 344 415 454 457 477 452 571

Coriander 282 297 301 361 365 374 378 381 386 395 398 422 457 459 473 481 517 524 535 566 577 584 585 587 602 604 606 609 653

Cornflour/cornstarch 193 499 500 736

Cornmeal 116 137 139 146 341 450

Couscous 156 376 458 478 508 576 580 585

Cranberries 99 104 125 131 143 207 320 331 433 702 723 726

Cremini mushrooms 349 425 430 443 515 547 557

Crushed nuts 697

Cucumber 136 213 277 287 291 293 294 306 335 348 355 439 458 490 532 533 560 562 585 587 596 602 621 681

Curry powder 261 292 300 346 377 378 409 417 423 431 434 454 460 472 483 509 566

D

Dark chocolate 326 666 723

Date syrup 139

Dijon mustard 272 276 278 385 355 370 528 541

Dill 115 256 264 265 291 306 490 524 583 683

Dried basil 156 276 453 490 506 630

Dried cranberries 104 125 143 433 702 723

Dried herbs 191 606

Dried oregano 156 347 360 384 410 411 437 445 453 471 474 476 490 491 492 507 556 558 580 586 590 592 597 603 604

Dried porcini mushrooms 390

Dried sage leaves 251

Dried shiitake mushrooms 154

Dried tomatoes 501 513 559 576 598

Dry white wine 552 569

E

Edamame 359 369 551 563

Eggplant 252 259 263 269 353 360 368 388 400 401 404 431 449 453 506 523 531 577 579 580 586 650

Enchilada sauce 571 592

F

Farfelle Pasta 464

Fennel seeds/powder 247 297 432 459 604

Fennel bulb 281 291 301 528 529 530 537

Flaxseeds 97 98 103 106 115 118 122 124 136 134 143 148 152 153 160 168 192 212 220 221 225 242 249 332 473 474 516 521 606 684 686 729

The Plant Based Cookbook For Beginners
650 Easy, Quick, & Simple Plant Based Vegan Diet Recipes With A 31 Day Meal Plan To Lose Weight & Live A Long Healthy Life

755

Frozen bananas 179 217 685 710
Frozen blueberries 128 137 147 684
Frozen mango 190 215 244 312 330 717 748
Frozen peas 401 431 472 481 483 509 552
Frozen spinach 432
Frozen tater tots 185

G

Garam masala 385 436 454 459 481 504 537 577 605
Garbanzo beans 287 484
Garlic 109 110 112 120 150 153 155 236 245 247 248 251 255 256
   259 261 262 263 269 271 273 275 277 280 284 285 286 287
   290 295 296 298 299 304
Garlic paste 591
Garlic powder 101 140 160 184 191 206 247 252 254 260 264
   265 270 340 341 363 422 427 449 455 460 464 473 483
   486 492 493 502 568 578 592 598 600 670
Garlic salt 421
Ginger ground 103 132 135 138 151 174 311 315 365 439 457 643
   686 694 706 707 712
Ginger paste 591
Gnocchi pasta 565 593
Gochujang 451
Golden potato 593
Grape tomatoes 400
Grapeseed oil 522 538
Green apple 172
Green bell peppers 380 384 425 446 482 484 502 573 603
Green chiles 340 537 571
Green beans 357 379 404 406 430 523 553 591 623
Green olives 580
Green onions 101 112 140 146 154 155 156 243 287 294 296 297
   298 302 359 363 364 366 369 383 389 395 399 413 415 419
   421 426 441 443 444 445 472 478 481 488 491 493 499 505
   508 509 516 517 518 531 533 537 538 541 543 545 548 549
   550 560 563 566 571 573 575 602 607 631 633
Ground cinnamon 103 104 107 108 114 116 124 125 126 130 133
   134 135 138 139 141 142 151 173 174 200 308 313 322 324 331
   332 415 417 434 437 457 543 560 576 609 617 618 619 635
   640 642 643 686 710 712 738 741
Ground coriander 374 378 381 386 398 457 459 525 566 524
   566 602 604 606 609
Ground cumin 109 263 334 342 349 353 374 376 377 378 389
   396 399 400 406 415 418 437 438 445 457 459 492 505 514
   522 524 560 566 576 585 590 592 594 604 606 609 610 616
   629 634
Ground flax 97 103 106 114 118 122 124 133 134 142 143 152 168
   192 659
Ground ginger 103 132 135 138 151 174 311 315 365 457 643 686
   694 706 707 711
Ground nutmeg 99 134 135 138 141 151 308 311 324 356 635 643
   712
Ground oats 643
Ground turmeric 115 120 155 194 308 311 374 381 386 389 396
   398 426 431 459 462 470 475 479 480 481 483 537 543 548
   577 616 619 686 710 748

H

Hemp seeds 134 144 156 158 220 222 230 244 250 304 331
Hot sauce 112 231 258 277 337 348 447 471 472 476 505 516
   613
Hummus 245 259 337 353 364 487 501 545 740

I

Italian salad dressing 266

J

Jerk seasoning 560

K

Kalamata olives 306 552
Kale 156 245 264 266 272 273 274 277 282 284 286 297 305
   345 355 373 382 390 393 398 433 520 530 534 536 539
   549 554 559 565 612 631
Ketchup 425 455 473 477
Kiwi 161 197

L

Leek 248 281 301 390 391 423 565 645
Lemon juice 102 123 136 159 165 169 171 172 198 201 242 244
   248 260 261 262 265 266 268 269 273 277 237 291 293 297
   298 301 304 305 306 336 357 363 373 385 394 395 397 405
   416 418 420 424 426 428 438 450 457 469 480 487 490
   496 499 504 508 512 519 529 530 535 540 541 552 556 564
   570 572 574 589 599 601 602 603 606 618 637 645 646 646
   648 650 652 665 668 676 681 684 688 691 699 700 706 711
   723 737 744 747 748 749 750 751
Lemon zest 124 133 139 144 242 297 298 305 330 362 395 397
   428 450 490 519 556 566 570 572 584 588 647 665 676 684
   688 699 744 749
Lime juice 158 231 236 254 282 288 294 296 340 346 351 352
   362 377 383 385 421 423 441 445 455 456 471 488 509 512
   513 514 521 522 523 528 531 539 542 545 548 560 563 566
   583 590 594 602 605 629 658 662 704 737
Lime zest 158 361 423 605 737
Lettuce leaves 136 265 276 338 350 352 364 422 498

M

Mango 117 158 161 188 190 197 215 241 244 288 312 330 485 560
   577 622 653 710 717 748
Maple syrup 96 97 98 102 103 106 107 108 111 113 116 117 118 121
   122 123 130 131 132 135 137 138 144 151 152 157 158 159 163
   164 166 173 174 176 178 181 188 189 192 193 194 196 199 202
   217 218 221 224 229 234 235 239 242 246 247 252 272 273
   284 300 302 308 310 311 314 315 316 317 321 322 325 327
   329 331 339 363 384 395 417 434 455 456 469 481 485 493
   502 541 567 568 591 631 637 639 641 655 656 658 662 663

756

The Plant Based Cookbook For Beginners
650 Easy, Quick, & Simple Plant Based Vegan Diet Recipes With A 31 Day Meal Plan To Lose Weight & Live A Long Healthy Life

676 682 684 388 689 693 694 695 696 697 698 699 700 702 703 704 705 707 711 712 713 715 718 722 723 725 728 731 733 735 737 739 742 744 746 748

Matcha tea powder 162 240 327

Mejdool dates 172

Microgreens 171

Mint 168 181 287 293 303 326 328 352 365 386 395 431 548 585 589 601 637 658 700 705 719

Mirin 361 392 443 533 550

Molasses 226 422 427 528 707 712 729

N

Noodles 296 352 356 357 358 369 372 383 391 393 429 432 441 443 446 448 469 470 471 477 479 493 518 521 526 532 533 538 541 548 549 550 551 563 628

Nutmeg 97 99 102 134 135 138 141 144 151 164 188 192 224 226 239 251 308 311 324 325 356 412 432 464 469 511 520 560 568 602 635 643 698 707 712 718 730

Nutritional yeast 101 110 115 140 153 156 160 206 243 247 248 254 257 560 266 273 276 304 342 416 429 432 453 470 494 496 564 569 598 677 678 679 681 740

O

Oat flour 99 106 135 144 149 151 152 164 204 225 473 474 682 734

Oat milk 107 229 491 701 715

Oats 98 99 102 103 105 106 107 113 125 127 129 130 131 132 133 134 139 141 142 143 144 145 156 163 164 165 174 175 189 199 200 202 207 218 220 221 224 229 233 271 311 364 438 473 474 491 591 643 655 680 682 684 690 692 695 706 708 715 738 740 744

Olives 287 350 368 387 501 513 580

Onion powder 101 140 247 254 256 260 264 270 340 343 421 438 470 473 477 493 494 560 560 590 594 670

Orange bell pepper 415 555

Oranges and Orange juice 143 232 267 288 289 294 296 299 303 316 331 336 345 349 371 478 485 560 622 751

Orange zest 108 125 132 143 178 232 288 289 294 299 300 478 543 587

P

Panko breadcrumbs 360 421 516

Paprika 153 247 254 255 256 259 260 384 457 470 471 473 481 486 492 503 507 522 550 552 560 567 568 571 592 594 634 670 683

Parsley 120 185 256 263 264 270 280 287 293 295 297 298 303 304 305 306 340 353 362 363 368 371 377 387 388 394 395 399 406 408 411 416 417 424 428 429 434 435 438 440 458 464 467 468 488 490 498 508 515 516 525 541 552 554 558 570 578 580 584 585 586 588 589 596 606 614 628 634 646 647

Parsnips 290 373 376 386 399

Pasta 298 465 470 490 495 496 513 515 525 526 558 563 569 598

Penne pasta 391 442 501 579 599

Pea greens 338

pea protein powder 190 225 229

Peanut butter 130 178 179 181 189 195 204 206 209 210 219 221 225 238 267 296 456 479 493 502 577 591 656 657 666 667 675 680 682 687 693 732 733

Peanuts 131 296 338 358 372 499 521 523 549 566 609 566 682 687 732

Pearl tapioca 117 720

Pearl barley 390

Pecans 134 173 174 176 193 351 460 667 676 706 707 728 741 748

Pesto 156 337 446 495 496 497 512

Pine nuts 362 400 406 496 519 520 557 662

Pineapple 215 240 309 330 475 509

Pineapple juice 197 309 475 500 673 622 676

Pitted dates 102 127 139 162 214 308 666 675 676 722 723 741 743

Plain flour 196 588

Popped popcorn 732

Potatoes 120 140 150 254 283 290 342 346 416 423 464 481 486 504 561 574 584 586 593 614 646 653 671 677

Potato starch 677 678

Powdered sugar 686

Pumpkin pie spice 143 166 187 193 204 205 229 728 734 741 746

Pumpkin puree 138 151 166 187 193 229 319 568 707 728 734 746

Pumpkin seeds 134 156 164 397 539 738 740 741

Purple cabbage 304 448

Q

Quinoa 121 199 289 297 306 364 395 398 433 434 457 466 540 573

Quinoa flour 619

R

Raisins 100 111 121 126 131 134 144 145 174 195 209 299 363 534 632 643 680 710

Rapeseed oil 196 386 410 522 538

Raspberries 108 139 147 208 220 332 665 685 699

Raw sugar 550

Red bell pepper 110 115 140 146 153 251 287 296 345 347 348 351 353 357 358 366 368 375 377 380 411 415 415 472 473 474 478 481 483 492 493 505 523 552 555 566 573 590 592 603 604 621

Red cabbage 288

Red chili flakes 368

Rice vinegar 302 451 493 502 521 527 531 532 533 538 555 562 563 591 596

Red Potatoes 115

Russet potato 149 248 440

The Plant Based Cookbook For Beginners
650 Easy, Quick, & Simple Plant Based Vegan Diet Recipes With A 31 Day Meal Plan To Lose Weight & Live A Long Healthy Life

757

758

The Plant Based Cookbook For Beginners
650 Easy, Quick, & Simple Plant Based Vegan Diet Recipes With A 31 Day Meal Plan To Lose Weight & Live A Long Healthy Life

W

Walnuts 99 102 106 114 119 124 126 132 141 143 165 192 212 281
311 390 417 418 425 525 547 557 567 659 666 675 692 693
699 713 717

White beans 216 260 262 428 507 634

White mushrooms 379 432

White long-grain rice 211 355 406 482 484 500 604

White miso 438 443 531 533 534 541 551

White pepper 101 519 588

White vinegar 350 492

White wine 264 347 386 433 511 552 569 588

White wine vinegar 264 347 386 433 588

Whole-wheat flour 100 103 114 119 122 124 137 146 148 174 187
188 192 204 212 220 226 227 241 356 360 430 446 447 488
515 567 593 611 654 688 689 729

Y

Yellow mustard 266 473 477 494

Yellow onion 109 149 269 283 379 429 447 454 461 467 473
474 482 484 527 552 557 564 568 571 590 602 651

Yellow bell pepper 110 153 508 603

Yellow squash 376 380 383 444

Z

Zucchini 124 140 149 153 162 192 224 227 239 282 347 358 362
376 383 391 392 394 404 410 429 438 444 446 447 461 479
488 497 523 540 558 569 573 586 590 592 616 627 628

The Plant Based Cookbook For Beginners
650 Easy, Quick, & Simple Plant Based Vegan Diet Recipes With A 31 Day Meal Plan To Lose Weight & Live A Long Healthy Life

759

Printed in Great Britain
by Amazon

78256230R00429